MASS MEDIA 95/96

Second Edition

Editor

Joan Gorham
West Virginia University

Joan Gorham completed her undergraduate work at the University of Wisconsin and received masters and doctoral degrees from Northern Illinois University. Dr. Gorham currently teaches courses in mass media effects, nonverbal communication, interpersonal communication, and communication in the classroom at West Virginia University. She serves as editor of *The Speech Communication Teacher,* and she is author of *Commercial Media and Classroom Teaching* as well as numerous articles on communication in instruction. She regularly teaches graduate classes dealing with media literacy for teachers throughout the state of West Virginia.

Annual Editions
A Library of Information from the Public Press

The Dushkin Publishing Group, Inc.
Sluice Dock, Guilford, Connecticut 06437

Cover illustration by Mike Eagle

The Annual Editions Series

Annual Editions is a series of over 60 volumes designed to provide the reader with convenient, low-cost access to a wide range of current, carefully selected articles from some of the most important magazines, newspapers, and journals published today. Annual Editions are updated on an annual basis through a continuous monitoring of over 300 periodical sources. All Annual Editions have a number of features designed to make them particularly useful, including topic guides, annotated tables of contents, unit overviews, and indexes. For the teacher using Annual Editions in the classroom, an Instructor's Resource Guide with test questions is available for each volume.

VOLUMES AVAILABLE

Africa
Aging
American Foreign Policy
American Government
American History, Pre-Civil War
American History, Post-Civil War
Anthropology
Archaeology
Biology
Biopsychology
Business Ethics
Canadian Politics
Child Growth and Development
China
Comparative Politics
Computers in Education
Computers in Business
Computers in Society
Criminal Justice
Drugs, Society, and Behavior
Dying, Death, and Bereavement
Early Childhood Education
Economics
Educating Exceptional Children
Education
Educational Psychology
Environment
Geography
Global Issues
Health
Human Development
Human Resources
Human Sexuality
India and South Asia
International Business

Japan and the Pacific Rim
Latin America
Life Management
Macroeconomics
Management
Marketing
Marriage and Family
Mass Media
Microeconomics
Middle East and the Islamic World
Money and Banking
Multicultural Education
Nutrition
Personal Growth and Behavior
Physical Anthropology
Psychology
Public Administration
Race and Ethnic Relations
Russia, the Eurasian Republics, and Central/Eastern Europe
Social Problems
Sociology
State and Local Government
Third World
Urban Society
Violence and Terrorism
Western Civilization, Pre-Reformation
Western Civilization, Post-Reformation
Western Europe
World History, Pre-Modern
World History, Modern
World Politics

Cataloging in Publication Data
Main entry under title: Annual Editions: Mass media. 1995/96.
    1. Mass media—Periodicals. I. Gorham, Joan, *comp.* II. Title: Mass media.
ISBN 1–56134–340–4   301.16'05

Second Edition

Manufactured in the United States of America

Printed on Recycled Paper

Editors/ Advisory Board

EDITOR

Joan Gorham
West Virginia University

ADVISORY BOARD

STAFF

To the Reader

In publishing ANNUAL EDITIONS we recognize the enormous role played by the magazines, newspapers, and journals of the *public press* in providing current, first-rate educational information in a broad spectrum of interest areas. Within the articles, the best scientists, practitioners, researchers, and commentators draw issues into new perspective as accepted theories and viewpoints are called into account by new events, recent discoveries change old facts, and fresh debate breaks out over important controversies.

Many of the articles resulting from this enormous editorial effort are appropriate for students, researchers, and professionals seeking accurate, current material to help bridge the gap between principles and theories and the real world. These articles, however, become more useful for study when those of lasting value are carefully *collected, organized, indexed,* and *reproduced* in a *low-cost format,* which provides easy and permanent access when the material is needed. That is the role played by *Annual Editions.* Under the direction of each volume's *Editor,* who is an expert in the subject area, and with the guidance of an *Advisory Board,* we seek each year to provide in each *ANNUAL EDITION* a current, well-balanced, carefully selected collection of the best of the public press for your study and enjoyment. We think you'll find this volume useful, and we hope you'll take a moment to let us know what you think.

We live in a mediated society, one in which the forms and formats of mass media continue to evolve as audiences shift and technologies change. The 5 largest U.S. newspapers have a combined daily circulation of over 6 million. The average American reads 11.6 different magazine issues per month. Ninety-five percent of Americans report listening to the radio at some point each day. The average household receives 27 television stations and has television on about 47 hours per week. Except for school, the church, and the family, no institution has a greater potential for shaping American values than the media. And, just as schools and parents have been blamed for a variety of society's ills, media have taken their fair share of heat.

The mass media are a part of the fabric of American society. Learning how to critically evaluate media messages—asking Who created this message? What is their agenda? What are they leaving out? How does what I am seeing or hearing reflect and/or shape real-world realities?—is a part of being literate in today's society. The organization of these readings reflects this media literacy perspective. Unit 1 provides an introduction to concerns that have been raised about the effects of mass media, particularly television, on audience perceptions and behavior. Units 2 through 4 explore influences that shape media messages. Units 5 through 9 are concerned with the implications of explicit and implicit media lessons.

Although newspapers, magazines, books, radio, and film have evoked their share of critical commentary, it was television that opened the door to widespread concern about media effects. Television established itself as a mass medium with unexpected speed. It took 80 years from the time the telephone was invented until it was available in 80 percent of American homes, 25 years for radio to enter 80 percent of homes, and 10 years for television to reach 80 percent of the population. Its rapid acceptance as the most massive of mass media, its combination of auditory and visual messages, its mesmerizing quality, and the nature of its communicating over limited airways presented a combination of circumstances that led to particular concern and critical examination of television's social impact. Consequently, these readings often use television as a reference point in describing how mass media messages are shaped and interpreted.

The articles in this anthology have been chosen to address the influences of media insiders and financial and regulatory pressures on media content and to critically examine trends in both informational and entertainment media. Most of the articles, even those that are primarily descriptive rather than editorial, include an element of critical commentary and draw conclusions or make recommendations with which you may disagree. I encourage you to debate these issues, drawing from both the information and insights provided in the articles as well as your own experiences as a media consumer.

This is the second *Annual Editions* collection of readings on mass media. It will be continually updated to reflect changing trends and to respond to the feedback and advice you, as a reader, provide. Those involved in producing this anthology are sincerely committed to including articles that are timely, informative, and interesting. Please complete and return the article rating form on the last page of the book to give us your suggestions and let us know your opinions.

Joan Gorham
Editor

Contents

Unit 1

Living with Media

Five selections discuss the range of critical commentary that has been directed toward mass media and their potential effects on society as a whole.

The concepts in bold italics are developed in the article. For further expansion please refer to the Topic Guide and the Index.

Unit 2

The Source's Perspective: A Push from the Right . . . a Pull to the Left

Four articles explore the idea that media messages are created by individuals who have the potential to incorporate their own biases in selecting, interpreting, and crafting those messages.

Unit 3

Commercial Considerations: Advertiser Influence on Media Messages

Four selections explore advertiser influences on newspaper, magazine, film, and television content.

The concepts in bold italics are developed in the article. For further expansion please refer to the Topic Guide and the Index.

Unit 4

Legal and Regulatory Restraints on Media Content

Four selections examine how media is held
accountable to various legal and regulatory restraints.

Unit 5

Information and Influence: Concerns with What We Learn from News Media

Five articles discuss mass media as a news source and the responsibilities they have with regard to possible inaccuracies, distortions, and a bad news bias.

Unit 6

The Power of Images

Three articles explore the power of images and raise questions of their effects—from engendering emotional responses to reinventing reality.

The concepts in bold italics are developed in the article. For further expansion please refer to the Topic Guide and the Index.

Unit 7

Ethical Questions

Five selections explore how presenting newsworthy information can be complicated by considerations of what is morally right and wrong.

Unit 8

Media and Politics

Four articles examine how mass media have impacted on the way American political leaders are elected and the way they govern.

The concepts in bold italics are developed in the article. For further expansion please refer to the Topic Guide and the Index.

Unit
9

Implicit Lessons:
Concerns with What
We Learn from
Entertainment Media

Eight selections explore how entertainment media
provide both explicit and implicit lessons and how
these lessons have shaped or have been shaped by
society.

The concepts in bold italics are developed in the article. For further expansion please refer to the Topic Guide and the Index.

The concepts in bold italics are developed in the article. For further expansion please refer to the Topic Guide and the Index.

Topic Guide

This topic guide suggests how the selections in this book relate to topics of traditional concern to mass media students and professionals. It is useful for locating articles that relate to each other for reading and research. The guide is arranged alphabetically according to topic. Articles may, of course, treat topics that do not appear in the topic guide. In turn, entries in the topic guide do not necessarily constitute a comprehensive listing of all the contents of each selection.

Living with Media

It has been estimated that the average child will have watched 5,000 hours of television by the time he or she enters first grade and 25,000 hours by the end of high school—more time than would be spent in a classroom earning a college degree. Guided by television, today's children are exposed to more information about the world than any other generation in history. They are also exposed to an estimated 350,000 commercials by age 18, and they have explored values, role models, cultural myths, and social issues through the media. This fascination with television is not restricted to childhood; 1993 figures from Nielsen Media Research indicate that women over the age of 55 log an average of 6 hours and 19 minutes of television viewing each day, while men over the age of 55 watch 5 hours and 29 minutes per day.

Questions of whether and to what extent media influence our behaviors, values, expectations, and ways of thinking are difficult to answer. While one bibliographer has compiled a list of approximately 3,000 citations of English-language articles focusing just on children and television (and all written within the last 35 years), concerns raised by critical commentary have not been unequivocally supported by research. Isolating media as a causal agent in examining human behavior is a difficult task, complicated by the challenge of understanding the complexities of the mind, differences in the context in which media are consumed (e.g., the personal, nonmedia experiences of the consumer; the extent to which media content is actively vs. passively processed), the difficulty of finding representative control groups who have not been exposed to media, and the challenge of determining long-range effects. Thus, while researchers have found it difficult to prove that mass media *are* responsible for significant changes in individual consumers and in society as a whole, they have also found it difficult to prove that they are *not* linked to such changes.

The media have been blamed for just about everything from a decrease in attention span to an increase in street crime to undoing our capacity to think. In *Amusing Ourselves to Death* (Penguin, 1986), social critic Neil Postman suggests that the cocktail party, the quiz show, and popular trivia games are reflections of society's trying to find a use for the abundance of superficial information given us by the media—and useful for little else than attempts to impress one another with small talk. Peggy Noonan, a former network writer who worked as a speechwriter during the Reagan administration, has observed that experiences are no longer "real" unless they are ratified by television (which is why, she says, half the people in a sports stadium watch the game on monitors rather than watching the field). Marie Winn's memorable description of a child, transfixed by television, slack-jawed, tongue resting on the front teeth, eyes glazed and vacant (*The Plug-In Drug*, Penguin, 1985) has become an oft-quoted symbol of the passivity encouraged by television viewing.

The articles in this section were chosen to give readers a feel for the range of critical commentary that has been directed toward mass media. In "Television: The Shared Arena," Joshua Meyrowitz focuses on the influences of television's version of reality on cultural change. By increasing awareness of differences among members of formerly isolated and distinct groups, television creates dissatisfaction and a demand for change; by presenting "backstage" and "close-up" views, television alters attitudes toward adult authority, male and female roles, and political leadership. "More than ever before," notes Meyrowitz, "the postmodern era is one in which *everyone* else seems somewhat familiar—and somewhat strange." Marie Winn ("The Trouble with Television") focuses not on television content but on how it is used and its effects on how children are raised.

In contrast, Douglas Gomery ("As the Dial Turns") and Bennett Daviss ("TV as Boob Tube: Bad Rap") contend that critics are too quick to blame media, particularly television, for society's evils. Daviss summarizes an extensively researched 1988 report of the U.S. Department of Education in which Daniel Anderson, a professor of psychology at the University of Massachusetts, concluded that scientific research has not, on the whole, provided convincing evidence that television has a mesmerizing effect on children, that it overstimulates them, or that it reduces attention span. John Leonard ("Why Blame TV?") suggests that "normal people" do not use television the way critics assume they do and, in fact, learn a great deal from its content. Countercritics such as these argue that culture is more likely to drive the media than to be driven by them; the popularity of mass media depends on their reflecting and preserving the status quo. They note that people who watch a lot of television often do so for a reason. They may be of lower socioeconomic status, they may be more passive in nature, socially alienated, or less intelligent—all factors that are as, if not more, likely to be actual causes of effects attributed to their television viewing.

It is both logical and prudent that society should want to arm itself against potential harm. Given its rapid growth as the "massest" of media, it is not surprising that critics have focused on television in their search for simple answers to complex problems that have come with the

TOPIC AREA	TREATED IN:	TOPIC AREA	TREATED IN:
New Technologies	2. As the Dial Turns 17. Tangled Webs They Weave 25. Photographs That Lie	**Prosocial Effects**	5. Why Blame TV? 41. Frankenstein Must Be Destroyed 42. Ethical Dilemmas of Prosocial Television
News Photography	19. Make-Your-Own Journalism 23. What the Jury Saw 24. When Pictures Drive Foreign Policy 25. Photographs That Lie 28. Feeding Frenzy	**Radio**	16. Media Accountability for Real-Life Violence 34. Power of Talk
News Reporting	6. Power Structure of the American Media 18. Media Con Games 19. Make-Your-Own Journalism 20. Media Pervasiveness 21. Summer's Top Crime Drama 22. Old News Is Good News 24. When Pictures Drive Foreign Policy 25. Photographs That Lie 27. Legislating Ethics 28. Feeding Frenzy 32. Churning Whitewater	**Ratings**	2. As the Dial Turns
		Right to Privacy	28. Feeding Frenzy 30. To "Out" or Not to "Out"
		Social Learning Theory	39. Don't Blame TV 41. Frankenstein Must Be Destroyed
Newspapers	10. Advertiser Influence 13. Newspaper Advocacy Advertising 24. When Pictures Drive Foreign Policy 27. Legislating Ethics	**Television**	1. Television: The Shared Arena 2. As the Dial Turns 3. Trouble with Television 4. TV as Boob Tube 5. Why Blame TV? 9. Sitcom Politics 16. Media Accountability for Real-Life Violence 19. Make-Your-Own Journalism 21. Summer's Top Crime Drama 24. When Pictures Drive Foreign Policy 28. Feeding Frenzy 36. Battle for Your Brain 38. Gendered Media 39. Don't Blame TV 40. Violence on TV 42. Ethical Dilemmas of Prosocial Television
Political Influence	1. Television: The Shared Arena 6. Power Structure of the American Media 24. When Pictures Drive Foreign Policy 31. Bad News Bearers 32. Churning Whitewater 33. Trouble with Spots 34. Power of Talk		

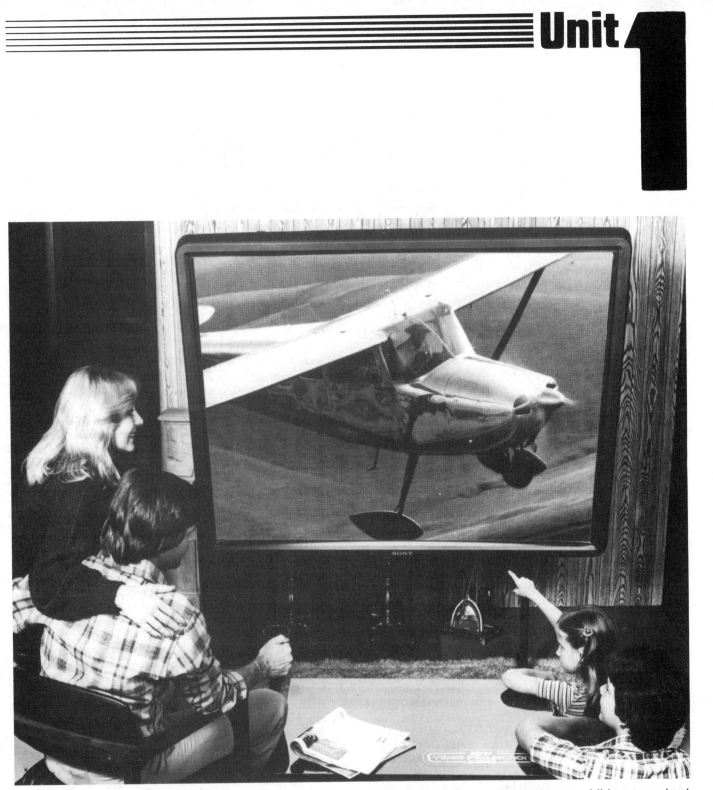

television age. However, the degree to which media drive social change, as opposed to merely responding to it, is an issue still clearly open to debate.

Looking Ahead: Challenge Questions

Canadian communications specialist Marshall McLuhan predicted that mass media would create a "global village" of shared hopes and dreams. Is there a downside of media—particularly television—providing an arena of shared experiences? To what degree are media influential in driving cultural change?

How has television affected the way children are raised and the way families interact?

How solid is the evidence that supports cause-effect relationships central to criticisms of mass media effects? To what degree can scientific research resolve questions of media effects? Do you find the arguments of media critics or countercritics more compelling? Why, or why not?

What are the implications of new technologies that expand consumers' choice and control of media offerings?

TELEVISION: THE SHARED ARENA

Joshua Meyrowitz

Joshua Meyrowitz is professor of communication at the University of New Hampshire. He is the author of the award-winning book No Sense of Place: The Impact of Electronic Media on Social Behavior *(Oxford University Press).*

In 1950, only 9 percent of U.S. homes owned television sets. Little more than twenty-five years later, only 2 percent of households were without one. In a remarkably short time, television has taken a central place in our living rooms and in our cultural and political lives. On average, a U.S. household can now receive thirty channels; only 7 percent of homes receive six or fewer stations. Some 95 percent of homes own a color TV, 63 percent own two or more sets, and 64 percent own a videocassette recorder.

Television is the most popular of the popular media. Indeed, if Nielsen research and other studies are correct, there are few things that Americans do more than they watch television. On average, each household has a TV on almost fifty hours a week. Forty percent of households eat dinner with the set on. Individually, Americans watch an average of thirty hours a week. We begin peering at TV through the bars of cribs and continue looking at it through the cataracts of old age.

Plato saw an important relationship between shared, simultaneous experience and a sense of social and political interconnectedness. Plato thought that his Republic should consist of no more than five thousand citizens because that was the maximum number of people who could fit in an arena and simultaneously hear the voice of one person. Television is now our largest shared arena. During the average minute of a typical evening, nearly a hundred million Americans are

tuned in. While a book can usually win a place on the lists of the top fifty fiction or nonfiction bestsellers for the *year* with 115,000 hardcover sales, a prime-time network program with fewer than fifteen million viewers for *each episode* is generally considered a failure.

Even the biggest best-sellers reach only a fraction of the audience that will watch a similar program on television. It took forty years for *Gone With the Wind* to sell twenty-one million copies; fifty-five million people watched the first half of the movie on television in a single evening. The television miniseries *Roots* was watched, in part or whole, by approximately 130 million people in only eight days. Even with the help of the television promotion, fewer than five million copies of *Roots* sold in eight years.

The television arena, like a street corner or a marketplace, serves as an environment for us to monitor but not necessarily identify with. Reading a newspaper requires an investment of money and reading effort, and at least some minimal identification with its style and editorial policy. We have to reach out for it and embrace it—both literally and metaphorically. But with television, we simply sit back and let the images wash over us. While we usually select reading material that clearly reflects our own self-image, with TV we often feel we are passively observing what other people are like.

Most of us would feel uncomfortable stopping at a local store to pick up the current issue of a publication titled *Transvestite Times* or *Male Strippers' Review*, or a magazine on incest, child abuse, or adultery. But millions of viewers feel quite comfortable sharing their

homes with transvestites, male strippers, and victims and perpetrators of incest, or almost anyone else who appears on *Donahue*, *Oprah*, or *Geraldo*. Ironically, our personal dissociation with TV content allows for the most widespread sharing of similar experience in the history of civilization.

In the 1950s, many intellectuals were embarrassed to admit that they owned a television set, let alone that they spent any valuable time watching it. But the massive saturation of television into virtually every U.S. home now imbues the activity of watching television with multiple layers of social significance. One can watch popular programs not merely to see the program but to see what others are watching. To watch television may not be to stare into the eyes of America, but it is to look over its shoulder and see what Americans see. Watching television —with its often distorted versions of reality—does not allow us to keep our finger on the pulse of the nation so much as it allows us to keep our finger on the pulse the nation is keeping its finger on. With television, it somehow makes sense for a viewer to watch the tube avidly while exclaiming, "My God, I can't believe people watch this stuff!"

Even though many people watch it alone, television is capable of giving each isolated viewer a sense of connection with the outside world and with all the other people who are watching. During major television events—whether fictional or nonfictional—such as the final episode of M*A*S*H or the explosion of the *Challenger*, one is likely to find that more than one out of every two people one sees on the street the next day has had a similar experience the night before. Regardless of specific content, then, television often serves a social function similar to the weather: No one takes responsibility for it, often it is quite bad, but nearly everyone pays attention to it and sees it as a basis of common experience and conversational topics. Perhaps this is why even pay cable households spend more than half their viewing time watching "regular" network programming and why the most frequent use of VCRs is for time shifting of programs broadcast by network-affiliated stations.

For many people, someone or something that does not appear on television does not fully exist in the social sense. The Watergate scandals became "real" not when the *Washington Post* reported the stories but when network television news reported that the *Washington Post* reported the stories. Similarly, civil rights and anti-Vietnam War protests became social realities not when demonstrators took to the streets but when the protests were viewed on television. And although most of our early presidents were seen by only a few of the voters of their day, it is now impossible to imagine a serious candidate who would not visit us all on TV. And so it is that politicians, salespeople, protestors, and terrorists all design their messages in the hope of capturing the television eye.

TOO CLOSE TO THE SET

Despite its ubiquity, the impact of television is not yet seen very clearly. For one thing, most of us watch television too closely—not in the way that mothers warn their children about, but in the sense of evaluating television primarily on the basis of whether we like or don't like its programs. Even scholars tend to reduce the impact of television to its past and current programming and to the motives of the institutions that control it. The overwhelming majority of television research and criticism has focused on the nature of the programs, their imitative or persuasive power, their aesthetic value or bankruptcy, the range of meanings that viewers can draw from them, or their underlying economic and political purposes.

These are important but insufficient questions. The effects of a new communication technology cannot be understood fully by looking only at the medium's typical content and patterns of control. To see the limits of such an approach, we need only to consider what its use in the

fifteenth and sixteenth centuries would have revealed about the impact of the printing press, then spreading through Western culture. A content/institutional approach to printing probably would have led observers to conclude that books had two major effects: 1) the fostering of religion (most early books were religious in content) and 2) the strengthening of central religious and monarchal authorities (who controlled much of what was printed). The underlying, but ultimately more significant, long-term effects of the printing press—such as the growth of individual thinking and science and the spread of nationalism and constitutional systems —would remain invisible.

This is not to suggest that the short-term, surface effects are inconsequential. Just look at William Carter. He printed a pro-Catholic pamphlet in England in 1584 and was promptly hanged. Similarly, our current information environment is choked and narrowed by the way television is controlled.

The television business is not structured to deliver quality programming to viewers but rather to deliver viewers to advertisers. We are sold to advertisers in lots of a thousand. The real programming on television is the commercial. That is where the time, the money, and the competition are. That is where the most creative television "artists" (if we want to use that term) are working. The TV shows —whether news or entertainment or "infotainment"—are simply the bait.

We are misled when we are told that program ratings are part of an audience-centered, "democratic" process that allows us to "vote" for shows. In fact, we are usually offered forced choices among advertiser-friendly programs. This is why TV ratings systems rarely ask whether or why we like or dislike a show or what we would like to see instead. Most ratings simply measure how many of what type of people are there for the ads.

Even if networks can draw millions of viewers to a program, the last thing they want to do is put the audience in a mood that does not mix well with consumption of the advertised products. One of the most-watched programs in televi-

sion history, *The Day After*, for example, was an ad failure. After all, what companies would want their products associated with nuclear holocaust? In fact, as one vice-president of the network confided to me, the airing of *The Day After*—as bland a treatment of its subject as it was—almost led to a stockholder suit against ABC because the network could have made more money airing a rerun of a program such as *The Harlem Globetrotters Visit Gilligan's Island*.

But to reduce television to a cultural nuisance or to a slickly disguised salesperson, as some analysts do, is to miss what is happening in our culture because of television and how it—not merely through its content but also as a certain form of shared experience—reshapes our attitudes and behaviors.

The effects of new media of communication arise not solely from their content but also from the new ways in which the medium packages and transmits information. Writing and print, for example, were able to foster the rise of individual thinking and science because they literally put information in the hands of individuals and because they allowed for the recording and wide-scale distribution of ideas that were too complicated to memorize (even by the people who came up with them). Even as William Carter swung from the gallows by regal decree, printing was quietly working against its apparent masters, ultimately secularizing the culture and encouraging the overthrow of monarchies. Similarly, the impact of television cannot be reduced to programs that come through the tube or to the institutions that control it. There are effects apart from, and even in opposition to, these forces.

The most significant long-term effects of television may also lie in its manner of packaging and transmitting information and in the ways that it undoes some of the systems of communication supported by print. Television has changed "who knows what about whom" and "who knows what compared to whom." As a result, it has changed the way we grow from childhood to adulthood, altered our sense of appropriate gender

---

Television dilutes the innocence of childhood by undermining the system of information control.

behavior, shifted our perceptions of our political and other leaders, and affected our general sense of "them" and "us."

VIDEO NURSERY

As printing and literacy spread through Western culture, literate adults discovered they could increasingly keep secrets from preliterate and semiliterate children. Adults used books to communicate among themselves without children overhearing. Clerics argued for the development of expurgated versions of the classics, and the notion of the innocence of childhood began to take hold, eventually spreading to the lowest classes with the growth of universal education.

Childhood was to be a time of innocence and isolation. Children were protected from the nasty realities of adult life. Unable to read, very young children had no access to the information available in books. Young children were presented with an idealized version of adult life. Children were slowly walked up the ladder of literacy with a new, somewhat less idealized view of adult life presented to them at each step of reading ability.

Television dilutes the innocence of childhood by undermining the system of information control that supported it. Television bypasses the year-by-year slices of knowledge given to children. It presents the same information to adults and to children of all ages. Children may not understand everything they see on television, but they are exposed to many aspects of adult life that their parents (and traditional children's books) would have once protected them from.

Parents often clamor for more and better children's television. But one could argue that there is no such thing as "children's television," at least not in the sense that there is children's literature. Children's literature is the only literature that children can read, and only children read it. In contrast, studies since the early days of television have found that children often prefer to watch programs aimed at adults. And adults often watch programs aimed at children—about a third of the audience for *Pee Wee Herman's Playhouse* is over eighteen.

At some point during the last decade, each of the following has been among the most popular programs in *all* age groups, including ages two to eleven: *Dallas, The Muppets, The Dukes of Hazzard, Love Boat, The A-Team, Cheers, Roseanne,* and *The Golden Girls.* Thus, children have

been avid viewers of adult soap operas, and adults have found pleasure in a children's puppet show.

In both fictional and nonfictional programs, children learn that adults lie, cheat, drink too much, use drugs, and kill and maim each other. But perhaps the most dramatic revelation that television provides to young children is that parents struggle to control children.

Unlike books, television cannot be used easily by adults as a tool to discuss how to raise children. A parental advice book can be used by adults to communicate among themselves about what to tell and not to tell children. But the same conversation on television is usually overheard by thousands of children, who are thereby exposed to the very topics suggested for secrecy and to the "secret of secrecy" itself—the fact that adults are anxious about their parental roles and conspire to keep secrets from children.

Even seemingly innocent programs reveal significant secrets to children. When the first TV generation watched programs such as *Father Knows Best* and *Leave It to Beaver,* for example, they learned that parents behaved one way in front of their children and another way when they were alone. In front of their children, the TV parents were calm, cool, and collected, but away from their kids, they were anxious and concerned about their parental behavior. Because we often reduce the effects of TV to imitation, we forget that while the children *on* such programs were innocent and sheltered, the children *watching* the shows often saw how adults manipulated their behaviors to make it appear to their children that they knew best. This is a view that undermines traditional parental authority by making children less willing to take adult behavior at face value. It is no wonder, perhaps, that the children who grew up watching *Father Knows Best* became concerned with the "credibility gap"; that is, the difference between what people proclaim publicly and what they say and feel privately.

Subsequent situation comedies, such as *One Day at a Time,* shocked many viewers because the parents in the shows revealed their fears and anxieties about parenting in front of their children and because the child characters on the shows were no longer sheltered or innocent. But in terms of what *child* viewers learned about the concerns of parents, there was relatively little new information. The third phase of family shows, including *The Bill Cosby Show* and *Family Ties,* offers a compromise between the two ear-

lier family visions: The line between parents and children has been partly reestablished, but the children are more sophisticated than early TV children and the parents are both less surefooted in front of their children and less conspiratorial away from them.

In a book culture, control over the flow of information is literally placed in parents' hands. Parents can easily give some books to children and withhold others. Parents can read one book while their children sit in the same room reading another. Television is not so cooperative. Parents often find it difficult to censor their children's viewing without censoring their own, and parents cannot always anticipate what will happen on TV the way they can flip through a book. A father may think he is giving his daughter a lesson in science as they watch the *Challenger* take off, only to discover that he has exposed her instead to adult hubris and tragedy.

Most television programs are accessible to children in a way that most book content is not. The visual/aural form of television allows children to experience many behaviors and events without the skill of decoding written sentences. And it is much simpler for children to wander off *Sesame Street* and slip beyond *Mr. Rogers' Neighborhood* into grownup television than it is for children to buy or borrow books from a grown-up library or bookstore. Television takes our children across the globe before we as parents even give them permission to cross the street.

As children's innocence declines, children's literature and children's programming have changed as well. Some children's books now discuss sex and drugs and other once-taboo topics, and war and divorce have recently visited *Mr. Rogers' Neighborhood.*

This does not mean that adults should abdicate their authority over children or even give up trying to control children's viewing of television. Adults are more experienced and more knowledgeable. But it does mean that the old support system for unquestioned adult authority has been undermined by television. In a television culture, children are more suspicious of adult authority, and many adults feel somewhat exposed, finding it more difficult to pretend to know everything in front of their children. The result is a partial blurring of traditional child and adult roles. Children seem older and more knowledgeable, and adults now reveal to their children the more childish sides of themselves, such as doubts, fears, and anxieties. Thus, we are seeing more adultlike children and more childlike adults, behavior styles characteristic of preliterate societies.

GENDER BLENDER

Our society once tried to maintain a clear distinction between the male realm and the female realm. The Victorians spoke of the "two spheres": a public, male world of brutal competitions, rationality, and accomplishments; and a private, female world of home, intuition, and child-rearing. Men were to suppress their emotions and women were to suppress their competitiveness. The ideal of separate spheres was quite strong in our society when television became the newest home appliance.

Yet even as television situation comedies and other programs featured very traditional gender roles in the two separate spheres, television, as a shared arena, was beginning to break down the distinction between the male and the female, between the public and the private realms. Television closeups reveal the personal side of public figures and events (we see tears well up in the eyes of a president; we hear male voices crack with emotion) just as most public events have become dramas that are played out in the privacy of our kitchens, living rooms, and bedrooms. Television has exposed even homebound women to most of the parts of the culture that were once considered exclusively male domains—sports, war, business, medicine, law, politics—just as it has made men more aware of the emotional dimensions and consequences of public actions.

When Betty Friedan wrote in *The Feminine Mystique* that women in 1960 felt a "schizophrenic split" between the frilly, carefree image of women in women's magazines and the important events occurring in "the world beyond the home," most of her examples of the latter were unwittingly drawn from the top television news stories of the year. By 1960, television was present in nearly 90 percent of U.S. homes. Similarly, other feminist writers have described changes in the 1960s by writing metaphorically of the "breaking of boundaries" (Gloria Steinem), "a sudden enlargement of our world" (Elizabeth Janeway), and of women having "seen beyond the bucolic peacefulness of the suburbs to the war zone at the perimeter" (Barbara Ehrenreich and Deirdre English). But these writers seem unaware of how closely their metaphors

describe the literal experience of adding a television to a suburban household.

The fact that early TV programs generally portrayed active men and passive, obedient women had no more of an imitative effect on women viewers than the innocent child characters on *Father Knows Best* had on child viewers. Television, it is true, suggested to women how society thought they should behave, just as etiquette books had for centuries. But television did something else as well: It allowed women to observe and experience the larger world, including all-male interactions and behaviors. Indeed, there is nothing more frustrating than being exposed constantly to adventures, activities, and places that you are told are reserved for someone else. Television also demystified the male realm, making it and its inhabitants seem neither very special nor very intimidating. No wonder women have since demanded to integrate that realm.

Television's impact has been greatest on women because they have traditionally been more isolated. But men are affected as well, partly because women have demanded changes in their behavior and partly because television emphasizes those traits traditionally ascribed to women: feelings, appearance, emotion. On television, "glorious victories" and "crushing defeats" are now conveyed through images of blood and limp bodies and the howls of survivors. Television has helped men to become more aware of their emotions and of the fact that emotions cannot be completely buried. Even at televised public hearings, it is hard to ignore the facial expressions, the yawns, the grimaces, the fatigue.

The way men react to public issues is also being subtly feminized. Men used to make fun of women for voting for candidates because of the candidates' appearance rather than their stands on the issues. But recent polls show that millions of men, as well as women, will now vote for a candidate they disagree with on the issues, if they "personally like" the candidate. About a third of Ronald Reagan's votes came from such supporters.

Television is one of the few public arenas in our culture where men routinely wear makeup and are judged as much on their personal appearance and "style" as on their "accomplishments." If it was once thought that women communicated and men accomplished, it is telling that our most successful recent president was dubbed the "Great Communicator" and was admired for his gentle voice and manner and his moist-eyed emotional appeals.

With television, boys and girls and men and women tend to share a great deal of similar information about themselves and the "other." Through TV close-ups, men and women see, in one month, many more members of the opposite sex at "intimate distance" than members of earlier generations saw in a lifetime. Further, unlike face-to-face interactions, in which the holding of a gaze may be construed as insulting or as an invitation to further intimacy, television allows one to stare and carefully examine the face, body, and movements of the other sex. Television fosters an easy and uninvolved intimacy.

Just as women have become more involved in the public realm, men are becoming more involved in the private realm, especially in the role of fathers. Traditional distinctions cannot be erased in a generation, of course. But dramatic changes have taken place in a remarkably short time. In 1950, only 12 percent of married women with children under six worked; by 1987, 57 percent did. Recent studies also show that men are now more likely to turn down overtime pay or travel and relocation offers in order to spend more time with their families.

In spite of its often sexist content, television, as an environment shared by both sexes, has made the membranes around the male and female realms more permeable. As a result, the nature of those two realms has been blurring. We are witnessing more career-oriented women and more family-oriented men; we are developing more work-oriented homes, and there is increasing pressure to make the public realm more family oriented.

PRESIDENTIAL PIMPLES

Just as television tends to mute differences between people of different ages and sexes, so does it tend to mute differences between levels of social status. Although television is certainly an important weapon in the arsenal of leaders, it often functions as a double-edged sword. Unlike other media, television not only allows leaders to reach followers, it also allows followers to gain unprecedented access to the close-up appearance and gestures of leaders.

"Leadership" and "authority" are unlike mere power in that they depend on performance and appeal; one cannot lead or be looked up to if one's presence is unknown. Yet, paradoxically, authority is weakened by excess familiarity. Awe survives through "distant visibility" and "mystified presence." One of the peculiar ironies of our age is that most people who step forward into the television limelight and attempt to gain national visibility become too visible, too exposed, and are thereby demystified.

The speaker's platform once lifted politicians up and away from average citizens, both literally and symbolically. In newspaper quotes and reports, the politician—as flesh-and-bones person—was completely absent. And on radio, politicians were disembodied voices. But the television camera now lowers politicians to the level of the common citizen and brings them close for our inspection. In recent years, we have seen our presidents sweat, stammer, and stumble—all in living color.

Presidential images were once much better protected. Before TV coverage of press conferences, newspapers were not even allowed to quote a president without his explicit permission. As late as the start of the Eisenhower administration, *The New York Times* and other publications had to paraphrase the president's answers to questions. In earlier administrations, journalists had to submit their questions in advance and were forbidden from mentioning which questions the president refused to answer. Presidential advisors frequently corrected presidents' answers during meetings with the press, and such assistance went unreported. In the face of a "crisis," our presidents once had many hours, sometimes even weeks or months, to consult with advisors and to formulate policy statements to be printed in newspapers. Now, standing before the nation, a president is expected to have all relevant information in his mind—without notes and without consultation with advisors. A president must often start a sentence before the end of the sentence is fully formed in his mind. Even a five-second pause for thought can seriously damage a leader's credibility. The apparent inarticulateness of all our recent presidents may be related more to the immediacy of television than to a decline in our leaders' mental abilities.

In language, the titles "president," "governor," and "senator" still call forth respect. But the close-up TV pictures of the persons filling those offices are rarely as impressive. We cannot help but notice the sweat on the brow, the nervous twitch, the bags under the eyes.

Television not only reduces our awe of politicians, it increases politicians' self-doubt and lowers self-esteem. A speaker's nervousness and mistakes usually are politely ignored by live audiences and therefore soon forgotten by the speaker as well.

But with videotape, politicians have permanent records of themselves mispeaking or anxiously licking their lips. Television may be a prime cause of the complaints of indecisive leadership and hesitant "followership" that we have heard since the mid-1960s.

In the 1950s, many people were shocked that a genuine hero, Dwight Eisenhower, felt the need to hire a Hollywood actor to help him with his television appearances. But now we are much more sophisticated—and more cynical. We know that one cannot simply *be* the president, but that one has to *perform* the role of "president." The new communication arena demands more control on the part of politicians, but it also makes the attempts at control more visible. Many citizens lived through twelve years of FDR's presidency without being aware that his legs were crippled and that he often needed help to stand. But we are now constantly exposed to the ways in which our presidents and presidential candidates attempt to manipulate their images to create certain impressions and effects.

The result is that we no longer experience political performances as naive audiences. We have the perspective of stage hands who are aware of the constructed nature of the drama. Certainly, we prefer a good show to a bad show, but we are not fully taken in by the performances. Rather than being fooled, we are willingly entertained, charmed, courted, and seduced. Ironically, all the recent discussions of how effectively we are being manipulated may only point out how visible and exposed the machinations now are.

I am not suggesting that television has made us a fully informed and aware

vision news is often molded, television is having other effects due to its immediacy and visual nature.

Most of our information about other countries once came through the president and State Department, often after careful planning about how to present the information to the public. This allowed the government to appear to be in control of events and always to have a ready response. In many instances, we now experience events at the same moment as our leaders, sometimes before them. The dramatic images of the fall of the Berlin Wall and other changes in Eastern Europe were watched by the president, the secretary of state, and millions of other Americans at the same moment. The immediacy of television often makes leaders appear to be "standing on the sidelines" rather than taking charge or reacting quickly.

Television's accessible, visual nature also works to level authority. Average citizens gain the feeling that they can form their own impressions of Mikhail Gorbachev, Philippine "People Power," and other people and events without depending on official interpretations. Once formed, the mass perceptions constrain our leaders' presentation of events. Ronald Reagan found he needed to temper his talk of the "Evil Empire" as the public formed a positive perception of Gorbachev. And the televising of Filipinos facing down Marcos' tanks made it difficult for Americans to accept our president's suggestion that the reported results of that country's election should stand because "there was cheating on both sides." President Reagan might have changed his rhetoric on these topics in any case, but the public's direct access

---

Television may be a prime cause of the complaints of indecisive leadership and hesitant "followership" that we have heard since the mid-1960s.

---

electorate. Indeed, relatively few Americans realize how selective an image of the world we receive through television news. When the same sort of occurrences take place in El Salvador and in Nicaragua, or in Poland and in Chile, they are often covered in completely different ways, often in keeping with preexisting news narratives concerning each country. But regardless of the ways in which the content of tele-

to the television images made it appear that Reagan was following rather than leading the nation.

The speed of television affects authority in relation to domestic events as well. The videotape of the attempted assassination of Ronald Reagan aired on television *before* a coded transmission about the event was received by Vice President Bush aboard his airplane. Several years later, Reagan had no immediate reaction to the *Challenger* explosion, because millions of Americans saw the *Challenger* explode before he had a chance to watch it on videotape. In both cases, the gap between the experience of the event and a unified administration response made the administration appear temporarily impotent.

As our leaders have lost much control over the flow of information—both about themselves and political events—they have mostly given up trying to behave like the imperial leaders of the past. We now have politicians who strive to act more like the person next door, just as our real neighbors seem more worldly and demand to have a greater say in national and international affairs.

SHARED PROBLEMS

The recognition of television as a new shared arena solves a number of mysteries surrounding television viewing, including: why people complain so bitterly about TV content but continue to watch so much of it; why many Americans say they turn to television for "most" of their news even though the script for an average evening network news broadcast would fill only two columns of the front page of *The New York Times*; why people who purchase videotape machines often discover that they have little interest in creating "libraries" of their favorite television programs.

The shared nature of the television environment creates many new problems and concerns over media content. Content that would be appropriate and uncontroversial in books directed at select audiences often becomes the subject of criticism when presented on television. When television portrays the dominant and "normal" white, middle-class culture, minorities and subcultures protest their exclusion. Yet when television portrays minorities, many members of the majority begin to fear that their insular world is being "invaded." The nature of the portrayal of some groups becomes a catch-22. If homosexuals are portrayed in a negative and stereotypical manner, for example, gay rights groups protest. If homosexuals are portrayed as normal people who simply have a different sexual orientation, however, other viewers object to television "legitimizing" or "idealizing" homosexual life.

Similarly, television cannot exclusively present content deemed suitable only for young children because adult viewers demand more mature entertainment and news. Yet, when truly mature content is placed on television, many parents complain that the minds of child viewers are being defiled.

Without the segregation of audiences, a program designed for one purpose may have quite different effects. An informational program for parents on teenage suicide may not only help some parents prevent a death, it may also encourage a previously nonsuicidal teenager to consider the option. Similarly, a program on how to outwit a burglar may make some home owners more sophisticated about protecting their homes against professional criminals at the same time that it makes unsophisticated burglars more professional.

Even a choice between happy endings and realistic endings becomes controversial on television. When programs end happily, critics argue that serious issues are trivialized through thirty- or sixty-minute formulas for solving major problems. Yet when realistic endings are presented—a criminal escapes or good people suffer needlessly—critics attack television for not presenting young children with the ideals and values of our culture.

When looked at as a whole, then, it becomes clear that much of the controversy surrounding television programming is not rooted in television content per se but in the problems inherent in a system that communicates everything to all types of people at the same time.

As a shared environment, television tends to include some aspect of every facet of our culture. Fairy tales are followed by gritty portrayals of crime and corruption. Television preachers share the airwaves with female wrestlers. Poets and prostitutes appear on the same talk shows. Actors and journalists compete for Nielsen ratings. But there is little that is new about any of the information that is presented on television; what *is* new is that formerly segregated social arenas are blurred together. Information once shared only among people of a certain age, class, race, religion, sex, profession, or other subgroup of the culture has now been thrown into a shared, public forum —and few are wholly satisfied with the mishmash.

A substantial part of the social significance of television, therefore, may lie less in what is on television than in the very existence of television as a shared arena. Television provides the largest simultaneous perception of a message that humanity has ever experienced. Through television, Americans often gain a strange sort of communion with each other. In times of crisis—whether an assassination or a disaster—millions of Americans sit in the glow of their TV sets and watch the same material over and over again in an effort, perhaps, to find comfort, see meaning, and feel united with the other faceless viewers.

Even when video cassettes and other activities pull people away from broadcast and cable television, the shared arena is not destroyed. The knowledge of its existence functions in many ways like the knowledge of the "family home" where relatives can spontaneously gather at times of crisis or celebration. The shared arena does not have to be used every day to have a constant psychological presence.

MAJORITY CONSCIOUSNESS

The shared arena of television does not lead to instant physical integration or to social harmony. Indeed, the initial effect is increased social tension. Informational integration heightens the perception of physical, economic, and legal segregation. Television enhances our awareness of all the people we cannot be, the places we cannot go, the things we cannot possess. Through exposure to a wider world, many viewers gain a sense of being unfairly isolated in some pocket of it.

Shared experiences through television encourage members of formerly isolated and distinct groups to demand equal rights and treatment. Today's "minority consciousness," then, is something of a paradox. Many people take renewed pride in their special identity, yet the heightened consciousness develops from the ability to view one's group from the outside; that is, it is the result of no longer being fully *in* the group. The demand for full equality in roles and rights dramatizes the development of a mass "majority," a single large group whose members do not want to accept any arbitrarily imposed distinctions in roles and privileges. The diminutive connotation of the term *minority* does not seem to refer to the small number of people in the group, but rather to the limited degree of access the members feel they have to the larger society. The concept of minority as it is sometimes applied to women—the majority of the population—is meaningless in any other sense.

Ironically, many minority group members express their special desires to dissolve into the mainstream, to know what everyone else knows, to experience what everyone else experiences. When gays, blacks, Hispanics, women, the disabled, and others publicly protest for equal treatment under the law, they are not only saying: "I'm different and I'm proud of it," they are also saying, "I should be treated as if I'm the same as everyone else." As gay politician Harry Britt of San Francisco has said: "We want the same rights to happiness and success as the nongay." In this sense, many minorities proclaim their special identity in the hope of losing at least part of it.

Television makes it seem possible to have integration, but the social mechanisms are not always in place. The potential for gaining access to the male realm, for example, is much greater for some women than for others. The feminist movement has primarily advanced upper- and middle-class women—often through the hiring of lower-class women to clean house and mind children. For many segments of our society, television has raised expectations but provided few new opportunities.

The shared information environment fostered by television also does not lead to the identical behavior or attitudes among all individuals. Far from it. What is increasingly shared is a similar set of *options*. The choice of dress, hairstyle, speech pattern, profession, and general style of life is no longer as strongly linked as it once was to traditionally defined groups.

Michel Foucault argued convincingly that the membranes around prisons, hospitals, military barracks, factories, and schools thickened over several hundred years leading up to the twentieth century. Foucault described how people were increasingly separated into distant spheres in order to homogenize them into groups with single identities ("students," "workers," "prisoners," "mentally ill,"

etc.). The individuals within these groups were, in a sense, interchangeable parts. And even the distinct identities of the groups were subsumed under the larger social system of internally consistent, linearly connected, and hierarchically arranged units. While Foucault observed that modern society segregated people in their "special spheres" in order to homogenize individuals into components of a larger social machine, he did not observe the current, postmodern counterprocess. As the membranes around spatially segregated institutions become more informationally permeable, through television and other electronic media, the current trend is toward integration of all groups into a relatively common experiential sphere—with a new recognition of the special needs and idiosyncrasies of individuals. Just as there is now greater sharing of behaviors among people of different ages, different sexes, and different levels of authority, there is also greater variation in the behaviors of people of the same age, same sex, and same level of authority.

A GLOBAL MATRIX

*I*n many instances, the television arena is now international in scope. Over four hundred million people in seventy-three countries watch the Academy Awards; "Live Aid" reached 1.5 billion people in 160 countries; Eastern European countries monitor Western television; Westerners watched Romanian television as capturing the TV station became the first goal of a revolution; the world watched as Chinese students in Tiananmen Square held English protest signs in front of Western TV cameras. The shared arena of television is reinforced through worldwide phone systems, satellites, fax machines, and other electronic media.

But this larger sense of sharing with "everybody" is too wide and diffuse, too quickly changing, too insubstantial. Metaphors aside, it is not possible to experience the whole world as one's neighborhood or village. Even discounting the numerous political, economic, and cultural barriers that remain, there is a limit to the number of people with whom one can feel truly connected. Electronic sharing leads to a broader, but also a shallower, sense of "us."

The effect of this is both unifying and fractionating. Members of the whole society (and world) are growing more alike, but members of particular families, neighborhoods, and traditional groups are growing more diverse. On the macro level, the world is becoming more homogeneous, but on the micro level, individuals experience more choice, variety, and idiosyncrasy. We share more experiences with people who are thousands of miles away, even as there is a dilution of the commonality of experience with the people who are in our own houses and neighborhoods. So the wider sense of connection fostered by electronic media is, ironically, accompanied by a greater retreat to the core of the isolated self. More than ever before, the postmodern era is one in which *everyone* else seems somewhat familiar—and somewhat strange.

As traditional boundaries blur—between regions, between nations, between East and West—there is a rise in factional and ethnic violence within areas that formerly seemed relatively homogeneous. Along with increased hope for world peace, the shared arena may stimulate new types of unrest. As the threat of world war recedes, we are faced with an increase in skirmishes, riots, and terrorism. Whether the era we are now entering will ultimately be viewed as a time of unprecedented unity or a period of unprecedented chaos remains to be seen.

AS THE DIAL TURNS

DOUGLAS GOMERY

Douglas Gomery, a professor in the College of Journalism at the University of Maryland, is the former senior researcher at the Wilson Center's Media Studies Project. He is author of nine books, including Shared Pleasures *(1992), which recently earned a prize from the Theater Library Association.*

I t was a defining moment in American history, albeit one run over and over, like an episode of "Star Trek." Into the tidy living room of a young family's suburban home, usually just days before Christmas, came the electronic marvel. The old mahogany radio set, already seeming a bit antique, was shoved into a corner, and two hefty deliverymen struggled to position the bulky new console across from the couch, between the easy chairs. Everyone gathered around as the first test pattern came on. Then the fun began—perhaps with giggling children on "Howdy Doody" or the Top 40 beat of "Dick Clark's American Bandstand" or the stars on "Ed Sullivan's Toast of the Town" or the magnificent coronation of Queen Elizabeth II. Thus was a new age born.

Pictures flowing through the air. That miracle had been much sought after and anticipated since movies and radio transformed American popular culture during the first quarter of the 20th century. And like those two earlier marvels of mass communication, and with many times more power, television has so refashioned and reshaped our lives that it is hard to imagine what life was like before it.

During the Great Depression and World War II, families gathered in crowded city apartments or in the parlors of distant farms to listen to the radio. But TV was instantly and unalterably linked with midcentury America's rising suburban ideal. Indeed, certain TV offerings, such as "Ozzie and Harriet," became synonymous with the ideal. Along with closely cropped lawns, two cars in the driveway, and a single earner so well paid that no one else needed to work, TV became a symbol of the "good life" in modern America.

The TV boom was delayed first by the war and then for several years after 1948 by what might be called "technical difficulties." By 1948, the number of stations in the United States had reached 48, the cities served 23, and sales of TV sets had passed sales of radios. Coaxial cables also made possible fledgling networks, relaying live shows (there was no tape then) from the East to the Midwest. But as more and more stations went on the air it became clear that the Federal Communications Commission (FCC) had not allowed enough geographic separation between stations to prevent serious interference. The agency froze TV-station allotments and redrew the maps. It was only on April 14, 1952—with the FCC's Sixth Report and Order—that TV as we know it first began to flow to all sections of the United States.

So rapid and complete was TV's friendly takeover of the American imagination that when Lucille Ball gave birth to her second son the "same" night in January 1953 that her Lucy Ricardo character on "I Love Lucy" gave birth to "Little Ricky," it caused a national sensation, including an article in *Life* and a cover story in *TV Guide,* itself newly born.

U biquity may be the medium's leading characteristic. In 1950 far less than 10 percent of Americans owned sets. Those were folks lucky enough to have the $500 that a black-and-white receiver cost at a time when $3,000 was considered a good yearly salary and $5,000 would buy a splendid Cape Cod in Levittown. But TV's allure was powerful. By 1955 about two-thirds of the nation's households had a set; by the end of the 1950s there was hardly a home in the nation without one. By 1961, when Newton Minow, the newly appointed chairman of the FCC, proclaimed television a "vast wasteland," there were more homes in the United States with TV than with indoor plumbing. In less than a generation, the TV set had gone from being an expensive, somewhat experimental gadget to a home appliance considered more indispensable than the toaster or washing machine. With the possible exception of the videocassette recorder (VCR) in the 1980s, no other electronic gadget has been adapted so widely and with such alacrity.

T oday, 99 percent of all households possess at least one TV, and most have two or more. There are nearly 200 million sets in use. More American homes have TVs than have telephones. (One study of the tiny minority of people who spurn TV found that the archetypal naysayer is a university professor of literature, wedded professionally to the printed word.) We take them to the beach, plug them into our automobiles, and even strap them on our wrists when we go jogging. Now a company called Virtual Vision promises to make TV even more omnipresent. Its $900 wraparound TV eyeglasses can be worn anywhere; they project an image that appears to float about 10 feet in front of the wearer.

In the space of only a few decades, watching TV seems to have become one of life's essential activities—along with eating, sleeping, and working. TV has become the Great American Companion. Two-thirds of Americans regularly watch television while eating dinner. The A. C. Nielsen Company, which monitors sets in a carefully selected nationwide sample of 4,000 households, regularly reports that the TV is on about seven and a half hours a day—virtually all of the time remaining if one subtracts eight hours for sleep and eight hours for work. Collectively, the nation tunes in to a staggering 250 billion hours per year. If one assumes that the average hourly wage is $10, that time is worth *$2.5 trillion*. If we could collect just $1 per hour we could wipe out the yearly federal budget deficit.

Figuring out who is actually watching the tube and when he or she is doing so is tricky. Nielsen's method shows when a set is on and what channel it is tuned to, but many studies have found that during much of the time the TV is on, no one is watching. Researchers have developed People Meters to try to determine who is watching, but these gadgets rely on viewers to "punch in" when they sit down in front of the set and "punch out" when they leave—hardly a foolproof method. As best as researchers can determine, the average person "watches" about four hours per day, varying by season (more in winter, less in summer), age (kids and senior citizens view the most), and race (African Americans and Hispanics watch more than whites).* When are the most Americans watching? Prime time (8 to 11 P.M., Eastern Standard Time) on Sunday nights in the depths of winter.

TV is one of the things that bring us together as a nation. Thanks to television, the Super Bowl has become our greatest national spectacle, watched in at least 40 million homes. (By contrast, Ross Perot's first "town meeting," which was wildly successful compared to other political broadcasts, was watched in only 11 million homes.) Such peak moments generate mind-boggling revenues. Advertisements during the 1993 Super Bowl, which NBC sold out a month before kickoff, cost in the neighborhood of $28,000 per second. Nevertheless, because virtually the entire nation assembles to watch this single game in January, advertisers such as Pepsi, Budweiser, and Gillette gladly ante up, and others have found

---

*African Americans and Hispanics watch more TV than whites because they have lower incomes, on average. TV is, after all, just about the cheapest form of entertainment available. Only as one gets richer can one afford the luxury of fancy meals, nights at the theater, and other forms of diversion.

> ## TV in America
>
> There are more TV sets in the United States than there are bathtubs or showers. There are more American homes with television than with indoor plumbing.
>
> •
>
> An average American living to age 65, at present levels of TV viewing, will have spent nine years of his life watching TV.
>
> •
>
> When children aged four to six were surveyed, "Which do you like better, TV or your daddy?" 54 percent said "TV."
>
> •
>
> Why is there no Channel 1 on your television set?
> The FCC took the frequency away from TV broadcasters in May 1948 for use by the military.
>
> •
>
> Twenty-seven million people watched the first televised presidential inauguration of Dwight Eisenhower on January 20, 1953. It was upstaged, though, the night before, when 44 million people tuned in for the birth of "Little Ricky" Ricardo on "I Love Lucy."
>
> •
>
> A 1979 Roper Poll of 3,001 couples showed that the leading cause of marital disputes was disagreement about which TV shows to watch.
>
> •
>
> If you were guilty of every crime shown on American TV in just one week, you'd go to jail for 1,600 years. Unless you had Perry Mason for your attorney.
>
> Reprinted from *The Official Couch Potato Handbook*, copyright © 1982, 1983, 1988 by Jack Mingo. Published by Last Gasp Publications, San Francisco, Calif. Reprinted with permission.

it a perfect showcase for major new products. It was during Super Bowl XVIII in January 1984 that Apple introduced the world to the Macintosh personal computer. (The Los Angeles Raiders beat the Washington Redskins, 38 to 9.)

TV is a multibillion-dollar business. Sales of new sets alone come to about $7 billion per year. Advertising revenues amount to more than $30 billion, still collected in large part by the major broadcast networks—ABC, NBC, CBS, and, since 1986, Fox. Prime-time ads generate some $4 billion, and billions more come from morning, soap opera, news, and late-night offerings. Cable TV in 1992 received ad revenues in excess of $3 billion, and another $2 billion came from subscribers who paid for the privilege of watching its millions of advertisements.

Buying and selling television shows was a $25-billion business last year, principally done by the major Hollywood studios. TV shows, from the latest episodes of "Roseanne" to 1960s-vintage series such as "Bewitched," are also one of the nation's biggest exports. If once it was said that the sun never set on the British Empire, now it never sets on "I Love Lucy." The U.S. trade in sitcoms and soap operas shaves some $4 billion per year off America's chronic trade deficit, a contribution exceeded only by that of the aerospace industry.

The TV industry itself is split in two. As a result of antitrust policy decisions during the Nixon administration, the networks are barred from owning Hollywood studios, and the studios are barred from owning networks—with one famous exception. To promote the development of a fourth network, the FCC in 1986 allowed Fox to create a limited TV network while owning a major Hollywood studio, Twentieth Century-Fox. As a rule, the networks can only show (not own) TV's valuable series. These complex rules are now being phased out and should be gone by the end of the century. Then we are likely to see a spate of mergers joining Hollywood studios and the TV networks.

Despite all the hype and hoopla that attend its doings, TV is a mouse among industries, a relatively small collection of enterprises whose earnings, even if lumped together, are still smaller than those of either Exxon or General Motors alone. TV's cultural influence likewise tends to be exaggerated. The medium is so pervasive that whenever critics confront a vexing social problem, they blame TV. Crime on the rise? It must be TV's fault. Scholastic Aptitude Test scores dropping? Blame the boob tube. Now it is said that TV-induced passivity is literally killing us. A recent study in the *American Journal of Health Promotion* concluded that couch potatoes are twice as likely to develop high levels of serum cholesterol as those who rarely watch television.

Our anxiety about TV increases as the nation changes. More and more children in this divorce-ridden society watch TV unsupervised. "Behold every parent's worst nightmare: the six-year-old TV addict," says *Time* magazine—who takes Bart Simpson as a role model, one might add.

Violence on television is probably the public's main concern. A recent Times-Mirror survey found that 80 percent of adults think that television violence is harmful to society. More than 1,000 studies have been carried out to search for links between TV viewing and violent behavior. Under pressure from Congress, the networks recently agreed to provide warnings before their most violent offerings. One mother declared in the *Washington Post* recently: "I find myself curiously unmoved by television producers covering themselves with a First Amendment flag. As far as I'm concerned, they have abrogated their rights to freedom of speech by being so resolutely unconcerned about the impact of what they put on television. That includes the 100,000 acts of violence . . . that the average child will have watched by the end of elementary school."

In 1992 the American Psychological Association concluded that televised violence can sometimes stir aggressive behavior in certain kinds of disturbed viewers. Most researchers probably would concur. But this is a narrow case. Whether video violence has a significant impact on the general public is quite another matter, and the pile of studies published so far has not produced a consensus. It is clear that heavy viewers of televised violence are more likely to engage in aggressive behavior than are light viewers, all other things being equal. But it may be that people with a predisposition toward violence are more likely to watch action/adventure programming to begin with, not that watching makes them become violent.

To regard some of the more extreme claims about the impact of TV skeptically is not to dismiss the challenge posed by the medium. By the time an average American child enters the first grade, she or he has seen at least 5,000 hours of TV and by all accounts has fallen in love with the medium. New video diversions soon appear, such as Nintendo (which has sold an astonishing 25 million machines in the United States). According to a 1991 National Assessment of Educational Progress study, nearly three of every four fourth graders admit to watching more than three hours of TV every day. By the end of

high school, teens have seen some 19,000 hours of TV—and an equal number of televised homicides. We do not need hundreds of studies to know that the time children spend spaced out in front of the tube is time they are not devoting to homework or baseball or daydreaming or any number of other more worthwhile activities.

There are legitimate fears about the effects of TV on young children. But once children learn how to use TV—how to pick acceptable shows to watch, for example, or to substitute videotapes when nothing good is on—only excess seems to prove harmful. Putting a positive spin on this, critics such as Ellen Wartella, dean of the College of Communication at the University of Texas, argue that the accumulated "effects research" suggests that classes in "visual literacy" for the young are a better bet than more radical measures to control what is aired.

Technology, meanwhile, is rapidly changing the very nature of the television challenge. In the very near future, for example, it even promises a partial solution—a technological fix—to the problem of children's excessive TV watching. Soon consumers will be able to purchase digital TV sets that can be selectively "deprogrammed," allowing adults to block certain programs from their children's eyes and ears.

For 30 years after the FCC's landmark

Sixth Report and Order, TV changed very little. During the last 10 years, however, it has been transformed. Roughly two of three households are now connected to cable television, and that proportion is steadily growing. Cable households have access, on average, to 30 networks rather than the traditional three. A generation ago, five of six viewers tuned into one of the Big Three networks; today only three of six do. The medium, in other words, is now more diverse. And we have changed not only what we watch but the way we watch it. Armed with remote controls, another relatively new piece of technology, viewers now "graze" or "surf" across cable's never-ending channels, from all-documentary formats (Discovery) to channels aimed at African Americans (Black Entertainment Network), from an alphabet soup of movie channels (AMC, TNT, TBS, and HBO) to all-weather and all-consumer news. We are promised all-crime, fashion, military, book, and (horror of horrors!) game-show channels in the near future. We can even shop by cable TV—and we do so to the tune of $2.2 billion annually. Soon, in all likelihood, we will do our banking and pay our bills through TV as well.

It was not only cable that overthrew the Big Three and transformed the TV experience. During the 1980s, the VCR took America by storm, occupying only one of every five households in 1985 but four of five today. Last year Americans rented an amazing 3.5 billion videos, which works out to an average of one a week for each household. Videotape rentals are now a $12-billion industry.

TV Around the World

The Japanese watch more TV than anyone (U.S. viewers are a close second). In Japan, the national TV craze is called ichioko-so-hakuchi-ka or "the complete idiotization of 100 million people."

•

Iceland, not generally considered a repressive country, has a TV-free day every Thursday "to reduce disruption to family life."

•

Sesame Street is so popular in Pago Pago that the government once considered naming the island's main street after it.

•

Bonanza is the most widely syndicated TV series. It has 250 million viewers in 85 countries.

•

A UNESCO Study found that TV-owners worldwide sleep an average of 13 minutes less per night than non-owners.

•

TV was banned in South Africa until 1975. The government was afraid it might threaten the precarious apartheid system there. Even as late as 1988, TV sets cost double what they would elsewhere to keep them out of the homes of black citizens.

1. LIVING WITH MEDIA

Impossible as it may seem, more technological change is coming. By the end of the century we will have digital high-definition television with movie-quality images, and in the next century, if not sooner, we will acquire the ability to summon (for a fee) an electronic newspaper on our screens and search through the biggest libraries in the world for information.

Already, these far-reaching changes have injected an undemocratic element into what was once in many ways a most democratic medium. Everybody could watch Neil Armstrong walk on the moon or Richard Nixon tender his resignation. That was because a TV set by the early 1970s cost only a third as much as the first '50s sets had. Cable TV offers no such bargains. The average monthly bill is $30 and climbing, despite recent congressional attempts to roll back prices. As a result, poor Americans subscribe to cable at half the rate of their wealthier counterparts, going without a whole slew of information and entertainment, from C-SPAN to local-access TV to ESPN. Many also go without VCRs. Add in the cost of videotape rentals and new gadgets (such as VCR Plus) and watching TV can suddenly become a $1,000-per-year-habit.

It is typical of the American attitude toward TV that, much as we may criticize the medium, we are also troubled by the fact that some Americans do not have equal access to it. Television has become the greatest entertainment and information machine of all time. Love it or leave it, we all—rich and poor, the powerful and the underclass—use it to educate ourselves in various ways and to define a common culture. Nielsen's Top 10 tells us what is "in." "Murphy Brown" elicits the wrath of former Vice President Dan Quayle. "Monday Night Football" defines the quintessential male-bonding night at the bar. "Jeopardy" teases Ph.D. candidates away from their dissertations to see if they are really smart. "Sixty Minutes," the single show virtually everyone agrees is entertaining and enlightening, has become as a consequence the most popular program in TV's history—and surely the one we all hope never to be caught on.

Television is like the fabled uncle who came to dinner and never left: It is difficult finally to decide how we feel about it. In one recent survey people were asked how much money it would take to convince them to give up TV for a year. Almost half refused for anything less than $1 million! After a half-century-long love-hate relationship, we are just not sure if the story of TV in America will have a happy ending. But we do know that TV—probably in some advanced version we have yet to imagine, and surely not as all-consuming or as controlling as its current critics believe it to be—will be forever with us.

THE TROUBLE WITH TELEVISION

Marie Winn

Marie Winn has written 12 books for parents and children, including Children Without Childhood *(Pantheon Books, 1983). She has two children and one television set, which is only used on special occasions.*

Of all the wonders of modern technology that have transformed family life during the last century, television stands alone as a universal source of parental anxiety. Few parents worry about how the electric light or the automobile or the telephone might alter their children's development. But most parents do worry about TV.

Parents worry most of all about the programs their children watch. If only these weren't so violent, so sexually explicit, so cynical, so *unsuitable*, if only they were more innocent, more educational, more *worthwhile*.

Imagine what would happen if suddenly, by some miracle, the only programs available on all channels at all hours of day and night were delightful, worthwhile shows that children love and parents wholeheartedly approve. Would this eliminate the nagging anxiety about television that troubles so many parents today?

For most families, the answer is no. After all, if programs were the only problem, there would be an obvious solution: turn the set off. The fact that parents leave the sets on even when they are distressed about programs reveals that television serves a number of purposes that have nothing to do with the programs on the screen.

Great numbers of parents today see television as a way to make child-rearing less burdensome. In the absence of Mother's Helper (a widely used nineteenth-century patent medicine that contained a hefty dose of the narcotic laudanum), there is nothing that keeps children out of trouble as reliably as "plugging them in."

Television serves families in other ways: as a time-filler ("You have nothing to do? Go watch TV"), a tranquilizer ("When the kids come home from school they're so keyed up that they need to watch for a while to simmer down"), a problem solver ("Kids, stop fighting. It's time for your program"), a procrastination device ("I'll just watch one more program before I do my homework"), a punishment ("If you don't stop teasing your little sister, no TV for a week"), and a reward ("If you get an A on your composition you can watch an extra hour of TV"). For parents and children alike it serves as an avoidance mechanism ("I can't discuss that now—I'm watching my program"), a substitute friend ("I need the TV on for company"), and an escape mechanism ("I'll turn on the TV and try to forget my worries").

Most families recognize the wonderful services that television has to offer. Few, however, are aware that there is a heavy price to pay. Here are eight significant ways television wields a negative influence on children and family life:

1. TV Keeps Families from Doing Other Things

The primary danger of the television screen lies not so much in the behavior it produces—although there is danger there—as in the behavior it prevents: the talks, the games, the family festivities and arguments through which much of the child's learning takes place and through which his character is formed. Turning on the television set can turn off the process that transforms children into people.[1]

Urie Bronfenbrenner's words to a conference of educators almost two decades ago focus on what sociologists call the "reduction effects" of television—its power to preempt and often eliminate a whole range of other activities and experiences. While it is easy to see that for a child who watches 32 hours of television each week, the reduction effects are significant—obviously that child would be spending 32 hours doing *something* else if there were no television available—Bronfenbrenner's view remains an uncommon and even an eccentric one.

Today the prevailing focus remains on improving programs rather than on reducing the amount of time children view. Perhaps parents have come to depend so deeply on television that they are afraid even to contemplate the idea that something might be wrong with their use of television, not merely with the programs on the air.

2. TV Is a Hidden Competitor for All Other Activities

. . . Almost everybody knows that there are better, more fulfilling things for a family to do than watch television. And yet, if viewing statistics are to be believed, most families spend most of their family time together in front of the flickering screen.

Some social critics believe that television has come to dominate family life because today's parents are too selfish and narcissistic to put in the effort that reading aloud or playing games or even just talking to each other would require. But this harsh judgment doesn't take into consideration the extraordinary power of television. In reality, many parents crave a richer family life and are eager to work at achieving this goal. The trouble is that their children seem to reject all those fine family alternatives in favor of television.

To be sure, the fact that children are likely to choose watching television over having a story read aloud to them, or playing with the stamp collection, or going out for a walk in the park does not mean that watching television is actually more entertaining or gratifying than any of these activities. It does mean, however, that watching television is easier.

In most families, television is always there as an easy and safe competitor. When another activity is proposed, it had better be *really special;* otherwise it is in danger of being rejected. The parents who have unsuccessfully proposed a game or a story end up feeling rejected as well. They are unaware that television is still affecting their children's enjoyment of other activities, even when the set is off.

Reading aloud is a good example of how this competition factor works. Virtually every child expert hails reading aloud as a delightful family pastime. Educators encourage it as an important way for parents to help their children develop a love for reading and improve their reading skills. Too often, however, the fantasy of the happy family gathered around to listen to a story is replaced by a different reality: "Hey kids, I've got a great book to read aloud. How about it?" says the parent. "Not now, Dad, we want to watch 'The Cosby Show,' " say the kids.

It is for this reason that one of the most important *Don'ts* suggested by Jim Trelease in his valuable guide *The Read-Aloud Handbook* is the following:

> Don't try to compete with television. If you say, "Which do you want, a story or TV?" they will usually choose the latter. That is like saying to a 9-year-old, "Which do you want, vegetables or a donut?" Since *you* are the adult, *you* choose. "The television goes off at eight-thirty in this house. If you want a story before bed, that's fine. If not, that's fine too. But no television after eight-thirty." But don't let books appear to be responsible for depriving children of viewing time.[2]

3. TV Allows Kids to Grow Up Less Civilized

. . . It would be a mistake to assume that the basic child-rearing philosophy of parents of the past was stricter than that of parents today. American parents, in fact, have always had a tendency to be more egalitarian in their family life than, say, European parents. For confirmation, one has only to read the accounts of eighteenth- or nineteenth-century European travelers who comment on the freedom and audacity of American children as compared to their European counterparts. Why then do parents today seem far less in control of their children than parents not only of the distant past but even of a mere generation ago? Television has surely played a part in this change.

Today's parents universally use television to keep their children occupied when they have work to do or when they need a break from child care. They can hardly imagine how parents survived before television. Yet parents *did* survive in the years before TV. Without television, they simply had to use different survival strategies to be able to cook dinner, talk on the telephone, clean house, or do whatever work needed to be done in peace.

Most of these strategies fell into the category social scientists refer to as "socialization"—the civilizing process that transforms small creatures intent upon the speedy gratification of their own instinctive needs and desires into successful members of a society in which those individual needs and desires must often be left ungratified, at least temporarily, for the good of the group.

What were these "socialization" strategies parents used to use? Generally, they went something like this: "Mommy's got to cook dinner now (make a phone call, talk to Mrs. Jones, etc.). Here are some blocks (some clay, a pair of blunt scissors and a magazine, etc.). Now you have to be a good girl and play by yourself for a while and not interrupt Mommy." Nothing very complicated.

But in order to succeed, a certain firmness was absolutely necessary, and parents knew it, even if asserting authority was not their preferred way of dealing with children. They knew they had to work steadily at "training" their child to behave in ways that allowed them to do those normal things that needed to be done. Actually, achieving this goal was not terribly difficult. It took a little effort to set up certain patterns—perhaps a few days or a week of patient but firm insistence that the child behave in certain ways at certain times. But parents of the past didn't agonize about whether this was going to be psychologically damaging. They simply had no choice. Certain things simply *had to be done,* and so parents stood their ground against children's natural struggle to gain attention and have their own way.

Obviously it is easier to get a break from child care by setting the child in front of the television set than to teach the child to play alone for certain periods of time. In the first case, the child is immediately amused (or hypnotized) by the program, and the parent has time to pursue other activities. Accustoming children to play alone, on the other hand, requires day-after-day perseverance, and neither parent nor child enjoys the process very much.

But there is an inevitable price to pay when a parent never has to be firm and authoritative, never has to use that "I mean business" tone of voice: socialization, that crucial process so necessary for the child's future as a successful member of a family, a school, a community, and a nation is accomplished less completely. A very different kind of relationship between parent and child is established, one in which the parent has little control over the child's behavior.

The consequences of a large-scale reduction in child socialization are not hard to see in contemporary society: an increased number of parents who feel helpless and out of control of their children's lives and behavior, who haven't established the parental authority that might protect their children from involvement in such dangerous activities as drug experimentation, or from the physical and emotional consequences of precocious sexual relationships.

4. Television Takes the Place of Play

. . . Once small children become able to concentrate on television and make some sense of it—usually around the end of their second year of life—it's not hard to understand why parents eagerly set their children before the flickering screen: taking care of toddlers is hard! The desperate and tired parent can't imagine *not* taking advantage of this marvelous new way to get a break. In consequence, before they are three years old, the opportunities of active play and exploration are hugely diminished for a great number of children—to be replaced by the hypnotic gratification of television viewing.

Yet many parents overlook an important fact: children who are suddenly able to sustain attention for more than a few minutes on the TV screen have clearly moved into a new stage of cognitive development—their ability to concentrate on TV is a sign of it. There are therefore many other new activities, far more developmentally valuable, that the child is now ready for. These are the simple forms of play that most small children enjoyed in the pre-television era: cutting and pasting, coloring and drawing, building with blocks, playing games of make-believe with toy soldiers or animals or dolls. But the parent who begins to fill in the child's time with television at this point is unlikely to discover these other potential capabilities.

It requires a bit of effort to establish new play routines—more effort, certainly, than plunking a child in front of a television screen, but not really a great deal. It requires a bit of patience to get the child accustomed to a new kind of play—play on his own—but again, not a very great deal. It also demands some firmness and perseverance. And a small amount of equipment (art materials, blocks, etc.), most of it cheap, if not free, and easily available.

But the benefits for both parent and child of *not* taking the easiest way out at this point by using television to ease the inevitable child-care burdens will vastly outweigh the temporary difficulties parents face in filling children's time with less passive activities. For the parent, the need for a bit more firmness leads to an easier, more controlled parent-child relationship. For the child, those play routines established in early childhood will develop into lifelong interests and hobbies, while the skills ac-

quired in the course of play lead to a sense of accomplishment that could never have been achieved if the child had spent those hours "watching" instead of "doing."

5. TV Makes Children Less Resourceful

. . . Many parents who welcome the idea of turning off the TV and spending more time with the family are still worried that without TV they would constantly be on call as entertainers for their children. Though they *want* to play games and read aloud to their children, the idea of having to replace television minute-for-minute with worthwhile family activities is daunting. They remember thinking up all sorts of things to do when they were kids. But their own kids seem different, less resourceful, somehow. When there's nothing to do, these parents observe regretfully, their kids seem unable to come up with anything to do besides turning on the TV.

One father, for example, says, "When I was a kid, we were always thinking up things to do, projects and games. We certainly never whined to our parents, 'I have nothing to do!' " He compares this with his own children today: "They're simply lazy. If someone doesn't entertain them, they'll happily sit there watching TV all day."

There is one word for this father's disappointment: unfair. It is as if he were disappointed in them for not reading Greek though they have never studied the language. He deplores his children's lack of inventiveness, as if the ability to play were something innate that his children are missing. In fact, while the *tendency* to play is built into the human species, the actual *ability* to play—to imagine, to invent, to elaborate on reality in a playful way—and the ability to gain fulfillment from it, these are skills that have to be learned and developed.

Such disappointment, however, is not only unjust, it is also destructive. Sensing their parents' disappointment, children come to believe that they are, indeed, lacking something, and that this makes them less worthy of admiration and respect. Giving children the opportunity to develop new resources, to enlarge their horizons and discover the pleasures of doing things on their own is, on the other hand, a way to help children develop a confident feeling about themselves as capable and interesting people.

It is, of course, ironic that many parents avoid a TV Turn-Off out of fear that their children won't know what to do with themselves in the absence of television. It is television watching itself that has allowed them to grow up without learning how to be resourceful and television watching that keeps them from developing those skills that would enable them to fill in their empty time enjoyably.

6. TV Has a Negative Effect on Children's Physical Fitness

. . . Not long ago a study that attracted wide notice in the popular press found a direct relationship between the incidence of obesity in children and time spent viewing television. For the 6–11 age group, "children who watched more television experienced a greater prevalence of obesity, or superobesity, than children watching less television. No significant differences existed between obese, superobese, and nonobese children with respect to the number of friends, their ability to get along with friends, or time spent with friends, alone, listening to the radio, reading, or in leisure time activities," wrote the researchers. As for teenagers, only 10 percent of those teenagers who watched TV an hour or less a day were obese as compared to 20 percent of those who watched more than five hours daily. With most other variables eliminated, why should this be? The researchers provided a commonsense explanation: Dedicated TV watchers are fatter because they eat more and exercise less while glued to the tube.[3]

7. TV Has a Negative Effect on Children's School Achievement

. . . It is difficult if not impossible to prove that excessive television viewing has a direct negative effect on young children's cognitive development, though by using cautionary phrases such as "TV will turn your brain to mush" parents often express an instinctive belief that this is true.

Nevertheless an impressive number of research studies demonstrate beyond any reasonable doubt that excessive television viewing has an adverse effect on children's achievement in school. One study, for instance, shows that younger children who watch more TV have lower scores in reading and overall achievement tests than those who watch less TV.[4]

Another large-scale study, conducted when television was first introduced as a mass medium in Japan, found that as families acquired television sets children showed a decline in both reading skills and homework time.

But it does not require costly research projects to demonstrate that television viewing affects children's school work adversely. Interviews with teachers who have participated in TV Turn-Offs provide confirmation as well.

Almost without exception, these teachers testify that the quality of homework brought into class during the No-TV period was substantially better. As a fifth grade teacher noted: "There was a real difference in the homework I was getting during No-TV Week. Kids who usually do a good job on homework did a terrific job. Some kids who rarely hand in assignments on time now brought in surprisingly good and thorough work. When I brought this to the class's attention during discussion time they said, 'Well, there was nothing else to do!' "

8. Television Watching May Be a Serious Addiction

. . . A lot of people who have nothing but bad things to say about TV, calling it the "idiot box" and the "boob tube," nevertheless spend quite a lot of their free time watching television. People are often apologetic, even shamefaced about their television viewing, saying things like, "I only watch the news," or "I only turn the set on for company," or "I only watch when I'm too tired to do anything else" to explain the sizable number of hours they devote to TV.

In addition to anxiety about their own viewing patterns, many parents recognize that their children watch too much television and that it is having an adverse effect on their development and yet they don't take any effective action to change the situation.

Why is there so much confusion, ambivalence, and self-deception connected with television viewing? One explanation is that great numbers of television viewers are to some degree addicted to the *experience* of watching television. The confusion and ambivalence they reveal about television may then be recognized as typical reactions of an addict unwilling to face an addiction or unable to get rid of it.

Most people find it hard to consider television viewing a serious addiction. Addictions to tobacco or alcohol, after all, are known to cause life-threatening diseases—lung cancer or cirrhosis of the liver. Drug addiction leads to dangerous behavioral aberrations—violence and crime. Meanwhile, the worst physiological consequences of television addiction seem to be a possible decline in overall physical fitness, and an increased incidence of obesity.

It is in its psychosocial consequences, especially its effects on relationships and family life, that television watching may be as damaging as chemical addiction. We all know the terrible toll alcoholism or drug addiction takes on the families of addicts. Is it possible that television watching has a similarly destructive potential for family life?

Most of us are at least dimly aware of the addictive power of television through our own experiences with the medium: our compulsive involvement with the tube too often keeps us from talking to each other, from doing things together, from working and learning and getting involved in community affairs. The hours we spend viewing prove to be curiously unfulfilling. We end up feeling depressed, though the program we've been watching was a comedy. And yet we cannot seem to turn the set off, or even *not* turn it on in the first place. Doesn't this sound like an addiction?

NOTES

1. Urie Bronfenbrenner, "Who Cares for America's Children?" Address presented at the Conference of the National Association for the Education of Young Children, 1970.
2. Jim Trelease, *The Read-Aloud Handbook.* Penguin, 1985.
3. W. H. Dietz and S. L. Gortmaker, "Do We Fatten Our Children at the Television Set? Obesity and Television Viewing in Children and Adolescents." *Pediatrics* 75 (1985).
4. S. G. Burton, J. M. Calonico, and D. R. McSeveney, "Effects of Preschool Watching on First-Grade Children." *Journal of Communications* 29:3 (1979).

TV as Boob Tube: Bad Rap

Bennett Daviss

Television & Families

Bennett Daviss is a freelance writer living in New England.

The image is etched so deeply in our imaginations that it's almost become archetypal: A child sits, mouth agape, transfixed by a television set, accepting and absorbing everything that flickers over the screen. He doesn't hear the telephone ring; he doesn't hear his mother call him for supper. He sits helpless, addicted to a medium that is destroying his ability to concentrate, shriveling his imagination, and leaving him incapable of reading, homework, or any other activity that demands complex and sustained mental involvement. The child's mind is being shaped to fit the tube.

It's a powerful and frightening image, one that frames our anxious relationship with the world's most potent communications tool. But that image is based on nothing more than anecdotes, a few well-publicized surmises, and a handful of inconclusive research studies, many of them flawed. That's the conclusion of an exhaustive report sponsored by the U.S. Department of Education—the most thorough review ever undertaken of almost 40 years' research into the effects of television on children's mental development. Its verdict: there's no real evidence to support the popular idea that television makes kids dull. But there's also none to prove that it doesn't.

"It's a mistake, based on the evidence so far, to condemn the medium," says Dr. Daniel Anderson, professor of psychology at the University of Massachusetts at Amherst and a 16-year student of the effects of television on children. At the request of then-Secretary of Education William Bennett, Anderson and graduate student Patricia Collins spent nearly two years sifting through 165 studies from around the world and summarizing their findings in *The Impact on Children's Education: Television's Influence on Cognitive Development,* published in April 1988. "If the claims of the critics are true," Anderson says, "the effects of television are akin to those of lead poisoning. At this point, though, we don't think an alarm should sound over the influence of the medium—the idea that, in itself, watching television is a harmful thing. People have pushed that idea, but any convincing evidence is simply lacking. In some cases, alarmists' claims are flatly contradicted. In some areas of concern, there is no body of evidence; in others, the research that has been done just isn't very good."

Anderson cites two key wellsprings of the myth that television necessarily harms children's mental development. "First and foremost," he says, "in the early and mid-1970s several popular books were written taking a negative view of television. They were based on very little hard evidence, but they were convincingly written and they had a great deal of influence. One called *The Plug-In Drug* did more than any other to establish the idea that television is, in and of itself, a harmful medium." The book, which has survived more than a dozen printings and is still influential, marshals anecdotal evidence and conjectures from experts to argue that viewing creates "a changed state

of consciousness" and transforms children into "television zombies." Author Marie Winn implies that the small screen bears substantial blame for social ills ranging from falling SAT scores to the drug epidemic.

"The deeper reason," Anderson adds, "is that this society's intellectual elite has always been suspicious of popular media, even though that view hasn't been supported by research. Every mass medium popular with children has been blamed for the problems of childhood—dime novels, comic books, movies, radio, television, and video games. Our local newspaper ran an editorial in the early 1800s declaring that children should only read geography and the Bible; novels were thought to weaken their moral fiber."

Since his report was published nearly 18 months ago, Anderson has had some direct experience with myth-making. His study circulated quietly among scholars and administrators for several months until the *Washington Post* printed an article about it last fall. Based on the *Post*'s piece, the Associated Press published a national wire story that focused on a single sentence from Anderson's summary: "There is no evidence that homework done during television viewing is of lower quality than homework done in silence." According to Anderson, the AP article gave readers the impression that his paper "was promoting the idea that kids should do their homework in front of the television set, which was a complete misunderstanding of what we were saying. Newspapers wrote editorials denouncing us, and I got all sorts of angry letters." Stunned by such erroneous reports, Anderson took to the media to detail the ways in which his study exposes the seven most common misconceptions about television.

First, the report says, "Despite popular stereotypes of children just sitting and staring at the television, it is common for children to engage in other activities while viewing." Researchers find that kids typically look away from the television screen more than 100 times an hour to play, talk, read, eat, do their schoolwork, primp, or nap. "Observations of children spending time with television do not conform to the popular descriptions of the 'zombie' viewer," Anderson states. He points to several studies in which "the child is always seen as a passive recipient who is 'controlled' by factors such as rapid cutting, changes in color, and movement." Typically, the studies describe children as "fixated" and portray them as "involuntary" viewers. Anderson dismisses the claims: "Systematic research has not verified these notions."

Second, he takes on the question of alertness, attacking the kind of generalizations made, for example, in Kate Moody's 1980 *Growing Up On Television*. The author wrote, "Television does not arouse active attention; rather, TV viewing suppresses it." Anderson discloses that her evidence supporting the judgment "is anecdotal and is based on interviews with . . . 'experts' including . . . other journalists, a hypnotist . . . and a botanist." Actually, most of the studies on alertness reveal that kids are quite involved in the shows they watch. A 1987 report, for example, found that five-year-olds watching *Sesame Street* recalled 92 percent of the material that adults considered key in understanding the stories. Other studies discovered that many of those 100 or more looks away from the television each hour are used to speculate with family members about characters' motives and what turns the story might take—hardly evidence of "suppressed" attention. Writes Anderson: "Television viewing is, in many ways, as cognitively active as reading."

Third, Anderson tackles the notion of "overstimulation." Both Winn's and Moody's books quote the renowned pediatrician T. Berry Brazleton's claim that "television creates an environment that overwhelms and assaults the child" with rapidly shifting images, flashes of light and color, and so on. Most children, Brazleton says, cope with such over excitement by dulling their minds. However, the theory holds, some don't. In the April 1976 *Journal of American Psychiatry,* physician Mathew Dumont writes, ". . . the constant shifting of visual frames in television is related to the hyperkinetic syndrome. . . . the hyperactive child is attempting to recapture the dynamic quality of the television screen by rapidly changing his perceptual orientation. . . ."

Anderson aims special scorn at one of the most often-cited studies of television's complicity in creating hyperactive kids. In the prestigious *Journal of Communication* in October 1975, psychologist Dr. Werner Halpern published a paper he called "Turned-On Toddlers," in which he claimed that hyperactivity among a group of two-year-olds was "directly traceable to *Sesame Street.*" Unfortunately, Halpern didn't bother to explain how, or offer any quantifiable data or controls. "The paper is completely inadequate in a scientific sense," Anderson laments, "but it got a tremendous amount of publicity and is cited in virtually all popular books about the effects of television. It was a really dumb paper, but it gave the whole idea a scientific veneer.

Fourth, Anderson vanquishes the idea that the time kids spend in front of television is stolen from more valuable and constructive pursuits. After reviewing relevant research, Anderson was able to state that "there is no consistent or strong evidence that television viewing displaces valuable cognitive activities." Most frequently, television-watching claims time from radio, comic books, and the movies, none of which have "been demonstrated to be more intellectually valuable than TV viewing.

"Everyone seems to imagine that if kids weren't watching television, they'd be doing their math homework or solving brainteasers," he adds. "Actually, they're just as likely to be out behind the garage smoking cigarettes or sitting on the lawn poking holes in the ground. There's a tendency to think about the negative effects of television without putting television in context."

The one "valuable cognitive activity" television may lessen is reading. Research in Canada and El Salvador indicates that children learn reading faster and more efficiently when their homes or towns don't have television. Other research shows that children who are light viewers tend to have better vocabularies than those who watch more TV, and Anderson also found reports suggesting that up to 10 or 12 hours of television a week—less than average—may actually help kids strengthen their reading skills and that, in any event, differences in reading abilities between light and heavy viewers tend to disappear as children grow. Although some kids may think watching TV is easier than reading and thus watch more than they read, no research has shown that television itself is any more responsible for that attitude than, for example, parents' own reading habits. "We found that kids weren't reading much before television and they're not doing much now," notes co-author Collins. "It doesn't mean that more reading wouldn't be good. It's just that TV isn't the culprit." Overall, then, "the effect of television on reading achievement appears to be small if it is, in fact, real," Anderson concludes.

Sixth, he found a smattering of evidence that "weakly indicates" that television might shorten children's attention spans, "yet the importance, generality, and nature of the effect is unknown." He points out, for example, that no one has answered the question of whether television shapes a child's attention span, or if the child's attention range was shortened by other factors and then "transferred" as an existing pattern to television-watching. On the other hand, Anderson admits that one study "convinced us that, under some circumstances, television can help kids' attentional skills." As an example, he cites the kind of puzzle that appears regularly in the Sunday comics pages and challenges kids to "find the 16 animals hidden in this farmyard scene"; camera zooms and other video techniques can help children learn to focus their attention on particular points in a scene by using the lens as a simulated focus of the viewer's own attention. Although he admits that "potential negative influences" on attention span "should be considered at least possible," he's quick to add that "the evidence just isn't there to support broad-brush claims and no one has really looked for it yet."

Finally, Anderson probes the often-repeated charge that television dulls kids' imaginations. It's a formidable case. When they're watching TV, kids can't "stop the action"—as they can when they're reading or fantasizing—to analyze or reflect on what's taking place, critics argue. In addition, by presenting a parade of concrete visual images, the small screen eliminates a child's need to supply his or her own. Just as bad television supplies entire populations of children with the same images and frames of reference, shrinking the number of imaginative new ones among kids in general.

Here, as in other areas, the evidence waffles. Some researchers have found that children use television's images as a launching pad for parallel fantasies while they watch. Others observed that youngsters were more imaginative in supplying endings to audiotaped stories than to videotaped ones. One study claims that children played less creatively after heavy television exposure than before it, while another reports that the most imaginative boys in a particular group of boys were also the heaviest viewers. "Television does not appear to interrupt the development of fantasy play or imaginativeness," Anderson sums up. "In fact, its incorporation as a common cultural experience into group play in preschool settings may help in forming friendships, promoting role-playing, and adding variety to play."

Ultimately, Anderson and Collins discovered that the evidence of television's effect on children's mental powers is simply too sparse to be in any way conclusive. "On the whole," they wrote, "there is no evidence that television, as a medium, either enhances or detracts from development of the intellect. In saying that television does not apparently damage a child's intellect, though, we're not also saying that TV is good for children."

Everyone seems to agree with Anderson and Collins that the evidence, when taken together, points in different—even opposite—directions. But that doesn't mean all observers share the report's value-free verdict. Some believe the medium's effects are more insidious and more progressive than the single sum of all the studies reviewed indicates. Among them: Dr. Jerome Singer and his wife Dorothy, co-directors of Yale University's Family Television Research and Consultation Center and two of the leading researchers in the area of children and television.

"Professor Anderson has not measured what sense children make of all of the rapid-fire shifts, cutaways, and interruptions that characterize U.S. commercial television," Dr. Singer points out in an April *New York Times* essay. "Several studies done at Yale and elsewhere suggest that children who are heavy viewers of television do not become more sophisticated about the medium. Compared to light viewers, they seem to have accumulated less general knowledge, they seem less able to follow the plots of TV dramas, they seem more prone to accept as possible the train-stopping or building-high leaps of superheroes, and they're less capable of explaining the function of commercials. Heavy viewers are also less likely to show imaginativeness or creativity. The fragmentary nature of television interferes with reflective thought and the careful mental repetition of the information presented. Modern cognitive psychology suggest[s] that such processes are a necessary condition for the development of consciously accessible, voluntarily organized learning."

Singer backs his assertions with two decades of personal research. In a 1979 *Psychology Today* article, the Singers wrote, "Can television enhance or inhibit imagination in young children? We think the latter is true, and are increasingly disturbed about the emphasis in American television on extremely short action sequences, frequent interruptions, and drastic changes in the visual field. . . . [I]t seems possible that [producers] are actually creating a psychological orientation in children that leads to a shortened attention span, a lack of reflectiveness, and an expectation of rapid change in the broader environment." As evidence, they offer the results of one of their own studies. A group of preschoolers was dosed daily with the tot-paced, very interactive *Mr. Rogers' Neighborhood.* After two weeks, the Singers say, those children showed more imagination and more positive relationships with other kids than did a group watching a similar amount of the hectic *Sesame Street.*

Others, though, think Anderson and Singer are simply wrong to search for measurable scientific data. "Anderson's criticisms of many of the studies confirmed my skepticism of this kind of experiment generally," says *The Plug-In Drug* author Marie Winn. "I'm doubtful that any of these questions are going to be resolved through 'scientific' research." Indeed, Anderson and Collins do admit that an array of variables have to be anticipated and controlled in performing objective research on something as subtle and personal as television viewing. Instead, says Winn, "I rather favor a common-sense kind of approach" to gauging the ways in which television sculpts kids' minds.

For example, Anderson writes that "there are numerous possible explanations of the fact" that children who don't watch TV read better than those who do; he adds that to blame television itself for certain of the children's deficits "is purely conjecture at this point," based on the scant available data. Winn's evidence is both more visceral and less ambiguous. "I've heard from hundreds of teachers that when they read children a story without showing them pictures, the children are at a loss," she says. "They ask, 'What does the princess look like?' or

'What does the woodcutter's cottage look like?' They lack the practice, and therefore the ability, to visualize for themselves. Teachers who've bridged the entry of television say that children were better at visualizing before there was television. This is the kind of evidence that is more indicative to me." It's also the kind that less and less often can be measured objectively. After all, where can scientists still go to find children who don't watch television?

Ultimately, though, those who scrutinize the medium professionally do agree on a key point: regardless of the hardware's effects, the messages that the hardware delivers play a key role in shaping young viewers' ideas about themselves and the world. "It's clear that kids don't watch television with blank minds," Anderson Says. "The evidence has grown, even since our report, that children take information from books. If parents would be alarmed to see their children reading pornography or Nazi propaganda, they ought to be just as concerned about what kinds of television programs their children are watching." Adds Dr. William Dietz, a pediatrician at Boston's New England Medical Center and a member of the American Academy of Pediatrics' subcommittee on children and television: "The conclusion that television viewing isn't mindless means that what children see presented on television, they're likely to incorporate into their own attitudes and behavior. That should strengthen the hand, and the resolve, of those actively engaged in trying to shape children's programming."

Too often, though, children's viewing isn't being shaped. Cartoon shows such as *Mutant Ninja Turtles* or *Masters of the Universe* don't offer much in the way of portable wisdom, and parents often don't help their kids interpret or modulate messages implicit in the deviant or sexual behavior common in adult programs. "Even if the content itself isn't memorable, things you learn in childhood become deeply ingrained," Anderson emphasizes.

"These messages form the ways in which you think about the world. Traditionally, societies use stories to teach their children about expectations, about ways to deal with life's problems, about the values supported by the culture. Stories become metaphors, lessons used throughout life. Too few people are paying attention to the fact that television has become today's storyteller, and there's very little burden on producers to offer stories that reflect the most appropriate moral and ethical values of our society."

What message, then, should producers themselves draw from Anderson's research? "The audience is actively trying to comprehend what they see, and what they comprehend will stay with them," he say[s]. "In every minute of their shows—even if they're intended purely as entertainment—producers are teaching kids, perhaps through formal techniques and clearly through content. It's a tremendous responsibility—and I hope they feel it."

Why blame TV?

The boob tube has little to do with our violent culture

John Leonard

As violence escalates in our everyday lives, a familiar scapegoat has reappeared: violence in the media. In a recent study sponsored by the Corporation for Public Broadcasting, 82 percent of the respondents said television is too violent. A call-in survey conducted last winter by NBC News found that a majority of people favored censorship of any program containing violence. And in the Mother Jones *article we've reprinted here, Carl Cannon gives evidence—some of it quite compelling—of the connection between what we see and what we do. But does television really inspire our trigger-happy fellow citizens, ask Todd Gitlin and John Leonard, or is the violence that threatens to ruin us the logical result of a frontier society that has lost its social and ethical moorings?*

Like a warrior-king of Sumer, daubed with sesame oil, gorged on goat, hefting up his sword and drum, Senator Ernest Hollings looked down November 23 from a ziggurat to intone, all over the op-ed page of the *New York Times*: "If the TV and cable industries have no sense of shame, we must take it upon ourselves to stop licensing their violence-saturated programming."

Hollings, of course, is co-sponsor in the Senate, with Daniel Inouye, of a ban on any act of violence on television before, say, midnight. Never mind whether this is constitutional, or what it would do to the local news. Never mind, either, that in Los Angeles last August, in the International Ballroom of the Beverly Hilton, in front of 600 industry executives, the talking heads—a professor here, a producer there, a child psychologist and a network veep for program standards—couldn't even agree on a definition of violence. (Is it only violent if it hurts or kills?) And they disagree on which was worse, a "happy" violence that sugarcoats aggressive behavior or a "graphic" violence that at least suggests consequences. (How, anyway, does television manage somehow simultaneously to *desensitize* and to *incite?*) Nor were they really sure what goes on in the dreamy heads of our children as they crouch in the dark to commune with the tube while their parents, if they have any, aren't around. (*Road Runner?* Beep-beep.) Nor does the infamous scarlet V "parent advisory" warning even apply to cartoons, afternoon soaps, or Somalias.

Never mind, because everybody agrees that watching television causes anti-social behavior, especially among the children of the poor; that there seems to be more violent programming on the air now than there ever was before; that *Beavis and Butt-head* inspired an Ohio 5-year-old to burn down the family trailer; that in the blue druidic light of television we will have spawned generations of toadstools and triffids.

In fact, there is less violence on network television than there used to be; because of ratings, it's mostly sitcoms. The worst stuff is the Hollywood splatterflicks; they're found on premium cable, which means the poor are less likely to be watching. Everywhere else on cable, not counting the court channel or home shopping and not even to think about blood sports and Pat Buchanan, the fare is innocent to the point of stupefaction (Disney, Discovery, Family, Nickelodeon). That Ohio trailer wasn't even wired for cable, so the littlest firebird must have got his MTV elsewhere in the dangerous neighborhood. (And kids have been playing with matches since, at least, Prometheus. I recall burning down my very own bedroom when I was 5 years old. The fire department had to tell my mother that the evidence pointed to me.) Since the '60s, according to statistics cited by Douglas Davis in *The Five Myths of Television Power*, more Americans than ever before are going out to eat in restaurants, see films, plays, and baseball games, visit museums, travel abroad, jog, even *read*. Watching television, everybody does *something else* at the same time. While our children are playing with their Adobe Illustrators and Domark Virtual Reality Toolkits, the rest of us eat, knit, smoke, dream, read magazines, sign checks, feel sorry for ourselves, think about Hillary, and plot shrewd career moves or revenge.

Actually watching television, unless it's C-Span, is usually more interesting than the proceedings of Congress. Or what we read in hysterical books like Jerry Mander's *Four Arguments for the Elimination of Television*, or George Gilder's *Life After Television*, or Marie Winn's *The Plug-In Drug*, or Neal Postman's *Amusing Ourselves to Death*, or Bill McKibben's *The Age of Missing Information*. Or what we'll hear at panel discussions on censorship, where right-wingers worry about sex and left-wingers worry about violence. Or just

From *Utne Reader,* May/June 1994, pp. 90-94. Excerpted from *The Nation,* December 27, 1993. © 1993 by The Nation Company, Inc. Reprinted by permission.

lolling around an academic deepthink-tank, trading mantras like "violence profiles" (George Gerbner), "processed culture" (Richard Hoggart), "narcoleptic joys" (Michael Sorkin), and "glass teat" (Harlan Ellison).

Of *course* something happens to us when we watch television; networks couldn't sell their millions of pairs of eyes to advertising agencies, nor would ad agencies buy more than $21 billion worth of commercial time each year, if speech (and sound, and motion) didn't somehow modify action. But what happens is far from clear and won't be much clarified by lab studies, however longitudinal, of habits and behaviors isolated from the larger feedback loop of a culture full of gaudy contradictions. The only country in the world that watches more television than we do is Japan, and you should see its snuff movies and pornographic comic books; but the Japanese are pikers compared with us when we compute per capita rates of rape and murder. Some critics in India tried to blame the recent rise in communal violence there on a state-run television series dramatizing the *Mahabharata*, but not long ago they were blaming Salman Rushdie, as in Bangladesh they have decided to blame the writer Taslima Nasrin. No Turk I know of attributes skinhead violence to German TV. It's foolish to pretend that all behavior is mimetic, and that our only model is Spock or Brokaw. Or Mork and Mindy. Why, after so many years of *M*A*S*H*, weekly in prime time and nightly in reruns, aren't all of us out there hugging trees and morphing dolphins? Why, with so many sitcoms, aren't all of us comedians?

But nobody normal watches television the way congressmen, academics, symposiasts, and Bill McKibbens do. We are less thrilling. For instance:

On March 3, 1993, a Wednesday, midway through the nine-week run of *Homicide* on NBC, in an episode written by Tom Fontana and directed by Martin Campbell, Baltimore detectives Bayliss (Kyle Secor) and Pembleton (Andre Braugher) had 12 hours to wring a confession out of "Arab" Tucker (Moses Gunn) for the strangulation and disemboweling of an 11-year-old girl. In the dirty light and appalling intimacy of a single claustrophobic room, with a whoosh of wind sound like some dread blowing in from empty Gobi spaces, among maps, library books, diaries, junk food, pornographic crime-scene photographs, and a single black overflowing ashtray, these three men seemed as nervous as the hand-held cameras—as if their black coffee were full of jumping beans, amphetamines, and spiders; as if God himself were jerking them around.

Well, you may think the culture doesn't really need another cop show. And, personally, I'd prefer a weekly series in which social problems are solved through creative nonviolence, after a Quaker meeting, by a collective or vegetarian carpenters. But in a single hour, for which Tom Fontana eventually won an Emmy, I learned more about the behavior of fearful men in small rooms than from any number of better-known movies, plays, and novels on the topic by the likes of Don DeLillo, Mary McCarthy, Alberto Moravia, Heinrich Böll, and Doris Lessing.

This, of course, was an accident, as it usually is when those of us who watch television like normal people are startled in our expectations. We leave home expecting, for a lot of money, to be exalted, and almost never are. But staying put, slumped in an agnosticism about sentience itself, suspecting that our cable box is just another bad-faith credit card enabling us to multiply our opportunities for disappointment, we are ambushed in our lethargy. And not so much by "event" television, like Ingmar Bergman's *Scenes from a Marriage*, originally a six-hour miniseries for Swedish television; or Marcel Ophul's *The Sorrow and the Pity*, originally conceived for French television; or Rainer Werner Fassbinder's *Berlin Alexanderplatz*, commissioned by German television; or *The Singing Detective*; or *The Jewel in the Crown*. On the contrary, we've stayed home on certain nights to watch television, the way on other nights we'll go out to a neighborhood restaurant, as if on Mondays we ordered in for laughs, as on Fridays we'd rather eat Italian. We go to television—message

We were a violent culture before television, from Wounded Knee to the lynching bee.

center, mission control, Big Neighbor, electronic Elmer's glue-all—to look at Oscars, Super Bowls, moon shots, Watergates, Pearlygates, ayatollahs, dead Kings, dead Kennedys; and also, perhaps, to experience some "virtual" community as a nation. But we also go because we are hungry, angry, lonely, or tired, and television is always there for us, a 24-hour user-friendly magic box grinding out narrative, novelty, and distraction, news and laughs, snippets of high culture, remedial seriousness and vulgar celebrity, an incitement and a sedative, a place to celebrate and a place to mourn, a circus and a wishing well.

And suddenly Napoleon shows up, like a popsicle, on *Northern Exposure*, while Chris on the radio is reading Proust. Or Roseanne is about lesbianism instead of bowling. Or *Picket Fences* has moved on, from serial bathers and elephant abuse to euthanasia and gay-bashing.

Kurt Vonnegut on Showtime! David ("Masturbation") Mamet on TNT! Norman Mailer wrote the TV screenplay for *The Executioner's Song*, and Gore Vidal gave us *Lincoln* with Mary Tyler Moore as Mary Todd. In just the past five years, if I hadn't been watching television, I'd have missed *Tanner '88*, when Robert Altman and Garry Trudeau ran Michael Murphy for president of the United States; *My Name Is Bill W.*, with James Woods as the founding father of Alcoholics Anonymous; *The Final Days*, with Theodore Bikel as Henry Kissinger; *No Place Like Home*, where there wasn't one for Christine Lahti and Jeff Daniels, as there hadn't been for Jane Fonda in *The Dollmaker* and Mare Winningham in *God Bless the Child*; *Eyes on the Prize*, a home movie in two parts about America's second civil war; *The Last Best Year*, with Mary Tyler Moore and Bernadette Peters learning to live with their gay sons and HIV; *Separate but Equal*, with Sidney Poitier as Thurgood Marshall; and *High Crimes and Misdemeanors*, the Bill Moyers special on Irangate and the scandal of our intelligence agencies; Graham Greene, John Updike, Philip Roth, Gloria Naylor, Arthur Miller, and George Eliot, plus Paul Simon and Stephen Sondheim. Not to mention—guiltiest of all our secrets—those hoots without which any popular culture would be as tedious as a John Cage or an Anaïs Nin, like Elizabeth Taylor in *Sweet Bird of Youth* and the Redgrave sisters in a remake of *Whatever Happened to Baby Jane?*

What all this television has in common is narrative. Even network news—which used to be better than most newspapers before the bean counters started closing down overseas bureaus and the red camera lights went out all over Europe and Asia and Africa—is in the storytelling business. And so far no one in Congress has suggested banning narrative.

Because I watch all those despised network TV movies, I know more about racism, ecology, homelessness, gun control, child abuse, gender confusion, date rape, and AIDS than is dreamt of by, say, Katie Roiphe, the Joyce Maynard of Generation X, or than Hollywood has ever bothered to tell me, especially about AIDS. Imagine, Jonathan Demme's *Philadelphia* opened in theaters around the country well after at least a dozen TV movies on AIDS that I can remember without troubling my hard disk. And I've learned something else, too:

We were a violent culture before television, from Wounded Knee to the lynching bee, and we'll be one after all our children have disappeared by video game into the pixels of cyberspace. Before television, we blamed public schools for what went wrong with the Little People back when classrooms weren't overcrowded in buildings that weren't falling down in neighborhoods that didn't resemble Beirut, and whose fault is that? *The A-Team?* We can't control guns, or drugs, and each year two million American women are assaulted by their male partners, who are usually in an alcoholic rage, and whose fault is that? *Miami Vice?* The gangs that menace our streets aren't home watching Cinemax, and neither are the sociopaths who make bonfires, in our parks, from our homeless, of whom there are at least a million, a supply-side migratory tide of the deindustrialized and dispossessed, of angry beggars, refugee children, and catatonic nomads, none of them traumatized by *Twin Peaks*. So cut Medicare, kick around the Brady Bill, and animadvert Amy Fisher movies. But children who are loved and protected long enough to grow up to have homes and respect and lucky enough to have jobs don't riot in the streets. Ours is a tantrum culture that measures everyone by his or her ability to produce wealth, and morally condemns anybody who fails to prosper, and now blames Burbank for its angry incoherence. Why not recessive genes, angry gods, lousy weather? The mafia, the zodiac, the *Protocols of the Elders of Zion?* Probability theory, demonic possession, Original Sin? George Steinbrenner? Sunspots?

The Source's Perspective: A Push from the Right . . . a Pull to the Left

In a speech preceding the dedication of the new home of the Stanford University Departments of Communication and Sociology, media expert Wilbur Schramm noted that, as a small town newspaper reporter, "the most important thing I learned is that news exists in the minds of men. It isn't an event, but something perceived after the event. . . . Hardly anything about communication is so impressive as the enormous number of choices and discards and interpretations that have to be made between [an] actual news event and the symbols that later appear in the mind of a reporter, an editor, a reader, a listener, or a viewer. Therefore, even if everyone does his job perfectly, it is hard enough to get the report of an event straight and clear and true."

Schramm's comments point to the tremendous impact of selectivity in crafting media messages. What gets into the media, and what does not, is influenced by choices made by individuals with personal opinions, causes, and biases. The process of making these decisions is called gatekeeping.

Gatekeeping is necessary. News operations cannot logistically cover or report every event that happens in the world from one edition or broadcast to the next. Entertainment operations cannot produce every script or synopsis that is submitted. Former NBC president Fred Silverman has estimated that each network receives about 1,200 series submissions per season, with single-episode pilots made for only 30 or 40 new programs, and less actually picked up for production. There are, in short, a lot more messages lined up for transmission than media channels can carry.

The concerns associated with the reality of gatekeeping relate to whether or not the gatekeepers abuse the privilege of deciding what information or viewpoints the mass audience receives. Simply being selected for media coverage lends support to an issue, an event, or an individual celebrity—the "masser" the medium, the greater the effect. Thus, the privilege of choice grants considerable power. The articles in this section center on the idea that media messages are created by individuals and organiza-

tions who have the potential of incorporating their own agendas and biases in selecting, interpreting, and crafting those messages. There is a relatively small number of voices that have ready access to media channels. Who are these people? Are their values and viewpoints representative of society as a whole? Is there a liberal bias among them? Or does a profit-oriented, essentially conservative power structure in American media tilt control toward the right?

Media writers—a term being used broadly here to include those who observe events, gather information, sit down in front of computer screens to create news stories or television or movie scripts, and put what has been written into the form that actually reaches the public—tend to be more liberal than the population as a whole. More journalists, particularly those working for the most prestigious and influential news groups, describe themselves as left of center and as Democrats than as political moderates or Republicans. The power structure in entertainment television is similarly dominated by liberals and idealists (see "Sitcom Politics").

Conservative media watchdog groups have provided evidence of what they perceive as a clearly liberal slant to media content, an outcome that might be attributed to both conscious intent and unconscious bias on the part of the writers. Some argue that news media characteristically cover liberal causes and candidates with a more positive "spin" or interpretation, while others have pointed to the treatment of interracial relationships, environmental issues, changes in family structures, secularism, materialism, and sexuality in both news and entertainment media as evidence of liberal bias.

On the other hand, mass media are businesses that are rapidly moving in the direction of control by huge corporations, many of whom have multimedia as well as nonmedia holdings. The chief executive officers of those corporations are almost without exception economic conservatives who value their relationships with the leaders of other powerful institutions, including the federal government. The mood of the country, whether people are spending or saving, whether they fear for the environment or fear for their jobs, whether they think times are good or bad, is influenced by news themes—and, in turn, influences the health of media owners' other corporate holdings. Arguments against liberal bias point to the influence of corporate owners on killing certain types of stories (Michael Wagner, an investigative reporter for the *Detroit Free Press* has noted, "If you look across the country, you

see papers doing a great job of covering prisons and juvenile crime and child abuse. But you don't see people asking how Exxon got to be bigger than five or six countries in the world") and on the reliance of news media on "official" government sources. This perspective is presented in the article "Power Structure of the American Media."

Finally, the media's marketplace orientation (see "Media Habits of Media Tycoons") and the influence of vocal conservative activist groups have been credited with keeping media messages close to a safe political center. These issues are further explored in articles in the following two units.

It is important to note that those who are critical of media's being either too liberal or too conservative would often commend their leaning in the opposite direction. Both camps acknowledge the power of media sources to influence public perceptions. The insight in terms of media literacy is that audiences recognize viewpoints as viewpoints, and they acknowledge gatekeeping effects in interpreting what they see and hear.

Looking Ahead: Challenge Questions

What characteristics of media operations influence their maintaining an implicit agreement to make gatekeeping decisions that favor government and corporate sources? Should information provided by "expert" sources be totally disregarded by news media? What would you consider an appropriate policy on how such information should be used?

Does the code of "objective journalism," which constrains a reporter from making interpretive comments or drawing inferences of her or his own in writing a news story, restrain bias?

What kinds of evidence support the argument that both news and entertainment media reflect a predominantly liberal bias?

What kinds of evidence support the argument that both news and entertainment media reflect a predominantly conservative bias?

How does the marketplace orientation of "media tycoons" affect choices they make regarding media content? To what degree do you find the business orientation of those who produce media (see "Media Habits of Media Tycoons") appropriate or inappropriate?

Do you believe that alternative media should be supported with taxes on commercial media revenues and/or other forms of government funding? Why, or why not?

Power Structure of the American Media

me•di•a pl of **medium** 2. an intervening thing through which a force acts or an effect is produced 3. any means, agency or instrumentality; specif., a means of communication that reaches the general public and carries advertising. *Webster's New World Dictionary*

Joe Stork and Laura Flanders

Joe Stork is the editor of Middle East Report. *Laura Flanders is Coordinator of the Women's Desk at FAIR, the national media watch group in New York.* Martha Wenger *provided additional research.*

In the lobby of Baghdad's Mansour Hotel, a year to the day after the beginning of the US-led war against their country, a group of Iraqi students were hawking souvenirs to visitors. Offering to translate a local newspaper story for a delegation of women from the US organization MADRE, one of the students enthusiastically paraphrased a few sentences from a two-column story on MADRE's delivery of milk and medicine to local hospitals. "The rest is nothing," he said, when asked to comment on the remainder of the piece. "Nothing but government propaganda."

In the United States it is not always so easy to be sure.

In Iraq, and other new states, the power structure of the national media is fairly obvious: it is largely identical with the state itself, under the supervision of a ministry of information. In many countries, the government owns and administers electronic media—television and radio—even where it does not exercise direct control, while print media is typically privately owned. The US is fairly unique in that virtually all media, electronic as well as print, is privately held, and overt censorship by the government is infrequent.

Mass media has emerged with the growth of modern political ideologies and the organization of societies globally in the form of nation-states. Along with other infrastructure, such as transportation and schools, it has played a role in the formation of those nation-states, reflecting the interests and perspectives of dominant groups. Mass media, as Eric Hobsbawm points out, have been an important means of making national symbols a part of everyday life, and "break[ing] down the division between the private and local spheres in which most citizens normally lived, and the public and national one."[1] In some instances mass media is a vehicle of overt propaganda. In every instance, the mass media functions as a handmaiden to power, and the power structure of the media is bound up with the locations of power in society at large. The media, which specializes in appearances, itself constitutes one of the least visible structures of power in modern society.

The media, by its very nature, selects and interprets. Most Americans say they get their news from television newscasts. As critic Jerry Mander put it, each night three men talk and 50 million people listen.[2] Just as in the physical world the medium of the atmosphere or conducting material changes the appearance of light or other phenomena that pass through it, so do the various communications media refract, deflect and alter the information that passes through as "news."

Economics of Media Power

One locus of power in any modern society is the state. In a developed capitalist economy such as the US, the other locus of power is economic: media is business—big business. The top media conglomerates—Time Warner, Gannett, Dow Jones, the New York Times Corporation—are firmly ensconced in the upper-middle range of the top *Fortune* or *Business Week* 500. Profit margins of 20 or 30 percent were common for media companies in the 1980s, and have been among the highest of any corporate sector.[3] No wonder Warren Buffet, a major owner of ABC and a shareholder in the Washington Post Company, said that even in the current recession media companies represent "economic marvels compared with American industry generally."[4]

Most media conglomerates have interests in both print and broadcasting. In 1982, Ben Bagdikian found that 50 corporations controlled half or more of the media business. By 1990, that number had shrunk to 23. The broadcasting business, which began as a private cartel in 1919, has never shed its founding characteristic. In 1919, Radio Corporation of America (RCA) was an "umbrella monopoly" under which General Electric, Westinghouse, AT&T and United Fruit divided the radio market and called their network the National Broadcasting Company. CBS appeared in 1927; ABC in 1943.[5]

The mythic image of the publisher/owner as tycoon—William Randolph Hearst/Citizen Kane in his palatial estate, Robert Maxwell on his behemoth yacht—is not far off the mark. "Journalism," the 19th century American editor Charles Dana once said, "consists in buying white paper at two cents a pound and selling it at ten cents a pound."[6] In 1990, at least four media execs drew over a million dollars in salary and bonuses, and more than a few others were not far behind. That's not counting the late Steve Ross, chairman of Time Warner, who got $78 million in salary and stock options in 1990—$48 million more than the combined salaries of the 600 *Time* employees he laid off in 1991.[7]

There is a contrasting myth of the media as having a fundamentally adversarial relationship with power and the state. This probably derives from the origin of newspapers in the pamphlets and information sheets of the 18th century published by radicals like Thomas Paine and William Cobbett. The cheap daily press was pioneered in the US (the first one-cent daily appeared in New York in 1833). What made the transition from pamphlet to newspaper possible was advertising, further linking the media to the interests of the commercial and financial classes. While there are many courageous reporters and editors risking life and livelihood around the world, the mass media as an institution is invariably closer to power than truth. The myth is from time to time replenished by events such as Watergate, and by the whining of politicians like George ("Annoy the Media") Bush when they are on a downhill trajectory. Much has been made of a recent survey indicating that a majority of reporters identified themselves as Democrats rather than Republicans. Apart from the questionable assumption that this places the reporters on the left politically, the fact remains that no such survey was taken of owners and publishers or boards of directors—as if that were somehow irrelevant (or perhaps irreverent).

The Politics of Media Power

The media's prime political function is at an ideological level—disseminating what Anthony Giddens calls public doctrines "by which dominant groups manage to sustain their power through persuading others of the legitimacy of their rule."[8] For the most part, this includes a deferential attitude toward power. One such "public doctrine" from the Middle East repertoire is the notion of a "peace process." The presumption that Washington is committed to a negotiated solution of the Arab-Israeli-Palestinian conflict is seldom if ever held up against the record.

Despite the formal separation of media and state in the US, here the media routinely purveys news from the perspective of the government. When it comes to foreign matters, the media reports not so much what goes on in the world as what the White House says goes on. The state does not control the media in any crude or direct way, but the government more than any other party sets the agenda and the tone—how a story is presented or an issue debated, or if it is presented at all. With all the attention to opinion polls in the presidential election campaign and the gulf war, for instance, who would imagine that four years of Nicaragua coverage in the *New York Times,* totalling more than 2300 articles, would include only 30 passing references in opinion polls? Perhaps this was because the polls showed the US public opposed two-to-one to the Reagan administration's provision of aid to the Contras.[9]

The mass media functions in relation to the state and other loci of power in some respects in the same way as an occasionally irascible pet to its master. Like the pet, the media requires the proper mix of muzzling, feeding and grooming, and must occasionally be brought to heel.

The obvious question in a discussion of media muzzling is censorship: who decides what we do not read (see, hear)? Pentagon control of media access in the invasions of Grenada and Panama and in the war against Iraq was blatant and effective. The US government, usually citing reasons of "national security," routinely withholds information from public disclosure.

Censorship also occurs at the level of ownership. NBC's *Today* show planned to do a story on the largest consumer boycott in the US—until they learned it was the one directed against NBC's corporate owner, General Electric (for production of nuclear weapons).[10] The reporter who compiled *Fortune*'s list of highest-paid executives quit in 1991 when executives of the magazine's parent, Time Warner, "interfered with his efforts to estimate the 1990 compensation of company chairman Steve Ross."[11]

Censorship can take the form of intimidation. Following a *60 Minutes* installment critical of Israel's handling of the October 1990 "Temple Mount massacre," CBS owner and chairman Lawrence Tisch called in reporter Mike Wallace and producer Don Hewitt for a tongue-lashing. (Wallace's version was subsequently confirmed by an independent Israeli judicial investigation.)

Other states and their partisans mount intimidation campaigns as well. When NBC broadcast a critical program on Israel's occupation policies in 1987, the Likud government banned NBC from interviewing Israeli officials, and only lifted the ban when NBC agreed to air Israeli objections to the program.

When the Public Broadcasting System scheduled "Death of a Princess" in 1980, a "docudrama" critical of the judicial system and treatment of women in Saudi Arabia, the Saudi government and Mobil Oil Company, a major PBS sponsor and partner in the Saudi oil industry, mounted a public and behind-the-scenes campaign to have the program scrapped. The show was aired, but was coupled with a panel discussion of "experts" whose main function was to clean up the Saudi image tarnished by the film. Partisans of Israel have used this technique whenever PBS dares to schedule a program reflecting a Palestinian point of view: campaign to get local affiliates to scrap the program, and insist on "equal time" wherever it is shown.

Feeding and Grooming

Who determines what we do see, read and hear? The US government employs some 13,000 persons, at a cost of some $2.5 billion per year, to do public and media relations. The Pentagon alone accounts for some 3,000 of these, at a cost of $100 million a year.[12] On an ordinary day, the White House and Pentagon each hold two briefings, the State Department one. These briefings in many respects set the agenda for foreign news coverage (including coverage by foreign correspondents based in Washington).

If the US government did not already have this in-house taxpayer-funded propaganda machine, it would have to hire a public relations firm like Hill and Knowlton, the way states like Saudi Arabia, Turkey, Morocco and the Emir of Kuwait (a.k.a. Citizens for a Free Kuwait) have done.[13] (Israel gets its PR advice from top Madison Avenue firms on a pro bono basis.)[14] The Kuwaitis paid H&K nearly $11 million for services like daily video feeds that were the source of most televised footage about the "Kuwaiti resistance," and for "focus groups" around the US to determine which rationales would generate greatest public support for the Bush administration's war policy.[15]

> "Israelis can learn a lot from watching how PR firms handle corporate crises. Johnson&Johnson was able to regain its market share on Tylenol within three to four weeks after seven people died taking tampered capsules, and the Tylenol scare got practically more national media than the Lebanon war. So clearly it was a case of Johnson&Johnson restoring America's faith in its product. Israel's up against the same problem."
>
> **Andrea Binder**, *American Jewish Congress staff person overseeing media relations training for Israeli officials. Source: Robert Friedman,"Selling Israel to America," Mother Jones, February-March 1987.*

Reporters and news programmers rely heavily on public relations feeds. As critics Martin Lee and Norman Solomon put it, most journalism is hard to distinguish from stenography. A special label, investigative journalism, has been coined to mark off those efforts that go beyond the official communiqué and the corporate press release.

Most daily newspapers are owned by media conglomerates like Gannett and Knight-Ridder. Hearst, which owns 13 newspapers, sends out several editorials a day to its subsidiaries. Some must be used; others are optional. The New York Times Co. owns 31 other dailies, and its news services have 600 outlets worldwide.

Reporters working in the Middle East rely on local feeders, who usually turn out to be "diplomatic sources" and other reporters. Part of the reason is that in many countries people can be arrested or worse for talking with a reporter. But it is also easier to do an assignment from the local five-star hotel. "If you looked at the phone books of correspondents in the Middle East," says one reporter who has worked there for a major US daily, "80 to 90 percent would be diplomats—Western diplomats. And people trade these names."[16]

The process through which information and analysis is filtered goes beyond the muzzlers and feeders to the components of the media itself. This is the process in which information is coded—in which one country's "naked aggression" becomes another's "peacekeeping mission." This is how a friendly monarch acquires a reputation as a "moderate."[17] Even logos and theme music are part of the process. John MacArthur, in his book on the media and the Gulf war, asked rhetorically why CBS did not introduce its Gulf crisis segments with some bars of Beethoven's *Pastoral* symphony, a three-dimensional United Nations logo, and a voice-over saying, "The quest for peace: CBS News brings you continuing coverage of the world community's efforts to avert war in the Persian Gulf."[18]

In the case of the print media, the newsweeklies reproduce the glitz and superficiality of electronic coverage. In the Gulf crisis, major dailies provided some critical accounts of official policy, but in terms of proportionality the result is much the same. The people who decide which stories to feature sometimes have strong views on an issue. Take the case of A. M. Rosenthal, whose columns on the Middle East in the *New York Times* reflect a political outlook akin to that of Ariel Sharon. As a columnist his perspective is transparent. For nearly 20 years, though, Rosenthal was managing editor and executive editor at the *Times*: he did not publish a word under his own name, but he assigned reporters and stories; he had a major say in what the *New York Times* published about Israel and the Middle East over several crucial decades, and how it said it. Rosenthal helped shape public perceptions of the region and US policy as events unfolded, and he will continue to shape the views of students and others who resort to the "newspaper of record" for an authoritative account of recent history.

For any party wishing to influence how a story is conveyed in the media, the three rules of thumb are: 1) get the first version; 2) get the headline; and 3) get the talk show. In addition to the formal networks embedded in the corporate structures of the US media, other, more informal networks contribute to the presentation and interpretation of the news. Less than two weeks before the presidential election, ABC's *Nightline* asked whether the media was being unfair to the president, and invited the Bush/Quayle campaign to the studio to produce a report on the day's news from their perspective—as if the news is not routinely presented from the White House point of view. The man who arranged the invitation was Bush's communications assistant, Dorrance Smith, formerly a *Nightline* executive producer. When Smith announced his move from ABC to the White House, the *Washington Post* described him as "a lifetime friend of the Bushes."[19]

Cults of Expertise

Since reporters are supposed to report, the media shops elsewhere for analysis and interpretation. On a foreign story of any importance, an interview with or guest appearance by a government official—a "player"—is almost obligatory. Next in line are "former players." Most active media "experts" are "former players." Few, if any, have any background as independent scholars. "The policy expert and adviser," writes James Smith in his book about think tanks, "if they aspire to be of use, must speak to power in a political and bureaucratic context; and they must speak a useful truth. Their claims to the truth must always be viewed in light of their relationship with power."[20]

In order to buttress their presentations with "credibility, authority, confirmation of objective truth," the media has cultivated a small group of "unofficial sources" who can be counted on to reinforce the perspective of the "official sources." Janet Steele found that "a relatively small group of unofficial sources" dominated the airwaves. Most of these came from think tanks like the American Enterprise Institute, Brookings and the Heritage Foundation. These institutions, many of them established in the last 20 years to advance conservative and right wing policy agendas, are largely corporate funded. It is not unusual to find a major institute such as the Center for Strategic and International Studies getting contributions from military contractors like Lockheed and from media companies like the New York Times, for whom the resident expert might write an op-ed promoting a particular arms procurement program. Steele documents the "operational bias" behind

> "Though unlike most Germans I had daily access to foreign newspapers...and though I listened regularly to the BBC and other foreign broadcasts, my job necessitated the spending of many hours a day in combing the German press, checking the German radio, conferring with Nazi officials and going to party meetings. It was surprising and sometimes consternating to find that notwithstanding the opportunities I had to learn the facts and despite one's inherent distrust of what one learned from Nazi sources, a steady diet over the years of falsifications and distortions made a certain impression on one's mind and often muddled it. No one who has lived for years in a totalitarian land can possibly conceive how difficult it is to escape the dread consequences of a regime's calculated and incessant propaganda."
>
> **William Shirer**, *The Rise and Fall of the Third Reich* (1960)

such media consultancy: The "experts" are trotted out to answer the unanswerable ("What is going to happen next?") and the transparently ridiculous ("What is Saddam thinking?"). The result is specious stereotyping. The "experts" are seldom asked hard questions about the policies that lie behind the current crisis, for often they are the people who were responsible for those policies or who endorsed them at the time.[21]

The think tanks and their experts serve a further purpose of lending an air of "balance," on the presumption that there are never more than two sides—liberal and conservative, or Democrat and Republican—to any issue. On the Middle East this approach produces some bizarre moments, as when an associate of the Washington Institute for Near East Policy is invited to intervene from a pro-Israeli slant (fair enough) and is "balanced" by a "Palestinian perspective" from the Brookings Institution![22]

The problem posed by the power of the media is not an intellectual one. The decision to escalate to war with Iraq was wrong for a lot of reasons, but not because the bombing of Baghdad was timed to coincide with US evening news shows. The problem is political: the policies that ruling circles impose. In a modern capitalist society, Gramsci has written, the state is charged with providing a balance between coercion and consent in securing citizen compliance with those policies, and acceptance of the dominant interests they serve. The mass media is a crucial institution in facilitating that balance, so that consent may generally play the larger role.

Notes

1 Eric Hobsbawm, *Nations and Nationalism Since 1780* (Cambridge: Cambridge University Press, 1990).

2 Jerry Mander, *Four Arguments for the Elimination of Television* (New York: William Morrow & Co, 1978).

3 Richard Harwood, "Journalism: A Look toward the Millenium," *Washington Post*, November 27, 1992.

4 Karen Rothmeyer, "The Media in Recession: How Bad Is It?" *Columbia Journalism Review*, September-October 1991, p. 25.

5 Ben Bagdikian, *The Media Monopoly* (Boston: Beacon Press, 1990).

6 Cited by Lewis Lapham, *Harper's*, May 1991.

7 Rothmeyer, pp. 23, 26.

8 Anthony Giddens, *Social Theory and Modern Sociology* (Cambridge: Polity Press, 1987), p. 256.

9 Martin Lee and Norman Solomon, *Unreliable Sources* (New York: Lyle Stuart, 1990), p. 138.

10 Fairness and Accuracy in Media (FAIR), *Extra!*, January-February 1991, p. 4.

11 *Extra!*, November-December 1991, p. 12.

12 Lee and Solomon, p. 104.

13 Susan Trento, *The Power House* (New York, St. Martin's, 1992).

14 Robert Friedman, "Selling Israel to America," *Mother Jones*, February-March 1987.

15 Morgan Strong, "Portions of the Gulf War were brought to you by...the folks at Hill and Knowlton," *TV Guide*, February 22, 1992.

16 Interview, November 1992.

17 On this filtering process, see Edward Herman and Noam Chomsky, *Manufacturing Consent* (New York, 1988).

18 John MacArthur, *Second Front: Censorship and Propaganda in the Gulf War* (New York: Hill and Wang, 1992), p. 86.

19 February 28, 1991.

20 James Smith, *The Idea Brokers* (New York: Free Press, 1991), cited in Janet Steele, "Enlisting Experts: Objectivity and Operational Bias in Television News Analysis of the Persian Gulf War," Media Studies Project (Washington: Woodrow Wilson International Center for Scholars, 1992), p. 13.

21 Steele, *passim*.

22 Steele, p.22.

Media Habits

of

Media Tycoons

Leo Bogart

Leo Bogart is author of Preserving the Press, The Age of Television *and other books on the media. This essay is adapted from a book he is completing on the subject of commercial culture.*

An ever-smaller number of ever-larger multi-media corporations account for a growing proportion of the flow of ideas and images that constitute American commercial culture. How do the executives who run these companies view what their organizations produce? How do they respond to it as media consumers themselves? The answers to these questions would certainly indicate what degree of social responsibility they exercise as they wield their awesome power to inform, persuade, and entertain. This essay examines the media habits of media tycoons in relation to the larger question of how mass media content is created for the market.

Creative Impulse and Business Needs

ABC's founder Leonard Goldensohn: "I fear that one of the most insidious by-products of the current merger mania may be the loss of a sense of stewardship, a value to which those of us in broadcasting have always been acutely sensitive. Because our business is more than a business. It is a public trust." Are such sentiments mere public relations? To what degree are they still common? The top managements of large multi-media companies can hardly be expected to share the kind of deep personal involvement in the ethos of an individual medium (like newspapers or movies) that characterized the media moguls of another era—men like William Randolph Hearst, Samuel Goldwyn or William Paley—whose first love was the product of the companies they had built, and who may have taken more pride in that product than in the profit, for which they also had a healthy respect. Today's media tycoons are less apt to be impresarios who rose from the professional ranks, and more likely to be generalists who happened to drift into the media business. Their talent may lie in administration or in their shrewdness as financiers. In the age of the media corporation, long-range considerations and civic or sentimental interests are not so easily tolerated.

"I do not compose music," said Gustav Mahler. "Music comes to me." Communications created to express personal impulses follow different conventions than those produced to order for sale in the market.

In *Defense of Poetry* Percy Bysshe Shelley wrote, "A man cannot say, 'I will compose poetry.' The greatest poet cannot say it. For the mind in creation is as a fading coal, which some invisible muse, like the inconstant wind, awakens to transitory brightness." Mass media, with their rigorous production schedules, require the muse to perform to order. Analogies to manufacturing help to sustain the illusion that impersonal forces are at work, obliterating the need for any moral judgments on the part of the participants.

2. SOURCE'S PERSPECTIVE

Media content is referred to generically as "software." Television programs called "products," "inventory," "projects," even as "brands." Below the top level of control, media, like all creative activities, are fraught with tension between the impulse for expression and the drive for profit. In newspaper publishing, this has been controlled through separation of the editorial and business functions (church and state, as editors refer to it). That separation has never existed in media devoted to entertainment rather than journalism. In multimedia companies, the line is difficult to draw.

Mass media's rigorous production schedules require the muse to perform to order.

There is a strong literary image of creative geniuses enchained by the masscult corporation, unable to express their true instincts, chafing as their great gifts are subordinated to serve sordid commercial purposes. Beyond question, many people working in or for media organizations despise their work, hate themselves for "selling out," and yearn for the time when they can retire to pursue, finally, their great destinies. Most, however, feel no such conflicts, and find that their career paths are well-chosen and satisfying.

People with a literary or artistic bent are not the only ones employed in media enterprises. There are jobs for accountants, mechanics, and statisticians. Their work may not be as central to the company's mission as that of the people who craft what appears in print or on the air, but they are a presence. As in any other kind of business, a major preoccupation of management is to keep all its employees productively occupied.

Thus there is a workaday rhythm in all these organizations that resembles that of any other institution in which human beings coordinate their activities to produce a complex assortment of products. The dominant tone is set by social interaction in relation to jobs, by aspirations, rivalries, romances, and achievements, by the pleasure people take and the small comforts they get in being with each other. It is, in short, the usual web of interpersonal connections in the work place rather than the joys or frustrations of the creative process that determines how most professionals in the communications field respond to their work.

The creative process can itself be a highly challenging one, even when it is applied to such minor tasks as the composition of an obituary notice or the preparation of a radio commercial script for a hardware store.

Some individuals take such mundane assignments with greater ease and pleasure than others, but the rewards inevitably go to those who do their best.

Rationale for Sell-Out

The demands of the workplace weed out those sensitive spirits who are unable to adapt to them. The rest, who may start as cynics or secret rebels, are inevitably caught in the machinery. They may simply find that they cannot market their skills for more pay or more comfortable working conditions. They may be intrigued by the exercise of crafts they increasingly master. They may be ensnared by the personal loyalties that bind them to a work group, or even to the enterprise itself. But whatever the motives, they come to accept the notion that what they are doing is good. And undoubtedly much of it is.

Former TV Network president: "For every witless show you pumped out you had something else you could be proud of. If you're talking programming, you want to have quality instead of all that really forgettable stuff. And you take pride in the good shows that you can produce."

We are accustomed to thinking of great talents as selling out when they choose to apply themselves to endeavors that do not match their own levels of excellence and integrity. Noble spirits enslaved to ignoble masters can always justify their decisions, and can in any case concentrate on technique if the substance of what they are working on does not accord with their real impulses.

Is it excellence of execution or seriousness of intent that distinguishes a valid creative expression from a phony one? Hacks can be deadly serious about their work; most become so to keep their sanity, even if they start out tongue in cheek. And convictions are easily acquired from one's surroundings if one has none to begin with.

Rationalization can be converted into honest belief in the value and importance of what one is doing. Few creative people in any medium spend a lifetime despising what they do. They may admit they are making compromises, but on balance they will tell you they are doing more good than ill, dispensing harmless amusement, advancing worthy causes through cryptic references in their copy, helping to preserve fine enterprises that might otherwise succumb to economic pressures.

Journalism has always attracted evangelical and investigative spirits of high purpose. Practiced at the incandescent level of an Emile Zola, it is a morally impelled vocation. Because the moral expectations made of creative individuals are so high, shame is often attached to the compromises that reveal them to be ordinary mortals.

Like rock stars proclaiming their social consciences at benefit concerts, producers of films and television programs sometimes see themselves as missionaries for social improvement. Their scripts are infused, often quite irrelevantly, with trendy themes of social uplift. To ascribe higher motives for what one does seems to be a deep-seated requirement of human nature, and perhaps especially of creative human nature.

Nothing about the process of self-justification is unique to the field of communication. Young people enter almost any field of employment with hesitations and misgivings, but come to like it and defend it as their sense of commitment increases. As common sense tells us and psychological theory confirms, there is a natural tendency for human beings to justify activities that they may have begun for wholly arbitrary and even irrational reasons.

There are individuals who despise what they do, and themselves for doing it, but most people retain their self-esteem by ascribing some genuine meaning or importance to the way they spend their energy and time. Arguments that may at first be adopted out of sheer defensiveness are quickly incorporated into a person's belief-system as they are repeated over and over. Even the producer of pornographic films knows that he is fighting prudery and bringing much needed pleasure to hundreds of thousands of lonely people.

Allan R., copy editor for a group of fetish-and-violence girlies: "What the hell, it's a living. And it's not that bad. Within the limited format, there's room for some experimentation and creativity. The pay is good, the atmosphere is relaxed, and the work isn't very demanding. I could do worse."

There is no form of communication that cannot be justified, and is not. Rationalization may apply not merely to the purposes of the enterprise as a whole, but to specific elements of its content. A newspaper's editorial policies may be dictated by its owner, but editorial writers, once they are assigned to articulate them, will quickly accept them as their own.

Only a fraction of communications content is devoted to controversial opinions, political or otherwise. Most creative assignments are fairly routine tasks that carry no particular emotional overhang. Here the prevailing values set by management are fed by subtle indirection into the flow of activities and judgments. Priorities, prejudices, no-no's, and tastes emerge as generally understood company policies, from the decisions, accolades and reprimands that are handed down from on high, case by specific case. Newcomers in an organization pick them up one by one from superiors and colleagues, just as they learn the uncodified protocols of office etiquette.

Creative expression always has some utilitarian motive. Is there any such thing as pure self-expression apart from its social rewards? How can we differentiate the social approval for artistic or intellectual performance from payment as a manifestation and symbol of social approval? Performers thrive on applause and praise but survive on more material compensation.

Many creative spirits who have been lured by material rewards of commercial culture share an ambiguity of feelings.

The dilemma of the artist accommodating to the harsh demands of the marketplace was nowhere made more explicit than in the golden era of Hollywood, which attracted such talented writers as William Faulkner, Aldous Huxley, F. Scott Fitzgerald, Dashiell Hammett, Lillian Hellman, Clifford Odets, and Nathaniel West. Thomas Mann said of this crew, which he observed at close quarters: "Anyone gambling on a career in movies was dependent on Satan's mercies."

In a letter to Edward Knobloch (August 21, 1921), Somerset Maugham wrote: "I look back on my connection with the cinema world with horror mitigated only by the fifteen thousand dollars."

Not all the creative spirits who have been lured by the material rewards of the commercial culture are as well known as Mann and Maugham, but many share the same ambiguity of feelings. (One who did not was George Bernard Shaw, who replied to a Hollywood invitation from Samuel Goldwyn, "Deeply regret collaboration impossible. You only interested in creativity. I only interested in money.")

A comedy producer: "I swear to you that artists like to be rewarded for their work at retail, and the freedom comes second."

Screenwriter Dorothy Kingsley: "I only wrote because I needed the money. I had no desire to express myself or anything like that."

"Virtue pays," said Mae West, "if you can find a market for it." It seems foolish to belabor creative individuals who adapt their talents to fit commercial requirements, or who sell them outright, like scriptwriters in a Hollywood "stable," when artistic geniuses have bowed to the same impulses and did not hesitate to earn their living working for popular media. Henry James wrote miscellaneous magazine pieces to earn money between commercially unsuccessful novels.

2. SOURCE'S PERSPECTIVE

He once said, on writing a play: "I have been governed by the one sordid and urgent consideration of the possibility of making some money."

The greatest of artists have freely acknowledged their willingness to follow market demands. Igor Stravinsky: "I do not wish to be buried in the rain, unattended, as Mozart was; . . . the very image of Bartok's poverty-stricken demise. . . was enough to fire my ambition to earn every penny that my art would enable me to extract from the society that failed in its duty toward Bartok as it had earlier failed with Mozart."

> **No one has made more scathing comments about the media than the people of the industry itself.**

Charlie Chaplin: "I went into the business for money, and the art grew out of it. If people are disillusioned by that remark, I can't help it. It's the truth."

Is it necessary to share the tastes of the mass audience in order to please it, or is it possible to be disengaged and guileful—planning, writing, painting, or otherwise creating to fit the pattern of the market against which one's own inner spirit is in rebellion? Commercial hack work requires a high degree of specialized skill that even highly talented individuals may find to be beyond their capacities. Dwight MacDonald relates that the poet and short story writer Delmore Schwartz "tried, twice, to sell out, and write a piece of junk that Liberty would crown with a $1,000 check [for its weekly 1,000 word short story]; both times he failed." He concluded, "Moral: You have to be sincere to sell out; it's like making money if your heart's not in it, the customer, or editor, sees through the imposture."

In *New Grub Street*, published over a century ago, George Gissing observes:

> Literature nowadays is a trade. Putting aside men of genius, who may succeed by mere cosmic force, your successful man of letters is your skillful tradesman. He thinks first and foremost of the markets; when one kind of goods begins to go off slackly, he is ready with something new and appetising. . . .It needs skill, mind you; and to deny it is a gross error of the literary pedants. . . .To please the vulgar you must, one way or another, incarnate the genius of vulgarity.

No one has made more scathing comments on the mass media than the talented people who come out of the industry itself. Media producers and entrepreneurs often express themselves as shocked by what they have to do to earn a living, and take pains to distinguish their own personal preferences from those of the public at large. Television producer Norman Lear, appearing on a televised panel discussion, once said he had not seen a new series that his studio had produced, and added, "I do not watch television."

Don Durgin, a former president of NBC-TV, remarked, "What you consider normal—normal honesty and dependability—is so rare in this business." One of his successors, Grant Tinker (then head of MTM productions), called poor television programming "a national crime" and said "someone should go to jail for it. . .probably network executives."

Yet another former NBC-TV president, Fred Silverman: "I'm disappointed at the lack of change and improvement in TV programming. My children aren't all that interested in watching TV. . . .I was responsible for some of the best programs and, unfortunately, some of the worst."

Silverman was once booted off the set of the game show *Password*, after asking a producer, "Who thinks up this crap anyway?"

Ben Stein, a television writer: "The business of television is the business of making easy money. . . The fact that you can get paid a million dollars in TV to do shit inspires you to do shit. There's no such thing as principle, only the deal."

Dick Wolf, producer of *Miami Vice* and *Law and Order*: "I have an eight-year old and a five-year-old child. They've never seen any of the shows I've ever produced. They shouldn't be watching them. They're not allowed to watch Saturday morning cartoons."

Media producers conscious of the shortcomings of what they produce are quick to point out that they are merely yielding to the pressures imposed upon them; they are only following orders. The blame lies elsewhere, with network or studio heads, with advertisers, with the ratings services. Television producers complain about their powerlessness, their lack of status as creative artists.

Norman Lear (before cable cut into the dominance of the networks):

> It is true that we who produce and write are responsible for physically producing violence, but the men and women in this community who make their living writing and directing television have only three theaters to sell their wares. So when you go to any of the three theaters (CBS,

ABC, NBC), you often find yourself writing what it is they are interested in buying. And if they are interested in buying a cop show or a private eye show, and within that context they are interested in as much action as they can get, then that's what you, as a craftsman, as a person with something to sell and a family to support, must do because that's what the buyer wants.

If the talented people who produce media content insist on passing the buck to the big shots, this suggests that their own criteria of excellence are different from those to be found in the front office. Anybody who self-consciously sells out presumably does so to someone else with different standards of judgment. Although the evidence is anecdotal, the media apparently do not always reflect the personal tastes or opinions of their creators. Do they mirror the values of those in charge? The only way to find out is to ask them, but they are not all that easy to pin down.

Tycoons As Consumers

Although the rank and file creators of media content are often uncomfortable or ambivalent about their tasks, few such qualms or scruples are evident among their masters. At the top, as in the ranks, there is a sense that the system operates on its own momentum and by rules that are beyond the power of individuals to alter. A limited number of powerful individuals run the large multimedia organizations. Some are reclusive or self-important, but a dozen agreed to talk to me about their own media habits and preferences. There is, as might be expected, no uniformity in their preferences or habits, but there are some recurrent themes.

Almost all are diligent students of the businesses they are in, spending vast amounts of office and private time to keep up with the output of their own and rival organizations. This dedication is symbolized by the wall of television monitors that dominates a network president's spacious office, with a paper-covered desk and a magnificent bare marble conference table. A four-way split screen carries CBS, NBC, ABC and CNN. The other large screen carries the local company-owned station. The sound is on full-blast as I enter the room. Yes, he tells me, the videos are on all day, though he mutes the sound when he has visitors or when he wants quiet. Apparently the noise does not bother him in his routine work. He also gets a feed of new program pilot tapes from Hollywood that he can look at. "I skim. And I watch at home in the evening. Do I watch for my own pleasure? Yes, I watch the news in various forms, and I'm a great fan of public television and A & E." (Evidently his personal viewing preferences are different from those that are satisfied by his own organization.)

Another network president, commenting on the monitors: "They're just humming away there like Muzak and after a while you just ignore them unless something catches your attention."

Some tycoons rise at five in the morning to examine the fresh day's newspapers, others take home videocassettes of the latest network releases or syndicated programs. Virtually all are regular readers of *The New York Times* and *The Wall Street Journal,* and compulsory scanners of the trade press.

"I read lots and lots of magazines. All of the news weeklies, *Forbes, Business Week, Ad Age, Professional Selling, Cable Week.* I see the *Columbia Journalism Review* and the *Harvard Business Review.* For fun I read *American Heritage, Smithsonian, Runner's World, World War II* magazine. I get *Fortune at* home."

Much of their reading, light and serious, is done on airplanes. One of them listens to management self-improvement audio tapes in his car on the way to work. While there is some disposition to disassociate themselves from popular tastes, their remarks reveal few traces of intellectual snobbery. In fact, there is an occasional self-deprecatory aside about their own vulgar interests. Apart from business-related subjects, their media exposure tends to conform to the habits of their social class. Not one mentioned reading a book of any heavy intellectual content, or having seen a film that might be considered avant-garde or off-beat. One major figure in the media world entertains himself with detective stories. Others are buffs of military history. One owns all twenty-one videotapes of the movie *Victory at Sea.* Another has 150 videos on the Second World War. Still another describes his book reading: "I read great trash. Anything with a swastika on the front, I usually read that." This is still a different case from that of Time Warner's late Steven Ross, who was reported never to read a book.

Several executives interviewed acknowledged that they are under extreme time pressures that restrict their exposure to new ideas, or to any ideas in depth.

Senior television executive: "Television is a lot less urgent than it used to be. In the course of business I have a certain amount of reading of scripts and treatments, and I have less time than I used to for other kinds of reading. I don't read as easily as I used to."

Some seem to husband their free time, while others expend it in chance and casual fashion, much like the public at large. A publisher of a large magazine: "I press the buttons and I stop at anything that looks interesting."

CEO of a station group: "I'm a big movie guy. I see

all the latest films, about two a week, going out to the theater. I like to watch the movies when they first come out. Hollywood picks up all the newest latest trends. They know what's going on in the world. We turn around and spend a lot of money on movies [to put on the air]."

Some media tycoons find it hard to separate their personal values from their business values. A senior television executive:

> Personal and professional is one and the same. In the old days everybody sat down and watched the *Ed Sullivan Show*. That kind of viewing has gone by the boards. The viewer's attention span is much shorter. There's a lot of grazing and inattentive viewing. They watch less intensely than they used to. I may be in the business, but my viewing isn't all that different. . . . You can watch a relatively little amount and still keep abreast of the programming. I make it a point to see each new show once relatively early in the season.

CEO of a multimedia company: "I have a set in the office, with a VCR attached, and I watch stuff that our folks are bicycling around the company. At home I'll look at business-related things like Michael Porter's Strategic Planning tapes."

Some media tycoons consume media voraciously, but not exclusively for their private delectation. Their social and business contacts are interwoven. Says a multi-media tycoon:

> As CEO I probably devote half my time to eyeballing, or meeting, or otherwise studying other media. Most of my reading and viewing is related to business or professional interests. My reading and viewing would total six or seven hours a day. I have four TV sets on all the time, to the networks and CNN. Trying to find ideas to use. If I go to see a movie that has nothing to do with business, I'll still think of business applications. Even if things are entertainment, I automatically translate it into the business at hand. In the media business, when you're awake you're at work.

Apart from what they ingest for professional or business reasons, their tastes are the middlebrow tastes of their counterparts in any business. Most are not bothered by commercialism, vulgarity, violence, and obscenity. It simply does not enter their thinking. They seem incapable of stepping aside from their own work and saying, "Here is where I'm forced to make compromises." They have no particular philosophy that

underlies what they do, or at least any that they can easily articulate. CEO of a station group:

> My taste is different from the average person's but I respect it. I would never be where I am today if I tried to program a television station to my liking. The first ten years in this business I tried to determine what's black and white; now I live in a sea of gray. By black and white I mean very strong opinions for or against. I don't interject myself into programming decisions. You just have to respect the ideas on the creative side. I just think anyone who feels strongly definitive today becomes argumentative. Things are moving so fast today that people shouldn't get too definitive in their opinions.

Other media tycoons clearly distinguish their personal preferences from those of the mass audiences for which their enterprises produce. A former television network president:

> Those people who aren't broadcasters born and raised simply don't have the same sense of responsibility as those with the bottom-line mentality. I don't think you can wrest CBS away from Larry Tisch and give it back to Frank Stanton. The whole thing goes back to the white hot competition in broadcasting today. If you just have three grand old networks plodding along and now you have all those new players doing competitive things, they're going to do what's calculated to get the viewer's attention, and he's going to eschew information and watch something witless and forgettable. Nobody should go to jail for it. The viewer can view whatever he wants. I just deplore it. Now with the new technology you would think you would have a lot of narrowcasting, with a giant menu of choices, but it isn't happening. I'm really bitching about the nature of the viewer. He's going to go for the junk food. Adding all of those other choices doesn't mean adding any new choices at all. . . The way I feel is negative. All of those opportunities we have to spend our time—as the quantity increases the quality of what we spend our time on decreases.

The CEO of a large multimedia company says he looks at the first seven minutes of the morning news "to tell me what I should know that's going on," but other than that sees no TV, except the Sunday morning programs, like *Meet the Press*. "I have no judgment about programs. I have no interest in them. It bores me. I try to look at the popular shows, but I can't follow them. I can't stand it." CEO of a major multi-media company:

TV is a medium of the lowest common denominator. Whoever can generate the greatest numbers wins. Cable has brought in narrowcasting, but it's still a mass medium. I think it's hard with commercial TV to produce anything but passive programming. TV is a passive medium. If you start highbrow stuff that doesn't have broad-based appeal your ratings will be off and you lose your mass audience. I think you're going to continue to see the lowest common denominator approach. It's just the nature of the beast. I think it's more a comment on America than on the media. We're a mirror of society.

A CEO of a multimedia company: "I usually found that when I went to network affiliates' meetings and watched the pilots of the new shows that I never found much that I liked. My tastes are not the same as those of the people who watch them."

Senior film executive: "You can personally like some things and you'll never make them because they don't have a commercial potential. Other things you might bend over backwards a little to push them. Is this something that someone would go to see? We're in a business and you can't run away from that. You have to look at things from the standpoint of whether they'll make a profit." A president of a large multi-media company:

When I was responsible for our broadcasting operations, I went to visit one of our television stations. I had a whole sheaf of questions I had written out on a yellow lined pad and the station manager had people running in and out of his office to find me the answers, all day long. When I went back to the hotel room before we were meeting for dinner I had our station on and the news show was quite well done. Then came this game show. I couldn't imagine why anyone would watch it. I could hardly believe how bad it was. When I talked to the station manager he said that was the highest rated show we have. People who are educated and have learned the joy of reading and thinking are going to spend a hell of a lot less time sitting on their ass eating peanuts and drinking beer and watching that crap.

A senior television executive: "I don't watch a lot

of television. I go cherry picking for the newest sporting event or other events. I dip around among the morning shows. I don't watch at all during the day. In the evening, the news, and maybe there'll be something that I'll watch—the beginning of Carson or *Nightline*. Series programming—I see almost none of it. I don't think I'm unusual."

It is possible to acknowledge taste differences while avoiding value judgments. A CEO of a large multimedia company, asked if there was ever any incongruity between his own tastes and his publications, replied, "All the time. I keep them separate. . .I think the unsuccessful publisher or editor is the one who attempts to dictate what people should be reading, what should be of interest to the people rather than developing a product that's relevant to their needs." Says a senior Hollywood executive:

I try to see at least one episode of most new shows. Very rarely would I watch more than one. I look to see what new ideas I can get, or to spot new talent, for things we may cast in the future. I see almost every new film that comes out, three or four a week. [What wouldn't you see?] The fifth *Rambo*, or other sequels. Some of the mindless violence, because I can't stand that stuff. I read. I read script material, and some books that I read for pleasure when I'm traveling. Both fiction and nonfiction. What I read for pleasure and for business overlaps. I read the trades, and seven or eight magazines. You're always looking at material you might be able to use. When I go to the theater in New York or London, I'm also looking to see if it would be a picture.

Intelligent, amiable and admirable though they may be, the people who run large media enterprises generally appear to regard the output of their own organizations as somewhat beyond their control. They certainly do not regard it as an extension of their personal interests or a reflection of their own preferences. Many of them stressed that they are in business to meet the public's tastes and demands, not to satisfy or impose their own. They are not unmindful of the cultural and political power their companies exercise, but they regard themselves as responsible custodians of a financial trust rather than as keepers of a sacred flame or as crusaders for enlightenment.

Cultural Democracy

Defenders of the mass media status quo like to fall back on the phrase "cultural democracy" to justify their pursuit of audience numbers, and to decry the imposition of other external criteria for judging content. This has always been the establishment view of mass media management. "How do you describe a good book?" Ralph Daigh of Fawcett's Gold Medal Books was asked forty years ago by a member of the House Select Committee on Current Pornographic Materials. The Committee had attacked paperbacks for "the dissemination of artful appeals to sensuality, immorality, filth, perversion, and degeneracy." Daigh replied, "A book is usually a good book if the public buys it in quantity." Pressed on this point, he added, "When the public buys a product in multimillion lots, that is an endorsement by the public, and it does connote that it is a good book."

For the majority of media executives who defend their output in spite of their personal distaste for it, the rationale is clear; they are in business to give the public what it wants.

David Sarnoff: "We're in the same position as a plumber laying pipes. We're not responsible for what goes through the pipe."

Marvin Antonowsky, at the time vice-president for programming at NBC: "The price of failure looms too large for us not to make the pragmatic decisions that are necessary, even though we may not like doing it."

Roger King, syndicator of *Oprah Winfrey, Wheel of Fortune*, and *Jeopardy*: "The people are the boss. We listen to the audience, see what they want and try to accommodate them. I know it sounds simplistic, but that's exactly what it is."

Roone Arledge, then president of ABC News and Sports: "I don't think it's our responsibility to sit and determine what people must see for their own good. If you don't recognize the forces that play on what people watch and what they don't, then you're a fool and should be in a different business."

Rupert Murdoch: "When the beaver gnaws down a tree, he isn't thinking of his vital ecological role either. But nevertheless he has one. And I think we have one too. . . .We destroy monopolies because we hope to make money for ourselves, but we enjoy it because it has clear social benefits as well."

Frank Stanton, in 1960: "A program in which a large part of the audience is interested is by that very fact a program in the public interest."

The majority of media executives are in business to give the public what it wants.

This last is a play on words, which confuses desire with well-being. It is like arguing that a child with an insatiable craving for chocolate or an adult with an incessant yen for cigarettes serves his own interests when he satisfies his wish. Yet, the proposition is central to the workings of commercial culture. The repercussions of what is read, seen or heard affect everyone, not merely the individuals who do the reading, viewing, listening. It is not merely the interests of its own audience that are engaged when a medium comes up for judgment.

Society as a whole has a stake in every form of media expression, inasmuch as this helps to shape the outlook and behavior with which all its members must coexist. The profit-centered rules of the marketplace are not necessarily the only ones, or even the most appropriate ones, that should apply to institutions that shape national values and character.

Democratic Media

EDWARD HERMAN

A DEMOCRATIC media is a primary condition of popular rule, hence of a genuine political democracy. Where the media are controlled by powerful and privileged elites, whether government leaders and bureaucrats or private sector elites, democratic political forms and some kind of limited political democracy may exist, but not genuine democracy. The media will, of structural necessity, select news and organize debate supportive of agendas and programs of the privileged. They will not provide the unbiased information and opinion that would permit the public to make choices in accord with its own best interests. Their job will be to show that what's good for the elites is good for everybody, and that other options are either bad or do not exist.

Freedom of Choice

Economists have long distinguished between "consumer sovereignty" and "freedom of consumer choice." The former requires that consumers participate in deciding what is to be offered in the first place; the latter is satisfied if the consumer is free to select among the options chosen for them by producers. Freedom of choice is better than no freedom of choice, and the market may provide a substantial array of options. But it may not. Before the foreign car invasion in the 1960s, U.S. car manufacturers chose not to offer small cars, because the profit margin on small cars is small. It was better to have choices among four or five manufacturers than one, but the options were constrained by producer interest. Only the entry of foreign competition made small cars available to U.S. buyers. Freedom of choice prevailed in both cases, but consumer sovereignty did not. The cost of *producer* sovereignty was also manifest in the policy of General

Motors Corporation, in cahoots with rubber and oil interests, of buying up public transit lines and converting them to GM buses or liquidating them.[1] The consumer of transportation services, if fully informed, might well have chosen to preserve and subsidize the electric transit option, but this sovereign decision was not open to them.

This distinction between sovereignty and free choice has important applications both to national politics and the mass media. In each case, the general population has some kind of free choice, but lacks sovereignty. The public goes to the polls every few years to pull a lever for slates of candidates chosen for them by political parties heavily dependent on funding by powerful elite interests. The public has "freedom of choice" only among a very restricted set of what we might call the "effective" candidates, effectiveness being defined by their ability to attract the funding necessary to make a credible showing.

At the level of mass communication as well, the dominant media with large audiences are owned by an overlapping set of powerful elite interests. There is a fringe media with very limited outreach that might support "ineffective" candidates, but because of their marginal status, they and the candidates they support can be easily ignored. As with the candidates, the populace has "freedom of choice" among the dominant set of mainstream media, but it lacks sovereignty except in a legalistic and formal sense (we are each legally free to start our own newspaper or buy our own paper or TV network. There is, of course, a wider array of choices on the fringe, but a large fraction of the population doesn't even know these fringe publications exist. The elite-dominated mass media, not surprisingly, find the political system admirable, and while sometimes expressing regret at the quality of the menu of candidates, never seriously question the

From *Z Papers*, January/March 1992, pp. 23-30. © 1992 by the Institute for Social and Cultural Communications, part of the Institute for Social and Cultural Change, Inc., 116 Saint Botolph Street, Boston, MA 02115. Reprinted by permission.

absence of citizen sovereignty as regards deciding on the effective options.

Naturally, also, the mass media hardly mention the undemocratic underpinning of the democratic process in the media itself. In fact, one of the most disquieting features of propaganda systems of the constrained democracies of advanced capitalism is that the consolidation of mass media power has closed down discussion of the need for radical restructuring of the media. It has also pushed such changes off the political agenda. As the "gatekeepers," the mass media have been in the enviable position of being able to protect themselves from debate or politics that threaten their interests, which illustrates the deeply undemocratic character of *their* role.

Arguably, the last great fight over structural change in the mass media was in 1934, when the FCC was created and broadcasting policy was fixed. At that time, an important lobbying effort pressed for the reservation of 25 percent of air channels for non-profit operations. This was defeated by the commercial lobby and upon the assurance by the commercial interests that they would service public interest needs.[2] As advertising grew, however, and entertainment and "noncontroversial" programming proved more profitable than public affairs and educational children's programming, the latter were gradually abandoned— but all on the quiet, as the gatekeepers determined![3]

Occasionally, issues like TV violence have aroused public opinion and caused the Congress to hold hearings and assail the TV networks, but the whole business has always been settled by appeals to corporate responsibility and self-regulation, and the assurance by the media barons of their deepest concern and commitment to rectifying the situation. In 1977, however, an unusually aggressive and naive House subcommittee actually drafted a report calling for investigation of the structure of the TV industry as a necessary step to attacking the violence problem at its source! As George Gerbner described the sequel:

> When the draft mentioning industry structure was leaked to the networks, all hell broke loose. Members of the subcommittee told me that they had never before been subject to such relentless lobbying and pressure. Campaign contributors were contacted. The report was delayed for months. The subcommittee staffer who wrote the draft was summarily fired. The day before the final vote was to be taken, a new version drafted by a broadcast lobbyist was substituted. It ignored the evidence of the hearings and gutted the report, shifting the source of the problem from network structure to the parents of America. When the network-dictated draft came to a vote, members of the full committee (including those who had never attended hearings) were mobilized, and the watered down version won by one vote.[4]

In short, the power of the "actual existing" highly undemocratic mass media is enormous. In alliance with an undemocratic system of political parties, it engineers consent or quiescence. The result is manifested mainly in apathy and an anger that is deflected away from primary establishment institutions.

Serving The Public's Needs

A democratic media can be identified by its structure and functions. In terms of structure, it would be organized and controlled by ordinary citizens or their grass-roots organizations. This could involve one or a few individuals or bodies serving local or larger political, minority, or other groups in the social and political arena. Media fitting these structural conditions would be bound to articulate demands of the general population because they are either part of it or instruments created to serve its needs.

In the mainstream system, the mass media are large organizations owned by other large organizations or shareholders and controlled by members of a privileged business elite. The ownership structure puts them at a distance from ordinary people. They are funded by advertising, and advertisers have to be convinced that the programs meet their needs. Thus in terms of fundamental structure, the mainstream media are not agents serving the general public: the first responsibility of mainstream media managers by law is to stockholders seeking profits; and as advertisers are the principal source of revenue, their needs come second. There is no legal responsibility to audiences at all; these must be persuaded to watch or buy, but by any means the gatekeeper chooses, within the limits of law and conventional standards of morality.

As regards function, a democratic media will aim first and foremost at serving the informational, cultural, and communications needs of the members of the public which the media institutions comprise or represent. The users would determine their own needs and fix the menu of choices either directly or through their closely controlled agents, and debate would not be limited to selected voices chosen by corporate or government gatekeepers. The sovereign listeners would not only participate in choosing programs and issues to be addressed, they would be the voices heard, and they would be involved in continuous interchanges with other listeners. There would be a horizontal flow of communication, in both directions, instead of a vertical flow from officials and experts to the passive population of consumers.

At the same time, a democratic media would recognize and encourage diversity. It would allow and encourage minorities to express their views and build their own communities' solidarity within the larger community. This would follow from the democratic idea of recognizing and encouraging individual differences and letting all such flowers bloom irrespective of financial capability and institutional power. This is also consistent with the ideal of pluralism, part of mainstream orthodox doctrine but poorly realized in mainstream practice. In the commercial media, minority voices are rarely heard except when serving a commercial message, and from on high, not in the terms decided upon within the community addressed. In Hungary, e.g., the new commercial media, "have a radio program for tourists from German-speaking countries, but none for hundreds of thousands of gypsies living in Hungary (7 percent of the population)."[5] The commercial media fail utterly in serving minority constituencies, tending toward the repetition of homogenizing mainstream cultural-market themes and serving diverse cultures in the same way as tourism serves indigenous peoples. The same criticism often applies to state controlled media.[6]

A democratic media would encourage people to know and understand their neighbors, nearby and at a distance, and to act and participate in social and political life. This is likely to occur where media structures are democratic, as these media will be open to neighbors who want to communicate views on problems and their communal resolution. Commercial media aim to entertain and divert, and tied in as they are to the dominant institutions, they serve the dominant elites and status quo, and avoid controversial messages of people aiming to disturb and initiate change. The commercial and state media treat the citizenry as passive recipients of entertainment-information as a commodity, offered them from above. They are not agents of a democratic citizenry, but of a business and state elite.

Democratizing The Media

There are two main routes to democratizing the media. One is to try to influence the mainstream media to give more room to now excluded ideas and groups. This could be done by persuasion, pressure, or by legislation compelling greater access. The second route is to create an alternative structure of media closer to ordinary people and grass-roots organizations that would replace or at least offer an important alternative to the mainstream media. This could be done, in principle, by private and popular initiative, by legislative action, or by a combination of the two.

The first route is of limited value, certainly, as a long run solution to the problem, precisely because it fails to attack the structural roots of the media's lack of democracy. If function follows from structure, the gains from pursuit of the first route are likely to be modest and transitory. Its small gains may, nonetheless, lead both activists and ordinary citizens to conclude that the mainstream media are really open to dissent, when in fact dissent is securely kept in a nonthreatening position. And it may divert energy from building an alternative media. On the other hand, the limited access obtained by pursuit of the first route may have disproportionate and catalyzing effects on elite opinion. This route may also be the only one that appeals to many media activists, and there is no assurance that the long run strategy of pursuing structural change will work.

The second route to democratization of the media is the only one that can yield a truly democratic media, and it is this route that I want to discuss at greater length. Without a democratic structure, the media will never serve a democratic function, even if, voluntarily or under pressure, they make concessions and gestures in that direction. The struggle for a democratic media structure is also of increasing urgency, because media structures have become less democratic in recent decades with the decline in relative importance of the public and non-profit broadcasting spheres, increased commercialization and integration of the mass media into the market, conglomeration, and internationalization. In important respects the main ongoing struggle has been to prevent further attrition of democratic elements in existing media structures.

This has been very much evident in Western Europe where powerful systems of public broadcasting, as well as non-profit local radio stations, have been under relentless attack by commercial and conservative political interests strongly influential in state policy. These changes have threatened diversity, quality, and relatively democratic organizational arrangements. In Eastern Europe and the Soviet Union, where state controlled media institutions are being rapidly dismantled, there is a dire threat that an undemocratic system of government control will be replaced by an equally undemocratic system of commercial domination.

It is obvious that a full-fledged democratization of the media can only occur in connection with a thoroughgoing political revolution and drastic alteration in the structure of power. Democratizing a national media would be very difficult in a large and complex society like the United States even with unlimited structural options, just as organizing a democratic polity here would be a bit more tricky than in a tiny Greek city state or autonomous New England town. The surest way to a democratic media would be to move back to the Articles of Confederation, and beyond—to really small units where people can interact on a personal level. For larger units, efficiency considerations would force centralization of national and international news gathering, processing, and distribution, and of cultural-entertainment productions as well. Funding would have to be insulated from business and government, but it could not be completely insulated from democratic decision processes. Maintaining involvement and control by ordinary citizens, while allowing a necessary degree of specialization and centralization, and permitting artistic autonomy as well, would present a serious challenge to democratic organization. As this is not on the immediate agenda, however, I am not going to try to spell out here the machinery and arrangements whereby these conflicting ends can be accomplished.

Some partial guidelines for the pursuit of democratic structural change in the media in the United States can be derived from the current debates and struggles in Europe, where the democratic forces are trying to hold the line (in Western Europe) and prevent wholesale commercialization (in the East). The democrats have stressed the deadly effects of privatization and commercialization on a democratic polity and culture, and have urged the importance of preserving and enlarging the *public* and *civic* spheres of the media. The public sphere is the government sponsored sector, which is far more important in Western Europe than in this country. It is funded by direct governmental grants, license fees, and to an increasing but controlled extent, advertising. This sphere is designed and responsible for serving the public interest in news, public affairs, educational, children's, and much cultural programming. It is assumed in Europe that the commercial sphere will pursue large audiences with entertainment (movies, sitcoms, cowboy-crime stories) and that its long term trend toward abandonment of non-entertainment values will continue.[7]

The civic sector comprises all the media that are non-commercial and non-government sponsored and funded, and which arise by individual or grassroots initiatives. This would include mainly local newspapers and journals, independent movie and TV producers, and radio broadcasters. The civic sector has virtually no TV presence in Europe, but radio broadcasting by non-profit organizations is still fairly important, sufficiently so to have produced a European Federation of Community Radios (FERL) to exchange ideas and coordinate educational and lobbying efforts to advance their ideals and protect their interests.

FERL has been lobbying throughout Europe for explicit recognition of the important role of the non-commercial, and especially the civic sector, in governmental and inter-governmental policy. It has urged the preservation and enlargement of this sector by policy choice. In France, the civic sector actually gets some funding from the state via a tax on commercial advertising revenues. This is a model that could be emulated elsewhere. It should be noted, however, that in the conservative political environment of the past half dozen years, the policies of the French regulatory authority, the Higher Broadcasting Council, has reduced the number of non-profit radio stations from 1,000 to under 300, and discriminated heavily in favor of religious and right-wing broadcasters as well.

Democratizing The U.S. Media

Democratizing the U.S. media is an even more formidable task than that faced by Europeans. In Western Europe, public broadcasting is important, even if under siege, and community radio is a more important force than in the United States. In Eastern Europe the old government-dominated systems are crumbling, so that there are options and an ongoing struggle for control. In the United States, commercial systems are more powerfully entrenched, the public sector is weak and has been badly compromised in the

Reagan-Bush years, and the civic sphere, while alive and bustling, is small, mainly local, and undernourished. The question is, what is to be done?

Funding

An extremely important problem for democratization is that the commercial sector is self-funding, with large resources from advertising, whereas the public and civic sectors are chronically starved. This gives the commercial media an overwhelming advantage in technical quality and polish, price, and publicity and distribution. An important part of a democratic media strategy must consist of figuring out how to obtain sizable and more stable resources for the public and civic sectors. The two promising sources are taxes on commercial media revenues and direct government grants. Commercial radio and TV are getting the free use of public airwaves to turn a private profit, and there is an important record of commercial broadcasting and FCC commitments to public service made in 1934 and 1946 that have been quietly sloughed off.[8] These considerations make a franchise tax, with the revenues turned over to the public and civic sectors that have taken on those abandoned responsibilities, completely justifiable.

The funding of the public and civic sectors from general tax revenues and/or license fees on receiving sets is also easily defended, given the great importance of these sectors in educational, childrens', minority group and public affairs programming. These services are important for democratic citizenship, among other aims.

In sum, local, regional and national groups interested in democratizing the media should give high priority to organization, education, and lobbying designed to sharply increase and stabilize the funding of the financially strapped public and civic sectors. Success in these endeavors is going to depend in large measure on the general political climate.

The Commercial Sector

The commercial sector of the media does provide some diversity, insofar as individual proprietors may allow it and advertisers can be mobilized in niche markets of liberal and progressive bent (*The New Yorker*, urban alternative press). The main drift of commercial markets, however, is deleterious to a democratic media, and while we may welcome the offbeat and progressive commercial media institutions, the main policy actions for this sector that progressives should support would be to limit further consolidation, conglomeration, and cross-ownership, and compel openings to excluded outsiders.

I do not believe that antitrust policy deserves major energies by media democrats, although these causes are worthy of support. I also favor "fairness doctrine" and quantitative requirements for local, public affairs, and childrens' programs for commercial radio and TV broadcasters. Part of the reason is straightforward: it is an outrage that they have abandoned public service in their quest for profit. A more devious reason is this: pressing the commercial broadcasters, and describing in detail how they have abandoned children and public service for "light fare," will help make the case for taxing them and funding the public and civic sectors.

The Public Sector

The Corporation for Public Broadcasting was brought into existence in 1967, with the acquiescence of the commercial broadcasters, who were pleased to transfer public interest responsibilities elsewhere as long as these were funded by the taxpayer. Public radio and TV both have been somewhat more open to dissent and minority voices than the commercial broadcasting media, partly a result of original design, but also because, despite their ties to government, they have proven to be somewhat more independent of government and tolerant of the controversial than the commercial broadcasters.

The independence and quality of the public sector depends heavily on the political environment. As long as it is kept on a short financial leash, underfunded, and worried mainly about attacks from the right, it will feature a William Buckley and McLaughlin, with McNeil-Lehrer on "the left," and offer mainly bland and cautious news and commentary plus noncontroversial nature and cultural events. Not surprisingly, it went into serious decline in the Reagan-Bush years. It needs a lot more money, longer funding periods, more autonomy, and less pressure from the right wing to perform well. There is an important role for the public sector in a system of democratic media, and its rehabilitation should definitely be on the democratic media agenda.

The Civic Sector

For real progress in democratizing the media a much larger place must be carved out for the civic sector. This is the nonprofit sector organized by individuals or grass roots organizations to serve the communications needs of the general population (as opposed to the corporate community and government). A top priority must be given to building this sector because only out of such democratically rooted structures are we likely to get a truly democratic communications service. Furthermore, the very process of building a media civic sector is important in the learning process of democracy and as part of community mobilization.

Alternative Press—There is an alternative local press in many cities in the U.S., usually distributed without charge and funded by advertising, but catering to a somewhat offbeat audience and providing an opening for dissent, within limits. This alternative press has a national Association of Alternative News Weeklies with 75 members and claims a readership of some four million. Its performance is spotty, but it fosters diversity.

It is possible to depend on advertising and to maintain alternative press substance. The costs of serious dissent may be heavy, however, and compromises are endemic. The *Village Voice* has provided significant dissent in the huge market of New York City. Even more interesting is the *Anderson Valley Advertiser* of Boonville, California, a local paper which has survived in a small town despite the radical perspectives of its editor. It has been subjected to advertising boycotts and is avoided regularly by some advertisers on political grounds, but its advertising penalties are partially offset by a wider readership generated by its exciting quality and vigor. *AVA* is a model of democratic newspaper work in its good local news coverage, its exceptional openness to letters and petitions, and the continuous and sometimes furious debates among readers and between readers and editors, that constitute a kind of town meeting on paper. A host of local issues are addressed, and national issues are debated in columns and letters, though no attempt is made to provide national and international news coverage. A thousand papers like *AVA* would make this a much more democratic country.

There is a national alternative press, led by *In These Times* and the New York *Guardian*. Between them they have a circulation of under 50,000, and despite their good quality and even greater promise, they struggle each year for readers and other subventions to keep afloat. These papers deserve support, and their continued existence and growth is important in a democratic media project. How to increase their outreach and strength is a puzzle that needs to be addressed.

Alternative Journals—There are a fair number of alternative journals in the United States, including *The Nation, Z Magazine, The Progressive, Mother Jones, Dollars and Sense, Monthly Review, Ms Magazine, Lies of Our Times, The Texas Observer, CovertAction Information Bulletin*, and others. Apart from *Mother Jones*, which has sometimes crossed the quarter million mark in circulation, based on large promotional campaigns, *The Nation* has the largest readership, with about 90,000. Most of the alternative journals have circulations between 2,000 and 30,000, and have chronic financial problems. By contrast, *Time* has a circulation of 4.2 million and *Reader's Digest* about 15 million. Some of the alternative journals could expand circulation with aggressive and large scale publicity and higher quality copy, but this would cost a lot of money. Not many of the U.S. billionaires are inclined to set up trust funds to help enlarge the circulation of alternative journals. Advertisers are also not bending over backwards to throw business their way.

Alternative Radio—Radio may be a more promising avenue for growth and greater outreach of alternative media than the print media. More people are prone to listen to radio and watch TV than read journals, or even newspapers, which are also harder to get into the hands of audiences. And radio broadcasting facilities are not expensive. Community radio made a large spurt in growth in the early 1970s, then tapered off, in part a result of the shortage of additional frequencies in the larger markets. Of the roughly 1,500 non-commercial radio licenses outstanding, half are to religious broadcasters. Many of the remaining 750 are college and university linked, and perhaps 250 are licensed to community organizations.

Many of the community stations have languished for want of continuity of programming and spotty quality. Discrete and sporadic programs do not command large audiences; building substantial audiences requires that many people know that particular types of programs are going to be there, day after day, at a certain time period. (This is why stations become "all news," or have talk shows all morning and rock music all afternoon.) There are also the usual problems of funding, as well as threats to licenses by more powerful commercial interests seeking to enlarge their domains. A national organization, the National Federation of Community Radios exists to advance and protect community radio interests.

Pacifica's five station network and News Service has done important work in providing an alternative and high quality radio offering and a sizable and loyal listenership. It deserves strong support and emulation. Radio Zinzine in Forcalquier, a small town of Upper Province in France, also provides an important model of constructive use of radio. Organized by the members of the progressive cooperative Longo Mai, Radio Zinzine, has given the local farmers and townspeople a more vigorous and action-oriented form of local news (as well as broader news coverage and entertainment), but also an avenue for communication among formerly isolated and consequently somewhat apathetic people. It has energized the local population, encouraged its participation, and made it more of a genuine community.

In a dramatic example of how democratic media can come into existence out of the needs of ordinary people who want to speak and encourage others to communicate, M'Banna Kantako, a 31-year-old black, blind, unemployed public housing resident in Springfield, Illinois organized Black Liberation Radio in 1986, out of frustration with the failure of the major media to provide news and entertainment of interest to the black community. Operating illegally on a 1-watt transmitter with a range of one mile, Kantako provides a genuine alternative for the black community. Kantako was ignored by the FCC and dominant media till he broadcast a series of interviews with blacks brutalized by the local police. Soon thereafter the FCC tried to get him off the air, and a court order was issued to close him down, but it remains unenforced. Undefended by the local media, Kantako has gotten considerable national publicity and support. Grass-roots organizers and student groups from 45 states and 4 foreign countries have contacted him, and several other "micro-radio" stations have gone on the air. This is genuinely democratic media: may it spread widely.

Alternative TV—The mainstreaming and commercialization of public TV was a factor in the upsurge of new and formerly dormant educational and other non-commercial TV channels in the 1980s designed to service the public interest function abandoned by the dominant PBS stations. (These stations were also helped along by tie-ins to cable, which permitted them to reach larger audiences with low power transmitters.) In an embarrassing episode for PBS, a PBS-sponsored report found that the new applicants-entrants would not be competing much with the older stations, as the older ones had moved to serve an upscale audience with a suitable menu. Meanwhile, the older stations have lobbied aggressively to prevent the new and refurbished ones sharing in government funding slotted for public TV stations. It goes without saying that the new stations deserve support as a democratizing force, although the older ones should not be written off—rather, they need reorganization and regeneration to allow them to throw off the Reagan era incubus and better serve a public function.

The growth of cable opened up democratic options, partly in the greater numbers of channels and potentially enlarged diversity of commercial cable, but more importantly in the frequent obligation of cable systems to provide public access channels and facilities. First imposed as a requirement by the FCC in 1972, partly as an impediment to cable growth by an FCC still serving the commercial broadcasters' interests, the movement was eventually institutionalized as part of negotiated agreements between cable companies seeking franchises and community negotiators. The cable companies were obliged to allow access to local community groups as part of their rationale for encroaching on "free" broadcasting TV, and getting local monopoly rights to boot, and community groups and activists took advantage of this strategic need to press local governments to bargain hard with cable companies in providing for access channels and facilities. In many cases the contracts called for provision of facilities and training to access users by the cable companies, and in some instances a percentage of cable revenues (1 to 5 percent) was contracted to be set aside to fund the access operations.

This important development offers a resource and opportunity that demands far more attention from media activists than it has gotten. Spokespersons for the public access movement call attention to the fact that there are some 1,000 sites where TV production takes place for access, over 2,000 access facilities, and that more than 15,000 hours of original material are transmitted over public access channels per week to an unknown but probably fairly sizable audience. The problems here, as with community radio, lie in the frequent absence of the continuity that makes for regular watching, and the lack of promotional resources. Some of the audience limits are inherent in the specialized focus of the programming (programs for the deaf, or for Vietnamese in their native language). The existing levels of participation and excitement are valuable, but the opportunities for growth are important and should be pursued. Furthermore, many cable contracts are up for renewal over the next few years and citizen mobilization is needed to protect cable access from attrition as well as to seek its enlargement.

A strenuous effort has been made by some media democrats to fill the programming gap with centrally assembled or produced materials, made available through network pools of video-tapes and by transmission of fresh materials through satellites. Paper Tiger TV has been providing weekly programs on Manhattan Cable for years, making these programs available to public access stations and movement groups wanting to use them in meetings.[9] An affiliated organization, Deep Dish Network, has tried to provide a national network for public access stations, encouraging local production, assembling and producing quality programs that are publicized in advance and transmitted via satellite to alerted individual dish owners, groups, and university and public access stations able to down-link the programs. There are some 3 million home satellite dish owners in North America who can receive Deep Dish offerings, and it is programmed on more than 300 cable systems as well as by many individual TV stations.

In addition to its notable 10-part Gulf Project series, that provided an alternative to mainstream TV's promotional coverage of the Gulf War, Deep Dish has had a major series on the Reagan-Bush era attacks on civil liberties, and it plans to transmit counter-celebratory programs on Columbus's conquest of the new world throughout 1992. On December 1, 1991, it transmitted an hour-long live program by Kitchen Center professional artists in conjunction with Visual AIDS, entitled Day Without Art, as part of a day of action and mourning in response to the AIDs crisis. Performed in New York City, there were live audiences receiving the program in eight cities, and a much wider audience call-in operation was part of the program. Group viewings and cable showings were encouraged in advance. Deep Dish also inspired Satellite University Network to put up six programs on Latino issues (immigration, abuses on the job, struggle for rights, history, etc.), and did a big outreach operation to get interested groups, universities, and public access stations to down-link the programs.

Deep Dish suffers from the sporadic nature of its offerings, which harks back to the basic problem of funding. An excellent case can be made for funding Deep Dish and similar services to the civic sector out of franchise taxes on the commercial stations or general tax revenues.

Technological Change—The sharp reductions in price and increased availability of VCRs, camcorders, fax machines, computers, modems, and desktop computer-publishing, have made possible easier communication among individuals, the lower cost production of journals and books, and new possibilities for TV production and programming. Of course, the telephone, mimeograph, offset printing and Xerox machines had the same potential earlier and were put to good use, but they never put the establishment up against the wall. In technological change, those with money and power tend to guide innovation and put technologies to use first, and frequently have moved on to something better by the time these things reach citizen access. Camcorders do not solve the problem of producing really attractive TV programs, let alone getting them shown and widely distributed. While books may be produced more cheaply with new desktop facilities, changes in commercial distribution—blockbusters, saturation advertising, deals with the increasingly concentrated distribution networks—may easily keep dissident books as marginalized as ever.

In perhaps the most dramatic illustration of the problem of catchup, the new communications technologies in the possession of the Pentagon and mainstream media during the Gulf War—video, satellite, computer—conferred a new and enormous power to mold images, block out history and context, and make instant history. "Image Industry Erodes Political Space," as John M. Phelan entitles his analysis of the new, centrally controlled communications technology.[10] And George Gerbner points out "past, present, and future can now be packaged, witnessed, and frozen into memorable moving imagery of instant history—scripted, cast, directed, and produced by the winners."[11]

The point is, it is important for democratic media advance that participants be alert to and take advantage of every technological innovation. The growth of dissident common carriers like Eco-Net and Peace-Net has been important in providing tools for research and means of alerting and communicating among activists. But the problems of reaching large audiences, as opposed to democratic activists being able to communicate more efficiently within and between small groups, remain challenging and severe.

Concluding Note

We are not living in an era of democratizing media. Instead, the main drift in the West has been toward increasing media centralization and commercialization and a corresponding weakening of the public sector. The civic sphere of non-government and non-commercial media has displayed considerable vitality but has been pressed to defend its relative position overall.

I have argued that the civic sector is the locus of the truly democratic media and that genuine democratization in western societies is going to be contingent on its great enlargement. Those actively seeking democratization of the media should seek first to enlarge the civic sphere by every possible avenue, to strengthen the public sector by increasing its autonomy and funding, and lastly to contain or shrink the commercial sector and try to tap it for revenue. Funding this sector properly is going to require government subvention. Media democrats should be preparing the moral and political environment for such financial support, while doing their utmost to advance existing democratic media.

Notes

1. R. B. Du Boff, *Accumulation and Power*, Armonk, N.Y.: M. E. Sharpe, 1989, p. 103.

2. See Robert McChesney, "The Battle for the U.S. Airwaves, 1928-1935," *Journal of Communication*, Autumn, 1990, pp. 29-57.

3. For descriptions of this process, see Erik Barnouw, *The Sponsor*, New York: Oxford, 1978; Edward Palmer, *Television and America's Children: A Crisis of Neglect*, New York: Oxford, 1988; Edward Herman, "The Externalities Effects of Commercial and Public Broadcasting," in Kaarle Nordenstreng and Herbert Schiller, eds., *New World Order? National Sovereignty and International Communication Revisited*, New Jersey: Ablex, forthcoming, 1992.

4. George Gerbner, "Science or Ritual Dance? A Revisionist View of Television Effects Research," *Journal of Communication*, Spring 1984, p. 170.

5. European Federation of Community Radios, *Final Report*, 3rd Congress May 16-20, 1991, p. 5.

6. In the North Italian province of Friuli, where two-thirds of the population speak Friulian, that language does not exist for the state-owned RAI. A community station, Radio Onde Furlane, has come into existence to service this 5 million person audience. See ibid., p. 5.

7. A major spokesperson for this form of critique and analysis has been Karol Jakubowicz, an official in the General Secretariat of Polish Radio and Television. See his background paper, "Post-Communist Central and Eastern Europe: Promoting the Emergence of Open and Plural Media Systems," 3rd European Ministerial Conference on Mass Media Policy, Cyprus, Oct. 9-10, 1991. Similar views are common among members of European Federal of Community Radios. See text below and document cited in note 5 above.

8. See items cited in note 2.

9. *Roar: The Paper Tiger Television Guide to Media Activism*, published in 1991 by Paper Tiger and the Wexner Center for Arts of Ohio State University, provides a short history of Paper Tiger plus other materials, including an excellent bibliography on the media and media activism.

10. *Media Development*, Fall 1991, pp. 6-8.

11. "Persian Gulf War: The Movie," in Hamid Mowlana, George Gerbner, and Herbert Schiller, eds., *Triumph of the Image: The Media's War in the Persian Gulf. A Global Perspective*, Boulder, Colo: Westwood Press, forthcoming.

SITCOM POLITICS

As Murphy Brown prepares to zap Dan Quayle, TV draws fire for its "liberal bias." Do the charges have merit?

RICHARD ZOGLIN

MAKING WISECRACKS about Vice Presidents is a venerable tradition on TV. But the gang-stomping of Dan Quayle at the Emmy Awards ceremony two weeks ago resembled a Rodney King beating by the Hollywood élite. Quayle, TV's favored whipping boy ever since he made *Murphy Brown* a campaign issue last May, was the butt of what seemed like every third joke onstage. Comedian Richard Lewis said he would "run away" if Quayle ever became President; Robin Williams, in a clip from the *Tonight* show, described Quayle as being "one taco short of a combination plate." Candice Bergen, accepting her Emmy for *Murphy Brown*, sarcastically thanked the Vice President. And Diane English, *Murphy*'s creator, capped the evening with a defense of single mothers that crossed the line into partisan meanness. "As Murphy herself said, 'I couldn't possibly do a worse job raising my kid alone than the Reagans did with theirs.' "

The audience laughed and applauded many of these lines. But the morning-after reaction was more troubled. At a campaign rally the next day, Quayle used the Emmy barrage to pound home his point that "Hollywood doesn't like our values." Many in the TV industry agreed that the whole display was, at the very least, poor public relations. "The Emmys fed into the myth that Hollywood is self-absorbed and self-indulgent," said producer Dick Wolf.

"They gave Bush and Quayle another 3 million votes." Even Bergen found the 3½-hour political diatribe in her honor a bit overboard. "It was a free-for-all, a disservice to TV," she said. "The Emmys didn't help Hollywood's profile."

Suddenly, that profile is a hot political issue. Quayle's attack on *Murphy Brown* (glamourizing her decision to have a baby alone, he charged, was symptomatic of Hollywood's scorn for traditional family values) has been the most widely quoted speech of the presidential campaign. Not far behind it is President Bush's swipe at another popular TV show: "We need a nation closer to *The Waltons* than *The Simpsons*."

These attacks have dovetailed with mounting criticism from less partisan observers. In a new book, *Hollywood vs. America*, critic Michael Medved argues that current movies and TV shows systematically disparage such values as patriotism, religious faith and marital fidelity. "Tens of millions of Americans now see the entertainment industry as an all-powerful enemy, an alien force that assaults our most cherished values and corrupts our children," he writes. "The dream factory has become the poison factory."

It's a strange sight. Conservative critics charge that the nation's most popular entertainment medium is out of step with the American people. Republican politicians think they can rack up political points by attacking shows that are watched and loved by millions. A Hollywood community that produced the most

conservative President of the century has, it is alleged, come under almost total domination by a clique of liberals. Is it all just political posturing? Or has television really crossed the line from entertainment into advocacy? Are the people who create TV shows too insulated from mainstream America, too liberal for prime time, too smug for their own good?

One thing, at least, is inarguable: entertainment TV is thrusting itself, and being thrust, into the political arena as never before. *Murphy Brown*'s season premiere, a surefire ratings blockbuster, will be a special hour-long episode in which Murphy responds to the Vice President. While harriedly tending to her new baby, she hears his remarks on TV and reacts with incredulity: "I'm glamourizing single motherhood? What planet is he on? I agonized over that decision." Later, she appears on her TV show to answer Quayle's charges: "Perhaps it's time for the Vice President to expand his definition and recognize that whether by choice or circumstance families come in all shapes and sizes. And ultimately, what really defines a family is commitment, caring and love."

TV's rebuttal to Quayle will not end there. An upcoming episode of *Hearts Afire*, a new sitcom set in Washington, features a scene in which a dull-witted conservative Senator (George Gaynes) sees *Murphy Brown* on TV for the first time. What has Dan Quayle got against that "good-looking woman?" he asks his chief aide (John Ritter). "Well, Senator, she had a baby out of wedlock," the aide says. "But she's not real, is she?" replies the Senator, echoing the snide chorus of derision that greeted Quayle's attack on "a fictional character."

TV is venturing into the political fray on other topics as well. The Simpsons chose the night of Bush's acceptance speech at the Republican Convention to make their reply to the President's gibe. "Hey, we're just like the Waltons," said Bart. "Both families spend a lot of time praying for the end of the Depression." The Clarence Thomas confirmation hearings were the subject of pointed comments on *Designing Women* last season. "The man does not belong on the Supreme Court," said one character. "He belongs in the national repertory theater." Even frivolous shows like *Freshman Dorm*, a CBS summer entry, reveal TV's heightened political consciousness. "Be careful what you wish for," said a black student. "I wanted a black Supreme Court Justice, and I got Clarence Thomas."

Prime time will draw even more heavily on the headlines this fall. The recession will be Topic A on *Roseanne*, as Dan Conner loses his job and the family must scramble to pay its bills. The Los Angeles riots will be the backdrop for episodes of several series, including *A Different World* and *Doogie Howser, M.D.* In *Doogie's* season opener, for example, the hospital staff spends a frantic shift caring for riot victims. Though the show takes no political stand on the riot or its causes, Doogie expresses his sympathetic sentiments at the end by paraphrasing Martin Luther King Jr. in his computer diary: "A riot is at bottom the language of the unheard."

Such topicality, of course, is not new for entertainment TV. More than 20 years ago, Norman Lear's *All in the Family* introduced the notion that situation comedies could provide social commentary while getting laughs. TV movies and drama shows like *L.A. Law* tackle virtually every headline-making issue that comes down the pike, from date rape to capital punishment. Nor has left-leaning political satire been unknown on network TV: *The Smothers Brothers Comedy Hour* in the late 1960s and *Saturday Night Live* starting in the mid-'70s took on Establishment targets with irreverent glee.

But never have prime-time entertainment shows been so bold about commenting on current affairs—or their creators been so willing to step outside their characters to engage in political debate. "I had no animosity toward Quayle," says Bergen, "but then this glint of a zealot appeared. With the recent poverty figures that have been released, and the highest levels of unemployment since 1984, making [Murphy's motherhood] a campaign issue is insane." Producer Diane English—

who even challenged Quayle to debate the issue, to no avail—draws a rather farfetched parallel between the Administration's campaign against TV and the '50s blacklist: "I really feel like I'm entering a new era of McCarthyism, where one day somebody is going to come up to me and say, 'Are you now or have you ever been involved in the television business?'"

The current wave of TV bashing is different from the attacks on excessive sex and violence launched in the past by conservative watchdogs such as the Rev. Donald Wildmon. Nor does it have much to do with recent right-wing charges that PBS programming—mainly a few independently produced documentaries—has a liberal slant. It goes straight to the hearts and mind-sets of the people who create the shows that most of America watches. In essence, it is an extension of an argument made by Ben Stein, a TV scriptwriter and former Nixon speechwriter, in his 1979 book, *The View from Sunset Boulevard*. Stein contended that, on subjects ranging from religion to the military, TV reflects the values of a pampered, predominantly liberal Hollywood élite.

It is hard to dispute the contention that TV's creative community, on the whole, has a liberal bent. Democratic activists are easy to find in Hollywood; Republicans (with a few exceptions, like Arnold Schwarzenegger, Charlton Heston and *Major Dad's* Gerald McRaney) tend to lie low. "There used to be a rule in Hollywood that you didn't mix your politics with your image," says one producer. "This wall came tumbling down for liberals but not conservatives. The conservative talents don't flaunt their politics."

A survey of 104 top TV creators and executives, conducted by the Center for Media and Public Affairs, a Washington watchdog group, found that the views of this TV "élite" are considerably more liberal than those of most Americans. For example, 97% of the respondents held a prochoice view on abortion, 86% supported the right of homosexuals to teach in public schools, and 51% do not regard adultery as wrong. "People in Hollywood are overwhelmingly left of center," says S. Robert Lichter, co-director of the center, "so it makes sense that they do material that is congruent with their point of view. So you get material on environmentalism, feminism, gay rights. You won't see old-fashioned patriotism, stories on religion, support for the military."

It is not at all certain, however, that liberal views translate into advocacy programming. Most producers insist that they avoid political commentary and strive for balance in presenting controversial issues. "We're here to entertain people, not become social activists," says Dick Wolf, executive producer of *Law & Order*. Steven Bochco, co-

creator of *L.A. Law* and *Doogie Howser, M.D.*, says, "Philosophically, I've been opposed to using my shows as political forum."

Diane English too insists her goal is to entertain, not sway voters. But she concedes she made the character of Murphy Brown "a liberal Democrat because in fact that's what I am." She sees TV's political role in somewhat grandiose, Madisonian terms. "The people in power, whether Democrats or Republicans, all have access to the airwaves. The opposing point of view is often not heard, and in this case, with 12 years of Republicans who are followed around by the press, with every word and every speech documented, perhaps Hollywood's liberal bent is kind of a natural balance to that."

The closest thing TV has to an advocacy producer is Linda Bloodworth-Thomason, creator of three current network shows: *Designing Women, Evening Shade* and the upcoming *Hearts Afire*. She and her husband Harry Thomason are Clinton friends and supporters (and part-time residents of Little Rock) who produced the biographical film that introduced the candidate at the Democratic Convention. "So-called serious newspeople miss the powerful potential of the entertainment forum as a means of influencing people's lives in a positive way," she says. "I have my own column on TV, and I take it as seriously as does Mike Royko or David Broder." Yet Bloodworth-Thomason denies that the TV community is a liberal monolith. "Entertainment corporations are owned by old, white, conservative, rich men," she says. "The artists they employ are more liberal. The slant of what the artists are allowed to put out will be determined by the profit factor. The bottom line is money."

Indeed, the structure of network television serves to keep entertainment from wandering too far from the safe political center. Advertisers, for example, shy away from any program that takes a controversial political stand or gets too explicit about sensitive subjects like homosexuality. No leading character in a prime-time TV series since *Maude* has had an abortion, mainly because of advertiser skittishness. "There's no issue today more contentious," says Joel Segal, executive vice president at McCann-Erickson/New York. "Nobody is interested in alienating large blocs of viewers."

Network executives, not surprisingly, have the same concerns. Censors monitor shows closely for any material that might be objectionable to a large (or at least vocal) segment of the audience. "It's the responsibility of good television to be topical, but it should not espouse any political candidacy," says CBS Entertainment president Jeff Sagansky. Still, success in the ratings (*Murphy Brown* commands the highest ad rates of any series on TV) can go a long way toward calming network nerves. "The viewers vote for *Murphy Brown* every week," says Sagansky, "and only vote for Dan Quayle every four years."

So does network TV reflect a liberal sensibility? Yes, a certain political correctness does prevail around the dial. The concerns of feminists, environmental activists and oppressed minorities are given sympathetic treatment; big corporations are usually portrayed as villains; government bureaucrats are typically inept or uncaring. But this is probably due less to political calculation than to dramatic necessity. Artists tend to gravitate toward humanistic concerns rather than institutional ones; pitting an underdog against the system always makes for a better story. This is not necessarily proof of liberal bias any more than the proliferation of TV shoot-'em-ups means that Hollywood producers support the N.R.A.

The irony is that one area where TV espouses unmistakably conservative values is the very one that Quayle chose to focus on: the family. Though single-parent households are common on TV (as they are in real life), the family bond is nearly always portrayed as strong and indispensable. If TV has any prevailing sin, it is its sunny romanticizing of that bond: no matter what the conflicts or crises, family love makes everything come out all right. If Dan Quayle were to look at TV a little more closely, he might find the stuff of Republican dreams.

—*Reported by Jordan Bonfante and Martha Smilgis/Los Angeles and Janice C. Simpson/New York*

Commercial Considerations: Advertiser Influence on Media Messages

Advertising is the major source of profit for newspapers, magazines, radio, and television, and advertising tie-ins are a common element in motion picture deals. While media writers may have the potential of reflecting their own agendas and social/political viewpoints as they produce media messages, they depend largely upon financial backing from advertisers who have their own interests to protect. Advertisers use media as a means of presenting goods and services in a positive light. They are willing to pay generously for the opportunity to reach mass audiences: in 1993 Proctor and Gamble spent $624 million to advertise on network television programs, General Motors spent $454 million, Phillip Morris $374 million, and PepsiCo $310 million. However, they are unwilling to support media that do not deliver the right kind of audience for their ads or that do not provide an appropriate "frame" within which to view them. The articles in this section explore advertiser influence on newspaper, magazine, film, and television content.

Mass advertising developed along with mass media; in fact, commercial media have been described by some as a system existing primarily for the purpose of delivering audiences to advertisers. While this may be an overly simplistic indictment, it reflects the marketplace orientation of the American media system, which depends on advertising revenue to offset enormous production costs and turn a profit. In October 1991, the average cost of a 30-second spot on the television show "Cheers" was $260,000, on "NFL Monday Night Football" it was $255,000, and on the television shows "Roseanne," "The Simpsons," and "60 Minutes" it was $200,000. A 30-second spot during the 1994 Superbowl cost just under $1 million. Advertising revenues provide approximately two-thirds of the income of a daily newspaper, which, in turn, devotes 50–75 percent of its space to advertisements. *Ms.* magazine began publishing without advertisements in June of 1990, a move that required raising subscription rates to $40 for 6 issues versus $16 for 10 issues of the old *Ms.* with advertisements.

Protecting advertising accounts can contribute to editorial decisions. For example, some advertising account executives admit that they consider a publication's overall trend in supporting their product category. In the article "Sex, Lies, and Advertising," Gloria Steinem reports being unable to attract advertisers of food products because *Ms.* does not regularly include food-oriented articles—and they also look at whether their brands or companies are featured favorably when they are mentioned in news or editorial copy. Editors at *Good Housekeeping,* which does not accept tobacco advertising, report still facing significant pressure against printing articles on the dangers of smoking because they stand to lose revenue from non-tobacco subsidiaries of the tobacco companies. Sometimes "news" or feature stories are developed specifically to attract or placate advertisers. Former *Vanity Fair* editor Tina Brown reversed a 1984 advertising slump by running a series of feature stories about fashion designers Bill Blass, Giorgio Armani, Ralph Lauren, Calvin Klein, and Yves Saint Laurent, who subsequently became loyal advertisers. In "Advertiser Influence," Philip Meyer explains advertiser pressures on newspaper publishers in terms of blurbs, BOMs ("Business Office Musts"), special treatment, keeping things out of the paper, and getting them in. Mark Crispin Miller, in "Hollywood the Ad," examines the influence of advertisers in cutting product placement deals with media producers, particularly those making movies.

Advertisers are sensitive to controversy, and they are prone to avoid supporting controversial media content. In 1989, when consumer groups threatened to boycott companies advertising on television's "Married . . . With Children" because they objected to the show's content, the companies looked carefully at whether it was in their best interests to remain associated with the program. Several advertisers withdrew; others refused to commit to further advertising unless they could screen and approve individual episodes. As a result, the Fox network asked the producers to tone down the scripts. For the same reason, NBC had a difficult time finding sponsors for its 1989 television movie "Roe v. Wade," which involved the controversy over abortion rights, and ABC canceled reruns of "Thirtysomething" (showing two gay men in bed discussing friends who had died from AIDS) and "Roseanne" (focusing on teenage drinking) because advertisers' boycotts of the first showings cost the network over $1.5 million in lost revenue.

Finally, advertisers' interest in not only how many but what kind of consumers select the media within which they advertise exerts influence on media content. Circulation data (for print media) and ratings data, such as that provided by the A. C. Nielsen and Arbitron organizations (for television and radio) are instrumental in determining rate scales for advertising sales. Advertisers are becoming increasingly attentive to the demographic data included in such reports, since age, gender, ethnic background, and income are factors that determine how a given consumer might respond to a product pitch. In television, programmers are able to assess a "premium program surcharge" for commercials aired during shows that attract the upscale viewers (especially women) advertisers most want to reach; thus, programming for that kind of audience becomes particularly attractive. Conversely, "Gunsmoke," which was still receiving very high ratings after 21 seasons, was canceled in 1975 because its viewers were becoming too old and too rural to attract sponsorship.

Whether or not the liberal, conservative, and marketplace agendas of media writers, owners, and advertisers tend to balance one another out is debatable. An optimistic perspective would conclude that, in the end, consumers are the primary gatekeepers since advertisers will support only what audiences desire. A more pessimistic perspective would point to the fact that even critically acclaimed media face uncertain futures if they do not appeal to enough consumers or to the right consumers.

Looking Ahead: Challenge Questions

Is advertiser influence on what goes into and what stays out of newspapers declining? How common are various forms of advertiser pressure on newspaper publishers, editors, and staff members?

How do responses to advertiser attempts to influence editorial copy affect a newspaper or magazine's credibility? What short-term and long-term considerations are salient in deciding where to draw the line between business realities and editorial integrity?

What is your response to the growing trend in advocacy advertising? Do you foresee implications for advertiser influence related to this kind of advertising? Should advocacy groups have the right to buy whatever advertising space they can afford for whatever messages they wish to communicate? Why, or why not?

Why did *Ms.* magazine decide to drop advertising? Why did it have problems attracting enough advertising revenue to break even? Gloria Steinem is highly critical of advertisers' relationships with *Ms.* and with women's magazines in general. Do you find anything defensible, from a business standpoint, in advertising policies as Steinem describes them?

What is subliminal advertising? Do product placement plugs within films have a subliminal effect on viewers? How have product placement trends affected the creative process and art of filmmaking?

Advertiser Influence

Philip Meyer

Philip Meyer is William Rand Kenan, Jr., Professor of Journalism at the University of North Carolina, Chapel Hill. A former director of news research for Knight-Ridder, he is author of The Newspaper Survival Book: An Editor's Guide to Marketing Research *(1985) and* Ethical Journalism: A Guide for Students, Practioners, and Consumers *(1987).*

Once in Miami I had a dispute with a car dealer. It was over a trivial matter, whether he or I was responsible for paying a small fee for the paperwork in our transaction. Perhaps it was the tropical heat that made it seem more important than it was. In any event, we were starting to raise our voices. Suddenly, looking at me suspiciously, he said, "Say, what kind of work do you do?"

I jumped at the opening. While I would certainly not use my newspaper connection to put pressure on this guy, I thought, there was nothing wrong with answering his question. Now he would have to watch his step. As casually as I could, I dropped the name of the *Miami Herald.* Then I waited to see how images of investigative reporters, consumer columns, and an outspoken editorial page would throw fear into his heart.

"Boy," he said. "You better watch your step. Do you know how much we spend on advertising in the *Herald* every week?"

I paid up and left, perhaps out of guilt for even thinking of using the newspaper in that way. It was not out of worry about jeopardizing the *Herald*'s advertising revenue. But the belief that buyers of advertising get some fringe benefits with their contracts or can use those contracts as le-

verage in other dealings with the newspaper or its personnel is a persistent one. It has some historical basis in fact—and, unfortunately, some present-day basis as well.

The first daily newspapers in the United States were established in the coastal cities, and social historian Michael Schudson has described them as "little more than bulletin boards for the business community." They were expensive and contained mostly ads, some editorial comment, and listings of ship arrivals and their contents. The few newspapers that were not business-oriented were the tools of political parties, factions, or candidates. Whether a paper was backed by a political or a commercial interest, an editor was subservient to that interest. And advertisers who bought space were concerned about advancing that interest as well as gaining any direct benefit from carrying their message to the small readership.

ADVERTISER INFLUENCE: THE MODEL

That equation changed when Benjamin Day founded the first of the penny papers, the *New York Sun,* in the late summer of 1833. Within three years, the *Sun*'s circulation reached 27,000, which was 26 percent more than the combined circulation of the eleven traditional papers, which still had their traditional formats and six-cent price. Day's innovations included editorial independence and a strong effort to build reader loyalty, and they were widely copied. Near the end of the fifth year, he was able to boast:

Since the *Sun* began to shine upon the citizens of New York, there has been a very great and decided change in the condition of the laboring classes and mechanics. Now every individual, from the rich aristocrat who lolls in his carriage to the humble laborer who wields a broom in the streets, reads the *Sun;* nor can even a boy be found in New York City or the neighboring country who will not know in the course of the day what is promulgated in the *Sun* in the morning.

Already we perceive a change in the mass of the people. They think, talk, and act in concert. They understand their own interest, and feel that they have numbers and strength to pursue it with success.

The daily newspaper business had found its market, and the model established by the penny press proved to be a lasting one. This model has two prime virtues. One is that it fulfills the First Amendment obligation to promote the free flow of information. The other is that it is economically sound.

From the business point of view, the model works like this: The newspaper attempts to reach as large an audience as possible, although quantity is not its only concern. It is especially interested in reaching the educated, the opinion leaders, the affluent, but it wants the masses as well. To do this, it sells its product cheaply, often not even recouping the cost of the paper it is printed on from the selling price, and it creates an editorial environment that readers perceive as trustworthy, reliable, and fair. The advertiser is drawn to this medium by three things: the number of people it reaches, their buying potential, and the climate of credibility. The newspaper's product, as Hal Jurgensmeyer of the University of Miami has pointed out, is influence.

In this model, there is no reason for the advertiser to exercise any control or influence over the editorial content. Indeed, to do so would be counterproductive, because it would undermine the independence that creates the trustworthy editorial environment that, in turn, gives the paper its influence. Advertisers pay money to the newspaper not because they support its editorial content, but because they hope to increase their sales. If business people did not profit from their advertising, they would stop doing it. As long as a dollar of advertising returns more than a dollar of increased sales, the rational advertiser will continue to spend that dollar no matter what the newspaper may do or say in its news and editorial columns—unless, of course, its content becomes so extreme that its credibility is damaged or destroyed. Newspapers of extremely low credibility, like the tabloids sold in supermarkets, have to make their money from circulation sales, not from advertising. (Peek inside a supermarket tabloid, and you'll see what I mean. The few ads they do have seem to be directed at people who will believe anything—for example, that there is a pill that will cause you to lose weight while you sleep.) A credible environment is what advertisers pay for, and they therefore have an economic stake in the integrity of the newspaper.

ADVERTISER INFLUENCE: THE REALITY

That's the model. Unfortunately, it is not always the reality. The literature of journalism criticism over the past twenty years is replete with instances of advertiser influence over what goes into and what stays out of newspapers. In nearly every case, however, the critic asserts that the situation is not as bad as it used to be. Perhaps. In 1984 I was a luncheon speaker at a meeting of the Kansas Press Association, and I recalled with ironic nostalgia my time on the copy desk of the *Topeka Daily Capital* in the 1950s, when brief stories about advertisers typed on yellow paper (meaning that they were not to be edited) and slugged "BOM" (for "Business Office Must") frequently crossed the copy desk. "Must" copy is material that *must* go in the paper, come what may. Of course, I added, that sort of thing doesn't happen nowadays—and the assembled editors and publishers rocked the room with howls of laughter.

Is advertiser influence declining or not? In order to be sure, we need some quantitative measures. There aren't very many. In 1967, the *Wall Street Journal* cited a survey of 162 business and financial editors, in which 23 percent said they routinely had to "puff up or alter and downgrade business stories at the request of the advertisers."

Some more recent data are available from the ASNE [American Association of Newspaper Editors] survey of 1982. In telephone interviews, editors were asked how frequently various kinds of ethical problems became so troublesome that they had to be discussed in the newsroom. One of the problems asked about was "pressure from advertisers: blurbs, business office musts, keeping things out of the paper or getting them in." (*Blurb* is newspaper jargon for a news item initiated by the business side of the paper on behalf of an advertiser.)

The responses indicated that advertiser pressure is a concern at least some of the time on papers read by 79 percent of the American public. For 46 percent, the frequency of such episodes is at least several times a year. For 26 percent, it is once a month or more. And for 9 percent, it happens every week. That's a lot of advertiser pressure.

Of course, the fact that such things are discussed may be a good sign. Back in Topeka [40] years ago, we didn't discuss it. We just sailed the copy right into print. In the 1982 survey editors, publishers, and staff members were asked a more specific question in a self-administered questionnaire:

> How often, to the best of your knowledge, does your paper publish editorial matter controlled by the business office on behalf of advertisers in the news columns (commonly known as "blurbs" or "business office musts")?

Publishers, editors, and staff members had somewhat different perceptions. The staffers were more likely to report awareness of BOM copy than editors, and the publishers reported the least awareness of all. If you believe the publishers, 21 percent of the reading public is exposed to blurbs in its news columns. According to editors, the number is 24 percent. According to staff members, it is 39 percent.

Such abuses are not, however, a daily occurrence. They happen with a frequency greater than once a month only to between 4 and 10 percent of the nation's newspaper readers, depending on whether you believe the publisher or the staff members.

The mere existence of the term *BOM copy* means that advertiser influence is institutionalized. How about more casual influences? How often, for example, does the publisher stroll into the editor's office and ask for special handling on an article about a company or organization that has some economic clout over the newspaper?

Not often, it turns out, but it does happen. By the publishers' own admission, it happens at newspapers read by 42 percent of the public. By the editors' estimate, it is 46 percent, and by that of the staff, 58 percent. The staff is just guessing, however, because an editor will try hard to keep these incidents invisible to the staff. Rather than pass the blame up to the publisher, most editors would prefer to be seen as arbitrary or currying favor themselves. Blaming the boss would be a mark of weakness. The fact that the editors and publishers are so close in their estimates suggests that a rate in the low forties is in the right ballpark. Remember, this is the estimate for the situation happening just once. According to the information supplied by both editors and publishers, the newspapers where such intervention happens more than once or twice a year reach only 14 percent of the total newspaper audience.

Special Treatment, Special Sections

That is still enough to supply an abundance of anecdotes for journalism critics. It is easier to find

examples of puffery than of suppression simply because the former are so visible. Here's a rare illustration of the latter. The *Twin Cities Reader,* a weekly based in Minneapolis, sent its music editor, Paul Maccabee, to cover a jazz festival sponsored by Kool Cigarettes. "Strange bedfellows, cigarettes and jazz," wrote Maccabee. "Duke Ellington died of lung cancer in 1974." He was fired. The publisher said he was afraid of losing the cigarette industry's four to five weekly pages of advertising.

Another example: At the *Houston Post* in the early 1970s, restaurant reviews were written by the advertising department—and only restaurants that advertised in the paper were reviewed. When the reviewer violated that policy and let his readers know about some restaurants that did not advertise, he was fired.

Newspapers have long been wary of using business names in news copy. In 1971 a large Boston department store, Jordan Marsh, was sued by a debtor who claimed undue harassment. When the debtor won a major ruling on a preliminary procedural issue, both the *Boston Globe* and the *Boston Herald-Traveler* reported the story—but without mentioning the name of the store.

The policy at some newspapers is to ban use of all business names, unless absolutely essential to the story, whether the reference is good or bad. The reasoning is that an unfavorable reference may annoy someone, and a favorable one—well, that's free advertising, and anybody who wants something good said about them in the paper should pay for it. The policy at least has the virtue of consistency, but it often makes for awkward writing. Bank robbers make their getaway in "a small car," not a Volkswagen. A news conference is held at "a downtown hotel," not at the Hilton.

Putting puffery into the newspaper is the more visible offense, and it can be demoralizing for staffers, particularly if they have to participate in it. In the late 1950s, when Al Neuharth was an assistant managing editor of the *Miami Herald* and I was a brand-new reporter, he dispatched me to the owners and managers of the Wometco Theater group so that I could gather material to fill the editorial columns of a special advertising section celebrating some anniversary of the company. I still remember the humiliation of being led around by the Wometco press agent, a cheerful little man who kept introducing me to everybody as "Paul." So depressed was I that I never bothered to correct him.

One such special advertising section almost got out of hand at the *Denver Post* in 1966. The business editor felt that he was being pressured by the ad manager to provide editorial coverage of a new shopping center equal to 25 percent of the ad space that the center was buying. He hadn't reached half that amount and had run out of things to say, he complained in a memo to his managing editor, William H. Hornby. It was all a mistake, said Hornby, and there was no policy of one free inch for every four paid.

Some better solutions to the special-section problem have been found: let the advertiser supply the editorial matter and then label it as advertising and use a distinctive type face to make it easily distinguishable from real news stories; or have the newspaper's advertising department write the copy and give it the same labeling.

Where an ongoing section is involved—a Sunday real estate section, for example—the trend today is toward solid, consumer-oriented reporting instead of puffery. Compare, for example, the *Philadelphia Inquirer*'s real estate section in the 1960s with its present-day counterpart. Before, the section's front page bannered stories on activities of local real estate developers and brokers. Now the boosterism is gone, replaced by a consumer-oriented approach, with information that house-hunting readers can use.

But a more subtle problem remains: the way in which the market for advertising influences what kind of news readers will get. Consider the weekly business sections that many newspapers began publishing in the late 1970s. The best of these sections cover business news with a depth and thoroughness never attempted before, and in so doing they have closed a historical gap in their service to their readers. What local business does has a visible effect on almost everyone in a community, its activities are news; but until recently, most newspapers behaved as though local government were the only source of power in the community, ignoring business even though it was sometimes a more important power center.

Did these new special sections spring into being because newspaper publishers suddenly awoke to the fact that there was a huge gap in their reporting on their communities? Not at all. What happened was that they awoke to the fact that they were missing out on a good way to make a buck.

The folks who woke them up were entrepreneurs who began utilizing the new technology of publishing, with its lower production costs, to start local business periodicals such as *Crain's Chicago Business Review*. When these independent journals entered a few markets and started selling advertising, the alert newspaper publishers wondered why *they* hadn't been getting that advertising. In direct response, some of the "Business Monday" newspaper sections appeared—and they worked. They provided a brand-new revenue stream that followed the penny-paper model in microcosm. A limited segment of readers, people interested in business, was drawn to the new section, and advertisers who wanted to reach that segment saw an efficiency there that could not be realized by ads that had the run of the paper. A

metropolitan daily is so fat that you can't expect every reader to look closely at every page, so it is not efficient for reaching a limited segment unless there is a section of editorial matter that attracts that limited segment. The "Business Monday" concept does this beautifully.

Another advertiser-supported editorial innovation is the zoned neighborhood section. By providing intensive local coverage of neighborhoods, these sections attract retail advertisers who want to reach specific neighborhoods without paying the cost of ads that appear in the full press run. A new service to readers is created, and it is financed by advertising revenue that is new and distinct, not just cannibalized from some other part of the paper. Everybody wins.

That's the good news. The bad news is that something that readers badly need may never be provided in the absence of a visible signal that it can be hooked to advertising. The major disappointment of my time on the corporate staff at Knight-Ridder was the failure of an experimental feature for children that I had helped recruit. It was called the "Dynamite Kids' Page," and the hope was that it would draw national advertising away from Saturday-morning television. It never did, and the page was dropped. An even more ambitious venture, a colorful Sunday supplement called "Three to Get Ready" and placed in a number of papers by a group of New York City entrepreneurs, met a similar fate. Both features would have been good for newspapers in the long run, because they would have taught children that print media can be fun and useful. Given more time, the advertisers might have come around. But business pressures sometimes dictate a short planning horizon, and the immediate attitudes of advertisers—or nonadvertisers—can have an effect on content that undermines the First Amendment theory on which newspapers rest their case for independence.

The Wall of Separation between Newsroom and Business Office

Joint efforts of news and advertising departments to create innovative products within the framework of the daily newspaper began comparatively recently. The historical pattern of abuses of business-office power on behalf of advertisers had led to the business-aversion rule in newsrooms and, on newspapers with strong editors, to a structural division between the news side and the business side. Under this ethic, the less the editor knew about what happened on the business side, the better. Insulated by this wall of separation from the machinations of the business office, the editor could make judgment calls without knowing how the financial fortunes of the newspaper would be affected. Publishers could be comfortable with this arrangement because it meant delegating ethical questions to the editor. The publisher was responsible only for hiring an editor of high moral standing; having done that, the publisher could devote full attention to maximizing profit. The public interest was somebody else's department.

And so the in-house atmosphere became adversarial, and those of us who worked on the news sides of such newspapers had no trouble believing that we were nobler than those grubby people who brought in the cash with which our salaries were paid. *We* were altruistic, looking out for the community's welfare. *They* were selfish, thinking only of the company's economic well-being. The symmetry of this dichotomy is appealing. Adherence to it is reflected quite clearly in the responses to this survey question . . . (the percentages represent editor responses):

> A business writer discovers that TV sets with built-in videotex decoders will be on the local market within sixty days, greatly increasing convenience and reducing costs for people who sign up for the local videotex service—which, incidentally, is not owned by your paper. The advertising manager calls the publisher and says local TV dealers are afraid they will be stuck with an oversupply of obsolete TV sets if the word gets out. Should the publisher:
> a. Order the story killed. (0 percent)
> b. Explain the problem to the editor with a recommendation that the story be delayed. (2 percent)
> c. Suggest to the editor that the story be doublechecked for accuracy. (36 percent)
> d. Help the ad manager pacify the retailers, but say nothing to the editor. (62 percent)

The majority position (d) reflects the wall-of-separation tradition, in which it is considered best to keep the editor ignorant of business-side problems. But is it the most rational position?

If you step back and look at the situation with the total newspaper in mind, you may arrive at a different answer. The retailers represent an important segment of the community, to whom significant damage could be done. Their interests need to be weighed against those of consumers. The equation is easy enough, particularly when First Amendment responsibilities are considered. When information damages some and benefits others, a strong presumption exists that the information should be provided and that the newspaper's duty is to its readers as consumers, not to the subset who would like to take advantage of

those consumers' ignorance. But where is the harm in doublechecking for accuracy? And is there not an important ethical benefit to be derived from doing so?

Where wrong information would be damaging to an individual or group, the need for accuracy, always at the top of any journalistic code of ethics in routine cases, is especially strong. If the editor does not know of the potential for damage in this case, he or she is likely to give it routine treatment even though it is normal to doublecheck where the damage potential *is* known. The wall of separation, designed to ward off evils of another kind, is working against the newspaper here.

There is, of course, the slippery-slope argument. Okay, this argument goes, the publisher would be justified in talking to the editor in this case, but if that conversation takes place, the next one will be more intrusive, the one after that even worse, and the advertising department will wind up dictating news content.

The argument assumes a weak editor and a malevolent publisher. Indeed, so does the wall-of-separation tradition. A principled publisher and a strong editor could work together to maximize the paper's ability to carry out both its profit-making and First Amendment missions. They could manage conflicts so as to minimize the damage to both sides more effectively than if each side were to pursue its own narrow interests. Cases like the example above highlight the weakness in the wall-of-separation tradition. Keeping key functions in separate, watertight compartments is not an efficient way to run a complicated operation like a newspaper. Indeed, the separation keeps the editors weaker than they need to be. An editor who understands the newspaper's financial situation is in a stronger position to fight for the resources needed to produce the kind of newspaper that readers deserve. . . .

Advertiser Pressure and Newspaper Economics

If a strong editor is an important ingredient in producing an ethical newspaper, a strong institution is even more important. Edwin A. Lahey, Washington bureau chief for Knight Newspapers in the 1950s and 1960s, put it bluntly when he said, "All I require of my publisher is that he remain solvent." A financially sound newspaper need not fear the whims of any given advertiser, and most advertisers need the newspaper too much to stay away. Most of the horror stories about newspapers knuckling under to advertiser pressure have to do with small, economically marginal publications, the 97-pound weaklings of journalism. Even among small papers, however, examples of moral courage can be found.

In 1969 two right-wing leaders, Fred C. Schwartz, head of the Christian Anti-Communist Crusade, and Benjamin Grob, an industrialist, took offense at a counterculture newspaper called *Kaleidoscope,* which was published in Milwaukee. Unable to attack it directly, they tracked down the printer, who turned out to be William F. Schanen, Jr., the owner of three weekly newspapers in Ozaukee County and a pioneer in the use of high-quality offset printing for small newspapers. They organized a boycott against Schanen's three weeklies, using a direct-mail campaign to urge people in Ozaukee County not to advertise in any of the three papers or to patronize anyone who did.

The boycott was highly effective, costing Schanen $300,000 in gross income during the first year. To save his company, he folded one of the three weeklies and sold another. He refused to stop printing *Kaleidoscope* on principle, although he himself did not approve of its content.

Schanen died in 1971, but his son, William Schanen III, continued the fight. As the counterculture's heyday waned, *Kaleidoscope* shut down for reasons unrelated to the boycott. That and his father's death contributed to bringing "the whole silly business to an end," the younger Schanen recalled. "We limped along, and then our circulation picked up . . . and every advertiser that pulled out was back within five years." But a shopper that had moved into the vacuum is still around, and the *Mequon Squire,* the paper sold during the boycott, is now a major competitor. Schanen looks back on the struggle as a successful defense of First Amendment principles. "I can't think of anything I'm prouder of," he said recently.

A similar boycott, launched at about the same time by a John Birch Society chapter against the *Denver Post,* had much less effect. For a dominant daily newspaper in a large metropolitan market, there is much less susceptibility to advertiser pressure.

The fact that advertiser pressures still exist where there is relative economic security may be related to causes that are as much social as economic. The ASNE survey showed that publishers who intervene in the news-editorial side to get special handling for an organization or an individual are as likely to do it for someone with whom they have strong social ties as they are for someone with economic clout. Table 1 shows the relative frequency of the two kinds of intervention as perceived by editors.

TABLE 1   Frequency of Publisher Intervention for Economic and Social Reasons

	Economic	Social
At least once a month	3%	3%
Several times a year	11	16
Less often	31	33
Never	54	48

The direct fear of economic retribution therefore may be less important than the publisher's desire to be helpful to his or her friends. The temptation is a strong one. Almost anybody who has worked for a newspaper in any capacity has felt it at one time or another. And this brings us to another large category of problems that comes under the general heading of fairness and balance—goals that are almost universally sought but are extremely difficult to attain.

Sex, Lies & Advertising

GLORIA STEINEM

Gloria Steinem was a founding editor of "Ms." in 1972 and is now its consulting editor. She is also at work on "The Bedside Book of Self-Esteem" for Little, Brown.

bout three years ago, as *glasnost* was beginning and *Ms.* seemed to be ending, I was invited to a press lunch for a Soviet official. He entertained us with anecdotes about new problems of democracy in his country. Local Communist leaders were being criticized in their media for the first time, he explained, and they were angry.

"So I'll have to ask my American friends," he finished pointedly, "how more *subtly* to control the press." In the silence that followed, I said, "Advertising."

The reporters laughed, but later, one of them took me aside: How *dare* I suggest that freedom of the press was limited? How dare I imply that his newsweekly could be influenced by ads?

I explained that I was thinking of advertising's media-wide influence on most of what we read. Even newsmagazines use "soft" cover stories to sell ads, confuse readers with "advertorials," and occasionally self-censor on subjects known to be a problem with big advertisers.

But, I also explained, I was thinking especially of women's magazines. There, it isn't just a little content that's devoted to attracting ads, it's almost all of it. That's why advertisers—not readers—have always been the problem for *Ms.* As the only women's magazine that didn't supply what the ad world euphemistically describes as "supportive editorial atmosphere" or "complementary copy" (for instance, articles that praise food/fashion/beauty subjects to "support" and "comple-

Suppose archaeologists of the future dug up women's magazines and used them to judge American women. What would they think of us—and what can we do about it?

ment" food/fashion/beauty ads), *Ms.* could never attract enough advertising to break even.

"Oh, *women's* magazines," the journalist said with contempt. "Everybody knows they're catalogs—but who cares? They have nothing to do with journalism."

I can't tell you how many times I've had this argument in 25 years of working for many kinds of publications. Except as moneymaking machines—"cash cows" as they are so elegantly called in the trade—women's magazines are rarely taken seriously. Though changes being made by women have been called more far-reaching than the industrial revolution—and though many editors try hard to reflect some of them in the few pages left to them after all the ad-related subjects have been covered—the magazines serving the female half of this country are still far below the journalistic and ethical standards of news and general interest publications. Most depressing of all, this doesn't even rate an exposé.

If *Time* and *Newsweek* had to lavish praise on cars in general and credit General Motors in particular to get GM ads, there would be a scandal—maybe a criminal investigation. When women's magazines from *Seventeen* to *Lear's* praise beauty products in general and credit Revlon in particular to get ads, it's just business as usual.

I.

When *Ms.* began, we didn't consider *not* taking ads. The most important reason was keeping the price of a feminist magazine low enough for most women to afford. But the second and almost equal reason was providing a forum where women and advertisers could talk to each other and improve advertising itself. After all, it was (and still is) as potent a source of information in this country as news or TV and movie dramas.

We decided to proceed in two stages. First, we would convince makers of "people products" used by both men and women but advertised mostly to men—cars, credit cards, insurance, sound equipment, financial services, and the like—that their ads should be placed in a women's magazine. Since they were accustomed to the division between editorial and advertising in news and general interest magazines, this would allow our editorial content to be free and diverse. Second, we would add the best ads for whatever traditional "women's products" (clothes, shampoo, fragrance, food, and so on) that surveys showed *Ms.* readers used. But we would ask them to come in *without* the usual quid pro quo of "complementary copy."

We knew the second step might be harder. Food advertisers have always demanded that women's magazines publish recipes and articles on entertaining (preferably ones that name their products) in return for their ads; clothing advertisers expect to be surrounded by fashion spreads (especially ones that credit their designers); and shampoo, fragrance, and beauty products in general usually insist on positive editorial coverage of beauty subjects, plus photo credits besides. That's why women's magazines look the way they do. But if we could break this link between ads and editorial content, then we wanted good ads for "women's products," too.

By playing their part in this unprecedented mix of *all* the things our readers need and use, advertisers also would be rewarded: ads for products like cars and mutual funds would find a new growth market; the best ads for women's products would no longer be lost in oceans of ads for the same category; and both would have access to a laboratory of smart and caring readers whose response would help create effective ads for other media as well.

I thought then that our main problem would be the imagery in ads themselves. Carmakers were still draping blondes in evening gowns over the hoods like ornaments.

Authority figures were almost always male, even in ads for products that only women used. Sadistic, he-man campaigns even won industry praise. (For instance, *Advertising Age* had hailed the infamous Silva Thin cigarette theme, "How to Get a Woman's Attention: Ignore Her," as "brilliant.") Even in medical journals, tranquilizer ads showed depressed housewives standing beside piles of dirty dishes and promised to get them back to work.

Obviously, *Ms.* would have to avoid such ads and seek out the best ones—but this didn't seem impossible. *The New Yorker* had been selecting ads for aesthetic reasons for years, a practice that only seemed to make advertisers more eager to be in its pages. *Ebony* and *Essence* were asking for ads with positive black images, and though their struggle was hard, they weren't being called unreasonable.

Clearly, what *Ms.* needed was a very special publisher and ad sales staff. I could think of only one woman with experience on the business side of magazines—Patricia Carbine, who recently had become a vice president of *McCall's* as well as its editor in chief—and the reason I knew her name was a good omen. She had been managing editor at *Look* (really *the* editor, but its owner refused to put a female name at the top of his masthead) when I was writing a column there. After I did an early interview with Cesar Chavez, then just emerging as a leader of migrant labor, and the publisher turned it down because he was worried about ads from Sunkist, Pat was

I ended up with an unsentimental education in the seamy underside of publishing that few writers see and even fewer magazines can publish.

the one who intervened. As I learned later, she had told the publisher she would resign if the interview wasn't published. Mainly because *Look* couldn't afford to lose Pat, it *was* published (and the ads from Sunkist never arrived).

Though I barely knew this woman, she had done two things I always remembered: put her job on the line in a way that editors often talk about but rarely do, and been so loyal to her colleagues that she never told me or anyone outside *Look* that she had done so.

Fortunately, Pat did agree to leave *McCall's* and take a huge cut in salary to become publisher of *Ms.* She became responsible for training and inspiring generations of young women who joined the *Ms.* ad sales force, many of whom went on to become "firsts" at the top of publishing. When *Ms.* first started, however, there were so few women with experience selling space that Pat and I made the rounds of ad agencies ourselves. Later, the fact that *Ms.* was asking companies to do business in a different way meant our saleswomen had to make many times the usual number of calls—first to convince agencies and then client companies besides—and to present endless amounts of research. I was often asked to do a final ad presentation, or see some higher decision-maker, or speak to women employees so executives could see the interest of women they worked with. That's why I spent more time persuading advertisers than editing or writing for *Ms.* and why I ended up with an unsentimental education in the seamy underside of publishing that few writers see (and even fewer magazines can publish).

Let me take you with us through some experiences, just as they happened:

■ Cheered on by early support from Volkswagen and one or two other car companies, we scrape together time and money to put on a major reception in Detroit. We know U.S. carmakers firmly believe that women choose the upholstery, not the car, but we are armed with statistics and reader mail to prove the contrary: a car is an important purchase for women, one that symbolizes mobility and freedom.

But almost nobody comes. We are left with many pounds of shrimp on the table, and quite a lot of egg on our face. We blame ourselves for not guessing that there would be a baseball pennant play-off on the same day, but executives go out of their way to explain they wouldn't have come anyway. Thus begins ten years of knocking on hostile doors, presenting endless documentation, and hiring a full-time saleswoman in Detroit; all necessary before *Ms.* gets any real results.

This long saga has a semihappy ending: foreign and, later, domestic carmakers eventually provided *Ms.* with enough advertising to make cars one of our top sources of ad revenue. Slowly, Detroit began to take the women's market seriously enough to put car ads in other women's magazines, too, thus freeing a few pages from the hothouse of fashion-beauty-food ads.

But long after figures showed a third, even a half, of many car models being bought by women, U.S. makers continued to be uncomfortable addressing women. Unlike foreign carmakers, Detroit never quite learned the secret of creating intelligent ads that exclude no one, and then placing them in women's magazines to overcome past exclusion. (*Ms.* readers were so grateful for a routine Honda ad featuring rack and pinion steering, for instance, that they sent fan mail.) Even now, Detroit continues to ask, "Should we make special ads for women?" Perhaps that's why some foreign cars still have a disproportionate share of the U.S. women's market.

■ In the *Ms.* Gazette, we do a brief report on a congressional hearing into chemicals used in hair dyes that are absorbed through the skin and may be carcinogenic. Newspapers report this too, but Clairol, a Bristol-

Myers subsidiary that makes dozens of products—a few of which have just begun to advertise in *Ms.*—is outraged. Not at newspapers or newsmagazines, just at us. It's bad enough that *Ms.* is the only women's magazine refusing to provide the usual "complementary" articles and beauty photos, but to criticize one of their categories—*that* is going too far.

We offer to publish a letter from Clairol telling its side of the story. In an excess of solicitousness, we even put this letter in the Gazette, not in Letters to the Editors where it belongs. Nonetheless—and in spite of surveys that show *Ms.* readers are active women who use more of almost everything Clairol makes than do the readers of any other women's magazine—*Ms.* gets almost none of these ads for the rest of its natural life.

Meanwhile, Clairol changes its hair coloring formula, apparently in response to the hearings we reported.

■ Our saleswomen set out early to attract ads for consumer electronics: sound equipment, calculators, computers, VCRs, and the like. We know that our readers are determined to be included in the technological revolution. We know from reader surveys that *Ms.* readers are buying this stuff in numbers as high as those of magazines like *Playboy;* or "men 18 to 34," the prime targets of the consumer electronics industry. Moreover, unlike traditional women's products that our readers buy but don't need to read articles about, these are subjects they want covered in our pages. There actually *is* a supportive editorial atmosphere.

"But women don't understand technology," say executives at the end of ad presentations. "Maybe not," we respond, "but neither do men—and we all buy it."

"If women *do* buy it," say the decision-makers, "they're asking their husbands and boyfriends what to buy first." We produce letters from *Ms.* readers saying how turned off they are when salesmen say things like "Let me know when your husband can come in."

After several years of this, we get a few ads for compact sound systems. Some of them come from JVC, whose vice president, Harry Elias, is trying to convince his Japanese bosses that there is something called a women's market. At his invitation, I find myself speaking at huge trade shows in Chicago and Las Vegas, trying to persuade JVC dealers that showrooms don't have to be locker rooms where women are made to feel unwelcome. But as it turns out, the shows themselves are part of the problem. In Las Vegas, the only women around the technology displays are seminude models serving champagne. In Chicago, the big attraction is Marilyn Chambers, who followed Linda Lovelace of *Deep Throat* fame as Chuck Traynor's captive and/or employee. VCRs are being demonstrated with her porn videos.

In the end, we get ads for a car stereo now and then, but no VCRs; some IBM personal computers, but no Apple or Japanese ones. We notice that office magazines like *Working Woman* and *Savvy* don't benefit as much as they should from office equipment ads either. In the electron-

You may be surprised to learn, as I was, that in the ratio of advertising to editorial pages in women's magazines, the ads average only about 5 percent more than in "Time," "Newsweek," and "U.S. News." That nothing-to-read feeling comes from editorial pages devoted to "complementary copy"; to text or photos that praise advertised categories, instruct in their use, or generally act as extensions of ads.

To find out what we're getting when we actually pay money for these catalogs, I picked random issues, counted the number of pages (even including letters to the editors, horoscopes, and so forth) that are not ads and/or copy complementary to ads, and then compared that number to the total pages. For instance:

Glamour, April 1990
339 pages total;
65 non-ad or ad-related

Vogue, May 1990
319 pages total;
38 non-ad or ad-related

Redbook, April 1990
173 pages total;
44 non-ad or ad-related

Family Circle, March 13, 1990
180 pages total;
33 non-ad or ad-related

ics world, women and technology seem mutually exclusive. It remains a decade behind even Detroit.

■ Because we get letters from little girls who love toy trains, and who ask our help in changing ads and box-top photos that feature little boys only, we try to get toy-train ads from Lionel. It turns out that Lionel executives *have* been concerned about little girls. They made a pink train, and were surprised when it didn't sell.

Lionel bows to consumer pressure with a photograph of a boy *and* a girl—but only on some of their boxes. They fear that, if trains are associated with girls, they will be devalued in the minds of boys. Needless to say, *Ms.* gets no train ads, and little girls remain a mostly unexplored market. By 1986, Lionel is put up for sale.

But for different reasons, we haven't had much luck with other kinds of toys either. In spite of many articles on child-rearing; an annual listing of nonsexist, multi-racial toys by Letty Cottin Pogrebin; Stories for Free Children, a regular feature also edited by Letty; and other prizewinning features for or about children, we get virtually no toy ads. Generations of *Ms.* saleswomen explain to toy manufacturers that a larger proportion of *Ms.* readers have preschool children than do the readers of other women's magazines, but this industry can't believe feminists have or care about children.

■ When *Ms.* begins, the staff decides not to accept ads for feminine hygiene sprays or cigarettes: they are damaging and carry no appropriate health warnings. Though we don't think we should tell our readers what to do, we do think we should provide facts so they can decide for themselves. Since the antismoking lobby has been pressing for health warnings on cigarette ads, we decide to take them only as they comply.

When women's magazines from *Lear's* to *Seventeen* praise beauty products in order to get ads, it's just business as usual.

Philip Morris is among the first to do so. One of its brands, Virginia Slims, is also sponsoring women's tennis and the first national polls of women's opinions. On the other hand, the Virginia Slims theme, "You've come a long way, baby," has more than a "baby" problem. It makes smoking a symbol of progress for women.

We explain to Philip Morris that this slogan won't do well in our pages, but they are convinced its success with some women means it will work with *all* women. Finally, we agree to publish an ad for a Virginia Slims calendar as a test. The letters from readers are critical—and smart. For instance: Would you show a black man picking cotton, the same man in a Cardin suit, and symbolize the antislavery and civil rights movements by smoking? Of course not. But instead of honoring the test results, the

3. COMMERCIAL CONSIDERATIONS

Philip Morris people seem angry to be proven wrong. They take away ads for *all* their many brands.

This costs *Ms.* about $250,000 the first year. After five years, we can no longer keep track. Occasionally, a new set of executives listens to *Ms.* saleswomen, but because we won't take Virginia Slims, not one Philip Morris product returns to our pages for the next 16 years.

Gradually, we also realize our naiveté in thinking we *could* decide against taking cigarette ads. They became a disproportionate support of magazines the moment they were banned on television, and few magazines could compete and survive without them; certainly not *Ms.*, which lacks so many other categories. By the time statistics in the 1980s showed that women's rate of lung cancer was approaching men's, the necessity of taking cigarette ads has become a kind of prison.

■ General Mills, Pillsbury, Carnation, DelMonte, Dole, Kraft, Stouffer, Hormel, Nabisco: you name the food giant, we try it. But no matter how desirable the *Ms.* readership, our lack of recipes is lethal.

We explain to them that placing food ads *only* next to recipes associates food with work. For many women, it is a negative that works *against* the ads. Why not place food ads in diverse media without recipes (thus reaching more men, who are now a third of the shoppers in supermarkets anyway), and leave the recipes to specialty magazines like *Gourmet* (a third of whose readers are also men)?

These arguments elicit interest, but except for an occasional ad for a convenience food, instant coffee, diet drinks, yogurt, or such extras as avocados and almonds, this mainstay of the publishing industry stays closed to us. Period.

■ Traditionally, wines and liquors didn't advertise to women: men were thought to make the brand decisions, even if women did the buying. But after endless presentations, we begin to make a dent in this category. Thanks to the unconventional Michel Roux of Carillon Importers (distributors of Grand Marnier, Absolut Vodka, and others), who assumes that food and drink have no gender, some ads are leaving their men's club.

Beermakers are still selling masculinity. It takes *Ms.* fully eight years to get its first beer ad (Michelob). In general, however, liquor ads are less stereotyped in their imagery—and far less controlling of the editorial content around them—than are women's products. But given the underrepresentation of other categories, these very facts tend to create a disproportionate number of alcohol ads in the pages of *Ms.* This in turn dismays readers worried about women and alcoholism.

■ We hear in 1980 that women in the Soviet Union have been producing feminist *samizdat* (underground, self-published books) and circulating them throughout the country. As punishment, four of the leaders have been exiled. Though we are operating on our usual shoestring, we solicit individual contributions to send Robin Morgan to interview these women in Vienna.

The result is an exclusive cover story that includes the first news of a populist peace movement against the Afghanistan occupation, a prediction of *glasnost* to come, and a grass-roots, intimate view of Soviet women's lives. From the popular press to women's studies courses, the response is great. The story wins a Front Page award.

Nonetheless, this journalistic coup undoes years of efforts to get an ad schedule from Revlon. Why? Because the Soviet women on our cover *are not wearing makeup.*

■ Four years of research and presentations go into convincing airlines that women now make travel choices and business trips. United, the first airline to advertise in *Ms.*, is so impressed with the response from our readers that one of its executives appears in a film for our ad presentations. As usual, good ads get great results.

But we have problems unrelated to such results. For instance: because American Airlines flight attendants include among their labor demands the stipulation that they could choose to have their last names preceded by "Ms." on their name tags—in a long-delayed revolt against the standard, "I am your pilot, Captain Rothgart, and this is your flight attendant, Cindy Sue"—American officials seem to hold the magazine responsible. We get no ads.

There is still a different problem at Eastern. A vice president cancels subscriptions for thousands of copies on Eastern flights. Why? Because he is offended by ads for lesbian poetry journals in the *Ms.* Classified. A "family airline," as he explains to me coldly on the phone, has to "draw the line somewhere."

It's obvious that *Ms.* can't exclude lesbians and serve women. We've been trying to make that point ever since our first issue included an article by and about lesbians, and both Suzanne Levine, our managing editor, and I were lectured by such heavy hitters as Ed Kosner, then editor of *Newsweek* (and now of *New York Magazine*), who insisted that *Ms.* should "position" itself *against* lesbians. But our advertisers have paid to reach a guaranteed number of readers, and soliciting new subscriptions to compensate for Eastern would cost $150,000, plus rebating money in the meantime.

Like almost everything ad-related, this presents an elaborate organizing problem. After days of searching for sympathetic members of the Eastern board, Frank Thomas, president of the Ford Foundation, kindly offers to call Roswell Gilpatrick, a director of Eastern. I talk with Mr. Gilpatrick, who calls Frank Borman, then the president of Eastern. Frank Borman calls me to say that his airline is not in the business of censoring magazines: *Ms.* will be returned to Eastern flights.

■ Women's access to insurance and credit is vital, but with the exception of Equitable and a few other ad pioneers, such financial services address men. For almost a decade after the Equal Credit Opportunity Act passes in 1974, we try to convince American Express that women are a growth market—but nothing works.

Finally, a former professor of Russian named Jerry Welsh becomes head of marketing. He assumes that women should be cardholders, and persuades his colleagues to feature women in a campaign. Thanks to this 1980s series, the growth rate for female cardholders surpasses that for men.

For this article, I asked Jerry Welsh if he would explain why American Express waited so long. "Sure," he said, "they were afraid of having a 'pink' card."

■ Women of color read *Ms.* in disproportionate numbers. This is a source of pride to *Ms.* staffers, who are also more racially representative than the editors of other women's magazines. But this reality is obscured by ads filled with enough white women to make a reader snowblind.

Pat Carbine remembers mostly "astonishment" when she requested African American, Hispanic, Asian, and other diverse images. Marcia Ann Gillespie, a *Ms.* editor who was previously the editor in chief of *Essence,* witnesses ad bias a second time: having tried for *Essence* to get white advertisers to use black images (Revlon did so eventually, but L'Oréal, Lauder, Chanel, and other companies never did), she sees similar problems getting integrated ads for an integrated magazine. Indeed, the ad world often creates black and Hispanic ads only for black and Hispanic media. In an exact parallel of the fear that marketing a product to women will endanger its appeal to men, the response is usually, "But your [white] readers won't identify."

It turns out Lionel executives *have* been concerned about little girls. They made a pink train and were surprised when it didn't sell.

In fact, those we are able to get—for instance, a Max Factor ad made for *Essence* that Linda Wachner gives us after she becomes president—are praised by white readers, too. But there are pathetically few such images.

■ By the end of 1986, production and mailing costs have risen astronomically, ad income is flat, and competition for ads is stiffer than ever. The 60/40 preponderance of edit over ads that we promised to readers becomes 50/50; children's stories, most poetry, and some fiction are casualties of less space; in order to get variety into limited pages, the length (and sometimes the depth) of articles suffers; and, though we do refuse most of the ads that would look like a parody in our pages, we get so worn down that some slip through. . . . Still, readers perform miracles. Though we haven't been able to afford a subscription mailing in two years, they maintain our guaranteed circulation of 450,000.

Nonetheless, media reports on *Ms.* often insist that our unprofitability must be due to reader disinterest. The myth that advertisers simply follow readers is very strong. Not one reporter notes that other comparable magazines our size (say, *Vanity Fair* or *The Atlantic*) have been losing more money in one year than *Ms.* has lost in 16 years. No matter how much never-to-be-recovered cash is poured into starting a magazine or keeping one going, appearances seem to be all that matter. (Which is why we haven't been able to explain our fragile state in public. Nothing causes ad-flight like the smell of nonsuccess.)

My healthy response is anger. My not-so-healthy response is constant worry. Also an obsession with finding one more rescue. There is hardly a night when I don't wake up with sweaty palms and pounding heart, scared that we won't be able to pay the printer or the post office; scared most of all that closing our doors will hurt the women's movement.

Out of chutzpah and desperation, I arrange a lunch with Leonard Lauder, president of Estée Lauder. With the exception of Clinique (the brainchild of Carol Phillips), none of Lauder's hundreds of products has been advertised in *Ms.* A year's schedule of ads for just three or four of them could save us. Indeed, as the scion of a family-owned company whose ad practices are followed by the beauty industry, he is one of the few men who could liberate many pages in all women's magazines just by changing his mind about "complementary copy."

Over a lunch that costs more than we can pay for some articles, I explain the need for his leadership. I also lay out the record of *Ms.:* more literary and journalistic prizes won, more new issues introduced into the mainstream, new writers discovered, and impact on society than any other magazine; more articles that became books, stories that became movies, ideas that became television series, and newly advertised products that became profitable; and, most important for him, a place for his ads to reach women who aren't reachable through any other women's magazine. Indeed, if there is one constant characteristic of the ever-changing *Ms.* readership, it is their impact as leaders. Whether it's waiting until later to have first babies, or pioneering PABA as sun protection in cosmetics, *whatever* they are doing today, a third to a half of American women will be doing three to five years from now. It's never failed.

But, he says, *Ms.* readers are not *our* women. They're not interested in things like fragrance and blush-on. If they were, *Ms.* would write articles about them.

On the contrary, I explain, surveys show they are more likely to buy such things than the readers of, say, *Cosmopolitan* or *Vogue.* They're good customers because they're out in the world enough to need several sets of everything: home, work, purse, travel, gym, and so on. They just don't need to read articles about these things. Would he ask a men's magazine to publish monthly columns on how to shave before he advertised Aramis products (his line for men)?

He concedes that beauty features are often concocted more for advertisers than readers. But *Ms.* isn't appropriate for his ads anyway, he explains. Why? Because Estée Lauder is selling "a kept-woman mentality."

3. COMMERCIAL CONSIDERATIONS

I can't quite believe this. Sixty percent of the users of his products are salaried, and generally resemble *Ms.* readers. Besides, his company has the appeal of having been started by a creative and hardworking woman, his mother, Estée Lauder.

That doesn't matter, he says. He knows his customers, and they would *like* to be kept women. That's why he will never advertise in *Ms.*

In November 1987, by vote of the Ms. Foundation for Education and Communication (*Ms.*'s owner and publisher, the media subsidiary of the Ms. Foundation for Women), *Ms.* was sold to a company whose officers, Australian feminists Sandra Yates and Anne Summers, raised the investment money in their country that *Ms.* couldn't find in its own. They also started *Sassy* for teenage women.

In their two-year tenure, circulation was raised to 550,000 by investment in circulation mailings, and, to the dismay of some readers, editorial features on clothes and new products made a more traditional bid for ads. Nonetheless, ad pages fell below previous levels. In addition, *Sassy,* whose fresh voice and sexual frankness were an unprecedented success with young readers, was targeted by two mothers from Indiana who began, as one of them put it, "calling every Christian organization I could think of." In response to this controversy, several crucial advertisers pulled out.

Such links between ads and editorial content was a problem in Australia, too, but to a lesser degree. "Our readers pay two times more for their magazines," Anne explained, "so advertisers have less power to threaten a magazine's viability."

"I was shocked," said Sandra Yates with characteristic directness. "In Australia, we think you have freedom of the press—but you don't."

Since Anne and Sandra had not met their budget's projections for ad revenue, their investors forced a sale. In October 1989, *Ms.* and *Sassy* were bought by Dale Lang, owner of *Working Mother, Working Woman,* and one of the few independent publishing companies left among the conglomerates. In response to a request from the original *Ms.* staff—as well as to reader letters urging that *Ms.* continue, plus his own belief that *Ms.* would benefit his other magazines by blazing a trail—he agreed to try the ad-free, reader-supported *Ms.* you hold now and to give us complete editorial control.

II.

Do you think, as I once did, that advertisers make decisions based on solid research? Well, think again. "Broadly speaking," says Joseph Smith of Oxtoby-Smith, Inc., a consumer research firm, "there is no persuasive evidence that the editorial context of an ad matters."

Advertisers who demand such "complementary copy," even in the absence of respectable studies, clearly are operating under a double standard. The same food

Elle, May 1990
326 pages total;
39 non-ad or ad-related

Lear's, November 1989
173 pages total;
65 non-ad or ad-related

companies place ads in *People* with no recipes. Cosmetics companies support *The New Yorker* with no regular beauty columns. So where does this habit of controlling the content of women's magazines come from?

Tradition. Ever since *Ladies Magazine* debuted in Boston in 1828, editorial copy directed to women has been informed by something other than its readers' wishes. There were no ads then, but in an age when married women were legal minors with no right to their own money, there was another revenue source to be kept in mind: husbands. "Husbands may rest assured," wrote editor Sarah Josepha Hale, "that nothing found in these pages shall cause her [his wife] to be less assiduous in preparing for his reception or encourage her to 'usurp station' or encroach upon prerogatives of men."

Hale went on to become the editor of *Godey's Lady's Book,* a magazine featuring "fashion plates": engravings of dresses for readers to take to their seamstresses or copy themselves. Hale added "how to" articles, which set the tone for women's service magazines for years to come: how to write politely, avoid sunburn, and—in no fewer than 1,200 words—how to maintain a goose quill pen. She advocated education for women but avoided controversy. Just as most women's magazines now avoid politics, poll their readers on issues like abortion but rarely take a stand, and praise socially approved lifestyles, Hale saw to it that *Godey's* avoided the hot topics of its day: slavery, abolition, and women's suffrage.

What definitively turned women's magazines into catalogs, however, were two events: Ellen Butterick's invention of the clothing pattern in 1863 and the mass manufacture of patent medicines containing everything from colored water to cocaine. For the first time, readers could purchase what magazines encouraged them to want. As such magazines became more profitable, they also began to attract men as editors. (Most women's magazines continued to have men as top editors until the feminist 1970s.) Edward Bok, who became editor of *The Ladies' Home Journal* in 1889, discovered the power of advertisers when he rejected ads for patent medicines and found that other advertisers canceled in retribution. In the early 20th century, *Good Housekeeping* started its Institute to "test and approve" products. Its Seal of Approval became the grandfather of current "value added" programs that offer advertisers such bonuses as product sampling and department store promotions.

By the time suffragists finally won the vote in 1920, women's magazines had become too entrenched as catalogs to help women learn how to use it. The main function was to create a desire for products, teach how to use products, and make products a crucial part of gaining social approval, pleasing a husband, and performing as a homemaker. Some unrelated articles and short stories were included to persuade women to pay for these catalogs. But articles were neither consumerist nor rebellious. Even fiction was usually subject to formula: if a woman had any sexual life outside marriage, she was supposed to come to a bad end.

In 1965, Helen Gurley Brown began to change part of that formula by bringing "the sexual revolution" to

By the time suffragists had won the vote, women's magazines were too entrenched as catalogs to help women use political power.

women's magazines—but in an ad-oriented way. Attracting multiple men required even more consumerism, as the Cosmo Girl made clear, than finding one husband.

In response to the workplace revolution of the 1970s, traditional women's magazines—that is, "trade books" for women working at home—were joined by *Savvy*, *Working Woman*, and other trade books for women working in offices. But by keeping the fashion/beauty/entertaining articles necessary to get traditional ads and then adding career articles besides, they inadvertently produced the antifeminist stereotype of Super Woman. The male-imitative, dress-for-success woman carrying a briefcase became the media image of a woman worker, even though a blue-collar woman's salary was often higher than her glorified secretarial sister's, and though women at a real briefcase level are statistically rare. Needless to say, these dress-for-success women were also thin, white, and beautiful.

In recent years, advertisers' control over the editorial content of women's magazines has become so institutionalized that it is written into "insertion orders" or dictated to ad salespeople as official policy. The following are recent typical orders to women's magazines:

■ Dow's Cleaning Products stipulates that ads for its Vivid and Spray 'n Wash products should be adjacent to "children or fashion editorial"; ads for Bathroom Cleaner should be next to "home furnishing/family"

features; and so on for other brands. "If a magazine fails for 1/2 the brands or more," the Dow order warns, "it will be omitted from further consideration."

■ Bristol-Myers, the parent of Clairol, Windex, Drano, Bufferin, and much more, stipulates that ads be placed next to "a full page of compatible editorial."

■ S.C. Johnson & Son, makers of Johnson Wax, lawn and laundry products, insect sprays, hair sprays, and so on, orders that its ads "*should not be opposite extremely controversial features or material antithetical to the nature/copy of the advertised product.*" (Italics theirs.)

■ Maidenform, manufacturer of bras and other apparel, leaves a blank for the particular product and states: "The creative concept of the ____ campaign, and the very nature of the product itself appeal to the positive emotions of the reader/consumer. Therefore, it is imperative that all editorial adjacencies reflect that same positive tone. The editorial must not be negative in content or lend itself contrary to the ____ product imagery/message (e.g. *editorial relating to illness, disillusionment, large size fashion, etc.*)." (Italics mine.)

■ The De Beers diamond company, a big seller of engagement rings, prohibits magazines from placing its ads with "adjacencies to hard news or anti/love-romance themed editorial."

■ Procter & Gamble, one of this country's most powerful and diversified advertisers, stands out in the memory of Anne Summers and Sandra Yates (no mean feat in this context): its products were not to be placed in *any* issue that included *any* material on gun control, abortion, the occult, cults, or the disparagement of religion. Caution was also demanded in any issue covering sex or drugs, even for educational purposes.

Those are the most obvious chains around women's magazines. There are also rules so clear they needn't be written down: for instance, an overall "look" compatible with beauty and fashion ads. Even "real" nonmodel women photographed for a woman's magazine are usually made up, dressed in credited clothes, and retouched out of all reality. When editors do include articles on less-than-cheerful subjects (for instance, domestic violence), they tend to keep them short and unillustrated. The point is to be "upbeat." Just as women in the street are asked, "Why don't you smile, honey?" women's magazines acquire an institutional smile.

Within the text itself, praise for advertisers' products has become so ritualized that fields like "beauty writing" have been invented. One of its frequent practitioners explained seriously that "It's a difficult art. How many new adjectives can you find? How much greater can you make a lipstick sound? The FDA restricts what companies can say on labels, but we create illusion. And ad agencies are on the phone all the time pushing you to get their product in. A lot of them keep the business based on how many editorial clippings they produce every month. The worst are products," like Lauder's as the writer confirmed, "with their own name involved. It's all ego."

3. COMMERCIAL CONSIDERATIONS

Often, editorial becomes one giant ad. Last November, for instance, *Lear's* featured an elegant woman executive on the cover. On the contents page, we learned she was wearing Guerlain makeup and Samsara, a new fragrance by Guerlain. Inside were full-page ads for Samsara and Guerlain antiwrinkle cream. In the cover profile, we learned that this executive was responsible for launching Samsara and is Guerlain's director of public relations. When the *Columbia Journalism Review* did one of the few articles to include women's magazines in coverage of the influence of ads, editor Frances Lear was quoted as defending her magazine because "this kind of thing is done all the time."

Often, advertisers also plunge odd-shaped ads into the text, no matter what the cost to the readers. At *Woman's Day,* a magazine originally founded by a supermarket chain, editor in chief Ellen Levine said, "The day the copy had to rag around a chicken leg was not a happy one."

Advertisers are also adamant about where in a magazine their ads appear. When Revlon was not placed as the first beauty ad in one Hearst magazine, for instance, Revlon pulled its ads from *all* Hearst magazines. Ruth Whitney, editor in chief of *Glamour,* attributes some of

I t's been three years away from the grindstone of ad pressures. . . . I'm just realizing how edges got smoothed down—in spite of all our resistance.

these demands to "ad agencies wanting to prove to a client that they've squeezed the last drop of blood out of a magazine." She also is, she says, "sick and tired of hearing that women's magazines are controlled by cigarette ads." Relatively speaking, she's right. To be as censoring as are many advertisers for women's products, tobacco companies would have to demand articles in praise of smoking and expect glamorous photos of beautiful women smoking their brands.

I don't mean to imply that the editors I quote here share my objections to ads: most assume that women's magazines have to be the way they are. But it's also true that only former editors can be completely honest. "Most of the pressure came in the form of direct product mentions," explains Sey Chassler, who was editor in chief of *Redbook* from the sixties to the eighties. "We got threats from the big guys, the Revlons, blackmail threats. They wouldn't run ads unless we credited them.

"But it's not fair to single out the beauty advertisers because these pressures came from everybody. Advertisers want to know two things: What are you going to charge me? What *else* are you going to do for me? It's a holdup.

For instance, management felt that fiction took up too much space. They couldn't put any advertising in that. For the last ten years, the number of fiction entries into the National Magazine Awards has declined.

"And pressures are getting worse. More magazines are more bottom-line oriented because they have been taken over by companies with no interest in publishing.

"I also think advertisers do this to women's magazines especially," he concluded, "because of the general disrespect they have for women."

Even media experts who don't give a damn about women's magazines are alarmed by the spread of this ad-edit linkage. In a climate *The Wall Street Journal* describes as an unacknowledged Depression for media, women's products are increasingly able to take their low standards wherever they go. For instance: newsweeklies publish uncritical stories on fashion and fitness. *The New York Times Magazine* recently ran an article on "firming creams," complete with mentions of advertisers. *Vanity Fair* published a profile of one major advertiser, Ralph Lauren, illustrated by the same photographer who does his ads, and turned the lifestyle of another, Calvin Klein, into a cover story. Even the outrageous *Spy* has toned down since it began to go after fashion ads.

And just to make us really worry, films and books, the last media that go directly to the public without having to attract ads first, are in danger, too. Producers are beginning to depend on payments for displaying products in movies, and books are now being commissioned by companies like Federal Express.

But the truth is that women's products—like women's magazines—have never been the subjects of much serious reporting anyway. News and general interest publications, including the "style" or "living" sections of newspapers, write about food and clothing as cooking and fashion, and almost never evaluate such products by brand name. Though chemical additives, pesticides, and animal fats are major health risks in the United States, and clothes, shoddy or not, absorb more consumer dollars than cars, this lack of information is serious. So is ignoring the contents of beauty products that are absorbed into our bodies through our skins, and that have profit margins so big they would make a loan shark blush.

III.

What could women's magazines be like if they were as free as books? as realistic as newspapers? as creative as films? as diverse as women's lives? We don't know.

But we'll only find out if we take women's magazines seriously. If readers were to act in a concerted way to change traditional practices of *all* women's magazines and the marketing of *all* women's products, we could do it. After all, they are operating on our consumer dollars; money that we now control. You and I could:

■ write to editors and publishers (with copies to advertisers) that we're willing to pay *more* for magazines with editorial independence, but will *not* continue to pay for those that are just editorial extensions of ads;

■ write to advertisers (with copies to editors and publishers) that we want fiction, political reporting, consumer reporting—whatever is, or is not, supported by their ads;

■ put as much energy into breaking advertising's control over content as into changing the images in ads, or protesting ads for harmful products like cigarettes;

■ support only those women's magazines and products that take *us* seriously as readers and consumers.

Those of us in the magazine world can also use the carrot-and-stick technique. For instance: pointing out that, if magazines were a regulated medium like television, the demands of advertisers would be against FCC rules. Payola and extortion could be punished. As it is, there are probably illegalities. A magazine's postal rates are determined by the ratio of ad to edit pages, and the former costs more than the latter. So much for the stick.

The carrot means appealing to enlightened self-interest. For instance: there are many studies showing that the greatest factor in determining an ad's effectiveness is the credibility of its surroundings. The "higher the rating of editorial believability," concluded a 1987 survey by the *Journal of Advertising Research,* "the higher the rating of the advertising." Thus, an impenetrable wall between edit and ads would also be in the best interest of advertisers.

Unfortunately, few agencies or clients hear such arguments. Editors often maintain the false purity of refusing to talk to them at all. Instead, they see ad salespeople who know little about editorial, are trained in business as usual, and are usually paid by commission. Editors might also band together to take on controversy. That happened once when all the major women's magazines did articles in the same month on the Equal Rights Amendment. It could happen again.

It's almost three years away from life between the grindstones of advertising pressures and readers' needs. I'm just beginning to realize how edges got smoothed down—in spite of all our resistance.

I remember feeling put upon when I changed "Porsche" to "car" in a piece about Nazi imagery in German pornography by Andrea Dworkin—feeling sure Andrea would understand that Volkswagen, the distributor of Porsche and one of our few supportive advertisers, asked only to be far away from Nazi subjects. It's taken me all this time to realize that Andrea was the one with a right to feel put upon.

Even as I write this, I get a call from a writer for *Elle,* who is doing a whole article on where women part their hair. Why, she wants to know, do I part mine in the middle?

It's all so familiar. A writer trying to make something of a nothing assignment; an editor laboring to think of new ways to attract ads; readers assuming that other women must want this ridiculous stuff; more women suffering for lack of information, insight, creativity, and laughter that could be on these same pages.

I ask you: Can't we do better than this?

Hollywood the Ad

Mark Crispin Miller

A prolific media critic, Miller often focuses on issues raised by the commercialism of the television, recording, and film industries. He is author of Boxed In: The Culture of TV *(1988), and* Seeing through Movies *(1990).*

"This approach to human beings strikes me as utterly cynical, and directly contrary to the democratic ideal." Such was the sharp response of Dr. Lewis Webster Jones, the head of the National Conference of Christians and Jews. Other clergymen agreed: this new technique could mean the twilight of democracy. It was not only God's ministers who sensed a threat. This technique, Aldous Huxley declared, made "nonsense of the whole democratic procedure, which is based on conscious choice on rational ground." The public protest was immense. The National Association of Radio and Television Broadcasters felt obliged to ban the use of the technique by any of its members, and the three major television networks also publicly rejected it. The New York State Senate unanimously passed a bill outlawing the technique. When KTLA, an independent TV station in Los Angeles, announced that it would soon start using the invention to discourage littering and unsafe driving, the station "received such a torrent of adverse mail," *Life* magazine reported, "that it cancelled the campaign."

Meanwhile, there were some who were not emitting "yelps of alarm," according to the *Wall Street Journal*. Indeed, certain forward-looking managers were rather taken with the idea, despite its dangers, or perhaps because of them. "Chuckles one TV executive with a conscious eye on the future," *Time* magazine reported in its coverage of the controversy, "'It smacks of brainwashing, but of course it would be tempting.'"

The invention that sparked the national panic, and that was also quietly thrilling certain corporate salesmen, was "subliminal advertising"—a phrase coined by the first of its practitioners, James M. Vicary, "a young motivational researcher and amateur psychologist," as the *Journal* called him. On September 12, 1957, Vicary, the vice-president of the Subliminal Projection Company, held a press conference to tout the results of an experiment that he had just concluded at a neighborhood movie theater in Fort Lee, New Jersey. For six weeks, using special equipment, he had flashed imperceptible allurements onto the screen during the theater's showings of *Picnic*, a Columbia release. Projected every five seconds for one three-thousandth of a second, those unnoticed coaxings, Vicary said, had dramatically boosted concession-stand sales of the items subliminally hyped on the big screen. Vicary had projected two terse bits of copy: "Hungry? Eat popcorn" and "Drink Coca-Cola."

BLATANT IMPOSITIONS

Today what matters most about Vicary's experiment is not his "findings"—which Vicary fabricated. His invention turned out to have had no effect at all on how much Coke or popcorn people swallowed, but was a mere sales gimmick to promote the Subliminal Projection Company itself. Although his "results" were valueless, the outrage stirred by his announcement is important. Back then the rumor that one movie had been temporarily polluted with an advertising pitch—"Drink Coca-Cola"—was enough to elicit a great wave of angry protest. That was in 1957. Let us now look at two clips from movies of the 1980s—movies that nobody protested.

In *Murphy's Romance*, released by Columbia in 1985, Sally Field is a youngish divorcée, poor but plucky, who has just moved with her sweet pre-adolescent son to a friendly little Texas town. At the start of the film she wanders into an old-fashioned drugstore, owned, we soon discover, by James Garner, a very benevolent curmudgeon ("Murphy"). On her way in, Field passes, and so we see (she's moving slowly so that we'll see), not one but *three* bright Coca-Cola signs (the merry red, the bold white script)—one on each front window, one on the front door. And then, as Field plunks herself down cutely at the soda counter, and as the seemingly brusque but really very kindly Garner comes to serve her, there is the following exchange:

Field: I'll have a banana split. No, I won't. I'll have a Coke.
Garner: A Coke?
Field: A lemon Coke.

Much is later made of Garner's cherished 1927 Studebaker, which sits out front; Garner refuses to put it elsewhere, despite a daily parking ticket. Although this business does say something obvious about Garner's character ("That Murphy! Stubborn as a mule!"), the car's visual function is to say "Drink Coca-Cola," because it shares the frame with, and is the same deep merry red as, those three prominent Coca-Cola signs. (The movie, incidentally, has a happy ending.)

Toward the beginning of *Who's Harry Crumb?*, a 1989 Columbia release, John Candy sits next to Jim Belushi on a bus. A fantastically inept detective, Candy is on his way to meet his employers in a big kidnapping case. Here, in all its comic brilliance, is the entire scene with Belushi:

Candy (eating cherries, offers one): Cherry?
Belushi (reading): No fruit, thank you.

Candy pulls a can of Diet Coke (silvery cylinder, red block letters) out of his bag.

Candy: Coke?
Belushi: No, thank you.
Candy: Mix 'em together, ya got a cherry Coke. Ah ha ha ha ha ha! A cherry Coke, ha ha ha ha!

Later, dining with his wealthy clients, Candy pours a can of Diet Coke into a brandy snifter full of ice cream, holding the (silvery) can up high so that its (red) name is not just legible but unavoidable.

What is the difference between James Vicary's ploy and these later cinematic tricks to make an audience "Drink Coca-Cola"? In 1957 Vicary tried to boost his business by implanting a commercial message in a Columbia release (and then by making false claims for the failed experiment). In 1982 Coca-Cola bought 49 percent of Columbia Pictures and began at once to plug (its own) products in (its own) movies—trying, just like Vicary, to profit by turning movies into advertising.

(The company kept it up until it sold Columbia Pictures to Sony, in 1989.) Certainly there is a difference in degree. Whereas Vicary's method was a furtive imposition on the movie, used in only one theater, and only temporarily, the come-ons embedded in Coke's movies are there forever, in whatever prints or tapes you choose to see, because those messages are worked—overtly—right into the movies' scripts and mise-en-scène.

In this overtness, one might argue, these later exhortations to drink Coca-Cola differ crucially from Vicary's gimmick, because his appeal was "subliminal," whereas the later cans and signs beckon us openly, like illuminated billboards. Such a distinction, however, rests on too crude an understanding of subliminal effects—which result not from invisible implants but from words or images that are, in fact, explicitly presented yet at best only half perceived. These latter-day plugs for Coca-Cola, for example, work as subliminal inducements because their context is ostensibly a movie, not an ad, so that each of them comes sidling toward us dressed up as non-advertising, just as other kinds of ads now routinely come at us disguised as "magalogues" and "advertorials"; rock videos; "educational" broadcasts, newsletters, filmstrips, and posters; concerts, art exhibits, sporting events, magazines, newspapers, books, and TV shows; and a good deal of our daily mail—in short, as anything and everything but advertising.

The subliminal impact of the Coke plugs arises not only from their cinematic camouflage but also from the pleasant welter of associations that in each movie efficiently glamorize every Coca-Cola can or logo; Garner's personal warmth and fine old car, John Candy's would-be riotous antics (and, in each case, the very fact of stardom itself), are attractions serving as oblique (that is, subliminal) enhancements to the all-important product. Precisely because of this benefit Coca-Cola has understandably been very careful in its choice of cinematic vehicles—and has also used them to stigmatize the competition.

In *Murphy's Romance*, Field's nice son goes looking for a job; and while "Coca-Cola" sheds its deep red warmth throughout Murphy's homey store, in a big supermarket where the kid is told abruptly that he isn't needed, two (blue) Pepsi signs loom coldly on the wall like a couple of swastikas. In fact, the company used such tactics before it bought Columbia. In Costa-Gavras's *Missing*, a Universal picture made just before the purchase, Jack Lemmon plays a very decent father searching Chile for his son, who has been kidnapped by Pinochet's soldiers. In one scene this haggard, loyal dad, while talking things out, takes rare (and noticeable) solace in a bottle of Coke—whereas inside the nightmare stadium where the army does its torturing and murdering there stands a mammoth Pepsi machine, towering in this underworld like its dark idol.

Although Pepsico owns no movie studio (yet), its officers began fighting back at once. A special manager tackled the job of keeping Pepsi on the silver screen, and from that moment the spheric Pepsi logo (white/blue/red) became a film presence almost as prevalent as big handguns. In the movies Pepsi is the choice of a new generation—that is, of every generation. The suburban kids are drinking Pepsi in *Ferris Bueller's Day Off,* like the poor kids in *Stand and Deliver* and *Lean on Me,* and like the old folks in *Cocoon: The Return.* Jennifer Beals is drinking Diet Pepsi in *Flashdance,* Kathy Baker is buying Pepsi in *Clean and Sober,* in *Always* a brightly lit Pepsi logo lengthily upstages Holly Hunter, and in *Legal Eagles* Debra Winger keeps her Pepsi cold and blatant in a refrigerator otherwise full of blank containers. Pepsi glides through the Texas of the fifties in *Everybody's All-American,* pops into the cute Manhattan of *Crossing Delancey,* and drops in on Norman Bates's milieu in *Psycho II* and *Psycho III.* And Pepsico, too, has tried to move against its major rival, declining to place a Pepsi ad on the cassette of *Dirty Dancing* unless Vestron, the video company, cut every scene that showed a Coca-Cola sign. Vestron passed. (All these movies have happy endings.)

PRODUCT PLACEMENT

Such subliminal tactics are certainly not peculiar to the mighty cola rivals. They are also used today—aggressively—by every other major advertiser. Indeed, cinematic product placement became so common in the eighties that it now sustains a veritable industry. Formerly plugging was a marginal (if common) practice in the movie industry, the result of direct bartering between studio and advertiser. In the eighties the plugging process became "rationalized," as dozens of companies formed to broker deals between advertisers and film producers. Usually the advertisers—and sometimes the studios themselves—keep the brokers on retainer with an annual fee; the advertisers are then charged extra for specific "placements." In return for the plug the advertiser will help defray the ever-rising costs of filmmaking, not only by providing props or costumes but often—and more important—by mounting a tie-in promotional campaign that will sell the movie in many ads, in thousands of bright aisles, on millions of clean boxes.

The arrangement seems to work wonders for the budgets of all concerned. The advertisers love it: "More and more companies now recognize that movies are an alternative advertising and promotional medium," a plugster exults. And this offer is one that financially pressed filmmakers can't refuse. "Obsessed with the bottom line, studios no longer snub promotion tie-ins—much to the delight of marketers eager to reach the last captive media audience," *Incentive* magazine reports. An executive at Walt Disney Pictures and Television says, "Add the magic of movies to a promotion, and you can rise above the clutter to get people's attention."

Always in search of the perfectly closed-off setting, advertisers have for decades been eyeing cinema, whose viewers can't flip the page or turn their chairs away. It is this interest in a captive audience that has the marketers delighting in the movies—which, now crammed with plugs, offer about as much magic as you would find at K-Mart, or at Lord & Taylor. Watching them, there is no way that you "can rise above the clutter," because they *are* "the clutter."

Consider one of Sylvester Stallone's big hits, *Rocky III,* which showcases in passing Coca-Cola, Sanyo, Nike, Wheaties, TWA, Marantz, and Wurlitzer, and—in actual ads within the film (with Rocky, now a big celebrity, as endorser)—Nikon, Harley-Davidson, Budweiser, Maserati, Gatorade, and American Express. Or consider *Over the Top,* a box-office disaster in which Stallone plays a humble trucker who, estranged from his son, must win the lad back by taking first prize in a major arm-wrestling tournament. Even before the opening credits are over, the movie has highlighted Budweiser, Colgate shaving cream, and Michelin tires; and daubed across the side of Stallone's giant rig is a huge full-color ad for Brut cologne, which shows up grandly in the film's big landscape shots. (Brut and the film's producers had a tie-in deal.) Moreover, each of the many arm wrestlers who roar and shudder at the Big Event bears the imprint of some corporate sponsor, so that the movie displays not only Hilton Hotels, TWA, Alpine car stereos, Leaseway Transportation, Nintendo—and Pepsi—but also Volvo *and* Toyota, Nike *and* Adidas, and Valvoline, Duracell, Soloflex, and AlkaSeltzer. (Both films have happy endings.)

These are two examples of Hollywood's new commercialism at its most grotesque, and there are many others—for example, the . . . 007 entry, *License to Kill,* in which James Bond ostentatiously smokes Larks, a plug for which Philip Morris paid $350,000; or *Back to the Future II,* a very loud and manic "romp" that lovingly showcases the futuristic wares of at least a dozen corporate advertisers; or *The Wizard,* a children's movie that is essentially a long commercial for Nintendo; or, in what may be (you never know) the most glaring case of rampant plugging yet, the children's movie *MAC & Me,* a shameless *E.T.* knock-off in which a handicapped child befriends an alien, MAC, who lives on Coca-Cola. (In just over a month this movie grossed $34 million.)

The practice of plugging is just as obvious in movies that do not resemble comic books. Take *Bull Durham,* which begins with the cute rookie pitcher Nuke LaLoosh (Tim Robbins) on the mound, the Pepsi logo plain as day on the outfield wall behind him, its colors reproduced exactly on his uniform. As the film proceeds, it also plugs—repeatedly—Budweiser, Miller, Jim Beam, Oscar Mayer, and a host of Alberto-Culver products. (*Bull Durham* has a happy ending.) Or take *Mr. Mom,* a feeble "issue" comedy about the travails of a green house-husband, which showcases McDonald's, Domino's pizza, Terminix exterminators, Folgers coffee, Lite beer, Jack Daniels, Van Camp's chili, Ban deodorant, Windex, Tide, Spray 'n Wash, Borax, Clorox 2, and Downy fabric softener. (*Mr. Mom* has a happy ending.) Or, finally, take *Murphy's Romance,* which showcases (aside from Coke) Purina, Heinz 57 Steak Sauce, Wesson Oil, Nike, Huggies, Vanish toilet-bowl cleaner, Fuji film, and Miller beer. There are also *two* bottles of Ivory Liquid at Sally Field's kitchen sink, and at one point she asks James Garner, "Could I have two Extra-Strength Tylenol and a glass of water, please?" At another point she shouts enticingly, "Campbell's tomato soup!"

Such bald intrusions into dialogue are no longer rare. Usually the spoken plug comes in the form of a casual request: "Want a Coke?" Eliot asks E.T. "Gimme a Pepsi Free," Michael J. Fox tells the soda jerk in *Back to the Future*—and since they didn't have that choice back in 1955, the jerk's snide retort is really funny. To the advertisers, such a soft gag is ideal, especially if it quotes an established piece of copy. For instance, in *Vice Versa,* one of the late 1980s' several comedies about adults and children swapping bodies, the apparent child, in line at the school cafeteria, betrays his inner maturity in this way: "I don't suppose you have any Grey Poupon?" (All these movies have happy endings.)

TV programs, routinely interrupted by pure ads, need not themselves display the labels quite so often, or so dramatically (although they do display them). American movies nonetheless have a televisual counterpart: Brazilian soap operas, a daily spectacle in which the products play so large a role that some multinationals, among them Coca-Cola, sign annual contracts with Brazil's largest television network, TV Globo, to keep their products constantly written into the shows' ongoing "stories." Down there in Rio the practice, which the Brazilians call by the English word "merchandising," is defended just as Hollywood defends the practice here—by attesting to its powerful naturalism. "Most soap operas are about daily life in which people go shopping and drive cars and drink beer," TV Globo's head of product placement says. "That's why it is so natural."

Likewise, a Hollywood plugster argues that since films "are pushing more toward reality," plugging is imperative: "A can that says 'Beer' isn't going to make it anymore."

In a few . . . movies—the eerie satire *Heathers,* the exquisite *Drugstore Cowboy*—the subtle use of products does make the fictive milieu more believable than generic items would. Usually, however, product placement does not seem natural at all but is deliberately *anti*-realistic: its sole purpose is to enhance the product by meticulously placing it within the sort of idealized display that occurs nowhere in real life but everywhere in advertising—which is itself just such display. In the world as advertised, the label or logo always shines forth like the full moon, whereas in our world, where "people go shopping and drive cars and drink beer," the crucial symbols reach us (if at all) with none of that sudden startling clarity—for the very ubiquity of advertising has paradoxically also worked to hide it from us. To live the daily life in which people go shopping is to be bombarded into numbness; and it is this stupefaction that movie plugs, like advertising proper, have been devised to penetrate.

As such plugs are anti-realistic, so also are they anti-narrative, for the same movie-glow that exalts each product high above the clutter of the everyday also lifts it out of, and thereby makes it work against, the movie's story. Even when half turned toward us, coquettishly, or placed in some marginal position, the crucial can or box or bottle tends (as it were) to make a scene. An expert rhetorical missile in the first place, and with its force enhanced a thousandfold by advertising, the product cannot even sneak by without distracting us at least a little, its vivid, pleasant features calling, "*Hey!* It's *me!*"

And when shoved right into the spotlight, the product doesn't just upstage the actors but actually stops the narrative. In *Uncle Buck,* John Candy appears sitting on a sofa, holding a big box of Kellogg's Frosted Flakes at his side, as prominent and boldly hued as an armorial shield—and on that sight the camera lingers. At such a moment the loud package wipes out its co-stars and surroundings, becoming the only thing we notice. (*Uncle Buck* has a happy ending.)

The rise of product placement has, however, damaged movie narrative not only through the shattering effect of individual plugs but also—more profoundly—through the partial transfer of creative authority out of the hands of filmmaking professionals and into the purely quantitative universe of the CEOs. All the scenes, shots, and lines mentioned above represent the usurpation by advertising of those authorial prerogatives once held by directors and screenwriters, art directors and set designers—and by studio heads, who generally cared about how their films were made, whereas the managers now in charge are thinking only of their annual reports. "Hollywood has changed," says Ed Meyer, of the ad agency Saatchi & Saatchi DFS Compton. "Unlike the old days, the bankers and M.B.A.s are calling the shots."

Thus the basic decisions of filmmaking are now often made, indirectly, by the advertisers, who are focused only on a movie's usefulness for pushing products. Take the case of costume designers, who have often in the eighties been displaced by "promo-costuming"—an arrangement that, according to *Premiere* magazine, either showcases the wares of name designers (Oscar de la Renta did *Bright Lights, Big City;* Giorgio Armani did *The Untouchables*) or, more frequently, "involves manufacturers of such branded staples as jeans and sneakers, which have visible logos that make them much easier to promote." In 1987, for example, Adidas shod and clad many of the characters in some sixty movies.

The plugging process is as thorough and exacting as the work of those professionals whose skill it has long since superseded. The pre-production effort is exhaustive: "Friendly producers," the *Wall Street Journal* reports, "send scripts to [Associated Film Promotions] weeks and even months before filming starts, and the company analyzes them scene by scene to see if it can place a product—or advertising material, a billboard perhaps—on, under, or behind the stars." While the advertisers may not be as idealistic about movies as, say, David O. Selznick, they are just as dictatorial: "We choose projects where we have maximum control," says one plugster. "We break a film down and tell the producers exactly where we want to see our clients' brands."

Such subordination of the movie is essential to plugging, which is based on the assumption that the movie will in no way contradict—will, indeed, do nothing but enhance—the product's costly, all-important aura. The plug, in other words, must not just "foreground" the crucial name or image but also flatter it—that is, brightly reaffirm the product's advertising. When its brokers argue that plugging enhances realism, they are implying that reality is only where the products mean just what their advertising says they mean: "power" or "safety" or "old-fashioned goodness."

Now and then in the eighties an American movie has invoked products critically, or at least in a way that is poetically telling and not just promotional. In Garry Marshall's *Nothing in Common,* a surprisingly grim and moving (if uneven) comedy about a successful young adman (Tom Hanks) and his dying scoundrel of a father (Jackie Gleason), the same product appears in two shots—not to sell it but as a chilling metaphysical implication and a visual hint that father and son, despite their mutual loathing and antithetical lifestyles, are fundamentally alike. Placed casually in each man's kitchen—the one tidy and state-of-the-art, the other bare and slovenly—is a box of the same cereal: Life. (*Nothing in Common* does not have a happy ending.)

Such dark suggestiveness is precisely what advertisers do not want, and so they, or their brokers, will back away from any movie that might somehow cast a shadow on their advertising. For advertisers are obsessed not just with selling their own specific images but also with universalizing the whole hermetic ambience for selling itself—the pseudo-festive, mildly jolting, ultimately tranquilizing atmosphere of TV and its bright epiphenomena, the theme park and the shopping mall.

CROSSOVERS

Even if, armed with some marvelous zapping gizmo, you could sit and blast away every obvious product as it passed through the frame or glowed in close-up, today's Hollywood movie would still seem like an ad. This is in part because movies now tend to look and sound a lot like TV commercials, as if the major film schools were teaching not, say, the best movies out of Warner Brothers but the latest campaign by the Saatchi brothers. Like ads, movies now tend to have a perfectly coordinated total look, as if they'd been designed rather than directed—a tendency so marked, in some cases, that the movie and some well-known ad can hardly be distinguished. Thus *The Color Purple,* with its lush score, hazy golden images, and long climactic round of teary hugs, leaves you thinking not that you should read the novel but that you really ought to call your mother ("Reach out—"), while the parodic *Raising Arizona* uses precisely the same wide-angle distortion and hyped-up, deadpan acting that Joe Sedelmaier used in his famous ads for Federal Express ("When it abso*lu*tely, posi*tive*ly—"), while *Top Gun,* the blockbuster salute to navy fliers, is in its action sequences identical to those spectacular commercials that allured the young with "It's Not Just a Job: It's an Adventure!" or (yes!) "Be All You Can Be!"—expert recruitment propaganda that was probably well known to the film's director, Tony Scott, who came to the movie business as a famed director of TV ads, most notably for Diet Pepsi. (These three movies leave you feeling good.)

Such crossovers are the usual thing in today's media industry, many of whose filmmakers learned their craft (and continue to work) in TV advertising. Ten years ago a stellar group of such professionals migrated from the ad shops of London to the studios of Hollywood, where they helped to alter modern cinema. Like his brother Tony (who, the year after *Top Gun,* directed the repetitious *Beverly Hills Cop 2*), Ridley Scott is a prolific ad-maker, most notably for Chanel, W. R. Grace, and Apple Computer. He is also the auteur of the inspired and nauseating *Alien;* the brilliant *Blade Runner;* a thriller designed, as if by computer, to stroke lonely women, *Someone to Watch over Me;* and finally the unforgivable *Black Rain.* The ad-maker Hugh Hudson has turned out such gorgeous, empty films as *Chariots of Fire* and *Greystoke: The Legend of Tarzan, Lord of the Apes.* Having made hundreds of short ads, Adrian Lyne came to Hollywood and made such ad-like films as *Flashdance, 9-1/2 Weeks,* and also the gynophobic crowd-pleaser *Fatal Attraction.* Alan Parker, whose films include *Midnight Express, Fame,* and *Mississippi Burning,* is easily the most successful of the British émigrés, because the most adept at stirring our worst impulses. Many American ad-makers have also become filmmakers, including Stan Dragoti, the director of the "I Love New York" ads and the plug-ridden *Mr. Mom;* Howard Zieff, the director of Alka-Seltzer's "Spicy Meatball" ad and the incoherent *Private Benjamin;* and Joe Pytka, the director of numerous Pepsi ads and the deadly racetrack comedy *Let It Ride.*

Meanwhile, as more and more admen direct films, more and more filmmakers are directing television ads—simply in order to keep working, now that the huge costs of moviemaking have made it nearly impossible to get a project going. Directors can no longer afford to scorn the sixty-second pitch: "There *was* a stigma in the past," Jerry Bernstein, the head of the Association of Independent Commercial Producers, observed in 1988. "The feeling was [that the ad] was not a great art form." That feeling is passé, if not extinct, now that Robert Altman, Martin Scorsese (Armani), Federico Fellini, Jean-Luc Godard, Francis Ford Coppola (Fuji), John Frankenheimer, John Badham, Tony Bill (Bud Light), John Schlesinger, David Lynch, Penny Marshall (Revlon), David Steinberg, Stephen Frears, and Errol Morris (7-Eleven), among others, are making ads. Cinematographers, too, have turned to advertising: Sven Nykvist, Nestor Almendros, Gordon Willis, Eric Saarinen, and Vilmos Zsigmond, among others. And filmmakers have even been doing celebrity turns in ads: Richard Donner for Amaretto di Saronno, George Lucas for Panasonic (in Japan), Bernardo Bertolucci for Pioneer, Spike Lee for the Gap, and for Nike (which he plugs throughout his movies) in a commercial that he also directed.

If movies look like ads, then, the transformation may owe something to this exchange of personnel—which delights the powers of advertising, who want their ads to look like movies (so that the restless TV viewer won't zap them). "Advertisers and agencies want their commercials designed with the look of the hottest features," one ad producer says. Crossovers have helped erase the old distinctions between movies and commercials: "The two disciplines—feature films and commercial films—have blended together to the point now where it's just filmmaking," says a senior vice-president at the ad agency DDB Needham, in Chicago. It might seem that through this convergence each "discipline" would somehow benefit the other—but in the era of the VCR it is advertising that has affected cinema, and not the other way around. Now that most movies are produced with an eye toward their eventual re-release on videocassette for the home audience, and now that TV, moreover, has induced a universal taste for TV's pace and tone, the new "filmmaking" takes its lead primarily from those who create the small screen's most hypnotic images. "There's not a good filmmaker alive who doesn't look to us for inspiration," Bob Giraldi, the director of ad spots for GE, Sperry Rand, McDonald's, Miller Lite, and many other corporations, claimed in 1984.

GRABBERS

Just as the product plug halts or weakens the movie narrative, so has this general drift toward ad technique drastically reduced the movies' narrative potential, for cinematic narrative works through a range of visual conventions or devices, and the recent rise of ad technique has all but wiped out that earlier diversity, coarsening a various and nuanced form into a poundingly hypnotic instrument—a mere *stimulus,* and an ugly one at that.

There is, first, the all-important difference in scale. "This is just like doing a small feature," Ridley Scott assured his crew on the set of a Pepsi ad in 1984. "I see commercials as short films," Adrian Lyne told *Advertising Age* in 1985. But to suggest that commercials are just like movies, only smaller (in both space and time), is to negate the crucial ground of cinematic art: an expansive visual field, broad enough to imply a world beyond, behind, more varied than, the glamorous item in midframe. TV is, to say the least, different. Watching *The Last Emperor* on your set is like trying to survey the Sistine Chapel ceiling by peeping at it through a toilet-paper roll. TV, however, has reduced the movies not just by putting blinders on the viewers of wide-screen epics but also by establishing a compositional norm of close-ups, two-shots, and other setups whereby the action is (just as in advertising) repetitiously *foregrounded.*

Such is now the norm of cinema. Today there are few scenes shot in deep focus (as in Renoir and Welles, *Vertigo* and *The Godfather Part II,* or, for that matter, *The Night of the Living Dead*). Likewise, we rarely see the kind of panoramic composition that once allowed a generous impres-

3. COMMERCIAL CONSIDERATIONS

sion of quasi-global simultaneity, as (most elaborately) in the movies of Robert Altman and Jacques Tati, and that also, more subtly, enriches the frame in most great movies, whose makers have offered *pictures,* composed of pleasurable "touches" and legible detail. These moving tableaux often, as André Bazin argued, gave their viewers some choice, and required some (often minimal) interpretive attention. Only now and then, and in films that don't come out of Hollywood—Terry Gilliam's *Brazil,* Stanley Kubrick's *Full Metal Jacket*—do we perceive such exhilarating fullness. In contrast, today's American movies work without, or against, the potential depth and latitude of cinema, in favor of that systematic overemphasis deployed in advertising and all other propaganda. Each shot presents a content closed and unified, like a fist, and makes the point right in your face: big gun, big car, nice ass, full moon, a chase (great shoes!), big crash (blood, glass), a lobby (doorman), sarcasm, drinks, a tonguey, pugilistic kiss (nice sheets!), and so on.

Thus today's movie not only foregrounds but also serializes, for just as TV's narrowness has superannuated deep focus and the movies' (sometime) lateral complexity, so has the speedy pace of TV's ads superannuated most of cinema's earlier transitional devices. As John Frankenheimer (*The Manchurian Candidate,* Fiat, AT&T) told *Advertising Age* in 1988, "No longer do films use the fade to black and the slow dissolve the way they used to." This laconic, and correct, observation hints at a grievous cinematic loss, because the fade and the dissolve are no quaint old movie mannerisms. Rather, the dissolve is a succinct and often beautiful means of conveying the passage of time or the onset of a memory; although it has no exact linguistic counterpart, to drop it from the movies would be somewhat like dropping the past tense from verbal language. The fade to black works like a curtain to cover some event too painful or intimate for exhibition, or as a means of conveying loss of consciousness, or as a somber sort of visual cadence, a way of saying, "It's over: now consider what you've seen." In today's ad-saturated "filmmaking" these devices not only seem too slow but are, in different ways, too suggestive of mortality for the movies' bright mall atmosphere, and so they have been dumped in favor of that most basic of connectives, the simple cut, the overuse of which has helped transform the movies into ad-like serial displays.

Such displays show us nothing—not only because each image in the series is as unambiguous as a brand-new belt but also because the serial rush itself is mesmerizing, and so it blinds us to the flashing items that compose it. Large, stark, and fast, the mere contrast stuns us pleasantly—a response that is, as it were, subvisual, as the ad-makers know very well. Thus both marketing and advertising always aim directly at the lowest levels of the mass (that is, your) brain, seeking a reaction that is not just "positive" but unconscious and immediate. Although the pillars of the ad world still use the word "persuasion" to (mis)represent their business, the whole selling project now depends on moves that are less rhetorical than neurological. "Color goes immediately to the psyche and can be a direct sales stimulus," one typical package designer says. Such blithe and simplistic Pavlovianism is wholly characteristic of the ad-makers and marketers, who like it when we respond without even knowing it, much less knowing why. Thus Philip Dusenberry, of the ad agency BBDO, in New York, claims to have learned (from making Pepsi ads) "that it wasn't important that the viewer read every scene—just that they get the impact of the message."

That last remark could as easily apply to the movies, which now, like advertising, rely heavily if not exclusively on techniques that work directly on the nervous system. Of course, the movies have always used gratuitous tricks to keep viewers riveted: pointless close-ups of a baby's smile to get the women cooing, martial music to tense up the men, sad violins to get the whole house sniffling. Indeed, some of cinema's basic rhetorical devices, it could be argued, are inherently non-narrative, subvisual: crosscutting for suspense, say, or the weepy reaction shot (which moves the viewers to weep). The point, however, is not that such tricks are new but that they are now all-important—for their power has been fantastically augmented by computer science, Dolby sound, great strides forward in the art of mock mayhem, and other technological advances.

Music, for example, has long been overused by Hollywood, as James Agee noted in 1945. Watching John Huston's war documentary *San Pietro,* which he admired immensely, Agee found it "as infuriating to have to fight off the emotional sales pressure of the Mormon Choir as it would be if all the honored watches and nasal aphrodisiacs insisted on marketing themselves against a Toscanini broadcast." At its pushiest, movie music "weakens the emotional imagination both of maker and onlooker, and makes it virtually impossible to communicate or receive ideas. It sells too cheaply and far too sensually all the things it is the business of the screen itself to present."

Watching the movies that Agee found overscored, most people now would probably agree with him, since the aesthetic errors of the past are easy to laugh at decades later. What may be less obvious today is the persistent relevance of Agee's argument, for the movies have, as visual events, been largely devastated by their "music"—a vast and irresistible barrage of synthesized sound, a hyper-rhythmic full-body stimulus far more effective, and a whole lot louder, than the old choral yawpings or symphonic sweeps that now seem so corny. Starting somewhere out there and back to the left, the "music" thrums and zooms and jumps and jangles right on through you, clearing out your head with such efficiency that not only is it impossible to receive ideas but the whole movie, once over, seems to have gone in one ear and out the other—except that it's not just your head that has functioned as a throughway but every vital organ.

It is the Dolby system, sometimes enhanced by George Lucas's more recent THX Sound System, that gives the music such prostrating force. Even on cassette, however, the music works an antivisual effect (just as it does throughout TV's shows and ads), imposing an upbeat mood on images that are, per se, so mundane that they would bore or even depress you if the music weren't there telling you to dance. In *St. Elmo's Fire,* Emilio Estevez drives off in a car, and the music makes it sound as if he's just won gold at the Olympics. At the end of *Private Benjamin,* Goldie Hawn walks down a lonely road, and the score exults as if she were attending her own coronation. (Both those movies have happy endings.)

More and more, the movies' very images are also—paradoxically—nonvisual, because, like the music, they try to force our interest or reaction through a visceral jolt that stuns the mind and shuts the eyes. Some of the movies' latest grabbers are very old, like the gooey close-up of some wondering baby ("Awwww!"), a device no less sickening in *Ghostbusters II* (1989) than it was in *Bachelor Daddy* (1941). Generally, however, the latest grabbers are more technologically sophisticated and (a lot) more violent than those sentimental moments—and far more commonplace, now that movie narrative has been supplanted by such blinding jabs.

As special effects have since *Star Wars* become more mind-blowing and yet more believable, they have also grown more important to the spectacle—and have changed in tone. In many instances the effects now *are* the movie, whether it's *Indiana Jones and the Last Crusade* or *A Nightmare on Elm Street 3,* films you can sleep through for twenty minutes without then having to ask, "What did I miss?" And as the effects have become the whole show, they have ceased to represent some ambiguous looming force, uncanny or apocalyptic—as they did in the first *King Kong, The Day the Earth Stood Still,* and *2001: A Space Odyssey*—and have instead become the tools for a light show that both stimulates and reassures, like fireworks on the Fourth.

In other words, whereas the effects were once used by and large to fake some scary threat to all humanity, they now routinely fake, in one way or another, someone's annihilation—and it is *good.*

The wipe-out might be violent, as at the end of *Raiders of the Lost Ark,* when the Nazis are melted down or shriveled up by the wrathful ark light, or as in the horror movies, where, say, Jason burns, zaps, and mangles several teens, until some teen burns or zaps or mangles Jason. Whether the killing force is righteous or demonic, the spectacle of its, his, or her destructiveness or destruction invites your rapt gaze of wondering assent, just like those movies that present the wipeout as a sweet translation into outer space (that is, heaven): *E.T., Close Encounters of the Third Kind, Cocoon, Cocoon: The Return*—films whose (grateful) characters finally disappear into the all-important light show, just like the films themselves.

For all their visual sophistication, these effects are meant to move us beyond, or back from, visual experience, by either having us nearly *feel* those razors rake that throat or having us *feel* as if we, too, were dissolving in a celestial bath of light. The same kind of experience—antivisual, non-narrative—is commonplace even in films that have no supernatural or "alien" component. In the eighties the car chase, for instance, became the movies' main story substitute, offering the illusion of dreamlike forward speed and the gratifying sight, sound, and feeling of machinery bucking, squealing, blowing up—elements that have become so frequent that to catalogue them here would fill a page, since they compose whole sections not only of the cop films (*The Presidio, Cobra,* and two *Lethal Weapons,* the two *Beverly Hills Cops, Red Heat*) but also of many comedies, even ones that didn't need such filler (*Midnight Run, The Blues Brothers, Throw Momma from the Train*). The pleasure here is not visual but physically empathic—the centrifugal tug, that pleasing *crash!*: mock thrills that have only gotten punchier and more elaborate as the car stuff has become routine. Likewise, screen violence in general, a relentless story substitute, has become both commonplace and often horribly sadistic. (The movies named in the above two paragraphs all have happy endings.)

THE IMPERATIVE OF VIOLENCE

The empathic function of today's screen violence has changed the character of movie heroics. In *Bullitt* (1968) and *The French Connection* (1971), in *The Searchers* (1956), and in the movies of Sam Peckinpah, the violence, however graphic, was muted by a deep ambivalence that shadowed even the most righteous-seeming acts of vengeance, and that therefore suppressed the viewer's urge to join in kicking. In contrast, screen violence now is used primarily to invite the viewer to enjoy the *feel* of killing, beating, mutilating. This is most obvious in the slasher films, in which the camera takes the stalking murderer's point of view, but the same empathic project goes on throughout the genres. There is no point to Rambo's long climactic rage, or Cobra's, or Chuck Norris's, other than its open invitation to *become him* at that moment—to ape that sneer of hate, to feel the way it feels to stand there tensed up with the Uzi. The hero's inner kinship with the villain used to seem uncanny, as in Hitchcock's and Fritz Lang's movies, and in Clint Eastwood's excellent *Tightrope*—whereas Stallone's Cobra gets a charge out of being *exactly* like the psychopaths he chases, just as we are meant to feel *exactly* like him.

Moreover, it is not just the overt paeans to machismo that thus incite us but also films that seem politically unlike, say, *Rambo III*—and like *Mississippi Burning*. Hailed for having a plot based on a key event in the history of the civil rights movement, it actually has no plot, nor is it even slightly faithful to that history. The movie is, in fact, nothing more than one long grabber. After an hour of watching white trash inflict atrocities on helpless blacks (and a nice white woman), we watch the kick-ass Gene Hackman argue hotly with his FBI superior, the tight-assed Willem Dafoe, who has from the outset rebutted Hackman's vigilantist urgings with the boring creed of rules and regulations. They fight at length (shouts, punches; a gun is even pulled)—and then, suddenly, Dafoe just up and *changes*: "New rules. We nail 'em any way we can. Even your way." This absolute reversal, although absurd in terms of character, makes sense rhetorically, since it's now time to have the three of us (audience, Dafoe, Hackman) all fold into Hackman, who is thereby freed to punish all those ugly rednecks in the ugliest of ways—crushing their testicles, threatening them with castration, maiming them with straight razors, and otherwise permitting "us" to act, through him, just like the Klansmen we presumably detest, while the blacks remain helpless throughout. (*Mississippi Burning* has a happy ending.)

Over and over, conventional narrative requirements are broken down by the imperative of violence—which need not be inflicted by "us," through the movie's hero, but is just as often used *against* us, by the movie's anti-hero, for what matters above all, it seems, is that we feel the stimulus. Thus we are victimized by the "sight" of the vampires in *The Lost Boys* biting off bright red gobbets of their victims' heads ("Ow!"), and by the sight and sound of the good guy having his fingers broken (*Blade Runner, Blue Thunder*) or receiving a ballistic kick between the legs (*Shoot the Moon, Black Moon Rising*). Likewise, the movies now more than ever shock us with the old nonvisual trick of going "Boo!"—a crude startler once used mainly in horror films but now recurring in thriller after thriller (and often heightened by the deep "*lub*-dub-*lub*-dub" that stimulates your fearful heartbeat).

The primacy of stimulation has, in short, made the movies increasingly cartoonlike. In the cartoon world nothing stands between the wish to look at violence and the enactment of that violence: no demands of plot or character, no physical limitations (space, gravity), no mortality. Ingeniously, and with cruel wit, the cartoon presents a universe wherein the predatory are punished again and again for their appetite by the very hills and trees, the doors and crockery. Full of rage and purpose, those victim-predators get nowhere, and yet never die, pushing on forever, despite the anvils falling on their heads, the steamrollers flattening their bodies out like giant pancakes, the cannonballs caroming down their throats—torments at once severe and harmless, and which occur exclusively because we want to see them happen.

It is not just *Batman* and *Who Framed Roger Rabbit* that invoke the cartoon but all those movies that present a universe wherein the stimulus is gross, never-ending, and immediate, the human "characters" appearing just as easily tormentable, and yet (usually) as indestructible, as Wile E. Coyote or Yosemite Sam. Thus *Lethal Weapon II*, which begins with the old Looney Tunes theme playing over the familiar Warner Brothers logo, includes several scenes in which Mel Gibson casually brutalizes Joe Pesci—squeezing his badly injured nose, for instance. And thus in *Dragnet*, as a car runs over Dan Ackroyd's feet there is a sound as of the crushing of a bag of walnuts, and Ackroyd pales and winces. And thus Jason, although dead, keeps coming back to life, like Freddy Kreuger, like Michael Myers, and, for that matter, like the dead ballplayers in *Field of Dreams*, like the vanished old folks in *Cocoon: The Return*, like the dead E.T.—all of them coming back forever and ever, because the cartoon always has a happy ending.

SURPLUS WISH FULFILLMENT

The convergence of the movies with both ads and cartoons makes sense, because the ad and the cartoon each present a fantasy of perfect wish fulfillment: that is, wish fulfillment that seems both immediate and absolute, arising, on the one hand, from a purchase (which will make life perfect *now*) or, on the other hand, from the animated spectacle itself (in which the universe appears responsive to one's wishes). This effect has been compounded in the movies, which now purvey a wish-fulfillment fantasy as extreme as, and far more compelling than, any Coke spot or Tom and Jerry free-for-all.

NEWSPAPER ADVOCACY ADVERTISING:
Molder of Public Opinion?

". . . If used properly, [it] can be an ideal medium for bringing ideas to audiences that must make public-issue choices in a democratic manner."

Eugene H. Fram,
S. Prakash Sethi,
and Nobuaki Namiki

The authors are, respectively, J. Warren McClure Research Professor, Rochester (N.Y.) Institute of Technology; associate director, Center for Management, Baruch College of The City University of New York; and associate professor, California State University at Sacramento.

EVEN A CASUAL examination of the newspapers in major metropolitan areas gives the impression that a wide variety of groups are using advocacy advertising. They utilize newspapers to espouse certain viewpoints, promote specific causes, or motivate individuals to engage in or refrain from particular activities. Public issue or advocacy advertising is neither new nor peculiar to the U.S., but is more widespread and practiced in its most vociferous form here.

The increased activity has been spurred by developments in the legal and political arena, as well as an evolution in the way public interest groups and social activists choose to communicate their messages. A changing competitive business environment also has motivated trade unions and companies to channel communications through advocacy advertising.

Early in 1990, in *Austin v. Michigan Chamber of Commerce,* the Supreme Court rendered a decision that may impact the use of advocacy advertising. It upheld a Michigan law prohibiting corporations from using treasury funds for independent expenditures to advance or oppose political candidates. The Court clarified the limitations on the right of corporations to engage in free speech (*e.g.*, place advocacy adver-

tisements) by using treasury funds. It also reaffirmed its 1986 decision in *FEC v. Massachusetts Citizens For Life, Inc.* giving bona fide political organizations the right to engage in political speech and endorse candidates, but denying it to corporations. Now that the limitations have been clarified, more organizations may feel comfortable about using public issue advertising.

Other reasons for increased activity in advocacy advertising may be explained best through example. In the political arena, California state officials launched an aggressive anti-smoking ad campaign in the news media backed with a $28,000,000 budget raised through taxes on cigarettes. More states and cities are likely to follow. Leaders of ethnic groups, especially black organizations in inner-city locations, also have been fighting cigarette companies through billboard campaigns and other direct actions.

In the commercial arena, the chemical industry and various environmentally sensitive businesses have been supporting the "green movement" through advocacy campaigns. Nuclear power proponents, through the U.S. Council on Energy Awareness, have been promoting greater use of nuclear energy. Unions and businesses have warned the public in newspaper advertisements to be wary of foreign competitors.

Nowhere is the diversity of advocacy campaigns more apparent than in cases of highly controversial social issues involving activist groups. The efforts by pro-life and pro-choice organizations are but one example of this phenomenon.

Advocacy advertising by corporations and industries in the U.S. can be traced to 1908, the year AT&T launched a newspaper

ad campaign to educate the public on the virtues of a private monopoly. Another big spurt came in the years immediately following World War II, when many companies launched campaigns to promote the free enterprise system and economic literacy.

Growth in advocacy advertising also occurred during the 1972-73 oil crisis, when the oil industry used paid advertising to explain and defend its "obscene" profits. With only some minor modifications, similar campaigns still are conducted today by a variety of industries and other groups.

The most notable change from the mid 1970s to mid 1980s was the diversity of groups opting for advocacy advertising. New users included organized labor; all types of voluntary private organizations; government and governmental agencies; and foreign governments and groups. A study of advocacy ads in *The New York Times* op-ed pages for the 18-month period beginning Jan. 1, 1985, found that for-profit corporations and trade associations were responsible for 85% of them. Public interest groups and labor unions accounted for four percent.

In contrast, nonprofit and religious groups were responsible for 31% of all advocacy ads in 1989, while labor unions placed 11%. Additionally, nonprofit and religious groups comprised 75 of the total 187 sponsoring organizations.

A recent trend involves getting major companies to underwrite paid messages for nonprofit organizations. The latter usually produce the ads and give the company sponsor credit. In other cases, the business organizations provide plugs for the nonprofit causes in their own commercials. For instance, Marion Merrell Dow (makers of

From *USA Today* magazine, July 1993, pp. 90-92. © 1993 by the Society for the Advancement of Education. Reprinted by permission.

3. COMMERCIAL CONSIDERATIONS

Nicorette) has worked closely with the American Lung Association on developing anti-smoking commercials.

In an attempt to examine the magnitude and diversity of advocacy advertising, *The New York Times* and *The Washington Post* were obvious choices to consider because they are among the most influential newspapers in the U.S. and carry the largest number of such messages. These publica- tions are likely to best represent advocacy advertising as it currently is practiced.

Advocacy ads sponsored by two groups—for-profit organizations with their trade associations and nonprofit public in- terest organizations, including religious groups—were examined. This twofold at- tention was based on the fact that for- profit and nonprofit groups frequently have been adversaries in disputes involving ma- jor public policy issues. Moreover, for- profit groups have been among the heaviest users of advocacy advertising. Individual nonprofit groups do not possess the fin- ances to mount major advocacy campaigns. As a class, though, they appear to represent a fast-growing category of sponsors respon- sible for an increasingly larger proportion of total advocacy advertising.

Considerable confusion and misunder- standing exist as to what constitutes ad- vocacy advertising because, in a sense, all advertising is advocacy in nature. Moreover, even when the scope is narrowed by ex- cluding messages that promote a sponsor's products and services, questions remain. Advocacy advertising must be separated from traditional public relations / goodwill advertising, public service messages, and public-interest "educational" advertising.

Advocacy advertising is part of the genre of promotion known as corporate-image or institutional advertising. Specifically, it is the sector concerned with the propagation of the sponsor's ideas and the elucidation of controversial social issues related to public policy. It involves defending or pro- moting the sponsor's activities, *modus operandi,* and / or position on controversial public policy issues, as well as changing the public perception of the sponsor's actions and performance. Taking advantage of con- stitutional safeguards for the freedom of speech, the sponsor is asserting its right to speak out on issues of public importance.

Out of 661 ads that ran during 1989, a typical year, 288 appeared in *The Washington Post* and 373 in *The New York Times.* They were sponsored by a total of 187 organiza- tions. Forty-nine percent were placed by profit-making corporations and their sup- porting trade associations, constituting 38% of the 187 sponsors. Nonprofit social service groups and religious groups ran 30% of the ads, but accounted for 40% of all sponsors.

Both for-profit and nonprofit organiza- tions are utilizing advocacy ads to help win support for their views.

Almost one-third (32%) of the ads were one- or two-time placements by the vast majority (143) of individual organizations, indicating the contextual and temporal im- portance of these ads. About three-quarters of the sponsors were responding to im- mediate issues of extreme urgency—*e.g.,* a pending piece of legislation or court action.

A handful of sponsors (44 organizations) accounted for more than two-thirds (68%) of the 661 ads. Further analysis shows that 11 sponsors placed 45% of them. Mobil Oil Corp. led the list with 12%, followed by the American Federation of Teachers (eight per- cent). The average advocacy ad occupied half a page.

The content areas (*e.g.,* issues, message tone) of the advertisements were evaluated by independent reviewers, who would read them and make a judgment as to which of several target audiences they were being ad- dressed. Topics covered in 60% of the 661 advertisements related to a specific industry. These were sponsored by profit-making organizations, trade associations, and unions. The oil industry placed the most (12%), with Mobil Oil sponsoring 95% of the ads for this group.

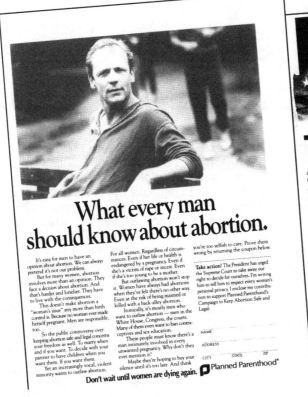

What every man should know about abortion.

It's easy for men to have an opinion about abortion. We can always pretend it's not our problem.

But for many women, abortion involves more than an opinion. They face a decision about abortion. And that's harder and lonelier. They have to live with the consequences.

This doesn't make abortion a "woman's issue" any more than birth control is. Because no woman ever made herself pregnant. Men are responsible, too.

So the public controversy over keeping abortion safe and legal concerns your freedom as well. To marry when and if you want. To decide with your partner to have children when you want them. If you want them.

Yet an increasingly vocal, violent minority wants to outlaw abortion.

For all women. Regardless of circumstances. Even if her life or health is endangered by a pregnancy. Even if she's a victim of rape or incest. Even if she's too young to be a mother.

But outlawing abortion won't stop it. Women have always had abortions when they've felt there's no other way. Even at the risk of being maimed or killed with a back-alley abortion.

Ironically, it's mostly men who want to outlaw abortion — men in the White House, Congress, the courts. Many of them even want to ban contraceptives and sex education.

These people must know there's a man intimately involved in every unwanted pregnancy. Why don't they ever mention it?

Maybe they're hoping to buy our silence until it's too late. And think

you're too selfish to care. Prove them wrong by returning the coupon below.

Take action! The President has urged the Supreme Court to take away our right to decide for ourselves. I'm writing him to tell him to respect every woman's personal privacy. I enclose my contribution to support Planned Parenthood's Campaign to Keep Abortion Safe and Legal:

NAME

ADDRESS

CITY   STATE   ZIP

Planned Parenthood®

Don't wait until women are dying again.

Restoring employee rights is good for America.

The rights of employees to organize and bargain collectively were systematically undermined in the Reagan-Bush years. Some in the business community and in Washington thought this "get tough" approach to employee rights would be good for the economy. It wasn't.

Wages and incomes fell. Consumer demand dropped. The economy slackened. And millions of good jobs with good wages were eliminated.

It's time, as President Clinton recently said, "to restore a needed balance in America's workplace." Restoring the balance — by restoring the rights of employees to organize and bargain collectively with their employers — is a key step toward rebuilding America.

Restoring employee rights is key to rebuilding the economy.

When employees are treated as partners instead of as replaceable parts, productivity and quality go up. The resulting increase in profits and wages generates new growth in consumer demand, investment, jobs, and tax revenues. Empowering workers makes the economy more powerful.

Restoring employee rights is key to reviving competitiveness.

We have fallen to 13th in the world in living standards. Industry after industry is losing out to more innovative foreign competitors. The countries that lead the world in workplace innovation,

economic competitiveness, and living standards all give employees more rights than we do. If America is to achieve real workplace innovation and become competitive again, employees need to be treated as real partners with real rights.

"It's time to restore a needed balance in America's workplace."
President Clinton

Restoring employee rights is simple.

Let's start by:
- Imposing stiff penalties on unfair employer labor practices.
- Outlawing the permanent replacement of strikers
- Letting workers join unions simply by a majority signing up, as workers in Canada and Europe do.
- Instituting binding arbitration in the case of first contracts.

Restoring employee rights costs the taxpayer nothing.

Restoring the right to organize and bargain collectively costs the taxpayer nothing. It puts spending power in the hands of ordinary Americans. It builds the economy. It translates into jobs at good wages. **It's good for America.**

Next in volume was the health care industry (seven percent), followed by defense, finance, and insurance, each contributing five percent of the year's total advertisements. When combined, these top five groups accounted for about one-third of the ads.

Other industrial sponsorship included pharmaceutical organizations (four percent), nuclear energy (three percent), and airlines (two percent). Most other industries only represented a fraction of one percent of total advertisements.

It would seem that the industries that employed advocacy advertising were active because they were facing important public policy issues—*i.e.*, changes in defense spending, banking concerns, and health care and insurance costs. The oil industry was the only exception, dominated by the long-standing Mobil series.

Approximately 45% of the advertisements contained messages targeted to government. Ten percent addressed government in general terms, 15% attempted to motivate the Executive Branch, and 20% had messages for Congress.

The audiences varied greatly by sponsor type. For example, while 29% of the for-profit group had copy directed toward Congress, only two percent of trade union and 10% of nonprofit group ads were directed there. On the whole, nonprofit sponsors had

less interest in government audiences, with about one-third of their ads targeted in that direction. By contrast, for-profit groups aimed approximately 60% of their message to government organizations.

Issues

The 661 advertisements covered 1,205 issues, separated into eight categories. Domestic and/or international economic and social welfare topics dominated, accounting for 60% of the total, followed by energy; pollution/conservation/environmental; political; international aid/human rights; consumer protection; and ethical/legal.

By far the most important primary objective was to get action—53% of all ads were written to mobilize public action in support of a public policy advocated by the sponsor. However, there was a difference in sponsors' objectives. Eighty-three percent of nonprofit social service ads urged public action, while profit-making firms seemed more interested in improving the company's image and public credibility.

Each of the two papers surveyed published an average of one advocacy advertisement per day. Although 187 different organizations placed one or more such ads, 11 sponsored nearly half of them. Three—Mobil Oil, the American Federation of

Teachers, and Partnership for a Drug Free America—were responsible for 25%.

Except for a few organizations with a long-standing program, advocacy advertising was utilized on an *ad hoc* basis, presumably with limited planning and forethought. Some 143 sponsors placed only one or two advertisements. Consequently, in terms of traditional advertising reach and frequency analysis, the vast majority of sponsors can expect very little long-term impact, even with full-page ads.

On the other hand, a sponsor could rationalize the use of advocacy advertising as a targeting instrument to influence specific groups at a given time. For instance, an advertisement in the *Washington Post* would be appropriate if the sponsor were interested in reminding certain Congressional representatives of their interest and influence at the time of a heated debate on a public policy issue.

It appears that use of advocacy advertising as a medium for education and information on a long-term basis is not expanding substantially. As a communications tool, it is being utilized primarily for immediate confrontational purposes. Nevertheless, if used properly, advocacy advertising can be an ideal medium for bringing ideas to audiences that must make public-issue choices in a democratic manner.

Legal and Regulatory Restraints on Media Content

If media messages are shaped by sources' biases and advertisers' agendas, they are also held accountable to legal and regulatory authorities whose involvement reflects a belief that the public sometimes requires protection from irresponsibility. The articles in this section deal with legal precedence and regulatory pressures that have been applied to media content and with the influence of citizens' action groups who act as media watchdogs.

Freedom of speech and of the press are regarded as fundamental American rights, protected under the U.S. Constitution. These freedoms, however, are not held without some restrictions. For example, it is commonly pointed out that freedom of speech does not extend to yelling "Fire!" in a crowded theater, since the resulting stampede for the exits would jeopardize the lives of the patrons. While legal and regulatory interpretations of what media may and may not do are in a constant process of change, there has evolved over time a set of general restrictions intended to keep those who have primary control over media content accountable for their actions.

Regulatory agencies, such as the Federal Communications Commission (FCC), exert influence over media access and content through their power to revoke or limit licenses to operate. They are primarily, though not exclusively, concerned with electronic media because of "spectrum scarcity," the limited number of broadcast bands available in any community. In addition, the courts exert influence over media practice through hearing and deciding cases of alleged violation of legal principles, such as protection of privacy or protection from malicious defamation. In general, legal principles are clear in their intent but vague in their parameters. By ruling on individual cases, legal precedence is established, providing historical guidelines under which specific actions have been judged in terms of their legality. Such rulings serve as warnings that similar actions are likely to elicit similar punishments if legal redress is sought. In some cases, both legal and regulatory sanctions against media providers are permissible for the same action. For example, both the Department of Justice and the FCC have the power to enforce Section 1464 of the U.S. Criminal Code, which bans obscenity. FCC penalties include license forfeiture and fines of up to $1,000 each day the offense occurs. The Justice Department can also prosecute and send a licensee to jail. In general, regulatory agencies are able to act more quickly than Congress or the courts in enforcing sanctions against media.

The first article in this section addresses the influence of activist groups who seek to influence "politically correct" treatment of issues with which they are concerned in the media. It is followed by a discussion of the controversy over pressures to "clean up television." The next article "If *I* Don't Like It, *You* Can't Watch It" illustrates the complexities of hammering out the parameters of both legal and regulatory precedence. If obscenity is illegal, what constitutes actionable obscenity? Under what circumstances is it appropriate for government agencies to protect the public from itself? Clearly, what some see as offensive, others seek out; if this were not so, there would be no market for "objectionable" media and they would not be produced. While there is general agreement that child pornography meets the criteria of obscenity (it is "patently offensive," "appeals to prurient interest," and has no "serious artistic, literary, political, or scientific value when taken as a whole"), are sanctions against the Oprah Winfrey show on which one guest discussed having sex with a dog equally necessary under the FCC mandate to serve "the public interest"?

Libel laws were designed to give individuals recourse against damaging statements made in the press. The courts have held that media are bound to make some mistakes in reporting facts, and that "malicious intent" must be proved to hold a reporter libelous. Legal precedence makes it particularly difficult for "public figures"— anyone in a position that attracts public attention—to prevail in either libel or invasion of privacy cases. Other laws that affect media content are concerned with copyright (which protects the copying of creative works without consent, beyond the "fair use" provision that allows small amounts of copying for educational and informational purposes), fraud (the U.S. Postal Service and the Federal Trade Commission [FTC] are empowered to initiate action against media that seek to defraud the public), and sedition (it is not legal to advocate violent overthrow of the government through the media). Shield laws, which vary from state to state, grant reporters the right to promise informants confidentiality, although they are regularly challenged. Regulatory restrictions, which tend to change with the regulatory climate of various administrations (the Reagan years began a trend toward deregulation; since the beginning of the Clinton administration, House and Senate debates suggest a move back toward regulation), limit individual organizations' media holdings, limit the amount of network programming allowed during prime-time hours, restrict advertising during children's programming, require stations to "actively promote" quality children's programming, and mandate that television and radio stations allow reasonable opportunities for individuals or groups to air rebuttals to attacks on their honesty, integrity, or character as well as to paid advertisements that deal with controversial issues of public importance.

The use of the courts in attempts to curb media vio-

lence presents a particularly interesting case study (see "Media Accountability for Real-Life Violence: A Case of Negligence or Free Speech?"). Laws regarding product liability have generally been defined through defective product cases, where a consumer uses a product as intended (e.g., follows the directions for applying a hair coloring product) and suffers damage as a result (all of her hair is on her pillow the next morning). Attempts to prosecute media organizations on the grounds of negligence have been complicated by the difficulty of establishing a direct cause-effect relationship between exposure to media violence and subsequent violent or dangerous acts. Nonetheless, the courts continue to accept cases that seek to apply product liability precedence to imitative violence, and media organizations continue to be required to defend themselves against assuming responsibility for responses to violent fare.

A final comment on the role of activist groups in exerting pressures on media providers. As is evident in the articles in this section, activist groups are instrumental in initiating lawsuits and Congressional hearings and in bringing perceived regulatory infractions to the attention of the FCC or FTC. In addition, they exert pressure directly on advertisers, writers, and owners. The degree to which their viewpoints represent the opinions of the general public is often questionable, but they illustrate the ability of citizens who understand the forces that shape media content to influence change.

Looking Ahead: Challenge Questions

How have conservative action groups proceeded in their attempts to eradicate what they consider objectionable media content? What actions have been taken by Congress and the FCC in response to concerns about indecency?

What are the arguments for and against the appropriateness of regulatory intervention in controlling indecent media content?

Why do you think the courts have been hesitant to hold media organizations accountable for violent acts said to be induced by violent media portrayals? Do the findings of product liability/negligence cases concerning media violence convince you that media violence should not be held responsible for causing real-life violence? Why, or why not?

Hollywood can no longer ignore watchdog groups

Terry Pristin

Los Angeles Times

HOLLYWOOD—Screenwriter and independent producer Jonathan F. Lawton did not realize he was asking for trouble when he created a character in his script "Red Sneakers" who leaves her older female lover for a man. But two prominent actresses rejected the role, saying that the story line might be deemed offensive to lesbians.

The actresses feared a reprise of last spring's assault on the allegedly homophobic screenplay for the upcoming movie "Basic Instinct," said Lawton, whose credits include the 1990 mega-hit "Pretty Woman" and the current "Pizza Man."

Unable to get a star for the leading role, Lawton brought his script to the Gay & Lesbian Alliance Against Defamation, one of several entertainment media watchdog groups that have sprung up in the last few years. He hoped the organization would applaud the script for including some positive gay characters.

But to his dismay, GLAAD agreed with the actresses (whom Lawton will not name), saying the screenplay promoted the view that a lesbian can be "cured" if she finds the right man. After a heated discussion, during which Lawton accused the organization of being "as bad as Jesse Helms," the screenwriter reluctantly agreed to make some changes.

In the revised script, the heroine is clearly a bisexual who relates to the older woman more as a daughter than a lover, and a romance between the older woman and another lesbian has been added. These modifications have "improved" the screenplay, according to GLAAD executive director Richard Jennings.

When it comes to political correctness in Hollywood these days, gay groups are perhaps the most visible but hardly the only advocates getting into the act.

Said Lawton, who has temporarily shelved "Red Sneakers" while he writes an action picture for director James Cameron: "Without a doubt, there's an enormous pressure to be politically correct, but it's very misserved. It ends up hurting projects more than it helps."

First circulated widely on college campuses a few years back, the term "politically correct" was initially used to disparage the movement to ban "hate speech," or language offensive to women and minorities. Reaching far beyond academia, it is now a catch-all way to refer to anything that smacks of liberal or leftist pieties.

When it comes to political correctness in Hollywood these days, gay groups are perhaps the most visible but hardly the only advocates getting into the act. Among other recent developments:

- Producers of movies with American Indian themes are working closely with Indian groups to head off the kind of criticism heaped on the recently released "Black Robe."
- Animal rights proponents, concerned about what one described as "an anti-wolf statement" in the Disney film "White Fang," persuaded producers to tone down a particular scene and include a disclaimer stating that there was no documented case in North America of a healthy wolf or pack of wolves attacking a human.
- Dubbing Spike Lee "a petit bourgeois Negro," a prominent black intellectual declared that the black filmmaker had no right to turn Malcolm X's life into a "commercial property."
- An advocate for the disabled warned Steven Spielberg in a letter released to the press that "Hook" may heighten children's fears of amputees. (But the film gets P.C. points for its ethnically diverse Lost Boys.)

From gays to American Indians to Asians to the disabled to environmentalists, Hollywood at the end of 1991 seems besieged by interest groups clamoring to put in their two cents, to register their disapproval, to redress historical wrongs and to help shape (or reshape) public images through the entertainment industry. Sometimes the advocates ask for—and are granted—the right to examine a screenplay; at other times they rely on sympathetic studio insiders to circulate copies.

Protests by aggrieved minority groups are almost as old as the movies themselves—dating back at least to "The Birth of a Nation," which sparked angry protests by the National Association for the Advancement of Colored People when it was released in 1915. And almost since the beginning of talkies, Hollywood has been prey to outside influence from conservative forces. The guardians of public morality began bearing down on the movie industry in the 1920s, leading to the creation of the Motion Picture Production Code. Strengthened in 1934 under pressure from the Catholic Church and other groups, it survived in one form or another until the 1960s.

In more recent years, the attempt to influence has traveled across the political spectrum. In 1979, for example, gay groups staged violent protests during the filming of "Cruising," William Friedkin's movie about the world of leather bars.

In the 1990s, there is evidence that these groups are gaining ground.

Although some filmmakers feel stifled, others say that listening to various interests is part of the cost of doing business in a democracy. They say that the influence of groups such as GLAAD is a welcome development after years in which minority groups have either been neglected or negatively portrayed.

Still others say the concerns about political correctness pale when pitted against Hollywood's general reluctance to take on weighty contemporary subjects.

"IF I DON'T LIKE IT, YOU CAN'T SEE IT"

Self-appointed guardians of our morality once again are striving to determine what Americans should be allowed to view, hear, and read.

Dave Berkman

Dr. Berkman is professor of mass communication, University of Wisconsin-Milwaukee.

"IF I don't like it, you can't watch it; if it offends me, you can't hear it." Such is becoming the increasingly realized result of a powerful alliance of religious fundamentalists and the Federal Communications Commission. Their aim is simple—only that which they define as "decent" shall modulate the carrier waves emanating from the transmitters of America's TV and radio stations.

The fundamentalists, who work in the private sector, accomplish their goal by threatening sponsors who buy time in what they consider "offensive" programming. The FCC, which, as a government agency, is bound by the proscriptions of the First Amendment, threatens to revoke broadcast licenses of offending stations—and, in the process, trash the Bill of Rights. All this is occurring in what we like to think of as a democratic America—whose right of free expression sets us apart from the rest of the world.

Some perspective is necessary because what is taking place in TV and radio is part of a larger attempt to limit what we see, hear, read, write, depict, utter, or otherwise express. Thus, while most of the current effort to censor and suppress is aimed at the broadcast media, which, because they are solely advertiser-supported and operate under government licenses, are those most vulnerable to such pressures, the other media—and indeed, the very arts—are targets of the censors as well.

Congress, responding to right-wing concerns, has passed legislation barring the National Endowment for the Arts (NEA) from funding works containing "depictions of sadomasochism, homoeroticism, the sexual exploitation of children, or individuals engaged in sex acts" and any material that somehow is judged to lack serious artistic value (read: makes a political point). A flap over the consequences of this legislation took place in November, 1989, when the NEA withdrew—and then, as a result of the ensuing protests within the artistic community, withdrew its withdrawal of—a grant to a New York City art exhibition because the text of the show's catalogue contained comments critical of, among others, Sen. Jesse Helms (R.-N.C.). According to the NEA chairman, John Frohnmayer, "political discourse ought to be in the political arena and not in [artistic works] sponsored by the Endowment." Shades of pre-*glasnost* Russia!

In the realm of non-broadcast media, the Blockbuster Video chain, fearing boycotts and picketing by Catholic and fundamentalist Christian groups, has refused to stock the home VCR version of "The Last Temptation of Christ." When the teenage girls' magazine *Sassy* ran an article that realistically discussed adolescent male sexuality, a host of advertisers withdrew their ads from that periodical after they were threatened by fundamentalist groups with consumer boycotts. (These, of course, are the same people most appalled by the rise in teenage pregnancy.) In Milwaukee, three Christmases ago, a local woman who decided that any tampering with the sanctity of Santa Claus is beyond the pale of permissibility successfully mounted a campaign that caused local theaters to withdraw a movie in which a slasher ran around in a Santa costume. (What was most disturbing here was that this act of censorship was treated as something admirable in the "cute" network coverage it received from NBC-TV and National Public Radio.) Then, let's not forget the threats, literally of a lethal nature, from another group of fundamentalists, in this case Muslims, which resulted in the two largest bookselling chains, Dalton and Walden's, temporarily removing Salman Rushdie's *Satanic Verses* from their shelves in 1989. Finally, there's the new law which prevents flag burning as an act of political expression.

The "Married . . . with Children" furor

Pressure from the religious right to "clean up TV" has been going on for some time—although it only hit the headlines in the spring of 1989 when Terry Rakolta, a suburban Detroit housewife, wrote a letter of complaint to the president of Coca-Cola, which resulted in the company's withdrawal of its advertising from the Fox Network series, "Married . . . with Children." Ironically, what passed almost unnoticed in the flurry of *The New York Times'* front-paged discovery of Rakolta, and her same-night appearance on a Ted Koppel *Nightline*, was that, while Coke may have cancelled its advertising in the program because of her complaint, it didn't cancel the series—something which, as the pre-Sony buyout owner of Columbia Pictures, whose TV division produces the series, it easily could have done if it really did share her sanctimonious concerns.

Rakolta objected to jokes about use by Peg Bundy, the mother on the series, of a vibrator as a substitute for her sexually inadequate husband. This is where Rakolta and I profoundly differ—she apparently is turned off by any non-Mom/Pop/Bud/Sis family depictions, while I sit there each Sunday evening in paroxysms of laughter at the antics of a family composed of a horny-bimbo-of-a-couch-potato-of-a-mother, whose kids have to forage for food; a dad who's an impotent loser with the IQ of his favorite VHF channel; and a slut-of-a-teenage-daughter who inherited her old man's brains and her old lady's hormones. Conversely, *I'm* offended by the goody-goody-two-shoes nature of that nice Huxtable family. Now it would seem to me that there's a fairly simple and democratic solution to the differences between Rakolta and those millions of others who, together with me, make "Married . . . with Children" the most viewed series on Fox—

she exercises her democratic right not to watch "Married," and I do the same with "The Cosby Show." If we did it my way, we all win—I watch what I want, she watches what she wants; I don't watch what I don't want, she doesn't watch what she doesn't want. However, what Rakolta wants is to have it *all* her way—she can watch what she likes, but *neither* of us can watch what she doesn't like!

What Rakolta and that majority of the sanctimonious among us—for the polls show that two out of three Americans support threats of boycotts against companies that buy time in "objectionable" programming—find fault with in my solution is that it doesn't take into account the fact that kids also are watching. As Rakolta recently complained, she was watching a daytime talk show, the topic of which was bestiality, with her eight-year-old daughter, "and I hadn't even explained sex between humans to [her]." How realistic is a viewpoint which holds that, if kids don't learn about sex from the media, they're never going to know "what all that 'funny stuff *down there*' is for"? Why should what is judged appropriate for *eight-year-olds* determine what I, who passed my eighth birthday 47 years ago, can have the choice of viewing? Does that majority of us who are adults *really* want to be limited to viewing only what the self-appointed guardians of our morality find acceptable for young children?

What Rakolta and her allies, such as the fundamentalist Rev. Donald Wildmon, together with the organizations he heads—Christian Leaders for Responsible Television (CLeaR-TV) and the American Family Association—want are media in which women adhere to their Biblically defined, secondary status, there is only heterosexuality (and that only within the sanctified confines of marriage), patriotism reigns supreme, and acceptance of Christianity is equated with patriotism. (Before his fall from grace, Jimmy Swaggert used to hold up the Bible and shout how it was the only constitution that a Christian America needed.)

The successes of the religious right already are such that NBC head Brandon Tartikoff has complained of fear-filled sponsors in a "feeding frenzy rushing to . . . say they [are] no longer going to sponsor a certain show." Twenty-three of the original 24 sponsors in the NBC docudrama, "Roe vs. Wade," withdrew their advertising from that program after anti-abortion groups which objected to the program threatened to initiate boycotts against them. Domino's Pizza announced that it has stopped advertising on "Saturday Night Live" because of a skit which ran on that series during 1988-89, featuring jokes about penises. ABC saw

$1,250,000 in advertising withdrawn from a November, 1989, episode of "thirtysomething" when sponsors who had purchased these spots learned that it included scenes of two gays in bed. Moreover, Lee Iacocca has warned the networks that, insofar as Chrysler's only concern in advertising on TV is to sell cars, they had better clean up their act—the clear message being that Chrysler will withdraw its spots from those shows whose themes, plots, character depictions, or humor might offend family car purchasers.

The FCC tilts to the right

As bad as the consequences for a free and robust television which the success of those in the private, predominantly fundamentalist sector may have, of far greater danger are the recent actions by the FCC, because, when it decides that what a station broadcasts is indecent, it can remove that station from the air. That is the message which the commission is communicating with the fines it has levied as punishments of radio stations offering so-called "shock" formats; sexually explicit rock music lyrics; and other programming it has judged "indecent."

The hypocritical cant behind these FCC actions makes them even more heinous. Ever since a Ronald Reagan-appointed majority took control of the commission in 1982 under the chairmanship of Mark Fowler, whose motto was "I'm not for deregulation, I'm for *un*-regulation," it has been FCC policy that *anything* goes. Radio and TV, like all other enterprises, should be subject only to the preferences and dislikes of the free marketplace. Until the Reagan years, any previous regulations which, for example, had limited the amounts of time a station could devote to advertising went by the wayside. Thus, the way was paved for all those hour-long "Get Thin/Get Rich/Grow Hair" kinds of programming which play late nights and weekend mornings, and even for stations that show nothing but commercials 24 hours a day—*i.e.,* the over-the-air shopping channels.

Indeed, so vehement has the commission been in adherence to its free marketplace philosophy, it even has refused to consider the effects of the advertising of potentially harmful products, such as sugared foods, on vulnerable pre-schoolers who, research shows, can not tell the difference between an ad and the programming content in which it is embedded. As far as this FCC is concerned, "No Commie-pinko-do-gooders are gonna interfere with the right of any five-year-old to decide what's good or not good to eat!"

While the philosophy underlying such a policy pleased the Bush/Reaganderthals who adhere to a free marketplace ideology, to the degree that it also might allow such a free marketplace to decide whether to accept program content that could offend the morality of another set of Administration allies—the traditionalist/fundamentalists—that spelled potential trouble. Such allegedly offensive program content, in fact, increasingly was being heard on radio stations whose formats offered so-called "shock jocks" like the "notorious" Howard Stern in New York City, or more "way out" contemporary rock music.

Needless to say, a Congress which would deny funding to indecent works of art did not miss a chance to come down against indecency in the realm of something as ubiquitous as broadcasting. Thus, after the FCC first warned the broadcast industry in 1987 that it would crack down on stations whose "indecent" content it did not approve, Congress enacted legislation, in effect mandating the commission to do—really, to do faster—what it already had begun.

So, the FCC under its new chairman, Alfred Sikes, citing the earlier 1987 warnings—and now with a legislative mandate (albeit one of questionable constitutionality) behind it—has begun its crackdown on "indecency" by fining four radio stations for broadcasting sexually explicit rock lyrics, skits, or comments.

Among the four were WXRK-FM, whose morning show featuring Howard Stern usually comes in second or third in the rat-ings among the 60 or so radio outlets that can be heard in the Metropolitan New York area. What was Stern's offense? He'd been the target of a complaint about a program in which he'd made references to penises, weiners, and orgasms.

Under the Supreme Court's rulings on what defines non-constitutionally protected expression, that which the prevailing standards in a given community would deem "indecent" can be barred. Perhaps my copy of the Constitution is an abridged version, but I can find nothing in the First Amendment that removes indecency from the absolute protections afforded all speech. In any event, the pressing question is how does an ostensibly free marketplace-dedicated FCC deign to punish any expression which is popular enough to command more listenership than all but one or two other choices out of some 60 options offered listeners in New York? Even if we all could agree that what Stern speaks *is* "indecent," why, with 59 other choices for those who might be offended by him, should we preclude those whose proclivities run to the "indecent" from indulging *their* preferences, indecent or otherwise? Nevertheless, the message to Stern's station, which, if cited again, could find its license permanently revoked—and to all the other 10,000-plus radio and 1,200 TV stations in America—is, shape up or suffer the penalties.

There are what, on the surface, would seem to be some deep ironies in all of this—although, upon examination, they turn out to be ironic only in a semantic, rather than in a substantive, sense. The favorite non-theological word in the vocabulary of the religious right, from which so much of the pressures to censor have emanated, is "freedom." However, as anyone who has ever watched a "Christian" TV channel for any period of time quickly will come to discern, is that, when a Falwell or a Wildmon speaks of "freedom," what he *really* means is the "freedom" of those who share his narrow beliefs as to what constitutes permissible personal conduct to force those limitations upon the rest of us.

The Reagan/Bush-ites on the Republican right like to speak of getting government off our backs. Here, too, any examination of what is meant by this reveals that what they want to get government off the backs of is not people, but capital—*i.e.,* government should do nothing to limit the uses of money. However, when it comes to conduct, whether in the realm of expression or in the bedroom, *that* may be subjected legitimately to whatever governmentally imposed injunctions are deemed necessary by the theologically rigid.

The possibility exists that, if the Rakoltas, the Wildmons, or the Reagan/Bush appointees to the FCC have their way, what we will end up with is the re-establishment of media reminicent in their blandness and lack of offense to what we viewed, read, and listened to in the 1950's.

Media Accountability for Real-Life Violence: A Case of Negligence or Free Speech?

A review of the U.S. court decisions on cases in which a child or young adult was the victim of violence that was said to have been induced by the media—from films to television to rock music—suggests that the courts have in general hesitated to hold media organizations accountable for inciting the violent acts of individuals.

Juliet Lushbough Dee

Juliet Lushbough Dee is Assistant Professor in the Department of Communication, University of Delaware. *The author gratefully acknowledges the help of Harvey L. Zuckman for providing information and inspiration for this article. She is also grateful to Melvin L. De Fleur and Everette E. Dennis for their invaluable assistance in criticizing earlier drafts, suggesting improvements, and providing encouragement in general.*

Television programs and motion pictures have been criticized by the public for "triggering" incidents of violence. These charges have been the strongest when the violent incident can be directly linked to a particular TV program or film by its apparent similarity. Are media organizations responsible for the potential effects of their products? What constitutes "proof" of the link between the media and subsequent actions of individuals? To what extent are media organizations liable?

In attempting to answer these questions, U.S. courts have struggled to bridge two trends in law over the last two decades: first, the expansion of the First Amendment's protection of free speech, characterized by increased intervention of courts to prevent genuine free speech issues from being decided by juries; and, second, the liberalization of tort law and a rush to strict liability, characterized "by the gradual erosion, if not elimination, of legislative and judicial impediments to recovery for dangerously defective products" (18, p. 77).

The past decade has seen a number of lawsuits in which a child or young adult has been the alleged victim of a violent act connected to a media portrayal. In these cases, child or adult plaintiffs or parents of deceased children have sued broadcasters, movie producers, rock musicians, game designers, or publishers for negligence.[1] In their suits they claimed that they themselves or a family member had been injured or killed in an incident instigated by a movie, an article, or a particular broadcast (or, in one case, violent television programs in general). As a rule, "courts have held that greater care must be exercised when dealing with children" (23, p. 384), and several courts have recognized demands for a high standard of care for children, who cannot be held to an adult standard of "reasonableness" (8, p. 10). For example, "a number of cases have held street vendors liable when children attracted to their product carelessly ran into the street and were injured by traffic" (23, p. 384).

This article focuses on an analysis of the legal arguments used in these cases. In the first six cases, someone was harmed by a third party whose dangerous conduct was allegedly triggered by the media. In the last nine cases, children or teenagers injured or killed themselves while enacting something they had read about, heard, played in a game, or seen on television. These fifteen cases raise important questions regarding the applicability of two legal concepts—negligence and incitement, as defined by First Amendment law—to the content of media and the foreseeability of its potential effects.

Before examining the facts of the cases, it is important to understand the legal definitions of negligence and incitement. Negligence is a theory of liability, legally defined as "the failure to use such care as a reasonably prudent and careful person would use under similar circumstances" (4, p. 930). For a broadcaster or publisher to be found negligent, a plaintiff would have to establish

(1) legal or "proximate" cause, defined as causation for which one might be held responsible legally; (2) a duty, which is an obligation recognized by law, requiring the actor to conform to a

From the *Journal of Communication*, Vol. 37, No. 2, Spring 1987, pp. 103-138. © 1987 by Oxford University Press, Inc. Reprinted by permission.

certain standard of conduct, for the protection of others against unreasonable risks; (3) a failure to conform to the standard required. This is commonly called the breach of duty (34, p. 150).

In tort law, which governs court decisions on negligence, defendants are negligent if their conduct poses "unreasonable" risks to others, as determined by judges or juries.

If an unreasonable risk of harm is probable or "foreseeable," then courts must weigh the gravity and likelihood of the danger against the "utility of the conduct" or the burden of requiring alternative conduct that would not result in a risk of injury. "Foreseeability" is clearly to some extent subjective, and "duty," "proximate cause," "reasonable," and "unreasonable" are slippery concepts; thus, "tort claims for negligence are somewhat malleable" (8, pp. 3–7). If defendants are found to be negligent, they are liable for damages claimed by the plaintiff. *Black's Law Dictionary* defines liable as "responsible, chargeable; answerable; compellable to make satisfaction, compensation, or restitution . . . bound to respond because a wrong has occurred" (4, p. 824). "Liability," a broad legal term, is defined here as the "condition of being responsible for a loss . . . evil, expense or burden" (4, p. 823).

Some attorneys have attempted to equate the free speech concept of "incitement" with the tort concept of "foreseeability." The concepts are not identical, however. "Incitement" implies that a high probability of danger is intended by the speaker; it is thus difficult to conceive of "inadvertent" incitement. Foreseeability, on the other hand, encompasses unintended consequences that are so predictable that they should have been anticipated (18, p. 77).

There is some ambiguity regarding incitement because it is not defined in the Constitution or any statute book. It is a concept that has been created by the Supreme Court in a series of cases interpreting the First Amendment, and it has come to be recognized, along with libel, slander, perjury, obscenity, and "fighting words," as an exception to the protections otherwise afforded by the First Amendment to free speech and a free press (*New York Times,* August 5, 1978).

The Supreme Court has stated two clear conditions that would be necessary in tandem to produce a conviction for incitement. These conditions were elaborated in *Brandenburg v. Ohio* (395 U.S. 444, 89 S. Ct. 1827, 23 L. Ed. 2d. 430 [1969]), in which the Court overturned the conviction of a Ku Klux Klansman for a speech demanding "revengeance" against blacks. The Court held that the government may not stop speakers from advocating the use of force or breaking the law "except where such advocacy is directed to inciting or producing imminent lawless action and is likely to incite or produce such action."

The *Brandenburg* decision thus requires a contextual analysis of every situation in which speech might be punished and specifies two conditions that must be present together before a conviction for incitement can be upheld: the danger of lawless action must be immediate and likely, and the speaker must have intended to stimulate the illegal action. *Brandenburg* sets the First Amendment standard for arguing that speech has threatened a third party.

Whereas laws concerning negligence are part of the common law, court decisions concerning incitement are part of constitutional law based on the First Amendment and ultimately interpreted by the U.S. Supreme Court. Common law, summarized in the *Restatement of the Law of Torts* (2), is based on precedent. Courts have some flexibility in deciding common law cases: they may accept the precedent set in previous cases, modify it, distinguish the precedent from the current case, or overrule the precedent.

The U.S. Constitution, on the other hand, is the supreme law of the land; any law that conflicts with it is unenforceable. Supreme Court Justices do have some flexibility in interpreting the Constitution and in overruling precedents from previous decisions. Whereas the common law has evolved on a case-by-case basis over many centuries, however, the Constitution provides a concrete point of departure. Although incitement per se is not mentioned in the Bill of Rights, the Supreme Court has relied on its interpretations of the First Amendment in arriving at the *Brandenburg* decision.

Equipped with these definitions, let us analyze the applicability of negligence versus incitement law to the first four cases, in which a third party, whose conduct was allegedly triggered by the media, either injured or killed an innocent victim.

The earliest and perhaps most clear-cut case is *Weirum v. RKO General, Inc.* In 1970, Los Angeles rock music station KHJ, which drew 48 percent of the area's teenage audience, broadcast a promotional contest called the "Super Summer Spectacular." The object of the contest was to locate KHJ's disc jockey, known as "the Real Don Steele." Steele was driving to various locations in a KHJ car and would give $25 to the first person who could catch him at a stop and answer a question correctly. The KHJ car was spotted by 17-year-old Robert Sentner in one car and 19-year-old Marsha Baime in another. In the course of their pursuit of Steele, they reached speeds of up to 80 miles an hour and forced the car of Ronald Weirum on to the center divider, where it overturned and killed him. Marsha Baime stopped to report the accident. Robert Senmer paused momentarily to tell a passing police officer; then he continued to pursue Don Steele, found him, and collected the $25 prize. Weirum's wife and children sued KHJ and its owner RKO General for negligence (*Weirum v. RKO General, Inc.,* 15 Cal. 3d 40, 123 Cal. Rptr. 468, 539 P. 2d 36 [1975]).

A guiding principle of negligence cases is that "all persons are required to use ordinary care to prevent others from being injured as a result of their conduct" (8). The plaintiffs argued that KHJ had "breached its duty" to Ronald Weirum (and all Los Angeles drivers) by failing to use ordinary and due care to refrain from implementing a contest that could endanger their lives.

Using a traditional negligence analysis, the court unanimously upheld a verdict and judgment against RKO General. It found that KHJ's contest had "created an unreasonable risk of harm to the motoring public" and that the risk was foreseeable by KHJ, which had not used due care in preventing it.

Another principle of negligence law is that courts must determine whether the risk of injury is "unreasonable," because "virtually every act involves some conceivable danger." Courts impose liability "only if the gravity and likelihood of the danger outweigh the utility of the conduct involved" (*Weirum*, p. 42). In this case, the "utility" of the contest clearly did not justify the grave danger of a high-speed car chase.

RKO General had argued that the First Amendment provides absolute protection for speech, but the court rejected this argument. It said that the real issue was "civil accountability for the foreseeable results of a broadcast which created an undue risk of harm. . . . The First Amendment does not sanction the infliction of physical injury merely because achieved by word, rather than act" (*Weirum*, p. 48).

A second attempt to recover damages for alleged negligence was the well-known case of *Zamora v. Columbia Broadcasting System et al.* In this case, 15-year-old Ronny Zamora and his friend Darrell Agrella were looting the home of Zamora's 83-year-old neighbor Elinor Haggart. When she confronted them, Zamora shot and killed her with her own pistol. Although Ronny had been "ignored or beaten at home" (11, p. 70), his lawyer Ellis Rubin ignored his sad home life and argued that he was not guilty by reason of insanity. This was due to "prolonged, intense, involuntary subliminal television intoxication." Psychiatrist Michael Gilbert testified in Zamora's defense, saying that he watched six hours of television each day, mostly in the form of violent crime programs such as "Police Story," "Kojak," and "Helter Skelter." Gilbert said: "He watched thousands of shootings and in these shootings there have been no consequences. The implication is that death is just an incident in the total plot. He didn't know the consequence and nature of the act when he pulled the trigger" (38, p. 104).

Despite this novel defense, Zamora was convicted for murder. After his conviction, he and his parents sued all three television networks for negligence, charging that the networks had "breached their duty" to him "by failing to use ordinary care" to prevent him from being "impermissibly stimulated, incited and instigated" to imitate the violence he saw on television. Focusing upon the "remoteness" of the injury in relation to the ideas communicated by the networks (18, p. 78), the U.S. District Court in Miami dismissed Zamora's complaint, explaining that in Florida, "negligence unconnected with physical injury will not provide the basis for mental or emotional injuries" (*Zamora et al. v. Columbia Broadcasting System et al.*, 480 F. Supp. 199 [S.D. Fla. 1979]).

Because the plaintiffs did not attempt to identify a particular broadcast that had allegedly led Zamora to commit murder, and because their complaint is patently absurd, it is tempting to dismiss this case as a display of chutzpah. Ironically, however, this is one of only two cases (the other, *Herceg v. Hustler* is discussed below) in which a court came anywhere near considering the question of mass media effects on individuals:

One day, medical or other sciences with or without the cooperation of television programmers may convince the FCC or the Courts that the delicate balance of First Amendment rights should be altered to permit some additional limitations in programming. The complaint before the Court in no way justifies such a pursuit (*Zamora*, pp. 206–207).

In *State v. Nelson Molina,* **Zamora's attorney Ellis Rubin attempted to prove a second client "not guilty by reason of insanity" with a contributing factor of "television intoxication."** According to Rubin, the television broadcast of the theatrical movie *Love at First Bite,* a comedy take-off on the Dracula myth with "a lot of violence" in it (39), was a contributing factor in influencing 21-year-old Nelson Molina to hold down 10-year-old Karla Gottfried while her 16-year-old step-brother David Gottfried stabbed and shot her to death. Rubin said that since the Zamora trial, there had been "thousands" of studies on television violence, including the 1982 National Institute of Mental Health report (29), which, according to Rubin, asserts "a causal connection between television violence and aggressive conduct of viewers, especially teenagers" (39).

Assistant State Attorney Jay Novick, who assigned the Zamora case for prosecution and himself prosecuted the Molina case (*State of Florida v. Nelson Molina*, No. 84–2314B, 11th Jud. Dist., Dade County, Florida, 1984), commented:

Molina *came 100 giant steps closer to linking TV and murder than* Zamora *did in the sense that the "TV intoxication" argument was not immediately thrown out by the judge. . . . It is true that Nelson Molina had auditory dyslexia and was antisocial; he also had some temporal lobe damage in his brain; he is not a leader; he's a follower; he's susceptible to the influences of others, and maybe he was influenced by David Gored to help murder Karla Gottfried. But is he susceptible enough to influences from TV to assist in a murder? That's poppycock. . . . In fact, the jury quickly rejected the insanity defense; it only took several hours to come back with the verdict. So I think in* Molina *we put an end to the TV intoxication argument* (25).

Both Nelson Molina and David Gottfried received life sentences for the murder of Karla Gottfried, but Ellis Rubin is currently appealing the life sentence for Molina and will again use the "television intoxication" argument implicating *Love at First Bite.* The case will be heard in the Third District Circuit Court of Appeal in Florida.

The case of *Olivia N. v. National Broadcasting Company* **involved a specific television program that became the catalyst for an act of violence.** The case resulted from the broadcast of NBC's made-for-television movie *Born Innocent.* On its surface there was much to commend the program, both as drama and as social commentary. Starring 15-year-old Linda Blair of *The Exorcist,* it exposed the savage conditions in girls' reform schools. Writer Gerald DiPego based his script on extensive research.

Born Innocent was aired at 8 P.M. (EST) on September 10, 1974.[2] At 8:17 P.M.. there was a scene in which four teenage girls used a plumber's helper to sexually assault Linda Blair, the "new girl." Switchboards of NBC affiliates across the country lit up with calls from angry viewers. NBC ultimately received over 3,000 calls and letters, which ran twenty to one against the movie (6, p. 69).

Four days later a 15-year-old boy and three teenage girls were arrested for assaulting 9-year-old Olivia Niemi and her girlfriend, whom they had "raped" with an empty beer bottle (6, p. 69). When questioned by police, their leader Sharon Smith said she had gotten the idea from *Born Innocent*.

Niemi's mother sued NBC, seeking damages for its alleged negligence in airing the sexual assault scene. Her lawyer Marvin Lewis argued that NBC was negligent in promoting *Born Innocent* in tandem with the animal movie *Born Free* and in permitting such an explicit and gruesome scene to remain in the film, especially in view of the fact that it was aired at 8 P.M. (6, p. 287). He argued that NBC knew about research on the effects of violence on children and should have known that some persons might imitate the rape scene (8, p. 18). Lewis also based his argument on psychological tests indicating that if the film had not been aired, the teenagers would not have devised such an attack; he thus contended that the television scene had caused the crime.

According to NBC's attorneys, however, Smith said she was " 'just getting at white people for what they have done to me' " (6, p. 288). In addition, Smith's psychiatrist was prepared to testify that her stepfather's sexual abuse of the girl was a more significant cause of her aggression than the television drama. Evidence for this is found in the fact that while torturing the younger girls Smith added touches of her own that were not in the television movie (6, p. 288).

When the case came to court, the trial judge of the Superior Court of the City and County of San Francisco refused to judge the case on grounds of negligence; he would rule only on the question of incitement. After viewing the entire film, he found that *Born Innocent* "did not advocate or encourage violent and depraved acts and thus did not constitute an incitement" (*Olivia N. v. NBC,* 74 Cal. App. 3d 383, 141 Cal. Rptr. 511 [1977]). He thus did not impanel a jury and dismissed the case.

The California Court of Appeal reversed the dismissal and remanded the case to the Superior Court for trial. Superior Court Judge Robert Dossee, too, ruled that the trial must be limited to the question of whether the broadcast had "incited" the real-life assault. Judge Dossee applied the *Brandenburg* test: while it could be argued that *Born Innocent* resulted in "immediate lawless action," it is equally clear that NBC had not aired the drama with this intent (7).[3] Lewis admitted that he could not prove incitement but insisted that he would prove negligence. But Judge Dossee granted NBC's motion for a nonsuit on the ground that, as a matter of law, Lewis could not prove the required element of incitement mandated by *Olivia N.* This decision was affirmed by the California Court of Appeal, and the Supreme Court of California refused to hear an appeal (126 Cal. App. 3d 488, 78 Cal. Rptr. 888 [1981]).

A fifth case in which an innocent third party was allegedly harmed as a result of a television program or movie is *Bill v. Superior Court.* In this case Jocelyn Vargas, a minor, attended the violent "gang movie" *Boulevard Nights* and was shot while walking to a bus stop after seeing the film. Through her mother she sued Tony Bill, executive producer of the movie, as well as producer Bill Benenson, director Michael Pressman, and their production company, alleging that they

knew, or should have known, that said movie was a violent movie and would attract certain members of the public to view said movie who were prone to violence and who carried weapons . . . and were likely to cause grave bodily injury upon other members of the general public at or near the showing of said movie (*Bill v. Superior Court for the City and County of San Francisco*, 187 Cal. Rptr. 625 [1982]).

Their suit claimed that Bill and his colleagues "negligently failed to warn" Jocelyn of these facts and "negligently failed to take sufficient steps to protect patrons."

In fact, there was evidence that before the film opened in Los Angeles, Benenson and Pressman suggested to Warner Brothers, who distributed the film, that there should be guards outside the theater in Los Angeles. They suggested this because the press was linking *Boulevard Nights* to *The Warriors,* describing both as "gang movies," the inference being that some violence did attend the showing of *The Warriors* (*Bill,* p. 627). Vargas did not claim that the content of *Boulevard Nights* incited violence, however; she claimed only that it would attract people who were predisposed to violence, that Bill, Benenson, and Pressman knew that, and that, knowing this, they had a duty to warn and/or provide protection (*Bill,* p. 628).

But the court denied her claim and ordered summary judgment for the defendants, explaining that "liability in such situations would have a chilling effect upon the selection of subject matter for movies similar to the effect which concerned the court in *Niemi* (*Bill,* p. 629). The court conceded that there may well be circumstances in which a speaker could be found liable for failure to warn about the foreseeable reactions of third parties but explained that the duty to warn "arises from the existence of a prior threat to a specific identifiable victim" (*Bill,* p. 632). There was clearly no prior or specific threat to Vargas, however, and because of this and the obvious First Amendment considerations, the court ruled in favor of the defendants.

Five weeks before the shooting of Jocelyn Vargas in March 1979, a young man was stabbed near a movie theater that had been showing *The Warriors.* Sixteen-year-old Martin Yakubowicz was returning to his home on the subway at 10 P.M. when at a subway station he encountered Michael Barrett and three other members of a gang who had just seen *The Warriors.* Yakubowicz was not part of a gang but was casually acquainted with Barrett and a second youth. Barrett, who had become intoxicated during the film, threatened Yakubowicz, who tried to avoid any conflict. Without provocation, Barrett drew a hunting knife and stabbed Yakubowicz to death, shouting "I want you, Marty" over and over. Attorneys Don Lubin and Elizabeth Mulvey charged that Barrett was imitating a character in *The Warriors* who had shouted "I want you" as he stabbed another character to death (*Yakubowicz v. Paramount Pictures Corporation and Saxon Theater Corporation,* Complaint, Civil No. 81–6565, Mass. Sup. Ct., 1984, pp. 2–3). But Paramount's defense attorneys David Rosenberg and Frances Cohen argued that "there is no such scene in *The Warriors*" (Memorandum of Defendant Paramount Pictures Corporation in Support of Its Motion for Summary Judgment, Civil No. 81–6565, April 30, 1987, p. 8).

Despite the disagreement over this scene, Martin's father William Yakubowicz brought suit against Paramount and the Saxon Theater Corporation, at whose theater *The Warriors* had been shown. Lubin and Mulvey charged Paramount with incitement, arguing that the film was "directed to producing imminent lawless acts of violence." The advertisements for the film were designed to attract members of gangs and other viewers prone to violence; for example, one advertisement

> *depicted a mass of menacing youths brandishing baseball bats. . . . The text accompanying the picture states: "These are the Armies of the Night. They are 100,000 strong. They outnumber the cops 5 to 1. They could run New York City. Tonight they're all out to get the Warriors"* (*Yakubowicz,* Plaintiff's Response to the First Set of Interrogatories Propounded by Defendant Paramount Pictures to the Plaintiffs, p. 3).

Lubin and Mulvey also charged Paramount and Saxon Theater Corporation with negligence. They argued that both defendants "knew or should have known" of a fatal stabbing and fatal shooting in Oxnard and Palm Springs, California, by patrons of *The Warriors,* three days before Yakubowicz was stabbed to death. They added that Paramount was aware that *The Warriors* "had caused an unprecedented series of lawless violent acts at or near a substantial number of theatres at which the film was exhibited" (*Yakubowicz,* p. 3). The violence accompanying the film was thus foreseeable, and Paramount had breached its duty to warn both exhibitors and viewers of the film, and had "failed to take responsible steps to guard the safety of the general public" (p. 4).

Paramount's attorneys countered that "Barrett identified Yakubowicz with a group that had attacked Barrett on a prior occasion" (Memorandum of Defendant Paramount, p. 7). Citing *Bill* and *Olivia N.,* they argued that *The Warriors* portrays but does not advocate violence; thus, there can be no finding of incitement.

When the court rules in this case it will be interesting to see whether it follows the precedent set by *Bill* or concludes that the stabbing and shooting three days before Yakubowicz's murder provide grounds for claiming that Paramount was negligent in permitting further exhibition of *The Warriors*. Should the court apply the *Brandenburg* test, it will have to accept the plaintiff's contention that Paramount "intended *The Warriors* to induce viewers of the film to engage in imminent acts of violence" (*Yakuhowicz,* Plaintiff's Response, p. 1).

In each of the next nine cases, parents sued a broadcaster or publisher when their son or daughter was injured or killed in a situation where they had been influenced by a television program, record album, magazine article, game, or even textbook.

The first two cases involve children who injured themselves while trying to carry out science experiments described in their school textbooks. In *Carter v. Rand McNally* (C.A. 76–1864–F [D. Mass. 1980], unreported case cited in Trial, November 1981, p. 110) and *Bertrand v. Rand McNally* (C.A. 77–957–M [D. Mass. 1980], unreported case cited in *National Law Journal,* September 22, 1980, p. 3), eighth-grade chemistry students Carolyn Carter and Christine Bertrand were doing an experiment described in their textbook *Interaction of Matter and Energy,* published by Rand McNally. The experiment

involved the calibration of an alcohol thermometer. Although it did not call for the use of methyl alcohol, other experiments in the same section of the textbook did, and the girls misread the instructions and added methyl alcohol to a beaker of crushed ice over a lighted Bunsen burner. The methyl alcohol exploded into flames, causing a flash fire in which Carter suffered burns over 40 percent of her body and Bertrand suffered second- and third-degree burns (35). They claimed that their burns were caused by Rand McNally's having designed experiments that called for either methyl alcohol or a bunsen burner in the same section of the book and that the publisher failed to adequately warn students and teachers about the hazards of using methyl alcohol.

Rand McNally's attorney Lawrence O'Connor argued that over 400,000 copies of the book had been sold without any reports of similar accidents; furthermore, there was testimony that the girls had been engaged in "tomfoolery and roughhousing" during the experiment (41, p. 3). But a Springfield, Massachusetts jury awarded them $155,000 in a judgment against Rand McNally. This was the first case in which a textbook publisher was found liable for injuries suffered by students conducting an experiment described in the book. But courts are divided on the question of imposing liability for inadequate warnings in textbooks, as is seen in the case of *Walter v. Bauer et al.*

Fourth-grader Christopher Walter was following the instructions in his textbook *Discovering Science 4,* which directed him to use a ruler and a rubber band in an experiment designed to demonstrate pitch. But the ruler was propelled into the boy's eye, causing damage that required two surgeries (*Walter v. Bauer et al.,* 109 Misc. 2d 189, Sup. 439 N.Y.S. 2d 821 [1981], p. 822). His father John Walter sued the Charles E. Merrill Publishing Company, using a products liability theory. He claimed strict liability in tort on the basis that the textbook experiment was inherently defective because it created an unreasonable risk of harm by placing "dangerous instrumentalities," the ruler and rubber band, in the hands of fourth graders, and because the textbook failed to give any warning about the dangers of the experiment (*Walter,* p. 821). But the court refused to find the publisher liable, arguing that

> Discovering Science 4 *cannot be said to be a defective product, for the infant plaintiff was not injured by use of the book for the purpose for which it was designed, i.e., to be read. More importantly perhaps, the danger of plaintiff's proposed theory is the chilling effect it would have on the First Amendment Freedoms of Speech and Press. Would any author wish to be exposed to liability for writing on a topic which might result in injury? . . . How to cut trees; How to keep bees?* (p. 823).

Walter's father appealed the decision, but the New York Supreme Court upheld the original ruling that a publisher could not be held liable for defective design and failure to warn in a products liability line of reasoning. Thus, this decision directly contradicts the jury decision awarding damages to Carolyn Carter and Christine Bertrand in a case with essentially identical facts. Because all are lower court decisions, however, subsequent rulings would be difficult to predict.

A case involving entertainment content rather than textbooks is *Walt Disney Productions et al. v. Shannon et al.*

Eleven-year-old Craig Shannon was watching "The Mickey Mouse Club Show" when an actor said: "Our special feature on today's show is all about the magic you can create with sound effects." Another actor demonstrated how to reproduce the sound of a rotating car tire by putting a BB inside a "large round balloon," filling it with air and rotating the BB inside the balloon. When Shannon saw this demonstration, he put a piece of lead nearly twice the size of a BB into "a large, skinny balloon." He blew up the balloon, it burst, and the lead shot into his eye, partially blinding him.

He brought suit against the producer of "The Mickey Mouse Club Show," Walt Disney Productions, Inc.; its syndicator, SFM Media Services; and the broadcaster, Turner Communications. Shannon's lawyer charged the defendants with negligence, contending that the show's actor had invited Shannon to do something that posed a foreseeable risk of injury. The Fulton Superior Court of Georgia granted the defendants' motion for a nonsuit on First Amendment grounds and dismissed the case. But the Court of Appeals reversed, ruling that the defendants were negligent and were liable for Shannon's partial blindness (*Shannon v. Walt Disney Productions*, 156 Ga. App. 545, 275 S.E. 2d 121 [1981]). After Shannon won in the Court of Appeals, the Supreme Court of Georgia granted *certiorari* (a writ seeking review).

The court acknowledged that the actor's encouragement did pose a foreseeable risk of injury. However, it identified Shannon's plight as a "pied piper case"; in order to win such cases, plaintiffs must prove the existence of two conditions: "an express or implied invitation extended to the child to do something posing a foreseeable risk of injury, and . . . the defendant must be chargeable with maintaining or providing the child with the instrument causing the injury" (*Walt Disney Productions Inc. v. Shannon et al.*, 276 S.E. 2d [hereinafter referred to as *Shannon*,] pp. 580–581). In adding the second condition, the Georgia court made it virtually impossible for a plaintiff to win a pied piper case against a broadcaster unless it could be proven that the broadcaster had supplied the audience with materials that posed a foreseeable risk of injury. (A pied piper interpretation of the law in the *Weirum* case might have found RKO General not liable for Weirum's death because it did not supply teenagers Sentner and Baime with their cars.)

The Georgia court does refer to both *Weirum* and *Olivia N.*, but it appears to view both as incitement cases, even though *Weirum* was decided on grounds of negligence:

> In our opinion, Weirum v. RKO General, Inc. . . . as well as Olivia N. v. NBC] . . . constitute authority for the proposition that a tort defendant can be held liable if the defendant incited, within the meaning of Brandenburg, a third party to commit a crime against the plaintiff. There is nothing in what the plaintiff was allegedly invited to do here that was "imminently lawless." Therefore, even assuming the correctness of the holdings in RKO and Olivia N. under the facts present there, we hold that these decisions are inapposite . . . (*Shannon*, p. 582).

The passage leaves the impression that the *Brandenburg* test was used in *Weirum*, although, as stated above, incitement was never mentioned in that decision. Nonetheless, the court seems to be trying to distinguish the *Shannon* case from *Weirum* on the grounds that "The Mickey Mouse Club" was not inviting children to do something that was "imminently lawless," as the *Brandenburg* test would require for a finding of incitement.

Rather than deciding the case on the basis of *Brandenburg* however, the court used the "clear and present danger" doctrine articulated by Oliver Wendell Holmes in *Schenck v. United States* (249 U.S. 47) in 1919:

> The most stringent protection of free speech would not protect a man in falsely shouting fire in a theater and causing a panic. . . . The question in every case is whether the words used are used in such circumstances and are of such a nature as to create a clear and present danger that they will bring about the substantive evils that Congress has a right to prevent (p. 52).[4]

By shifting its language from "foreseeable risk of injury" to "clear and present danger" of injury, the court moved the case from the realm of negligence to First Amendment law. Although the court admitted a "foreseeable risk of injury" to be present, it concluded that a "clear and present danger of injury" was absent (*Shannon*, p. 583), partly because, of the 16 million children estimated to be watching "The Mickey Mouse Club" that day, only one was reported injured. (Had this logic been applied in *Weirum*, the court might have concluded that there was not a clear and present danger to Los Angeles drivers because only two teenagers among over a million listeners [40] were found to be speeding in response to the KHJ broadcast.)

In *Shannon*, the court concluded with an observation that to find in favor of the plaintiff would open a First Amendment Pandora's box that would "have a seriously chilling effect on the flow of protected speech through society's mediums of communication" (p. 583).

The next case, that of *DeFilippo v. NBC*, **involved a 13-year-old regular viewer of Johnny Carson's "Tonight Show."** In this particular broadcast, Carson announced that after the commercial break, stuntman Gar Robinson would help him do a stunt that involved dropping through a trapdoor with a noose around his neck. At this point, Robinson said: "Believe me, it's not something that you want to go and try. This is a stunt ***." The audience laughed, and Robinson continued: "I've seen people try things like this. I really have. I happen to know somebody who did something similar to it, just fooling around, and almost broke his neck" (*DeFilippo v. National Broadcasting Company et al.*, 446 A. 2d 1036 [R.I. 1982], pp. 1037–1038). After the commercial break, Carson was "hanged" without injury.

Several hours after the broadcast, the parents of Nicholas DeFilippo found their son hanging from a noose in front of the television set, which was still on and tuned to NBC. They brought suit against NBC and its affiliate WJAR for negligence. Their attorneys, Thomas Pearlman, Morton Marks, and William Gosz, proposed two theories of recovery. The first was that NBC was negligent in permitting the stunt to be broadcast and that they "negligently failed to adequately warn and inform . . . plaintiff of the dangers of this program" (*DeFilippo*, p. 1038). The second theory was that the broadcast "had been intentionally shown with malicious and reckless disregard of . . . Nicky's welfare" and that NBC had "placed their financial interests above those of . . . the deceased minor" (p. 1038).

Later the plaintiffs added a products liability argument to their first two causes of action. In supporting their claim of negligence, they relied primarily on *Weirum,* claiming that the broadcast media should be liable for the foreseeable results of their actions and that, under the doctrine of *Weirum,* the question of foreseeability should be determined by a jury.

The products liability line of reasoning assumed, first, that television programs are a commercial product, placed in a competitive commercial market. Product liability laws require that any product which could be dangerous must be accompanied by a warning. Gar Robinson's warning was given in a jovial, joking atmosphere and was "feeble, light-hearted, incomplete, and inadequate. The entire tenor of the scene was such as to challenge a teenage boy to imitate the hanging . . . himself" (30, p. 40).

A product requiring an adequate warning of danger involved in its use is in a "defective condition" if it is marketed without such a warning, even if it is perfectly made. Because Robinson's warning was inadequate, this argument continues, the program was "defective" or "unreasonably dangerous." If a consumer is injured by a defective or unreasonably dangerous product, the manufacturer must bear the cost of the injury under the doctrine of "strict liability in tort." This doctrine has been upheld in a number of cases, including *Turcotte v. Ford Motor Company* (494 F.2d 173 [1st Cir. 1974]), which dealt with Ford's defective Pintos.

The trial justice of the Superior Court of Rhode Island was intrigued with the products liability argument but ultimately rejected it, holding that the broadcast was not a product. He distinguished *DeFilippo* from *Weirum* on the grounds that in *Weirum* "there was explicit incitement," but because stuntman Gar Robinson had warned people not to try the hanging, it could not be considered an incitement. He then held as a matter of law that the First Amendment barred recovery for the DeFilippos and ruled in favor of NBC. On appeal, the Supreme Court of Rhode Island upheld the lower court's ruling. It cited the *Olivia N.* case and echoed the reasoning in *Shannon:* because Nicky DeFilippo was apparently the only person who imitated the stunt hanging, the court concluded that the broadcast was not an incitement. "To permit plaintiffs to recover on the basis of one minor's actions would invariably lead to self-censorship by broadcasters in order to remove any matter that may be emulated and lead to a lawsuit" (*DeFilippo,* p. 1041). Even Morton Marks, who authored the case for the plaintiffs, acknowledged that if he and his colleagues had won their case based on negligence and product liability, "it would have created enormous problems for broadcasters. NBC would have had to employ additional lawyers to scrutinize content, even more than Standards and Practices already does" (22).

Like *DeFilippo,* the *Nezworski* case also involved a boy who hanged himself by accident while trying to imitate a stunt he had seen on television. Whereas Nicholas DeFilippo was 13 years old and was watching a talk show targeting an adult audience, Jeremy Nezworski was six years old and was watching a children's cartoon, "The Scooby Doo Show." Jeremy and his four-year-old brother Brad watched an episode of this cartoon in which a character put a pillowcase over his head and a rope around his neck in a sort of mock hanging. Jeremy

immediately tried to imitate the stunt and killed himself by accident. His mother Suzanne Nezworski sued ABC and Hanna-Barbera Productions, producers of "The Scooby Doo Show," charging them with negligence on a products liability theory similar to that in *DeFilippo.* Her complaint defined the negligent conduct as "presenting a program . . . for children, which program was unfit for children, failing to warn parents of the dangers of viewing this program, presenting violent scenes in such a manner as to mislead children as to the consequences . . ., and failing to heed reports . . . and warnings as relates to children's programming" (*Nezworski v. ABC and Hanna-Barbera Productions et al.,* Complaint and Jury Demand, 683–108 NO, June 8, 1983, p. 3). Her complaint further charged that ABC and Hanna-Barbera had breached their duty to provide children with programming that would not present an unreasonable risk of harm to them, and that the violent acts in the cartoon "could reasonably have been anticipated to be misunderstood by the intended viewing audience" (Complaint, pp. 3–4).

David Vinocur, the attorney for ABC and Hanna-Barbera, cited *Zamorn, Olivia N.,* and *DeFilippo* and moved for a summary judgment, arguing that "a television program is an intangible" (Brief in Support of Motion for Summary Judgment, 683–202 NO, January 31, 1984, p. 11) and not a product subject to product liability laws. He further argued that "The Scooby-Doo Show" did not constitute incitement within the meaning of *Brandenburg* (p. 8).

In response, Charles Goodman, who represented Suzanne Nezworski, cited Supreme Court rulings that have distinguished First Amendment rights of broadcasters from those of the press, such as *Red Lion Broadcasting Company v. FCC* (89 S. Ct. 1794 [1969], p. 1806) and *FCC v. National Citizens Committee for Broadcasting et al.* (98 S. Ct. 2096 [1978]); in the latter case the Supreme Court ruled that "there is no unabridgeable First Amendment right to broadcast comparable to the right of every individual to speak, write or publish" (p. 2114). Goodman added that the existence of 43 organizations in the United States concerned with violence in television programming indicates "substantial concern nationwide for the danger to children involved in media broadcasting" (Brief in Opposition to Motion for Summary Judgment, 683–202 NO, January 31, 1984, p. 4).

In an out-of-court settlement (Order of Dismissal, 683–202 NO [Circuit Court, Gogebic County, Michigan, 1984]) the defendants paid an undisclosed sum of money to Suzanne Nezworski. Part of the settlement agreement included a gag order on all parties; therefore, none of the attorneys who worked on this case were willing to comment on it. As a result, one can only speculate that (a) ABC and Hanna-Barbera were afraid they might lose if the case went to a jury, (b) ABC and Hanna-Barbera were reasonably certain of winning the case but were afraid of negative publicity it would engender, or (c) ABC and Hanna-Barbera chose to settle out of court for economic reasons in what insurance companies refer to as a "nuisance settlement," meaning that they estimate the costs of litigation and simply choose to pay the plaintiff less, without admitting any wrongdoing. Whatever the rationale, this is the only one of the fifteen cases discussed here in which a broadcaster chose to settle out of court rather than continuing to press for a summary judgment on First Amendment grounds.

Pulling v. TSR Hobbies **involved a 16-year-old player of the game Dungeons and Dragons.** Irving Lee Pulling, a junior in a public high school program for gifted students in Virginia, was (along with other students) encouraged by his English teacher Susan Peckitt to play the fantasy role-playing game in which players assume the identity of characters they create themselves. There is no time limit; a game may continue for months or even years. Another English teacher, Scott Hutchison, was the Dungeon Master, and after the game had continued for several months, he put a "curse" on Irving Pulling which said: "Your soul is mine, and I choose the time. At my command, you'll leave the land" (*Pulling v. TSR Hobbies, Inc., TSR Inc., E. Gary Gygax, Scott T. Hutchison, and Susan B. Peckitt,* Motion for Judgment, June 8, 1984, p. 7). Pulling was apparently experiencing "extreme emotional and psychological stress" from playing the game (Petition for Appeal, No. L-68-84, June 8, 1984, p. 3) and wrote about his disturbed feelings in his English exam in Susan Peckitt's class:

> *Oh, forget it. I'm above man now and I grow weary of this world. I'm tired of man's stupidity, corruption and murder and condemnation of those who believe differently from him. This is the last paper I will ever write. GOODBYE.* (Motion for Judgment, Exhibit K).

A few hours after Hutchison placed the "curse" on Pulling, he committed suicide by shooting himself in the chest with a pistol.

His mother Patricia Pulling sued Dungeons and Dragons manufacturer TSR Hobbies (TSR stands for Tactical Strategies Research; it is a war toys firm) and E. Gary Gygax, who designed the game, charging them with "negligent design and negligent failure to warn" (Motion for Judgment, p. 14). She claimed that Gygax and TSR Hobbies "either knew or should have known that the game could affect a child's perception of reality." Like the plaintiffs in *Walter, DeFilippo,* and *Nezworski,* she followed a products liability line of reasoning, arguing that TSR Hobbies "failed to give an adequate warning of . . . the game's dangers" and that "injury could be reasonably anticipated" (Motion for Judgment, p. 14).

To show that Dungeons and Dragons is designed to become an obsession with its players, she quoted the *Dungeon Master's Guide,* which says that the game "will slowly evolve into a compound of your personality and those of your better participants" and added: "To be most effective, the player is encouraged to merge his own personality with that of his character in the game" (Motion for Judgment, pp. 3–4).

In addition to charging the defendants with negligence, she also charged them with "intentional infliction of emotional distress" (Petition for Appeal, p. 11). In support of these charges, she quoted extensively from the *Players Handbook, Dungeon Master's Guide, Monster Manual, Deities and Demigods,* and *Eldritch Wizardry,* citing numerous references to sadomasochism, assassination, murdered players becoming "undead" by being "resurrected or reincarnated," homicidal mania, and suicidal mania (Petition for Appeal, p. 3). She also quoted Dr. John Holmes, an editor of the basic Dungeons and Dragons manual, who published an article suggesting that he was aware of the problem that "some players begin to think of their characters as real persons with a separate existence of their own. . . . When one of these alter egos gets killed, the game player sometimes suffers psychic shock and may go into depression" (16). Pulling thus argued that Holmes admitted that the emotional distress the game causes in some adolescents is foreseeable; she also quoted from his book *Fantasy Role-Playing Games:*

> *No one who does not play Dungeons and Dragons can understand the shock that comes with the violent death of one's character. It is a little piece of the player that gets killed. . . . Obviously, for the very young player, the death of a character . . . may be a bit too much. The thoughtful Dungeon Master provides for this—the rules allow resurrection and reincarnation, for this is after all, a world of fantasy!* (17, p. 79, quoted in *Pulling,* Petition for Appeal, p. 14).

Attorneys Harvey Chappell and David Kohler, who represented TSR Hobbies, filed a demurrer (a motion to dismiss the case), arguing that Dungeons and Dragons was protected expression under the First Amendment. They cited *Zamora, Olivia N., Bill, Shannon, Walter,* and *DeFilippo,* stressing that Pulling would have to prove incitement, which she had not attempted to argue (TSR's and Gygax's Brief in Opposition to Petition for Appeal, pp. 10–14). Judge Richard Taylor sustained the demurrer on First Amendment grounds and dismissed the case (Final Order, No. L-68-84, Circuit Court of Hanover County, Virginia, September 17, 1984). Pulling appealed to the Virginia Supreme Court, but her appeal was denied on procedural grounds (Record No. 850026, Supreme Court of Virginia, 1985).

Like *DeFilippo, Herceg v. Hustler* **involved a boy who hanged himself by accident.** In this case, 14-year-old Troy Dunaway hanged himself after reading an article on "autoerotic asphyxia" entitled "Orgasm of Death" in *Hustler* magazine; the magazine was found at his feet, opened to the article. His mother Diane Herceg sued *Hustler* for negligence, claiming that its article was both an "attractive nuisance" and a "dangerous instrumentality or defective product." With regard to the question of negligent publication, the court said: "No court has held that the written word is an attractive nuisance which would impose a special duty on defendant magazine. . . . A magazine article is easily distinguishable from items such as gun powder, fireworks, gasoline and poison which have an obvious physical effect" (*Herceg v. Hustler Magazine, Inc.,* 565 F. Supp. 802 [S.D. Tex. 1983], motion to dismiss denied, 583 F. Supp. 1566 [S.D. Tex. 1984]).

The court thus held that the claim was barred under the First Amendment but added that Herceg could attempt to show that the *Hustler* article "was 'directed to inciting or producing' the death, which would entitle [them] to relief" (p. 805). Thus encouraged, Herceg's attorneys Michael Essmyer and Clinard Hanby refiled the suit on grounds of incitement.

At trial, *Hustler's* attorney Jack Price pointed out that the article began with the warning "DO NOT ATTEMPT this method" (28, pp. A3–A5). Price argued that the article was "educational" and "warned more than 30 times that autoerotic asphyxia often results in death" (27, p. 17D). In addition to giving examples of people who had died this way, it referred to the practice as "neither healthy nor harmless" and concluded with the warning that "auto-asphyxiation is one form of sex play you try only if you're anxious to wind up in cold storage with a coroner's tag on your big toe" (28, pp. A3–AS).

But Essmyer and Hanby argued that the article was part of a series called "Sexplay," which *Hustler* described as "informative articles to increase your sexual knowledge, to lessen your inhibitions and ultimately to make you a much better lover" (28, pp. A3–AS). Judge Woodrow Seals expressed uneasiness about the plaintiffs' argument, noting parallels between this case and *DeFilippo*, but they argued that stuntman Gar Robinson did not explain specifically how to do the stunt hanging, whereas the *Hustler* article amounted to a "how-to" on autoerotic asphyxia (10).

The jury found in favor of Herceg and Andy Vines, who had suffered the emotional trauma of finding the deceased Dunaway. The jury awarded Herceg $169,000 and Andy Vines $13,000 in general and punitive damages.

Hustler appealed the ruling, citing *DeFilippo, Olivia N.,* and *Zamora,* among other cases. It emphasized the fact that its article was based on an earlier article on adolescent asphyxia in the *Journal of Child Psychiatry* (36), arguing that if that journal and other publications such as *Vanity Fair* could publish articles on autoerotic asphyxiation, it was unfair to punish *Hustler* for writing about the same subject. *Hustler* also raised the possibility that "thousands of youngsters were deterred by the warnings" not to attempt autoerotic asphyxiation (*Herceg* Reply Brief for Appellant, No. 85-2833, p. 9).

Hanby and Essmyer acknowledged that the article contained a number of warnings not to try autoerotic asphyxiation, but "interspersed with the warnings were glowing descriptions of the 'high accompanied by giddiness, lightheadedness and exhilaration' " and " 'the overpowering feeling of pleasure and oblivion'. . . . Many parts of the article imply that 'you can get away with it—if you're good at it' " (Brief for the Appellees, No. 85-2833, pp. 2–9). Furthermore, unlike the *Journal of Child Psychiatry,* "Hustler knew that its magazine was read by minors . . . and would have had to close its eyes not to foresee that a child would ignore a warning, especially when the activity warned against was presented in such a glowing, exhilarating light" (p. 17). Hanby and Essmyer conceded that *Brandenburg* was "probably not applicable to a *civil* lawsuit for *nonpolitical* speech" (p. 17) and urged the Court of Appeals to consider a new approach that would permit a finding of liability for negligent speech similar to that imposed in a defamation suit (pp. 7–8).

Nonetheless, the Court of Appeals reversed the trial court ruling, finding that *Hustler* had not intended for teenage boys to hang themselves; thus the article did not constitute incitement. The court cited a libel case, *Gertz v. Welch* (418 U.S. 323, 94 S. Ct. 2997, 41 L. Ed. 2d 789 [1974]), which held that "Under the First Amendment, there is no such thing as a false idea. However pernicious an opinion may seem, we depend for its correction not on the consciences of judges and juries but on the

competition of other ideas" (*Herceg v. Hustler Magazine, Inc.,* 814 F.2d 1017 [5th Cir. 1987], p. 1020).

But Judge Edith Jones dissented in part, arguing that *Hustler* should be found negligent because its article was an "attractive nuisance" (p. 1030). She cited the 1986 findings of the U.S. Attorney General's Commission on Pornography that "there is a direct causal relationship between exposure to sexually violent materials and anti-social sexual violence" (quoted on p. 1027). It bears repeating that she and the *Zamora* court are the only judges who have mentioned research on mass media effects in their opinions.

The case of *McCollum v. Osbourne* involved a 19-year-old fan of rock singer Ozzy Osbourne. John McCollum had listened to Osbourne's records since he was 14. In 1984 he apparently listened to two of Ozzy Osbourne's songs, "Suicide Solution" and "Paranoid," for five hours while drinking heavily, after which he committed suicide by firing a .22 caliber revolver into his right temple. His parents Jack McCollum and Geraldine Lugenbuehl sued Osbourne and CBS Records for negligence, asserting that the lyrics of the two songs had been a proximate cause of their son's death. Their attorneys Thomas Anderson and Doug Miller followed a products liability line of reasoning, alleging that the defendants had distributed "a defective product," specifically "defective music and lyrics" (*McCollum v. Osbourne et al.,* First Amended Complaint, C571832, December 4, 1985, p. 12). The complaint reproduces the lyrics of the songs, which include "All day long I think of me, but nothing seems to satisfy/If I lose my mind, if I don't find something to gratify/Can you help me? Oh, shoot out my brains, oh yeah!. . . . And so as you hear these words, that in you now, if I state/I tell you to end your life, I wish I could mine; it's too late" (quoted in *McCollum,* Memorandum of Points and Authorities in Support of Demurrer of CBS, Inc. to First Amended Complaint, C571832, April 11, 1986, pp. 5–6). CBS argued that the line "shoot out my brains" was misquoted, that in fact it was "occupy my brain," and the line "I tell you to end your life" is actually "I tell you to enjoy life" (p. 3).

Another song, "Suicide Solution," includes these lyrics: "Wine is fine but whiskey's quicker; suicide is slow with liquor/Take a bottle, drown your sorrows; then it floods away tomorrows/Breaking laws, knocking doors, but there's no one at home/Make your bed, rest your head, but you lie there and moan/Where to hide, Suicide is the only way out/Don't you know what it's really about?" (quoted in First Amended Complaint, C571832, December 4, 1985, p. 5).

Referring to the last three lines, Anderson and Miller charged that John McCollum had indeed "made his bed and rested his head on his pillow when he shot himself." They charged that Ozzy Osbourne and CBS Records knew or should have known that the lyrics "could produce an uncontrollable impulse to . . . commit suicide . . . in accordance with the lyrical instructions of said music and lyrics" (p. 11). They added that McCollum's death was a "proximate result of defendants' slow malicious destruction of [his] mind . . . from the time of the purchase of the various Ozzy Osbourne rock albums . . . up until the moment of his suicide" (p. 25).

In response, CBS attorneys William Vaughn and Douglas Abendroth cited *Olivia N., Bill, DeFilippo, Shannon,* and *Zamora,* among other cases, and pointed out that the plaintiffs did not even attempt to argue that Osbourne's music had incited McCollum's suicide. They explained that the song "Suicide Solution" actually condemns alcohol abuse, which it equates with suicide. Osbourne's songs constitute passive speech "in a fixed medium," and courts "have uniformly refused to find in such works the 'call to action' and 'imminence of action' necessary to constitute 'incitement'—since their message is answerable by more speech" (Demurrer of Defendant CBS, Inc. to Plaintiff's First Amended Complaint; Demurrer of Defendant John "Ozzy" Osbourne to Plaintiff's First Amended Complaint; Motion of Above Defendant to Strike Portions of First Amended Complaint, C571832, August 7, 1986, p. 41). Vaughn and Abendroth also cite numerous examples of characters expressing the desire to commit suicide in music and literature, such as Hamlet, Romeo and Juliet, Anna Karenina, Willy Loman, Sylvia Plath in real life, and the theme song "Suicide is Painless" from *M*A*S*H* (pp. 46–48).

During oral argument, Judge John Cole of the Los Angeles Superior Court made it clear that he had serious doubts about McCollum's case. He noted that the "products liability theory is creative, but there is no product to which the doctrine can be applied" (p. 2). But Anderson shifted his argument from negligence to incitement, arguing that both "Paranoid" and "Suicide Solution" constitute "a call to immediate action" (Reporter's Transcript of Court Proceedings, C571832, August 7, 1986, p. 8). He also introduced a new theory, suggesting that the two songs contained a "low frequency cycle . . . that reduces the mind's ability to resist a suggestion" (p. 9). Judge Cole said: "If there is something on that record that affects the subconscious, that has nothing to do with the First Amendment" (p. 35), and he gave Anderson leave to amend the complaint.

Anderson and Miller consulted the Institute for Bio-Acoustics Research, which did a computer analysis of "Suicide Solution" and claimed that there is a 28-second instrumental interval containing "masked" lyrics: "Ah know people/ You really know where it's at/You got it/Why try, why try/Get the gun and try it/Shoot, shoot, shoot" (repeated for about 10 seconds; Notice of Motion and Motion for Leave to File an Amended Complaint; Memorandum of Points and Authorities; Declaration of Thomas T. Anderson in Support Thereof and Proposed Amended Complaint, C571832, October 7, 1986, p. 6).

The attorneys observed that these words are not included with the lyrics of "Suicide Solution" on the album jacket of *Blizzard of Oz;* thus, they are "intentionally concealed from any person who reads the album jacket or the copyrighted version of 'Suicide Solution'. . . . Ozzy Osbourne knew that the words incited one to [commit] suicide and therefore intentionally left them off the album jacket" (Second Amended Complaint, C571832, October 7, 1986, pp. 11–12). They added that the words are sung at one and a half times the normal rate of speech but are perceptible enough to be heard if one concentrates (Notice of Motion and Motion for Leave to File an Amended Complaint, p. 6). They argued that these masked lyrics constitu-

ted "a call to immediate action," thus meeting the *Brandenburg* test for incitement (Reporter's Transcript of Court Proceedings, December 12, 1986, p. 1).

The Institute for Bio-Acoustics Research further claimed that the song had certain tone patterns similar to "hemisync" tones produced in a psycho-acoustic process patented by Robert Monroe in 1975; this process supposedly produces simulated human brain waves to promote relaxation and sleep, help listeners process information, and increase the rate of learning. Anderson and Miller argued that the masked lyrics and hemisync tones made McCollum more susceptible to the idea of shooting himself (Second Amended Complaint, C571832, October 7, 1986, pp. 14–15). They added that it was not just Osbourne's music which incited McCollum "but his entire presence. . . . He once bit the head off of a live bat while he was performing on stage" (p. 6).

CBS attorneys Vaughn and Abendroth accepted, for the sake of argument, the assertion that the masked lyrics were there, but countered: "If this seemingly random assortment of words which plaintiffs claim to hear has any meaning at all, it is certainly a prime example of poetic obscurity and literary indirection. . . . This is not a 'call to action' or 'incitement' within the meaning of *Brandenburg*" (Memorandum of Points and Authorities of Defendant CBS, Inc., in Opposition to Motion for Leave to File an Amended Complaint, C571832, December 11, 1986, p. 14). They responded to the allegation about hemisync tones with the argument that to dissect music and then maintain that some elements are protected speech and others are not "is a step along the path that would eventually lead to such absurd propositions as 'most of the words and music are protected, but the drum beat is not because it . . . overenhanced the message'" (p. 26). Ozzy Osbourne flatly denied the existence of the masked lyrics and the hemisync tones (Defendant Osbourne's Memorandum of Points and Authorities in Opposition to Plaintiff's Motion to Seek Leave to File a Second Amended Complaint, Declaration of Michael J. O'Connor in Support Thereof, C571832, December 12, 1986, p. 4). His attorney Michael O'Connor argued that to "impose a duty upon Mr. Osbourne . . . is to require him and other artists to foresee the occurrence of and be responsible for the unexpected behavior of all individuals who might . . . consider themselves 'fans'" (p. 16).

In their reply to the Osbourne and CBS Records briefs, Anderson and Miller urged that the "law of torts is anything but static, and the limits of its developments are never set. *When it becomes clear that the plaintiff's interests are entitled the legal protection against the conduct of the defendant, the mere fact that the claim is novel will not of itself operate as a bar to the remedy*" (Reply to Defendant's Memorandum of Points and Authorities in Opposition to Plaintiff's Motion to Seek Leave to File a Second Amended Complaint, C571832, December 17, 1986, p. 5; italicized sentence quoted from 34, Section 1, pp. 3–4). They tried to combine arguments of negligence and incitement, concluding that Osbourne and CBS Records "should be held liable negligently for . . . inciting McCollum to commit suicide" (p. 16).

Judge John Cole ultimately sustained the defendants' demurrers and dismissed the case on First Amendment grounds (Order of Dismissal, C571832, Los Angeles Superior Court, 1986). In his decision, he acknowledged that the masked lyrics, "Get the gun and try it, Shoot, shoot, shoot," come

> closest of all . . . to an urging to take immediate action, argued to be without First Amendment protection under cases such as Weirum v. RKO General. . . . But these words cannot be so closely parsed as to distinguish them from the general proposition that "the central concern of the First Amendment in this area is that there be a free flow from creator to audience of whatever message a (recording) might convey" [Olivia N. v. NBC]. . . . It could not be argued that the language would be actionable if in a book or magazine. Neither can it be so argued here. Further, no duty exists to support negligence causes of action (p. 1).

Ozzy Osbourne and CBS Records were successful in the Los Angeles Superior Court, but attorneys Anderson and Miller are currently filing an appeal with the California Supreme Court.

Like *McCollum v. Osbourne*, **Vance and Roberson v. Judas Priest involved young men who attempted suicide after listening to "heavy metal" rock music.** But while John McCollum did not survive to explain his motivation in shooting himself, James Vance did survive a suicide attempt to claim that the music had induced him and his friend Raymond Belknap to try to kill themselves. Vance, age 19, and Belknap, age 18, apparently barricaded themselves in Belknap's room one afternoon, drinking beer, smoking marijuana, and listening to Judas Priest's 1978 album *Stained Class* for six hours with the volume turned all the way up. When Belknap's sister banged on the door, they jumped out the first-floor window, taking a shotgun with them. In a church playground, Belknap hugged Vance, put the barrel of the sawed-off shotgun under his chin, and pulled the trigger, killing himself instantly. Having made a suicide pact with Belknap, Vance reloaded and held the gun under his chin but must have flinched; he survived with his face horribly disfigured (20, p. 1). Vance, who was unemployed, apparently told police that he and Belknap had often discussed "the benefits" of suicide. "They also considered obtaining automatic weapons for the purpose of committing mass murder" in their small town of Sparks, Nevada (20, p. 4).

Vance and Belknap's mother Aunetta Roberson filed suit against Judas Priest and CBS Records for negligence, claiming that it was foreseeable that "peculiarly susceptible" persons among the rock group's cultlike following, such as Vance and Belknap, "would listen to this music and thereafter commit harm to themselves" (*Vance v. Judas Priest et al.*, No. 85–5844, Complaint, July 10, 1986, p. 4). The lawsuit quotes from the song "Hero's End," including these lyrics (pp. 4–5): "He would take you with him where the music's been before/As you merge with power surge./If you were in its way, you have no choice, no, but to/Hear its voice and would live hypnotized and in a dream/ But one so strong so long becomes mean./Why do you have to die to be a hero?"

Attorneys Timothy Post and Ken McKenna, representing Vance and Roberson respectively, charged that these lyrics "encouraged the followers to commit suicide," and the hypnotic beat of the music combined with the lyrics had mesmerized Vance and Belknap "into believing the answer to life was death. The lyrical instructions of the music . . . created an uncontrollable impulse to commit . . . suicide" (pp. 3–5). McKenna added that Belknap, after listening to the music, became "unable to control his will" (*Roberson v. Judas Priest et al.*, No. 86–3939, Amended Complaint [Wrongful Death], July 2, 1986, p. 6). Post and McKenna also pursued a products liability argument, charging that the album was a defective product and that CBS Records was negligent in not putting a warning or printing the lyrics on the album cover, which might have alerted parents (*Vance v. Judas Priest et al.*, No. 85–5844, Complaint, July 10, 1986, p. 7).

CBS Records attorney Suellen Fulstone filed a motion to dismiss the case (*Roberson v. Judas Priest et al.*, Motion to Dismiss, No. 86–3939, August 20, 1986). Citing *DeFilippo, Shannon, Olivia N., Bill, Walter* and *Zamora*, among other cases, she argued that the plaintiffs' claim was barred by the First Amendment. Not only did the lyrics of "Hero's End" fall "far short of the 'incitement' required to satisfy *Brandenburg*," she claimed; "in all fairness, they can hardly be taken to advocate suicide even in the most abstract terms" (p. 6). She added that the content of speech is "not actionable under any products liability theory" (p. 16).

In opposing CBS Records' motion to dismiss the case, Post and McKenna insisted that the First Amendment "simply is not involved," that theirs is a "standard, garden-variety tort action seeking to enforce responsibility for creating a defective product" (*Roberson v. Judas Priest et al.*, Points and Authorities in Opposition to Motion to Dismiss, No. 86–3939, September 22, 1986, p. 8). They emphasized their argument of "intentional infliction of emotional distress," citing *Hyde v. City of Columbia* (637 S.W. 2d 151 [Mo. App. 1982], *cert. denied*, 459 U.S. 1226, 1983), in which the Missouri Court of Appeals found a newspaper liable for negligence when a woman previously kidnapped by an unknown man still at large was terrorized by him on seven occasions after he saw her name and address in the newspaper. They suggested that Judas Priest had intentionally inflicted emotional distress on "a discrete adolescent audience, among whom susceptibility to the suggestion of the performers was clearly foreseeable" (p. 20).

In her reply brief for CBS Records, Fulstone argued that *Hyde* had nothing to do with the "development and distribution of an abstract creative work," repeated that the plaintiffs would have to argue incitement, which they had not tried to do, and urged that the case be dismissed (*Roberson v. Judas Priest et al.*, Reply Points and Authorities in Support of Motion to Dismiss, No. 86–3939, November 21, 1986, pp. 3A). But District Judge Jerry Whitehead is allowing the case to trial on May 2, 1988 (*Vance v. Judas Priest/Roberson v. Judas Priest et al.*, Order Denying Motion to Dismiss, No. 86–5844 and No. 86–3939, Second Judicial District, Washoe County, Nevada, 1986). CBS petitioned the Nevada Supreme Court to intervene, but it denied the petition (*CBS, Inc. v. Second Judicial District Court of Nevada et al.*, No. 17772, Supreme Court of Nevada, 1986).

The cases discussed here raise important questions about the applicability of negligence versus First Amendment law with regard to media accountability. Several legal analysts support the relevance of the concept of negligence to the accountability of media organizations. Writing about the *Olivia N.* case, Lambert (19) argues that imposing liability on NBC for stimulating the assault on Olivia Niemi "may indeed have a chilling and possibly salutary impact on the electronic media. But hasn't that always been a prime purpose of the law of torts, its prophylactic purpose, to chill and hence discourage tort-feasors?" (19, p. 79). Miller (23) agrees, arguing that "when a child or a third party is injured as a result of the child's imitative act of television violence, the broadcaster should be held subject to liability" (p. 381). Reminding us that courts have upheld a higher standard of "reasonable care" for children, she asserts that "broadcasters should recognize children's attraction to television and [eliminate] the exhibition of acts of violence that are likely to be imitated" (23, p. 384). This argument follows the "attractive nuisance" doctrine, which imposes a duty of care on landowners to protect trespassing children because of their inability to appreciate danger (23, p. 386). Miller also supports her case by citing an adult's liability for giving a potentially dangerous article to a child. "Similarly, if a broadcaster gives a child a dangerous idea that he or she is likely to imitate, the broadcaster should be held subject to liability for the very same reasons" (23, p. 385).

But the problem with an argument that connects "dangerous articles" and "dangerous ideas" is the word "idea"; clearly, ideas are precisely what the First Amendment is designed to protect. As Hoffman, who supports the First Amendment claims, suggests, virtually any book or television program creates a "foreseeable" risk that readers or viewers will imitate what they see or read. "A proper policy analysis should . . . recognize that it is for this very reason that no legal duty should ordinarily be imposed. We fool only ourselves if we say that liability should not be imposed because books do not incite or because no harm is foreseeable" (18, p. 80). Thus, although many of the cases discussed here contain sufficient evidence to create a jury issue on the foreseeability of harm, whether it is called foreseeability or a clear and present danger,

> the cure for any such harm would be so much worse than the disease. . . . Each citizen in a free society is deemed to have the judgment and responsibility to decide which theories and ideas to accept, not because we assume that everyone will exercise that judgment wisely or responsibly, but that we are . . . far better off leaving these matters to the marketplace of ideas than to legislature, judge or jury (18, p. 81).

The issue of "foreseeability" has been particularized to apply to cases where *direct* antecedents to the violent act can be traced. Thus the Florida court dismissed the *Zamora* case on grounds of the "remoteness" of Ronny Zamora's crime from the collective programming of the networks over ten years. But remoteness" is not a proper basis to dismiss claims in the *Olivia N., Bill, Shannon, DeFilippo,* or *Herceg* cases, however, where plaintiffs were able to identify specific programs or articles that led to the injuries, since "the amount of research supporting the connection between television violence and antisocial behavior

would almost certainly be considered sufficient to state a jury question in claims against broadcasters and publishers [and] is not significantly less reliable than the type of expert opinion evidence used to get a jury in routine tort litigation" (18, p. 79). So, clearly, a key legal issue in attributing a link between media violence and real-life violent acts is the consideration of what such an attribution would mean for the protection of free expression.

Are court rulings on obscenity or indecent programming, other free speech issues, applicable in the negligence suits discussed here? The Supreme Court recognized a special interest in protecting children when applying the First Amendment in *Ginsberg v. New York,* in which the Court held that "exposure to material containing nudity impaired the morals and ethics of the young and was a clear and present danger" (23, p. 396). If the sale of material containing nudity to a 16-year-old constitutes a clear and present danger to the public, challenges Miller, "then educating children in subjects such as weaponry, rape and arson is equally such a danger" (23, p. 397).

Children were again the ostensible subject of the case of *FCC v. Pacifica Foundation* (438 U.S. 726 [1978]). The Supreme Court upheld the FCC ruling that WBAI-FM in New York City had violated federal law when it broadcast George Carlin's "Seven Dirty Words" monologue (31, pp. 511, 525–526) because it had been broadcast "at times of the day when there is a reasonable risk children may be in the audience" (31, p. 525). The Supreme Court opinion noted that broadcasting had traditionally received the least First Amendment protection of all media because it is "uniquely pervasive," it can affect people in the privacy of their own home, prior warning cannot completely protect listeners or viewers, and "children may obtain access to broadcast material" with relative ease (31, p. 526). Would it not be inconsistent of courts, Miller again suggests, "to be more concerned about a child's exposure to 'naughty words' than they are about a child's assimilation of aggressive behavior? The latter has a much greater potential for damage, both to the child and to society" (23, p. 398).

In ruling on the *Olivia N.* case, however, the California court acknowledged the four arguments above as outlined in *Pacifica* but said that "the effect of the imposition of liability could reduce the U.S. adult population to viewing only what is fit for children" (14, p. 933). The court added that "the narrowness of the *Pacifica* decision precludes its application [in *Olivia N.*]" (14, p. 934). Finally, the court said that reliance on *Pacifica* as a precedent in *Olivia N.* was misplaced because "*Pacifica* deals with regulation of indecency, not the imposition of general tort liability" (14, p. 934). In deciding the *DeFilippo* case, the Rhode Island court mentioned *Pacifica* in passing but did not find it to provide a basis for tort liability against broadcasters (DeFilippo, p. 1039).

There are other examples of cases in which speech is not protected by the First Amendment, as in *Chaplinsky v. New Hampshire* (315 U.S. 568 [1942]). In this case the U.S. Supreme Court formulated the "fighting words doctrine": it upheld the conviction of a Jehovah's Witness who called a police officer a "damned Fascist" and "a God damned racketeer," concluding that words likely to cause the average person to fight or to incite an immediate breach of the peace are not protected by the First Amendment. Concludes Miller, "If the social interest in order and morality overrides the usual right of free speech [in *Chaplinsky*], it should impose liability [in *Olivia N.*]" (23, p. 394).

If libel is subject to tort law, why is other speech immune?

A number of scholars (8, 23, 42) have argued that in *Gertz* the U.S. Supreme Court has adopted a negligence standard for determining media liability in defamation cases involving private persons. Zuckman (42) maintains that in *Gertz* the court was clearly saying that tort liability of the media was alive and well in the face of First Amendment claims.

It is certainly true that the U.S. Supreme Court allows private parties to sue the press for libel and for invasion of privacy. Public figures have to prove actual malice—that a libelous statement was published with the knowledge that it was false or with a reckless disregard for the truth. Proving malice in such a libel suit might correspond to proving intent in an incitement case. But private figures merely have to prove that publishers are negligent, that they have failed to exercise ordinary care. The Supreme Court thus approved a negligence standard for libel law despite the very real danger of self-censorship and the chilling effect of libel suits by both public and private figures (32).

In a defamation case, the broadcast would be the direct cause of injury to a person's reputation, whereas in the case of imitated violence, the broadcast would be the indirect cause of the injury. Despite this clear difference, however, Miller maintains that if legal cause can be established, "there is no reason to impose liability in one instance and allow First Amendment protection in the other" (23, p. 395).

Abrams (1) agrees with Zuckman that media should be held liable for libel because the First Amendment does not protect false, defamatory statements about private persons. He argues that, although it is false, libelous speech is not protected, but "unreasonable" speech probably is. Thus the negligence test of "unreasonableness" should never be applied: "We do not punish speech merely because we think it unreasonable. . . . In the end, the negligence model leaves everything to *ad hoc* judgments of juries and judges" (1, p. 10). He thus implies that the *Brandenburg* decision is specifically applicable in such cases.

Zuckman, however, questions the relevance of the *Brandenburg* ruling with regard to cases such as *DeFilippo;* he recalls that *Brandenburg* was directed toward speech that advocates violence or overthrowing the existing social order, assuming that such advocacy may incite "imminent lawless action," such as a riot: "But what has this to do with a state permitting a private common-law tort action to provide recompense for personal injuries caused by someone negligently communicating with others?" (42, p. 9). He further argues that to permit recompense for personal injuries caused by words spoken or broadcast "neither forbids nor proscribes negligent communications" (42, p. 9). Liability should be imposed "if and only if

such communications result in harm to others. Since negligent expression is neither proscribed nor forbidden by penalty of law, the 'incitement' test, which is designed to limit proscription of free speech, is totally inappropriate here" (42, p. 9).

Miller agrees with Zuckman that the *Brandenburg* incitement standard is badly misapplied in these cases. Furthermore, the courts "have ignored the judicial recognition of different standards for children in all areas of law" (23, p. 398). Either the definition of incitement should be modified to deal adequately with broadcasts aimed at children or, preferably, it should not be applied at all "because it blindly protects the broadcaster from liability while ignoring the real issues of duty and causation that should be addressed" (23, p. 399).

Drechsel likewise comments that to apply an incitement test "is almost the same as creating an absolute bar to liability" (8, p. 18). In contrast, Abrams argues that *Brandenburg* provides a completely adequate First Amendment standard for determining when speech genuinely leads to harm to innocent third parties.

Are children "competent to reject" speakers' solicitations?

Like Abrams, Haiman believes that the *Brandenburg* decision provides the best incitement test the Supreme Court has devised thus far, but he adds that situations in which listeners or viewers are not absolutely responsible for their own behavior should be extremely rare. Those who advocate illegal action should not be accountable for behavior of listeners who are "competent to reject their solicitations," even in highly charged situations where listeners may voluntarily abandon reflective thought (15, p. 278). "Unless deceived, coerced or mentally deficient, human beings are not inanimate objects who are 'triggered' by others. . . . A democratic society simply cannot, in proper keeping with its philosophy, operate on the premise that its citizens are incapable of resisting seductive inducements to criminal behavior" (15, pp. 278–283).

Haiman does not deny that viewing a scene of torture may serve as a model to be imitated, but he says that the danger lies in assuming without proof that such scenes are the single or inevitable cause of particular illegal acts" (15, p. 175). He cites the examples of Heinrich Pommerenke, a mass slayer of women in Germany, whose crimes were allegedly triggered by Cecil B. DeMille's *The Ten Commandments,* and John George Haigh, the British vampire who sucked his victims' blood through soda straws, apparently inspired by "the 'voluptuous' procedure of—an Anglican High Church Service" (15, p. 175). These grisly examples certainly support Haiman's argument in favor of the part of the *Brandenburg* test which holds that the communicator must intend to incite illegal action. To find Cecil B. DeMille or a priest administering communion guilty of inciting these horrors would be unreasonable.

Thus, those who follow through on a speaker's incendiary suggestions must have "powerful motivations of their own to do so, without which the incitements to which they were exposed from others" would fall on deaf ears (15, p. 283). In the *Zamora* and *Olivia N.* cases, there is no question that Ronny Zamora and Sharon Smith had "powerful motivations of their own" to commit murder and assault, respectively. The sad fact is that children who are abused become abusers (21, pp. 20–22).[5]

Whether Michael Barrett, who murdered Martin Yakubowicz, or the gang members who shot Jocelyn Vargas in the *Bill* case were victims of child abuse is not known, but one might assume that their formative years were less than ideal. (Nelson Molina, on the other hand, had been "over-indulged" but not abused [26], although to conclude that *Love at First Bite* provided the sole motivation for assisting in a murder would require some logical pole-vaulting.)

Haiman's point that listeners are "competent to reject speakers' solicitations" is of course applicable in *Olivia N.* (Smith and her cohorts could have chosen not to terrorize the two younger girls), *Bill* (the person who shot Jocelyn Vargas at the bus stop could have chosen not to) and *Yakubowicz* (Michael Barrett could have chosen not to imitate the stabbings in *The Warriors*). But Haiman is discussing moral decisions not to commit violence against an innocent third party. What would he say about a child who is shown how to do something which seems fun and harmless—would he argue that 11-year-old Craig Shannon was "competent to reject" the encouragement to put a BB in a balloon?

Indeed, of the fifteen cases discussed here, the *Shannon* and *Walter* decisions raise the most disturbing questions regarding the courts' attempt to fit these cases into the "incitement" mold. In both cases, young boys were instructed by respected authorities, a school textbook and "The Mickey Mouse Club Show" respectively, to try experiments that led to serious injury or loss of their eyes. One cannot help wondering why the Charles Merrill Publishing Company did not foresee the danger of directing nine-year-olds to try an experiment with a ruler and rubber band. The fact that there were two reversals in the *Shannon* case brings to mind the old judicial maxim that hard cases make bad law.

One can easily agree with the finding of negligence in the *Weirum* case in view of KHJ's irresponsibility in creating a clearly foreseeable risk to Los Angeles drivers. One can accept the *Zamora* and *Olivia N.* decisions in view of the fact that a major cause of both Ronny Zamora and Sharon Smith's reprehensible crimes was not television violence but the fact that both had been abused as children. One can accept the *Bill* decision in view of the fact that to hold movie producers liable for violence erupting outside movie theaters would probably have such a chilling effect on expression that the public would be deprived of seeing *West Side Story* as well as *The Warriors*. One can accept the *DeFilippo* decision in the view of the fact that Gar Robinson did warn viewers not to attempt the stunt, however light-heartedly. Even if there had been no warning at all, one could argue as in *Olivia N.* that NBC was not guilty of incitement because its intent was to entertain; it had no intention of inciting viewers to re-enact the stunt. To find NBC negligent for broadcasting the stunt hanging would set a precedent with grave First Amendment implications. Had the court found NBC liable for instigating DeFilippo's death, the gate would be open for any individuals suffering injury to seek damages against the networks by claiming that they had hurt themselves or were hurt as the result of seeing a particular television program.

One must also admit certain parallels between *DeFilippo* and *Herceg*: both involved content in which the primary purpose was to entertain, however raunchy and bizarre *Hustler's* article was. In both cases there were warnings not to attempt the type of hanging presented. ABC and Hanna-Barbera's decision to settle *Nezworski* out of court may have been a tacit admission that "The Scooby Doo Show" was the catalyst for Jeremy Nezworski's accidental hanging, but because there was no court decision, no legal precedent was set.

With regard to Irving Pulling, who shot himself after playing Dungeons and Dragons, there is arguably serious cause for concern in view of the fact that Dr. Thomas Radecki, founder of the National Coalition on Television Violence, has documented over 90 suicides and murders linked to Dungeons and Dragons and has requested a congressional hearing concerning this game (24). On the other hand, in both *Pulling* and *McCollum,* the two boys apparently had access to loaded guns in their homes, leaving one to at least question the parents' wisdom in making the weapons so accessible. Dungeons and Dragons and Ozzy Osbourne's music are no doubt as offensive to some people as *Hustler's* article on autoerotic asphyxiation, but for courts to conclude that they constituted incitement would again have an undeniable chilling effect on freedom of expression. The same arguments could apply to *Vance* and *Roberson*.

In short, one can accept the court decisions in all the cases discussed here with the exception of the *Walter* and *Shannon* cases, where children were expressly invited to use a ruler and rubber band or to make "magic" with sound effects and encouraged to put BB's in balloons in *Shannon*. *Shannon* seems to resemble *Weirum* more closely than do the other cases: in both situations a broadcaster encouraged young listeners or viewers to engage in actions posing risks that were foreseeable and that in fact resulted in death and partial blindness, respectively. Indeed, is there really so much difference between the facts of *Walter* and *Shannon* and the case of Carolyn Carter and Christine Bertrand? Wasn't Christopher Walter merely following the directions in his textbook when the rubber band somehow became a slingshot for the ruler? Wasn't Craig Shannon simply following the directions of the "Mickey Mouse Club" actor, just as the two girls were following the directions in their textbook? Of course, the courts in *Walter* and *Shannon* had undeniable and legitimate First Amendment concerns in both cases. To have found the textbook publisher or Walt Disney Productions liable for negligence would doubtless have had a chilling effect on any number of how-to books and television programs. But if they were not legally negligent, were they simply stupid and thoughtless?

Thus far, experts in the field appear to view negligent publishing or broadcasting cases as an aberration rather than a trend. Anderson has commented that "The *Weirum* case involved such egregious circumstances—encouraging teenagers to drive around the Los Angeles freeways involved such a clearly foreseeable risk—that I think this case is limited to its facts" (3). Gillmor (13) agrees with Anderson that *Brandenburg* really doesn't fit the cases discussed here because "it was originally intended for cases in which a speaker incites a crowd to violence." Like Anderson and Gillmor, Drechsel (9) agrees that *Brandenburg* "is not really applicable in terms of the factual situation in these cases, but it's the only Supreme Court decision that the lower courts have to turn to." Blasi (5) agrees with Dreschel that "there may well be more suits of this nature, but not enough to show a trend." He distinguishes *Weirum* from the subsequent cases, however, because, while in *Weirum* a direct relationship can be shown between the speaker and the audience, in the subsequent cases the connection rests on the portrayal of images or ideas.

But how could there be blanket protection for the expression of ideas? This question "raises a concern that the courts, when struggling to articulate the reasons a televised rape scene is an 'expression of ideas' while a chemistry book experiment is not, would actually be deciding which ideas are worthy of protection" (18, p. 85). Perhaps the courts should resolve these cases by use of a policy-oriented duty analysis, applied on a case-by-case basis" (18, p. 88), rather than a mechanistic extension of the First Amendment to tort law. Hoffman charges that the First Amendment immunity provided by the courts in *Olivia N., Shannon,* and *DeFilippo* merely substitutes an "incitement" formula for that of "foreseeability" (18, p. 89).

Given the preponderance of evidence *of* television effects research, both Hoffman (18) and Miller (23) maintain, it is "foreseeable" that children will imitate violent acts or dangerous stunts they see on television, even though this research was referred to only in the *Zamora* case. Whereas Miller argues that this evidence should be used to find broadcasters negligent for airing acts of violence which children imitate, Hoffman argues that freedom of expression must have a preferred position in all but the most unconscionable cases such as *Weirum.* The courts have seemed to follow this latter course.

But despite the lack of resolution in the courts' stance on these cases, media accountability for violent acts will probably remain a judicial rather than a legislative issue for many reasons. First and most simply, neither Congress nor the FCC can make blanket rulings that impose prior restraint on broadcasters. As Rowland has convincingly demonstrated, "no congressional subcommittee . . . ever seriously contemplated major structural change in American broadcasting" (37, p. 286). More evidence of media effects is also unlikely to change the situation. Having "everything to gain from reducing its accountability" for negative effects of violence on television, the television industry has co-opted many research efforts by promoting studies and researchers who "would minimize any claim of effects" (12, p. 166).

Thus, the courts are likely to continue to provide the major avenue for the clash between negligence and First Amendment rights of media organizations. Because common law theories of tort liability are tailored to deal with the facts of a particular case, judicial redress for acts of violence compelled by media depictions provide the most narrowly drawn, and therefore most likely, means for forcing the media to respond to concerns about violent programming (33, p. 344). Noting that "judges and juries have been reluctant to award damages every time someone is injured in an imitative violence scenario," Prettyman and Hook conclude that at some point "the Supreme Court will have

to make clear whether *Brandenburg* is broad enough to encompass the imitative violence cases or whether a completely different standard should be applied" (33, p. 382).

These cases surely differ from a moral if not legal standpoint with reference to imitative violence. The problems *of* children innocently following textbook instructions or imitating stunts they see on television or read about in magazines, as in *Shannon, Carter and Bertrand, Walter, DeFilippo, Nezworski,* and *Herceg,* and the problems *of* copycat violence, as in *Olivia N., Bill,* and *Yakubowicz,* provide the testing point of these two doctrines. The problems of older teenagers who commit violence to themselves, ostensibly with a media catalyst, as in *Pulling, McCollum,* and *Vance* and *Roberson,* comprise a different type of copycat violence.

The increase in the number of cases to come to the courts in the 1980s may in part be attributable to the development of common law through test cases as well as an increase in individuals turning to the courts for redress of grievances against the media. But it is critical that these test cases all involve children or young adults. While cases of media-incited violence among adults have been difficult to prove, even in the aggregate, children have provided a rallying cry for social fears about the harmful effects of the media since even before *Seduction of the Innocent* in the 1950s. In the long run, this testing of media accountability may be yet another in a series of attempts to find direct and therefore remediable solutions to the problems of violence in our society.

NOTES

1. Cases in which adults over 20 have sued for negligent publishing have been reviewed elsewhere (8, 18).
2. This was the first time *Born Innocent* aired, although it has been aired many times since its first broadcast in 1974. In subsequent showings, however, the rape scene was cut.
3. Television writer Gerald DiPego was shocked and horrified by the *Olivia N.* case. His intention in writing *Born Innocent* was to raise public awareness about conditions in reform schools.
4. Holmes formulated this doctrine in *Schenck v. U.S.* In the case, Charles Schenck encouraged young men to become draft resisters, claiming that being drafted was a violation of Amendment XIII, which abolished slavery, and that World War I was a cold-blooded venture in the interest of the chosen few on Wall Street. Holmes and the U.S. Supreme Court concluded that Schenck's words presented a "clear and present danger" to national security and Schenck was convicted under the 1918 Sedition Act (32).
5. According to Ed Magnuson (in *Gertz*), "Child abuse perpetuates itself. In a great preponderance of cases—estimates run as high as 90%—the abusive parent was abused as a child."

REFERENCES

1. Abrams, F. "Negligent Programming? Some First Amendment Ramifications." *Communications Lawyer* 1(1), Winter 1983, pp. 1, 8–9.
2. American Law Institute. *Restatement of the Law of Torts.* St. Paul, Minn.: American Law Institute, 1939.
3. Anderson, D. Stanley. Rosenberg Centennial Professor of Law, University of Texas Law School. Telephone interview, August 8, 1985.
4. Black, H. C. *Black's Law Dictionary: Definitions of the Terms and Phrases of American and English Jurisprudence, Ancient and Modern.* St. Paul, Minn.: West, 1979.
5. Blasi, V. Professor of Law, Columbia University. Telephone interview, January 14, 1986.

6. Cowan, G. *See No Evil: The Backstage Battle over Sex and Violence on Television.* New York: Simon & Schuster, 1978.

7. DiPego, G. Personal interview, Santa Monica, California, January 14, 1979.

8. Drechsel, R. "Media Tort Liability for Physical Harm: Problems in Legal Duty and Cause." Paper presented to the Law Division of the Association for Education in Journalism and Mass Communication, August 3, 1985.

9. Drechsel, R. Telephone interview, August 13, 1985.

10. Elliott, J. "Magazine Faces Suit over Article on Sex Act." *Houston Post,* July 26, 1985.

11. Footlick, J. K. "The Trials of TV." *Newsweek,* October 10, 1977.

12. Gerbner, G. "Science or Ritual Dance? A Revisionist View of Television Violence Effects Research." *Journal of Communication* 34(3), Summer 1984, pp. 164–173.

13. Gillmor, D. M. Telephone interview, January 15, 1986.

14. Gillmor, D. M. and J. A. Barron. *Mass Communication Law: Cases and Comment.* St. Paul, Minn.: West, 1984.

15. Haiman, F. S. *Speech and Law in a Free Society.* Chicago: University of Chicago Press, 1981.

16. Holmes, J. E. "Confessions of a Dungeon Master." *Psychology Today,* November 1980, pp. 84–94.

17. Holmes, J. E. *Fantasy Role-Playing Games: Dungeons, Dragons and Adventures in Fantasy Gaming.* London: Arms and Armour Press, 1981.

18. Hoffman, J. M. "From Random House to Mickey Mouse: Liability for Negligent Publishing and Broadcasting." *Tort & Insurance Law Journal* 21, Fall 1985, pp. 6589.

19. Lambert, T. F. "Television and the First Amendment." *Journal of the Association of Trial Lawyers of America* 37, 1978, p. 65.

20. McCabe, M. "Rock Bank Faces Trial in Teen Suicide Case." *San Francisco Chronicle,* December 16, 1986, pp. 1, 4.

21. Magnuson, E. "Child Abuse: The Ultimate Betrayal." *Time,* September 5, 1983, pp. 20–22.

22. Marks, M. Telephone interview, January 17, 1985.

23. Miller, N. "Media Liability for Injuries that Result from Television Broadcasts to Immature Audiences." *San Diego Law Review* 22(1), 1985, pp. 377–400.

24. National Coalition on Television Violence. "Dungeons & Dragons, Fantasy Role Playing Linked to 90 Deaths: Groups Plead for Hearing." Press release, May 12, 1987.

25. Novick, J. Assistant State Attorney, Miami, Florida. Telephone interview, April 3, 1987.

26. Novick, J. Assistant State Attorney, Miami, Florida. Telephone interview, May 8, 1987.

27. Obbie, M. "Magazine Sued for Provoking Youth's Death: Boy, 14, Killed Self Trying Sexual Practice." Houston *Post,* October 22, 1985, pp. A3–A5.

28. Obbie, M. "Hustler Article 'Extremely Responsible,' Doctor Says: Psychiatrist Hired by Magazine Testifies in Lawsuit over Channelview Boy's Death." *Houston Post,* October 24, 1985, p. 17-D.

29. Pearl, D., L. Bouthilet, and J. Lazar (Eds.). *Television and Behavior: Ten Years of Scientific Progress and Implications for the Eighties,* Volume 2: *Technical Reviews.* National Institute of Mental Health, U.S. Department of Health and Human Services (DHHS Publication No. ADM 82–1196), 1982.

30. Pearlman, T. J. and M. J. Marks. "Broadcast Negligence: Television's Responsibility for Programming." *Trial* 16(8), August 1980, pp. 40–43, 71.

31. Pember, D. R. *Mass Media Law.* Dubuque, Ia: Wm. C. Brown, 1984.

32. Picard, R. G. "Media Self-Censorship: 'The Public Will Never Know.' " In M. Emery and T. C. Smythe (Eds.), *Readings in Mass Communication: Concepts and Issues in the Mass Media.* Dubuque, Ia: Wm. C. Brown, 1983, pp. 521–525.

33. Prettyman, E. B. and L. K. Hook. "The Control of Media-Related Imitative Violence." *Federal Communications Law Journal* 38(3), 1987, pp. 317–382.

34. Prosser, W. and J. Wade. *Cases and Materials on Torts.* Minneola, N.Y.: Foundation Press, 1971.

35. Reuter, M. "Rand McNally to Pay Damages in School Textbook Mishap." *Publisher's Weekly,* September 26, 1980, p. 42.

36. Rosenblum, S. and M. Faber. "The Adolescent Sexual Asphyxia Syndrome." *Journal of Child Psychiatry* 18(3), 1979, pp. 546–558.

37. Rowland, W. D. *The Politics of TV Violence: Policy Uses of Communication Research.* Beverly Hills, Cal.: Sage, 1983.

38. Tilden, M., Programming Assistant, KHJ Radio, Los Angeles, California. Telephone interview, January 16, 1985.

39. "TV on Trial." *Broadcasting,* November 5, 1984, p. 35.

40. "TV on Trial: R. Zamora Case." Newsweek, September 12, 1977, pp. 104–105.

41. Tybor, J. R. "Jury Blames Text for School Fire." *National Law Journal,* September 22, 1980, pp. 3, 12.

42. Zuckman, H. L. "There Is Tort Liability for Negligent Programming." *Communications Lawyer* 1(1), Winter 1983, pp. 1, 89.

The tangled webs they weave

Digital technology is driving the media, telecommunications and computer industries together. But whether this communications "convergence" lives up to its full promise will depend less on boffins than on bureaucrats and bohemians.

IN A loft apartment in New York's Tribeca district, Kenny Miller is having a multimedia interaction. On cable television he is watching a live programme produced by his friend, David Levitt; over the telephone he is asking Mr Levitt to "perform for us". Instantly the picture changes and Mr Levitt's giddy falsetto bubbles from the box, singing an ode to Mr Miller. The camcorders, audio mixers and Macintosh computers strewn around the loft look on in mute fascination.

Is this the future of television? In an embryonic form, it is. Mr Miller is the technical director of the "new media" division at Viacom, a cable-TV firm currently waging a takeover battle for Paramount Communications. Mr Levitt used to teach at the Massachusetts Institute of Technology's Media Lab. They are now among the architects of the multimedia age.

That this age is close at hand became clear on October 13th, when one of America's Baby Bell telephone companies, Bell Atlantic, and its largest cable-TV firm, Tele-Communications Inc (TCI), said they had agreed to one of the biggest-ever corporate mergers. This was the latest and most spectacular sign that firms in media, computers and telecommunications are betting billions on the multimedia revolution. The fight for Paramount is another. Yet, crucial as such deals are, people like Mr Miller and Mr Levitt matter too. Without them, the revolution will not happen at all, let alone be televised.

If the exchange between Mr Miller and Mr Levitt was primitive, it was at least tangible—and thus rare. The most

extraordinary thing about the multimedia boom is that so many moguls are spending such vast sums to develop digital technologies for the delivering of programmes and services which are still largely hypothetical. The talk is of fibre-optic networks broadcasting 500 channels; of "teleputers" that will change the way that commerce is pursued and leisure enjoyed; of a global information industry that John Sculley, chairman of Apple Computer, reckons will one day be worth $3.5 trillion.

Beneath all this techno-bluster, it is still far from clear how profitable the communications "convergence" will be, or for whom. That will depend mainly on the answers to two questions. First, how will governments regulate the building and maintenance of the glittering new networks? Second, and more critical, what exactly will the networks deliver? Bosses fret about the first question, but the decision is out of their hands. Over the second they have more control, but are fairly clueless. Messrs Miller and Levitt have a clue. And that is why they matter.

If the 1980s were a time for media tycoons, the 1990s are for self-styled visionaries. These gurus see a dawning digital age in which the humble television will mutate into a two-way medium for a plethora of information and entertainment: movies-on-demand, video games, databases, educational programming, home shopping, telephone services, telebanking, teleconferencing, even the complex simulations of "virtual reality". This souped-up TV will itself be a powerful computer. And it will, says Gerald Levin, boss of Time Warner, the

world's biggest media group, let consumers tune in to "anything, anywhere, anytime".

Optics and digits

What is behind such grand prophecies? Primarily, two technological advances: digitisation (including digital compression) and fibre optics. Both are indispensable to the high-speed networks that will deliver snazzy new services to homes and offices. Digitisation means translating information—video, audio or text—into 1s and 0s, a form in which it is easier to send, store and manipulate. Compression squeezes this information so that more of it can be sent using a given amount of transmission capacity, or bandwidth: ten channels, say, in the space previously occupied by one.

Fibre-optic cables are producing a vast increase in the amount of bandwidth available. Made of glass so pure that a sheet of it 70 miles (110km) thick would be as clear as a window-pane, a solitary strand of optical fibre the width of a human hair can carry 1,000 times as much information as all radio frequencies put together. This expansion of bandwidth helps make two-way communication, or interactivity, possible.

Neither digitisation nor fibre optics is new. But it was only this year that America's two biggest cable-TV owners, TCI and Time Warner, said they would spend $2 billion and $5 billion respectively to deploy both technologies in their systems, which together serve a third of America's 60m cable homes. Soon, some TCI subscribers will be wired to receive 500 channels rather than the customary 50; Time Warner will launch a trial "full-service network" in Florida with a range of interactive services.

These two announcements signalled the start of a mad multimedia scramble in America, home market to many of the world's biggest media, publishing, telecoms and computer companies, almost all of which have entered the fray. The reasons are simple: greed and fear. Greed for new sources of revenue; fear that profits from current businesses may fall as a result of re-regulation or cut-throat competition.

So far—the Paramount battle notwithstanding—most firms have rejected the hostile takeovers that marked the media business in the 1980s. Instead, they have favoured an array of alliances and joint ventures akin to Japan's loose-knit *keiretsu* business groupings. TCI's boss, John Malone, evokes "octopuses with their hands in each other's pockets—where one starts and the other stops will be hard to decide".

Mr Malone suggests that the alliances represent a new model of corporate structure. Others see mere marriages of convenience in which many participants, such as Time Warner, are cash-poor, burdened with spectacular debts from the last phase of industry restructuring. None wants to miss out on any futuristic markets—long-distance surgery, say, or virtual sex. But none has much idea which services consumers will want. In so uncertain a climate, alliances spread costs and risks.

This is especially true where expensive, emerging technologies are involved. Different industries are leading in different areas, and will need to build on one another's strengths. So cable-TV firms, which lack expertise in the switching technology needed for anyone-to-anyone communication, are teaming up with telephone firms. The Bell Atlantic-TCI deal is huge but hardly unique: Nynex, a Baby Bell, has invested $1.2 billion in Viacom; US West, another Bell, put $2.5 billion into Time Warner; and on October 12th Rupert Murdoch said that News Corporation might be looking for an alliance with a telecoms firm. Telephone companies have formed consortiums with electronics companies, and technophobic Hollywood is embracing anyone who knows what "broadband interactive network" means.

Silicon Valley is under siege. Cable and telephone firms are linking with computer makers to develop hardware and operating software for interactive networks. Rivals such as Apple and IBM are working together. The market for a cable box to make dumb TVs smart is being chased by a gaggle of alliances: one includes Time Warner and the computer industry's hottest shop, Silicon Graphics; another features Microsoft, Intel and General Instrument.

This hunting in packs will probably continue at least until it is clear which technol-ogies and systems will form the standard for interactive-TV. No one wants to spawn another Betamax. But even then, picking the winning technology will be no guarantee of easy money. Fat profits will come only if and when consumers are willing to pay for the experiences that new technology makes possible. "The public doesn't give a damn about the technology," says Mr Malone. "People will want to know what services and programmes the network has to offer."

Building the perfect beast

Yet before the network can offer anything at all, it has to be built. The speed at which that happens will largely depend on the least high-tech force of all: government.

America is not alone in building fibre-optic networks. Japan hopes to have a national one in place by 2015; Singapore is wiring itself to be an "intelligent island". But America is home to the firms leading the multimedia parade. And as the only place where "information highways" have been a political issue, it offers a study of how communications policy and multimedia do—and do not—mix.

When Americans heard Al Gore banging on during the presidential campaign about how digital highways were a vital piece of infrastructure, many assumed that they were to be built from scratch and that the government would build them. Neither was correct. Thousands of miles of optical fibre already connects most American cities. What is missing are the local links to carry signals from the superhighway to the home (or to the curb, where coaxial cable or wireless technology can take over). The government could never afford the $50 billion-plus to lay this fibre. That was always going to be the job of cable-TV or telecoms firms.

Cable firms hope to steal slices of the $12 billion video-rental market (with pay-per-view films) and the $80 billion local telephone market. The Baby Bells are hungry, too. Pressure on their monopolies from nimble competitors has left them keen to attack long-distance carriers and rival Bells, and to send video down their lines. Pitched battles between the two industries are often predicted. But so far they have preferred to cuddle rather than cudgel.

Co-operation and competition both depend in turn on regulation. Traditionally, cable and telephone firms have been prohibited from invading one another's markets. This was plausible—perhaps even desirable—in an earlier day. But technology and competition are now making nonsense (and not only in America) of regulatory structures which treat these two converging industries as if they were entirely distinct.

Thinking on regulation is changing in America, albeit slowly and often incoherently. Some congressmen propose following Britain, where cable firms have spent hugely to build fibre-optic networks since being allowed to provide telephone service.

The Bells might accept such a plan so long as they, for their part, were allowed to provide video—pointing the way towards a grand compromise that legislators hope would allow each household to choose between at least two multimedia delivery systems.

Others question whether deregulation would indeed promote competition. They fear that the Bells (with combined revenues of $82 billion) would crush the cable firms (revenues: $21 billion). Alternatively, the two camps might co-operate, as in the recent series of deals between cable firms and the Bells. This might well be the most efficient way to get the networks built, but it raises the spectre of mega-monopolies in television and telephone service. (A federal judge recently brushed such concerns aside by ruling it unconstitutional for Bell Atlantic to be barred from providing video. The decision could be overturned on appeal.)

Other vexing issues await. Should network-builders be forced to provide "universal service", connecting every house on demand? Should prices for basic services be mandated? Should the system be open for anyone to put content on? Or should network operators alone be left to decide which services and programming they accept? Will technical standards be available to the public, or will they be proprietary?

When earlier versions of these questions were raised during development of the cable-TV, telecoms and computer industries, the answers varied widely. Multimedia thus reopens a debate which will be echoed around the world—especially in countries with telephone monopolies or state-owned broadcasters—and on which growth and profitability will depend. "How can I figure out the right capital expenditure," asks one frustrated American cable boss, "when it might be years before Congress and the courts get their acts together?"

Massaging the medium

A fair question. But to see what may lie beyond these issues, assume a network. Consider the viewer, confronted with 500 channels—or 5,000, or just one—linked to a computer stocked with every imaginable piece of software. Will he be baffled? Or just bored? Avoiding both these outcomes will be multimedia's biggest challenge.

Adrift in a sea of channels, viewers will first need help navigating. They will also need to be convinced that what they might see is worth paying for. "Just as software and system services drive the computer industry," writes Nicholas Negroponte, an academic at MIT's Media Lab, in *Wired*, a clever new techno-media magazine, "programming and intelligent browsing aids will drive the television industry."

Back to Mr Miller. His employer, Viacom, has a venture with StarSight, a small firm that is designing an electronic TV guide. The competition will include TCI, which, betting that a well-known brand name will be an advantage, has teamed up with Mr Murdoch's News Corp, which owns *TV Guide* (the paper version), to make a browsing aid based on the magazine's format. Bell Atlantic is developing an easy-to-use system called "Stargazer".

The real question, though, is not so much what such menus will look like, as what they will offer. One sure bet is "movies-on-demand". Video shops make 80% of their sales on 10% of their titles. Yet it is a "law of nature," notes Mitch Kapor, former boss of a computer-software firm, Lotus, and now a public-interest lobbyist on high-tech issues, that "regardless of how many

Cannibal's feast

Market sizes, 1992 estimates, $bn

	United States	Britain
Telephone services	150	35
Mail order/home shopping	70	6
On-line information services	35	7
Home video rental	12	2
Video games*	5	1

Source: Oppenheimer & Co; Euromonitor; ICC Key Note; press reports
*Hardware and software

copies of a hot movie a video store has, there's never one left on the shelf when you get there". Video-on-demand preys on this frustration. At first, popular films will be shown simultaneously on several channels, but with staggered start-times so viewers can tune in when they wish. Eventually, viewers should be able to see most movies at most times without leaving home.

Beyond that, the outlook is less clear. Champions of multimedia point to other rich markets which their creature might devour (see table). But doing so will not be easy. Anyone who has watched America's tacky home-shopping channels knows they are no immediate threat to conventional retailing. The history of electronic newspapers and other on-line information services has been disappointing enough to make even fervent proselytisers for multimedia wary of predicting success for services beyond movies-on-demand.

Luring consumers will require programming that is visually arresting, intelligent and easy to use. Home-shopping will probably have to grow much more sophisticated in its presentation, perhaps whisking viewers off to a virtual Versace where they can watch clothes being modelled on images of their own bodies. Educational software will need to mix video, sound and text in ways which seduce children and parents alike.

These "killer applications" will probably not come from boffins. Instead, they will come from a new breed of high-tech bohemians—call them techno-bohos—who combine computer skills with story-telling and/or artistic flair. Some even have business savvy. Before Viacom, Mr Miller advised big firms on computer systems as well as designing interactive art installations.

Yet his position at Viacom is rare. Most techno-bohos work not for big media or computer firms, but for the small video-game and software houses which promise to be central to multimedia's future. The success of Nintendo and Sega in infiltrating homes around the world indicates that people may well also pay to have games piped in through networks. Moreover, the creators of such games are already perfecting the skills needed to bring video, animation, sound and narrative together effectively.

Their magic is much in demand: Chevron Oil recently hired Maxis, a video-game software house, to make simulation games for training its refinery workers. Game-making acumen should also help craft educational and reference programmes which will add mightily to multimedia's respectability and so reinforce its appeal.

True, most programmes of this sort, made for CD-ROM machines hooked up to computers, have so far been visually crude and textually uninspired. But the exceptions hint at what may come. Knowledge Adventure, a Californian start-up, produces sharp-witted educational programmes for children. Another Californian firm, Voyager, makes music-appreciation discs such as "Multimedia Beethoven". Hong Kong-based InterOptica specialises in travel. Its

"Astonishing Asia" lets users explore images and information on everything from strange rituals to even stranger stimulants.

Such firms may one day emerge as the Walt Disneys of multimedia, and are attracting corresponding curiosity from the industry's behemoths. Apple has agreed to distribute InterOptica's CD-ROM discs; AT&T and Paramount have stakes in Knowledge Adventure; in May, Viacom bought a tiny video-game house, ICOM Simulations. Analysts at Salomon Brothers reckon that multimedia software will gradually consolidate into a handful of big "studios".

The Hollywood parallel goes deeper. Historically, the media industry's winners have been those able to control both programming and distribution. That precedent helps explain why Mr Levin of Time Warner, a cable giant with film and publishing interests, is one of multimedia's biggest boosters; and why Mr Malone is trying to grab as much programming as he can. It also leads some media *savants* to predict that Nynex's role in the Paramount battle will not be the last instance of a telecoms firm pursuing a film studio or TV network.

History is not destiny. Governments may decide to treat interactive networks as pieces of public infrastructure and to limit how much "content" their owners can control. Even if that does not happen, the multimedia industry may still not turn into a digital Hollywood, dominated by vertically integrated giants. Once bandwidth is in effect unlimited, and especially if there are competing delivery systems—based on telephone-line, cable and wireless systems—demand for programming will be immense. Successful programmers, even small ones, may have so much leverage that they can treat distributors as mere middlemen.

Either way, says Adrian Slywotzky, of Corporate Decisions, a Boston-based management consultancy, the next few years will determine the shape of multimedia. "In the computer industry, the genetic code was set in 1979-83; everything that's happened since was set in motion then." In multimedia, the chromosomes are being configured now.

Information and Influence: Concerns with What We Learn from News Media

With the advent of television, Canadian communications specialist and educator Marshall McLuhan predicted the coming of a "global village" in which communication media would transcend the boundaries of nations: "Ours is a world of allatoneness. 'Time' has ceased, 'space' has vanished. We now live in . . . a simultaneous happening." In naming CNN founder Ted Turner its 1991 Man of the Year, *Time* magazine noted that, a generation later, CNN has begun to make McLuhan's prophecy come to pass. The availability of a worldwide, 24-hour news network has changed news from something that *has happened* to something that *is happening*. As president, George Bush was quoted as having said to other world leaders, "I learn more from CNN than I do from the CIA."

The reporting of news and information is not the most widespread use of media; most people use media primarily for entertainment. It was not, in the beginning, considered an important function within media organizations. The first "newspapers" focused more on political advocacy and editorializing than on attempting to provide a comprehensive or objective overview of newsworthy events. Television news was originally limited to 15-minute broadcasts presented as a public service. Over the years, however, news operations became central to network status; organizations whose only claim to fame was producing the "I Love Lucy" television show did not get invited to lunch at the White House. News operations became intensely competitive, locked in head-to-head popularity races in which the loss of one ratings point could translate into a loss of $10 million in advertisement revenue. Television news also had a substantial impact on newspaper readership and content. Unable to compete with the immediacy of television reports of breaking events, newspapers moved toward placing more emphasis on feature and special-interest stories.

News, by definition, is timely: it is "news," not "olds." Decisions regarding what stories to play and how to play them are made under tight deadlines. Satellite broadcasting, lightweight electronic field equipment, computer-generated graphics, and sophisticated access to archive information have dramatically decreased the time required to access, package, and disseminate news. However, reporters and editors have less time to investigate, reflect, and evaluate. Within the news ranks, the worst sin is often being the second source to break a story. The *Washington Post*'s Bob Woodward has suggested that one cause for an increase in what he calls "dud stories" is

a decline in reporters' skepticism and their desire to move with stories when they break without a research delay. Consider the media coverage of the 1994 O. J. Simpson murder case, in which the media blitz arguably set a record for air and cable time. In an effort to provide coverage of any angle that would heighten the public's interest, the media sacrificed much of the objective balance considered to be paramount to major news organizations (see "Summer's Top Crime Drama, Continued").

Both news reporters and news consumers have a tendency to accept information without questioning sources. According to author Irving Fang, television news anchors are hired for their ability to do five things: speak clearly, impart a sense of the news, convince viewers that they know what they are talking about, keep a newscast running smoothly, and maintain contact with the audience. Television stations have been known to hire research firms to measure galvanic skin response of randomly chosen viewers in an attempt to determine the success of various newscasters in getting an emotional response during their reports. Those who do, stay on; those who do not are fired. Despite these employment criteria, newscasters are consistently given very high credibility ratings by the public. In a 1986 *Times Mirror* poll, 67 percent of respondents gave President Ronald Reagan (who was enjoying a period of solid public support) a high credibility rating, while 81 percent rated newscaster Dan Rather as highly credible. (An earlier *Times Mirror* poll ranked Walter Cronkite's credibility not only higher than the president's but higher than the pope's!) What news reporters tell us is often perceived as believable simply because it is in the news. The media confer their own credibility; reporters who quote a "leading educator" or a "source close to the president" are rarely questioned about who those sources actually are. Accordingly, in "Media Con Games," Martin Lee and Norman Solomon advise critical news consumers to be alert to ways news media deliberately or inadvertently distort facts and issues.

The difference between news and opinion is often lost on the average reader or viewer. There is a difference between an editorial and straight news copy, between the evening news and the program "60 Minutes," between a documentary and a "based on" made-for-television movie. Yet, perceptions of events are often drawn from a combination of these sources. Even the choice of wording in a news story has an impact: Did the candidate receive an "enthusiastic" response or a "polite" one? Was the drop

in unemployment "an encouraging" 0.5 percent or "only" 0.5 percent? These interpretations are known as news "spin," which is also evident in the selection of stories and where they are placed in a news report.

A final concern addressed in these readings is the tendency of news media themselves to blur the lines that have traditionally separated the informing, influencing, and entertaining functions of media. In "Make-Your-Own Journalism: The Trend toward Fabricating the News," Ted Smith presents several cases that illustrate a trend for fabricating the news in the interest of supporting an editorial point. Congressman Robert Dornan (R-California) has suggested that the term "news media" is becoming an oxymoron as competition among news operations pulls them toward an "info-tainment" mentality. News writers do not consider tabloids such as the *Star* or the *National Enquirer* worthy of being called news media, but they understand their attraction.

The share of Americans who rely on television for news has been growing steadily for three decades. According to several studies, Americans say, by a ratio of two to one, that they would believe what they see on television over what they read in a newspaper if reports seem to conflict. As television devotes more time to news-type programming, so have media critics devoted more space to discussing concerns associated with news coverage.

In *The Evening News* (Doubleday, 1990), Arthur Hailey observes that people watch the news to find out the answers to three questions: Is the world safe? Are my home and family safe? Did anything happen today that was interesting? Given cursory answers to those questions, many viewers feel they are "keeping up"—although the total amount of news delivered in a half-hour newscast would, if set in type, hardly fill the front page of a daily newspaper.

Even news veteran David Brinkley has stated that news programs should not bore people any more than is necessary. Following that philosophy, television news presents primarily headlines. The ability to bring the public those headlines as they happen is the strength of broadcast news; however, depending only on television as a news source can create a false sense of being informed.

Looking Ahead: Challenge Questions

What are some of the "con games" for which active and skeptical news consumers should be constantly on alert? Why do journalists engage in these practices?

What are some implications of the tendency for journalists to blur the line between reporting and editorializing? Is there any justification for fabricating, such as in the examples discussed by Ted Smith (see "Make Your Own Journalism"), in presenting news?

Why is the line between information and entertainment functions of media eroding? Is this a cause for concern? Do you perceive any desirable outcomes of this trend? What is your own opinion of info-tainment media?

MEDIA **CON** GAMES

MARTIN A. LEE AND NORMAN SOLOMON

Martin A. Lee and Norman Solomon are associated with Fairness and Accuracy in Reporting (FAIR), a New York-based media watch group. This article is adapted from their book, "Unreliable Sources: A Guide to Detecting Bias in News Media," published by Lyle Stuart.

At one time or another, we've all read a newspaper story or seen a news broadcast that we know misses the real story. Perhaps we have been present at an event, only to find the next day's news account bears little resemblance to our first-hand experience. The more we understand about the world, the more often we see how the news media deliberately or inadvertently fudge the facts and distort key issues.

Reading between the lines and seeing through media con games aren't natural talents; they're acquired skills. Most of us aren't experts in the nuances of international diplomacy, military strategy, corporate mergers and leveraged buyouts, or a hundred other topics the media report on regularly.

"Of course, it is possible for any citizen with time to spare, and a canny eye, to work out what is actually going on," said novelist Gore Vidal, "but for many there is no time, and the network news is the only news even though it may not be news at all but only a series of flashing fictions intended, like the avowed commercials, to keep docile huddled masses, keep avid for products addled consumers."

One can learn to be a more critical consumer of the news. Toward this end, it helps to survey a wide range of news media, especially publications that question conventional wisdom. The irascible media critic I.F. Stone used to read everything he could get his hands on. He pointed out the mainstream media's contradictions and omissions in his journal, *I.F. Stone's Weekly*, which tweaked the nose of the

American establishment during the 1950s and 1960s.

Stone's method is easy to apply to today's media. One doesn't have to be an expert on macroeconomics, for example, to figure out that something is amiss when a *New York Times* headline reads, APRIL JOB GROWTH EASED DECISIVELY, STIRRING CONCERN, and a *USA Today* headline two days later says, JOBLESS RATE INCREASE SEEN AS GOOD NEWS. Or compare New York *Newsday*'s headline of April 13, 1989—CITY SCHOOL DROPOUT RATE IS UP—to *The New York Times* on the same day, DROPOUT RATE UNCHANGED, DESPITE MORE SPENDING.

Mixed messages sometimes appear in the same newspaper. On April 30, 1989, the *St. Louis Post-Dispatch* headlined on two different pages: JESSE JACKSON HINTS AT RUNNING FOR D.C. MAYOR and JACKSON HAS NO PLANS FOR MAYOR RACE. Conflicting assertions ran on the same page of *The New York Times* (June 15, 1989); the headline stated, UGANDA AFTER ITS YEARS OF TERROR: A NEW STABILITY, but the subhead disclosed, 300 REBELS REPORTED KILLED IN CLASH WITH UGANDA ARMY.

For those who read more than one daily paper, it can be instructive to compare how the same wire service report is presented in different outlets. For example, an Associated Press dispatch in the *San Juan Star*, Puerto Rico's English-language paper, on August 20, 1989, led as follows: "Police used whips and dogs to disperse hundreds of blacks, including Archbishop Desmond Tutu, during mass protests on Saturday at two whites-only beaches." *The New York Times*, meanwhile, ran a watered-down version of the same AP dispatch: "South African police dispersed hundreds of blacks during protests today at two whites-only beaches." Whoever edited the AP copy for *The Times* took a bite out of the article, omitting any reference to police dogs.

Sometimes, important wire stories are picked up by certain newspapers and ignored by others. On July 22, 1989, the *San Juan Star* ran a lengthy AP dispatch with the headline, NORTH CONTRA-SUPPORT NETWORK LINKED TO DRUGS IN COSTA RICA. According to this report, a Costa Rican congressional commission found that a Nicaraguan contra support network created by Lieutenant Colonel Oliver North had been involved in cocaine trafficking in Costa Rica. A short item in *The Washington Post* the next day noted that Costa Rica officially barred North, Richard Secord, and former U.S. national-security adviser John Poindexter from entering its territory because of their role in fostering the contra drug connection. None of this information was reported by *The New York Times* or the major television networks, even though they all subscribe to AP.

What follows is a run-down of some media con games for which active and skeptical news consumers should be constantly on the alert:

LOADED LANGUAGE

This category of media distortion could include a peculiar—or politically dubious—use of a word or phrase that might stand reality on its head. Or it might entail the selective applications of phrases that, when compared in different contexts, display a pattern of bias.

For example, in its coverage of anti-government demonstrations in then-Communist-ruled East Germany, the *San Francisco Examiner* described protesters throwing rocks at police as engaged in "civil disobedience." When is the last time the *Examiner* or other mainstream media used the phrase "civil disobedience" to describe Palestinian youths in the Occupied Territories throwing rocks at Israeli soldiers?

Serge Schmemann's front-page article

From *The Progressive*, July 1990, pp. 16-20. © 1990 by Martin A. Lee and Norman Solomon. Reprinted by permission of the authors.

in *The New York Times* was headlined, MOSCOW CAUTIONS NATO ON REPLACING MISSILES IN EUROPE; WEIGHS VIOLATING TREATY. The article asserted that the Soviet Union was "prepared to violate the American-Soviet treaty banning medium- and short-range nuclear missiles from Europe" if NATO upgraded its own missiles. Two days later, A.M. Rosenthal beat the same drum in his *Times* opinion column: "Gorbachev's Foreign Minister warned that Moscow was ready to violate a U.S.-Soviet treaty. . . ."

Compare this language to a *Times* news story by Michael R. Gordon: "The Bush Administration has not said whether it accepts the strict reading of the ABM treaty . . . or whether it endorses a much more permissive reading of the agreement developed by the Reagan Administration." In *Times*speak, the Soviets *violate* arms treaties; the U.S. Government merely *reinterprets* them—permissively.

Permissive readings were in vogue in the U.S. media a few years ago when President Reagan was pushing the Star Wars program. Accepting Reagan's "broad" interpretation of the Anti-Ballistic Missile (ABM) Treaty, *Nightline* host Ted Koppel derided as a "clever move" a Soviet journalist's insistence that the 1972 treaty prohibited Star Wars deployment. Apparently, Koppel was unfamiliar with Article 5 of the ABM Treaty, which states in no uncertain terms that each party must not "develop, test or deploy ABM systems or components which are sea-based, air-based, space-based, or mobile land-based."

The Washington Post argued in favor of giving "humanitarian aid" to the Nicaraguan contras. However, according to the Geneva Conventions and Protocols and the International Red Cross, the right to "humanitarian aid" is not available to members of a military force. It must be distributed by humanitarian groups, not an interested party such as the U.S. Government. Such aid must be applied impartially to all civilians who need it, not just those on one side. These criteria automatically disqualified the contras. But one wouldn't know this from *The Washington Post* and other U.S. media, which ignored international legal standards as they endorsed more aid to the contras.

How the press labels a political group often says more about the journalist doing the labeling than about the group itself. *New York Times* correspondent Serge Schmemann, reporting on the results of municipal elections in Berlin, stated, "Both the extreme Left and the extreme Right gained. . . . The left-wing Alternative List, as the West Berlin chapter of the Greens is called, gained about two percentage points, getting 11.7 per cent of the vote. . . . But most surprising was the 8 per cent of the popular vote garnered by the Republican Citizens Party, a Far Right group" that campaigned on a racist anti-immigrant platform.

Calling the antinuclear, ecology-oriented Greens an "extreme" political party says a lot about bias at *The Times*. Schmemann never explains in what way the Greens are "extreme"—a term laden with negative connotations. By lumping the nonviolent Greens together with a neo-Nazi party, he implies a moral equivalence between the so-called extremes. Such smear tactics are particularly reprehensible in view of the fact that the Greens have long been at the forefront of antiracist, anti-Nazi movements in Germany and elsewhere in Western Europe.

Even worse than "extreme" or "radical" in U.S. political discourse is the label "communist." A *New York Times* story by Jonathan Fuerbringer referred matter-of-factly to "the communist regime of Nicaragua." The characterization was biased and inaccurate, as Fairness and Accuracy in Reporting (FAIR) noted in a letter to *The Times*. "What communist regime allows approximately half of the economy to remain in the private sector as in Nicaragua—a higher percentage than in Mexico or Brazil?" After complaints from readers, *The Times* ran a terse correction: "While Nicaragua is Marxist, it does not operate on the Soviet model of communism."

In contrast to "Marxist" Nicaragua, *The Times* and other U.S. media routinely refer to neighboring states as "the democratic countries in Central America." During Mikhail Gorbachev's visit to Cuba in 1989, Cable News Network (CNN) correspondent Tom Mintier wondered whether Gorbachev would prevail upon Fidel Castro to stop subverting "the budding democracy in El Salvador," a nation where government-sponsored Death Squads make a mockery of the rule of law.

Times writers habitually refer to "the Marxist government of Angola," as if this were the official title of that country's governing body. But Angolan officials do not call themselves "the Marxist government of Angola." To them, Angola is simply Angola. *The Times* and other U.S. mass media, however, never referred to General Augusto Pinochet's regime as "the Fascist government of Chile" or to the apartheid regime as "the racist government of South Africa."

UNATTRIBUTED ASSERTIONS, SUSPICIOUS SOURCES

Unattributed assertions are often of questionable validity. For example, *CBS Evening News* anchor Dan Rather, introducing a story about a Palestine Liberation Organization conference in Algiers, said,

"Bert Quint reports that the show was orchestrated by Moscow." How did Quint manage to figure out Moscow's role in this affair? Obviously no one stood up and began waving a conductor's wand. Quint's claim that Moscow "orchestrated" the PLO conference was not attributed to any source. When questioned by FAIR, a CBS producer conceded that the word "orchestrated" may have been ill-chosen.

Occasionally reporters need to speak with sources "off the record" or on a "not-for-attribution" basis. This makes it possible for people to provide news without risking their jobs, safety, or reputations. Sources need to know they can trust a journalist before sharing confidences. This is especially true for whistleblowers in government or corporate spheres.

Unfortunately, journalists often grant anonymity to people who should be publicly accountable. Instead of a bond of trust, the relationship becomes an indentured contract, as reporters look to governmental and corporate elites for their daily dose of news.

By "suspicious sources," we mean instances when reporters cite unidentified sources, as in "top U.S. officials say. . . ." or "according to Western diplomats. . . ." This happens so often that it's difficult to know who's really talking and why.

One should be alert to journalists' use of unnamed official sources. If the unnamed source is a whistleblower speaking accurately and truthfully about his or her boss or agency, the information can be considered a "leak," and in all likelihood the reporter will be serving the public interest. If, on the other hand, the unnamed source is the voice of a government agency and there's no legitimate reason for the source to be unnamed, the information can be considered a "plant," and in all likelihood the reporter will be serving the interest of the agency, not the public.

There is ample reason for suspicion whenever unnamed intelligence sources are invoked: "CIA officials warned. . . ." or "U.S. intelligence experts believe. . . ." When unnamed intelligence sources are cited, lies and disinformation often follow. For example:

Relying on unnamed U.S. intelligence sources, most major media reported in November 1984 that Soviet MIG fighter jets were being unloaded in Nicaragua. The story turned out to be a hoax.

James LeMoyne of *The New York Times* quoted unnamed "American officials" who claimed that the Medellín cocaine cartel "has close ties . . . to some Sandinista officials in Nicaragua." How do American officials know this? And why didn't they want to be publicly associated with their remarks? Perhaps it had something to do with the fact that the U.S. Drug Enforcement Administration publicly debunked allegations of a Sandinista drug connection, as reported by *Times* correspondent Joel Brinkley.

Another dubious practice involves imbalanced sources. Reporters don't usually interject their own opinions into stories; this would be a blatant violation of journalistic codes, which stipulate that reporters must remain "objective." Instead, the media transmit bias by the way they choose their sources. An article about an important foreign policy or domestic issue might quote only official U.S. sources—named and unnamed. The kind of "experts" the media feature in print and broadcast news reports—and the kind who are left out—narrowly frame the spectrum of public opinion.

New York Times correspondent Paul Lewis utilized suspicious sources in an article headlined, U.S. HUMAN RIGHTS GROUP FACES A KEY TEST. Lewis began with the following: "An American-led campaign to make the U.N. Human Rights Commission a less political and more effective watchdog against oppressive governments is facing its most critical test in years, diplomats say." Lewis cited only unnamed "Western diplomats" and "experts" in his fifteen-paragraph piece, except for a single comment attributed to U.S. delegate Vernon Walters.

Lewis snubbed opposing views but dutifully repeated the assertion that the United States was simply trying "to get the [United Nations] commission working in a less political manner." In view of strenuous U.S. efforts to initiate U.N. investigations of its enemies while blocking probes of allied countries, independent human-rights experts objected to Lewis's gullible portrayal of the United States as a neutral watchdog. Lewis ignored "the substantial role the U.S. has played in politicizing U.N. human rights work," wrote Human Rights Watch deputy director Ken Roth in a letter to *The Times*. "It is misleading to portray the U.S. as the champion of impartiality when its own participation in the commission has been so politically charged."

Reports about nuclear weapons and disarmament often quote U.S. and Soviet officials without including comments from representatives of peace and antinuclear groups. When nongovernment sources are included, they tend to be conservative rather than progressive critics. These patterns are rampant throughout the mainstream news media. On several *MacNeil/Lehrer* discussions of nuclear-weapons issues in the late 1980s, for example, the most dovish "expert" interviewed was Senator Sam Nunn of Georgia, a Pentagon booster.

When U.S. media occasionally present dissenting views on foreign policy, it is usually the leaders—the elites—of foreign countries who are invited to render their opinions, not representatives from popular U.S. movements. These opposing views are foreign by definition, and often anti-American by implication. When U.S. officials square off with their Soviet or Iranian counterparts, it may seem that we're getting a balanced discussion of the issues at stake, but the choice of official experts frames the debate in a biased manner. A U.S. audience is likely to be more receptive to the views of American officials who are pitted in debates against leaders of "enemy" states. Missing are the voices of citizen-action groups in the United States that oppose various aspects of American foreign policy.

STENOGRAPHY OR JOURNALISM?

It happens all the time: A Government official says something, reporters take down every word, and whatever is said—whether truth or lie—ends up as a sound bite on the evening news or a quote in hundreds of newspapers and magazines. Many journalists apparently believe that officials are there to dish out the facts, and reporters merely have to come and get them.

Of course, journalists have an obligation to report what high-level officials say. But a good reporter should also indicate when an official says something of questionable veracity or when an official out-and-out lies. Unfortunately, reporters rarely note when official statements cannot be corroborated.

Journalists often act more like stenographers than reporters, duly transcribing lies, half-truths, disinformation, and propaganda without attempting to put remarks in perspective or pointing out when something is amiss. Journalists continue to do this even when U.S. officials have been publicly discredited. A classic example:

In December 1989, CNN and other prominent American news media reported that several months earlier two high-ranking representatives from the Bush Administration—National Security Adviser Brent Scowcroft and Deputy Secretary of State Lawrence Eagleburger—had secretly visited Beijing and met with China's hardline leaders. The July 1989 meeting occurred only a few weeks after the Chinese government massacred hundreds of prodemocracy demonstrators in Tiananmen Square. It was embarrassing for Secretary of State James Baker to admit that he "misled" the public about Bush's covert China diplomacy. But this hardly tarnished his reputation with the Washington press corps.

A few days after news of the China visit was disclosed, the U.S. invaded Panama. True to form, reporters eagerly conveyed Baker's explanation for the military assault—to promote democracy in Panama.

Such noble rhetoric didn't square with U.S. support for the Chinese tyrants who crushed the democracy movement in their country. But instead of asking Baker why they should believe him about Panama when he had lied about China, journalists merely repeated what the Secretary of State said.

THE KISSINGER-HAIG DISEASE

The Kissinger-Haig disease stems from U.S. journalists' unhealthy reliance on official sources and experts, to the exclusion of critical, nongovernmental dissenting views. Advanced stages of this illness afflict the Sunday snooze shows: ABC's *This Week with David Brinkley*, NBC's *Meet the Press*, and CBS's *Face the Nation*.

ABC *Nightline* host Ted Koppel has a bad case of the Kissinger-Haig disease; the two former Secretaries of State were the most frequent guests on *Nightline* during a forty-month period surveyed by FAIR. "Whenever anything significant happens, the networks round up the usual suspects," remarked *Newsday* media critic D.D. Guttenplan. "Newspaper reporters often operate the same way."

Former U.S. officials often go into business as private consultants after leaving the Government. Henry Kissinger, for example, served as a paid consultant in dealings with China's rulers before and after the June 1989 Tiananmen Square massacre. His firm, Kissinger & Associates, represents multinational corporations that profit from a friendly investment climate in China. Kissinger also heads China Ventures, a company engaged in joint ventures with China's state bank. But none of these connections was mentioned when Kissinger, posing as an independent foreign-policy expert, apologized for Chinese government atrocities and urged the Bush Administration not to impose economic sanctions against that country.

PASSIVE PHRASES, GLOSS-OVER EUPHEMISMS

These linguistic techniques can impart a subtle bias to news coverage. While the press sometimes has a penchant for hype and sensationalism, reporters and editors frequently choose words that end up neutralizing controversial events. Euphemistic phraseology can convey a skewed impression about current events.

Some U.S. reporters invoked passive phrases and gloss-over euphemisms in writing about the 1973 military coup in Chile. They often said that Chilean President Salvador Allende "died" in the presidential palace, when he was murdered by the armed forces. According to *The New York Times*, Allende's policies caused "chaos" which "brought in the military."

This obscures the fact that the U.S. Government and corporations like ITT were instrumental in fomenting chaos and backing the coup. The notion that "chaos" prompted the Chilean military to move in and restore order implicitly downplays and neutralizes the brutality of the coup, in which tens of thousands of people were killed, tortured, and "disappeared."

Heinous acts of repression by the military government in U.S.-allied Turkey—including the torture, murder, and incarceration of trade unionists and other serious human-rights abuses—*The Washington Post* characterized as merely "controversial measures." Turkey's military despot pursued a "down-to-earth approach" as he sought to deal with "the rough and tumble of everyday politics," according to *The Post*.

Referring to political violence in El Salvador, the *Christian Science Monitor* stated euphemistically, "Death and destruction still loom high in the saddle in El Salvador," without indicating who—in this case, the U.S.-backed Salvadoran government—was responsible for tens of thousands of political killings in that country.

The use of passive phrases and gloss-over euphemisms results in what Michael Parenti has described as the "scanting of content." "By slighting content and dwelling on surface details, the media are able to neutralize the truth while giving an appearance of having thoroughly treated the subject," Parenti wrote in *Inventing Reality: The Politics of the Mass Media*.

CONTRA COMMON SENSE

This category of media manipulation involves obvious and gross misstatements of fact that defy common sense.

For example, the lead sentence of a *New York Times* article by Matthew Wald in the aftermath of the Exxon oil spill in Alaska stated: "What man has done and has tried fecklessly to undo here for almost a month, nature is doing instead." The article was based on Exxon assertions that two-thirds of the millions of gallons of oil spilled by the tanker *Exxon Valdez* "is gone, most by natural action." Where did all the oil go? Did it magically disappear through the hole in the atmosphere's ozone layer? Why give any credence whatsoever to an absurd Exxon public-relations ploy?

The Miami Herald reprinted an article by *New York Times* science writer Jane

Brody headlined, 'CHEMOPHOBIA' MAY BE AS BAD AS CHEMICALS. Reports of health hazards in common foods containing pesticides and environmental chemicals are causing "chemophobia," according to Brody. "But this mounting 'chemophobia' is, in turn, raising fears among many scientists [who] say few people appreciate the benefits of chemicals or the potential negative consequences of rapidly spreading chemophobia."

Brody continues with a whopper: "According to the best available scientific estimates [which she never cited in her article], 99.9 per cent of carcinogens in the diet come from natural sources [which she never identified]. Synthetic chemicals account for only 0.01 per cent of the carcinogens Americans consume." Another insult to common sense. What was Brody trying to say? That food laced with pesticides and other chemical poisons is healthier than organically grown produce? When we called to ask Brody to supply evidence to back up her statements, we were told she doesn't respond to inquiries from readers.

THE NUMBERS RACKET

The numbers racket is a category of media bias that includes rigged statistics, inflated or deflated estimates of attendance at political demonstrations, contradictory tallies, and numerical tricks. For instance:

Each month, the Federal Bureau of Labor Statistics (BLS) releases national unemployment figures. These statistics, dutifully reported by mass media, hide the true extent of unemployment in the United States. Not counted are people without jobs who haven't looked for work for over a month because the prospects are discouraging, as well as those who are forced to retire early. Moreover, the BLS inflates the number of employed by counting those who work only one hour a week.

The BLS actually compiles two sets of statistics. The bureau's "U-7" rate, which factors in "discouraged" employment-seekers and early retirees, is a much more accurate reflection of unemployment percentages in the United States. Thus in 1986, when the media reported the average national unemployment rate was 6.2 per cent, 14.3 per cent of the labor force actually experienced unemployment. The U-7 rate is available to journalists, who typically ignore the higher figures.

"In the end," wrote former *New York*

Times labor correspondent William Serrin in *The Nation*, "the press almost always takes the easy way out and uses the conventional numbers, a tendency historically encouraged by the Government because it puts the best face on unemployment."

The headline of an unsigned *New York Times* story on December 31, 1989, read, 15,000 JEWS AND PALESTINIANS JOIN JERUSALEM PEACE RALLY. The figure cited in the headline was based on Israeli police estimates. In fact, the number of demonstrators was significantly higher, as the unidentified *Times* correspondent noted in the fifth paragraph of the article: "The Peace Now movement, which organized the rally, put the number at closer to 35,000. With crowds ten to twelve deep along much of the route, the Peace Now figure did not seem inflated." Then why was the deflated number featured in the headline?

During the mid-1980s, journalists frequently repeated State Department claims that Nicaragua hosted some 2,500 to 3,500 Cuban military personnel and 6,000 Cuban civilians. *The New York Times* upped the figure to 3,500 to 5,000 Cubans in combat support roles in Nicaragua.

But when a Cuban general, Rafael del Pino Diaz, defected to the United States in the summer of 1987, he indicated that only 300 to 400 Cuban military personnel were posted in Nicaragua (the amount claimed all along by Cuba and Nicaragua). Although the U.S. Government and the media trumpeted del Pino Diaz as the most important military defector in Cuban history, *Times* correspondent Bernard Trainor ignored his assessment of the level of Cuban support for Nicaragua. Trainor continued to write about "thousands of Cuban military advisers in Nicaragua."

Some prefer to blame the media's inadequacies on lousy reporters. But the institutional framework in which journalists try to do their job is also at fault. The most serious and pervasive distortions in the U.S. media are the result not only of deadlines, inadequate space, poor judgment, a lack of skill, or the idiosyncratic nature of professional news people. Such factors cannot explain the larger patterns of bias that persist.

"Despite the wonders of communications technology," says British journalist Ed Harriman, "the news often seems little more than folklore, a steady stream of nursery tales for adults."

MAKE-YOUR-OWN JOURNALISM

The Trend toward Fabricating the News

Ted Smith

Ted Smith is associate professor of journalism at Virginia Commonwealth University in Richmond, Virginia.

On February 8, 1993, Americans were treated to an unusually candid look at the realities of contemporary journalism. The occasion was a two-hour press conference called by General Motors to announce that it had filed suit for defamation against NBC.

At issue was a one-minute segment of a story titled "Waiting to Explode?" aired on the network's *Dateline NBC* video newsmagazine during "sweeps week" in November 1992. The central claim of the story was that GM pickup trucks made between 1973 and 1987 are unsafe because their "sidesaddle" fuel tanks have a tendency to rupture and burn in side-impact collisions. The contested segment seemed to offer dramatic proof of the claim: It showed the results of a test crash commissioned by NBC in which a GM pickup burst into flames after being struck in the side by a car.

GM contended that the test was rigged. In a meticulously documented presentation, GM general counsel Harry Pearce argued that, contrary to NBC's claim that the pickup's fuel tank had been "punctured," X-ray photos showed it had remained intact. The fuel leak occurred because the tank had been deliberately overfilled and was fitted with a nonstandard replacement gas cap that flew off on impact. Worse, NBC had virtually guaranteed that any fuel leak would become a fire by attaching model-rocket engines to the underside of the truck and igniting them by remote control an instant before the crash. Finally, additional videotapes shot by onlookers at the scene showed that what appeared to be a blazing holocaust in the NBC footage was in fact only a fifteen-second flare-up that burned little more than grass.

The network, which had stonewalled GM at every step of its investigation, initially stood firm. While admitting that "sparking devices" had been used in the test, NBC News President Michael Gartner insisted that the story was "fair and accurate." But his defiance was short-lived. The following night, *Dateline* cohosts Jane Pauley and Stone Phillips ended their program by announcing that a settlement had been reached. They then read detailed statements in which the network conceded the validity of the GM complaints and apologized to both the company and its viewers.

All things considered, NBC had little choice but to capitulate. Aside from the strength of GM's case, it was faced with widespread criticism from other journalists, who, intent on preserving their own credibility, condemned NBC's reporting as an egregious but isolated violation of professional norms.

HISTORY OF FABRICATIONS BY TELEVISION NEWS

Among the most vociferous of the critics was Don Hewitt, executive producer of CBS' *60 Minutes*, who affirmed that NBC "knowingly did violence to the truth" but insisted, "It's not something that anybody at *60 Minutes* would do."

To Walter Olson, this sounded a bit like a "Gary Hart Memorial Dare." Writing in the June 21 issue of *National Review*, he presented evidence of a long history of spectacular fabrications in television exposés of allegedly unsafe vehicles. Among his examples:

In 1978, at the height of the Ford

Pinto controversy, ABC's *20/20* used footage of a fiery rear-end crash from a 1967 test conducted by UCLA researchers to illustrate its claim that full-size Fords were also likely to explode when hit from behind. What the original 1968 research report noted but ABC failed to report is that the test was designed to investigate how fire from a crash would affect the passenger compartment of a car. An incendiary device had been used to produce the explosion.

Meanwhile, on *60 Minutes*, a 1980 story purported to show that the small "CJ" model Jeep had a tendency to roll over in J-turns—described as "a fairly gentle right-hand turn that a driver might make if he was going into a parking lot"—and in the kind of evasive maneuvers that would be needed to avoid an unexpected obstacle in the road. Among the many things that CBS did not tell its viewers: The Jeeps shown toppling over in its tests had weights hanging out of sight in their wheel wells and, in the evasive maneuver tests, had been turned by their robot drivers at rates two to three times faster than that of the average human driver.

The following year, in an Emmy Award–winning story, *60 Minutes* claimed that if the most common type of rim used on heavy truck tires is dislodged, it "fires off like a shell out of a cannon," killing or maiming anyone unlucky enough to be in its path. The claim was illustrated with dramatic footage of a test in which an exploding rim annihilated two dummies. CBS did not report that the rim had exploded only after approximately 70 percent of its locking device had been shaved away by the testers.

More recently, a 1986 story focused on the alleged problem of "sudden acceleration" in the Audi 5000. In seeking to explain this phenomenon, *60 Minutes* cited an expert who claimed that "unusually high transmission pressure" could be the cause and then illustrated his claim with footage of a test in which an Audi gas pedal is seen to "go down by itself," in Ed Bradley's words. Bradley did not point out that the pedal's mysterious movement was the result of compressed air or fluid being forced into the transmission from a tank apparently located just out of sight of the camera on the passenger seat of the car.

PRÉCIS

Today's print and electronic journalists often distort the facts of the news in a variety of ways.

For example, out-and-out fabricated events have appeared with some regularity on network television news, as with NBC's test collision last year on a General Motors pickup truck that had been rigged to explode.

Such fabrications also appear in print. However, more common than falsehoods of journalists' own creation are news reports that embody the false or misleading claims of other sources. In coverage of foreign affairs, this abuse often takes the form of uncritical reports of hostile propaganda.

In coverage of domestic affairs, the most common falsehoods are the advocacy data generated by the ubiquitous "studies" conducted by special interest groups to influence public opinion and public policy.

Other journalistic abuses involve the convenient mislabeling of images on television and in still photos and the withholding of crucial information that journalists feel does not fit the way they wish to present a story (as in the TV broadcast of the Rodney King beating).

This trend has been spurred by a change in the core values of journalism. Today's journalists are no longer content to serve as mere conduits of information. Instead, they have adopted the more active and exciting role of "Champions of the People."

MISLEADING VIEWERS THROUGH MISLABELING IMAGES

As these examples suggest and as many others could confirm, fabricated events have appeared with some regularity on network television news. But fabrications are only one of a range of abuses that continue to occur with some frequency in both print and broadcast coverage. One of the most common abuses is *mislabeled images*.

The classic example occurred in a 1968 CBS documentary titled *Hunger in America*. In one particularly dramatic scene, viewers were shown a tiny baby lying in a San Antonio hospital and told that it was dying before their eyes of starvation. But as a local newspaper subsequently reported, the baby in question had been born prematurely after its mother was injured in a fall, and it died of complications arising from prematurity; neither the baby nor its mother was malnourished. Although repeatedly informed of this error by Accuracy in Media and others, CBS used the same footage, without comment or correction, to illustrate a story on hunger on its May 1, 1983, newscast.

A more recent example comes from a January 1993 story on *60 Minutes* that maintained that a valuable Army medical research project in Louisiana had been canceled because of pressure from animal rights extremists. At one point, while the narrator spoke of "a brutal confrontation with animal rights activists" in Louisiana, viewers were shown footage of an impassioned animal rights demonstration. But as Rep. Bob Livingston (R-Louisiana) pointed out in a detailed denunciation of the story delivered on the floor of the House, the demonstration viewers saw took place in a different state and did not concern the specific issue in question; in Louisiana, there had been no "confrontation" over the project, "brutal" or otherwise. Although apprised of the error by Livingston in March, CBS rebroadcast the story without correction on July 25.

Perhaps the most blatant recent instance of mislabeling comes, once again, from NBC. In a feature story on its January 4, 1993, evening newscast, NBC argued that logging in Idaho's Clearwater National Forest is, among other things, polluting streams and killing fish. It illustrated this claim with two film clips. One showed a man in a stream netting what correspondent Robin Lloyd described as fish that had been killed by pollution; the other showed several large

> *Fabricated events are only one of a range of abuses that continue to occur with some frequency in both print and broadcast coverage. One of the most common abuses is mislabeled images.*

fish floating belly up in a pool. In fact, the fish in the first clip were not dead but stunned, and the man netting them was a biologist engaged in studying their health; the fish in the second clip were dead, but the pool they were floating in was located somewhere in the South, not in Idaho.

Although alerted to these errors almost immediately, NBC did not broadcast a correction until February 24, and then only after it had received widespread publicity, including a denunciation by Sen. Larry Craig (R-Idaho) in a speech shown nationally on C-SPAN.

ABUSES OF THE EDITING PROCESS

Given the severe limitations of time and space within which all journalists must work, it is inevitable that various forms of *editing abuses* will occur. In the case of television, these limitations are constant and acute, and the abuses are correspondingly abundant.

Consider, for example, the tape of the Rodney King beating, which almost certainly has been shown more often than any other footage in the history of television news. It is worth remembering that the tape records only the last few minutes of a long and complex series of events. Nevertheless, it is still far too long for the needs of television and so is almost always presented in a heavily edited form.

Because the tape is ostensibly *about* police brutality, the edited versions show only one or more phases of the beating,

Editing abuses are part of the larger category of crucial omissions, in which a journalist is aware of information that is vital to a story but chooses not to report it.

cut out from the whole and strung together to form a continuous sequence. Unfortunately, this editing both intensifies the violence and eliminates certain significant scenes.

In one of these, from the very beginning of the tape, King appears to lunge aggressively at the police. This action was the central focus of the successful defense of the officers in their first trial, but it is doubtful even today whether more than a small fraction of the American public has seen it. For those who have not seen it, the jury's verdict could well seem indefensible, and it is an open question how much this editing contributed to the Los Angeles riots.

Other editing abuses are more mundane. The most common of them occur when individuals are quoted in the news, and almost everyone who has been quoted frequently can provide examples of the problem. Serious abuses of this kind tend to occur in investigative reports designed to expose some flaw in an individual or organization.

As a result, it is now standard practice for anyone who suspects he might be the subject of such a report to record all conversations and interviews with the journalists involved. This practice appears to have been popularized by the Illinois Power Company, which was the subject of a scathing critique in a 1979 *60 Minutes* story about alleged construction problems at one of the company's nuclear power facilities. Armed with its own videotapes of all interviews conducted with corporate officials, the company was able to produce a rebuttal that clearly documented several serious distortions in the CBS report.

Officials of the Newmont Gold Company, one of two targets of a 1989 *20/20* exposé of the supposed hazards posed by the use of cyanide in gold-mining operations, took a more aggressive approach. Having concluded (correctly) that their views would not be presented fairly, they sent transcripts of all interviews with corporate spokesmen to four hundred newspaper editors before the program aired.

OMITTING CRUCIAL INFORMATION

Editing abuses are part of the larger category of *crucial omissions*, in which a journalist is aware of information that is vital to a story but chooses not to report it.

Coverage of the April 25, 1993, gay rights march in Washington provides an especially clear example of the practice. Organizers of the march hoped that it would build the legitimacy of their movement by showing homosexuals to be decent, conventional, and essentially normal individuals, and this was the image that was dutifully projected by most of the major news media, including network television and the *New York Times*.

But, as the *Washington Times* stressed in its coverage and as unedited pictures on C-SPAN clearly confirmed, this image was made possible only by the systematic exclusion of the more bizarre and provocative activities of the participants: men locked in passionate embraces or exposing themselves to the crowds, caresses shared by topless lesbians, flamboyant transvestites marching in combat boots and dresses, leather-clad figures with whips.

Another clear example can be found in a *20/20* story broadcast on December 8, 1992. As part of their effort to show that the U.S. Customs Service's drug interdiction program is ineffective, a team of ABC reporters flew a small aircraft from Mexico to Arizona. Once over U.S. territory, they descended to 250 feet and dropped a bag containing a taco to be retrieved by another team on the ground.

As it happened, the exercise fooled no one. A Customs Service plane observed the drop and was right behind the ABC aircraft when it landed in Tucson; other agents were on hand to greet ABC reporters when they drove up to retrieve the bag.

None of this was mentioned in the *20/20* story. Ignoring the evidence of its own test, it concluded that the interdiction program is a costly failure.

THE MEDIA'S CREATION AND PROPAGATION OF FALSEHOODS

A final and ubiquitous form of abuse occurs when journalists, through accident, ignorance, or design, report what can be charitably described as *falsehoods*. In some cases, the journalist is the source of the false information. For example, on September 28, 1980, the *Washington Post* published a front-page story titled "Jimmy's World." Written by *Post* reporter Janet Cooke, it featured the plight of an eight-year-old heroin addict she called "Jimmy." The following April, after the story had been awarded a Pulitzer Prize for local news reporting, it was discovered that little "Jimmy" did not exist.

Six years later, Cooke's editor Bob Woodward created his own example of the genre. In his 1987 book *Veil*, which was excerpted for a front-page series in the *Washington Post*, Woodward described a dramatic bedside interview in Georgetown University Hospital with former CIA Director William Casey, in which Casey supposedly admitted his complicity in the Iran-Contra scandal. However, Woodward has never offered any cogent explanation of how he was able to gain access to Casey, whose family maintained a constant vigil at his bed in a room guarded twenty-four hours a day by the CIA. Nor has Woodward explained how he was able to conduct an interview with a dying man suffering from severe aphasia and therefore physically incapable of communicating with anyone.

On television, journalistic falsehoods seem to appear most frequently in historical, scientific, and economic material. For example, a PBS documentary entitled *The Liberators* focused on the history of the 761st Battalion, an all-black tank unit that fought with Patton's Third Army in Europe at the end of World War II. First broadcast on Veterans Day 1992, the documentary credits the 761st with leading Patton's Normandy breakout, relieving the 101st Airborne Division at Bastogne, and liberating the death camps at Buchenwald and Dachau. Although the men of the 761st fought with honor and distinction, these were not among their accomplishments. At first staunchly defended by PBS and its New York affiliate WNET-TV, the film was withdrawn from circulation in February 1993 for a "full review of all the issues raised." The review, completed in September, found there was no evidence the 761st had done what *The Liberators* had portrayed it as having done.

In addition to falsehoods of their own creation, journalists also disseminate the false or misleading claims of other sources. In coverage of foreign affairs, this abuse often takes the form of uncritical reports of hostile propaganda. For example, a brief item on the March 30, 1987, CBS evening newscast reported that

> a Soviet military publication claims the virus that causes AIDS leaked from a U.S. Army laboratory conducting experiments in biological warfare. The article offers no hard evidence but claims to be reporting the conclusions of unnamed scientists in the United States, Britain, and East Germany. Last October, a Soviet newspaper alleged that the AIDS virus may have been the result of Pentagon or CIA experiments.

CBS clearly did not bother to check the accuracy of the story. If it had, it would have found that the story had been exposed by the State Department five months before as part of a Soviet disinformation campaign. Unfortunately, there is some evidence that a variant of that campaign has succeeded. Reports that AIDS was created and spread by U.S. government agencies as part of a genocidal plot against minorities are common in some segments of the minority press, and fragmentary poll data suggest that as many as 30 percent of black inner-city residents believe them. Some of these reports cite the 1987 CBS story as a source.

In coverage of domestic affairs, the most common falsehoods are the advocacy data generated by the ubiquitous "studies" conducted by special interest groups to influence public opinion and public policy. For example, in 1982 the late home-

In addition to falsehoods of their own creation, journalists also disseminate the false claims of other sources. In coverage of foreign affairs, this abuse often takes the form of uncritical reports of hostile propaganda.

less advocate Mitch Snyder used an informal survey of urban shelters to estimate that the total number of homeless could reach 3 million by 1983. By all accounts, this is a grotesquely exaggerated figure. A 1990 Census Bureau project that deployed 15,000 people nationwide to conduct an actual count of the homeless found a total of 229,000, and no serious study has produced a figure above 700,000. Snyder himself suggested that his estimate was groundless. Testifying before Congress in 1984, he said: "These numbers are in fact meaningless. We have tried to satisfy your gnawing curiosity for a number because we are Americans with Western little minds that have to quantify everything in sight, whether we can or not." Nevertheless, his estimate is still routinely reported in the news media, including recent network newscasts on ABC (December 27, 1992), CBS (December 26, 1992), and NBC (June 10, 1993).

Similarly, on March 26, 1991, the Washington-based Food Research and Action Center (FRAC) announced the shocking finding that an estimated 5.5 million American children under twelve are "hungry" and an additional 6 million are "at risk of hunger." These estimates were derived from what FRAC described as "the most comprehensive childhood hunger study ever conducted in the United States." In reality, that study was grossly and obviously flawed. Its estimates were produced by combining the findings of seven small, local surveys conducted by hunger advocacy groups and projecting the results to the nation as a whole. Worse, its definition of hunger had nothing to do with physical malnutrition and was construed so broadly that almost

any family living on a budget would be classified as at least "at risk of hunger." Nevertheless, a recent study has found that the FRAC estimates were reported by ABC, CBS, PBS, *Newsweek*, all of the major wire services, and thirty-six of the forty largest daily newspapers in the country. Further, the coverage was not merely favorable but often exaggerated the findings. For example, Dan Rather introduced the study—which was the lead item on the March 26 CBS evening newscast—with a chilling (and absurd) statement: "A startling number of American children [are] in danger of starving."

The point of these examples is to suggest that much of the supposedly factual information reported by the news media is false or misleading. In some ways, this should not be a very surprising conclusion. In addition to an enormous literature on the problems of contemporary journalism produced by a wide variety of critics over the past twenty-five years, media watchdog groups such as Accuracy in Media and the Media Research Center have documented literally thousands of examples of bias and abuse (including nearly all of those cited here). Further, such distortions have been evident in all media throughout the history of journalism, and their occurrence has long been accepted as part of the price that must be paid for freedom of the press.

On the other hand, given a well-educated, professional corps of journalists ostensibly committed to the most stringent standards of accuracy, fairness, and objectivity, it is reasonable to ask why such gross distortions are common in media coverage and, in the opinion of many knowledgeable observers (including a growing body of concerned journalists), are actually increasing in number. Nor is it easy to understand why these distortions are so seldom acknowledged or corrected.

REASONS FOR THE EROSION IN JOURNALISM'S QUALITY

Although the issues involved are complex, the declining quality of journalistic coverage can be largely attributed to three interconnected factors.

Journalism is the only institution in American society that is routinely exempted from the critical scrutiny of the press.

The first consists of a subtle but profound change in the core values of journalism. Under the older model, which is still the "official" view of the profession, journalists were assigned an essentially passive role in which their principal duty is to provide a factual account of the flow of events and the conflict of ideas. But this view has gradually been replaced over the last three decades by a new "social responsibility" model in which journalists, no longer content to serve as mere conduits of information, have adopted the more active and exciting role of "Champions of the People," whose principal duty is to assist in perfecting society by searching out problems, inequities, and abuses that must be resolved. Unfortunately, this essentially critical posture carries with it the constant temptation to subordinate mere factuality to the seemingly greater good of improving society and a corresponding tendency to judge the quality of reporting primarily in terms of its impact. Thus, it is no accident that the most serious reporting abuses are generally seen in the kind of crusading investigative journalism that typifies the new social responsibility model.

The two remaining factors tend to exacerbate the inherent weaknesses of the new model. Both print and broadcast media have been faced for some years with increasing competition for a dwindling audience. As in the past, this situation has created additional pressures to emphasize the coverage's impact over its quality. It must also be noted that in a world of increasing complexity and specialization, journalists are still educated as generalists. As a result, they often lack the skills and training needed to accurately evaluate the information they receive. These deficiencies become acute as journalists adopt a more active role.

Two additional factors help to explain why journalists so seldom acknowledge or correct their errors. First, the extensive protections afforded to journalists by our society ensure that there are few occasions when anyone has the power to force them to make corrections, and thus they seldom do. The only exceptions occur when a credible lawsuit is filed (as in the *Dateline NBC* incident) or when an error is so widely publicized that such things as credibility or professional standing are placed at risk (as in the case of the Janet Cooke story). But this level of publicity is rare.

Second, the press has gradually evolved into a unitary, closed, and remarkably homogeneous institution made up of individuals bound together by a set of shared professional norms. Among these norms is an implicit but powerful "gentleman's agreement" to the effect that professional journalists should avoid public criticism of their colleagues. As a result, journalism is the only institution in American society that is routinely exempted from the critical scrutiny of the press.

THE LIKELIHOOD OF REFORMS

This analysis suggests that substantial improvements in the quality of reporting are likely only given changes in certain core values and norms of the profession. But there is no evidence that journalists have any desire to make those changes, and they cannot be imposed from without.

However, modest improvements do seem possible. One obvious possibility would be to reform journalism education. If journalists are to function as critics, they should be trained in the critical skills. Foremost among these is the ability to accurately evaluate quantified or statistical research and therefore recognize the flawed advocacy data that underlie so many of the fabrications and falsehoods in the news.

Pending these reforms, the best alternative would be to create an independent, nonpartisan center for research evaluation that could provide journalists with timely and objective assessments of the studies that purport to be newsworthy.

Media Pervasiveness

James F. Hoge Jr.

James F. Hoge Jr., is Editor of Foreign Affairs.

GLOBAL REACH AND PICTURE POWER

The dramatic increase in live television reporting of international crises began just five years ago with the satellite coverage of the Tiananmen square demonstrations. CNN pioneered such real time coverage and other broadcasters adjusted rapidly upon seeing its power. Print journalism also modified its style to intensify emotional and on-the-spot depictions, often at the expense of analysis. These capabilities of modern media to be immediate, sensational and pervasive are unsettling the conduct of foreign affairs. This would be so were the Cold War still underway, but in the shapeless aftermath of a clear-cut superpower rivalry the impact of media's immediacy is magnified. The technology that makes possible real-time, global coverage is truly revolutionary. Today's correspondents employ lap-top computers, wireless telephones that transmit directly to satellites and mobile satellite dishes to broadcast vivid pictures and commentary from the scenes of tragedy and disorder without the transmission delays, political obstructions or military censorship of old.

For policymakers, the nonstop coverage of CNN (also coming in the future from the BBC and others) presents opportunities to constantly monitor news events and disseminate timely diplomatic information. Despite these benefits, politicians are more concerned than elated by global, real-time broadcasting. They worry about a "loss of control" and decry the absence of quiet time to deliberate choices, reach private agreements and mold the public's understanding. They point with nostalgia to how those opportunities helped President John F.

Kennedy respond safely to the discovery of Soviet missiles in Cuba. In an era when satellite intrusiveness was still a government monopoly, Kennedy was able to sustain secrecy for six days of crucial negotiations. Television in 1962 was sufficiently underdeveloped that Defense Secretary Robert McNamara did not turn on a television set during the two weeks of the crisis.

Today's pervasive media increases the pressure on politicians to respond promptly to news accounts that by their very immediacy are incomplete, without context and sometimes wrong. Yet friend and foe have come to expect signals instantly, and any vacuum will be filled quickly by something. Former Secretary of State George Shultz suggests the dilemma in his observation that live television "puts everybody on real time, because everyone is seeing the same thing."

The new norm of responding to crises with immediate statements results in anxious scrambles like that of the U.S. government upon learning of President Boris Yeltsin's closure of the Russian parliament last October. Alerted early in the day to the crackdown, the State Department's upper echelon suspended normal business to focus on what the secretary of state and the president should say on television by 4 p.m. In another era, the diplomatic norm would have been "the less said the better" until far more was known.

THE RIGHT LESSONS

The difficulties of adjusting to this new age, however, are compounded when all manner of problems, with separate causes, are attributed to media pervasiveness. Key among these are an absence of perceivable government strategy and changes in the composition of America. In hindsight, the Cold War provided a gauge for determining the importance of events by how much they affected America's secu-

rity versus that of its superpower rival. The parameters of press coverage tended to be those of the country's foreign policy—the containment of communism and Soviet expansionism. The press was often critical, but of the execution of policy more than the aims.

With the old gauge lost, policymakers and the media alike are struggling to understand the new international order of risks and opportunities. They are doing so with a less attentive audience. The eyes of the American public are focused on domestic problems more than on the dismaying unruliness that so quickly succeeded the euphoria at the end of the Cold War. Surveys such as those done by the Times Mirror Center for the People & the Press document strong public sentiment that the nation earned the right to address its societal ills by having borne the expense of containment for so long.

In the absence of persuasive government strategy, the media will be catalytic.

For policymakers, adjusting to media pervasiveness must start by drawing the right lessons from the chaos of recent years. If policy-makers want to set the agenda and not leave it to the media, they must have an agenda. The existence of policy that can command public support against emotional swings stirred up by television imagery is key. In the absence of persuasive government strategy, the media will be catalytic. This is the process we have witnessed repeatedly of late, when a crisis erupts and, in the absence of any clear statement of interests and threats, the press raises humanitarianism above more concrete national interests as an exclusive justification for action and intervention. The resulting annoyance of policymakers was pointedly expressed in British Foreign Secretary Douglas Hurd's jab at foreign correspondents during a speech last September: "They are founding members of the 'something must be done' club."

The power of pictures has been repeatedly demonstrated in several post–Cold War incidents. In April a hitherto impotent NATO swiftly imposed a limited ultimatum in the Bosnian conflict after a mortar shelling of a Sarajevo marketplace caused horrifying civilian casualties. Observers on the scene questioned why this particular loss of life—no greater than others occurring in Bosnia—led to action against the Serbian siege. In good part, the answer was television. A CNN crew happened to be out and about the city that Saturday morning. National Security Advisor Anthony Lake's "enlargement" speech of last September identified the problem and the antidote: "Public pressure for our humanitarian engagement increasingly may be driven by televised images, which can depend in turn on such considerations as where CNN sends its camera crews. But we must bring other considerations to bear as well: cost; feasibility; the permanence of the improvement our assistance will bring; the willingness of regional and international bodies to do their part; and the likelihood that our actions will generate broader security benefits for the people of the region in question."

The antidote is more easily identified than applied, as illustrated by the response to those television images of the shelling in Sarajevo. Threatened NATO air strikes, while benefiting the city's citizens, provoked major policy uncertainties and may point to the danger of media-driven initiatives. State and Defense Department officials disputed the further applicability of limited intervention. Subsequent air strikes against Serbian positions around the Muslim enclave at Gorazde resolved the question only briefly. For a time the Bosnian Serbs continued shelling and advancing their tanks on the United Nations "safe haven." Next steps—whether toward negotiations or further intervention—remained uncertain.

A similar absence of articulated policy contributed to the public's harsh reaction against continued American involvement in Somalia after 18 U.S. soldiers were killed. In his waning days as president, George Bush reacted to televised pictures of starving Somalians by commit-

ting U.S. armed forces to a limited and supposedly doable assignment of famine relief. When the assignment expanded in the early Clinton administration to include warlord hunting, it provoked a devastating firefight in the streets of Mogadishu. In truth the probability of hostilities was inherent from the beginning. While adversaries were still fighting, no humanitarian operation could remain free of the conflict. And the American public was unprepared to accept casualties where vital U.S. interests were not at stake.

The enduring impression on public attitudes was made by the violent suppression of student demonstrations in Beijing's Tiananmen square. Images of students demanding free expression, of a lone protester facing down a tank, followed by reports of violent repression after the television cameras were barred from the area, drastically altered U.S. opinion, starting at the top. Bush administration press secretary Marlin Fitzwater fingered the media's impact in this 1991 observation, recorded in the *Chicago Tribune*: "We were the first government to respond, labeling it an outrage and so forth, and it was based almost entirely on what we were seeing on television. We were getting reporting cables from Beijing, but they did not have the sting, the demand for a government response that the television pictures had."

Rapidly, American public and political support evaporated for acquiescence to China's expected evolution from economic improvement to political liberalization. Congress, and then candidate Bill Clinton, reacted spasmodically and linked improvement in China's human rights record to continued tariff preferences. One year into his presidency, Clinton realized the tight linkage of those issues threatened to damage a number of U.S. interests. At the deadline for renewing China's most-favored-nation tariff preferences, Clinton substantially decoupled trade and human rights policies. The power of television imagery and the campaign rhetoric it provoked remained to be offset by selling the new realism to the public.

THE WRONG LESSONS

With the passage of time, we are seeing the application of lessons learned by the military from America's first televised war in Vietnam. Many of today's officers

subscribe to the belief that television coverage turned the public against the war, thus undermining the chances for victory. They cite images of bloodied GIS, body bags, indecisive battles and civilian casualties. These lessons, which are influencing the military's media policy, are wrong in important ways.

The American public, in fact, supported the Vietnam War and its "containment" justification for a full five years. Attributing disenchantment to bloody televised images ignores findings that fewer than two percent of television presentations during the war showed any blood. The fact, not the image, of body bags was the important factor. University of Michigan researchers found a positive correlation between the decline of support in specific communities and the number of dead soldiers returned home. (Long before the television age, a similar correlation led to mounting protest in Great Britain against the Boer War.) Support for the Vietnam intervention fell below 50 percent only after President Lyndon Johnson implied in a March 1968 speech that he considered the war unwinnable.

From its understanding of Vietnam came the military's subsequent emphasis on quick resolutions, limited media access and selective release of "smart" weapons imagery. The public, however, will not remain dazzled when interventions become difficult. As in Vietnam, public attitudes ultimately hinge on questions about the rightness, purpose and costs of policy—not television images.

AND ALL THE REST . . .

Media pervasiveness must be put in the context of other societal changes lest its contribution to the difficulties of making post–Cold War policy be overstated. Policymakers must adjust to these fundamental changes, but they cannot do so if they mistakenly blame those complicating effects on the power and practices of the media.

First, there is the much-discussed "inward turning" of the American people. Released from the "nuclear terror" factor, Americans feel free to concentrate on home and neighborhood. Their attention to external problems is hard to get and once obtained is hard to rally behind assertions of leadership. President Clinton, ruefully but not altogether seriously, has envied his predecessors' use of the

Cold War as a battle cry. More seriously, the president has consciously downplayed his involvement in foreign policy to focus "like a laser beam" on the domestic platform that won him the election. Public opinion surveys indeed do confirm a marked lapse in public support for foreign initiatives, except for economic ones that promise jobs. Clinton has paid heed. Trade and economics are the primary subjects around which he has attempted to forge an explicit international strategy.

To attitudinal shifts and presidential disinterest must be added the effects of America's changed economic makeup. Making national foreign policy is complicated by the increasingly specialized stakes in the global economy of the country's regions. Further complexity comes from the pursuit by local and state governments of their parochial and often competing overseas interests. On this intricate economic map must be overlaid changes in the nation's demography. Immigration and birthrate patterns are creating a more pluralistic population. As groups enlarge and prosper, they exert more political pressure on U.S. foreign policy leaders to pay attention to their places of origin. Each issue-based constituency develops well-endowed interest groups to compete for government and media attention.

VOX POPULI

To properly weigh the potential of media pervasiveness for harmful versus constructive effects requires factoring in how the public responds to the media. Image-provoked bursts of public compassion or anger can induce government paralysis or overreaction. It need not be so. Television images usually have a short shelf life, and their emotional effects can be tempered by reason. But that requires political leadership that constructs supportable policy, explains it and knows when to stand fast behind it.

A common bias of informed elites is that the general public's disinterest in world affairs makes it vulnerable to sensationalized media. It is true that the public is inattentive to the fluxes and flows of international affairs when there is no direct security threat. But a sometimes overlooked aspect of media pervasiveness is its ability to quickly inform an audience swollen large in times of crisis. At such moments the massive flow

of information will contain the sound and the unsound, the responsible and the irresponsible. In an information-rich society, the public develops intuitive skills for parsing information and its sources. Readers and viewers weigh some, but not all, of it seriously and will listen to leadership skilled in the art of persuasion.

It is an imperfect process and hard for policymakers to manage, particularly when technology is augmenting media capabilities. Citizens and leaders adjust by steps, sorting out and familiarizing themselves with the new. The process has occurred with every major change in communications capability such as photography in the Civil War, the telegraph, telephone, radio and most recently television. Media pervasiveness is disruptive. But, over time it can democratize information, thereby giving the public a greater voice in policy debates.

The unusual and the violent remain basic ingredients of news; discord is recorded, peacefulness is not.

How much and how well are the media informing the public about international affairs? The trends are mixed. During the recent recessionary years, media executives acted on declining public interest to cut back foreign news. Newspapers trimmed space allocated for foreign news and closed or left overseas bureaus vacant. Of late, there are noticeable shifts. Some newspapers are expanding their foreign coverage. The Associated Press, although filing shorter stories for tighter news holes, now has 90 overseas bureaus, and CNN has 20. For both services, these represent the biggest such commitments in their histories. The three main television networks, which still command the largest audiences, also show signs of reconsideration. But it comes after an eight-year period in which the new corporate owners of all three networks drastically reduced the number of full-time overseas correspondents and camera crews. As never before, network news divisions rely on freelance video footage and commentary from foreign stringers, some of whom have dubious connections. When regular correspondents are used, too often they are "parachuted" into the latest strife to

air knowing reports via satellite within hours.

While the means of covering international news are being revolutionized, journalistic practices hew to tradition. The unusual and the violent remain the staples of news. Discord draws attention, while peacefulness goes unrecorded. Issues and places engaging America's interests are covered the most. Newspapers, no longer able to be first with news, still report the "what" of events but the elite ones incorporate the "why" as well. Television showcases violence with inadequate attention to context, giving those who rely on the medium a limited, distorted and unremittingly threatening picture of the world.

SETTING THE AGENDA

In the American system of governance, it is the president who sets foreign policy, with rare exceptions. For the most part, secretaries of State and Defense and security advisors counsel and implement. The news media may influence but mostly follows the politicians' agenda. To sell policy to Congress and the public, a president and his aides must employ the forum of their time. In the world of today and tomorrow that puts a premium on adjusting to media pervasiveness—with all its pitfalls and potential—thorough preparation, considered statements in place of off-the-cuff remarks (a Clinton propensity) and communications training are essential tools of office.

Even then, mistakes or contradictory signals will be aired and immediately assessed by allies and adversaries, all of whom have instant access to globe-straddling media. But public miscues generate a recognition of necessary corrections more quickly than the private errors of traditional diplomacy. Openness might occasionally let secrets out; it will as often make mistakes plain. While buffering sensitive negotiations is more difficult than in J.F.K.'s time, it is still possible.

The problem today is that the management of crises and the attempts at agenda-setting appear confused, uncertain and too reliant on overnight polling results. Remedy can come only from the top, from presidential leadership that clarifies and convinces. Then the odds will improve that the constructive potential of media pervasiveness will outweigh its harmful effects.

The Summer's Top Crime Drama, Continued

Walter Goodman

On display in the opening days of the summer season's hit television crime mini-series, along with the pictures of that 15-inch hunting knife, those splashes of blood on the walkway and O. J. Simpson's head of hair, is the nexus of money, celebrity and power that is driving both the conduct of his case and its treatment by television. The orgy of coverage, already notable in the history of a medium that goes in for orgies, and with plenty more promised, exposes a collusion between television professionals and courtroom professionals that is flattering to neither.

Having gotten past a risibly tedious inventory of evidence (Q. "Item No. 1 contains two bindles of hair?" A. "It contains two swatches. But 1C contains a bindle"), the preliminary hearing makes a terrific show.

The trial form is inherently dramatic, of course, and this proceeding has already offered a dog that barked (take that, Holmes!); a man who says he sold a stiletto-type knife to the accused ("He paid with a $100 bill.

He wanted it sharpened."); a mysterious envelope and mysterious tapes (stay tuned), and O. J. Simpson himself listening to the account of the discovery of the bodies of the two people he is accused of killing. Was

---

As the Simpson story moves into court, coverage plays to the crowd.

Simpson the man moved, or was O. J. the performer playing to the camera when his cheek muscle jumped and he looked toward the ceiling and seemed to sigh and took a sip of water offered by Robert L. Shapiro, his lawyer and the author of an article titled "Using the Media for Your Advantage."

(Viewers could not see the pictures of the corpses, since they were purposely positioned out of camera range in the interests of family-friendly television. Would any network have resisted carrying them if they had been available? Possibly

not, but be assured the anchors would have cautioned viewers that something harsh was coming up, which might have been taken as an invitation to more intense watching. Anyhow, with the findings on blood and hair yet to be admitted into evidence, who can turn away?)

So it is audience-grabbing theater, with some instruction in the workings of the law. But is this one of those events of true national significance—on the order, say, of the assassination of President John F. Kennedy or the landing on the moon or the war with Iraq—that demand every bit of television time and talent that can be mustered? By the standards of show business, the hour after hour of the Simpson case on all four major networks plus CNN and Court Television are resoundingly justified; the ratings prove it. But that is precisely the problem for anyone who believes that news standards are or ought to be different from entertainment standards.

If the Simpson saga has not already set a record for air and cable time, it could do so . . . [as] the

(REUTERS/BETTMANN)

Surrounded by camera crews, Robert Shapiro, attorney for O. J. Simpson, is shown arriving at Simpson's preliminary hearing.

preliminary hearings resume. Thus does coverage breed coverage and competition breed redundancy. This lavish expenditure of resources comes from institutions that have cut back on documentaries about matters that may affect viewers' lives long after the Simpson episode has gone the way of the Bobbitt episode. While reducing foreign bureaus, the networks have been investing in news magazines, most of which have lately been providing weekly updates on O. J. & Company. You can't tell one from another, except for the faces that front them, and it is not always easy to tell a television news magazine from a television tabloid.

The expenditure of news talent is prodigious. All the famous personages are contributing their presences and prestige to the occasion, pausing during longueurs to discuss in earnest tones the impact of their saturation coverage on any trial that may yet occur. These are people who are hauled out on ceremonial occasions to personify the more responsible side of television. Many are invited to speak at college graduations or at journalism schools, where they may instruct the young that television news does its duty when it

draws attention to consequential happenings that may otherwise be insufficiently understood, not when it succumbs to the hour's sensation.

And gathered around them are troops of experts: defense lawyers, former prosecutors, forensic specialists, DNA researchers, professors of this and that. Any millionaire trying to hire a legal team in Los Angeles or New York will just have to wait until

---

A newspaper can still outbid a television show in the venality stakes.

---

the show is over. These eminences do not come cheap, and you can feel sympathy for Jose Camacho, the knife salesman who sold his story to The National Enquirer for a paltry $12,500. At least Mr. Camacho, who seemed very embarrassed on the stand, had some information to peddle; the unembarrassable experts are trading in speculation.

(Print journalists may take satisfaction from the revelation that a newspaper can still outbid a television show in the venality stakes, "Hard Copy" not having offered Mr.

Camacho as much as the Enquirer: Q. "You wanted to sell your story to the highest bidder, right?" A. "Sure." Why Mr. Camacho, one of several witnesses who brought a flavor of the city to the courtroom, shared the money with his two bosses, keeping only a third for himself, remains unexplained, or maybe it explains why they are bosses and he is a salesman.)

When it comes to big names known to television viewers, the defense is right up there with the networks. No doubt Alan Dershowitz and F. Lee Bailey were chosen for their legal acumen, but in the contest now going on, instant national recognition cannot hurt. (Mr. Dershowitz has reportedly been muzzled for the time being, and one observer suggested that he was hired to shut him up, but the name carries weight with the audience.) The rules in behalf of the defense in criminal trials, so admirable when the defendant is a down-and-outer with a court-appointed lawyer, take on a perverse aspect when he is rich as O. J. Simpson.

A law-school dean assists Mr. Shapiro in cross-examination, and you can be sure that any expert proffered by the prosecution, like the lightly credentialed city employee who testified about the quantity of blood and number of hairs needed for testing, will be countered by the world's leading expert on such arcana, the man with a 50-page curriculum vitae who helped write the book on which the prosecution witness relies. (Last week the impression was left that the great expert's current opinion on hair swatches or bindles or follicles was different from what his book says, but it is a sorry expert who cannot come up with a plausible explanation for any such discrepancy.)

The experts recruited by the networks and the experts recruited by the defense make a mighty high-profile, high-powered cast. Their connection with previous television spectaculars, bearing names like Menendez, Brando, von Bulow and Tyson, are mentioned by television reporters with a kind of awe. It's a tube-happy world. The famous knife was apparently bought during a break from the filming of a television pilot. A witness brought on to help establish the time of the murder explained that he walks his dog each evening between the Dick Van Dyke show and the Mary Tyler Moore show. When Peter Jennings announces an intermission for lunch in Los Angeles, he reminds viewers that "General Hospital" can be seen in its entirety.

Prosecution and defense traded charges of grandstanding.

As for the prosecutors, making their debut on the nation's screens in the biggest legal extravaganza of all time, they find themselves in the attractive role of underdog, which could yet work to their advantage. And even if their case goes the way of so many prosecution cases in Los Angeles, they should have lucrative futures as defense lawyers or, even better, television experts.

Perhaps the courtroom surprises tossed in by the defense, like the mysterious envelope (big enough to contain a hunting knife) and the mysterious tapes, would have been produced in a similar way even if no camera were operating, but commentators suggested that these were flourishes for the audience, including the people who will sit on the jury for any trial. Prosecution and defense traded charges of grandstanding.

Whatever anyone's intentions, the lavish coverage compels all parties to play to the crowd, just as the crowd compels the lavish coverage. With the adversaries in an exhibitionist alliance, the silent Mr. Simpson aside, it's almost an all-win game: networks are getting good ratings; the defense team, the prosecutors, the experts, the witnesses, even the municipal court judge can expect to benefit from their hours on screen, and America has a choice of six or so channels on which to enjoy the revels.

As for sure losers, there are only one's hopes of what television news might be and dreams of what a fair trial ought to be.

Old News Is Good News

BILL MOYERS

Bill Moyers is a well-known analyst for PBS.

LONG A KEEN OBSERVER OF AMERICA'S CULTURAL AND POLITICAL WARS, BILL MOYERS SPEAKS HERE ABOUT THE DANGER HE SEES IN THE BLURRING OF THE LINE BETWEEN ENTERTAINMENT AND "STRAIGHT" NEWS.

Mine is the reporter's perspective—one small fish in that vast ocean we call the media. I want to put in a word for the craft, for reporting, the old-fashioned kind.

When I began working for *Harper's* in 1970, I thought I understood what the word "news" meant, where information stopped and entertainment began; what newspapers did that was different from television. Since then, we have witnessed a media explosion, the effect of which is like standing at ground zero seconds after the explosion of the atomic bomb. Walter Lippmann told us that journalism is a picture of reality people can act upon. What we see today is a society acting upon reality refracted a thousand different ways.

Where is America's mind today? It's in the organs, for one thing. Now folks can turn on a series called *Real Sex* and watch a home striptease class; its premier was HBO's highest-rated documentary for the year. Or they can flip over to NBC News and get *I Witness Video.* There they can see a policeman's murder recorded in his cruiser's camcorder, watch it replayed and relived in interviews, complete with ominous music. Or they can see the video of a pregnant woman plunging from a blazing building's window, can see it several times, at least once in slow motion. Yeats was right: "We have fed the heart on fantasies, and the heart's grown brutal from the fare."

I wonder if *Real Sex* and *I Witness Video* take us deeper into reality or insanity? How does a reporter tell the difference anymore in a world where Oliver Stone can be praised for his "journalistic instincts" when he has Lyndon Johnson tell a cabal of generals and admirals: "Get me elected and I'll get you your war."

Rolling Stone dubs all this the "New News." Straight news—the Old News by *Rolling Stone's* definition—is "pooped, confused, and broke." In its place a new culture of information is evolving— "a heady concoction, part Hollywood film and TV, part pop music and pop art, mixed with popular culture and celebrity magazines, tabloid telecasts, cable and home video." Increasingly, says the magazine, the New News is seizing the function of mainstream journalism, sparking conversation and setting the country's social and political agenda. So it is that we learn first from Bruce Springsteen that the jobs aren't coming back. So it is that inner-city parents who don't subscribe to daily newspapers are taking their children to see the movie *Juice* to educate them about the consequences of street violence; that young people think Bart Simpson's analysis of America more trenchant than many newspaper columnists; that we learn just how violent, brutal and desperate society is, not from the establishment press, but from Spike Lee, Public Enemy, the Geto Boys and Guns N' Roses.

Walter Lippmann told us that journalism is a picture of reality people can act upon. What we see today is a society acting upon reality refracted a thousand different ways.

From *New Perspectives Quarterly*, Vol. 9, No. 4, Fall 1992, pp. 35-37. © 1992 by the Center for the Study of Democratic Institutions. Reprinted by permission.

The Politics of Culture

JANN WENNER

Editor and publisher of Rolling Stone *magazine, Jann Wenner has had his hand on the pulse of America's cultural scene for a quarter century. Since his magazine took a direct hit in Bill Moyers' critique of the media, we asked him to respond to charges that publications such as his contribute to the decline of Western civilization.*

Around the world and in our own country, the battles being waged have more to do with culture than with politics. Mainstream media in the U.S. ignored cultural news throughout the 1960s and '70s, yet it has been the cultural events of those years — changing sexual and family values, growing cynicism and alienation among the young, ethnic and cultural tensions, etc. — that have come to define the political values of the '90s in the U.S.

The so-called "entertainment media" have been following these changes all along. In fact, *Rolling Stone* was founded on the premise that cultural news was important political news. We saw early on that cultural, artistic and, ultimately, political styles all take shape in the popular-culture cauldron.

People can debate high-brow versus low-brow culture, or rail against the entertainment media's frivolity. But the fact remains that though rap and riots, sexual roles and family values are finally being covered in the traditional press, all these issues were explored much earlier, in much greater depth and with more feeling in the entertainment media.

The mainstream press is now having to play catch-up, and it's going to be an uphill battle because it has for so long misinformed the public by misreading what's really on people's minds. Worse, they have repeated the most fallacious remarks by politicians about what's really at stake in this country, without examining those remarks — which, by the way, is the role the great newspapers *used* to play so well.

In a way, the traditional press is coming full circle. After years and years of missing the story and losing its readership, this political season the press — particularly *The New York Times* and *Newsweek* — have really focused on the issues. They have gone into great depth on economic issues and they are no longer allowing politicians to make statements that are merely repeated and left unchallenged.

Television coverage, on the other hand, continues to be abysmal. With regard to the Democratic and Republican conventions this summer, the television anchors and reporters simply stood in the way of what TV does best, which is to present the news unfiltered. During both conventions, talking heads focused on the technicalities of speeches and how they were delivered rather than what was said. A very limited number of people actually had anything valuable to add to the political proceedings. Certainly no one needed a pompous Dan Rather telling them what was going on. These "personalities" need to get out of the way and let Americans see and judge the political process for themselves.

DE-MASSIFYING THE MEDIA | No one should lament the fact that a decentralization and defusion of news has taken place. Such a change does not mean that we will now depend on *Us Magazine* to tell us about economic issues, or Bart Simpson to enlighten us about foreign affairs. It's not an either/or proposition. Pure political reporting is extremely important and cannot be replaced. But I daresay that these days Bart Simpson is more attuned to the American people's cynicism about the values and priorities of this country than any number of other programs that are on the air.

As news outlets have decentralized — through cable and alternative press publications — there has also been an integration of cultural and political news. It seems that the mainstream media have finally realized that they cannot understand the workings of this country unless they understand the politics of culture. This integration of cultural and political news — the trend so many journalistic purists lament — is a welcome change, as far as I'm concerned. Such admixing — think of *Murphy Brown,* Ice T, or Oliver Stone's *JFK* on the "entertainment" side — has given access to those whose voices and perspectives were rarely heard in the traditional press but whose critiques of American values and priorities are shared by millions of people. Whether the issue is police brutality, single-parenthood or government cover-ups, it has often been the "entertainment media" that has pushed the debate onto America's political agenda.

I don't want to seem a moralist. The public often knows what's news before we professionals do. But there's a problem: In this vast pounding ocean of media, newspapers are in danger of extinction. I don't mean that they're going to disappear altogether—but I do feel that we are in danger of losing the central role the great newspapers have historically played in the functioning of our political system.

Once newspapers drew people to the public square. They provided a culture of community conversation. The purpose of news was not just to represent and inform, "but to signal, tell a story and activate inquiry." When the press abandons that function, it no longer stimulates what the American philosopher John Dewey termed "the vital habits" of democracy—"the ability to follow an argument, grasp the point of view of another, expand the boundaries of understanding, debate the alternative purposes that might be pursued."

I know times have changed, and so must the newspapers. I know that while it's harder these days to be a reporter, it's also harder to be a publisher, caught between *Sesame Street* and Wall Street— between the entertainment imperatives that are nurtured in the cradle and survival economics that can send a good paper to the grave.

I sense we're approaching Gettysburg, the moment of truth, the decisive ground for this cultural war—for publishers especially. Americans say they no longer trust journalists to tell them the truth about their world. Young people have difficulty finding anything of relevance to their lives in the daily newspaper. Non-tabloid newspapers are viewed as increasingly elitist, self-important and corrupt on the one hand; on the other, they are increasingly lumped together with the tabloids as readers perceive the increasing desperation with which papers are now trying to reach "down-market" in order to replace the young readers who are not replacing their elders.

Meanwhile, a study by the Kettering Foundation confirms that our political institutions are fast losing their legitimacy; that increasing numbers of Americans believe they are being dislodged from their rightful place in democracy by politicians, powerful lobbyists and the media—three groups they see as an autonomous political class impervi-ous to the long-term interests of the country and manipulating the democratic discourse so that people are treated only as consumers to be entertained rather than citizens to be engaged.

That our system is failing to solve the bedrock problems we face is beyond dispute. One reason is that our public discourse has become the verbal equivalent of mud wrestling. The anthropologist Marvin Harris says the attack against reason and objectivity in America today "is fast reaching the proportion of a crusade." America, he says, "urgently needs to reaffirm the principle that it is possible to carry out an analysis of social life that rational human beings will recognize as being true, regardless of whether they happen to be women or men, whites or blacks, straights or gays, Jews or born-again Christians." Lacking such as understanding of social life, "we will tear the United States apart in the name of our separate realities."

Taken together, these assumptions and developments foreshadow the catastrophe of social and political paralysis. But what's truly astonishing about this civic disease is that it exists in America just as a series of powerful democratic movements have been toppling autocratic regimes elsewhere in the world. While people around the globe are clamoring for self-government, millions of Americans are feeling as if they have been locked out of their homes and are unable to regain their rightful place in the operation of democracy. On the other hand, those same millions want to believe that it is still in their power to change America.

The Center for Citizen Politics at the University of Minnesota reports that beneath America's troubled view of politics "is a public that cares very deeply about public life. This concern is a strong foundation for building healthy democratic practices and new traditions of public participation in politics."

People want to know what is happening to them, and what they can do about it. Listening to America, you realize that millions of people are not apathetic; they want to signify; and they will respond to a press that stimulates the community without pandering to it; that inspires people to embrace their responsibilities without lecturing or hectoring them; and that engages their better natures without sugarcoating ugly realities or patronizing their foibles.

> Once newspapers provided a culture of community conversation. When the press abandons that function, it no longer stimulates what the American philosopher John Dewey termed "the vital habits" of democracy.

The Power of Images

We tend to accept pictures as the most objective reflection of reality; after all, a photo does not lie. But, as Richard Nixon has pointed out, while a picture does not lie, it may not tell all the truth.

When an interview subject is shot dwarfed behind a huge desk, or against an unflattering background, an editorial comment is being made. When heroes are shown composed and calm and enemies are shown frowning, agitated, and nervous, editorial comments are being made. Most of us can go through boxes of family photographs and find some we like and many we find unflattering, having frozen an expression that was fleeting in reality but seemingly characteristic when captured on film. The choice of images used by news media, some of which are used over and over, taps into powerful affective responses on the part of news audiences.

Technically, pictures can lie, or at least mislead, and we frequently see examples of their doing so. A blue-screen or chromakey process allows television weather reporters to stand in front of a blank blue screen, while their maps are photographed by a different camera. Television cameras translate colors into red, blue, and green chromiance channels for transmission; thus, masking out the blue channel leaves a "hole" behind the announcer that is filled in by the second camera's image when the two shots are superimposed. (If the announcer should be wearing a jacket in the same clear blue that reads exclusively on the blue chromiance channel, her or his body will also disappear.) The forecaster watches television monitors hidden at the sides of the blue background, which allows sweeping gestures in the general area of temperatures or isobars shown on the map. In truth, he or she is not in front of a map at all.

A similar process called rotoscoping, in which computers black out designated parts of photographs, allowed a 1991 Diet Coke commercial to show Humphrey Bogart, Louis Armstrong, and James Cagney hanging out in a 1990s nightclub. Rotoscoped images from old movies, with the backgrounds removed, were stripped into contemporary scenes shot with stand-ins, photographed with the same lenses and lighting, and painted by computer (or colorized) to blend in. George Lucas's Industrial Light & Magic, a company founded in 1975 to design the special effects for the movie Star Wars, has pioneered a process called digital composing or "morphing" (for metamorphoses) in which film images are reduced to numerical codes that can be manipulated by computer. One image can melt into another, as when the liquid metal man took on different identities in the Terminator 2 movie, or when people of different genders and races melted into one another in Michael Jackson's video Black and White.

This kind of photo magic is not seen in news reporting; however, digital technology makes more subtle manipulations both easy and tempting (see "Photographs That Lie: The Ethical Dilemma of Digital Retouching"). It is not uncommon to remove unattractive backgrounds or unwanted people to make a photo ready to grace the cover of a newsmagazine. A news reporter, broadcasting in front of a blue screen, can appear to be presenting first-hand accounts of an event superimposed behind her or him. Reenactments of events not actually captured by a photojournalist are labeled as such, but often photographed in a grainy, awkwardly composed style similar to what might have been captured by a hidden camera. Audiences may be informed that the images are staged, but their apparent reality carries the same impact and credibility of any other picture. News crews outside the studio with a single camera may concentrate on shooting an interview subject, then later shoot "cut-ins" of the interviewer asking the questions that are edited into the final footage. The possibility exists that differences in inflection, or subtle differences in wording the questions, can alter the way the responses are interpreted. Reporters on television's "60 Minutes" have been accused of intentionally altering the context of a subject's remarks through this process.

Early filmmakers quickly discovered the impact of relational cutting, an editing process that affects audiences' responses and adds implied meanings to a story. Serial images are interpreted in combination rather than separately. When shots of a happy group of kids at a birthday party are intercut with shots of a sad and lonely child, the joy of the birthday celebration is interpreted in conjunction with the sadness of the child who is left out. Similarly, news coverage of the president at a posh golf course followed by footage of striking workers or homeless children can—intentionally or unintentionally—communicate symbolic meanings to viewers.

Sometimes photojournalists or news editors take certain liberties in providing images that capture the essence of what was felt in observing an event. As early as the Civil War, Alexander Gardner's battlefield photos were enhanced with the addition of bodies when woodcuts were made for printing. Although he denied restaging the event, it is commonly believed that Joe Rosenthal's Pulitzer prize-winning photo of marines raising the flag over Iwo Jima was of a reenactment, using an 8-foot by 4-foot flag to replace the smaller one that was planted first.

Obviously, the symbolism of the picture struck a chord—the moment portrayed (large flag and all) was sculpted into a Washington, D.C. monument. Photographer Eddie Adams' 1968 footage of the police chief of Saigon killing a captive Viet Cong officer was aired on American television with a gunshot from a sound effects record edited in to enhance the effect. Adams has always felt uncomfortable that the drama of the gunshot was used in place of an explanation that placed the action in context. The ultimate interpretation of the image was that America was supporting a decadent South Vietnamese regime, not that the act might have been justified. Some critics argue that this was precisely what was intended by liberal journalists with an antiwar agenda.

Earlier in this century, social reformers Jacob Riis and Lewis Hine were instrumental in moving Americans to action through their dramatic photographs of the conditions in immigrant tenements and of children at work in terrible conditions in factories, mines, and mills (a fact widely denied by employers). Dorthea Lange, Arthur Rothstein, and Walker Evans portrayed the human toll of the Great Depression in photographs that today remain the impression held in the minds of those who were not then alive. More recently, Alon Reininger's intimate photographs of the devastation wrought by AIDS have helped put a face on the disease, and the future of law enforcement was surely affected by what a video camera recorded of the 1991 police interaction with Rodney King in Los Angeles.

Selection, composition, editing, and technical effects combine to affect the meanings derived from photographic images. Pictures speak to us more loudly than words. They are an essential element of the news media's ability to communicate to mass audiences. But their messages are often felt more than interpreted, and they must be understood to be an extension of the subjective eye behind the lens.

Looking Ahead: Challenge Questions

If photographs draw their power from emotional more than intellectual interpretation, how can the choice of news photographs influence the course of history?

Are there different standards for appropriateness when using video in court (such as in the Rodney King trial) versus using segments from the same video in news reports of court proceedings?

What ethical dilemmas are posed by digital retouching of photographs? If your wedding photographs catch you with a bad hairstyle, would it be appropriate to have them retouched? What about digitally taking off your or your spouse's extra 20 pounds? Or digitally taking off the president's extra 20 pounds before putting him (or her) on the cover of *Newsweek*? What constitutes ethical use of digital technology?

WHAT THE JURY SAW DOES THE VIDEOTAPE LIE?

MICHAEL B. ROSEN

Michael B. Rosen is Associate General Counsel at Boston University.

With the videotape as evidence what more was needed? The beating of Rodney King was seemingly fortuitously captured by an amateur's use of his video camera. The videotape (or portions) were shown repeatedly on national television. After a lengthy trial of the police officers, the jury's verdict: acquittal. The national response to the verdicts: condemnation, outrage, and anger. Even President Bush decried the verdicts: "What you saw and I saw on the TV video was revolting. I felt anger. I felt pain." In Los Angeles, the anger fueled riots.

ABC-News reporter Dave Maresh tried to raise a question about the video itself:

"What George Holliday's video camera saw seemed as clear-cut as black and white: Rodney King suffering a merciless beating at the hands of Los Angeles police officers. . . . Video looks so real, so capable of bringing all of the sorrow and destruction of a riot scene right into your living room. But is it real? The most basic question of all and the hardest for viewers to answer."

The question that defied answer for many was how a verdict of acquittal could have been reached if the jury had seen the videotape. Was the jury racist? Was the prosecution inept? But the leading nature of the question is the assumption or premise that the videotape was clear and convincing evidence, beyond a reasonable doubt, of a beating rather than of police using reasonable force to subdue a potentially dangerous individual. Put another way, perhaps the most important question is whether television, through the medium of videotape, is—or should be—taken at face value in court.

In the Rodney King case, the videotape was shown over

and over again, including slow motion and stop-frame, and was used by defense counsel as well as by the prosecution as evidence in support of the positions being advocated.

The fact that the Rodney King beating was captured on videotape may have been unusual. But the planned or serendipitous videotaping of "live" events as evidence to both public opinion or a jury in a court of law will become increasingly commonplace. A noted litigator on issues involving the press, Floyd Abrams, states:

"The whole notion of how our society is changing because of these new cameras and the proliferation of the cameras is really a stunning one. For the first time in our history, we have people who don't work for the press, who don't work for the police, being the ones first on the scene."

As a medium for communicating emotional and evocative images, photography has a power that human, "live" testimony often lacks. As more accidents, crimes, arrests, or political demonstrations are captured by amateur or professional videocamera operators, will this improve the accuracy of court verdicts?

The basic story of the Rodney King case is familiar: A motorist — often minority — engages in some traffic infraction, major or minor. When asked to pull over by police, he fails to do so and a chase ensues. Other police officers join the case. The motorist is finally stopped and arrested. Between the time he is stopped and the time he is brought before a magistrate and charged with a crime, he has suffered serious bodily injury. The motorist charges that he has been beaten by the police after he was stopped. The police ascribe any injuries of the motorist to reasonable force used to subdue a potentially dangerous and violent person.

From the police viewpoint, a driver who has refused to stop when ordered to do so by police and has then endangered himself and others by driving away, often at high speed, represents a risk to the public's safety until the individual is in police custody. Having already shown a willingness to place others at risk by engaging in an attempt to drive away from the police, the motorist is an unknown risk to the police. Does he have a gun? Will he attempt to use violence to avoid being arrested? The use of *reasonable force* to place the individual in restraint and insure that he has no weapon is proper police procedure. If attacked or threatened by the motorist, the police may under appropriate circumstances even use *deadly force* to protect their lives or the lives of others.

But to many people, the issue is whether police have used excessive force to administer a "punishment" to the driver who was foolish enough to try to drive away. Frequently the above scenario is played out before no witnesses other than the immediate participants.

But in Rodney King's case there was an unexpected witness: the videocamera. Unknown to any of the participants, George Holliday used his videocamera to photograph and record some of the incident after the chase had stopped. The

81-second videotape segment was shown on nationwide television and what might have been a depressingly familiar story — motorist who led police of high speed chase alleges he was beaten by police — became a national outrage of documented police brutality.

The video segment shown on television — or the portions of the segment that found air time — appeared to show police officers raining blows with their batons on a helpless Rodney King who was either kneeling or lying on his face. Did the video lie? Regardless of one's opinion about the outcomes in the Rodney King case, the acceptance of video as virtual reality must be examined.

THE MIRROR WITH A MEMORY

In its infancy, photography was limited to still lifes. In the 1830s, in order to make a living while attempting to promote commercially his invention of the telegraph, Samuel F.B. Morse opened a portrait studio in New York, utilizing the latest methods of the master, Daguerre. But the rigors of the subjects having to sit from ten to twenty minutes, out of doors, on the roof of a building, in the full sunlight or indoors using mirrors to reflect the sunlight usually resulted in portraits with the eyes shut (or tears streaming down the cheeks). The photographic venture was unsuccessful for Morse and he was forced to close his studio (fortunately, the telegraph proved more successful). It was not until the year 1840 that John William Draper, a professor in New York, succeeded in taking the first known photographic portrait in which the subject's eyes were *open* — an amazing achievement for the time.

As photography became quicker and more portable, the ability of photographs to capture eloquently and movingly the drama of actual events was demonstrated by the photographic record of war. From Roger Fenton's "Valley of the Shadow of Death" in the Crimea in the 1850s to the photographs of Union and Confederate dead at Fredericksburg, Antietam, and Gettysburg by Mathew Brady, Alexander Gardner, and Timothy O'Sullivan, photography became evidence: a record of apparent objectivity.

Perhaps the power of the photograph lies in the fact that it is presented as an objective image of life but at the same time is known to be a partial and limited view, a snapshot, a frozen portion of time. The bodies lie before our eyes on the road to Antietam. That they are dead is assumed. We do not know how they died, but the fact of their death is the inescapable truth, more powerful than the verbal account of an eyewitness could ever be.

Still photographs are accepted routinely as evidence in ordinary life and in the courtroom. The ease with which they are accepted may stem from the fact that once they are authenticated by the photographer or witness who vouches for the accuracy of the representation contained in the photograph, they are *actual evidence*. But because they are limited in time, they are not self-explanatory. As in Alexander Gardner's famous photo of the dead at Antietam, we know only that they are dead, not how they died.

The transition from still photographs to videotape or other moving pictures does not always convince. Simply because the videocamera or motion picture camera can capture many still photos in succession does not mean that in viewing the multiple sequenced photos that make up a film we are convinced that we have seen all that there is to see. With the still photograph we know there is more beyond the lens.

Indeed, the carnage of the American Civil War had an unintended research by-product that led to the development of motion pictures: with amputation the usual surgery for wounds to limbs, the need for artificial legs that would actually enable a person to walk led a prominent Boston physician, Dr. Oliver Wendell Holmes (the father of the jurist) to put together in sequence photographs of people walking in order to capture with precision how human limbs move and bend when humans walk. Writing in the *The Atlantic Monthly* in 1863, Holmes said of his discovery that by using the "instantaneous photograph" in sequence, the actual motion of "human locomotion" could be studied. What Dr. Holmes called "the mirror with a memory" would soon be pushed to new uses.

E.J. Muybridge used multiple cameras to record a horse's gait. His photographs astounded conventional wisdom and showed that a horse's actual gait was totally different from that normally assumed and shown in paintings. The *Scientific American* in 1878 printed eighteen drawings taken from Muybridge's photographs and instructed its readers that if the illustrations were pasted on a strip and mounted on a topless drum known as a *zoetrope*, by rotating the drum, "the actual motions" of the horse could be seen. In 1880, Muybridge used a similar device to project the "motion pictures" onto a screen.

By 1893, the inventions by George Eastman of continuous film and Thomas A. Edison's patented camera for "taking a large number of photographs of a moving object in such a manner that any two successive pictures are almost identical in appearance" (U.S. Patent No. 403, 534) and his "apparatus for exhibiting photographs of moving objects" (U.S. Patent No. 493, 426) formed the basis for motion pictures.

Edison's own description in the 1893 patent of the projector made clear that he understood that it is the illusion of motion that is recorded and played back: "a single composite picture is seen by the eye, said picture giving the impression that the object photographed is in actual and natural motion."

Videotaped evidence is fine as far as it goes. If we want to see a witness testify so that we can judge his facial expressions and mannerisms as he speaks and he cannot be in court, a videotape of his statement can provide the missing factors. But when the events in question are in dispute, the videotape record is not unambiguous. It may be objective in that it

records what it was focussed upon. But without information as to the events beyond the lens, the record on the videotape is not self-explanatory.

THE MARION BARRY CASE

"They had the mayor using cocaine on video but it showed the theory of entrapment that the defense wanted to show." ABBE LOWELL, *former special assistant to the Attorney General and currently a Washington, D.C., attorney.*

U.S. District Judge Thomas Penfield Jackson, who presided over the trial in 1990, of Washington, D.C., Mayor Marion Barry, told a law school symposium that he had been disappointed that the jury did not convict "Barry of the more serious charges because he had "never seen a stronger government case." Key to the evidence as to one of the charges on which Barry was acquitted was an 80-minute videotape, made by secret camera installed in the Vista Hotel. The camera was installed by and operated by the FBI. The videotape showed Barry meeting with a woman in a room at the hotel. The fact that Barry smoked cocaine is shown clearly and unambiguously on the videotape. Laboratory reports and other trial testimony established beyond doubt that the substance being smoked was cocaine.

The jury's verdict of acquittal on this count demonstrated the jury's acceptance of the defense of entrapment: when the government goes to the time and expense to prepare for the commission of a crime, including renting the hotel room, providing the crack to be smoked, and having prepositioned camera crews there to film the scene, the defense may or may not establish entrapment as a matter of *law*. In the judgement of the jury the video was evidence of entrapment. Unless Barry could be lured to the set where the lights, camera, film crew and other accessories were ready to record the crime for posterity, and unless, once there, he could be convinced to do that which he may have done repeatedly elsewhere, there would be no movie to show to the jury — and to the nation as snippets on the national news shows.

In the Barry case, the jury listened to the evidence not merely as to what was on the film but to find out what the film showed. The circumstances surrounding the filming and the testimony of the participants all contributed to presenting the visual image in a fuller setting. The jury must have shared Thomas Edison's understanding that the film merely gives the "impression that the object photographed is in actual and natural motion." Having been lured to the hotel room and invited to smoke the crack cocaine, for the jury Barry was not seen in "actual and natural motion." We may all believe that the Mayor of Washington, D.C., should not use controlled substances. But are we prepared to say that the jury made the wrong decision as to the criminal charge on this particular count?

TRUTH OR PROPAGANDA
"One picture is worth a thousand words"

If one picture is worth a thousand words, what is the value of sixteen frames per second? To say that film is propaganda is not to say that what is seen is false. Some of the earliest and greatest propaganda films were those made by and for the Third Reich. The mass rallies showing thousands of Hitler Youth (*Hitlerjungend*), armed with shovels, pledging a frenzied fealty to the Führer, were not imaginary. They actually took place. The young people were not paid actors but fervent devotees of the Nazi cause. The fact that the cameras were rolling and the film taken shows a nation of young and old dedicated to the Führer, and this film could be distributed worldwide, were no accidents — it was often part of the reason for the rallies to be held in the first place.

We have neither time nor space here to explore the range of issues of film and propaganda. Some are discussed elsewhere in this issue in Professor Murray-Brown's article, "Desperate Deception." But in the context of videotape in court, the value of film as propaganda is clear.

The natural affinity of film and trials is immediately obvious to any attorney. If we think of a trial as an attempt by both sides to present a picture of reality, the value of film is apparent. Each side attempts to present to the "trier of facts" (jury, or sometimes a judge) evidence that will convince the trier of facts that one side's picture of the events in question is more believable than the other side's. While we can use euphemisms that the search is for truth, attorneys know that it is persuasion, not truth, that is the job of the attorney. (This is not a statement about the ethics of an attorney. Attorneys are — or are supposed to be — bound by ethical principles that impose obligations about presenting truth and not presenting known falsehoods to the court.) To bring a case to trial is, for the attorney, the effort to present a picture and to attempt to convince the trier of facts to adopt the client's position as the truth instead of the picture that the advocate on the other side will attempt to create. (The burden of and amount of persuasion may vary on a issue. For example, in a criminal case, the prosecution must establish its case "beyond a reasonable doubt." But it is still pictures of reality that must be presented to the jury.)

Increasingly, some savvy trial attorneys prefer the evocative effect of video over "live" testimony from a client to generate sympathy for or understanding of the client's position. In addition to the power that a video may have in showing pain, suffering, and other aspects of a client's life "after the accident," the risk that live testimony may falter can be eliminated. Inter-

viewed on CNN, Washington trial attorney John Coale put it succinctly:

"I'll take a video tape over a live witness any day. Sometimes we videotape on purpose and use that instead of a live witness, because studies have shown and my experience shows that . . . you capture the attention of a jury for a much longer time. It's just better. People are used to watching television. They're not used to evaluating testimony, but they are used to seeing the tube."

A whole jurisprudence has developed over the use of "Day-in-the-Life" videos. Used extensively in personal injury litigation to demonstrate the pain, suffering, and life impairments suffered by the alleged victim, these made-for-court videotapes of the injured person going about, or attempting to go about the tasks of living are often major factors in the jury's award of damages. As Milwaukee attorney J. Ric Gass has written:

"The reason that these videos are prepared is relatively straightforward: they effectively convey selected portions of an individual's life to a jury in a very powerful, extremely memorable and highly credible manner. The use of the graphic video and its typical presentation on a television set makes for a potent combination."

RODNEY KING:
THE TRIAL AND THE VIDEOTAPE

My biases should be made known: I do *not* believe that justice was done in Simi Valley and I believe that after the chase, Rodney King became victim, unlawfully punished by the police.

Most who have formed their opinion about the beating of Rodney King have done so based on the brief portions of the George Holliday videotape they may have seen on television as well as other press coverage. Most people have had neither the opportunity nor reason to examine the videotape with care or to review the trial testimony. It is easy to overlook the fact that much of the evidence at the Simi Valley trial came from sources other than the videotape. Fifty-six witnesses testified over the course of the seven-week trial, including observers (some of whom were police officers) as well as expert witnesses. The videotape (which in fact lasts more than nine-minutes) was shown both at full speed, slow motion, and frame-by-frame to illustrate the actions of the defendants and Rodney King.

It may overstate the obvious, but is has been decidedly unfashionable for any commentator to point out, as did Eric W. Rose and Steven S. Lucas in a nationally syndicated column published the day after the Simi Valley acquittals were announced, that, "for the jury, the videotape was one of many pieces of evidence to evaluate in a complex case. For the public, the videotape was the sole piece of evidence."

The discrepancies between what people thought they saw at

home and the evidence in court has been ably summarized in a controversial article by Roger Parloff in the June 1992 issue of the *American Lawyer*, titled "Maybe The Jury Was Right." Noting that "I can't remember a time when I have ever felt so hesitant to say what I believe," Parloff effectively compares the actual content of the video to the trial testimony to conclude that the Simi Valley jury had a basis for its acquittals.

To understand that video presents ambiguities rather than right and wrong is to remember the function of the jury, a function video cannot replace. We may disagree with the verdict of the jury, but, as Parloff argues meticulously with reference to the actual testimony introduced at trial and its relationship to what the video did and did not show, it is possible to understand the argument that the video supported the defense that the police acted to subdue King, not to punish him.

Those who have seen only the video would not know that it was not disputed that after his car was stopped, King refused to be searched for weapons or be handcuffed, that he danced around and, when two officers attempted to put handcuffs on him, he shook them off and stood up. That is not on the video; as Parloff makes clear, it was essentially uncontradicted testimony.

Those who have seen only the video would not know that Sergeant Koon then ordered King to get on the ground or he would fire a taser dart. He then fired the first dart. He repeated his instructions and warning and, when King did not get down, fired the second dart. That too is not on the video, but as Parloff tells us, is part of the uncontradicted testimony the jury heard.

The video starts after the second dart has hit; instead of being rendered immobile by the darts, King gets fully to his feet and rushes either at or toward Officer Powell. Powell swings his baton and hits King — possibly in the head, possibly in the neck or on the shoulder. The video is not clear. King falls to the ground. With the video out of focus and a car partially blocking the view, the video shows Powell raining blows onto King while King apparently continues to try to raise himself. As Parloff's article points out to an incredulous readership, the *prosecution's expert* on use of force did not find this to be unreasonable force.

King lies on the ground. When he moves or attempts to raise himself, he is hit with blows from the baton, pushed to the ground by an officer's foot, and kicked. It is not clear from the video that any of the baton blows from this point on hit King in the head.

The famous shot of Officer Briseno putting out his hand to stop Officer Powell is seen clearly on the video. Officers Powell and Wind are seen on the video poised over King with their batons, striking him when he attempts to get up, arguably in a least one case, continuing to do so after he is on the ground.

Regardless of how you define the offense, the issue the jury "decided" in Simi Valley was whether these officers should be *convicted of a crime* for using excessive force (and whether the commanding officer, Sergeant Koon, committed a crime by failing to prevent his subordinates from using excessive force). Again, as Parloff points out, what the video can never show and only testimony can present is the mindset of the officers. On many points their testimony was supported both by the video and by other testimony: King had shown a reckless disregard for life by forcing the high-speed chase. King had shown both extraordinary strength and unwillingness to submit peacefully to arrest. King had not been searched and could have been concealing a weapon (in addition to his own physical strength).

It is against that backdrop that the officers' defense went

Students of propaganda should not neglect the poster. In "Persuasive Images: Posters of War and Revolution" (Princeton University Press), authors Peter Paret, Beth Irwin Lewis, and Paul Paret demonstrate the flexibility and power of the medium in wartime. The posters reproduced here all come from the collection of the Hoover Institution of Stanford University. The uses to which the poster was put in wartime were many: to encourage men to enlist, to persuade women on the home front to save materials for the war effort, to inflame the general public toward even more hatred against the wicked foe, to stiffen the resolve of a side facing imminent defeat. There are images based on racism and some silences: the atrocities of the Nazis against the Jews found no expression on posters. There are a few lapses in the text of the book: for a few of the Russian posters, the translation is incomplete or, in one case, wrong (in #145, the Russian does not mean "Take your rifle and hand to the Polish front" but simply "Take your rifle to the Polish front"). Contexts provided for each poster underscore the role propaganda played in its creation and reception. The study of such posters may help to immunize some readers against the power of propaganda. One must be grateful to the compilers and to Princeton University Press for a collaboration that has produced a first-rate example of book-making.

beyond the lens to put a perspective on the video: in showing that King in fact did repeatedly either get to his feet or attempt to get to his feet; in the case of Officer Wind, to show that he never hit King in the head with his baton. The ability of the defense to present a context for the police officers' actions, a context of perceived threat and danger, was sufficient to convince the jury that there was reasonable doubt as to the prosecution's case.

The video did not lie; nor did it present the full story. The jury evidently accepted the argument made by Sargent Koon's attorney that Rodney King was at all times "in control" of the situation: he could have avoided or ended the beating simply by ceasing to resist the arrest.

The argument begs the question. If a police officer shoots a fleeing defendant because he did not stop after the officer has shouted, "Stop or I'll shoot," it may be true that the fleeing defendant was "in control" of the situation and could have avoided being shot if he stopped fleeing. But that does not answer the question as to whether the force used was excessive. The legal right of a police officer to use reasonable force or deadly force is not defined by whether an order has been disobeyed. Rather, the definition goes to the need to use force in the first place. An officer can command the fleeing purse snatcher to stop; he may use reasonable force to apprehend him. But, under principles of American law, he can't shoot and kill the purse thief on the ground that if he didn't the thief would get away. Yet at all times, the purse thief was "in control."

The argument that the person being arrested controls his fate was rejected by the Supreme Court as a justification for the use of deadly force on a nondangerous suspect. It is the police officer who is responsible for the amount of force used, not the suspect. Under the Constitution, according to the Supreme Court, "It is not better that all felony suspects die than that they escape . . . A police officer may not seize an unarmed, nondangerous suspect by shooting him dead." Writing for the majority in a 1985 case, Justice White stated "The use of deadly force is a self-defeating way of apprehending a suspect and so setting the criminal justice mechanism in motion. If successful, it guarantees that the mechanism will not be set in motion." *Tennessee v. Garner*, 471 U.S. 1 (1985).

But the fact that the "in control" argument proves too much is a legal distinction. Whether it was the composition of the jury, the quality of the advocacy, or simply the weight of the evidence, the jury in Simi Valley looked not only at the video but at the larger picture painted by the testimony and other evidence. The jury concluded that under the circumstances the defendant police officers found themselves in that evening, they would not or could not, from the vantage point of hindsight, find the officers guilty of a crime.

The Parloff article does a service by taking the time to show how the jury could have acquitted the defendants. And it is clear that the jury did not ignore the videotape, but relied on it, to confirm a view presented by the defense that the officers, acting out of fear of the unknown, did not use unreasonable force intended to cause "great bodily harm." The jury's hung verdict on the lesser count against Officer Powell *left open* the question as to whether he had unreasonably continued to beat King when it was not "necessary" to do so in order to subdue him.

The issue the American public judged through an inadequate viewing of the video was whether it was necessary to beat and continue to beat Rodney King. The jury in Simi Valley had a bigger picture presented through the seven-week trial and answered a different question. The videotape may be instrumental in "proving" that Rodney King was "in control" in that had he not resisted (or moved from pain and agony from the taser dart and prior blows), he would not have continued to have been beaten. The video shows this clearly. For the jury, that was consistent with the view that the use of force was not criminal.

But for society, the video left unanswered the question of whether police should beat a man who is on the ground every time he tries to get up until he is beaten into submission. Police officials across the country condemned the scenes shown on the video because modern police methods answer that question in the negative.

The media's repetitive showing of snippets of the video contributed to a mass judgement that was to a large extent uninformed by the full content of the video and, as the trial went on, the other evidence at trial. For many, the judgement was made once a portion of the video was seen, and repetition merely reinforced the judgement to the point of certainty. In these circumstances, the jury's verdict defied rational explanation because our collective judgement had already been formed.

When video is used in court, there are controls to prevent misuse, including control of the trial by the presiding judge as well as the natural checks and balances of the adversary system so that misleading use of a video can and will be pointed out by the advocates on the other side. On television we have no such controls and by sheer repetition alone an image is accepted as reality, as appearing to represent the impression that the object photographed is in actual and natural motion.

Videotape as a part of court proceedings is here to stay. We will always have to be vigilant to ensure that we do not mistake this illusion of "actual and natural motion" for the full story of what what lay beyond the lens. And for those concerned with the impact on police work of the proliferation of amateur video cameras, the best and last word belongs to my colleague Dean Edwin Delattre, who works with police across the nation:

"Since the savage beating of Rodney King . . . when working on ethics with police, I am now often asked, 'What should we do about video cameras out there?' The answer is not complex: . . . Do your job the right way, the way you have been trained — use only minimum necessary force and respect the people you serve — and you don't have to worry about cameras."

WHEN PICTURES DRIVE FOREIGN POLICY

Somalia raises serious questions about media influence.

Jacqueline Sharkey

Jacqueline Sharkey is a University of Arizona journalism professor and an award-winning investigative reporter. Christine Stavem and Anita Caldwell contributed research for this report.

THE IMAGES HORRIFIED THE NATION. Americans were stunned as television news programs aired footage of jeering Somalis dragging the body of a dead U.S. soldier through the streets of Mogadishu. Viewers also saw U.S. Army pilot Michael Durant nervously answering questions from his Somali captors, his eyes flicking toward them as he tried to gauge their reactions.

Those who missed the evening news saw the images in their local newspapers, many of which ran photos of the dead and captured Americans on their front pages.

After seeing the pictures, which were first shown on October 4 and 5, thousands of Americans called Capitol Hill to demand that U.S. troops be withdrawn. Newspapers that ran them were deluged with calls and letters from readers who were furious that the pictures had been published.

Members of Congress referred to the pictures—and the resulting calls—in angry speeches exhorting President Clinton to bring the troops home immediately. National security adviser Anthony Lake said the photographs made the president "very angry," and lent "a new urgency" to White House efforts to clarify U.S. policy toward Somalia.

The photographs and the reactions they evoked sparked a nationwide debate about the political and ethical implications of the pictures, and the media's influence on foreign policy.

Government officials, policy analysts and journalists are concerned about the powerful impact that photographs can have on public and congressional opinion. Dramatic images can oversimplify complex issues, commentators say. They fear that emotions raised by the pictures of the dead and captured U.S. soldiers, for example, might overwhelm other political and military factors that the Clinton administration needs to consider regarding Somalia. Some believe the situation is further complicated by the fact that the video footage was shot by Somali stringers whose political sympathies are unclear.

"What sort of policy making is it to have Washington's actions decided, even in part, on the latest affecting pictures on the evening news?" wrote the New York Times' Walter Goodman.

Some analysts, however, believe the photographs illustrate how the media increase the public's participation in foreign affairs by showing the results of governmental decisions.

The pictures "brought home to everybody in this country that something was wrong with the American policy," says Newsday's Patrick Sloyan, who won a Pulitzer Prize for his coverage of the Persian Gulf War and has reported from Somalia.

The photos also raise questions about the role of the media in the post-Cold War world, where the framework for formulating policy—and news coverage—on the basis of the East-West conflict has collapsed.

Diplomats and analysts say the crisis in Somalia, and the way that news organizations have covered it, is an example of the challenges facing the government and the media, at a time when the criteria for defining U.S. interests have not yet been formulated.

The situation is complicated, they say, by the media's capacity for showing real-time images of violence and conflict from any part of the world. This practice can distort public opinion and government priorities. Analysts also are concerned that U.S. coverage often lacks historical and cultural context that could give the public greater—and sorely needed—perspective.

THE PHOTOS FROM SOMALIA are only the most recent example of how visual images can affect foreign policy.

The U.S. public's horror at the on-camera execution of ABC newsman Bill Stewart in 1979 by a Nicaraguan national guardsman helped persuade the Carter administration to withhold support for dictator Anastasio Somoza—a decision that helped the Sandinistas overthrow him.

In the weeks after the Persian Gulf War, the American public's reaction to the pictures of Kurdish women and children killed and wounded by Saddam Hussein's forces as they tried to flee Iraq led President Bush to begin Operation Provide Comfort, sending U.S. forces to protect refugees.

Some commentators believe U.S. policy in Somalia has been driven principally by photographs. They say the pictures of starving children that appeared in the media last year contributed to the decision to send in U.S. forces.

On the day that U.S. troops departed for Somalia last December, retired diplomat George F. Kennan questioned why the American people and members of Congress had accepted President Bush's decision to send American forces to a distant land where the United States had no pressing national security interests.

"There can be no question that the reason for this acceptance lies primarily with the exposure of the Somalia situation by the American media, above all, television," he wrote in his diary, excerpted in the New York Times on September 30.

If U.S. policy, "particularly policy involving the uses of our armed forces abroad, is to be controlled by popular emotional impulses, and particularly ones provoked by the commercial television industry," he continued, "then there is no place...for what have traditionally been regarded as the responsible deliberative organs of our government."

Some journalists believe that view exaggerates the power of television. In responding to Kennan, CBS newsman Dan Rather wrote in a letter to the New York Times that "to give television credit for so powerful an influence is to flatter us who toil there—but it's wrong." Some reporters "may wish for the power to direct public opinion and to guide American policy—but they don't have it."

CNN executive Ed Turner made a similar point on the cable network's "Reliable Sources," which examines media issues.

"It's up to the president and the State Department to conceive policy and execute it, and if somehow we are driving them, then maybe we need some new officials in Washington," he said on the October 10 program.

But New York Times Washington Bureau Chief R.W. Apple Jr. said Turner's idea of how policy is formulated is "a fantasy." The "journalism of

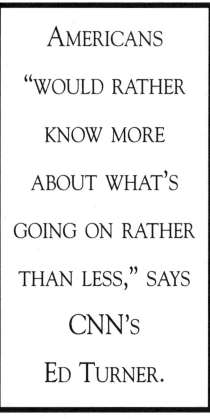

AMERICANS "WOULD RATHER KNOW MORE ABOUT WHAT'S GOING ON RATHER THAN LESS," SAYS CNN'S ED TURNER.

images," Apple said, has always had a "tremendous impact upon public opinion, and public opinion has always had a tremendous impact on government."

Some argue that this relationship has strengthened the democratic process by providing the public with information to evaluate foreign policy decisions.

Author and former New York Times reporter David Halberstam, who won a Pulitzer Prize for his coverage of the Vietnam War, says the image of starving children drove the United States to become more involved in Somalia, and now the pictures of U.S. casualties in Mogadishu have provided a "counterimage" that tells Americans "the price of this involvement."

Toronto Star correspondent Paul Watson says that's one reason he took the photo of the Somali crowd dragging the dead soldier. The photo was distributed in the United States by the Associated Press.

"I think it is important for the people who elect the politicians, and who should decide where their troops go, to know what happens to them," he said in an interview from his home in Johannesburg, South Africa.

CNN's Turner cited similar reasons for his network's decision to run footage of the dead and captured U.S. troops.

CNN had video of one dead soldier, plus that of Durant, shot by a CNN stringer. Video of another U.S. casualty being dragged through the streets had been shot by a stringer for Reuters, whose headquarters is in London.

The American people "have a right to see what their foreign policy is, how their tax dollars are being spent, what's happening to their troops," Turner said on "Reliable Sources." "It's fair and proper that they should understand what this kind of warfare is all about."

Using Foreign Stringers

Some journalists and policy analysts express concern that the footage had been shot by Somalis whose political affiliations were unclear, and who might be vulnerable to manipulation or intimidation.

U.S. news organizations have been relying on Somali personnel since pulling correspondents out of Mogadishu earlier this year, after several journalists were killed and others received kidnaping and death threats.

Former CBS and New York Times newsman Bernard Kalb, who has also worked for the State Department, challenged CNN's use of the videos. "How do we know we can trust the product that is being distributed?" Kalb asked Turner on "Reliable Sources."

"You don't," Turner replied. But he defended CNN's decision to use the footage. "You get this and you don't use it? We're in the job of reporting." Americans "would rather know more about what's going on rather than less."

Turner said in an interview that he didn't know whether the CNN stringer had ties to the clans fighting in Mogadishu, but that the stringer had been reliable in the past.

Reuters Editor in Chief Mark Wood says he presumed the stringer who took the video of the dead U.S. soldier had tribal ties to clan leader Mohammed Farah Aidid, but did not believe that had affected his coverage.

Wood says the stringer, Issa Mohammed, had worked for Reuters as a driver and assistant. When the news service pulled its staffers out, it handed Mohammed a camera and told him to shoot whatever looked important.

His videos have always seemed unbiased, Wood says. All Mohammed's footage has been scrutinized by Reuter personnel in Nairobi, Kenya, and in London because the news agency is aware he is not "a qualified journalist."

"We would rather have had a

skilled cameraman or journalist there," he says, "but having lost three people in one incident, we weren't prepared to risk any more lives."

That doesn't comfort Marvin Kalb, director of the Joan Shorenstein Barone Center on the Press, Politics and Public Policy at Harvard University. He thinks the increasing use of foreign nationals "is one of the more serious problems now facing television news."

Kalb says the networks "hand out camcorders to political activists in different parts of the world" because news departments don't have enough staffers or money to cover the story, or consider the situation too dangerous for U.S. journalists. Viewers don't know whether video from abroad comprises "honest pictures" or "pictures taken for political purposes," he says.

CNN's Ralph Begleiter recalled seeing a story from South Africa in which the black correspondent was an employee of the white minority government, a fact that many viewers did not know. News organizations need to tell the public "more about these people who are providing the news," he told a foreign policy forum sponsored by the Freedom Forum Media Studies Center at Columbia University.

Nevertheless, some journalists think concerns about foreign nationals can be exaggerated. "It's the news quality of the picture that counts," says Newsday's Sloyan. The videos of the dead and captured U.S. soldiers were "clearly taken with all the proper parameters for news photography."

Distorted Picture?

Another concern about the impact of the images on the debate about policy in Somalia is that they may present a distorted view of the situation.

"There is a great success story here that the television pictures don't always show," Rep. Richard Gephardt (D-Mo.) told reporters on October 5. Outside Mogadishu, "the food is being delivered.... There is a lot that has been accomplished."

USA Today senior diplomatic correspondent Johanna Neuman points out that the media had not shown pictures of the thousands of Somalis who had demonstrated in support of the United States after more than a dozen U.S. soldiers were killed during fighting in Mogadishu on October 3.

CNN's Turner acknowledged the lapse, and the network later ran reports about the demonstrations. Many

EVERETTE DENNIS BELIEVES "REAL-TIME COVERAGE IS A DISASTER IN TERMS OF ITS IMPACT ON FOREIGN POLICY."

newspapers ran stories and photos about the positive results of U.S. involvement in the weeks that followed, but it was too late to change many hearts and minds.

Rep. W.J. Tauzin (D-La.) echoed the feelings of many members of Congress when he cited the "ingratitude" shown by Somalis in the photos as a reason to bring U.S. troops home.

But some journalists say this attitude indicates that the Somalia coverage was distorted not by the photographs of the dead and captured U.S. soldiers, but by a lack of pictures that could have provided more context for understanding what happened to the American troops.

"The pictures that we don't have from Somalia are as significant as the pictures that we do have," says Dave Marash of ABC's "Nightline." "There have been a lot of casualties on the Somali side," but Americans seldom have seen photographs of those deaths.

Exaggerated Impact?

Policy analysts say that although the pictures of American casualties have been a catalyst for renewed debate about U.S. policy in Somalia, they have not controlled the discussion.

"Image in and of itself does not drive policy," Marvin Kalb says. "Image heightens existing factors."

These factors, such as the history of the region and chances of achieving clear objectives, have the decisive effect on policy making, Kalb says. He and

others point out the media have carried searing images of the situation in Bosnia for more than a year, but U.S. involvement has been limited to air operations, partly because both the public and government officials regard the situation as a complex ethnic conflict unrelated to immediate U.S. interests.

USA Today's Neuman, who is writing a book about television coverage of war, believes diplomats sometimes use dramatic images as an excuse to cover policy failures.

"I think that policy makers may be too quick to blame the picture or the media drumbeat when the evidence suggests that it's a failure of leadership," she says.

Nevertheless, she and others agree that television has altered forever the way in which foreign policy is formulated and conducted.

U.N. Ambassador Madeleine Albright, testifying about Somalia at a Senate Foreign Relations Committee hearing October 20, said, "Television's ability to bring graphic images of pain and outrage into our living rooms has heightened the pressure both for immediate engagement in areas of international crisis and immediate disengagement when events do not go according to plan. Because we live in a democratic society, none of us can be oblivious to those pressures."

Neuman says despite the drawbacks, communications technology has helped to "democratize information," giving the public a greater voice in policy debates. Television has meant "the end of elitism in diplomacy," she says. Government officials have to "talk to all of us now."

Air Force Reserves Maj. James Callard, who teaches U.S. foreign policy at Fort Lewis College in Durango, Colorado, says this information has given the public an opportunity to reevaluate the principles underlying U.S. foreign policy, including using military force to achieve political objectives.

Callard says the photographs of the dead and captured soldiers in Somalia have led people to ask not only how and where the armed forces will be used overseas, but why. As the public has gotten more access to information about these decisions, it is less willing simply to accept the government's word that the commitment of troops is justified.

Sen. John McCain (R-Ariz.), a prisoner of war during the Vietnam conflict and a leading proponent of a rapid pullout of U.S. forces in Somalia,

WHEN IS A PICTURE TOO GRAPHIC TO RUN?

The irony was chilling. The 22 print and broadcast journalists attending a seminar in early October on ethical decision making at the Poynter Institute in St. Petersburg, Florida, had spent part of the day discussing whether newspapers should run photographs of dead bodies. That night, footage of the dead U.S. soldier being dragged down a Mogadishu street was aired on the evening news.

The video—plus the photograph the next day in the St. Petersburg Times and numerous other newspapers—led seminar participant Phil Record, ombudsman at the Fort Worth Star-Telegram, to organize an informal survey of his colleagues. Twelve said they would have run the picture on page one—six in color and six in black and white. Five would have used it inside in black and white, three would not have used it, one was uncertain and one did not answer.

The hypothetical decisions at the Poynter symposium reflected those made in newsrooms across the country. Lou Gelfand, reader representative of Minneapolis' Star Tribune, found that of 34 major dailies, 11 used the photograph on the front page, including the New York Times and USA Today; 15 used it inside, and eight didn't use it.

The picture, taken by the Toronto Star's Paul Watson, was transmitted by the Associated Press with a warning that the soldier was unidentified and that his family might not have been notified. "The photo was so strong that it overrode any consideration" about the identification, says AP Managing Editor Darrell Christian.

Other journalists agreed. "That photo said more about the failure of U.S. policy in Somalia than all the news stories written in the past six months," wrote Arizona Republic columnist Steve Wilson, whose paper used the picture.

But some editors said the photo was too offensive. Sacramento Bee Ombudsman Art Nauman quoted Managing Editor Rick Rodriguez as saying "the picture was too graphic. It was an image that would stick in people's minds, unlike the television image that is fleeting."

Readers made the same points in criticizing the Florida Times-Union's decision to put the picture on page one. The Jacksonville paper received more than 300 complaints, according to Reader Advocate Mike Clark. He believes the paper broke "a compact of sorts" with readers by publishing a picture of an identifiable casualty whose family might not have been notified. The photo "turned readers away," and many of them "did not read a word of the coverage," he wrote in an October 6 column.

The overwhelming majority of readers who bombarded papers across the country with letters and phone calls thought the photo should not have been used. The Houston Chronicle logged about 500 phone calls, all but a handful criticizing the decision to publish the picture, says spokesperson Lainie Gordon.

Reader Franklin Thompson defended the Chronicle. "We should not condemn or lash out at the bearer of bad news, but at the individuals who create it," he wrote. "I prefer not to have important world issues censored."

But Larry Rivers, executive director of the Washington office of the Veterans of Foreign Wars, believes the central issue is not censorship, but respect for the dead. The public could draw conclusions about U.S. policy without the media "showing dead corpses of American servicemen being driven through the streets," he said on CNN's "Larry King Live."

Thousands of viewers and readers agreed. "As the mother of an Army M.P. lucky enough to have returned home safely from Somalia, I am horrified that another mother witnessed her son's picture as you printed it," Cathy J. Waters wrote in a letter to the Arizona Daily Star in Tucson.

In fact, Mary Cleveland of Portsmouth, Virginia, identified the soldier as her son after she saw the picture in Norfolk's Virginian-Pilot. Cleveland told a Virginian-Pilot reporter that running the picture was "not fair" and that "pictures like that should never be printed."

The managing editor of the Virginian-Pilot—whose readers include many military families—had written an eloquent defense of the paper's decision to use the picture on the day the photo was published. "We could not deny people so closely linked to events so far away the fullest understanding of what is happening and what others are seeing and reacting to," Cole C. Campbell wrote.

Campbell, now editor of the paper, stands by the decision. "By publishing the photos and the stories we are telling people what is going on, and that may contribute to public debate."

—J.S.

also says increased coverage of military operations is "not all bad."

"World War I wouldn't have lasted three months if people had known what was going on in that conflict," he said on CNN's "Crossfire" on October 14.

However, the nature of modern media coverage presents serious problems for foreign policy. Television's ability to show conflicts as they occur greatly reduces the time that governments have for deliberation and negotiation before the public demands action.

Everette E. Dennis, executive director of the Freedom Forum Media Studies Center, believes "real-time coverage is a disaster in terms of its impact on foreign policy."

Public opinion used to be formed over weeks or months, but now "it takes only hours for [it] to in some way be galvanized" to support "a particular policy or approach," Dennis says. "One of the obligations of leadership these days is to try to take a somewhat measured approach in the midst of all kinds of conflicting signals and visual images that might, in fact, be wrong."

But the media's emphasis on conflict makes this difficult. "For many viewers for whom this is the main source of news, the picture of the world is limited, threatening and deeply distorted," James F. Hoge Jr., editor of Foreign Affairs, wrote recently in Media Studies Journal.

Retired diplomat Jack F. Matlock Jr. says in the same journal that television's emphasis on violence means that important elements of foreign policy decisions receive little coverage. "Television is excellent at conveying a feel for violence, a feel for struggle, but not very good at conveying constructive things, institution-building. It's day-in, day-out work, with very little spot news."

But institution-building is at the heart of the Clinton administration's policy in Somalia, and commentators agree that this trend is one of many that the media must learn how to cover in the post-Cold War world.

Setting the Agenda

Questions about the pictures of the dead and captured U.S. soldiers—Did they have too much influence on policy? Did they present a distorted picture of U.S. policy?—reflect larger issues about how the media will set the agenda now that the East-West conflict has destroyed what Matlock calls the "navigation points" that guided foreign policy and news coverage for 40 years.

Some analysts believe the media—which in the past often allowed the government to set the agenda for foreign coverage—will develop independent criteria for evaluating which issues and events will define coverage in the wake of the Cold War.

However, several aspects of the Somalia coverage suggest that the media's priorities may not change much. The coverage shows that the media continue to focus on what Hoge calls "flashpoints of conflict" rather than reporting on political or economic trends.

The resulting emphasis on "parachute journalism"—dropping correspondents into trouble spots and expecting reports within hours—means Americans seldom receive the background or context that would enable them to evaluate U.S. policy in a meaningful way, commentators say.

For example, few stories about Somalia have discussed how the country became involved in the East-West conflict. During the 1970s and '80s the Soviet Union and the United States showered dictator Siad Barre with money and weapons, hoping to win his allegiance. These armaments "still fuel his hellish legacy," according to Nigerian journalist Tunji Lardner.

Most stories also don't mention that Aidid, whom many U.S. media now call a "warlord," helped overthrow the dictator Barre in 1991, thus becoming a hero to many Somalis.

"The Western press typically seems unaware of the historical record," Lardner wrote recently.

Many reporters still view Somalia through a Western prism.

They are unaware that some analysts believe the humanitarian intervention that their photos and stories supported is "humanitarian imperialism" that enabled the U.S. government to pursue its own policy initiatives under the guise of doing a good deed, says Freedom Forum research associate Jon Vanden Heuvel.

Some Somalis regard the United States as just "another player" in the political system, especially after the troops' mission was expanded from feeding the starving to nation-building, he says.

Information about historical and cultural factors might have enabled the public—and the government—to understand why some Somalis have been hostile to U.S. efforts to become involved in the country's political affairs.

But most news reports did not discuss these issues. Instead, the photograph of the crowd jeering the dead soldier has become a critical moment in U.S. policy, some commentators say.

The picture, says Marvin Kalb, is "not just an American body being dragged through the streets of Mogadishu," but "a symbol of American power being dragged through the Third World, unable to master the new challenges of the post-Cold War era."

Photographs That Lie

The Ethical Dilemma Of Digital Retouching

J. D. Lasica

J. D. Lasica is a features editor and columnist at the Sacramento Bee.

few years ago I wandered into a seminar touting the wonders that technology would bring to the photographs of tomorrow. Up on the screen, a surreal slide show was in progress. One slide showed Joan Collins sitting provocatively on President Reagan's lap. *Click.* Joan was now perching, elfishly, on the president's shoulder. *Click.* Reagan had grown a third eye. *Click.* Now he was bald. *Click.* And so on.

A representative from the Scitex Corporation, a Bedford, Massachusetts, company that manufactures digital retouching equipment, said that computers could now alter the content of photographs in virtually any manner. The slides had all been produced electronically—with no trace of tampering.

The audience, clearly dazzled, tossed off a dozen or so questions about whether the machines could do this or that. Finally a hand shot up. "Nobody's said a word about the potential for abuse here. What about the ethics of all this?"

"That's up to you," said the representative.

Welcome to journalism's latest ethical nightmare: photographs that lie.

In the past few years, this razzle-dazzle digital artistry has begun to turn up at the nation's largest newspapers, magazines and book publishing houses. The trend has a lot of people worried.

Consider what has taken place already:

• Through electronic retouching *National Geographic* slightly moved one of the Great Pyramids at Gîza to fit the vertical shape of its cover in 1982.

• An editor at the *Asbury Park Press*, the third-largest newspaper in New Jersey, removed a man from the middle of a news photo and filled in the space by "cloning" part of an adjoining wall. The incident prompted the paper to issue a policy prohibiting electronic tampering with news photos.

• The *Orange County Register*, which won a Pulitzer Prize for its photo coverage of the 1984 Summer Olympics, changed the color of the sky in every one of its outdoor Olympics photos to a smog-free shade of blue.

• The editors of the book *A Day in the Life of America* could not choose a cover photo from the thousands of pictures taken by the world's leading photojournalists. They solved the problem electronically by taking a photo of a cowboy on horseback, moving him up a hillside and, for good measure, enlarging the crescent moon. "I don't know if it's right or wrong," says co-director David Cohen. "All I know is it sells the book better."

• For one of its covers, *Popular Science* used a computer to place an airplane from one photo onto the background of another aerial photo. And a number of magazines have combined images of people photographed at different times, creating composites that give the false appearance of a single cover shot.

• The *St. Louis Post-Dispatch* used a Scitex computer to remove a can of Diet Coke from a photo taken of Ron Olshwanger, winner of the 1989 Pulitzer Prize for photography.

Faster than you can say "visual credibility gap," the 1980s may be the last decade in which photos could be considered evidence of anything.

"The photograph as we know it, as a record of fact, may no longer in fact be that in three or five years," warns George Wedding, director of photography for the *Sacramento Bee.*

Jack Corn, director of photography for the *Chicago Tribune*, one of the first papers to buy a Scitex system, says the stakes are enormous. "People used to be able to look at photographs as depictions of reality," he says. "Now, that's being lost. I think what's happening is just morally, ethically wrong."

Digital technology's impact will be no less dramatic in other areas.

Within a decade, consumers will be able to buy a hand-held digital camera that uses a microchip instead of film, allowing the owner to "edit" photos. Soon you'll be able to remove your mother-in-law from that otherwise perfect vacation snapshot.

In the cinema, some experts are predicting the day when long-dead movie stars will be re-animated and cast in new films. "In 10 years we will be able to bring Clark Gable back and put him in a new show," John D. Goodell, a computer graphics consultant, told the *New York Times*.

Beyond such fanciful applications of digital technology, Goodell raises a dark scenario: Consider what might happen if the KGB or a terrorist group used such technology to broadcast a fabricated news bulletin about a natural disaster or an impending nuclear attack—delivered by a synthetic Dan Rather.

More likely than an assault by the Islamic Jihad on our airwaves will be an assault on our trust in visual images. Will photos be admissible evidence in a courtroom if tampering cannot be detected? Can newspapers rely on the truthfulness of any photo whose authenticity cannot be verified? As the price of these machines comes down, what will happen when the grocery-store tabloids start using—or abusing—them?

In television, too, the potential for abuse is great. Don E. Tomlinson, assistant professor of journalism at Texas A&M University, foresees the day when news producers try to re-create news events that they failed to capture on camera using exotic technology whose use was once confined to cinematic special effects. Airing such a simulation on a nightly newscast could confuse viewers about whether they're watching the real thing.

Tomlinson goes so far as to suggest that an unscrupulous TV reporter might use digital technology to fabricate an entire story because of ratings pressure, for career advancement or simply to jazz up the news on a slow day. A shark lurking near a populated beach, for example, could be manufactured using file footage and a digital computer.

While digital machinations on television may pose the greatest threat to the credibility of visual images in the long run, today the war is being waged in print.

Ironically, publishers are snapping up these systems not for their photo-altering capabilities but for economic reasons.

Newspapers and magazines are using digital computers to achieve huge savings in labor and materials, enhance the quality of color photo reproduction, push back editorial deadlines (because of the time saved) and transmit color separations to remote printing plants via satellite.

Among the publications already employing the technology are *Time*, *Newsweek*, *U.S. News & World Report*, *USA Today*, *Newsday*, the *Atlanta Journal* and *Constitution*, the *Providence Journal-Bulletin* and, most recently, the *New York Times*. (Incidentally, while Scitex is the industry leader in producing these machines, it is not alone in the field. Crosfield Electronics of East Rutherford, New Jersey, and Hell Graphics Systems of Port Washington, New York, also manufacture digital retouching systems.)

"People have no idea how much alteration is going on," says Michael Morse of the National Press Photographers Association. "When you're looking at that *Redbook* or *Mademoiselle* or *Sports Illustrated* tomorrow, there's a good chance somebody has done something to that picture."

Of course, some of this photo modification is familiar terrain. Pictures have been faked since the earliest days of photography in the 1850s. Retouching photos by hand was once common practice in many newsrooms, and photographers can change the composition of a black-and-white print in the darkroom. But over the years, ethical standards have tightened. Today retouching a news photo is forbidden at most publications, and faking a photo can be grounds for dismissal.

As the tools of the trade change, however, the rules of the game evolve as well. Altering a photo has never been so fast and seamless. Digital systems allow an editor or art director to capture, display, alter, transmit and publish a picture without it ever seeing photographic paper.

A photographer in the field is now able to capture an image on a light-sensitive semiconductor chip and send it to the newsroom via telephone line, microwave or even satellite. The image—a collection of hundreds of thousands of pixels, similar to the makeup of a TV screen—is then reassembled on the video monitor of a picture editing station, or "electronic darkroom," where an editor can size it, crop it, enhance the contrast and tone and correct minor flaws. From there the image is sent to a color laser plotter, which converts the pixels into signals of zeros and ones (representing the densities of magenta, cyan, yellow and black printing inks) and produces a color separation. While conventional processing reads a transparency or photo by exposing it to light, electronic scanning creates an instant digital representation of an image. *Voilà*! A process that would normally take hours is accomplished in minutes. With a plaything this seductive, it's easy to understand the temptation to "improve" a news photo at the stroke of a few keys.

Rolling Stone magazine used a digital computer to erase a pistol and holster slung over the arm of "Miami Vice" star Don Johnson after he posed for a 1985 cover shot. Editor Jann Wenner, an ardent foe of handguns, ordered the change; using a computer saved the time and expense of having the cover re-shot.

Unquestionably, this high-tech process is here to stay. The question thus becomes: Where do you draw the line?

"If someone wants to remove a tree from a photo or move two people closer together, that's crossing the line," says Dennis Copeland, director of photography for the *Miami Herald*. "The media's image has been hurt because of those few people who've abused the technology."

While a spot survey of editors, art directors and picture editors at major newspapers nationwide found no one who supported the notion of using digital technology to tamper with the integrity of a documentary news photograph, there was far greater acceptance of using it to create conceptual or illustrative photos.

The distinction is far from academic. Documentary photographs aim to portray real events in true-to-life settings. Conceptual photos are meant to symbolize an idea or evoke a mood. Because a studio shot of, say, a truffle is more akin to a still life than to the hard-edge realism of photojournalism—indeed, because the shot is staged in the first place—art directors and page designers are given wide latitude in altering its content.

What is happening, many photographers and picture editors fear, is that the distinction between the two styles is blurring, partly due to the new technology. Scott Henry, chief photographer for the *Marin County* (California) *Independent-Journal*, detects in photojournalism "a quiet shift toward pictures as ornamentation or entertainment rather than reportage."

And George Wedding of the *Bee* says of tampered photographs, "Fabricated images that look authentic on first glance sometimes taint the believability of the pictures around them."

Wedding sees a trend toward increased reliance on conceptual photos, caused in part by the recent influx into newsrooms of art directors and designers who take their visual cues from art schools and the advertising field, where manipulation is the name of the game. "These people have not been taught the traditional, classic values and goals of documentary photojournalism," he says.

Joseph Scopin, assistant managing editor for graphics at the *Washington Times* (which uses the Scitex system), thinks those fears are overblown. "If you run a photo of someone holding a 4-foot-tall, 300-pound strawberry, it's pretty obvious to the reader we're playing with the images," he says.

Sometimes, however, the distinction can be lost on the reader.

The *Asbury Park Press* ran into that difficulty in 1987 when it ran a cover story in its "Health and Fitness" section on a new kind of beef with lower cholesterol. Says Nancy Tobin, the paper's design director, "We had a head-on shot of a cow munching hay and a studio shot of a beautiful salad, and [we] combined the two images on Scitex. People came up to us afterward and said, 'How'd you get that cow to eat that salad?' We labeled it *composite photo illustration*, but some people were left scratching their heads."

Readers may grow more accustomed to digital photography's use as it spreads from the feature sections to the rest of the paper. Last summer the *Hartford Courant* ran a Page One color photo that showed how the city's skyline will look after several new skyscrapers go up; the feat was accomplished with *Newsday*'s Scitex equipment. Experts say it won't be long before newspapers' real estate pages display computer-created photos, rather than rough "artist's conceptions," of planned developments.

But some observers worry that increased use of digital retouching will make readers skeptical about the integrity of even undoctored images.

"People believe in news photographs. They have more inherent trust in what they see than what they read," says Kenneth Kobre, head of photojournalism studies at San Francisco State University. "Digital manipulation throws all pictures into a questionable light. It's a gradual process of creating doubts in the viewer's mind."

It was precisely that concern that led *National Geographic*, the magazine that moved a pyramid, to rethink its position. Jan Adkins, former associate art director, explains: "At the beginning of our access to Scitex, I think we were seduced by the dictum, 'If it can be done, it must be done.' If there was a soda can next to a bench in a contemplative park scene, we'd have the can removed digitally.

"But there's a danger there. When a photograph becomes synthesis, fantasy rather than reportage, then the whole purpose of the photograph dies. A photogra-

pher is a reporter—a photon thief, if you will. He goes and takes, with a delicate instrument, an extremely thin slice of life. When we changed that slice of life, no matter in what small way, we diluted our credibility. If images are altered to suit the editorial purposes of anyone, if soda cans or clutter or blacks or people of ethnic backgrounds are taken out, suddenly you've got a world that's not only unreal but surreal."

Adkins promises that, at *National Geographic* anyway, "the Scitex will never be used again to shift any one of the Seven Wonders of the World, or to delete anything that's unpleasant or add anything that's left out."

But even if other publications begin to show similar self-restraint, critics warn, digital technology is making additional inroads that threaten the credibility of visual images.

Already, there are a half dozen software programs on the market, such as "PhotoMac" or "Digital Darkroom" for the Macintosh, that allow the user to edit photographs digitally. The programs retail for about $700.

And then there is the digital camera, a sort of hand-held freeze-frame video camera that should be in stores within a decade, at a price within reach of the average buyer. What disturbs many people about this device is that the original image exists in an electronic limbo that can be almost endlessly manipulated. The camera differs from Scitex digital retouching equipment, which works with an original photo or negative.

"The term *photographic proof* may already be an archaic term," says the *Bee*'s Wedding. "You used to be able to hold up a negative and see that the image is real. With the advent of digital technology, you're going to hold up a floppy disk and you're not going to see anything."

Adds Tobin of the *Asbury Park Press*: "This is scaring everyone, because there's no original print, no hard copy. From the moment the shutter is snapped, it exists only as a digitized electronic impulse. Talk about the ability to rewrite history! It literally will be possible to purge information, to alter a historic event that occurred five years ago because no original exists.

There's enormous potential for great wrong and great misuse."

Scitex spokesperson Ned Boudreau says the digital industry addressed such concerns long ago. "To hear the critics tell it," he says, "it's like we've unleashed Joe McCarthy all over again. We haven't."

He says safeguards, such as an archiving system that stores originals where no one can get at them, can be built into the digital equipment. At present, however, manufacturers do not provide such options unless requested.

John Derry, director of graphic services for Chromaset, a San Francisco creative-effects studio that has used digital retouching for dozens of corporations' advertising campaigns, thinks Americans will learn to accept the technology as it becomes pervasive. "Maybe it's generational," he says. "My mother could never tell the difference between videotape and movies, between the hard, sharp edge of Johnny Carson and the soft look of motion picture film.

"As we move into this new technology, perhaps there will be people who won't be able to discern electronically manipulated images from undoctored images. But I think most of us are already pretty savvy about this stuff. If you show someone a picture of Reagan punching Gorbachev, most people won't think it's real. They'll think, Oh, look at this doctored photo. How'd they do that?"

None of this assuages the critics of digital technology, but even its detractors concede this much: It's not the technology itself that's the culprit. Machines aren't ethical or unethical; people are.

"You've got to rely on people's ethics," says Brian Steffans, a top graphics photography editor at the *Los Angeles Times*. "That's not much different from relying on the reporter's words. You don't cheat just because the technology is available."

Wedding of the *Bee* is less sanguine about the future of news photography: "I hope that 10 years from now readers will be able to pick up a newspaper and magazine and believe what they read and see. Whether we are embarking on a course which will make that impossible, I don't know. I'm afraid we have."

Ethical Questions

Gatekeeping decisions are complicated by considerations of not only what is newsworthy but what is morally right and morally wrong in accessing and presenting information. Sometimes being "fair" compromises telling a whole story. Sometimes being "truthful" is insensitive. Sometimes being "interesting" means being exploitive. The first two articles in this section present general perspectives on ethical practice. They are followed by examples of specific situations that raise ethical questions for discussion.

In "Ethics and Society," Louis Day examines the challenge of balancing obligations when the rights or desires of one person or group conflict with those of others. Some media organizations seem to have a greater concern for ethical policy than do others and have found it appropriate to attempt to articulate clearly defined guidelines for practice (see "Legislating Ethics"). However, rules rarely can be applied without considering specific aspects of a particular case. Outright fabrication of facts is considered unethical; communicating the essence of what several people said by creating composite quotes from "anonymous sources" falls into a grayer area. Lying, cheating, and stealing are considered unethical; impersonating a sympathetic lawyer to get inside a criminal operation sometimes wins journalistic commendations.

When Pennsylvania state treasurer R. Budd Dwyer ended a 1987 press conference by putting a gun in his mouth and killing himself, news crews from stations around the state were left with extremely dramatic film footage—and a question of whether the probability of offending viewers' sensitivities and causing pain to Dwyer's family were too great to justify its use. When Ted Bundy murdered Caryn Campbell in Colorado in 1975, her Dearborn, Michigan, family did not realize it would have to reexperience their pain for almost 14 years, until Bundy's execution in 1989, as broadcasters reminded their viewers of the local angle in almost every story on the Bundy case. Many news stories deal with tragedy. What is the appropriate "rule" regarding sensitivity to subjects and those who love them (see "Feeding Frenzy")?

One of the regularly debated issues in media circles is the coverage of rape. Those that believe the name of the victim should be withheld contend that rape is a particularly personal and traumatic crime and that disclosing a victim's name would be victimizing her twice. Others feel that being a victim of rape will never lose its stigma until it is treated like any other crime; thus, the potential hurt today's victim may feel will be justified by a change in future attitudes toward rape. A similar argument has been applied in the practice of "outing" homosexuals, particularly those in prominent positions, in the interest of gay rights (see "To 'Out' or Not to 'Out' "). When, if ever, should long-term objectives come into play in making decisions about what constitutes news?

What responsibility does a news organization have when the subject of a story threatens to kill him- or herself if the story runs? What about when the police request that a story not run in order to avoid compromising an ongoing investigation? Publishing information on details of the investigation might protect the next potential victim, but what if a killer finds out the police are getting close and changes her or his pattern? What if there would have been enough clues at the next crime scene to nail down a conviction? Writers struggle with the public's right to know, their sense of responsibility in informing readers/viewers, and their culpability if someone is hurt because of a story. Conversely, journalists are aware that terrorists *want* news coverage. Failure to keep the public abreast of information on terrorist situations and hostage dramas denies them legitimate news, and it may lead to retribution on the part of the terrorists. However, providing coverage of such dramas feeds directly into their reason for existence.

Is it ethical for journalists to cover stories on issues about which they have strong personal views, or does such practice compromise objectivity? What about their relationship with sources? Is it fair to become a "friend" to win trust? What standards apply in deciding to honor a subject's request, after the fact, that a piece of information not be used, or that it appear without attribution? What kind of promised favors are defensible as reasonable reimbursement for information? Is it fair to break through an interviewee's guard with nine innocent questions and go for the jugular with the tenth? If so, what kind of setup is demanded when editing the comments, since surely the tenth response will be central to the story?

None of these are easy questions, and none of them have pat answers. As William Henry observes in his article "To 'Out' or Not to 'Out,' " "Whether it is staking out Gary Hart's bedroom, probing the background of an alleged rape victim, or pondering the number of months that passed between marriage and childbirth for the wives of Ronald Reagan and televangelist Pat Robertson, the press almost always strikes some people as having gone too far." In the final analysis, no code of conduct can or does prescribe behavior in every possible situation.

Looking Ahead: Challenge Questions

To whom do media practitioners owe allegiance in making ethical judgments? Who, besides the subject of a story, is affected by such judgments?

How would you define the rules of "ethical practice"? To what degree do your rules provide guidance for making decisions in the various case examples included in this unit's articles?

Ethics and Society

Louis A. Day
Louisiana State University

The Need for a System of Ethics

In August 1988 the *Seattle Post-Intelligencer* notified a Superior Court judge, Gary Little, that it was about to break a story detailing allegations that he had had sexual relations with boys. Other local news organizations were preparing similar stories. The day before the story was to be published, Little committed suicide. Some accused the press of "hounding the man to his death," especially in light of the fact that he had expressed his intention of leaving public life.[1] One reader blamed this outpouring of criticism of the press on a moral relativism in which judgments are "not as clear cut as they once were."[2] Richard Cunningham, a journalism professor who reviewed this case in *The Quill,* agreed: "It seems to this writer, at least, that it *can* be frightening for journalists and others to sail on a boundless sea without traditional anchors."[3]

Society and Moral Anchors

As this case illustrates, society is not always a gentle taskmaster when it comes to passing judgment on its moral agents. The standards against which society scrutinizes individual

---

The reading and viewing public. . . . expect journalists to report the truth, even when there is no formal agreement to do so.

---

and institutional behavior are embedded in its code of moral conduct, its system of ethics. But if Cunningham is correct—if we are morally adrift without traditional anchors—that is sufficient justification to explore the following question: Why does society really *need* a system of ethics? There are at least four reasons that merit attention.

The Need for Social Stability First of all, a system of ethics is necessary for social intercourse. Ethics is the foundation of our advanced civilization, a cornerstone that provides some stability to society's moral expectations. If we are to enter into agreements with others, a necessity in a complex, interdependent society, we must be able to trust one another to keep those agreements, even if it is not in our self-interest to do so.[4] Professional athletes who demand to renegotiate their contracts before they have expired may breed contempt and mistrust in the front office and the belief among the fans that they are placing self-interest over the interests of the team. The reading and viewing publics likewise expect journalists to report the truth, even when there is no formal agreement to do so. When reporters fail in this expectation, public confidence is eroded.

Certainly, episodes like the Janet Cooke affair, in which the *Washington Post* returned a 1981 Pulitzer Prize for feature writing after a young reporter admitted that she had fabricated the story, can undermine the credibility of the media. The embarrassing episode began when the *Post* published a dramatic account of an eight-year-old heroin addict, identified by Cooke as "Jimmy." Jimmy was depicted as a third-generation heroin addict, and the article painted a bleak picture of his home environment in southeast Washington, where he lived with his mother, an ex-prostitute, and her lover, Ron. According to this depressing account of Jimmy's world, Ron was a drug dealer, who was also responsible for Jimmy's addiction. Cooke even described a scene in which Jimmy got "fixed up" with an injection of heroin.[5]

The article angered and upset Police Chief Burtell Jefferson, who threatened to have Cooke and the *Post* editors subpoenaed if they did not reveal Jimmy's true identity. Washington's mayor even ordered a search for the child. But Cooke told her editors that Ron had threatened to kill her if she told anyone who he was. The editors stood by their reporter and succeeded in holding Washington officials at arm's length. In the meantime, the *Post* entered the Cooke article in the Pulitzer competition.[6]

Cooke's journalistic deception began to unravel after she won the prize. The *Toledo Blade,* in preparing a "hometown-girl-makes-good" story, discovered some discrepancies in the biographical information transmitted by the Associated Press from the Pulitzer form. *Post* editors were then informed, and Cooke soon confessed that the "Jimmy" story was a fabrication based on a composite of young addicts whom she had heard about from social workers. Cooke resigned, and the *Post* returned her Pulitzer Prize.[7]

Fortunately, such instances are rare, but just one well-publicized ethical indiscretion can undermine respect from an already skeptical public. To the credit of the *Post,* the newspaper's ombudsman moved swiftly to make a full disclosure to the readers.[8]

The Need for a Moral Hierarchy Secondly, a system of ethics serves as a *moral gatekeeper* in apprising society of the relative importance of certain customs. It does this by alerting the public to (1) those norms that are important enough to be described as moral and (2) the "hierarchy of ethical norms" and their relative standing in the moral pecking order.

There is a need for a system of ethics that identifies moral customs and practices.

All cultures have many customs, but most do not concern ethical mores.[9] For example, eating with utensils is customary in Western countries, but the failure to do so is not immoral. Standing for the national anthem before a sporting event is a common practice, but those who remain seated are not behaving unethically. There is a tendency to describe actions of which we disapprove as immoral, although most of our social indiscretions are merely transgressions of etiquette. A system of ethics identifies those customs and practices where social disapproval is significant enough to render them immoral.

However, even those values and principles that have the distinction of qualifying as moral norms are not all on an equal footing. From time to time in this book I will refer to certain ideas, such as the commitment to truth and proscriptions against stealing, as *fundamental* societal values. This distinction suggests that some are more important than others. Trespassing, for example, although not socially approved, is generally viewed less seriously than lying. This may explain why the journalistic practice of invading private property to get a story, though not applauded in all quarters, does not usually meet with the same degree of condemnation as the use of outright deception.

The Need to Resolve Conflicts Thirdly, a system of ethics is an important social institution for resolving cases involving conflicting claims based on individual self-interest.[10] For example, it might be in a student's own interest to copy from a classmate's term paper. It is in the classmate's best interest to keep her from doing so. Societal rules against plagiarism are brought to bear in evaluating the moral conduct inherent in this situation.

The Need to Clarify Values Finally, a system of ethics also functions to clarify for society the competing values and principles inherent in emerging and novel moral dilemmas. Some of the issues confronting civilization today would challenge the imagination of even the most ardent philosopher. A case in point is the battle over animal rights, a movement that has confronted researchers with this discomforting question: do the human benefits of animal research outweigh the suffering of the creatures themselves?[11] This issue also poses a thorny public relations problem, particularly for those companies using animals to test commercial products.

An ethical system encourages debate and the airing of differences over competing moral principles. In so doing, it crystallizes society's attitudes about ethical dilemmas and often leads to adjudication (if not a satisfactory resolution) of disputes. This point is illustrated by a brouhaha that erupted at the University of Massachusetts at Amherst in April 1986. According to a *Newsweek* account of the incident, a guest lecturer suggested that gay men were "20 times more likely to commit mass murder, to shoplift, to cheat and to molest children."[12] Was this statement harassment or a legitimate exercise of free speech? The debate at the school, which lasted for several weeks, centered on the competing societal values of civility and free expression. Although no agreement was reached on which principle should prevail,[13] a dialogue was fostered that encouraged a rational deliberation of the issues.

In another case, the *St. Cloud Daily Times,* in Minnesota, published the names of five juvenile football players who had been suspended from school for drinking. Some school officials and the parents of the players filed a complaint with the Minnesota News Council. The complainants felt that the boys had suffered enough. However, the council voted 10 to 2 in favor of the newspaper, because "rightly or wrongly, high school football generates considerable public interest, and the players, even though youngsters, achieve a high profile within their communities."[14]

The Particular Needs of Media Practitioners

If a system of ethics provides moral cohesion for society's individual members and institutions, media practitioners are in particular need of one. Why? First of all, they are the primary source of information in a democracy. They stand at the crossroads between the citizens and their political, economic, and cultural institutions. Accurate and reliable information is the lifeblood of the democratic process, whether it be political intelligence offered up by journalists or the economic messages of advertisers. Society has a right to expect a certain level of ethical behavior from its media institutions, and when this conduct is not forthcoming, a crisis of confidence occurs between these institutions and the public.

In addition, codes of ethics are generally the hallmark of professionalism. . . . [V]irtually every area of media practice—journalism, advertising, public relations, and even the entertainment industry—has some kind of ethical code. But the lack of any form of enforcement mechanism has caused some critics to question whether media practitioners are truly part of a professional enterprise.

Media practitioners, particularly journalists, are also influential in that they touch the lives of all of us. Thus, they should serve as role models for society and should reinforce society's ethical expectations. Audience members, especially those who are young and impressionable, often take their ethical cues from media personalities. When a television journalist, for example, uses deception to get a story without a compelling reason for doing

so, this message is not lost on the audience. Each ethical indiscretion further erodes society's confidence in the media. . . .

The Two Levels of Moral Duty

When individuals emerge from their primitive stages of moral development and enter society, they assume certain obligations. The ethics system is not a smorgasbord from which one can pick and choose moral delicacies. Society imposes certain responsibilities on its constituents as a condition of membership. These responsibilities are known as moral duties. Although there are many kinds of moral duties, for the sake of simplicity they can be divided into two categories: general and particularistic.

General ethical obligations are those that apply to all members of society. Some are pri-

---

A duty is often imposed on media practitioners to avoid certain conflicts of interest because of their unusual role within society.

---

mary (or fundamental), in that they take precedence over other principles and should be violated only when there is an overriding reason for doing so.[19] Prohibitions against stealing, cheating, lying, and breaking promises are examples of fundamental duties. Others bind all of us, even though they do not occupy such a prominent position on the hierarchy of values as our primary general obligations. These secondary obligations, such as prohibitions against gambling and trespassing, have a weaker claim to moral permanence than our fundamental duties and are more likely to be violated or perhaps subordinated to competing interests. Charity bingo games and legalized state lotteries are two classic examples.

There is, of course, substantial disagreement among philosophers over the extent of our general obligations. Some believe, for example, that there is a moral duty to assist others in distress, to be a good samaritan. Others continue to ask, "Am I my brother's keeper?" and question whether such good deeds are really a general moral obligation. However, one could probably get agreement among philosophers and nonphilosophers alike that two general obligations underlie all others: to treat others with the respect and moral dignity to which they are entitled and to avoid intentionally causing harm to others.[20] You will notice that the latter duty is based on *intentional* harm, not *foreseeable* harm. For example, reporters know that scandalous revelations will harm others, but their *intent* is not to harm but to inform the public about matters of public interest. Even if their revelations are unwarranted, few journalists would embark on a story with the underlying motive of causing personal injury.

Particularistic obligations are determined by membership within a specific group, pro-

---

Journalist's obligations must be based on more general obligations of society.

---

fession, or occupation. Practicing Roman Catholics, for example, have a moral duty to refrain from using artificial birth control. Doctors have a duty to maintain a confidential relationship with their patients, and attorneys have a responsibility to mount a vigorous defense for their clients, even if they believe them to be guilty. These are moral obligations that do not bind the rest of us.

A duty is often imposed on media practitioners to avoid certain conflicts of interest because of their unusual role within society. This obligation was apparently ignored several years ago when more than 5,000 media representatives and guests accepted invitations to visit Disney World for three days.[21] Although some insisted on paying their own way, others accepted Disney's offer to underwrite all expenses. The reporters and media executives who attended planned extensive coverage for Disney World's 15th anniversary, an event that might otherwise have gone unnoticed.[22] For Disney and central Florida this arrangement was a publicity bonanza. For critics, including those inside the media, it was an ethical debacle. Michael Gartner, president of the American Society of Newspaper Editors, summed it up: "If Disney World wants to do this, it's fine, but I am disappointed that so many reporters and editors aren't troubled by the acceptance."[23] The editor of the *New York Times*, A. M. Rosenthal, lamented: "I thought we had cleaned ourselves up and we haven't. It is astonishing."[24]

Particularistic obligations for media practitioners, like those in other professions, are sometimes based on the more general societal obligations. Journalism's commitment to truth and fairness is a case in point. But occasionally the general and particularistic obligations collide, causing heated debate about which should prevail. Suppose, for example, that a reporter is covering a war in which American troops are fighting alongside those of an ally. The journalist is invited by the enemy forces to inspect evidence of allied atrocities. But instead of producing the evidence, the enemy sets up an ambush of American troops. Should the reporter cover the ambush?

This was the hypothetical scenario presented in early 1989 to Peter Jennings of ABC News and Mike Wallace of "60 Minutes," who were participants on a 10-part Corporation for Public Broadcasting series, "Ethics in America." Jennings originally said he would not cover the ambush as part of his job and that he would warn the American troops. Wallace strongly disagreed and contended that reporters should cover this story just as they would any other. As the discussion progressed, Jennings moved closer to Wallace's position, but after wrestling with this moral dilemma, Wallace acknowledged his uncertainty. This hypothetical case produced an outpouring of interest and commentary within the journalistic community because of its graphic illustration of the conflict between reporters' journalistic (particularistic) obligations and their general duty as American citizens.[25]

It was a real-life drama, not a hypothetical scenario, that brought charges of journalistic callousness against a television photographer and sound technician. On March 4, 1983, Cecil Andrews, an unemployed roofer with a history of mental instability, phoned WHMA-TV in Annistan, Alabama, and said: "If you want to see somebody set himself on fire, be at the square in Jacksonville in ten minutes." The photographer, Ronald Simmons, and the sound technician, Gary Harris, were on duty that night and notified the police. Simmons and Harris were then sent to the scene, but the police were nowhere in sight. The two rolled their camera as Andrews attempted to set himself on fire. Harris eventually intervened, but not before Andrews had been severely burned.[26]

When the story came to national attention, Simmons and Harris were criticized by their professional peers for having failed to intervene in an effort to prevent the suicide attempt. The station's news director, Phillip

Cox, who had dispatched the two men, maintained that they had done what was expected of them. Simmons, the cameraman, echoed this sentiment: "My job is to record events as they happen." Harris, the sound man, declared, "My conscience is clear." But the station's general manager, Harry Mabry, expressed concern and said that his station's procedures had been reviewed following the incident.[27]

On that day the technology of television prevailed over what some perceived as the obligation of any citizen. But the troubling ethical issues raised by the collision of such conflicting moral duties persist, as evidenced by the retrospective disagreement even among the station's staff.

Deciding among Moral Duties

The duties just explored orchestrate our relations with one another and with society. Our moral calculations affect other humans, regardless of whether these individuals are known personally to us or are members of that amorphous mass known as the public. Thus, our ethical judgments must take into account *all* parties, including ourselves, to which we owe allegiance.

Ralph Potter, of the Harvard Divinity School, has referred to these duties as "loyalties" in constructing his own model for moral reasoning.[28] Lawyers, for example, have obligations to their clients, their professional colleagues, the judicial system, and society at large, as well as to their own sense of ethical conduct. Teachers have loyalties to the students, par-

---

It is an article of faith in many news organizations that advertisers should exercise no influence over editorial or news content.

---

ents, academic colleagues, school officials, and the community at large. Sometimes these loyalties conflict, increasing the tension in the moral-reasoning process. The authors of *Media Ethics: Cases and Moral Reasoning*, make this observation:

Many times while doing ethics, direct conflicts arise between the rights of one person or group versus those of others. Policies and actions inevitably must favor some to the ex-

clusion of others. Often our most agonizing dilemmas revolve around our primary obligation to a person or social group. Or, we ask ourselves, is my first loyalty to my company or to a particular client?[29]

The moral agent's responsibility consists of giving each set of loyalties its share of attention before rendering an ethical determination. Thus, as media practitioners we must identify those parties that will be most affected by our actions. . . .[30]

1. Individual conscience
2. Objects of moral judgment
3. Financial supporters
4. The institution
5. Professional colleagues
6. Society

First of all, we should follow the adage "Let your conscience be your guide." Our *conscience* often tells us, if we are willing to listen, the difference between right and wrong. In other words, we should feel personally comfortable with our decision or at least be able to defend it with some moral principle. Being able to look ourselves in the mirror without wincing from moral embarrassment is a sign of our virtue.

The *objects of moral judgment* are those individuals or groups most likely to be harmed or affected directly by our ethical decisions. For example, racial and ethnic minorities are the objects of moral judgment when films depicting them are based on stereotypes. Certain specialized audiences should also be taken into account, as when a sexually explicit program is aired during the time of the day when children are most likely to be watching or listening. A public official whose womanizing catches the fancy of the media would also be in harm's way, much to the delight of his political opponents. It may seem strange to suggest that a loyalty is owed to such unsavory topics of news coverage. But there is a duty to take into account the interests of others, even if we believe that the target of our action deserves punishment or public scorn.

Media practitioners also must be loyal to their *financial supporters*, who pay the bills and make it possible to compete in the marketplace. These include advertisers as well as individual subscribers. There will always be tension between the lure of profits and the ethical mandate to operate in the public interest, but the industry must sometimes strive to find an accommodation between them. This is not to suggest, of course, that the media must compromise their contract with society to present objective news coverage because of objections and pressure from advertisers or stockholders. It is an article of faith in many news organizations that advertisers should exercise no influence over editorial or news content. Thus, these loyalties to financial supporters must be carefully weighed, and in some cases the moral duty to society must override other considerations.

Allegiance to one's own *institution* is a noble gesture under most circumstances, because company loyalty is usually valued in corporate circles. Reporters often take pride in the news organizations for which they work and are concerned as much about their institutions' credibility as about their own. However, blind loyalty can work to the detriment of the company. For example, a PR executive who recommends to management that the company "stonewall" the press concerning the effects of an environmental disaster is disserving the company as well as the public. It should be noted that loyalty to one's organization may also take into account the stockholders (if any), because they are interested in the financial well-being of the company as well as in protecting their investments. Of course, media executives tend to be more concerned about the duties owed to investors than those owed to lower level employees.

A practitioner's allegiance to *professional colleagues* is often powerful and unfaltering. When rendering a moral judgment, two questions are relevant: How will my actions reflect on my professional peers? Are my actions in keeping with the expectations of my colleagues? Suppose that a television news producer decides to air graphic death scenes from a satanic ritual. Public protests would suggest that this ill-advised decision might reflect poorly on all broadcast journalists. On the other hand, reporters often look to the expectations and practices of their colleagues for moral support to legitimize their actions. Protection of news sources is a case in point, and some reporters have gone to jail rather than breach these confidential relationships and risk the ostracism of their peers.

For media practitioners obligation or loyalty to *society* translates into a sense of social responsibility. It goes without saying that ethical decisions cannot be made without factoring the public interest into the equation. Because our own sense of moral propriety, that is, our conscience, is based on societal norms, our obligations to ourselves and society are often in concert. This is not always the case, however, as when reporters publish the contents of a stolen classified government document revealing American duplicity in foreign relations. In this case their consciences might override the concern for social prohibitions against stealing. However, if their motivations for releasing this information are related to self-interest (personal recognition, increased ratings, and the like), they have acted unethically.

Considerations of societal duties are more complex than they appear. In the real world society is not some monolithic entity but consists of many different groups, among which choices sometimes have to be made: news sources, public figures, minorities, senior citizens, children, the handicapped. It is the balancing of these interests that presents a real challenge to media practitioners in the rough and tumble world of a diverse civilization. . . .

Notes

1. Richard P. Cunningham, "The Press as Moral Arbiter," *The Quill,* November 1988, p. 16. Six years earlier, in 1982, the Washington Commission on Judicial Conduct had admonished Judge Little for having had out-of-court contact with juvenile offenders, but its decison was kept private.

2. Ibid.

3. Ibid.

4. Jeffrey Olen, *Ethics in Journalism.* Englewood Cliffs, N.J.: Prentice-Hall, 1988, p. 3.

5. For a discussion of this case see H. Eugene Goodwin, *Groping for Ethics in Journalism,* 2d ed. Ames: Iowa State University Press, 1987, pp. 166–69.

6. Ibid., 167.

7. Ibid., 168.

8. For a discussion of this case see William L. Rivers and Cleve Mathews, *Ethics for the Media.* Englewood Cliffs, N.J.: Prentice-Hall, 1988, pp. 232–33.

9. See John Hartland-Swann, "The Moral and the Non-Moral," in Tom L. Beauchamp, *Philosophical Ethics: An Introduction to Moral Philosophy.* New York: McGraw-Hill, 1982, pp. 7–10.

10. Olen, *Ethics in Journalism,* 3.

11. See "Of Pain and Progress," *Newsweek,* December 26, 1988, pp. 50–59.

7. ETHICAL QUESTIONS

12. "Everything but Shouting 'Fire,'" *Newsweek,* October 20, 1986, p. 70.

13. Ibid.

14. Quoted in "Using Names of Boozing Boys," *The Quill,* September 1988, p. 9.

19. See Olen, *Ethics in Journalism,* 2–3. One author refers to these as prima facie duties in Beauchamp, *Philosophical Ethics,* 188–90.

20. See Bowie, *Making Ethical Decisions,* 100.

21. James C. Clark, "Many Reporters Couldn't Say No," *1986–87 Journalism Ethics Report,* Society of Professional Journalists. Chicago: National Freedom of Information Committee, Society of Professional Journalists, 1987, p. 4.

22. Ibid.

23. Ibid.

24. Ibid.

25. See "More on Jennings, Wallace, and the 'North Kosanese,'" *The Quill,* April 1989, pp. 5–7.

26. William A. Henry III, "When 'News' Is Almost a Crime," *Time,* March 21, 1983, p. 84. For a discussion of this case, see Gail Marion and Ralph Izard, "The Journalist in Life-Saving Situations: Detached Observer or Good Samaritan?" *Journal of Mass Media Ethics,* 1, no. 2, Spring-Summer 1986, p. 62.

27. Henry, "When 'News' Is Almost a Crime."

28. See Ralph Potter, "The Logic of Moral Argument," in Paul Deats (ed.), *Toward a Discipline of Social Ethics.* Boston: Boston University Press, 1972, pp. 93–114.

29. Clifford G. Christians, Kim B. Rotzoll, and Mark Fackler, *Media Ethics: Cases and Moral Reasoning,* 2d ed. White Plains, N.Y.: Longman, 1987, p. 17.

30. Some of these categories are derived from those developed by Christians, Rotzoll, and Fackler in *Media Ethics,* 17–18.

Legislating Ethics

Will detailed codes make newspapers more honorable and help them regain public confidence? Or are they an invitation to a libel suit?

Alicia C. Shepard

Alicia C. Shepard, a former reporter for the San Jose Mercury News, is a Washington, D.C.-based writer. She wrote about the impact of newspaper diversity efforts on white men in our November 1993 issue.

Last winter the Kansas City Star got a hot tip: Municipal employees were selling city-owned asphalt mix to a privately owned gas station. The Star sent a reporter to the scene. The station operator asked the reporter for $30 to cover the payment, the reporter agreed and the asphalt was dumped.

Once the city was notified, it quickly picked up the purloined asphalt mix and later fired two employees. In journalistic terms, it was a slam dunk. Only the story was never written. Star editors considered the reporter's decision to provide cash a serious ethical mistake.

"At this moment, the Star became a part of the story it was there to report," Editor and Vice President Arthur S. Brisbane wrote in a column. "It is our job to witness and publish—not to participate in the making of the news."

After that incident and another involving a conflict of interest, Star editors decided to take a close look at the various guidelines used by departments around the newsroom and consolidate them. "It surprised us that some things we thought were common knowledge weren't," Managing Editor/News Mark Zieman says.

The Star is not alone. From the tiny Napa Valley Register in California, which doesn't have formal written guidelines, to the Hartford Courant, which is updating its seven-year-old code, newspaper editors are talking about ethics. Should they have a written code like doctors, lawyers and a growing number of businesses?

Few newspapers are vehemently opposed to written codes. Yet less than 100 newspapers have them, according to a survey by the Associated Press Managing Editors (APME). More editors now believe written codes—not just broadly stated principles—are necessary and are writing or considering their own.

Many say a strong ethics code will enhance credibility in an industry that has been losing public confidence. They say reporters need to know the ground rules and that a code should be written down and discussed; editors can't just assume reporters—who change jobs relatively often—will know the guidelines.

But how specific should such codes be? Editors like Zieman say if they aren't very detailed, they're meaningless. Others, like Managing Editor Earl Maucker of Fort Lauderdale's Sun-Sentinel, say if the documents have too many rules, they won't be followed. And some media lawyers think writing a detailed ethics code is the equivalent of handing a plaintiff's libel attorney a manual on how to win.

Many papers loosely rely on codes offered by the American Society of Newspaper Editors (ASNE) and the Society of Professional Journalists (SPJ). But some say those codes are too vague and outdated.

The APME leadership is lobbying for a highly detailed, controversial code that was circulated at the group's annual meeting last September in Minneapolis. Eight members of APME, headed by David V. Hawpe, editor of Louisville's Courier-Journal, spent a year researching and writing guidelines on deception, fact-checking, freebies, conflicts of interest, confidential sources, electronic polls, gifts and pre-publication review of articles.

Hawpe's group wants ethics codes written down and, rather than languishing in editors' top drawers, published in papers and regularly discussed with the staff. The entire APME membership will vote in September on whether to accept the proposed code. APME leaders aren't seeking to set industrywide standards; rather, they are offering their code as a prototype for papers to adopt or consider when modifying or creating their own codes.

While the APME code was generally well received at the organization's annual meeting, sections that call for systematic fact-checking when feasible and condemn the use of deception except as a last resort are drawing the most criticism.

APME leaders see their new code as a vehicle to encourage everyone—the public, journalists and lawyers—to consider the need for clearly defined standards and what their effect would be. The debate—to have or not to have, to be specific or not—has encouraged them. Discussion is exactly what they wanted to create when they wrote their five-page Declaration of Ethics.

7. ETHICAL QUESTIONS

Regaining Public Confidence

Journalism "is among the most ethically sensitive of crafts," says Hawpe, whose paper has yet to adopt a comprehensive code. "But there is a need for an ongoing conversation about ethics. That's what this is all about."

Hawpe and Gannett News Service Editor Robert Ritter, a driving force behind the code, believe a newspaper's greatest asset is not its staff or advertising lineage, but its credibility. And newspaper credibility has been on a downhill slide for a long time. According to a Los Angeles Times poll in March 1993, only 17 percent of the American public believes the media do a very good job—down from 30 percent in 1985.

Ritter hopes adopting strict, specific ethics codes will help recapture public confidence. As president of APME last year, he began giving serious thought to a strong ethics code when he realized the organization had not taken a hard look at its own in 18 years. A lot had changed.

Journalists stumble all the time into territory that has no ethical road map. Technology alone has created a mushrooming set of dilemmas. Many existing codes offer no advice on how to handle electronic polling results or what to do about the rapidly growing field of computer-assisted journalism.

Tabloid-style broadcast "news" programs like "Hard Copy" and "A Current Affair," where the line between fact and fiction is often blurred, are causing problems for newspapers.

So are media mistakes and their subsequent negative publicity.

"There was a tremendous amount of talk earlier this year about breaches in ethics in television and newspapers," Ritter said in October. He pointed to the explosion staged by "Dateline NBC," USA Today's use of a misleading photograph of gang members in Los Angeles, and questions raised when the New York Times, in a story about attorney general-nominee Kimba Wood, quoted an unnamed source—Wood's husband.

Conversation led to action. APME ethics chairman Hawpe sent out 1,500 surveys last spring to newspaper editors. More than 570 replied. Some 43 percent said they feel under greater pressure than ever about ethical issues, while 71 percent said corporate pressure for profit has a greater effect on news coverage than in the past. They also said it's now harder to avoid giving advertisers special treatment.

Before writing the new 3,000-word code, Ritter and Hawpe held all-day

> ## "There was a tremendous amount of talk...about breaches in ethics in television and newspapers."
>
> *Robert Ritter, editor,*
> *Gannett News Service*

seminars in Hartford, Nashville, Kansas City and Sacramento. They recruited ethicist Michael Josephson to assemble groups of politicians, executives, reporters, community activists and members of the public to talk about how newspapers do their jobs.

"They don't understand how we go about our work and how we edit our work," Ritter says. "They don't think we have much regard for privacy. They don't understand why journalists choose not to participate in the community or understand the difference between off and on the record. What we see as arm's length, they see as arrogant."

In July, the APME ethics group began revising its code and presented it at the organization's annual meeting, where actor Tom Selleck spoke on its behalf. Selleck, a target of the tabloid press, has donated money won from lawsuits to the University of Southern California to develop media ethics programs.

Selleck participated in a lively panel discussion with journalists, a lawyer, a businessman and a local politician. Of the nine panelists, only two—Fort Lauderdale's Maucker and AP attorney Richard Winfield—opposed the code.

Maucker says it's too detailed to be worthwhile. "It's simply not realistic to expect our staff to follow every line and

every paragraph and every nuance," Maucker says. "So what good is it?"

The editor believes that newsroom directives should be very clear but also contain some flexibility. "I agree a code should be in writing but you can't cover every contingency nor should you attempt to," Maucker says.

Winfield, who handles AP's libel suits, calls detailed codes "toxic" because they provide too much courtroom ammunition to newspaper adversaries.

Others on the panel disagreed. "When we deal with the newspapers, we don't know what the standards are," said Michael Wright, chairman and CEO of Supervalu Inc., a large food wholesaler. "They don't check facts or get quotes that support the facts of a pre-existing premise and they ignore quotes to the contrary.... I think it's desperately needed."

Seeking Feedback

Before APME members decide later this year whether to adopt the code and recommend it to member papers, Hawpe wants feedback. He hopes newspapers around the country hold debates and consider what they want in an ethics code. Parts of APME's code are likely to be revised before the vote.

"I would be surprised if that detailed a code indeed becomes the code adopted by APME," says Jennifer Carroll, managing editor for the Lansing State Journal in Michigan and a vice chair of APME's ethics committee.

Brigham Young journalism professor Ralph Barney would vote to reject the code. Barney, the co-author of "Doing Ethics in Journalism," says the more specific a code is, the more dysfunctional it becomes.

"It's always dangerous to be specific because there always seem to be exceptions," he says. "The question is, shall people think for themselves on the basis of general principles or just follow the rules?... These codes are almost insulting for thoughtful people, but they are useful for ignorant people."

Another journalism professor, Lee Wilkins at the University of Missouri, also would cast a nay vote. "What I don't like—and it's why I'm not fundamentally a strong supporter of codes—is they too often take on the easy issues, like no freebies and always tell the truth," she says. "They don't have the capacity to change over time. In most organizations, somebody has to make a real extreme boner to have a code rewritten."

APME's proposed code has many

provisions that are standard procedure at most newspapers. Many are the "easy" ones Wilkins refers to: The draft would forbid accepting gifts, insist reporters pay their own way and avoid any financial interest or conflicts with newsmakers. But the code goes further than many when it comes to community involvement.

"We think journalists shouldn't be involved in any organization they cover, shouldn't participate in demonstrations or sign petitions," Ritter says. "Nor should they serve as decision makers or fundraisers in community organizations."

Strict ethics codes like APME's aren't easy to swallow for small-circulation papers. Larger newspapers absolutely prohibit taking freebies of any sort. But it's not so simple for managing editors like Doug Ernst of the 21,000-circulation Napa Valley Register in California. His paper has no formal code and often struggles with how to handle free tickets to cultural and athletic events.

"If you don't take the tickets, you don't get to go," Ernst says. "Then we don't get the news into the paper and that's not fair to readers.... If I take the tickets and I bash them, is that fair? We get those problems all the time."

Editors at small newspapers, however, are not without a sense of humor. "I joke our ethics code is that nobody is allowed to accept gifts of less than $50 because they demean the newspaper," says Chris Powell, managing editor of the 50,000-circulation Manchester Journal Inquirer in Connecticut.

As for deception—using trickery, misrepresentation, hidden cameras or tape recorders—the APME draft calls the practices "outside the bounds of generally accepted journalistic behavior." It does provide five exceptions when deception may be used if there is no other way to get a story of crucial public interest.

Critics say there are too many loopholes for this approach to be effective. Editor & Publisher cited the deception provision—and the code's detailed standards—as reasons to reject the APME draft.

If undercover techniques are used, the proposed code mandates that a paper must run a sidebar explaining why the editors thought it was appropriate.

In fact, disclosure sidebars are a theme throughout the draft. If you use a confidential source, explain why the source must remain unidentified. If a picture is posed or altered, explain why. If a poll is done, explain how it was taken and its limitations—no more simply describing it as unscientific. If someone on the paper has a financial conflict, reveal it.

"The theory behind the code is the general notion that whatever you are going to do, be as open and as accountable as possible," says Josephson.

Accuracy is another major issue. "Newspapers," says the draft, "should develop and use safeguards to avoid error. These should include systematic verification of facts and quotations and corroboration of critical information." This section draws the most criticism, especially from libel attorneys.

Fact-checking, according to the code's authors, can be anything from replaying a taped interview to reading a quote back to the source or calling a second party to verify it.

"Any story where someone is put in a bad light, we have an obligation to double-check and make sure we're damn right," says Michael Waller, edi-

But Will Reporters Use Them?

Ethics codes may be a hot topic for editors. But what about the people on the front lines, the reporters? If their newspaper has one, have they read it? Do they consult it? Is it any help?

Conversations with a handful of reporters around the country suggest that dictionaries are consulted far more often. Reporters interviewed say they rely on their own instincts when questions of ethics arise. Some do consult codes, some can't (when there isn't one), and some don't even know if their paper has one.

John Mintz, a business reporter who has been at the Washington Post for 11 years, is one of the latter. (The Post has a code.) "It's not absolutely necessary to have written codes but it is to have ethical standards," he says. "It's real important to know the general things that are expected, especially for young reporters."

Dan Meyers, a reporter with the Philadelphia Inquirer's Denver bureau with 18 years of experience, says an ethics code would have helped him when he was starting out. "Why not have a code?" he asks. "I say this as a sinner, not a bishop. I broke plenty of rules when I was young, partly because no one had ever laid out the ground rules. There were things I did then that I wouldn't do now."

Judy Fahys, a business reporter at the Salt Lake Tribune for more than year, had to check with an editor to determine whether her paper has a code. It doesn't.

"A written ethics code would be of value if only for the reason that as a reporter my job is to hold different people accountable," Fahys says. "I don't think I should be different and not be held accountable. . . . I write stories about lawmakers taking free lunches. Why should I take a lunch and a lawmaker not? A lot of reporters set their own limits."

Rather than dash to the ethics code, many reporters consult their editors when faced with a dilemma.

"I find myself having conversations with editors when I perceive a gray area," says Craig Gilbert, a political reporter for the Milwaukee Journal with 12 years of experience. "But I have a pretty good idea in my mind what's improper and proper."

Says Joseph Williams, a Miami Herald reporter with a decade of experience who wasn't sure the Herald had a code (it does): "Generally you know this is something you should or shouldn't do. If there's a question, then I ask an editor."

Reporters interviewed seem to agree codes do help in such situations as whether to accept a free meal or tickets. But even that provision can sometimes be unclear. "Say a source offers you dinner at his house," says Fahys. "I know they are not doing it to influence me, but is that acceptable or not? I think the real value of an ethics code is not what it says, but the process of developing [it]."

One thorny issue is differentiating between a journalist's roles as reporter and citizen. "That's one that really comes down to individual cases," says Meyers, "which is why it's difficult to write an absolute prohibition" on community involvement. —A.C.S.

tor of the Hartford Courant and an APME code author. "Why would anyone object strenuously to this section?... Corroborating critical information is what we should be doing now even without a code."

Alice Neff Lucan, a newspaper lawyer in Washington, D.C., thinks that provision is elitist. "Small newspapers—especially weeklies—cannot do many of the things the code would require," such as double-checking facts, because they don't have the staff, Lucan says. "It works well at the Louisville Courier, but don't put this down the throat of my clients."

No one disagrees with the notion of corroborating facts. What concerns lawyers like the AP's Winfield, however, is how the code could be used against the paper if facts aren't double-checked.

"If a newspaper doesn't have a fact-checker or doesn't verify quotes for an article," he says, "it gives the plaintiff's lawyer the opportunity to challenge the absence of a systematic veri-

Rules of the Game

Highlights of the Associated Press Managing Editors' proposed ethics code:

ACCURACY: Newspapers should develop and use safeguards to avoid error. These should include systematic verification of facts and quotations and corroboration of critical information.

ALTERATION OF QUOTES: While some newspapers may impose a stricter standard, there may be little or no actual harm in altering quotes in the following limited circumstances:

(1) Correcting grammar that could make the statement confusing or would make the speaker appear foolish;

(2) Avoiding dialect that is not essential to the story.

ALTERATION OF PHOTOS: The actual content of a photograph should not be altered or manipulated, except for illustrative purposes, in which case the image must be clearly labeled to indicate it has been altered.

HONESTY: Deceptive practices such as misrepresentation, trickery, impersonation and use of hidden tape recorders or cameras in news gathering can seriously undermine a newspaper's credibility and trustworthiness. These practices are outside the bounds of generally accepted journalistic behavior.

An editor confronted with a decision to exceed those bounds should meet the following minimum conditions:

(1) Public importance: The expected news story must be of such vital public interest that its news value clearly outweighs the damage to trust and credibility that might result from the use of deception.

(2) Alternatives: The story cannot reasonably be recast to avoid the need to deceive.

(3) Last resort: All other means of getting the story must have been exhausted.

(4) Editorial approval: The decision to use deception must be approved at the highest level of the newsroom after thorough discussion.

(5) Disclosure: The deceptive practices and the reason they were used must be disclosed in print at the time the story is published.

As a final caution, an editor should ask these questions:

(A) Was the decision to deceive discussed as thoroughly and broadly as feasible, and do other staffers generally accept the decision?

(B) Will readers and staff members tend to agree that the story justified the deception?

POLLS AND SURVEYS: Newspapers should clearly distinguish between scientific polls and non-scientific surveys such as reader call-ins or write-ins and person-on-the-street inquiries that are reported in statistical terms. This must be done in a way that is likely to be understood by the average reader.

PROMISES: (1) Journalists should not promise anything outside the scope of their authority. Promises made in such circumstances cannot be considered binding on the newspaper. Senior editors should ensure that staff members understand the limits of their authority.

(2) Promises made to a news source regarding conditions of use or attribution (including such designations as off the record, on background, not for attribution and embargoed) or pre-publication review of any sort should be kept by the newspaper or the information should not be used.

CONFLICTS OF INTEREST: (1) Journalists should avoid situations that compromise their newspapers, whether actual or apparent. They should not be involved in the news they cover. They should avoid signing petitions, participating in demonstrations or serving in a decision making capacity or fundraiser for organizations that generate significant news.

(2) Journalists should not accept favors or gifts, subsidized or free travel, accommodations, special discounts, tickets to sports or entertainment events, or other benefits from news sources or organizations that the newspaper may cover.

(3) Contests: Stories, photographs and illustrations should not be published for the purpose of winning awards or prizes.

FAIRNESS: (1) Opportunity to reply: In reporting any statements that could injure the reputation of an individual or group, those affected must be given the earliest opportunity to reply.

(2) Courtesy and compassion: Special care should be taken to treat sensitively those who are unaccustomed to dealing with the press.

(3) Developments: When stories have been prominently displayed, fairness requires that substantial subsequent developments be covered and similarly displayed.

DIVERSITY: (1) Editors must make concerted, sustained efforts to recruit, retain and develop staffs that reflect the variety of the communities they serve.

(2) Journalists should conduct themselves in a way that underscores a commitment to fair treatment for all people. Membership in discriminatory clubs and organizations undermines a journalist's credibility.

fication and to show the newspaper violated the national standard set by a prominent and prestigious organization. Therefore, the newspaper has been at fault. Write your check. In the real world, that's how it works."

Keep it General

Winfield and Lucan, like many of their colleagues, prefer a broadly written ethics code. Specifics, they say, complicate things for libel cases and don't work in a field where no code can anticipate every dilemma.

"It's the whole tone of the code that I don't like," Lucan says. "It speaks in terms of shoulds, must, never. You can't do that in journalism."

George Freeman, the New York Times' assistant general counsel, agrees and opposes any written code.

"Reporters understand that ethics is not something that can be put on two pieces of paper," Freeman says. "It's a matter of tradition, journalistic ethics and responsible journalistic procedures. Those aren't susceptible to being described in black and white."

Media lawyers cite instances where codes have been used against newspapers, but there are no statistics on the subject, according to Henry R. Kaufman, general counsel for the Libel Defense Resource Center in New York City.

Lucan cites a $370,000 actual malice verdict won by a neurosurgeon in Denver against a weekly newspaper called Westword. In that case, the plaintiff's attorney introduced the SPJ ethics code and claimed the paper violated it.

To prove libel, a plaintiff's lawyer must show actual malice—that the paper knew the information was false and published it anyway. That's tough to prove, says libel defense attorney David J. Bodney in Phoenix. Recognizing that, he says, plaintiffs' lawyers now try to turn actual malice cases into negligence cases, which are easier to win.

"The biggest boost they've got to win a jury over is an alleged violation of an ethical canon," says Bodney, who is handling Westword's appeal. "That's burned indelibly into a jury's memory."

But Bryan Morgan, the lawyer who defended Westword, says the in-

> "Reporters understand that ethics is not something that can be put on two pieces of paper."
>
> *George Freeman, assistant general counsel, New York Times*

troduction of an ethics code in this case made no difference. "I don't think the jury paid any attention to the ethics code or to the journalist experts who testified," he says.

Make it Specific

Morgan believes that if a paper is going to have a code, it should be specific. A vague code "leaves the impression that journalists don't have any rules to play by," Morgan says, "and the only way to make the bastards play by the rules is to sue them."

Some journalists concur.

"If lawyers and doctors were to conduct their professions the way we do, with nothing in writing except vague generalities," says the Courant's Waller, "we would be on our high horse about how lackadaisical that is. That appears to be a double standard."

Another reason to have a specific code, Louisville's Hawpe says, is to make sure reporters and editors clearly understand the newspaper's policies. If they do and they follow them, say APME code supporters, then no one has to worry about going to court. "The staff needs to know specifically how to

operate," Hawpe says. "Should they record a conversation? If so, should they tell the person? It's an obvious obligation on our part to provide that kind of guidance with precision, specificity and clarity."

Josephson predicts ethics codes will become more common. "By the turn of the century, I believe 90 percent of newspapers will have codes," says the ethicist, who also helps businesses write codes. "It's just not rational anymore to leave to chance that a reporter, an editor or a photographer will know and understand the policies of the paper. The thing that has stopped code growth is news people hate rules and authority. They love to say: 'It depends.' "

But simply adopting a code is not enough. It must be an integral part of a newspaper's routine, says John Sweeney, ombudsman of the Wilmington News Journal, which has been publishing its code in the paper—without attracting lawsuits—for over a decade.

Recently Sweeney began conducting training sessions with News Journal staff members. They talk about decisions the paper has made and get reporters and editors to justify them. He also uses American Press Institute videos on ethical dilemmas, such as whether the name of Patricia Bowman, who said she was raped by William Kennedy Smith, should have been used. Such discussions have greater value, Sweeney believes, than a written code.

Los Angeles Times media critic David Shaw is in favor of ethics codes but doesn't want their value exaggerated. "I don't think an ethics code would change our credibility, our behavior would," he says. "I think [the public] would think better of us if we'd stop sticking microphones in the faces of mothers of accident victims, or stop going ape over whether Bill Clinton or Gary Hart can keep their fly zipped. That has less to do with a written code and more to do with behavior.

"If we think we've solved our credibility problem by writing [ethics codes] down and passing them out to new employees, we're crazy."

Feeding Frenzy

GINGER CASEY

Ginger Casey is a reporter and moderator for KQED-TV, San Francisco.

IT WAS Jan. 17, 1989, when the call came in. Some guy armed to the teeth with semiautomatic weapons had gone crazy at a schoolyard in Stockton. He'd opened fire on a playground full of kids, killing five and wounding 30 before killing himself. MacNeil-Lehrer wanted someone to go in and cover the story from the second-day angle — how the town was handling the aftermath, anything new the police had come up with about this guy, why someone would kill innocent children, that kind of thing.

It was a plum assignment, really. No chasing bits and pieces of information, no holing up at the command center. It was more of a think piece, an overview.

The crew and I rode up in the van. We got the usual hospital shots at St. Joseph's, of harried emergency room workers. They were in the special mechanical overdrive that allows people to do their jobs in a crisis, but all of them were deeply shaken at the thought that someone had done this to kids . . . my God, barely-out-of-diapers kids, who learned hopscotch and horror in an afternoon.

I was able to find one of the school psychologists, but she looked as if she herself needed professional help. "Why did he have to kill himself?" she asked. "He denied us justice." She stared at her hands.

It was good stuff, but our real work wouldn't begin until the next morning. The big thing we were all waiting to hear was whether or not the school would reopen. Would any kids venture out on the playground? If they did, we wanted to be the first ones there.

Stockton is not a major news center. While it has its own paper and several radio stations, there are no big TV stations there, only small news bureaus serving a few Sacramento stations. News is something brought in by antenna or cable, or the occasional out-of-town crew covering some "spot" event.

So for the people who lived near the school, the scene the next morning must have been simply overwhelming. I know that when my two colleagues and I turned the corner and saw the school, we all gasped — and we've been doing this kind of work for years.

There were hundreds of journalists crowded onto the school lawn, spilling over onto the sidewalks and street. You couldn't even see them all. Up and down the street, remote vans and satellite trucks hunkered and roared like feeding elephants, trunks extended to the sky. I counted 60 cameras.

Sixty cameras. Where in God's name did they all come from?

Until just a few years ago, the media crowd at a major news story was fairly predictable. Local TV and print reporters would be there, the three network crews, possibly one or two wire service reporters. It usually meant a crowd of about 20 to 25 people, figure two or three to each camera (reporter, camera person and possibly a sound engineer). Local reporters would claim sovereignty, feeling they owned the story, all the while enviously eyeing the networks' expensive equipment and better-dressed journalists.

Times have changed. Independent news agencies and tabloid TV shows have sprung up. Satellite trucks and live gear now enable any station to have a local presence on a national story. Why wait for Dan or Peter or Tom to tell you on the network news when you can send your own anchor team or reporter to the event? Be there yourself, and show off the bells and whistles of your new technology!

The big granite slab inscribed with the school's name — it looked eerily like a giant tombstone — was littered with used Styrofoam coffee cups. One was perched inside a wreath of flowers someone had placed on the sign during the night.

Technicians and reporters called out to each other in recognition, laughing with delight to be working the same story again. "Hey Tom! How the hell are 'ya? Jesus, I haven't seen you since the Sacramento landlady!" These horrific events, when newsroom budgets are thrown to the wind and journalists are sent on expensive out-of-town trips, are reunions of a sort.

A funny thing happens when you cover a major news event. The event itself becomes the backdrop; the picture is swallowed by the frame, and the whole thing acquires an air of unreality. When you look at something through the lens of a camera, or interpret it using note pads and microphones, it doesn't seem quite as authentic — or disturbing — as when you come armed only with your senses. The hardware serves as a kind of shield of denial, a way to create structure — however illusory — out of chaos.

Making structure out of chaos — isn't that what our job is supposed to be about? Show the folks back home the gruesome details, but within the comforting, bite-sized confines of the medium. Frame the fire so it burns from edge to edge of the screen, show the bombs landing on rooftops and watch as buildings explode like smashed toys, shoot the burned-out neighborhood so it looks like Dresden, go sound up full on a wailing parent. Present the event in precise order: tight shot, medium shot, wide shot, soundbite, more pictures. For a story like Stockton, use some "symbol" shots — a single sneaker if you can find one, or an empty swing blowing in some desolate wind.

But the most important component, at least for the reporter, is the "stand-up," the moment when you are standing in front of the camera, the electronic oracle of the event. This is the time to look sage, wise, appropriately moved. They call these news packages "wraps." It's a good word for what reporters do: wrap everything up in a neat package.

I have a theory that a lot of journalists go into this profession because they need that structure. At some deep level, they are corralling their own wild stallions when they bring sense to an insane event. I joke with my friends that there are some people in this business who, if they couldn't cover a fire, would probably set one. When the news sirens start to wail, some of us go into heat.

Those sirens beckon us perilously close to the rocks. And sometimes we crash.

The school administrator stood in front of the building, obviously nervous as he faced the mob of reporters, photographers and sound technicians. "Why did you decide to open school today?" someone shouted. The man swallowed. "After discussing it with the psychologist and other administration officials, we decided it would be in the best interest of the children to try to return to our normal routine," he said. A half-dozen cameras and reporters dropped out of the crowd, and a half-dozen more dropped in. "Why is school open today?" someone shouted.

Ah, the voice on the video. So important to a boss back at the station that your voice is heard above the melee, asking the cogent question. Serious points for an ambitious reporter. Enough to drive him to ask the question even if it has been answered four times already. The principal looked around, confused. "We, uh, we discussed it with the psychologist and other administration officials and felt it would be in the best interest of the children to try to return to our normal routine." More cameras out, more cameras in. A shout came from the back. "Why did you decide to open the school today?"

Suddenly a yellow school bus pulled around the corner. The school administrator was spared. The group had found a car target, and swarmed toward it, microphone poles extended, cameras clicking, reporters and photographers jockeying for position.

"Please stand back from the bus!" the school administrator shouted. "Please stand back! Off the sidewalk, please!" The crowd ignored him and surged forward as the bus pulled to the curb. Its lone passenger, a small boy with glasses, stared through a side window at the approaching mob. He was barely tall enough to see all the way over the windowsill. His eyes grew enormous.

As the crowd pushed forward and reached the door of the bus, the driver pulled away again. Quickly. The crowd began to move down the street toward the remote vans, leaving the school administrator alone on the sidewalk repeating over and over, "Please stand back! Please stand back!"

I was tapped on the shoulder. It was a woman I had worked with at a station in Los Angeles. She had been sent up to cover the story. "Christ, do you believe it?" she asked, looking over the crowd. "What a zoo. It makes me sick." We'd been talking for a few moments when suddenly she said, "Oh, God, Ginger, I just hope no one gets a kid. I'm a mother. I can't stand it." Well then, I told her, don't get one. "You know how it is," she said. "If someone gets a kid, then I have to."

She was right, of course. If someone got a kid, she would have to, as well. It's the way the game works. You don't want your competition to have any angle you don't have, and crying kids on camera were powerful images. If having your voice heard at a news conference scored points, so did interviewing a child. Your boss would tell you that you "kicked ass." Your résumé tape would look terrific.

As she walked away, I saw that several reporters had already broken from the crowd and were going door to door down the block looking for witnesses. Those with any shame at all at least had the decency to pretend to be sheepish; younger, less experienced reporters boldly knocked on doors with a sense of entitlement. I knew what they would say; I had said it myself at one time, and had even half convinced myself I believed it. "Sharing this terrible tragedy will help others"; "There are so many people concerned"; "At a time like this, it sometimes helps to talk." As if the media were some kind of cultural confessional.

Yes, I knew all the tricks. I had learned to hide my excitement when I found someone naive enough to share their pain with me. And I swallowed the shame of knowing that their tragedy would be a good career move for me.

Back in front of the school, reporters were lined up shoulder to shoulder like bowling pins for their "live shots," all of them using the front of the school as the backdrop. The coffee cups had been moved off the school marker. I hoped it was because someone had realized the disrespect; I suspected it was because the flowers were crucial to the shot. Technicians stood ready at their tripods, pools of cables snaking back along the sidewalk to the vans. The reporters were framed so no other reporters were seen doing their respective live shots. That's considered bad form: You're supposed to look as if you are the only one "live" on the scene, the solitary witness for the folks back home, spouting the inevitable opening lines: "Still more questions than answers here this morning, Dave" . . . "Officials are still trying to figure out what triggered this terrible tragedy" . . . "The one man who could explain what happened here is dead by his own hand." And the tried-and-true classic, "As the residents of this tiny town struggle to pick up the pieces of their lives . . ."

At the top of the hour, they all began, a chorus of live shots beamed home through mountaintop repeaters and satellites, ending up neatly boxed in someone's living room. Within minutes it was over, as reporters soberly signed off, promising

more details as "this terrible tragedy unfolds."

It had to happen, of course. Some parents were going to bring their kids to school. They were going to try their best to carry on, to pretend that after the previous day the world still made sense. As I watched from the edge of the crowd, an Asian woman came around the corner, holding onto her child's tiny hand. Someone let out a yell.

I should preface what happened next with a short disclaimer. Most of the people who were at that school that day were, no doubt, dedicated, hard-working professionals. Most of what they were doing was proper: collecting information, digging for facts, trying to package their reports and get them back to the station in a timely manner. If the crowd had been smaller, they probably would never have done what they did. But they did.

I remember thinking how much the crowd looked like an amoeba as it began to roll toward the woman and her child. Not everyone even knew what they were heading for, only that the mass they were a part of had found something to focus on. A kind of feeding frenzy takes over at highly charged events, and reporters don't necessarily act, but react.

The woman froze and pulled her child closer to her and then turned and began to run, pulling her child with her. The crowd ran after her.

Many of the children who attended the school were Cambodian refugees, who endured God-only-knows-what to come to this country. The day before, whatever sense of safety they might have had vanished in a stream of blood and bullets. And here they were being chased by a mob, microphone poles extended like weapons, cameras trained on them, people shouting at them to stop. Some reporters even tried to interview them as they fled, yelling "Did you see it? Did you see it?"

Chances are you didn't see any of this at home. In fact, I'd say it's a safe bet that you didn't. There is a tacit agreement in this business never to pull back the curtain, never to show you the little man pulling his bells and whistles. What you see is the great and powerful Oz. When I read my script to MacNeil-Lehrer over the phone, I was told they hadn't sent me to cover the role of the media, that it was incidental to the story.

In the world of TV news, viewers see only the product of journalism, not its process. They're never told that television is a lens that both shapes and reflects. And we journalists find it easy to ignore this awkward truth, too. We never see the consequences of our presence at an event, and even more rarely do we even think about it. When we do, we have lofty philosophical discussions about whether the way we cover the news has conditioned our audience, if we have corrupted them with sensationalism. We ponder if we should force the media to "pool" coverage in these situations and limit the number of cameras.

There are good arguments on the other side, of course. We're giving people what they want. Limiting press access can lead to censorship. The First Amendment gives us a constitutional right to do our jobs.

All true. But what I learned on the playground that day is that we also have a moral and ethical responsibility that goes beyond providing objective reporting. It's the responsibility to be gentle to those in pain, and compassionate. It's the responsibility to know when we have overstepped our bounds as witnesses. And it's the responsibility, in the end, to hold the mirror up, not just to the news event, but to ourselves.

When a story subject threatens suicide
"I'm going to kill myself!"

The story was wrapped up and ready for broadcasting. But the story could prompt the story's subject to take his life.

Mike Jacobs

Mike Jacobs anchors the 10 p.m. news and heads the investigative unit at WTMJ-TV in Milwaukee.

One story, two ethical decisions and a threat of suicide: a combination that would create a lively discussion in any newsroom.

It started as an intriguing tip: Two years ago, a suburban cop was fired because he was stopping teenage boys, threatening to give them speeding tickets, and then letting them go in exchange for sex. But the police chief did not refer the case to the district attorney for possible charges, avoiding embarrassing publicity for the department. Now, two years later, and in the wake of other allegations about a troubled police department, our sources wanted us to know about this episode.

We located two of the victims, and they confirmed what had happened. One victim, now 24 years old, even agreed to talk about it on camera, without having his identity concealed. He described, in detail, the sexual contact in the officer's apartment when he was 19 years old.

But a few days later, the young man called us back. He'd changed his mind. He did not want to be on TV.

Ethical decision #1: Should we air the interview? He did the interview voluntarily. We had it "in the can." He was not retracting his statement, simply asking that we not use his name or picture. We decided to use the interview, masking the man's identity electronically. We did so because he was, essentially, a sexual assault victim, and we routinely withhold the names of such victims. Furthermore, it was his information that was important, not his identity.

I told him...that nothing he'd done was worth dying for.

Ethical decision #2 proved to be a lot more difficult. A week later, we tracked down the former officer, living in a small town 150 miles away. We surreptitiously took pictures of him working in his yard and then approached him for an interview.

When we told him why we were there, he broke down and asked to speak to me alone. He tearfully confessed to what he'd done, told me he'd tried to put that ugly period behind him, and assured me he'd had no contact with teenagers since then. He said he'd been receiving counseling from a minister. And then he asked if we were going to put his story on TV.

When I told him we were, he said, and I'll never forget his words: "Well, you've just made up my mind. I'm going to get my shotgun and go out into a farm field and kill myself. I hate myself for what I've done. My parents don't know why I left town. And I can't stand the thought of them finding out."

I spent the next hour trying to talk the man out of committing suicide. I told him he shouldn't do anything foolish since there was a chance the story might not air, that nothing he'd done was worth dying for. I coaxed. I cajoled. I pleaded. It was,

perhaps, the most difficult hour of my life.

He finally assured me he wouldn't do anything until he'd heard from me. We left and went straight to his church. We told his minister about the suicide threat. The minister agreed to visit the man immediately.

We drove back to the newsroom for discussions with news management and the station attorney. Legally, the story was clean. We had all the facts nailed down, including a confession.

Journalistically, we had a good story. But ethically, we had a problem. Could we tell this story, knowing it might cause a man to take his life?

We wrestled with other questions as well: Was it still a story since the incidents had happened a few years ago? If so, what was the most important part of the story? And was this man still using his authority to take advantage of teenagers?

We came up with these answers:

Because the officer had resigned, he was no longer in a position to use his badge to take advantage of teenagers. He had assured me he was not involved in activities that put him in contact with young people. And we knew, if we did a story, the D.A. would investigate to find out if he was telling the truth (and letting him know he was being watched).

We decided it was still a story. But we believed an equally important part of the story was the fact that the police chief had

From *FineLine*, October 1989, pp. 1, 8. *FineLine*, the newsletter on journalism ethics. Reprinted by permission.

allowed the officer to resign, without referring the case to the D.A.

Yet, we did not want to do a story that might result in a man's suicide.

We decided to air the story, withholding the former officer's identity. We electronically altered our videotape of the man working in his yard so he could not be recognized. We notified him in advance, through his minister. In our story, we told the viewers about the sexual incidents.

And we explained how the police chief had handled the case.

The D.A. immediately launched an investigation. Months later, after interviewing everyone involved, the D.A. decided he was not going to prosecute the former officer so long as he had no further contact with teenagers. The D.A. criticized the police chief for the way he had handled the case. But the D.A. ruled the chief had not acted criminally.

The police chief, declaring himself cleared of criminal wrongdoing and citing his age, 55, immediately resigned.

The former officer did not kill himself.

We believe we handled this case responsibly. But there is a larger issue: Can the threat of suicide be enough to kill a story? If so, some important stories probably would go unreported. Each case, we decided, must be based on its own set of facts.

To "Out" or Not to "Out"

The press wrestles with a thorny issue: When is it appropriate to reveal the private lives of public officials?

William A. Henry III

When the *Village Voice* was offered a free-lance article last month that purported to expose the homosexuality of a high Pentagon official, editors of the radical New York City weekly decided to reject the piece as an unwarranted invasion of privacy. Last week the same editors permitted a *Voice* columnist to summarize the allegations, complete with the official's name. The rationale for the turnaround: the man's identity had been so widely circulated by other news organizations that continued restraint would have been "a futile exercise."

But at the Washington *Post*, editors chose to cover the controversy without citing the official by name. Explained Karen DeYoung, the *Post*'s assistant managing editor for national news: "Our policy is that we don't write about personal lives of public officials unless the personal aspects begin influencing the way they perform their jobs." The paper canceled a Jack Anderson column, normally a featured item, because it named the man, even though editors assumed many of Anderson's 700-plus clients would run the story, making the *Post*'s discretion largely symbolic.

The hottest ethical issue for journalists these days is where to draw the line between two colliding rights, the individual's right to privacy and the public's right to know—and then,

having drawn the line, how to avoid being pulled across it by cunning manipulators or by the competitive urge on a breaking story. In the case of the Pentagon official, the press coverage was not prompted by any crime, scandal or even news event. It was entirely brought about by gay activists pursuing a political agenda. They had no grudge against the official. Many professed to admire him. But they were determined to embarrass the Pentagon about its exclusion of gays from the armed services. To them, it was hypocritical for Defense Secretary Dick Cheney to retain a high civilian official, knowing—or at least not caring—that he was gay, while continuing to enforce antigay rules that apply to the uniformed ranks.

The activists had an arguable point about the apparent double standard within the Pentagon. But their tactics are controversial, and the readiness of much of the nation's news media to carry the story about the official raised serious questions about journalistic ethics and quality control. The article exposing the official was printed last week by the *Advocate*, a Los Angeles-based gay magazine published every two weeks. In a blatant bid for publicity and newsstand sales, the magazine faxed dozens of advance copies to mainstream journalists. The cover line referred to "outing" the official, a gay neologism for exposure of a homosexual by other homosexuals. The author, Mi-

chelangelo Signorile, pioneered the tactic in the defunct New York City gay magazine, *OutWeek*.

Most of the people Signorile quoted had only hearsay knowledge. Their main "evidence" was that the official had supposedly been a regular customer in years gone by at a predominantly gay Washington bar. The few sources who claimed first-hand knowledge about him were generally permitted to remain anonymous. Even some unnamed sources knew nothing themselves but were merely quoting still more obscure acquaintances: in one anecdote an unidentified man said an apparent one-night stand, picked up in a bar, told him of having "dated" the official.

Hardly any serious newspaper, magazine or network would accept so loosely sourced a story from its own staff. Yet few journalists tried to verify the claims in the *Advocate* before repeating its main point. Syndicated columnist Anderson and his partner Dale Van Atta compounded the damage with a claim that the official "is considering resigning because of accusations that he is a homosexual." Instead, Van Atta admits, the official directly said in an interview he had no plans to quit. Asked to explain this contradiction, Van Atta lamely contended, "I said he was considering resigning, and that's a far cry from saying he was seriously considering it."

Though many major dailies declined to name the official, countless

From *Time*, August 19, 1991, p. 17. © 1991 by Time Inc. Magazine Company. Reprinted by permission.

smaller papers ran the Anderson-Van Atta column. Among them was Pennsylvania's Harrisburg *Patriot,* from which the item was in turn excerpted for a Pentagon news summary distributed to 10,000 employees. Other dailies covered the outing debate. The Detroit *News* named the official twice in news stories; the New York *Daily News* identified him in a gossip column. All four TV news networks decided not to use the official's name, but secondary outlets used it, including cable channel CNBC, a corporate sibling of NBC piped into nearly 44 million homes,

and New York station WPIX. Reasons ranged from sympathy with the gay activists' arguments to CNBC program executive Andy Friendly's observation, "Everybody's talking about this topic."

Whether it is staking out Gary Hart's bedroom, probing the background of an alleged rape victim or pondering the number of months that passed between marriage and childbirth for the wives of Ronald Reagan and televangelist Pat Robertson, the press almost always strikes some people as having gone too far. For others, whose political cause is

being advanced either intentionally or inadvertently, the deplorable can suddenly seem delightful. But the real question is not just who benefits from a media decision. Rather, it is whether the media behave thoughtfully and ethically. If news organizations, in the zeal to keep up with competitors, compromise their standards and let themselves be manipulated, they imperil their credibility and integrity—and ultimately everybody loses.

—*Reported by Linda Williams/ New York*

Media and Politics

America's political system is based on the choices of its people. A candidate's success in being elected to public office depends on his or her ability to communicate to mass audiences; thus, mass media have always been central to the political process.

There is little question that television has changed politics. Although it is true that images have always been important to some degree—getting on the cover of a newsmagazine, for example, has traditionally required that a striking vertical-composition shot be provided for the photographers covering a story—television has made visual images particularly powerful. Martha Cooper explains that television combines sound and picture to present an aesthetic rather than a logical experience, using a narrative rather than a discursive approach. Discursive presentations are sequential and linear. With print media, we read each sentence from beginning to end before going on to the next. With oral material, such as radio, we perceive only one piece of information at a time. People tend to be analytical about discursive material, to look for what assertions are being made and how they are supported.

By contrast, narrative material may present information out of sequence. A photograph, a painting, or a television picture requires the viewer to shift focus to analyze the foreground, the background, the different elements of the image. People's reaction to narrative material emphasizes the aesthetic or affective response rather than the informative value. Candidates for public office often find themselves evaluated in terms of appearances as much as on the substance of their words. A selection of comments made about contenders in the past several years includes criticism of the following sort: Gerald Ford lost the 1976 Carter-Ford debates because he made less eye contact with the camera; Paul Simon's earlobes were too big and his droning voice did not match his perky bow tie; Al Gore looked like he belonged in the cast of "Dynasty" more than in the White House; Bruce Babbitt could not work up a convincing smile; Jimmy Carter smiled too much to be taken seriously enough to win a second term; and Michael Dukakis was the Ice Man who could not compete with George Bush, the Nice Man.

Politicians are not supposed to admit that they like or know how to use television, but, ever since Dwight Eisenhower's administration in the 1950s, advertising agencies have been routinely engaged to assist with political campaigns. Campaign managers, such as the late Republican party advisor Lee Atwater, are acutely aware of "packaging" the candidate, much like any other product. Their response to criticism is that they are simply doing what is necessary to get today's candidate elected.

They did not, they argue, invent the game; they just know its rules and help their candidates play to win.

Section 315 of the Communications Act of 1934 provides that all legally qualified candidates for office be afforded equal opportunity to use broadcast media to communicate their messages to the public. It further states that broadcast licensees shall not censor the content of material broadcast under this provision. (Broadcasters were initially concerned about their responsibility for libelous comments made in these uncensored messages; however, their exemption from being sued for libel under such conditions has been upheld by the Supreme Court.) When candidates appear on bona fide newscasts or news interview programs, the necessity to provide equal time is not applied, though most broadcast operations attempt to even out coverage of candidates even in exempt categories.

Besides being given equal access to broadcast time, Section 315 specifies that all candidates be given the opportunity to buy advertising time at the same rate. During the 45 days before a primary and the 60 days before a general election, advertising must be made available to all candidates at the station's "lowest unit charge" (in other words, the cheapest rate available to any advertiser in a given time period). Paid political advertising provides an opportunity for candidates to make points that might have been ignored or downplayed in "free" news coverage of the campaign. However, such advertising has become a controversial element of campaigns for several reasons, including its tendency to go for knee-jerk emotional responses and its increasingly negative tone (see "The Trouble with Spots").

Daily news coverage of candidates on the campaign trail provides a different kind of information than do interviews, debates, and the substantive elements of the campaign itself. When reporters cover the campaign as news, they do most of the talking. Sometimes in the background a candidate is seen orating and, at the last minute, the sound picks up a few of her or his own words. These snippets are called sound bites. They often run only six or seven words—in 1968 the average sound bite for presidential candidates on network news was 42 seconds; in 1992 it was less than 9 seconds—and are selected for their news value, not necessarily their ability to capture the essence of what the campaign addressed that day. Campaign staffs engage regularly in "spin patrol," a process of trying to influence the slant reporters will take in interpreting both campaign news and noncampaign news, such as the state of the economy, that might affect voter attitudes.

Once in office, news "spin" affects public perceptions

of how a political leader is doing (see "Bad News Bearers"). Activist groups who wish to unseat an incumbent leader in the next election often continue their efforts to influence news stories that raise questions regarding character and competence throughout the term of office. An example of such strategic maneuvering is described by Trudy Lieberman in "Churning Whitewater."

The media have a fascination with politicians as personalities. The implicit agreement between politicians and the press that kept Warren Harding's, Franklin Roosevelt's, Dwight Eisenhower's, John Kennedy's, and Lyndon Johnson's adulteries out of the public eye no longer holds. It is arguable that disclosures such as these give voters valuable insight into the character of the candidates under consideration, and this is often a point made by reporters who bring such stories forward. It is also arguable that the interest generated by such stories overrides the public's focus on what is important: where candidates stand on issues. News media tend to be highly conscious of this criticism and very committed to providing a forum for candidates to discuss issues, but they are also sensitive to competitive pressures.

The media are not without blame in either sensationalizing or trivializing politics, but they are also not entirely responsible for these trends. As author Richard Zoglin has pointed out, catchy campaign slogans and the practice of oversimplifying issues were not invented by television people. Successful leaders have always had to adapt to the medium of their time. They must be able to forge an emotional bond with the people. Perhaps, to a certain degree, it is appropriate that politicians who will need to use media to communicate themes and dreams while in office "audition" for that role as a part of running for office.

Looking Ahead: Challenge Questions

How can news spin influence a political leader's success both during the campaign for office and while serving in office? Do you think the press has been fair in its coverage of the Clinton administration?

How has the increased use and sophistication of political advertising spots affected the political process? Are all of the changes that have been associated with this trend undesirable? Has the process of selecting political leaders become better, worse, or simply different?

Is knowledge of a political candidate's personal conduct relevant to your voting decision? Should this information be available to the public? How should it be treated by mainstream news media?

Call-in talk shows have increased access to the broadcast airways. Since the 1992 election, these shows have assumed a particularly political slant. In his article "The Power of Talk," Howard Fineman muses, "This may all be great broadcasting, but is it good government?" Do such shows enhance or compromise democratic ideals?

Bad News Bearers

The media really were mugging Bill Clinton.
Here's the proof.

Christopher Georges

Back in the Democrats' glory days (before they were elected), the Clinton image warriors figured out how to win the message crusade. Swallowing their pride–or what was left of it–the Democrats brilliantly plagiarized from the Reagan-Deaver-Gergen-Ailes gospel of media maintenance: a line of the day, a coordinated theme, populist images. And to their own surprise, it worked.

So when the new team of eager-Deavers took over America in January, it only made sense to stay on the same page. After all, if Reagan could pull the wheelchairs out from under the elderly and still, thanks to gushy photo ops and a pliant press, appear as the old folks' champion, smooth-talking Clinton–with the right communications plan–should also be able to have his way. Certainly the parallels between the Clinton and Reagan media strategies have limits, but the Carvillites made no secret of the fact they wanted to keep up the Deaver magic. That meant limiting national media access to the Boss; frowning on presidential news conferences (Reagan had only 21 in his first three years); giving preference to local media markets; catchy visuals; sell, sell, sell; and so on.

Given all that, why did the media–before moderately toning down its belligerence in late June–savage Clinton in his first four months in office? To hear the media tell it, the bad news is all the administration's doing. After all, they say, Clinton's bumbling decisions–from A(ir Clinton) to Z(oë)–would do in even the

most popular of politicians, and if that explanation doesn't convince you, the media have offered a dozen or so alternatives, including: Clinton's communications team has been arrogant; the White House press office has gone over the heads of the White House press corps; George Stephanopoulos smirked too much; and so on.

It's hard to argue with all that. And, to a certain degree, they're right (except perhaps for the smirk). But as the press ruminates on the slapstick communications effort, the conventional wisdom tells only half the story. Could it possibly be that the negative tone and content of the coverage has something to do with the press itself?

Not to worry; this won't parrot the tired administration line (any administration, that is) that the media are biased against it. They're not. But unlike administrations from Nixon's to Bush's, the Clinton crowd may be onto something. After being Deaverized, then Hortonized, and then mulling it over for the past few years, the presidential press has at long last taken on a fiercer, less trusting tone–a tone not heard in these parts since the nastiness of Watergate. "The press has a learning curve. The '88 campaign seared them," says Larry Sabato, author of *Feeding Frenzy* and professor of government at the University of Virginia. "The barbs are sharper; the coverage is tighter. They're going for the jugular."

Although reporters and editors are loath to admit it, a day-by-day comparison of Clinton White House reporters' dispatches with those of the media that covered the past administration confirms Sabato's claim. But it's not just that the press is tougher on Clinton than on any recent administration, but tougher in a very specific way: Because it's constantly looking for

Research assistance for this article was provided by Danny Franklin, Spencer Freedman, Nicholas Joseph, Jennifer Levitsky, and Genevieve Murphy.

the con, the press won't take the bait on the Rockwellian images or be soothed by promises or be bullied by press officers. And if the media sense that they are getting the Reagan/Deaver treatment, woe be it to the messenger—whether it's the president or his flacks.

That, of course, is a step in the right direction. But like just about everything else that involves the press, it's turned into a caricature. In its zeal to expose presidential hooey, the media see—and report—slickness where it may not exist. Almost nothing that comes out of the White House, the press seems to be saying, should be taken at face value; hypocrisy could lurk in any and every press release. For Beleaguered Bill, that means his message of the day, even the noblest ones, such as PAC reform, is portrayed as a deception; it means that compromise—any compromise—becomes at best a broken promise, at worst a ruse; presidential trips, even a summit with Yeltsin, are described as Hollywood-style sales campaigns; progress, like the announcement of a national service program, is presented as an unfulfilled pledge; and even pathetic gaffes and loose-lipped friends become "evidence" of slickness. It means, in short, that in the press' zeal to avoid being snookered, it has neglected a crucial part of its job: an objective rendering of the news.

HARD PRESSED

And just how unobjective have the media been? Consider, for example, that for Bush, 74 percent of the evaluative comments made by TV reporters on evening news broadcasts during the first three months of his administration were positive, according to the Center for Media and Public Affairs. (The only group more likely to comment favorably on Bush was Republicans, with an 80 percent rating.) For Clinton, just 21 percent of the comments made by reporters have been positive. In fact, all other groups except Republicans—and that includes interest groups and foreign sources—were more likely to make positive remarks about Clinton than journalists were.

But numbers tell only a small part of the story. For a better picture of the media's double-standard, we'll have to go to the videotape, starting with a comparison of the way the national media handled four similar issues for the new administrations in 1989 and 1993:

National Service: Like Clinton in 1992, Bush in 1988 campaigned aggressively for national service. Bush's ambitious campaign rhetoric called specifically for a full-blown domestic peace corps. Once elected, however, Bush announced that his plan was—to be

kind—less comprehensive: In fact, it consisted merely of creating the "Points of Light" foundation, funded with a paltry $25 million federal outlay.

The program, which was unveiled with a splashy photo-op at a New York youth center, where the Bushes touchingly cradled babies and related to a once-stabbed teenager, was trumpeted with glowing reports on all three networks. In fact, ABC News devoted an entire *American Agenda* segment to a weepy piece on the youth center and the Bush plan. NBC's John Cochran opened his piece with the Bushes entering the center to a cheering crowd: "President Bush chose New York to finish what he started at the Republican convention last summer, when he said volunteer groups could be 'a thousand points of light,'" and closed it saying that if the program is "far from the Great Society, that's fine.... The last thing [Bush] wants is a federal bureaucracy."

> *For Beleaguered Bill, the messages of the day, even the nobelest ones, such as PAC reform, have been portrayed as deceptions; compromise—any compromise—has become at best a broken promise, at worst a ruse; even pathetic gaffes and loose-lipped friends become "evidence" of slickness.*

Clinton's plan, like Bush's, fell short of his campaign promise—but it came a whole lot closer. In fact, Clinton's $7 billion proposal not only calls for real money, but is expected to involve 100,000 youths by 1997. (Keep in mind, by the way, that John F. Kennedy's Peace Corps enrolled fewer than 16,000 volunteers at its peak in 1966.) How did the press react to the Clinton announcement, which, like Bush's, was presented in a made-for-TV photo-op at a youth center? CBS's Dan Rather offered a two-line news-read drily announcing the plan and then led into the day's White House report: a feature detailing how Clinton had cunningly evaded his pledge to cut the White House staff by 25 percent through a bookkeeping maneuver. NBC's Andrea Mitchell, on the other hand, did offer a national service feature—but focussed on the plan's drawbacks. "Five million students now have college loans and could have assumed they'd be eligible," she reported, "but Clinton's plan would cover only a fraction of them." She added that "some critics worry that Clinton's proposal, small as it is, could be a boondoggle." After a scholar slammed the program, Mitchell closed: "Once again, Clinton has proved that there is big difference between what he promised as a candidate and what he can deliver as president." The print press was even less generous: *The Washington Post's* front page story led not with the plan but by stating that Clinton had, in preparing the program, buckled to a special interest, watering it down from the original version. "Despite the grand words . . ." *The Wall Street Journal* reported, and "though smaller than the president had led audiences to expect, the program was introduced with a Clintonesque flair."

Education Reform: Clinton's campaign pledges for education reform, while ambitious, still did not match the scope of those made in 1988 by Bush, who had, after all, pledged to become our education president. What did Bush eventually present in April 1989? Not only was his "reform" package mostly a compendium of pilot programs, but he had reneged on his most basic promise: to increase the level of spending for education. In fact—in a move that would certainly be labeled a Slick Willie in 1993—the Bush plan, which was trumpeted as a 2 percent spending increase was, in reality, with inflation factored in, an education cut.

The coverage? Again, it was universally favorable. Not one of the networks and few of the major papers noted the gap between the plan and the promise. Even worse, all three networks fell for the funding level charade, parroting the administration line that spending was upped. ABC News' Brit Hume, for example, featured a Democratic governor—who the Bush people had conveniently offered up for this very occasion—who praised the plan as "a strong new commitment." In print, *The Los Angeles Times'* front page story led saying that the Bush plan "backs up his campaign pledge to become the 'education president' . . . [with] a program intended to 'make excellence in education not just a rallying cry but a classroom reality.'"

Four years later, almost to the day, Clinton proposed a plan that, while it fell short of his campaign pledge, was not only more comprehensive than Bush's, but also closer to the rhetoric of his campaign (such as promising increased funding, which he came through on). Even so, *Time* labeled the plan "pallid," saying it "avoids all the toughest issues" and charged Clinton with breaking yet another campaign pledge. Other news organizations, such as *The Boston Globe,* stated falsely that Clinton was trying to fob off Bush's old plan as his own. And on TV, consider the negative tone of NBC's report, the thrust of which was that "some teachers today were skeptical," and which featured two

teachers and an education expert, all of whom criticized the plan. "Probably just another level of paper that will have to come down," says one teacher. "We'll have to fill out something."

PAC and Lobby Reform: In 1988 Bush not only campaigned for PAC reform—as did Clinton in 1992—but also came through with a plan in his first 100 days. Coverage of the Bush program was straightforward and positive. ABC News' Ann Compton, for example, said that the plan came as a "surprise" to Congress and labeled it a "PAC attack." *The Washington Post's* story led calling the Bush plan "a wide-ranging package of ethics proposals for the three branches of government and . . . broad reform in campaign financing laws." Even the paper's editorial page labeled it "a workmanlike and valuable job."

Yet while Clinton's plan is without question bolder, more comprehensive, and more detailed, the press, from *The New York Times* to *Newsweek,* has focussed largely on the Clinton con—that is, how the president and the Democrats have continued, even as they have proposed reform, to take money from special interest donors. CBS News' Rather, for example, offered: "Candidate Clinton said he would deliver . . . on election campaign reform. Today, President Clinton came out with his plan for what is called campaign reform . . . Correspondent Eric Enberg looks past the photo op. . . ." Enberg's report jabbed at Clinton for hypocrisy and noted that while Clinton was proposing reform, he and other Democrats were still taking thousands of dollars from "fat cats" and "influence brokers." That's good reporting, of course, but where were Enberg and the rest of the probing pack in 1989 when Bush proposed his reforms? Hadn't Bush and the Republicans continued to take money from PACs and lobbyists too?

The Populist Con: For presidents, the populism dance comes with the job. So when horse-shoe-playing-Bush—who was about as elitist as presidents get these days—played the game, the press reacted about as expected. "No longer the Yale yuppie with a silver spoon in his mouth," NBC's Andrea Mitchell reported in April of 1989, "no longer the attack dog of the campaign. The new image: a guy who could live in your hometown." The same month, *Newsday* reported that in place of the "the Reagan glitz and glamour . . . have come a tumble of children, grandchildren, and in-laws the likes of which the White House has not seen since the days of John F. Kennedy. There are newborn puppies in the parlor and a freshly dug horseshoe pit in the back yard." In the meantime, the press dutifully ignored, for example, Bush's Kennebunkport trips, which routinely caused traffic backups and even interfered with the livelihood of local lobstermen, just as they had looked the other way when Ronald Reagan spent $50,000 of taxpayer money on planes and helicopters for a weekend excursion to Rancho del Cielo.

But for Clinton (even before the hair-care fiasco), the media made an outright mockery of his man-of-the-peoplism (despite his far more humble roots), from the White House jogging track to *The Washington Post's* photo spreads whenever an administration biggie buys a pricey home.

PHOTOSLOP

It's not, however, just what the press has been reporting, but what it hasn't. Apparently in a feverish attempt to avoid becoming ventriloquist dummies for the Clintonites, the media have routinely glossed over and even taken pot-shots at the president's message in cases where a little Reagan-era flacking might have been entirely legitimate. A few examples:

▶ When Clinton took his act to California on May 18 to hype his jobs and defense conversion programs—neither of which had received air time on NBC—Andrea Mitchell's report not only ignored the Clinton proposals, but rambled through one negative image after another. After opening with a shot of presidential hecklers ("You broke your promise"), she reminded viewers of how Clinton said he had found himself "surprised" at the size of the deficit when he came into office. Mitchell then commented on his Hollywood connections ("To fix the president's image, the Hollywood producer who staged all those campaign bus trips showed up today"), before closing by saying that if Clinton has his way, we are all likely to face higher taxes.

▶ CBS took that same set of events and butchered the message even further. Also virtually ignoring Clinton's proposals (the jobs plan is mentioned only in reference to Clinton's troubled relationship with Congress), Susan Spencer's story covers: Clinton's ditching his middle class tax cut pledge; a soundbite from a woman who asks Clinton about his plan to convert defense industries to civilian projects ("What is it supposed to convert us into, except jobless, homeless, and hungry?"); high unemployment in California; and the "you broke your promise" hecklers.

▶ One of Clinton's fleeting moments of glory in May came when the House Ways and Means Committee passed his tax package. But NBC's Mitchell had other images in mind: "Today was mostly good news," she starts, and then explains why it was really a "black letter day." She proceeds to take us through a two minute tour of the dark side of the Clinton presidency. Clinton's tax package, she explains, will hit small

business owners hard; the president is being attacked by Ross Perot; "Many view [Clinton] as a tax-and-spend Democrat"; "the president's ratings in the business community have plummeted"; Clinton's deficit reduction fund is, according to Republicans, a "shell game," and according to an independent analyst, a "gimmick." She closes relatively mercifully, saying the "point of [the economic plan] is to make the President *appear* more accountable, more concerned about deficit reduction."

▶ One of the President's few foreign policy highlights came on April 15, when he rallied seven nations to pledge $28 billion in new aid to Russia. CBS' Dan Rather granted this news a 10-second read before turning to correspondent Susan Spencer, who then proceeded with a full feature on the administration's ill-fated value-added tax trial balloon.

▶ Similarly, the administration's program to provide free vaccines for every child in America merited a short news read from NBC's Tom Brokaw, who provided neither an explanation of the plan nor any other detail. The feature report that followed, however, took viewers to New Haven to explain how "free vaccines won't alone solve the problem." On ABC, a story about the vaccine plan didn't take viewers that far. The network's report on the compromise that led to the final vaccine plan—a compromise that experts agreed made the plan more affordable and more closely targeted to the truly needy—focussed almost exclusively on Clinton's waffling; the piece ignored both the substance of the plan and its improvement. "The White House has now backed away from the one health care proposal the President has already made," reported correspondent Brit Hume. "On immunization, Mr. Clinton did more than just compromise—he agreed to a major overhaul of his plan. If this happens on health care, what emerges from Congress may not much resemble what Mr. Clinton sends up there."

WITH FRIENDS LIKE THESE...

Obviously, something's bugging the media. Of course, the press is not monolithic. Even so, if you talk to enough reporters, a pattern emerges. For one, their prickliness towards the Clinton administration is, to a degree, personal. Most reporters are closer personally and politically to Democrats, which means that the press' standards with Democrats are generally higher. (Jimmy Carter was victimized by the double-standard problem as well.) At the same time, the natural reporter-Democrat bond means, ironically, that many reporters may be more willing to take liberties that offend their Democrat administration sources; some reporters admit (although not for attribution) that they feel more compelled to tread gently when dealing with Republican sources simply because they fear losing access.

Personalities aside, there's a more Clinton-specific reason why some reporters have been eager to paint the president as a con-man: They, rightly or wrongly, believe it. "He's not straightforward," explains Julia Malone, White House correspondent for Cox newspapers. "This feeling is not only of him, but his staff." Adds another White House reporter, who asked not to be quoted by name, "He's incredibly charming, but he lies. That's right, Clinton lies. Reporters hate that. I sympathize with his efforts, but it's easy to find yourself being angry with him."

Of course, no White House reporter who wants to keep his job until the next photo-op would dare let such an assessment slip into copy. So some do the next best thing: They show it, or at least try to. This helps explain why the media made such a hoo-ha about the travel story, the hypocrisy on PAC and lobbying reform, and the ersatz populism. They show it in dozens of smaller, subtler ways as well. On June 1, for example, *The New York Times* devoted an entire article to explain that Clinton had stepped out the previous day to play *three* holes of golf. Why an entire story for three holes? "The White House," the piece notes a few paragraphs in, "concerned about Mr. Clinton's image these days, had spent much of the day trying to avoid any mention of a presidential golf outing." The piece then takes the unusual step of explaining how the story was reported: "Mr. Stephanopoulos said early in the day that the President was going to Quantico, Va., to present awards at a golf tournament, and he insisted that he did not actually play golf. 'He had too much work,' he said. But Mr. Stephanopoulos called back to say there had been some 'confusion' and that the President did play."

ROSE-COLORED WINDOW

To truly understand the media's recent edginess, however, you have to go back to the seventies. Watergate and Vietnam made the media realize that they were being manipulated by the communications gurus, and that turned a previously fangless press nasty. Into this minefield stepped Ford and then Carter. But by the time Reagan was elected, the cynicism shtick had grown old; the press—perhaps reflecting the mood of the nation, or weary of being labelled unpatriotic—mellowed its tone.

The timing couldn't have been better for the Deaverites who were not only able to sell upbeat images of their man's ability where he was making progress

(such as in dealing with the Soviets) but also in areas where he wasn't, such as officiating at the Special Olympics (he had proposed cutting the budget for the disabled), and dedicating senior citizens projects (he had proposed cutting federal housing subsidies for the elderly). The media, of course, eventually caught on to the Reagan video game and grew progressively more savvy about being manipulated. But old habits die hard, and as Willie Horton proved, by 1988 the press was still malleable. Media cynicism remained, moreover, at bay for the most part during the first two years of the Bush administration, thanks in part to Bush's unique communications strategy—government by press conference. Although the conferences gave the appearance of an open and active president, the reality (as pointed out in a *Washington Monthly* article in December 1991) was that the briefings, which rarely covered any ground Bush did not want covered, were merely a back-door method of making the president appear tough and active.

How did the press react to Clinton's National Service program announcement? CBS's Dan Rather offered a two-line news-read drily announcing the plan and then led into the day's White House report: a feature detailing how Clinton had cunningly evaded his pledge to cut the White House staff by 25 percent through a bookkeeping maneuver.

But by the third year of Bush's presidency, none of that seemed to matter. Coverage of the President turned decidedly sour. Part of the reason was, of course, the sinking economy. But it's also true that the untold numbers of seminars, articles, and books self-reflecting on the presidential cons of the past few years were beginning to sink in. The result was to throw the skepticism machine back into high gear.

That helps explain not only the press's prickly aversion to any form of phoniness—real or perceived—in the current administration, but the harsh treatment Bush received in his last year as president. (By Campaign

1992, the old tricks were no longer working: Bush's sudden incarnation as a "reformer" might have flown in 1989, but it drew only mockery in 1992. The press even dug up and hit him for his failure to meet those long-forgotten campaign promises.)

Clinton benefitted from a cheerleading media during the second half of the campaign, but when he moved into the White House, he faced what was for the most part a new set of reporters—a group that continued its work on Clinton where it had left off on Bush.

In one sense, we should be grateful for the media's tougher tone. "No one," says *The New York Times*'s Andrew Rosenthal, who covered the Bush White House, "wants to be played for a chump." That's true, of course, but it's also true that avoiding the presidential hustle doesn't require leaving fair play behind.

CHURNING WHITEWATER

Trudy Lieberman

Trudy Lieberman is a senior editor at Consumer Reports.

"The mainstream media (to which we mail *ClintonWatch* regularly) is now beginning to parrot much of the information and analysis we break." — *ClintonWatch*, November 1993

"Citizens United has been a powerful force behind the exposure of the biggest story to hit Washington D.C. since Watergate." — *Citizens Agenda*, February 1994

Whether or not the story turns out to be more than an extended fishing expedition, it is already clear that the frenzied media are feeding on bait dangled by a master of media manipulation

In a cluttered office tucked away in one of the many red-brick office condominiums that ring Washington, D.C., David Bossie, source par excellence to journalists dredging the Whitewater swamp, handles one of the eighteen calls he says he gets each hour. This one is from Bruce Ingersoll, a staff reporter for *The Wall Street Journal*. The discussion centers on bonds. "I have a whole file on bond transactions," Bossie tells Ingersoll. "I will get a report on what I find. I know you are trying to move quickly on this. You want to come out before *they* come out." A few minutes later Bossie says, "I don't know what I have to give you," but promises to spend the next couple of hours going through materials. "You're on deadline, I understand that." He then points Ingersoll in another direction. "Have you done anything on Beverly? [Presumably that is Beverly Bassett Schaffer, former Arkansas Securities Commissioner.] You guys ought to look into that. There will be lawsuits against the Rose law firm," he adds.

"Lot 7," Bossie tells me between calls, is the next big story. "ABC and *U.S. News & World Report* are looking at Lot 7. We're the only ones that have the abstract. Wade [Chris Wade, a real estate agent who sold some of the Whitewater lots] dumped the property and got something from the Clintons."

The phone rings again. Bossie addresses the caller as "Judge." "That judge who called," Bossie explains later, "called me in August and said he had a friend, [another judge named] David Hale, who was in trouble because of Bill Clinton." It was this phone call and the charges that Hale later made through Bossie's organization, Citizens United, that fueled David Bossie's zealous investigation into Whitewater. Bossie's efforts have, in turn, generated daily page-one headlines — and another chapter in the saga of American pack journalism. "I'm the information bank," he says.

Bossie, the twenty-eight-year-old political director for Citizens United, a conservative Republican operation, runs an information factory whose Whitewater production lines turn out a steady stream of tips, tidbits, documents, factoids, suspicions, and story ideas for the nation's press and for Republicans on Capitol Hill. Journalists and Hill Republicans have recycled much of the information provided by Citizens United into stories that have cast a shadow on the Clinton presidency.

Bossie, who says he works sixteen hours a day on Whitewater, earned his Republican stripes as the national youth director in Senator Robert Dole's 1988 presidential campaign, and then moved on during the 1992 Bush campaign to become executive director of the Presidential Victory Committee. His boss, Floyd Brown, worked as Dole's Midwest political director during the 1988 campaign, but is best known for producing the Willie Horton commercial that helped sink the presidential ambitions of Democrat Michael Dukakis.

Brown, with Bossie as a principal researcher, wrote *"Slick Willie": Why America Cannot Trust Bill Clinton*, a 192-page paperback released during the 1992 presidential campaign. At the time, the press paid little attention to the book's revelations, including a preview of the current Whitewater scenario.

Since the Arkansas judge's telephone call last August, Citizens United has collected thousands of facts and documents on Whitewater and packaged it all to catch the attention of the press and to restoke the story whenever it threatened to die down.

Bossie and Brown have been briefing people since October — "the top fifty major publications, networks, and editorial boards," Bossie says. "We've provided the same material on the Hill both on the House and Senate side." An equal opportunity source, Bossie says he would gladly provide documents to Democrats, but they haven't asked.

Francis Shane, publisher of Citizens United's newsletter, *ClintonWatch*, hesitates to say exactly whom they've worked with — "We don't particularly like to pinpoint people" — but he does say, "We have worked closer with *The New York Times* than *The Washington Times*." Jeff Gerth, *The New York Times*'s chief reporter on Whitewater, hesitated to talk on the record. He did say, "If Citizens United has some document that's relevant, I take it. I check it out like anything else."

Most of the information is found in five thick packets stacked up around the Citizens United offices, four of them neatly bound and bearing the Citizens United emblem — an eagle and a flag — on the front. There's the volume titled "Arkansas Bond Deals with Stephens Inc.," which, among other things, details the potential problems Citizens United perceives with a 1989 Arkansas Student Loan Association bond issue. "Truly there are many areas of this issue which need further investigation," the volume points out. Bossie himself says, "They were making sweetheart deals through bonds," and then he adds, "The ones working on this are *Money* magazine and *The Bond Buyer*." A second volume covers Bill and Hillary Rodham Clinton's tax returns from 1980 through 1990; a third details lawsuits involving James McDougal; a fourth is a collection of real estate abstracts; and a fifth is a package titled "Whitewater Documents," which contains an assortment of deeds, mortgages, checks, letters, reports, balance sheets, and press releases. Citizens United has also compiled an eighteen-page list of "Criminal statutes relating to potential Whitewater Crimes," complete with legal citations.

ClintonWatch, a newsletter dedicated to "Proving Character Does Count in a President," is sent to all media and contains tales and tidbits that have found their way into the nation's news. The organization's official newsletter, *Citizens Agenda*, sent to its 11,000 subscribers periodically, offers a morsel or two and boasts about the group's success in siccing the media on to the Whitewater story. Citizens United's newest infor-

AP/WIDE WORLD

mation effort is a *Whitewater Fax Bulletin*, also called *ClintonWatch*, which is fed to the media almost daily. "Nobody seems to have all the answers, but by sharing our information with members of the media, we can start putting pieces together ... We are making new discoveries every day," Brown said in launching his new fax service in early March. One of the first *Fax Bulletins* was aimed at stirring up interest in Lot 7, which Bossie had told me was the next big story.

Floyd Brown, who created the Willie Horton ads in 1988, proudly announces another campaign for another election: a phone number that played recordings of alleged conversations between then-candidate Bill Clinton and Gennifer Flowers.

The March 1994 issue of *ClintonWatch* characterized the organization's impact on Whitewater press coverage this way: "We here at *ClintonWatch* have been working day and night with the major news media to help them get the word out about the Clintons and their questionable dealings in Whitewater and Madison Guaranty." Of course, Citizens United is not the only source of information on Whitewater. And reputable reporters do their own digging and doublechecking. Still, an examination of some 200 news stories from the major news outlets aired or published since November shows an eerie similarity between the Citizens United agenda and what has been appearing in the press, not only in terms of specific details but in terms of omissions, spin, and implication. Here are four cases in point.

David Hale talks

Citizens United takes full credit for blowing the Whitewater story wide open with what it calls Floyd Brown's "exclusive news-making interview with Arkansas Municipal Judge David Hale." Hale, who owned Capital Management Services, a Small Business Administration-approved lending company, claims he was pressed by then Governor Clinton to make a loan of $300,000 to Susan McDougal, one of the Clintons's Whitewater partners, who, he said, did not qualify. Part of this loan allegedly found its way into the coffers of the Whitewater Development Corp.

The November 1993 issue of *ClintonWatch* recounts much of what Hale told Brown in a feature called "Clinton Fingered in Loan Cover-Up." As that issue was making its way to the news desks of the nation's media, Citizens United began arranging interviews for Hale with various news organizations. "Everything Hale has done [with the media] has gone through us," Shane told me.

On November 2 *The New York Times* and *The Washington Post* broke the Hale story. Both deny that Brown was the source. "Mr. Hale asserted in interviews with reporters," that Clinton had personally pressed him to make the $300,000 loan, the *Times* article said. A few days later *The Washington Times* featured in its news columns a copy of the $300,000 check payable to Susan McDougal and signed by Hale. That check is in Bossie's Whitewater document collection labeled exhibit "B-1."

Over the next several weeks, virtually all of the major media carried Hale's version of the loan transaction, but few looked into his political connections, his motives, or his credibility. Many referred to interviews they had had with Hale himself. On November 7, for example, the *Los Angeles Times* said, "In a series of interviews, Hale provided this account ...." On November 11, NBC reported: "Now this man, a former local judge under indictment on an unrelated case, has told NBC News ...." The November 15 issue of *Newsweek* mentioned a "telephone interview" with Hale. On December 15, ABC's *World News Tonight* noted, "This is David Hale, until recently a Little Rock investor ...."

Hillary seeks power of attorney

In the same story that featured the $300,000 check, *The Washington Times* lobbed another grenade: it printed a copy of a letter Hillary Clinton wrote to McDougal on November 28, 1988, asking for power of attorney over Whitewater matters. The *Times* portrayed the letter as proof that, despite their disclaimers, the Clintons were active in the management of Whitewater.

The letter filtered through the press. In January *USA Today* credited *The Washington Times*'s disclosure with keeping the Whitewater issue alive, and *The Wall Street Journal* in a March 18 story on the "scrappy 12-year-old broadsheet" noted the paper's power-of-attorney "scoop." A Nexis search turns up thirty-one news organizations that cited the power of attorney letter. Some used it to show the Clintons were more than passive investors in Whitewater; a few amplified the facts. *The Boston Globe*, for example, reported that Hillary Clinton obtained the power of attorney; *USA Today* noted, correctly, that she didn't. The letter seeking power of attorney is in the Citizens United file as exhibit "K-1."

The fact that Hillary Clinton asked for power of attorney in 1988 is intriguing, but does it prove the Clintons's long-standing involvement? Or could there have been other explanations? For example, was McDougal, who had experienced health problems, incapable of cleaning up the mess Whitewater supposedly had become?

The Sheffield Nelson tapes

Newsweek's February 7 issue revealed that Sheffield Nelson, a Little Rock attorney who ran against Clinton for governor in 1990, had taped conversations with McDougal. In those conversations, McDougal claims that the Clintons had not been truthful about their Whitewater losses, and is quoted as saying, "I could sink [the claim of a $69,000] loss quicker than they could lie about it .... And Bill Clinton knows it." *Newsweek* said the tape was obtained from "independent sources" but had been "authenticated" by Nelson. Several newspapers picked up *Newsweek*'s findings.

Two weeks later Representative Jim Leach, the ranking Republican on the House Banking Committee, handed to the press additional portions of the Sheffield Nelson tapes — giving the "sink and lie" quote even wider circulation. The *Los Angeles Times* in a story crediting Leach with release of the tapes did note that a portion of Nelson's interview with McDougal "was previously provided to some reporters by sources who asked not to be identified."

CNN picked up the story, named Leach as the source of the tapes, and cited "new evidence resurrecting some of the most serious questions about President Clinton's role in the Whitewater controversy." CNN showed viewers a $6,300 Whitewater check for payment of a mortgage taken out by Hillary Clinton, which it said "appears to back up at least part of the McDougal tape," but did not explain how. Nowhere in the broadcast did CNN demystify the implied connection between the mortgage payment and

---

"Everything Hale has done [with the media] has gone through us," says *Clinton-Watch*'s publisher

McDougal's taped statement. (Exhibit "J-9" in the Citizens United collection shows a "Whitewater Development Co. check #130, reflecting a $6,361.65 interest payment on H. Rodham. #23039.")

NBC waited until mid-March to do its version of the Nelson tape, which it said "NBC News has obtained." It, too, gave prominence to the "sink and lie" quote. But NBC used a different check to back up McDougal's allegation on the tape, that the Clintons did not lose money on Whitewater. NBC said that among the Clintons's losses for 1982 was a check for $20,744. NBC noted that the White House said the money was for repayment of a Whitewater-related loan. On camera, McDougal said the check was repayment for a personal loan. (Exhibit J-4 in the Bossie Whitewater collection notes: "Bill Clinton check #621 for $20,744.65 to Madison Bank & Trust noted as repayment of note." ABC had shown the same check five weeks earlier.)

In his press conference at the end of March, Clinton admitted the check was not a Whitewater loss, but a loan, which he had forgotten about, taken out to help his mother buy a cabin.

Was Citizens United a source for NBC's piece? *ClintonWatch* publisher Shane says only, "We have a close relationship with them. We've worked with all the networks. Ira [producer Ira Silverman] does a good job." An incident reported in the *Arkansas Democrat-Gazette* reveals how close that relationship is. In January, the paper said that former Arkansas Securities Commissioner Beverly Bassett Schaffer accused Bossie and an NBC crew of ambushing her outside her office and then stalking her after she refused to grant an on-camera interview. Silverman was quoted as saying the incident was the result of "aggressive journalism," noting that Bossie was in Arkansas "for another aspect of NBC's investigation" into Whitewater. Silverman says, "I talk to them [Citizens United] along with everyone else. Back in October and November it was difficult to develop sources." He added that early on Bossie provided sources.

The only reporter who acknowledged a connection between Citizens United and the tape was John Aloysius Farrell of the *The Boston Globe,* who reported that conservative activist Floyd Brown "is up to his old tricks .... This week Brown released a typical nugget to the press: a tape of a spring 1992 visit by Clinton's partner in Whitewater Development Co., James McDougal, to the law offices of GOP attorney Sheffield Nelson."

Vince Foster solicits the FDIC

In 1989, Vince Foster wrote to the FDIC seeking legal work for the Rose law firm from the government, which was beginning to clean up the savings and loan mess. The government was trying to recoup some of its losses by suing Frost & Co., a Little Rock accounting firm that had been hired by the state to examine the books of Madison Guaranty. The government contended that Frost had issued a misleading report about Madison's financial condition. In his letter, Foster said the firm does not represent any savings and loan, although the firm apparently had previously represented Madison Guaranty, a potential conflict of interest. Rose got the job.

The Washington Post, citing FDIC records, broke the story of Foster's letter on November 3, three and a half months after his suicide. It was picked up later that month by *The Washington Times* and publications covering the thrift industry. *The Wall Street Journal* mentioned it in a mid-December editorial.

But it wasn't until early January, after Citizens United featured Foster's letter in *ClintonWatch*, that it received prominent play in the media. The newsletter said that the Rose firm had settled its $60 million suit against Frost for $1 million and then "billed the government $400,000 for its trouble." It also emphasized a point *The Washington Post* had made in passing. It quoted from Foster's letter: "[t]he firm does not represent any savings and loan association in state or federal regulatory matters," but added this embellishment: "(note the use of the present — not the past — tense)."

From January 1 to the end of March, twenty-three news organizations referred to the Foster letter — more than triple the number that picked up the story after the November 3 *Washington Post* piece. Many, including *The Atlanta Journal-Constitution*, *The Dallas Morning News*, *The Arizona Republic*, and *The Boston Globe*, mentioned the $400,000 fee highlighted in *ClintonWatch*. *Newsday*, on January 16, called attention to Foster's use of the present tense in his letter.

All of the surveyed papers quoted the same portion of Foster's letter. Only the Minneapolis *Star Tribune* gave the letter a fuller presentation. It added this from the letter: " ... while there may be individual transactions or situations where a conflict of interest would arise, we believe that the firm would not be ethically disqualified from serving as fee counsel." The paper goes on to point out that Foster does not mention Rose's past involvement with Madison.

The *Star Tribune* story was only one of two stories during that period that we found which brought some balance to the charges flying about

Stories were peppered with such phrases as "eyebrows are raised," "questions persist," "scandalous odors" the Clintons, and to question what the fuss was all about. The other was a January 31 *Business Week* story, which pointed out that the "Whitewater case could end with a whimper, not a bang," because, among other reasons, the government has already investigated many of the dealings of James McDougal and come up empty handed, a point that should have been made in other stories. (Recently, the *Chicago Tribune* and *The Wall Street Journal* featured stories exploring the link between Bossie and Brown and the Whitewater story.)

In mid-February, the FDIC cleared the Rose law firm of conflict of interest in the Frost & Co. matter. William Safire referred to FDIC investigators as "whitewashers." Republicans prevailed on the FDIC to reopen the case.

Back in October, *ClintonWatch* exhorted the Washington news media to "end their endless babbling about Camelot and get down to the business of investigating the legal, ethical, and moral shortcomings of the Clinton administration."

Whitewater is about character, publisher Fran Shane tells me. "The American people have elected a president with 43 percent of the vote. He is a man of no character. He may have to tell the people he didn't come clean. We're saying Bill Clinton may not be worth saving."

Many news organizations explain the importance of Whitewater in similar terms. Take *Time*, for instance. In a January 24 story laced with references to documents that also appear in Bossie's Whitewater collection, the magazine pronounced that "the investigation concerns the much larger issue of whether a President and First Lady can be trusted to obey the law and tell the truth."

The character issue can be turned on the press, which has shamelessly taken the hand-outs dished up by a highly partisan organization, with revenues of more than $2 million a year, without identifying the group as the source of their information.

Of course, journalists get leads and documents from all kinds of sources, savory and otherwise. Then the good journalist goes on to corroborate, amplify, and analyze the facts, and judge whether Fact A really does connect to Fact B. Those elements were missing from most of the pieces we examined.

Some stories did point out that no crimes and no illegalities had been committed. Often they nevertheless went on to string together assorted facts, without the connective tissue. Instead, the stories were peppered with such phrases as "those interviewed also wonder aloud," "eyebrows are raised," "questions persist," "scandalous odors," and "ethically suspect sweetheart deal." This approach had the effect of implying guilt by innuendo. The bigger the pile, the guiltier the Clintons must be.

As of this writing in early April, it appeared that Citizens United was still conducting outreach. A briefing led by Floyd Brown for the Washington press corps was held at the National Press Club on March 15 " to discuss information and documentation regarding Whitewater." According to Shane, the experience was like "trying to explain it to the learning disabled." Apparently, though, Citizens United was getting through. The next day the *Arkansas Democrat-Gazette* reported that Brown handed out a "treasure trove of information" to reporters, "who grabbed them up like goodies."

THE TROUBLE WITH SPOTS

Edwin Diamond and Stephen Bates

Edwin Diamond is Professor of Journalism at New York University, where he directs the News Study Group, and he is the media columnist for New York Magazine. *His previous books include* The Media Show: The Changing Face of the News, 1985–1990. *Stephen Bates, a lawyer, is a fellow at the Woodrow Wilson Center for Scholars in Washington, D.C. He is the author of* If No News, Send Rumors: Anecdotes of American Journalism.

So far we have been analyzing the effects of a given spot in a given race. More significant, ultimately, are the systemic effects of political advertising on the general strategy of campaigns, the overall styles of electoral politics, the kinds of candidates chosen, and the shifting sources of their support. The media men argue that they have helped displace at least some of the old politics and party power—the political bosses, in Robert Goodman's words, who "handed all the money around." Now, says Goodman, "Anybody can run for office if they can get enough backing to get on the tube. They don't have to pay party dues any more; they don't have to come up through the ranks; they don't have to kiss the butts of party bosses or newspaper publishers. They can do their own thing." Gerald Rafshoon also claims that the media campaigns have opened up politics. "I think it is better if you can raise some money to be able to go directly to the people, through television, than to have to go through middlemen." While there are abuses in the system, Rafshoon says, they are not as great as they were before, "when people didn't really know the candidates."

Charles Guggenheim, however, thinks we only have traded one set of troubles for another. We asked him, Is the system of campaigning better or worse than when Guggenheim began working in presidential politics in 1956? "Better *and* worse," he replied. "Adlai Stevenson was not nominated by going through the primaries. He wasn't nominated by a bunch of kids who worked like hell for him in New Hampshire. Harry Truman made up his mind he wanted Stevenson nominated, and he was nominated. One man decided. Who was going to be his vice-president? That decision took place in some smoke-filled room. Who knows what was traded off. If we were there in 1956, we'd be talking about that problem. Now we're talking about new problems."

In our interviews, monitoring, and analysis we found that these new problems within the campaign system group under ten headings:

1. High Costs of Campaigning. After the 1950 congressional elections, in which television played a relatively minor role, William Benton, who founded a major advertising agency before he became a U.S. senator from Connecticut, told a reporter: "The potentialities of television are so great that they could revolutionize politics. The terrifying aspect is the high cost, the expense of which could well determine election or defeat." In 1968, a few weeks before his death, Robert Kennedy was interviewed by Walter Cronkite. The CBS newsman asked Kennedy to respond to charges that he had tried to buy the Indiana primary election. A testy Kennedy responded, "We would all cut down eighty percent of our expenditures if television wasn't so expensive. If television would make all of this time available to us, as a public service, then there wouldn't be any great expense in a political campaign."

The exact numbers are elusive and often resist comparison, but clearly campaign spending has risen sharply, and television advertising has contributed to the rise. From 1912 to 1952 each national party committee spent about the same amount of money per vote cast in national elections. Thereafter, concurrent with the introduction of television, campaign expenditures skyrocketed; by 1968 the committees were spending three times as much per vote as they had sixteen years earlier. Moreover the share of campaign spending going to television has increased at an even faster rate, at the expense of other campaign methods: while total political spending (adjusted for inflation) has tripled since 1952, the amount spent on television has increased at least fivefold. Many local campaigns of course don't use TV—the district is too small, the cost too high, and/or available stations reach beyond district boundaries. In local or statewide races using television heavily, the proportion of the budget devoted to TV can go as high as 90 percent.

Is this too much? For perspective, United Airlines spent more to advertise its friendly skies in 1986—$110 million—than was spent by all the candidates for House and Senate seats in the same year—$97 million. Herbert Alexander, the political scientist and campaign-spending specialist, argues that "election dollars should be regarded as the tuition Americans are willing to pay for their education in politics." If the major function of a political campaign is to educate the electorate concerning the alternatives available, then perhaps we should more properly ask whether *enough* money is being spent. In a 1982 report commissioned by the U.S. Senate, Harvard's Institute of Politics concluded that, at least at the presidential level, candidates lack the financial resources to meet "the vast demands of a national campaign." Of the many problems related to campaign finance, the study termed this insufficiency "the most troublesome."

Some critics argue that, total spending levels aside, campaigns spend too much on television. But again, viewing a campaign as an educational process, TV is a good buy. By one estimate, reaching a TV viewer in 1983 cost less than half a

From *The Spot! The Rise of Political Advertising on Television,* Third Edition, 1992, chapter 16, pp. 368–383, by Edwin Diamond and Stephen Bates. © 1992 by the Massachusetts Institute of Technology. Reprinted by permission.

cent, reaching the same person by a newspaper ad cost one and a half cents, and reaching the same person by direct mail cost around twenty-five cents. In primaries, and especially in the highly contested Iowa and New Hampshire curtain raisers, the education process proceeds with a vengeance; *Congressional Quarterly* estimates that the presidential candidates in 1980 spent $13.89 a vote in Iowa and $8.90 in New Hampshire. Still, restricting or abolishing polispots would by itself not reduce overall spending levels. The money would go into other, less efficient forms of communication.

True, campaign costs could be reduced by making broadcasters provide free airtime. "In order to perform the most important transaction in a democracy, we have to pay a ransom to those people that we've loaned the airwaves to," says Robert Squier, adding: "It's unconscionable." Currently, broadcasters must help subsidize campaigns by charging federal candidates lower rates than other short-time advertisers pay. In our view, mandating any additional subsidy would conflict with the basic tenets of American broadcasting: Stations are privately owned, and the owners are supposed to make programming decisions without government intervention. There is also a practical consideration. With VCRs, cable, and other competing media, broadcasting in the 1990s exists in a different economic climate than in the days of the 1970s and 1980s, when owning a TV station was likened to having a license to print money. Broadcasters, in short, need the cash.

The more pointed question about the high cost of running for office has to do with the sources of money rather than the amounts. At times it seems that politics has become solely a rich man's game. This idea was driven home by the best bumper sticker of 1980, distributed by Arch Moore's gubernatorial campaign against Jay Rockefeller in West Virginia: "Make him spend it all, Arch." Money is and always has been, in Jess Unruh's phrase, the mother's milk of politics. Campaign finance reforms have sought to lessen its preeminent role. But the Supreme Court overturned the part of the reforms that would restrict a candidate's contributions to his own campaign. The unintended consequence, then, has been to make individual contributors less important relative to a candidate's own wealth. Politics, as a result, is at least as much a rich man's game as ever—a problem that reaches well beyond political advertising.

2. The Death of the Parties. Candidates used to need the blessing of party leaders in order to run, and once running, they needed the help of party workers. That began to change in the 1950s, with the entry into politics of people like Rosser Reeves from ad agencies and later with the rise of the independent media specialists. Expertise slipped from the party's grasp as new political tools became available, and the parties failed to adapt. Candidates no longer need parties in order to run, and if they can be elected without their party's help, they may see little need to be loyal. A certain political cohesion is lost, and governance becomes more difficult.

Like the problem of money, the problem of weakened parties predates television. The decline of the parties began with the Progressive Era, when reforms cut into one of the parties' strongest tools, patronage (incumbent parties still have prizes to pass around, of course, as readers of New York City news-

papers were reminded by the Koch administration's scandals of 1986). But television certainly has contributed. Candidates and elected officials can now reach the public directly, through newspapers and the evening news as well as advertising. News coverage in particular has encouraged a move toward "democratization" of the presidential nominating process. Voters—in some states they need not even be registered Democrats or Republicans to participate in primaries—increasingly have selected the delegates to national conventions and, by extension, the parties' nominees. In the process incumbent officials have often been shut out—officials who have a particular stake in the outcome, in that they must run on the same ticket with the presidential nominees. As with campaign finance reforms, the adjustments to the party system have created several unintended consequences. Reforms designed to eliminate corruption and to open up the process to the public have instead continued to weaken the parties. In 1988 the process started to reverse, as both parties took measures to give elected officials greater influence on party matters.

While television has contributed to the problem, we believe it can also contribute to the solution. Both parties, but especially the Republicans, have adapted the television medium and the newer communications technologies to the changing politics. The Republican National Committee sponsors seminars for Republican candidates on television techniques, direct mail, polling, and other media tools. It also now maintains a résumé videotape from each of several Republican media consultants, so that candidates can get a feel for the work done by different media firms. The committee also sponsors TV advertising of its own, including the 1980 spot starring the Tip O'Neill look-alike and 1988 ads reminding voters of "Carter-era" inflation, unemployment, gas lines, and malaise. The Republican Senate Committee now produces programs featuring Republican senators, for cable systems and local TV stations. All these signs of life suggest that television can have a reviving effect on the parties.

3. The Rise of the Hired Gun. Beginning in the 1960s candidates turned to independent consultants. The consultants, as their critics say, get paid to win; they have no incentive to worry about the behavior of their candidates once in office, or about the level of political debate, or about the quantity of voter participation. One of the most influential critics is Curtis Gans, who heads the Committee for the Study of the American Electorate. Gans says that many of the media managers are "very nice, very bright, but not responsible to anybody. They do twelve campaigns at once, and they do the same for each person." Politicians have always had aides, coat holders, advisers, hangers-on, and kitchen cabinets. But, while the retinues in the old days stayed with the politician in office, the new consultants serve the candidate only through the election, and then again, two or four or six years later, should they be called on. The media managers have a guaranteed payday, win or lose. The political retinue get their payday only with victory, in the form of jobs and influence. The media managers need victory also, though: too many losses and their business phones stop ringing.

On the whole, then, are outsiders more likely to counsel a winning-is-the-only-thing strategy, while insiders, or the candidate's conscience, urge the candidate to hold true to principles? Will they behave like amoral mercenaries? Not usually, we believe. The media managers are less involved in the petty rivalries, the jockeying for power, the ego contests (including the inner struggles of the candidates themselves), the backstabbing—and they are more likely to be objective in their judgments. The consultants often perform more responsibly than the retinue. And in any case, the voter can only judge candidates on the basis of their campaigns—*vide* the faltering John Glenn campaign in early 1984—or of their characters—*vide* Hart and Donna Rice in 1987. The average voter didn't know the inside-baseball details of Roger Ailes's philosophy of communications or Susan Estrich's leadership style, nor should the voter have cared. It's the candidate's campaign and overall persona that count. Responsibility, finally, for strategy and tactics rests with the name on the ballot. We talked with two dozen of the best-known political consultants, media and otherwise. There are dozens more, many of them talented, unknown, eager for experience and exposure. Candidates need not bend themselves and their candidacies to suit a particular consultant. They can always get a new helper.

4. The Arrival of the Outsider. The media consultant isn't the only new player in politics. Candidates themselves, no longer beholden to party leaders, find that they need not work their way up through party ranks—or in fact up through any particular ranks at all. The potential has always been present, but mainly for military leaders (Presidents Jackson, Harrison, Taylor, and Grant, as well as, posttelevision, Eisenhower). But today men and women with no previous electoral experience run for office more and more frequently, coming from business (Frank Lautenberg, Lew Lehrman), from academe (Daniel Patrick Moynihan, S. I. Hayakawa, John Silber), from the space program (Harrison Schmitt, John Glenn), and from Hollywood (Shirley Temple Black, Clint Eastwood, Sonny Bono, Ronald Reagan). The most consistently effective political advertising, as we saw, is that promoting name identification. A candidate can, with sufficient funds, swamp the electorate with his name and face; some can go on to win office. If the concept of political outsiders in government seems unappetizing to us today, the opposite would have been true for the Founding Fathers—for them, political insiders were to be guarded against. The national legislature, in their vision, would be composed largely of farmers, leaving their fields for a couple of years to serve their country. The principal difference today is that media-propelled outsiders rarely return voluntarily to their fields.

5. Depressed Voting. Turnout in presidential elections has declined since 1960; barely more than half of eligible citizens voted in 1988, the lowest in forty years. This is the same period when the amount of money spent on television political advertising has tripled in constant dollars. Many campaigns have taken money from participation-oriented activities such as canvassing and phone banks and put it into spots. And the spots themselves, in the view of some critics, do not inspire voting. "These are campaigns that drive people away from the polls," says the columnist David Broder.

But it is extremely difficult to untangle the various factors that may be depressing voter turnout. Some evidence indicates that letter writing, petition signing, protesting, and other forms of participation have increased while voting has gone down; people may simply be turning to alternative means of expressing their political views. Some consultants we interviewed, notably Eddie Mahe, argue that the decline in voting is more apparent than real, a temporary artifact of demography. In the 1960s and 1970s the baby-boom generation reached voting age and shrank turnout figures (a reduction that increased when the voting age was lowered from twenty-one to eighteen, swelling the ranks of younger voters), because young people traditionally vote at a lower rate than older people. As that population cohort ages, by this reasoning, voting turnouts will increase. Furthermore, the political scientist Richard E. Neustadt has suggested that the high voting rates of the past reflected something other than civic-mindedness. In the nineteenth and early twentieth centuries, campaigns were lively entertainment. People may have followed politics, says Neustadt, "because they didn't have anything else to do in those boring times."

As for spots' impact on turnout in particular elections, the evidence goes both ways. Though consultants are loath to admit it, some negative ads are intended to reduce turnout. Keeping the opponent's supporters from voting is easier than getting them to switch sides, and it often creates a margin of victory. But an ad that goes too far may rile the opponent's supporters into turning out in greater numbers than otherwise. In the 1988 campaign for U.S. Senate from Ohio, George Voinovich aired a spot claiming that the incumbent, Howard Metzenbaum, was "soft on child pornography." The wild shot helped bring Metzenbaum supporters to the polls; Voinovich later admitted that, had he been a regular voter, the spot might have provoked him to pull the Metzenbaum lever.

A strident ad battle may also alert inattentive citizens and, in turn, increase turnout. At the close of a blistering campaign for governor of Florida in 1986, the conventional wisdom held that voters would show their disgust by staying home; instead 61 percent came to the polls, six points above the state's average for off-year elections. In 1990, Jesse Helms's antiquotas spot—which constituted a not-so-veiled slam against his black opponent, Harvey Gantt—had the effect of raising the turnout among blue-collar whites who, earlier polls had shown, were inclined to stay home on election day. The caustic spots of the 1988 presidential campaign may not have increased turnout, but a CBS survey suggests that they didn't decrease it either. The poll found that citizens who were disenchanted with the tone of the Bush-Dukakis race were mostly voters; nonvoters tended to be unperturbed.

Other factors also enter the equation. For some citizens, nonvoting may be a declaration of satisfaction with the status quo. Nonvoting may also reflect the judgment that candidates are indistinguishable; the successes of Jesse Jackson in 1984 and Pat Robertson in 1988 demonstrate that nonvoters will register and vote when they perceive that a candidacy represents their interests. In any event, it's worth remembering that universal participation would not necessarily change electoral outcomes. A 1991 study by Stuart Rothenberg found that nonvoters, who once were disproportionately Democratic, now are increasingly

Republican; a turnout of 100 percent would not have altered the outcome of the 1976 election or any one since. Finally, some evidence suggests that the problem is not turnout among registered voters, but rather getting voters registered to begin with. Among registered voters, turnout in the United States isn't much different from turnout in other Western democracies. But only in the United States does the entire burden of registration fall on the individual rather than on the government.

Television has been blamed for a variety of developments in American society. But correlation—the simultaneous expansion of television and of nonvoting—does not indicate causation. For now, at least, the vote is still out on whether media campaigns have contributed significantly to lower voter turnouts.

6. The Disengaged Citizenry. Even if citizens are still voting, perhaps their hearts are no longer in it. In their landmark 1963 study *The Civic Culture,* the social scientists Gabriel A. Almond and Sidney Verba found that Americans felt proud of their political system, obligated to participate in it, and competent to make a difference through it. But in 1991, a Kettering Foundation study diagnosed "serious cancers in the body politic," particularly the voters' "pervading sense of impotence." The study laid part of the blame on negative advertising. The same year, the Markle Commission on the Media and the Electorate reported that Americans behave as if "presidential elections belong to somebody else, most notably presidential candidates and their handlers." This study also singled out negative spots for fostering a "cynical, passive and uninformed" electorate.

No doubt voters have grown more dispirited. As late as the 1950s, substantial majorities of Americans believed that the government was trustworthy and that they as individuals could make a political difference. According to polls, these two crucial benchmarks, trust and efficacy, declined slightly in the mid-1960s and then plummeted in the mid-1970s. But it's hardly the sole fault of television or negative advertising. The consultants didn't produce Vietnam or Watergate. The fact that television's effects are small compared to real-world events is, of course, only a partial defense. Our worry, as we will discuss shortly, is that the primacy of polispots may have turned politics into a sort of spectator sport.

7. The Constraints of Brevity. How can a candidate possibly say anything substantive in thirty seconds? Referring to sound bites as well as spots, Michael Dukakis sourly concluded that the 1988 campaign had been about phraseology rather than ideology. But in our study of 1,050 spots, we found that quite a bit can be said in thirty seconds. John Deardourff, tired of the argument that brevity equals vacuity, once offered this script at a Harvard conference:

> I believe that the question of abortion is one that ought to be reserved exclusively to a woman and her doctor. I favor giving women the unfettered right to abortion. I also favor the federal funding of abortions through Medicaid for poor women as an extension of that right to an abortion, and I oppose any statutory or constitutional limitations on that right.

After reading the script aloud, Deardourff said: "That's twenty-four seconds. I don't know how much more one needs to know about that subject in order to form an opinion." If most campaigns avoid burdening their spots with such specifics, the reason is strategy, not the limits of the medium. John Lindsay's 1972 presidential campaign broadcast a thirty-second spot in Florida that gave the candidate's positions on, among other issues, gun control (for), abortion (for), and school prayer (against). Lindsay's media manager, David Garth, later said that the spot "probably lost the entire population of Florida."

Conciseness counts in politics generally, and not just in spots. We remember Lincoln's two-minute Gettysburg Address, not the two-hour oration that preceded it. Then as now, in the words of an Aspen Institute study, "effective leaders are typically those with an ability to popularize complex issues by reducing them to short-hand labels." American politics produced bumper-sticker wisdom and tight sound bites long before there were automobiles or radio-TV: "Tippecanoe and Tyler too" rang true, and it rhymed.

Brief ads do have one shortcoming. In thirty seconds, a candidate cannot hope to answer a half-true attack spot. In the 1988 Bush furlough ad, the voice-over says that Dukakis "gave weekend furloughs to first-degree murderers not eligible for parole" while the text on the screen tells viewers that "268 escaped" and "many are still at large." But as reporters discovered, only 4 of the 268 escapees were first-degree murderers, and only 3 escapees—none of them murderers—were still at large. This truth might have been difficult for the Dukakis campaign to explain in thirty seconds. What kept Dukakis from doing so, however, was not the constraints of brevity; it was the incompetence and misdirection of the campaign itself—plus the decision to try to get public attention off an issue that, even without the Bush campaign's misleading gloss, was bound to cost Dukakis votes.

Just as short is not invariably shallow, long is not invariably thoughtful. Longer spots often are no more than feel-good music videos, concentrating on the candidate's background and family with only passing mention of issues. They also attract a smaller audience. Carroll Newton, the ad agency executive who worked in the Eisenhower and Nixon campaigns, once calculated that a half-hour unit of programming would lose at least a third of the time-slot's usual audience; a fifteen-minute program would lose a quarter of the audience; a five-minute spot would lose from 5 to 10 percent; and a thirty- or sixty-second spot would lose nothing. In the 1990s, with TV remote controls and cable options, long-form programming would lose even more viewers. Thus, these telecasts end up preaching to the already converted—which is important, but which is not the only goal. Finally, the goal of informing undecided but interested voters may best be attained by combining different media. In 1988, the Pete du Pont and Pat Robertson campaigns both aired spots that urged viewers to read newspaper inserts for additional details about the candidates' stances.

8. The Sleaze Stands Alone. Critics have long blamed the messenger of political advertising for the presumed down-and-dirty state of political discourse. Arthur Schlesinger, Jr., for example, has said that television "has had an effect of draining content out of campaigns."

The argument overromanticizes the past. Perhaps the most "unscrupulous" and "ill-informed" campaign, according to

Daniel Boorstin, predated television by three hundred years: the promotion of the American colonies, which attracted would-be adventures by promising limitless food, gold, even fountains of youth. A century later, Abigail Adams wrote that the 1800 Jefferson-Adams campaign could "ruin and corrupt the minds and morals of the best people in the world." According to campaign accusations in the years that followed, Martin Van Buren was a transvestite; Grover Cleveland, a wife-beater; and Theodore Roosevelt, a drug addict. Television, in fact, may have forced campaigns to clean up their acts, coming as they do into the modern American home.

True, dirty campaigns sometimes sway voters, particularly when the other side doesn't respond. "If you put a negative spot on the air today and the opponent doesn't answer it, it's believed to be true," says Doug Bailey. But the consultants pride themselves on their ability to execute lightning-fast responses. "When a client of ours is attacked," boasts Robert Squier, "the people of that state are going to get some kind of response the next day."

In the 1988 presidential campaign, Dukakis tried answering Bush and, as Ed McCabe testified, gave Bush a double bounce. A TV set shows the Bush ad with Dukakis in the tank. Dukakis turns off the TV and feistily declares: "I'm fed up with it. Never seen anything like it in twenty-five years of public life—George Bush's negative television ads, distorting my record, full of lies, and he knows it." As the Harvard sociologist Kiku Adatto pointed out, it was a measure of the times that the candidate demonstrated his toughness by turning off a television. The Dukakis campaign also tried to convince reporters that particular factual assertions in Bush ads were inaccurate and that the furlough issue was irrelevant and racist. But the counterattacks were blunted by a Dukakis ad featuring a Hispanic man who had murdered while on parole from federal prison. Dukakis seemed unable to choose between dismissing the furlough issue and trying to use it against Bush.

Attacking the attackers became a popular technique after 1988. During the 1989 Republican primary for governor of Virginia, a Marshall Coleman spot attacked Paul Trible as, among other things, a turncoat with plans to raise taxes. The spot ends: "Today Paul Trible is in trouble again. No wonder he's running negative ads." In reality, Trible had not been airing negative ads. Coleman's media man, the ineffable Robert Goodman, had created a straw man, or straw ad, and then demolished it. Coleman won the Republican primary and faced Douglas Wilder in the general election. Wilder's media consultant, Frank Greer, proceeded to out-Goodman Goodman with spots that attacked Coleman for sleazy campaigning. Tracking polls found that the antimud stuck. Wilder narrowly won.

9. The Debasing of Political Argument. Critics also accuse political commercials of impeding thoughtful discussion of the issues. The examples should be familiar by now: Daisy, "Castro" thanking Senor Sasser, "Governor Reagan couldn't start a war; President Reagan could," the revolving-door prison. Where Lincoln and Douglas once debated slavery, now talking fish and talking cows praise incumbents. The messages are conveyed in viewers' living rooms, where defenses may be down, via manipulative production techniques.

Of course, television has changed the conduct of the political game. A century ago a few thousand voters might learn a candidate's arguments directly, through speeches or leaflets. Fewer than twenty thousand people witnessed one of the Lincoln-Douglas debates of 1858. The same constraints applied to the era's equivalent of negative ads, too. The vicious slanders on Lincoln were spread by crude printing presses and newspapers of limited circulation. Today spots can bring the candidate and his positive or negative message to hundreds of thousands, even millions of voters, and do so repeatedly. That mammoth audience will include supporters, leaners, and opponents. A mean-spirited attack that attracts half-engaged fence sitters, as we have seen, may repel previously solid voters or provoke the opponent's supporters to go to the polls. This mass audience makes the television campaign partly self-correcting, certainly more so than other media of the modern campaign, such as direct mail. Some of the most vicious attacks of the late 1980s came in letters to targeted mailing lists—a giant step backward to the crude leaflets of the 1800s.

TV may be more demanding of voters than these other media. The consultants rely on all sorts of production techniques to convey facts and feelings. David Garth sometimes supersaturates his spots with audio and visual information. Ads often employ metaphors: the bear in the woods, torn Social Security cards, spattering mud, Pinnochios, weather vanes. Efficient communication, as E. D. Hirsch has pointed out, requires shared reference points. Today, many of those reference points are visual. And important as information is, emotion is also part of the voting choice. Voters want to feel a connection to the candidate and his candidacy. As Roger Ailes told us, "You can present all the issues you want on the air, and if at the end the audience doesn't like the guy, they're not going to vote for him." Viewers of the 1980 Carter-Reagan debate, Ailes contended, remembered four things: Carter's bizarre reference to his daughter Amy; Reagan's line, "There you go again"; Reagan walking over to shake hands with Carter at the end; and Reagan in general looking comfortable, while Carter "looked constipated." Two of the best spots of 1988, made by Ken Swope for Dukakis during the Democratic primaries, had little to do with information and a lot to do with emotion. One showed small children cavorting in front of an enormous, *Patton*-style American flag. On the soundtrack is "America the Beautiful," beginning on a child's toy piano and then slowly building to a full orchestra. The other spot shows a homeless man huddled over a steam grate. The camera pulls back to reveal, immediately behind him, the White House. The voiceovers are forgettable, but the images linger.

In technique, such spots are no more manipulative, no more insidious, than ads that promise good times with beer or remind you to call home. After forty years of experience with television, Americans are inured to the razzle-dazzle of production values. A jump cut may sustain some viewers' interest, but it won't suspend their disbelief. The politicians use TV for the same reason that Budweiser and AT&T do: That's where the consumer-voters are. On any given autumn night during the week, 120 million Americans are watching.

But even though spots don't cloud the mind, they may in some sense sap the political will. Television has not only amplified the candidate's voice; it has also affected the nature of political discourse. To the extent that polispots are made to resemble life-style cola commercials, they may be taken no more seriously than the rest of television advertising. When they become just one more entertainment to watch, it may become harder and harder for the audience to regard them as important. This is especially true when there is no other campaign visible to the viewer—when, as the consultant Robert Shrum has said, a political rally consists of three people around a television set. The result may be a distancing between candidate and citizen, with voting perceived as just one more activity being commended to us by television's faraway purveyors of goods and services.

The problem may be more basic than any one spot or series of spots. Forty years of television experience may have inured us not only to production values but to the immediacy of politics as well; something fundamental may have been lost when campaigns switched from "live" to "taped." The obvious solution, however—to divorce politics from TV—doesn't hold up. Since the 1950s the voting classes have increasingly stayed home to be entertained, a trend encouraged by demographics (the suburban migration), by improved at-home options (radio, television, VCRs), and at least partly by fear (crime in the streets). Taking politics away from television would take campaigns outdoors again. But, absent broader social changes, most voters wouldn't follow.

10. Who Governs? Finally, critics contend that spots have diminished the stature of our elected officials. Negative TV campaigns generate "unnecessary turnover in public office," according to Curtis Gans. Fearing that they may be next, elected officials must constantly watch their backs. Democratic Congressman David Obey told the *New York Times* that "the main question" in a representative's mind each time he votes is "What kind of a 30-second spot are they going to make out of this vote?"

While, as we've noted, spots do sometimes produce unjust results, we doubt that "unnecessary turnover" in public office tops most people's list of the major problems facing the republic. In recent years, over 80 percent of senators and over 95 percent of members of Congress have won reelection. Nine House seats changed hands in 1988, the lowest in American history. Incumbents can count on receiving more money in contributions than challengers (about twice as much), as well as heavier media coverage. Then there is the franking privilege, the videotaped reports sent to local TV stations and cable outlets, and now the promise of video reports mailed directly to constituents—all of which increase name recognition and support. By deploying a negative spot, a challenger is seeking to overcome some of the incumbent's institutional advantages.

The Power of TALK

Call-in democracy ignited the presidential race. Now it's shaking up government, rattling Clinton—and driving Washington's agenda.

HOWARD FINEMAN

Let's talk about the power of talk, of calling in to your favorite show:

■ A Florida man goes on CNN's "Larry King Live." He says his wife died of cancer because she used a cellular phone. There is no scientific study on the question. The cellular industry scoffs and declines to put a spokesman on the show. Big mistake. The lines light up. By last Friday—eight days after "King"—a share of stock in Motorola, Inc., the biggest maker of cellular phones, has dropped 20 percent. The federal government, at the industry's urging, gears up to study the issue.

■ It's two days before Bill Clinton's Inauguration. On public radio in Washington, host Diane Rehm goes to the "open phones." Much of her audience is, literally, inside the Beltway, people who might be sympathetic to Zoë Baird's child-care problems. The lines light up. Opinion makers and politicos are listening. The verdict: Zoë's got to go. "If that's the feeling here," Rehm muses, "what's happening in Sioux City?" Washington begins to get the message. Three days later Baird withdraws.

■ On Tuesday the Joint Chiefs of Staff meet with Secretary of Defense Les Aspin in the "Tank," their Pentagon conference room. The topic: whether to allow avowed homosexuals in the military. The Chiefs are against it on military grounds. But they have other arguments. Top brass are not known for the common touch, but they tell

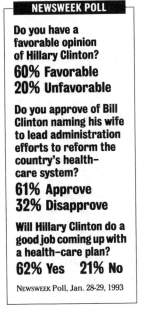

NEWSWEEK POLL

Do you have a favorable opinion of Hillary Clinton?

60% Favorable
20% Unfavorable

Do you approve of Bill Clinton naming his wife to lead administration efforts to reform the country's health-care system?

61% Approve
32% Disapprove

Will Hillary Clinton do a good job coming up with a health-care plan?

62% Yes   21% No

NEWSWEEK Poll, Jan. 28-29, 1993

the president: look at the polls, listen to the radio. Three days later Clinton moves far more cautiously than he had wanted, merely ordering the services to quit asking new recruits if they are gay.

Talk-show democracy changed politics in the presidential race last year, bringing candidates phone to phone with voters. With his vision of teledemocracy and his surprisingly strong showing in November, Ross Perot woke up the establishment to the voters' anger. Now comes the next step: call-in government. Having tasted power, voter-callers want more; having risen

through talk, Clinton is being rattled by it. "People want two-way talk," says King. "They say, 'We want to talk to our government!'" Americans can do it through the burgeoning phenomenon of call-in shows, led by King, Rush Limbaugh and Brian Lamb on C-Span, and mirrored locally by dozens of tart-tongued, influential hosts. These shows, in turn, generate tidal waves of switchboard-clogging calls and letters-to-your-congressman. Call-in government is a needed jolt to sclerotic Washington. But it also raises the specter of government by feverish plebiscite—an entertaining, manipulable and trivializing process that could eat away at the essence of representative democracy.

It's hot: It's probably inevitable. Call-in shows are a fast-growing format, accounting for nearly 1,000 of the nation's 10,000 radio stations. "Larry King Live" is the highest-rated show on CNN. This week he switches his 15-year-old late-night radio call-in show to afternoon "drive time" on more than 300 stations, quadrupling his radio audience. Television networks, which experimented with call-in formats during the campaign, are studying ways to use them again. "You're going to see a lot more call-in on the networks," predicts King. "It's hot and they know it."

Technology and demographics are the agents of change. Cheap satellite time allows local hosts like Mike Siegel of Seattle to go national with ease. Many mobile-phone services now have special deals with call-in shows, enabling motorists to punch a single button to dial in. King's new show will be carried live on United Airlines planes, most of them equipped with phones. Two decades ago baby boomers turned on, tuned in and dropped out of politics. Now, says Atlanta radio consultant Jon Sinton, they are tuning in again, abandoning rock for talk. Flying to the coast, or idling on a clogged freeway, they can get in touch using the same cellular technology King's guest told them to worry about. "Now you can call Larry and get cancer at the same time," jokes Sinton.

Politicians are getting with the program, literally. New York Gov. Mario Cuomo is a pioneer; he's hosted a regular call-in show for years. Other local politicians are dong the same. At the Democratic National Committee, new chairman David Wilhelm is laying plans for Clinton and other administration officials to make themselves available for call-ins. If he needs any advice, he can ask Susan Estrich. A former Harvard law professor, she ran Michael Dukakis's famously out-of-touch campaign in 1988. She left Cambridge, Mass., for Los Angeles, where she now teaches law—and hosts a call-in show. "Anybody who ever spent five minutes in radio," she says, "could have told you that gays in the military would strike a chord."

You could have learned the same lesson by watching C-Span. Though it is available in 58 million homes, its audience is rarely more than 2 million. But a new survey shows that an astounding 98 percent of its viewers voted in 1992, and the network provides instant feedback from them. During breaks in the Baird hearings, C-Span's Lamb fielded viewer calls in his deadpan manner. The voices grew angrier with each break—and they were being heard by the same Capitol insiders who were watching the hearings. "In the old days people would have had to wait for details on Baird," says lamb. "Now it's in real time."

The next layer of the call-in system is CNN. Increasingly the network is including viewer call-in segments in its news shows to complement King's prime-time appearances. The network's ratings rose sharply during the election year and stayed there. CNN's newest star is White House communications director George Stephanopoulos, whose boyishly evasive briefings garner high daytime ratings. "He's getting some of our highest numbers," says a CNN official. CNN is likely to continue carrying Stephanopoulos—and wrap call-ins around him.

NEWSWEEK POLL

Should homosexuals be able to serve in the armed forces?

CURRENT
53% Yes   42% No

11/92
48% Yes   44% No

Should the military temporarily stop asking about inductees' sexual orientation while the new administration consults about changing policy on gays in the military?

44% Yes   48% No

NEWSWEEK Poll, Jan. 28-29, 1993

Until recently, and with the important exception of Ralph Nader, Democrats and their allies largely ignored the power of talk broadcasting. Conservatives have always understood and relied on it. While Franklin Roosevelt sold his New Deal in radio "fireside chats," Father Coughlin and Gerald L. K. Smith developed their own vast audiences of naysayers. Long

before he became president, Ronald Reagan sharpened his antigovernment message on the radio. Pat Buchanan honed his combative style as a call-in host in Washington. "The fact is that liberals feel empowered and conservatives don't," says Limbaugh.

If conservatives feel any sense of "empowerment" these days, it's due in large part to Limbaugh. His show is the most listened-to in talk radio (15 million tune in each week on 560 stations). His best-selling book, "The Way Things Ought to Be," has sold 2 million copies in hardback; his TV call-in show is fast approaching Letterman-Leno ratings, and a new newsletter has 170,000 subscribers. Only nominally a call-in affair, Limbaugh's show offers group therapy for mostly white males who feel politically challenged and who would rather hear Rush's voice than their own. But they react. In Sacramento, Calif., last week, a Democratic lawmaker banned Limbaugh's show from the internal broadcasting system in the California capitol. Limbaugh, who began his broadcasting in Sacramento, put the issue to his listeners. Within minutes, calls poured in. His show was back on the system that same day.

As famous as King, Limbaugh and Lamb have become, the roots and power of call-in

---

Look Who's Talking

Ross Perot didn't invent rule by phone, he merely tapped into a network that's been giving millions of Americans someone to talk to for years. Last week the phone lines crackled with discussion about Bill Clinton, Zoë Baird and gay soldiers. But a survey of some leading chat shows reveals that there was still plenty of room for local news, gossip—and ego.

MICHAEL JACKSON, Los Angeles
Hot Topic: Gang violence
Audience: 1,150,000
Political Slant: Liberal
Pet Peeve: Proposed license fee for L.A. hiking trails

MIKE SIEGEL, Seattle
Hot Topic: Gays in the military
Audience: 800,000
Political Slant: "Pragmatist"
Pet Peeves: Seattle's "politically correct" police chief, crack houses

IMHOTEC GARY BYRD, New York
Hot Topic: Haiti
Audience: 1 million
Political Slant: Liberal, Afrocentric
Pet Peeve: Double Standards

JERRY WILLIAMS, Boston
Hot Topic: Local water rates
Audience: 250,000
Political Slant: "Pragmatic"
Pet Peeves: Big government, high taxes

LARRY KING, Washington
Hot Topics: Foreign-policy hot spots, gas taxes
Audience: 8,520,000
Political Slant: Nonpartisan
Pet Peeve: Long-winded callers

RUSH LIMBAUGH, New York
Hot Topic: Clinton's promises
Audience: 15 million
Political Slant: Conservative
Pet Peeves: Liberals, "Feminazis," tree-hugging environmentalists

BRIAN LAMB, Washington
Hot Topic: White House press access
Audience: (Not available)
Political Slant: "Completely neutral"
Pet Peeve: People who call more than once a month

DIANE REHM, Washington
Hot Topic: Zoë Baird
Audience: 100,000

Political Slant: Liberal
Pet Peeves: Callers who disregard women's rights

ROE CONN, Chicago
Hot Topics: Mike Ditka, the Chicago Bears, the "Home Alone" family
Audience: 500,000
Political Slant: Liberal
Pet Peeve: The recession

DAVID GOLD, Dallas
Hot Topics: Zoë Baird and gay soldiers
Audience: 138,000
Political Slant: Conservative
Pet Peeves: Liberal media and big government

Special Features
New York celebs **Don Imus, Howard Stern** and **Bob Grant** have mass appeal, attracting a million listeners a week each. **Malin Salu,** whose New York call-in show is in Spanish, and Washington African-American conservative **Armstrong Williams** wield influence in their communities. Veteran hosts **Bob Hardy** (St. Louis) and **Brad Davis** (Hartford) draw big audiences interested in consumer and community affairs.

democracy are local. Call-in shows first turned political in New York and Boston, cities in which arguing in public about politics—or anything else—is a way of life. The recent history of call-in clout begins with 35-year veteran Jerry Williams in Boston, who in 1989 teamed up with Ralph Nader and others to protest a congressional pay raise. They succeeded in delaying it six months. Williams, Siegel and others founded the National Association of Radio Talk Show hosts—a kind of Continental Congress of call-in government.

Talk-show hosts can get results—and have been doing so for years before Rush Limbaugh arrived. In Seattle, Siegel took his microphone to a crack house and got it shut down. In Boston, Williams helped derail the state's seat-belt law, the proposed location of a state prison and numerous legislative pay increases. In 1986, he got 2,000 people to show up on Beacon Hill in a snowstorm to decry a Dukakis tax increase. "It's nothing new," Williams says of the Limbaughs of the world. "It is they who have been asleep."

With Nader in the lead, others outside the conservative movement are exploring the power of talk radio. National Public Radio has launched a successful call-in show, "Talk of the Nation." It's now heard on more than 70 stations, most in major markets. Jim Hightower, a feisty Democrat and former agriculture commissioner in Texas, is launching a national show he says will attack an establishment the right rarely touches: Wall Street and big corporations. He's resisting pleas to turn the program into a call-in ("I don't want to be chained to a studio"), but if he is going to be true to his populist roots, he may have no choice.

Secular religion: This may all be great broadcasting, but is it good government? Perot, who's busy wiring his "town halls," obviously thinks so. So do many of the 19 million Americans who voted for him. Conservatives think it's grand—a more accurate reflection of grass-roots opinion than the evening news. Radio consultant Sinton agrees—even though he is advising Hightower and calls Limbaugh "Hitler Light." "The grass roots are basically conservative," says Sinton. "And our medium, radio, is much more representative of America than others." Free expression is America's secular religion. Tuning in—and calling in—is just a high-tech way of honoring it.

But it can be honored too much. What King calls the "hum" of talk radio can be misleading. Only the most devoted and outraged of listeners call—rarely more than 2 or 3 percent of an audience. Politicians who react slavishly can be deceived. "It's a potential early-warning sign, like radar in Greenland," says Democratic polltaker Harrison Hickman. "You don't launch a strike based on that evidence alone." And its effects can be oversold. "Talk shows didn't get rid of Zoë Baird," says Limbaugh. "She got rid of herself."

The more troubling question is whether America needs a government of its angriest voices. "Only the people who feel most strongly call us," says Rehm. "But they aren't the only ones who vote." Dial-in democracy is attracting the same forces of manipulation that prey on other levers of power; interest groups on the right and left have the technology and determination to patch themselves into the national conversation. The intensity, speed and entertainment value of talk radio has a downside in a society already plagued by long-lasting problems and a short attention span. Ratings count and boredom is the enemy. There's enormous pressure to keep the "board lit" by moving to the next hot topic.

But it's obvious how this controversy will come out. On CNN last week, "Crossfire" debated the pros and cons of dial-in democracy. The weekend shows discussed it. Rehm has scheduled a call-in show about . . . call-in shows. So all you need to do now is pick up the phone and give your opinion.

With DONNA FOOTE *in Los Angeles,* PATRICIA KING *in San Francisco,* MARK STARR *in Boston and* GINNY CARROLL *in Houston*

Implicit Lessons: Concerns with What We Learn from Entertainment Media

Mass media provide both explicit and implicit lessons, both of which contribute to consumers' knowledge and attitudes. Explicit lessons are central to informational media, although they are often embedded in entertainment media as well: in television's "Mister Rogers' Neighborhood," Fred Rogers teaches children to share while Big Bird of "Sesame Street" teaches them to count; comic books include drug awareness messages; crime dramas teach viewers that they have the right to remain silent when arrested. Implicit lessons are regarded with more suspicion, at least in part because they tend to shape audience attitudes and behaviors without their consciously being aware of these effects. The readings in this unit look at how such learning occurs, and what the lessons are.

Nicholas Johnson, a former chairman of the Federal Communications Commission (FCC), has noted, "Every moment of television programming—commercials, entertainment, news—teaches us something." While we may seek out entertainment media as a means of escape into a fictional world, portrayals of gender roles, family interaction, ethnic minorities, and so forth have the potential of affecting social reality. In "The Make-Believe Media," Michael Parenti argues that, in a modern mass society, people rely to a great extent on media to provide insight into how things are, and how they should be: What are politicians like? What is the life of the rich and famous like? What is romance like? Children, in particular, have limited experiences with which to compare media images and are especially vulnerable to accepting stereotypes. Parenti believes that adults are also more affected than they realize.

There are two major theories of how media lessons influence social behavior. Social learning theory holds that media have a direct effect on behavior by providing role models that we emulate. Cultivation theory suggests that media portrayals influence our attitudes, which subsequently affect our actions. In both of these models, influence is strongest when media consistently present the same stereotypes, and when personal experience with the object of the stereotype is limited or absent. It is easy to generalize that media should stop providing negative role models and start providing positive ones, should stop distorting reality and start reflecting it. It is much more difficult to operationalize such advice in specific terms.

Media portrayals of gender roles, family life, and ethnic minorities have changed over the years. Television's Bundys of "Married . . . With Children," the Conners of "Roseanne," and the Simpsons are a far cry from the Cleavers of "Leave It to Beaver," the Bradys, or even the Huxtables of "Cosby" fame. Beavis and Butt-head and Bart Simpson are less compliant and more cynical than were earlier television youth. Some argue that these new portrayals simply reflect changes in social norms and attitudes; others claim they provide the role models and shape the attitudes that drive such changes (see "Battle for Your Brain"). In "Gendered Media: The Influence of Media on Views of Gender," Julia Wood contends that media images of male/female roles and interactions have harmful social learning and cultivation effects. In contrast, Jeff Greenfield (see "Don't Blame TV") argues that media have little influence on significant trends in social norms.

Other articles in this section address concerns with the negative themes prevalent in Hollywood films and with media sex and violence. Michael Medved provides evidence of an antireligious, antifamily, anti-America bias in movies (see "Hollywood's Poison Factory: The Movies' Twisted Image). Various researchers have reported that at least 80 percent of all commercial television programs contain violence, that there are an average of 10.8 violent acts per hour in music videos, and that children's cartoons contain an average of 32 acts of violence per hour (the "winner" in a 1991 study was the Fox network's "Dark Water," with 109 violent acts per hour). Planned Parenthood reports that Americans are exposed to more than 9,000 scenes of suggested sexual intercourse, sexual comment, or innuendo in an average year of television viewing. (None of the networks, however, accept condom ads.) What are the implications of these trends?

The final articles in this section directly address the issue of why the enrichment of entertainment media, if one believes that should occur, is a complex goal. William Brown and Arvind Singhal explain the "Ethical Dilemmas of Prosocial Television." How does one define what is "prosocial" when people do not have common moral, ethical, and cultural values? Who should decide which social beliefs and behaviors are to be promoted?

Looking Ahead: Challenge Questions

Is it true that "popular entertainment is basically propaganda for the status quo"? How is it that adults as well as children are affected by what is presented as fiction?

To what degree do media portrayals of women, men, families, religion, patriotism, ethnic minorities, sex, and violence reflect changing social norms? To what degree do they shape social norms? Why has each been criticized? With which criticisms do you agree? Disagree?

What is your response to Beavis and Butt-head? Do you find them humorous? Why, or why not? Do you agree with John Leland's explanation for their appeal?

Should there be more prosocial lessons in entertainment media?

The Make-Believe Media

Media images influence how we appraise a host of social realities

Michael Parenti

Michael Parenti is a political scientist, lecturer, and social commentator. He is the author of Inventing Reality: The Politics of the Mass Media; Democracy for the Few; The Sword and the Dollar: Imperialism, Revolution, and the Arms Race; *and* Make-Believe Media: The Politics of Entertainment (St. Martin's Press), *from which this article is adapted.*

Make-believe. The word connotes the playful games and fantasies of our childhood—a pleasant way of pretending. But in the world created by movies and television, make-believe takes on a more serious meaning. In some way or other, many people come to believe the fictional things they see on the big and little screens. The entertainment media are the make-believe media; they make us believe.

Today, instead of children's games, storytelling, folk tales, and fables of our own making, we have the multibillion-dollar industries of Hollywood and television to fill our minds with prefabricated images and themes. Nor are these just idle distractions, for such images often have real ideological content. Even if supposedly not political in intent, the entertainment industry has been political in its impact, discouraging critical perceptions of our social order while planting pictures in our heads that have been supportive of U.S. militarism, armed intervention abroad, phobic anti-communism, authoritarian violence, consumer acquisitiveness, racial and sexual stereotypes, vigilantism, simple-minded religiousity, and anti-working-class attitudes.

Remarking on the prevalence of media-induced stereotypes of African-Americans, Ellen Holly put it well: "Again and again, I have seen black actors turned down for parts because they were told that they did not look the way a black person should or sound the way a black person should. What is this business of 'should'? What kind of box are we being put into? I have seen black writers told that the black characters they put down on a page were not believable because they were too intelligent."

Studies show that women, too, are put in a box: portrayed mostly in subsidiary roles and depicted as less capable, effective, or interesting than the more numerous white male principals. To be sure, things have changed somewhat. Women can now be seen playing lawyers, judges, cops, executives, professionals, and sometimes even workers, but the questions of gender equality and the fight for feminist values are seldom joined. Likewise, the struggles of sleep-starved, underpaid single mothers trying to raise their children and survive in an inhospitable environment are not usually considered an appropriate theme for prime-time television or Hollywood.

Working people of both genders and whatever ethnic background are still underrepresented in the media. With few exceptions, such as the movie *Norma Rae,* they play minor walk-on roles as waiters, service people, gas station attendants, and the like in an affluent, upper-middle-class, media-created world. Blue-collar people are portrayed as emotional, visceral, simple-hearted and simple-minded, and incapable of leadership or collective action against the injustices they face in their workplace and community. Their unions are depicted as doing more harm than good for them. Given the hostility that network and studio bosses have manifested toward organized labor in the entertainment industry, it is small wonder that labor unions are almost always portrayed—if at all—in an unsympathetic light.

Generally speaking, whether it's a movie about factory workers, cops and crime, or the invasion of galactic monsters, it is individual heroics rather than collective action that save the day. Solutions and victories are never won by ordinary good people, organizing and struggling for mutual betterment, but by the hero in self-willed combat, defying the odds and sometimes even the authorities to vanquish the menace and triumph.

In great supply as heroes of the

make-believe media are the purveyors of violence and macho toughness: the military man, cop, counterinsurgency agent, spycatcher, private investigator, and adventurer. From Dirty Harry to Rambo, it's all helicopter gunships, screeching car chases, and endless shoot-em-ups and punch-em-outs. Check the movie ads in your newspaper and count the number of weapons displayed. Flip your television dial during prime time and count the number of guns or fistfights or other acts of violence and aggression. They are even more numerous than the commercials.

To be sure, iconoclastic opinions and images get through now and then. Liberal and even strongly progressive themes can be found in an occasional movie or television episode. Underdog and dissident voices are heard for rare moments. But these are the exceptions. As media critic Erik Barnouw concludes: "Popular entertainment is basically propaganda for the status quo." And sociologist Hal Himmelstein believes that television has become "one of our society's principal repositories of [conventional] ideology."

Do these media images and themes have any real effect on us? Indeed they do. In modern mass society, people rely to a great extent upon distant image-makers for their cues about a vast world. In both entertainment and news shows, the media invent a reality much their own. Our notion of what a politician, a detective, a corporate executive, a farmer, an African, or a Mexican-American is supposed to be like; our view of what rural or inner city life should be; our anticipations about romantic experience and sexual attractiveness, crime and foreign enemies, dictators and revolutionaries, bureaucrats and protestors, police and prostitutes, workers and communists—all are heavily colored by our exposure to movies and television shows.

Many of us have never met an Arab, but few of us lack some picture in our minds of what an Arab is supposed to be like. If drawn largely from the mass media, this image will be a

> *In modern mass society, people rely to a great extent upon distant image-makers for their cues about a vast world. In both entertainment and news shows, the media invent a reality much their own.*

stereotype—and most likely a defamatory one. As Walter Lippmann noted almost 70 years ago, stereotypic thinking "precedes reason" and "as a form of perception [it] imposes a certain character on the data of our senses." When we respond to a real life situation with the exclamation "Just like in the movies!" we are expressing our recognition and even satisfaction that our media-created mental frames find corroboration in the real world.

The media images in our heads influence how we appraise a host of social realities, including our government's domestic and foreign policies. If we have "learned" from motion pictures and television series that our nation is forever threatened by hostile alien forces, then we are apt to support increased military spending and warlike interventions. If we have "learned" that inner-city denizens are violent criminals, then we are more apt to support authoritarian police measures and cuts in human services to the inner city.

Audiences usually do some perceptual editing, projecting something of their own viewpoint upon what they see. But this editing itself is partly conditioned by the previously internalized images fed to us by the same media we are now viewing. In other words, rather than being rationally critical of the images and ideologies of the entertainment media, our minds—after prolonged exposure to earlier programs and films—sometimes become active accomplices in our own indoctrination.

We are probably more affected by what we see than we realize. Jeffrey Schrank notes that 90 percent of the nation's adult viewers consider themselves to be "personally immune" from the appeals of television advertisements; yet, this same 90 percent accounts for about 90 percent of all sales of advertised products. While we might think it is always other people (less intelligent than ourselves) who are being manipulated by sales appeals and entertainment shows, the truth might be something else.

Media critic Jerry Mander argues that electronic images are "irresistible," since our brains absorb them regardless of how we might consciously perceive such images. Children believe that what they are seeing on television and in the movies is real; they have no innate capacity to distinguish between real and unreal images. Only as they grow older, after repeated assurances from their elders, do they begin to understand that the stories and characters on the big and little screens do not exist in real life. In other words, *their ability to reject media images as unreal has to be learned.*

The problem does not end there, however. Even as adults, when we consciously know that a particular media offering is fictional, we still "believe" it to some extent—that is, we still accumulate impressions that lead to beliefs about the real world. When drawing upon images in our heads, we do not keep our store of media imagery distinct and separate from our store of real-world imagery. "The mind doesn't work that way," says Mander.

The most pervasive effect of television—aside from its actual content—may be its very existence, its readily available, commanding, and often addictive presence in our homes, its ability to reduce hundreds of millions of citizens to passive spectators for major portions of their lives. Television minimizes interactions between persons within families and communities. One writer I know only half-jokingly claims, "I watch television mainly as a way of getting to know my husband and children." Another associate of mine, who spent years in Western agricultural regions, relates how a farmer once told her:

9. IMPLICIT LESSONS

"Folks used to get together a lot. Now with television, we see less of each other."

Claims made about the media's influence sometimes can be unduly alarmist. It is not all a matter of our helpless brains being electronically pickled by the sinister tube. But that is no excuse for dismissing the important impact the media do have. The more time people spend watching television and movies, the more their impressions of the world seem to resemble those of the media. Academic media critics George Gerbner and Larry Gross found that heavy television users, having been fed abundant helpings of crime and violence, are more likely to overestimate the amount of crime and violence that exists in real life. They are also more apt to overestimate the number of police in the United States, since they see so many on television. "While television may not directly cause the results that have turned up in our studies," conclude Gerbner and Gross, "it certainly can confirm or encourage certain views of the world."

In sum, it is not just a matter of the entertainment industry giving the people what they want but of playing an active role in creating those wants. As any advertiser knows, supply not only satisfies demand, it helps create demand, conditioning our tastes and patterning our responses. The single greatest factor in consumption is product availability. For every ounce of quality programming and quality movies made

> **The most pervasive effect of television—aside from its actual content—may be its very existence . . . its ability to reduce hundreds of millions of citizens to passive spectators for [most] of their lives.**

available to us, the media also give us a ton of mind rot.

Those who produce images for mass consumption exercise an enormous power, but they are not omnipotent. They are not entirely free from public pressure. The viewing audience is sometimes more than just a passive victim. There are times when popular agitation, advances in democratic consciousness, and changes in public taste and educational levels have forced the media to modify or discard the images that are served up. The public has to keep fighting back. We got rid of Amos 'n' Andy and Sambo; we can get rid of Dirty Harry and Rambo.

More important than eliminating the bad shows is demanding better ones—for our children and ourselves.

Viewing movies like *Glory* and television series like "Roots" are a far better way to learn about the African-American experience than watching shows like "The Jeffersons." A movie like *Salt of the Earth* tells us more about the realities of the labor struggle and blue-collar life than the clownlike Archie Bunker on "All in the Family." A film like *Born on the Fourth of July* tells us more about the heart-wrenching realities of war than all the John Wayne and Rambo flicks put together. Better entertainment can be produced that is not only intelligent and socially significant but also capable of attracting large audiences. But at present there is not enough of it, and the little there is usually gets poorly distributed and modestly advertised—if at all.

There is nothing wrong with mindless relaxation in front of a viewing screen now and then. What is wrong is when it becomes a way of life, preempting our experience and taking over our brains, providing us with a prefabricated understanding of what the world is supposed to be. And this it does for too many people. A better awareness of how we are manipulated by the make-believe media might cause us to waste fewer hours of our precious lives in front of both the big and little screens and allow us more time for reading, conversing, relating to our friends and families, criticizing social injustice, and becoming active citizens of our society and the effective agents of our own lives.

Battle for Your Brain

Stupidity, served with knowing intelligence, is now TV's answer to real smarts. And no one serves it like the crude and rude Beavis and Butt-head.

John Leland

It is television at its most redeeming. A whale swims gracefully across the screen as the narrator mourns its imminent destruction. Watching in their living room two boys, about 14, are visibly moved. Their eyes widen, their nostrils twitch uncomfortably. One boy's lips stiffen around his wire braces. The only hope, the narrator says, "is that perhaps the young people of today will grow up more caring, more understanding, more sensitive to the very special needs of the creatures of the earth." It is a rich moment, ripe with television's power to make remote events movingly immediate. The boys can watch idly no longer. Finally one turns to the other and asks, "Uh, did you fart?"

The boys are Beavis and Butt-head, two animated miscreants whose adventures at the low end of the food chain are currently the most popular program on MTV. Caught in the ungainly nadir of adolescence, they are not nice boys. They torture animals, they harass girls and sniff paint thinner. They like to burn things. They have a really insidious laugh: *huh-huh huh-huh*. They are the spiritual descendants of the semi-sentient teens from "Wayne's World" and "Bill and Ted's Excellent Adventure," only dumber and meaner. The downward spiral of the living white male surely ends here: in a little pimple named Butt-head whose idea of an idea is, "Hey, Beavis, let's go over to Stuart's house and light one in his cat's butt."

For a generation reminded hourly of its diminished prospects, these losers have proven remarkably embraceable. "Why do I like 'Beavis and Butt-head'?" asks Warren Lutz, 26, a journalism major at San Francisco State. "You're asking me to think, dude." Created by beginner animator Mike Judge, 30, for a festival of "sick and twisted" cartoons last year, Beavis and Butt-head have become a trash phenomenon. T shirts, hats, key rings, masks, buttons, calendars, dolls are all working their way to malls; a book, a comic book, a movie, a CD and a Christmas special are in the works. David Letterman drops a Beavis and Butt-head joke almost nightly; later this fall the pair will become a semiregular feature on his program. As their notoriety reached Fort Lewis College in Durango, Colo., archeology students have started calling Jim Judge, Mike's father, Dr. Butt-head. "Whenever any . . . 8- to 12-year-olds find out I'm related to Beavis and Butt-head," he says, "I become a god to them." Beavis and Butt-head, whose world divides into "things that suck" and "things that are cool," are clearly the new morons in town.

They are also part of a much wider TV phenomenon, one that drives not just stupid laughs but the front-page battle now being waged for control of Paramount Pictures. It is the battle to play road hog on the Information Highway. As cable technology continues to expand our range of viewing options, the old boundaries of propriety and decency no longer apply. Beavis and Butt-head join a growing crowd of characters who have found a magic formula: nothing cuts through the clutter like a slap of bracing crudity. Nothing stops a channel surfer like the word "sucks."

Stupidity, served with a knowing intelligence, has become the next best thing to smarts. Letterman's signature "Stupid Pet Tricks" bit, now 11 years running, introduced a new voice to television: ironic, self-aware, profoundly interested in the ingrained dumbness of the tube. Instead of dumbing down, it made smart comedy out of the process of dumbing down—and it clicked. Barry Diller successfully built Fox into the fourth network on a shockingly *lumpen* cartoon family, the Simpsons, and an even more *lumpen* real one, the Bundys of "Married . . . With Children." Nickelodeon's cartoon "The Ren & Stimpy Show," the highest-rated original series on cable, follows the scatological adventures of a Chichuahua and a cat, sometimes not getting much farther than the litter box. The network's new contender, "Rocko's Modern World," wallows down a similarly inspired low road. Its first episode, in which a home-shopping channel called "Lobot-o-shop" pitched items like tapeworm farms for kids, beat "Ren & Stimpy" in the ratings. And the widely loved and hated radio host Howard Stern has taken his act to E! Entertainment Television. "There's a purity to [this] kind of ignorance," says "Beavis and Butt-head" writer David Felton, at 53 MTV's oldest staff member.

This Is Your Reel Life

Channel surf's up in Chicago. In a week, Windy City-zens can expand their minds with plenty of retro TV.

'BEWITCHED': Bothered and bewildered by the news? You'll be even more confused if, in channel-flopping, you spot two different Darrens.   5 times

'BONANZA': Can't find "Battlestar Galactica" on the dial but need a Lorne Green fix? Catch him on the Ponderosa in all his pre-Alpo splendor.   8 times

'CHARLIE'S ANGELS': Aaron Spelling's TV jiggle-magic made Farrah Fawcett a '70s star, featuring hot-pants-style karate and lots of teeth.   10 times

'DRAGNET,:   Duhn-duhn-duh,   duhn-duh-dah-dah-daaaaaah. Dunh-duh-dah, dun-duh-dah dah dah. Dunh-duh-duh, duhn-duh-dah dun.   11 times

'F TROOP': How the West was really won by "Gilligan's Island" types in army uniforms. And check out those very un-P.C. Indians.   7 times

'THE FLINTSTONES': Pre-Jurassic park rock! Watch Fred's weight unaccountably fluctuate from episode to Stone Age episode.   11 times

'GILLIGAN'S ISLAND': Bob Denver's panicky ensign makes Beavis look well adjusted. The real question: who is the Professor sleeping with?   5 times

'I DREAM OF JEANNIE': Monitor Hagman's hair: eraser-head to Sonny Bono and back again. Eden's harem pants would be cool with Doc Martens.   5 times

'LEAVE IT TO BEAVER': Good parenting? Ward and June try to shepherd the Beave through an idyllic '50s childhood. Result: the '60s.   10 times

'THREE'S COMPANY': This Carter-era ménage à trois hit No. 1 in the Nielsens. Was this the gay '70s, or what?   5 times

"Going back to the basic point where thinking begins. And staying there."

But they are not just any losers, this lineage of losers. They are specifically *our* losers, totems of an age of decline and nonachievement. One in five people who graduated from college between 1984 and 1990 holds a job that doesn't require a college education. If this is not hard economic reality for a whole generation, it is psychological reality. Loser television has the sense to play along; it taps the anxiety in the culture and plays it back for laughs. Homer Simpson works in a nuclear power plant. Al Bundy sells shoes. Beavis and Butt-head work at Burger World and can't even visualize the good life. In one episode, as an act of community service, they get jobs in a hospital. Sucking on IV bags, planning to steal a cardiac patient's motorized cart, they agree: "It doesn't get any better than this, dude."

The shows also all share a common language. When "Beavis and Butt-head" producer John Andrews, 39, needed to put together a writing staff, he first called Letterman head writer Rob Burnett for suggestions. "Most of this stuff is done by overeducated guys who grew up reading Mad Magazine, National Lampoon, and watching 'Animal House' and 'Saturday Night Live'," says Matt Groening, creator of the Simpsons. "Scripts are based on what comes out of the collective memory of the writers, which is mostly memories of sitting in front of a TV set growing up." More than just throwbacks to the intelligently dumb television of the Three Stooges and Ernie Kovacs, the current shows are broad immersions in pop culture, satirical and multitiered. They address an audience that can view reruns of "Gilligan's Island" and "I Dream of Jeannie" half as camp, half as the fabric of shared experience. "The smarter you are, the more you see single events on different levels simultaneously," says Fernanda Moore, 25, who likes "The Simpsons," "Ren & Stimpy" and "Beavis and Butt-head." A doctoral candidate at Stanford, Moore is the daughter we all crave and perhaps fear. "Dumb people I know," she says, "aren't self-referential."

Of course, this is only one way to watch the shows. Lars Ulrich, drummer in the band Metallica, was delighted one day to spot Beavis wearing a Metallica T shirt. Yet he was also alarmed. "I would have to say—as little as I want to say it—that I think there are people like that. I'm not sure dumb is the right word. I would go more in the direction of the word ignorant." Either way, as the channels open up, the ship of fools is now sailing at full capacity.

At MTV's offices in New York last week, the ship was running through some rough waters. MTV from the inside is a Marshall McLuhan rec room, a place where precociously creative young people invent cool ways to frame ugly heavy-metal videos. In the production area of "Beavis and Butt-head," these young people had a problem. "I don't know," said the show's creator, Mike Judge, in a voice hauntingly close to Butt-head's (Judge does the voices for most of the characters). The staff was watching an unfinished episode in which Bill Clinton visits Beavis and Butt-head's high school, and something just didn't feel real. As MTV political reporter Tabitha Soren introduced the president to the assembly on screen, Judge's face just lost its air. "Do you really think she could hear [Butt-head] fart from across the gym?" he asked. It was a pressing question; the show was set to air in less than a week. The staff was hushed. Finally someone offered, "If it was a big one she could." Judge considered. "No way."

The fast success of the show, along with the rapid production pace, has been a shock to Judge. Since he moved to New York from Dallas in February, he says, he hasn't met anyone except the people he works with. His office at MTV is spare, the walls empty except for a few

TV ADS FOR ACURA'S INTEGRA COME IN REGULAR AND EXTRAFUNKY. REGULAR AIRS ON '60 MINUTES,' FUNKY ON MTV.

pictures of Beavis and Butt-head and a snapshot of his daughter, Julia, almost 2. In his locker is a stuffed Barney dinosaur, a bottle of Jack Daniel's and a Gap jacket. "You know what's weird?" he says, with a gentle Southwestern accent. "Every now and then I'll say, 'Well, that's pretty cool,' and I can't tell if that's something I would have said before or if I'm doing Butt-head." In a file on his desk, he keeps a drawing of a black Beavis and Butt-head, renamed Rufus and Tyrone. At the moment he has no plans for them. For all their anti-P.C. offensiveness, Beavis and Butt-head have yet to cross the line into race humor. "Actually," says Kimson Albert, 22, one of four African-American artists on the show's staff, "the creator and producer are the most P.C. people."

Judge grew up in Albuquerque, N.M., by his own description "just the most awkward, miserable kid around." He played trumpet in the area youth symphony and competed on the swim team and made honor roll at St. Pius X High School. For kicks, he and his friends used to set fires, just to see how many they could keep going at once and still be able to stomp them out. Three years ago, after working at a couple of unhappy engineering jobs, Judge bought himself a $200 animation kit. His first short, "Office Space," aired on last month's season première of "Saturday Night Live." His third, completed in January 1992, introduced the characters Beavis and Butt-head. It was about torturing animals. He called it "Frog Baseball."

"I was a total animal lover," he says. "When I did the storyboard, I didn't want people to see what I was working on. I thought, 'I don't want to show this to anybody; why am I doing this?'" Even now Judge looks back on "Frog Baseball" with mixed feelings: "I never thought that's what I'd be known for."

Gwen Lipsky, 34, is MTV's vice president of research and planning. When she tested "Beavis and Butt-head" before a target audience last October, she noticed something peculiar. "The focus group was both riveted and hysterical from the moment they saw it. After the tape was over, they kept asking to see again. Then, after they had seen it again, several people offered to buy it from

me." Almost without exception, she says, the group members said Beavis and Butt-head reminded them of people they knew. "Interestingly, the people in the focus group who seem the most like Beavis and Butt-head themselves never acknowledge that the characters are them."

Susan Smith-Pinelo, 24, knows them well. A graduate of Oberlin, she is an artist working at what "Generation X" writer Douglas Coupland calls a McJob, as a receptionist at the Sierra Legal Defense Fund. "People laugh at Beavis and Butt-head, Wayne and Garth," she says. "Our generation can relate to this lunatic fringe of teenagers who have fallen out of society, live in a world of TV . . . It's kind of sick, but we like to laugh at them and say, 'I'm not a loser'."

Dick Zimmermann is not a twentysomething and is not amused. A retired broadcasting executive from Larkspur, Calif., Zimmermann, 44, won a state lottery worth nearly $10 million in 1988. Early last summer, while channel surfing, he caught Beavis and Butt-head in the infamous cat episode—touchy ground for anyone involved with the show. Even today it makes Judge uneasy. "They never did this thing with the cat," he says, defensively. "They just made a joke about it: what if you put a firecracker in Stuart's cat's butt." Five days after the show ran, when a cat was found killed by a firecracker in nearby Santa Cruz, Zimmermann put up a $5,000 reward and went to the press. The cause of death, he told Larkspur's Inde-

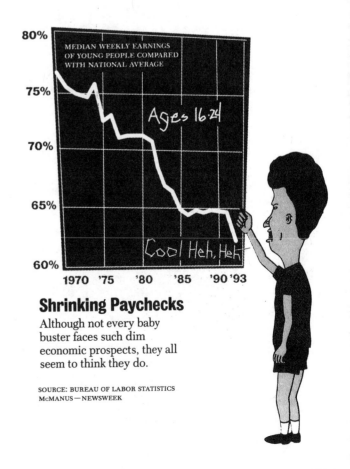

Shrinking Paychecks
Although not every baby buster faces such dim economic prospects, they all seem to think they do.

SOURCE: BUREAU OF LABOR STATISTICS
McMANUS — NEWSWEEK

pendent Journal in a front-page story, was "Beavis and Butt-head." Opening a hot line, he mounted a one-man campaign against the program. "I admit that shows like 'Cops' are obviously very violent," he told NEWSWEEK, "but at least there is the element of good triumphing over evil. The thing about 'Beavis and Butt-head' that caught my eye was the total lack of redeemability. [They] engage in arson, petty theft, shoplifting, auto theft, credit-card fraud, cruelty to animals and insects—not to mention their attitude toward women."

The infamous cat episode will never air again. Three other episodes are also out of circulation, and the show has softened considerably this season. All involved are particularly sensitive because the show runs in family hours: at 7 and 11 p.m. weekdays, and in the afternoon on Saturdays. "The sniffing-paint-thinner we probably shouldn't have done," Judge concedes. "But I'm new to this. I thought of this show as going on at 11, no one's ever going to see it. I think it should run once at 11. We have toned it down."

Gwen Lipsky contends that young kids don't watch the show, that 90 percent of the audience is over 12. But part of the show's appeal is that, yes, these are dangerous, irresponsible messages. "They'll do stuff that we want to do but don't have the guts to do," says, Alex Chriss, 14, who dropped his karate classes to watch Beavis and Butt-head. "On one episode they stole a monster truck and ran over a hippie guy singing save-the-earth songs. We go around mimicking them—not what they say, but how they say it."

Of course, such mimicry is not always harmless, and it is here that we probably need some parental caution. Beavis and Butt-head don't have it; confronted with an image of a nuclear family at the table, Butt-head asks, "Why's that guy eating dinner with those old people?" But other children do. Bill Clinton likes to watch "American Gladiators" with Chelsea; they enjoy the camp value together. And there are lessons to be learned, even from television that prides itself on not doling out lessons. "The whole point of [Beavis and Butt-head] is that they don't grow up," says Lisa Bourgeault, an eighth grader at Marblehead Middle School in Marblehead, Mass. "That's what's hip and cool. But *we* will."

Let's hope so. As our former vice president once put it, with an eloquence few scripted TV characters could match, "What a waste it is to lose one's mind, or not to have a mind." To which, like Beavis and Butt-head, we can only reply, "Huh-huh. Huh-huh. Cool."

With CAREY MONSERRATE *and* DANZY SENNA *in New York,* CARL HOLCOMBE *in San Francisco,* TIM PRYOR *and* MARK MILLER *in Los Angeles and bureau reports*

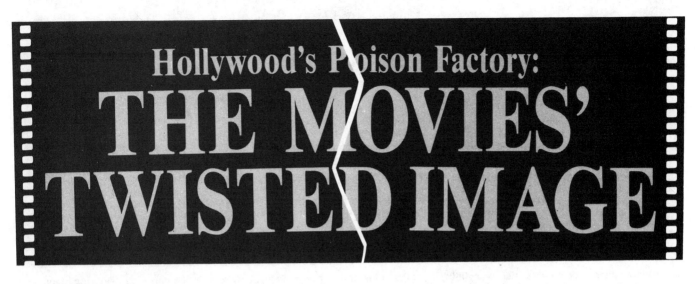

Hollywood's Poison Factory:
THE MOVIES' TWISTED IMAGE

"Why does Hollywood persist in making films that so constantly revel in the dark side, in gloom and despair, destruction and horror?"

Michael Medved

Mr. Medved, co-host of the weekly Public Broadcasting System program, "Sneak Previews," is the author of Hollywood vs. America: Popular Culture and the War on Traditional Values. *This article is adapted from an address to the Center for Constructive Alternatives, Hillsdale (Mich.) College.*

AMERICA'S long-running romance with Hollywood is over. For millions of people, the entertainment industry no longer represents a source of enchantment, magical fantasy, uplift, or even harmless diversion. Popular culture is viewed now as an implacable enemy, a threat to their basic values and a menace to the raising of their children. The Hollywood dream factory has become the poison factory.

This disenchantment is reflected in poll after poll. An Associated Press Media General survey released in 1990 showed that 80% of Americans objected to the amount of foul language in motion pictures, 82% to the amount of violence, 72% to the amount of explicit sexuality, and, by a ratio of three-to-one, felt that movies today are worse than ever.

In reality, you don't need polls or surveys to understand what is going on. When was the last time you heard someone say, "You know, by golly, movies today are better than ever!" Only Jack Valenti, the head of the Motion Picture Association of America, can make such statements with a straight face. There is a general recognition even among those Americans who still like to go

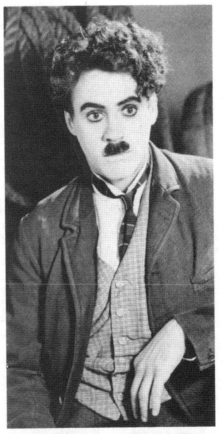

The 1992 film biography "Chaplin," starring Robert Downey, Jr., concentrated almost as much on the actor's struggles with McCarthyism and his self-imposed exile because of his left-wing politics as it did on his brilliant comedic talents.

to movies that their quality has declined. This has begun to register in disastrous box office receipts.

There is a dirty little secret in Hollywood. For movie attendance, 1991 was the worst in 15 years, the summer season the worst in 23. Forty percent of Americans report that they don't see a single film in the course of a year—a higher percentage than ever before. What Hollywood publicizes, of course, is total box office gross receipts, which look respectable, but are misleading because the ticket prices have been raised so much. If you actually count the number of warm bodies sitting in theater seats, movie attendance has declined markedly.

Major studios like MGM and Orion are teetering on the verge of collapse. Carolco, which produced "Terminator II," 1992's biggest hit, has scaled back all operations and fired one-third of its employees. This is clearly an industry in trouble.

Rather than searching for solutions, Hollywood looks for scapegoats. The most common line is: "It's the recession," but this ignores, among other things, the fact that, in the past, the movie business always has proven to be recession proof. Economic downturns generally saw the movie business profit as people sought escape.

What Hollywood insiders refuse to recognize is that the crisis of popular culture, at its very core, is a crisis of values. The problem isn't that the camera is out of focus, editing is sloppy, or the acting is bad. It is with the type of stories Hollywood is telling and the kind of messages it is send-

From *USA Today* magazine, September 1993, pp. 78-82. © 1993 by the Society for the Advancement of Education. Reprinted by permission.

Movie biographies once concentrated on uplifting portraits of historical figures. Today, they revel in the dark side, featuring gloom and despair, destruction and horror. In 1992, Twentieth Century Fox lost millions on "Hoffa," despite Jack Nicholson's Academy Award-nominated performance in the title role as the corrupt leader of the Teamsters Union.

ing in film after film. The industry is bursting with professionalism and prowess, but it suffers from a sickness of the soul.

Hollywood no longer reflects—or even respects—the values that most Americans cherish. Take a look, for example, at the 1992 Academy Awards. Five very fine men were nominated for best actor of the year. Three of them had portrayed murderous psychos: Robert DeNiro in "Cape Fear," Warren Beatty in "Bugsy," and Anthony Hopkins in "The Silence of the Lambs" (a delightful family film about two serial killers—one eats and the other skins his victims). A fourth actor, Robin Williams, was nominated for playing a delusional homeless psycho in "The Fisher King." The most wholesome character was Nick Nolte's, a good old-fashioned manic-depressive-suicidal neurotic in "The Prince of Tides."

These are all good actors, delivering splendid performances, compelling and technically accomplished. Yet, isn't it sad when all this artistry is lavished on films that are so empty, barren, and unfulfilling? Isn't it sad when, at the Academy Awards—the annual event that celebrates the highest achievement the film industry is capable of—the best we can come up with is movies that are so floridly, strangely whacked out?

I repeat: The fundamental problem with Hollywood has nothing at all to do with the brilliance of the performers, the camera work, or the editing. In many ways, these things are better than ever before. Modern films are technically brilliant, but morally and spiritually empty.

Anti-religious bias

What are the messages in today's films? For a number of years, I have been writing about Hollywood's anti-religious bias, but I must point out that this hostility never has been quite as intense as in the last few years. The 1991 season boasted one religion-bashing movie after another in which Hollywood was able to demonstrate that it was an equal-opportunity offender.

For Protestants, there was "At Play in the Fields of the Lord," a lavish $35,000,000 rainforest spectacle about natives and their wholesome primitive ways and the sick, disgusting missionaries who try to ruin their lives. For Catholics, there was "The Pope Must Die," which was re-released as "The Pope Must Diet." It didn't work either way. It features scenes of the Holy Father flirting with harlot nuns and hiding in a closet pigging out on communion wafers. For Jews, there was "Naked Tango," written and directed by the brother of the screenwriter for "The Last Temptation of Christ." This particular epic featured religious Jews operating a brutal bordello next door to a synagogue and forcing women into white slavery.

Most amazingly, there was "Cape Fear," which was nominated for a number of the most prestigious Academy Awards. It wasn't an original concept, but a remake of a 1962 movie in which Robert Mitchum plays a released convict intent on revenge who tracks down his former defense attorney. Gregory Peck portrays the lawyer, a strong, stalwart and upright man who defends his family against this crazed killer. In the remake, by "Last Temptation" director Martin Scorsese, there is a new twist—the released convict is not just an ordinary maniac, but a "Killer Christian from Hell." To prevent anyone from missing the point, his muscular back has a gigantic cross tattooed on it, and he has Biblical verses tattooed on both arms.

When he is about to rape the attorney's wife, played by Jessica Lange, he says, "Are you ready to be born again? After just one hour with me, you'll be talking in tongues." He carries a Bible with him in scenes in which he is persecuting the lawyer's fami-

Spike Lee's "Malcolm X," with Denzel Washington starring as the ex-convict turned black supremacist, was accused of stirring racial unrest, rather than providing entertainment.

ly, and he tells people that he is a member of a Pentecostal church.

The most surprising aspect of this utterly insulting characterization is that it drew so little protest. Imagine that DeNiro's character had been portrayed as a gay rights activist. Homosexual groups would have howled in protest, condemning this caricature as an example of bigotry. However, we are so accustomed to Hollywood's insulting stereotypes of religious believers that no one even seems to notice the hatred behind them.

The entertainment industry further demonstrates its hostility to organized religion by eliminating faith and ritual as a factor in the lives of nearly all the characters it creates. Forty to 50% of all Americans go to church or synagogue every week. When was the last time you saw anybody in a motion picture going to church, unless that person was some kind of crook, mental case, or flagrant hypocrite?

Hollywood even removes religious elements from situations in which they clearly belong. The summer of 1991 offered a spate of medical melodramas like "Regarding Henry," "Dying Young," and "The Doctor." Did you notice that all these characters go into surgery without once invoking the name of God, whispering one little prayer, or asking for clergy? I wrote a non-fiction book about hospital life once, and I guarantee that, just as there are no atheists in foxholes, there are none in operating rooms—only in Hollywood.

Religion isn't Hollywood's sole target. The traditional family also has received surprisingly harsh treatment from today's movie moguls. Look again at "Cape Fear." The remake not only changed the killer, it also changed the hero. This brings me to the second message Hollywood regularly broadcasts. The lawyer Gregory Peck plays in the original version is a decent and honorable man. In the remake, Nick Nolte's character is, not to put too fine a point on it, a sleazeball. He is repeatedly unfaithful to his wife. When she dares to question that practice, he hits her. He tries to beat up his daughter on one occasion because she is smoking marijuana. That a happily married, family-defending hero—the kind of person that people can identify with—is transformed into a sadistic, cheating, bitter man says volumes about the direction of American movies.

Did you ever notice how few movies there are about happily married people? There are very few films about married people at all, but those that are made tend to portray marriage as a disaster, as a dangerous situation, as a battleground with a long series of murderous marriage movies.

In "Sleeping with the Enemy," Patrick Bergin beats up Julia Roberts so mercilessly that she has to run away. When he comes after her, she eventually kills him. In "Mortal Thoughts," Bruce Willis beats up *his* wife and is killed by her best friend. In "Thelma and Louise," there is another horrible, brutal, and insensitive husband to run away from. In "A Kiss Before Dying," Matt Dillon persuades twin sisters to marry him. He kills the first one, then tries to murder the second, but she gets him first.

In "She-Devil," Rosanne Barr torments her cheating husband, Ed Begley, Jr. In "Total Recall," Sharon Stone pretends to be married to Arnold Schwarzenegger and tries to kill him. When he gets the upper hand, she objects, "But you can't hurt me! I'm your wife." He shoots her through the forehead and says, "Consider that a divorce." The ads for "Deceived," starring Goldie Hawn, say, "She thought her life was perfect," and, of course, her model husband turns out to be a murderous monster. "Deceived" is an appropriate title, because we all have been deceived by Hollywood's portrayal of marriage.

The trend even applies to television. *The New York Times* reports that, in the 1991-92 TV season, there were seven different pregnancies. What did six of the seven have in common? They were out of wedlock. The message is that marriage is outmoded, dangerous, oppressive, and unhealthy, but is it true?

The conventional wisdom is that the divorce rate in America stands at 50%, a figure used repeatedly in the media. Yet, the 1990 U.S. Census Bureau report has a category listing the number of people who ever have been married and who ever have been divorced. The latter shows that less than 20% have been divorced. The evidence is overwhelming that the 50% divorce rate is more than a slight overstatement—it is a destructive and misleading myth.

Nevertheless, Hollywood has been selling divorce for years. Remember "The Last Married Couple in America," starring Natalie Wood? That may be a Hollywood prophecy, but it is not the reality of the American heartland. In this matter, as in so many others, by overstating the negative, the film industry leads viewers to feel terrified and/or insecure, and their behavior is affected adversely. I know many people who say, "I'm reluctant to get married because I know there's a 50% chance I'm going to get divorced." Wouldn't it make a difference if they knew there actually was an 80% chance of staying together?

America-bashing

Another negative message is America-bashing. The U.S. is portrayed on movie and television screens as a nightmarish land where nothing is going right and evil powers dominate. Consider, for example, that full-color, breathless guided tour of the fetid fever swamps of Oliver Stone's paranoid imagination. In "JFK," Stone suggests a conspiracy so grand, so enormous, so corrupt that it involves absolutely every conceivable American institution and organization except the Camp Fire Girls.

Oliver Stone's nightmare increasingly has become Hollywood's dream of America. One of the ways my immigrant mother and my immigrant grandparents on my father's side learned about America was through movies. They glorified the American past, and some of them were very good, like "Drums Along the Mohawk" or "Young Mr. Lincoln." Today, if Hollywood made a movie about young Mr. Lincoln, he would be an abused child and grow up to be corrupt and power-lusting.

The American past, according to Hollywood, mainly is about the rise of evil businessmen and the "exploitative" capitalist system, or, alternatively, about the supposedly glorious 1960s. There are a plethora of phony 1960s nostalgia movies clearly made by people who are determined to glorify all those who protested against the Vietnam War and insult all those who actually fought it. Is there a more maligned and abused group of people than Vietnam vets? They always are portrayed as weird guys. If a screenwriter needs to come up with an explanation for why a character is a crazed killer, it is, "Oh, he was in 'Nam." Remember, 3,000,000 Americans fought in Vietnam and a mere handful are crazed killers.

The other era the movies tend to focus on obsessively is the 1930s, with those wonderful dramatic elements of negativity—the Depression and gangsters. The glories of our history? Forget it.

In 1985, there was an attempt to make a movie about the American Revolution that cost $35,000,000 and showcased Al Pacino, his Brooklyn accent firmly intact, as a soldier in the Continental Army. However, this movie made the Americans the bad guys! Did it take a genius to tell Warner Brothers that, if you make a movie about the Revolution that runs two and a half hours and makes the Americans the bad guys, no one will want to see it?

In 1991, the U.S. rallied with unanimity behind Operation Desert Storm. Many commentators predicted that there would be a glut of movies about it. Wouldn't Hollywood be eager to exploit the Gulf War? Not one presently is in production or even in development.

By contrast, there currently are five major studio projects in development about the Black Panther Party—that tiny, briefly fashionable gang of thugs who murdered many of their own members. An industry that thinks the American people are more interested in the Black Panthers than in the genuine heroes of our armed forces is one that is profoundly out of touch.

What is the motivation behind the

messages Hollywood is sending? Some people say, "Well, you know, the movie business is perfect capitalism; it's merely giving the people what they want."

However, an analysis of the controversial content of recent films and their corresponding box office performance shows that this is not the case. More than 60% of all feature films now are rated "R"—despite the fact that they consistently earn less money than those rated "G" or "PG." In 1991, PG-rated films drew a median box office gross three times larger than R-rated films, but Hollywood persists in making the majority of its releases as gore- and sex-drenched R-rated shockers. Is this an example of responding to the public?

The movie industry expresses its underlying values most clearly with those projects it considers serious "art"—films that make some philosophical or political statement. Consider the 1990 "Guilty by Suspicion," a dark, tragic tale of an idealistic, blacklisted left-wing director in the 1950s. How could Warner Brothers possibly assume it would make money on this very expensive Robert DeNiro project, especially when more than a half-dozen previous films about the horrors of the McCarthy era had failed miserably at the box office?

Or take a look at the three gigantically expensive film biographies that came out in 1992. One is about Jimmy Hoffa, played by Jack Nicholson. The second is about Malcolm X, directed by Spike Lee. The third is about Charlie Chaplin, specifically his struggles with McCarthyism during the 1950s and how he eventually had to flee to a self-imposed exile because of his left-wing politics.

If we can assume that the primary purpose of these movies, each of which cost tens of millions of dollars, is not to earn money, then what is it? Why does Hollywood persist in making films that so constantly revel in the dark side, in gloom and despair, destruction and horror? I'll try to offer a brief explanation, but someone versed in clinical psychology might be able to diagnose the situation better.

People in the movie business are motivated by a tremendous desire to be taken seriously. They don't want to be thought of as just entertainers. They want to be respected as "artists," and the view today is that, in order to be a serious artist—to make a statement—you have to be removed from the mainstream in your own country.

This view ignores all of Western history. Was William Shakespeare alienated from the Tudor monarchy? He wrote play after play glorifying Elizabeth's antecedents and became a court favorite. He was part of the establishment and was proud of it. When Johann Sebastian Bach wrote the imperishable music for which he is known, he did so for Prince Leopold, the elector of

Brandenburg, and the Church of St. Thomas in Leipzig. He composed more than 600 sacred cantatas and chorales, devotedly serving the religious hierarchy of his time.

In the past, most great artists served and respected the society they lived in. To be sure, they were not content with all its aspects, but they weren't off on the sidelines wearing black turtlenecks saying that life is meaningless and bleak or immersing crucifixes in their own urine. The "serious artist alienated from society" syndrome has ruined the visual arts, poetry, and classical music. It even has begun to destroy popular culture, which heretofore has been more in tune with ordinary people.

Today, to win the highest critical praise or receive Oscar consideration, you have to make a movie that says life is short and bitter and that it stinks. Mel Brooks recently made the least successful movie of his career, 'Life Stinks.' Pretend for a moment that you are the head of MGM and Brooks comes to you and says, "Hey, I have an idea for a fun comedy called 'Life Stinks.' Think that's gonna sell?" No, but it will help him get taken seriously as an "artist."

These are not bad people. They are very well intentioned. There isn't a single AIDS benefit that they will miss. If there is any kind of dinner to save the rainforests, they are there. They want to be loved. Nevertheless, they earnestly believe that the only way they will receive respect from those who "count"—critics, motion picture industry heavyweights, media, and intellectual elites—is to make brutal, bitter, America-bashing, family-bashing, religion-bashing movies.

What can the public do?

At a conference on popular culture and values, I was on a panel that included one-time Supreme Court nominee Robert Bork. The question of regulating the content of movies came up. Interestingly enough, Bork generally was in favor of government intervention—*i.e.,* censorship. He pointed out that all law is based upon moral judgments. Law exists to influence the moral behavior of its citizens.

This certainly is a convincing argument, but I don't think censorship is a good idea for one very simple reason: the government makes a mess of everything it does, and it would make a huge mess of determining what goes into movies! It always surprises me that conservatives, who understand that the government is remarkably inept, believe that state power somehow can be counted upon to raise the moral tone of our popular culture. Forget it; that is only wishful thinking.

This does not mean that we can't talk about values in movies. I have drawn a good

deal of criticism over the years because, as a professional critic, I try to consider the values and the message in movies—not just their technical excellence—and I speak out about this in the national press and on television. It is vital that those considerations should play a more prominent role in our public discussions of contemporary cinema. That is alternative number one to censorship. No film is morally neutral, fails to send a message, and doesn't change you to some extent when you see it. Movies have a cumulative, potent, and lasting impact.

Another alternative to censorship is corporate responsibility. The great business conglomerates making entertainment have to exercise a more mature sense of social and corporate accountability. We are living in an age when we increasingly are asking corporations to be responsible for their pollution of the air and the water. Why shouldn't they be responsible for the pollution of the cultural environment around us? In the same way that other activists use boycotts and stockholders meetings and every sort of public pressure, popular culture activists must develop a new sense of determination and resourcefulness. The impact of popular culture on our children and our future is too important an issue to leave in the hands of a few isolated movie moguls in Hollywood or politicians in Washington.

There are many indications that the entertainment industry may be eager to reconnect with the grass roots and entertain an expanded notion of its own obligations to the public. The industry has behaved responsibly in some areas. In the past few years, it changed its message about drugs. No longer is it making movies in which marijuana, cocaine, and other illegal substances are glamorized. Hollywood made a decision. Was it self-censorship? You bet. Was it responsible? Yes.

We can challenge the industry to adapt a more wholesome outlook, to send more constructive messages. We can clamor for movies that don't portray marriage as a living hell, that recognize the spiritual side of man's nature and glorify the blessings in life we enjoy as Americans and the people who make sacrifices to ensure that others will be able to enjoy them.

The box office crisis has put Hollywood in a receptive mood. Already two film corporations have committed to a schedule of family movies for a very simple reason—they are wildly successful. Only two percent of movies released in 1991 were G-rated—just 14 titles—but at least eight of them proved to be unequivocally profitable. (By comparison, of more than 600 other titles, *at most* 20% earned back their investment.) "Beauty and the Beast," my choice for best movie of 1991, was a stunning financial success. We need many more pictures like this, and not just animated features geared for younger audiences. Shouldn't it be possible to create movies with adult themes, but without foul language, graphic sex, or cinematic brutality? During Hollywood's golden age, industry leaders understood that there was nothing inherently mature about these unsettling elements.

People tell me sometimes, "Boy, the way you talk, it sounds as though you really hate movies." The fact is that I don't. I'm a film critic because I *love* movies. All the people who are trying to make a difference in this business love movies and love the industry, despite all its faults. They love what it has done in the past and its potential for the future. They believe that Hollywood can be the dream factory again.

When I go to a screening, sit in a theater seat, and the lights go down, there is a little something inside me that hopes against all rational expectation that what I'm going to see on the screen will delight, enchant, and entice me, like the best movies do. I began this article by declaring that America's long-running romance with Hollywood is over. It is a romance that can be rekindled, however, if this appalling, amazing industry once again can create movies that are worthy of love and merit the ardent affection of their audience.

Gendered Media: The Influence of Media on Views of Gender

Julia T. Wood

Department of Communication, University of North Carolina at Chapel Hill.

THEMES IN MEDIA

Of the many influences on how we view men and women, media are the most pervasive and one of the most powerful. Woven throughout our daily lives, media insinuate their messages into our consciousness at every turn. All forms of media communicate images of the sexes, many of which perpetuate unrealistic, stereotypical, and limiting perceptions. Three themes describe how media represent gender. First, women are underrepresented, which falsely implies that men are the cultural standard and women are unimportant or invisible. Second, men and women are portrayed in stereotypical ways that reflect and sustain socially endorsed views of gender. Third, depictions of relationships between men and women emphasize traditional roles and normalize violence against women. We will consider each of these themes in this section.

Underrepresentation of Women

A primary way in which media distort reality is in underrepresenting women. Whether it is prime-time television, in which there are three times as many white men as women (Basow, 1992 p. 159), or children's programming, in which males outnumber females by two to one, or newscasts, in which women make up 16% of newscasters and in which stories about men are included 10 times more often than ones about women ("Study Reports Sex Bias," 1989), media misrepresent

actual proportions of men and women in the population. This constant distortion tempts us to believe that there really are more men than women and, further, that men are the cultural standard.

Other myths about what is standard are similarly fortified by communication in media. Minorities are even less visible than women, with African-Americans appearing only rarely (Gray, 1986; Stroman, 1989) and other ethnic minorities being virtually nonexistent. In children's programming when African-Americans do appear, almost invariably they appear in supporting roles rather than as main characters (O'Connor, 1989). While more African-Americans are appearing in

---

MEDIA'S MISREPRESENTATION OF AMERICAN LIFE

The media present a distorted version of cultural life in our country. According to media portrayals:

White males make up two-thirds of the population. The women are less in number, perhaps because fewer than 10% live beyond 35. Those who do, like their younger and male counterparts, are nearly all white and heterosexual. In addition to being young, the majority of women are beautiful, very thin, passive, and primarily concerned with relationships and getting rings out of collars and commodes. There are a few bad, bitchy women, and they are not so pretty, not so subordinate, and not so caring as the good women. Most of the bad ones work outside of the home, which is probably why they are hardened and undesirable. The more powerful, ambitious men occupy themselves with important business deals, exciting adventures, and rescuing dependent females, whom they often then assault sexually.

From *Gendered Lives: Communication, Gender, and Culture* by Julia T. Wood, chapter 9, pp. 231-244, 250-259. © 1994 by Wadsworth Publishing Company, Inc. Reprinted by permission.

prime-time television, they are too often cast in stereo-typical roles. In the 1992 season, for instance, 12 of the 74 series on commercial networks included large African-American casts, yet most featured them in stereotypical roles. Black men are presented as lazy and unable to handle authority, as lecherous, and/or as unlawful, while females are portrayed as domineering or as sex objects ("Sights, Sounds, and Stereotypes," 1992). Writing in 1993, David Evans (1993, p. 10) criticized television for stereotyping black males as athletes and entertainers. These roles, wrote Evans, mislead young black male viewers into thinking success "is only a dribble or dance step away," and blind them to other, more realistic ambitions. Hispanics and Asians are nearly absent, and when they are presented it is usually as villains or criminals (Lichter, Lichter, Rothman, & Amundson, 1987).

Also underrepresented is the single fastest growing group of Americans—older people. As a country, we are aging so that people over 60 make up a major part of our population; within this group, women significantly outnumber men (Wood, 1993c). Older people not only are underrepresented in media but also are represented inaccurately. In contrast to demographic realities, media consistently show fewer older women than men, presumably because our culture worships youth and beauty in women. Further, elderly individuals are frequently portrayed as sick, dependent, fumbling, and passive, images not borne out in real life. Distorted depictions of older people and especially older women in media, however, can delude us into thinking they are a small, sickly, and unimportant part of our population.

The lack of women in the media is paralleled by the scarcity of women in charge of media. Only about 5% of television writers, executives, and producers are women (Lichter, Lichter, & Rothman, 1986). Ironically, while two-thirds of journalism graduates are women, they make up less than 2% of those in corporate management of newspapers and only about 5% of newspaper publishers ("Women in Media," 1988). Female film directors are even more scarce, as are executives in charge of MTV. It is probably not coincidental that so few women are behind the scenes of an industry that so consistently portrays women negatively. Some media analysts (Mills, 1988) believe that if more women had positions of authority at executive levels, media would offer more positive portrayals of women.

Stereotypical Portrayals of Women and Men

In general, media continue to present both women and men in stereotyped ways that limit our perceptions of human possibilities. Typically men are portrayed as active, adventurous, powerful, sexually aggressive, and largely uninvolved in human relationships. Just as consistent with cultural views of gender are depic-tions of women as sex objects who are usually young, thin, beautiful, passive, dependent, and often incompetent and dumb. Female characters devote their primary energies to improving their appearances and taking care of homes and people. Because media pervade our lives, the ways they misrepresent genders may distort how we see ourselves and what we perceive as normal and desirable for men and women.

Stereotypical portrayals of men. According to J. A. Doyle (1989, p. 111), whose research focuses on masculinity, children's television typically shows males as "aggressive, dominant, and engaged in exciting activities from which they receive rewards from others for their 'masculine' accomplishments." Relatedly, recent studies reveal that the majority of men on prime-time television are independent, aggressive, and in charge (McCauley, Thangavelu, & Rozin, 1988). Television programming for all ages disproportionately depicts men as serious, confident, competent, powerful, and in high-status positions. Gentleness in men, which was briefly evident in the 1970s, has receded as established male characters are redrawn to be more tough and distanced from others (Boyer, 1986). Highly popular films such as *Lethal Weapon, Predator, Days of Thunder, Total Recall, Robocop, Die Hard,* and *Die Harder* star men who embody the stereotype of extreme masculinity. Media, then, reinforce long-standing cultural ideals of masculinity: Men are presented as hard, tough, independent, sexually aggressive, unafraid, violent, totally in control of all emotions, and—above all—in no way feminine.

Equally interesting is how males are *not* presented. J. D. Brown and K. Campbell (1986) report that men are seldom shown doing housework. Doyle (1989) notes that boys and men are rarely presented caring for others. B. Horovitz (1989) points out they are typically represented as uninterested in and incompetent at homemaking, cooking, and child care. Each season's new ads for cooking and cleaning supplies include several that caricature men as incompetent buffoons, who are klutzes in the kitchen and no better at taking care of children. While children's books have made a limited attempt to depict women engaged in activities outside of the home, there has been little parallel effort to show men involved in family and home life. When someone is shown taking care of a child, it is usually the mother, not the father. This perpetuates a negative stereotype of men as uncaring and uninvolved in family life.

Stereotypical portrayals of women. Media's images of women also reflect cultural stereotypes that depart markedly from reality. As we have already seen, girls and women are dramatically underrepresented. In prime-time television in 1987, fully two-thirds of the speaking parts were for men. Women are portrayed as significantly younger and thinner than women in the population as a whole, and most are

JILL

I remember when I was little I used to read books from the boys' section of the library because they were more interesting. Boys did the fun stuff and the exciting things. My mother kept trying to get me to read girls' books, but I just couldn't get into them. Why can't stories about girls be full of adventure and bravery? I know when I'm a mother, I want any daughters of mine to understand that excitement isn't just for boys.

depicted as passive, dependent on men, and enmeshed in relationships or housework (Davis, 1990). The requirements of youth and beauty in women even influence news shows, where female newscasters are expected to be younger, more physically attractive, and less outspoken than males (Craft, 1988; Sanders & Rock, 1988). Despite educators' criticism of self-fulfilling prophesies that discourage girls from success in math and science, that stereotype was dramatically reiterated in 1992 when Mattel offered a new talking Barbie doll. What did she say? "Math class is tough," a message that reinforces the stereotype that women cannot do math ("Mattel Offers Trade-In," 1992). From children's programming, in which the few existing female characters typically spend their time watching males do things (Feldman & Brown, 1984; Woodman, 1991), to MTV, which routinely pictures women satisfying men's sexual fantasies (Pareles, 1990; Texier, 1990), media reiterate the cultural image of women as dependent, ornamental objects whose primary functions are to look good, please men, and stay quietly on the periphery of life.

Media have created two images of women: good women and bad ones. These polar opposites are often juxtaposed against each other to dramatize differences in the consequences that befall good and bad women. Good women are pretty, deferential, and focused on home, family, and caring for others. Subordinate to men, they are usually cast as victims, angels, martyrs, and loyal wives and helpmates. Occasionally, women who depart from traditional roles are portrayed positively, but this is done either by making their career lives invisible, as with Claire Huxtable, or by softening and feminizing working women to make them more consistent with traditional views of femininity. For instance, in the original script, Cagney and Lacey were conceived as strong, mature, independent women who took their work seriously and did it well. It took 6 years for writers Barbara Corday and Barbara Avedon to sell the script to CBS, and even then they had to agree to subdue Cagney's and Lacey's abilities to placate producer Barney Rosenzweig, who complained, "These women aren't soft enough. These women aren't feminine enough" (Faludi, 1991, p. 150). While female

viewers wrote thousands of letters praising the show, male executives at CBS continued to force writers to make the characters softer, more tender, and less sure of themselves (Faludi, 1991, p. 152). The remaking of Cagney and Lacey illustrates the media's bias in favor of women who are traditionally feminine and who are not too able, too powerful, or too confident. The rule seems to be that a woman may be strong and successful if and only if she also exemplifies traditional stereotypes of femininity—subservience, passivity, beauty, and an identity linked to one or more men.

The other image of women the media offer us is the evil sister of the good homebody. Versions of this image are the witch, bitch, whore, or nonwoman, who is represented as hard, cold, aggressive—all of the things a good woman is not supposed to be. Exemplifying the evil woman is Alex in *Fatal Attraction*, which grossed more than $100 million in its first four months (Faludi, 1991, p. 113). Yet Alex was only an extreme version of how bad women are generally portrayed. In children's literature, we encounter witches and mean stepmothers as villains, with beautiful and passive females like Snow White and Sleeping Beauty as their good counterparts.

Prime-time television favorably portrays pretty, nurturing, other-focused women, such as Claire Huxtable on "The Cosby Show," whose career as an attorney never entered storylines as much as her engagement in family matters. Hope in "Thirtysomething" is an angel, committed to husband Michael and daughter Janey. In the biographies written for each of the characters when the show was in development, all male characters were defined in terms of their career goals, beliefs, and activities. Hope's biography consisted of one line: "Hope is married to Michael" (Faludi, 1991, p. 162). Hope epitomizes the traditional woman, so much so in fact that in one episode she refers to herself as June Cleaver and calls Michael "Ward," thus reprising the traditional family of the 1950s as personified in "Leave It to Beaver" (Faludi, 1991, p. 161). Meanwhile, prime-time typically represents ambitious, independent women as lonely, embittered spinsters who are counterpoints to "good" women.

Stereotypical Images of Relationships Between Men and Women

Given media's stereotypical portrayals of women and men, we shouldn't be surprised to find that relationships between women and men are similarly depicted in ways that reinforce stereotypes. Four themes demonstrate how media reflect and promote traditional arrangements between the sexes.

Women's dependence/men's independence. Walt Disney's award-winning animated film *The Little Mermaid* vividly embodies females' dependence on males for identity. In this feature film, the mermaid quite literally gives up her identity as a mermaid in order to become acceptable to her human lover. In this children's story, we see a particularly obvious illustration of the asymmetrical relationship between women and men that is more subtly conveyed in other media productions. Even the Smurfs, formless little beings who have no obvious sex, reflect the male-female, dominant-submissive roles. The female smurf, unlike her male companions, who have names, is called only Smurfette, making her sole identity a diminutive relation to male smurfs. The male dominance/female subservience pattern that permeates mediated representations of relationships is no accident. Beginning in 1991, television executives deliberately and consciously adopted a policy of having dominant male characters in all Saturday morning children's programming (Carter, 1991).

Women, as well as minorities, are cast in support roles rather than leading ones in both children's shows and the commercials interspersed within them (O'Connor, 1989). Analyses of MTV revealed that it portrays females as passive and waiting for men's attention, while males are shown ignoring, exploiting, or directing women (Brown, Campbell, & Fisher, 1986). In rap music videos, where African-American men and women star, men dominate women, whose primary role is as objects of male desires (Pareles, 1990; Texier, 1990). News programs that have male and female hosts routinely cast the female as deferential to her male colleague (Craft, 1988; Sanders & Rock, 1988). Commercials, too, manifest power cues that echo the male dominance/female subservience pattern. For instance, men are usually shown positioned above women, and women are more frequently pictured in varying degrees of undress (Masse & Rosenblum, 1988; Nigro, Hill, Gelbein, & Clark, 1988). Such nonverbal cues represent women as vulnerable and more submissive while men stay in control.

In a brief departure from this pattern, films and television beginning in the 1970s responded to the second wave of feminism by showing women who were independent without being hard, embittered, or without close relationships. Films such as *Alice Doesn't Live Here Anymore, Up the Sandbox, The Turning Point, Diary of a Mad Housewife,* and *An Unmarried Woman* offered realistic portraits of women who sought and found their own voices independent of men. Judy Davis's film, *My Brilliant Career,* particularly embodied this focus by telling the story of a woman who chooses work over marriage. During this period, television followed suit, offering viewers prime-time fare such as "Maude" and "The Mary Tyler Moore Show," which starred women who were able and achieving in their own' rights. "One Day at a Time," which premiered in 1974, was the first prime-time program about a divorced woman.

By the 1980s, however, traditionally gendered arrangements resurged as the backlash movement against feminism was embraced by media (Haskell, 1988; Maslin, 1990). Thus, film fare in the 1980s included *Pretty Woman,* the story of a prostitute who becomes a good woman when she is saved from her evil ways by a rigidly stereotypical man, complete with millions to prove his success. Meanwhile, *Tie Me Up, Tie Me Down* trivialized abuse of women and underlined women's dependence on men with a story of a woman who is bound by a man and colludes in sustaining her bondage. *Crossing Delancey* showed successful careerist Amy Irving talked into believing she needs a man to be complete, a theme reprised by Cher in *Moonstruck.*

Television, too, cooperated in returning women to their traditional roles with characters like Hope in "Thirtysomething," who minded house and baby as an ultratraditional wife, and even Murphy Brown found her career wasn't enough and had a baby. Against her protests, Cybill Shepherd, who played Maddie in "Moonlighting," was forced to marry briefly on screen, which Susan Faludi (1991, p. 157) refers to as part of a "campaign to cow this independent female figure." Popular music added its voice with hit songs like "Having My Baby," which glorified a woman who defined herself by motherhood and her relationship to a man. The point is not that having babies or committing to relationships is wrong; rather, it is that media virtually require this of women in order to present them positively. Media define a very narrow range for womanhood.

Joining the campaign to restore traditional dominant-subordinate patterns of male-female relationships were magazines, which reinvigorated their focus on women's role as the helpmate and supporter of husbands and families (Peirce, 1990). In 1988, that staple of Americana, *Good Housekeeping,* did its part to revive women's traditional roles with a full-page ad ("The Best in the House," 1988) for its new demographic edition marketed to "the new traditionalist woman." A month later, the magazine followed this up with a second full-page ad in national newspapers that saluted the "new traditionalist woman," with this copy ("The New Traditionalist," 1988): "She has made her commitment. Her mission: create a more meaningful life for herself and her family. She is the New Traditionalist— a contemporary woman who finds her fulfillment in traditional values." The long-standing dominant-submissive model for male-female relationships was largely restored in the 1980s. With only rare exceptions, women are still portrayed as dependent on men and subservient to them. As B. Lott (1989, p. 64) points out, it is women who "do the laundry and are secretaries to men who own companies."

Men's authority/women's incompetence. A second recurrent theme in media representations of relationships is that men are the competent authorities who save women from their incompetence. Children's litera-

PAUL

I wouldn't say this around anyone, but personally I'd be glad if the media let up a little on us guys. I watch those guys in films and on TV, and I just feel inadequate. I mean, I'm healthy and I look okay, and I'll probably make a decent salary when I graduate. But I am no stud; I can't beat up three guys at once, women don't fall dead at my feet; I doubt I'll make a million bucks; and I don't have muscles that ripple. Every time I go to a film, I leave feeling like a wimp. How can any of us guys measure up to what's on the screen?

ture vividly implements this motif by casting females as helpless and males as coming to their rescue. Sleeping Beauty's resurrection depends on Prince Charming's kiss, a theme that appears in the increasingly popular gothic romance novels for adults (Modleski, 1982).

One of the most pervasive ways in which media define males as authorities is in commercials. Women are routinely shown anguishing over dirty floors and bathroom fixtures only to be relieved of their distress when Mr. Clean shows up to tell them how to keep their homes spotless. Even when commercials are aimed at women, selling products intended for them, up to 90% of the time a man's voice is used to explain the value of what is being sold (Basow, 1992, p. 161; Bretl & Cantor, 1988). Using male voice-overs reinforces the cultural view that men are authorities and women depend on men to tell them what to do.

Television further communicates the message that men are authorities and women are not. One means of doing this is sheer numbers. As we have seen, men vastly outnumber women in television programming. In addition, the dominance of men as news anchors who inform us of happenings in the world underlines their authority ("Study Reports Sex Bias," 1989). Prime-time television contributes to this image by showing women who need to be rescued by men and by presenting women as incompetent more than twice as often as men (Boyer, 1986; Lichter et al., 1986).

Consider the characters in "The Jetsons," an animated television series set in the future. Daughter Judy Jetson is constantly complaining and waiting for others to help her, using ploys of helplessness and flattery to win men's attention. The Rescuers, a popular animated video of the 1990s, features Miss Bianca (whose voice is that of Zsa Zsa Gabor, fittingly enough), who splits her time evenly between being in trouble and being grateful to male characters for rescuing her. These stereotypical representations of males and females reinforce a number of harmful beliefs. They suggest, first, that men are more competent than women. Compounding this is the message that a woman's power lies in her looks and conventional

femininity, since that is how females from Sleeping Beauty to Judy Jetson get males to assist them with their dilemmas (McCauley, Thangavelu, & Rozin, 1988). Third, these stereotypes underline the requirement that men must perform, succeed, and conquer in order to be worthy.

Women as primary caregivers/men as breadwinners. A third perennial theme in media is that women are caregivers and men are providers. Since the backlash of the 1980s, in fact, this gendered arrangement has been promulgated with renewed vigor. Once again, as in the 1950s, we see women devoting themselves to getting rings off of collars, gray out of their hair, and meals on the table. Corresponding to this is the restatement of men's inability in domestic and nurturing roles. Horovitz (1989), for instance, reports that in commercials men are regularly the butt of jokes for their ignorance about nutrition, child care, and housework.

When media portray women who work outside of the home, their career lives typically receive little or no attention. Although these characters have titles such as lawyer or doctor, they are shown predominantly in their roles as homemakers, mothers, and wives. We see them involved in caring conversations with family and friends and doing things for others, all of which never seem to conflict with their professional responsibilities. This has the potential to cultivate unrealistic expectations of being "superwoman," who does it all without her getting a hair out of place or being late to a conference.

Magazines play a key role in promoting pleasing others as a primary focus of women's lives. K. Peirce's (1990) study found that magazines aimed at women stress looking good and doing things to please others. Thus, advertising tells women how to be "me, only better" by dyeing their hair to look younger; how to lose weight so "you'll still be attractive to him"; and how to prepare gourmet meals so "he's always glad to come home." Constantly, these advertisements empha-

JOANNE

I'd like to know who dreams up those commercials that show men as unable to boil water or run a vacuum. I'd like to tell them they're creating monsters. My boyfriend and I agreed to split all chores equally when we moved in together. Ha! Fat chance of that. He does zilch. When I get on his case, he reminds me of what happened when the father on some show had to take over housework and practically demolished the kitchen. Then he grins and says, "Now, you wouldn't want that, would you?" Or worse yet, he throws up Hope or one of the other women on TV, and asks me why I can't be as sweet and supportive as she is. It's like the junk on television gives him blanket license for doing nothing.

size pleasing others, especially men, as central to being a woman, and the message is fortified with the thinly veiled warning that if a woman fails to look good and please, her man might leave (Rakow, 1992).

There is a second, less known way in which advertisements contribute to stereotypes of women as focused on others and men as focused on work. Writing in 1990, Gloria Steinem, editor of *Ms.*, revealed that advertisers control some to most of the *content* in magazines. In exchange for placing an ad, a company receives "complimentary copy," which is one or more articles that increase the market appeal of its product. So a soup company that takes out an ad might be given a three-page story on how to prepare meals using that brand of soup; likewise, an ad for hair coloring products might be accompanied by interviews with famous women who choose to dye their hair. Thus, the message of advertisers is multiplied by magazine content, which readers often mistakenly assume is independent of advertising.

Advertisers support media, and they exert a powerful influence on what is presented. To understand the prevalence of traditional gender roles in programming, magazine copy, and other media, we need only ask what is in the best interests of advertisers. They want to sponsor shows that create or expand markets for their products. Media images of women as sex objects, devoted homemakers, and mothers buttress the very roles in which the majority of consuming takes place. To live up to these images, women have to buy cosmetics and other personal care products, diet aids, food, household cleaners, utensils and appliances, clothes and toys for children, and so on. In short, it is in advertisers' interests to support programming and copy that feature women in traditional roles. In a recent analysis, Lana Rakow (1992) demonstrated that much advertising is oppressive to women and is very difficult to resist, even when one is a committed feminist.

Women's role in the home and men's role outside of it are reinforced by newspapers and news programming. Both emphasize men's independent activities and, in fact, define news almost entirely as stories about and by men ("Study Reports Sex Bias," 1989). Stories about men focus on work and/or their achievements (Luebke, 1989), reiterating the cultural message that men are supposed to do, perform. Meanwhile the few stories about women almost invariably focus on their roles as wives, mothers, and homemakers ("Study Reports Sex Bias," 1989). Even stories about women who are in the news because of achievements and professional activities typically dwell on marriage, family life, and other aspects of women's traditional role (Foreit et al., 1980).

Women as victims and sex objects/men as aggressors. A final theme in mediated representations of relationships between women and men is representation of women as subject to men's sexual desires. The irony of this representation is that the very qualities women are encouraged to develop (beauty, sexiness, passivity, and powerlessness) in order to meet cultural ideals of femininity contribute to their victimization. Also, the qualities that men are urged to exemplify (aggressiveness, dominance, sexuality, and strength) are identical to those linked to abuse of women. It is no coincidence that all but one of the women nominated for Best Actress in the 1988 Academy Awards played a victim (Faludi, 1991, p. 138). Women are portrayed alternatively either as decorative objects, who must attract a man to be valuable, or as victims of men's sexual impulses. Either way, women are defined by their bodies and how men treat them. Their independent identities and endeavors are irrelevant to how they are represented in media, and their abilities to resist exploitation by others are obscured.

This theme, which was somewhat toned down during the 1970s, returned with vigor in the 1980s as the backlash permeated media. According to S. A. Basow (1992, p. 160), since 1987 there has been a "resurgence of male prominence, pretty female sidekicks, female homemakers." Advertising in magazines also communicates the message that women are sexual objects. While men are seldom pictured nude or even partially unclothed, women habitually are. Advertisements for makeup, colognes, hair products, and clothes often show women attracting men because they got the right products and made themselves irresistible. Stars on prime-time and films, who are beautiful and dangerously thin, perpetuate the idea that women must literally starve themselves to death to win men's interest (Silverstein et al., 1986).

Perhaps the most glaring examples of portrayals of women as sex objects and men as sexual aggressors occur in music videos as shown on MTV and many other stations. Typically, females are shown dancing provocatively in scant and/or revealing clothing as they try to gain men's attention (Texier, 1990). Frequently, men are seen coercing women into sexual activities and/or physically abusing them. Violence against women is also condoned in many recent films. R. Warshaw (1991) reported that cinematic presentations of rapes, especially acquaintance rapes, are not presented as power-motivated violations of women but rather as strictly sexual encounters. Similarly, others (Cowan, Lee, Levy, & Snyder, 1988; Cowan & O'Brien, 1990) have found that male dominance and sexual exploitation of women are themes in virtually all R- and X-rated films, which almost anyone may now rent for home viewing. These media images carry to extremes long-standing cultural views of masculinity as aggressive and femininity as passive. They also make violence seem sexy (D. Russell, 1993). In so doing, they recreate these limited and limiting perceptions in the thinking of another generation of women and men.

In sum, we have identified basic stereotypes and

themes in media's representations of women, men, and relationships between the two. Individually and in combination these images sustain and reinforce socially constructed views of the genders, views that have restricted both men and women and that appear to legitimize destructive behaviors ranging from anorexia to battering. Later in this chapter, we will probe more closely how media versions of gender are linked to problems such as these. . . .

Pathologizing the Human Body

One of the most damaging consequences of media's images of women and men is that these images encourage us to perceive normal bodies and normal physical functions as problems. It's understandable to wish we weighed a little more or less, had better developed muscles, and never had pimples or cramps. What is neither reasonable nor healthy, however, is to regard healthy, functional bodies as abnormal and unacceptable. Yet this is precisely the negative self-image cultivated by media portrayals of women and men. Because sex sells products (Muro, 1989), sexual and erotic images are the single most prominent characteristic of advertising (Courtney & Whipple, 1983). Further, advertising is increasingly objectifying men, which probably accounts for the rise in men's weight training and cosmetic surgery. Media, and especially advertising, are equal opportunity dehumanizers of both sexes.

Not only do media induce us to think we should measure up to artificial standards, but they encourage us to see normal bodies and bodily functions as pathologies. A good example is the media's construction of premenstrual syndrome (PMS). Historically, PMS has not been a problem, but recently it has been declared a disease (Richmond-Abbott, 1992). In fact, a good deal of research (Parlee, 1973, 1987) indicates that PMS affected very few women in earlier eras. After the war, when women were no longer needed in the work force, opinion changed and the term *premenstrual tension* was coined (Greene & Dalton, 1953) and used to define women as inferior employees. In 1964, only one article on PMS appeared; in 1988–1989, a total of 425 were published (Tavris, 1992, p. 140). Drug companies funded research and publicity, since selling PMS meant selling their remedies for the newly created problem. Behind the hoopla, however, there was and is little evidence to support the currently widespread belief that PMS is a serious problem for a significant portion of the female population. Facts aside, the myth has caught on, carrying in its wake many women and men who now perceive normal monthly changes as abnormal and as making women unfit for positions of leadership and authority. Another consequence of defining PMS as a serious problem most women suffer is that it leads to labeling women in general as deviant and unreliable (Unger & Crawford, 1992), an image that fortifies long-held biases against women.

Menopause is similarly pathologized. Carol Tavris (1992, p. 159) notes that books describe menopause "in terms of deprivation, deficiency, loss, shedding, and sloughing," language that defines a normal process as negative. Like menstruation, menopause is represented as abnormalcy and disease, an image that probably contributes to the negative attitudes toward it in America. The cover of the May 25, 1992, *Newsweek* featured an abstract drawing of a tree in the shape of a woman's head. The tree was stripped of all leaves, making it drab and barren. Across the picture was the cover-story headline "Menopause." From first glance, menopause was represented negatively—as desolate and unfruitful. The article focused primarily on the problems and losses of menopause. Only toward the end did readers find reports from anthropologists, whose cross-cultural research revealed that in many cultures menopause is not an issue or is viewed positively. Women in Mayan villages and the Greek island of Evia do not understand questions about hot flashes and depression, which are symptoms often associated with menopause in Western societies ("Menopause," 1992, p. 77). These are not part of their experience in cultures that do not define a normal change in women as a pathology. Because Western countries, especially America, stigmatize menopause and define it as "the end of womanhood," Western women are likely to feel distressed and unproductive about the cessation of menstruation (Greer, 1992).

Advertising is very effective in convincing us that we need products to solve problems we are unaware of until some clever public relations campaign persuades us that something natural about us is really unnatural and unacceptable. Media have convinced millions of American women that what every medical source considers "normal body weight" is really abnormal and cause for severe dieting (Wolf, 1991). Similarly, gray hair, which naturally develops with age, is now something all of us, especially women, are supposed to cover up. Facial lines, which indicate a person has lived a life and accumulated experiences, can be removed so that we look younger—a prime goal in a culture that glorifies youth (Greer, 1992).

Body hair is another interesting case of media's convincing us that something normal is really abnormal. Beginning in 1915, a sustained marketing campaign informed women that underarm hair was unsightly and socially incorrect. (The campaign against leg hair came later.) *Harper's Bazaar*, an upscale magazine, launched the crusade against underarm hair with a photograph of a woman whose raised arms revealed clean-shaven armpits. Underneath the photograph was this caption: "Summer dress and modern dancing combine to make necessary the removal of objectionable hair" (Adams, 1991). Within a few years, ads promoting removal of underarm hair appeared in most women's magazines, and by 1922, razors and depilatories were firmly ensconced in middle America as evidenced by their inclusion in the women's section of the Sears Roebuck catalog.

Media efforts to pathologize natural physiology can be very serious. As we have seen in prior chapters, the emphasis on excessive thinness contributes to severe and potentially lethal dieting, especially in Caucasian women (Spitzack, 1993). Nonetheless, the top female models in 1993 are skeletal, more so than in recent years (Leland & Leonard, 1993). Many women's natural breast size exceeded the cultural ideal in the 1960s when thin, angular bodies were represented as ideal. Thus, breast reduction surgeries rose. By the 1980s, cultural standards changed to define large breasts as the feminine ideal. Consequently, breast augmentation surgeries accelerated, and fully 80% of implants were for cosmetic reasons ("The Implant Circus," 1992). In an effort to meet the cultural standards of beautiful bodies, many women suffered unnecessary surgery, which led to disfigurement, loss of feeling, and sometimes death for women when silicone implants were later linked to fatal conditions. Implicitly, media argue that our natural state is abnormal and objectionable, a premise that is essential to sell products and advice for improving ourselves. Accepting media messages about our bodies and ourselves, however, is not inevitable: We can reflect on the messages and resist those that are inappropriate and/or harmful. We would probably all be considerably happier and healthier if we became more critical in analyzing media's communication about how we should look, be, and act.

Normalizing Violence Against Women

Since we have seen that media positively portray aggression in males and passivity in females, it's important to ask whether media messages contribute to abuse of and violence against women. There is by now fairly convincing evidence (Hansen & Hansen, 1988) that exposure to sexual violence through media is linked to greater tolerance, or even approval, of violence. For instance, P. Dieter (1989) found a strong relationship between females' viewing of sexually violent MTV and their acceptance of sexual violence as part of "normal" relationships. He reasoned that the more they observe positive portrayals of sexual violence, the more likely women are to perceive this as natural in relationships with men and the less likely they are to object to violence or to defend themselves from it. In short, Dieter suggests that heavy exposure to media violence within relationships tends to normalize it, so that abuse and violence are considered natural parts of love and sex.

Dieter's study demonstrates a direct link between sexual aggression and one popular form of media, MTV. Research on pornography further corroborates connections between exposure to portrayals of violence against women and willingness to engage in or accept it in one's own relationships (Russell, 1993). Before we discuss this research, however, we need to clarify what we will mean by the term pornography, since defining it is a matter of some controversy. Pornography is not simply sexually explicit material. To distinguish pornography from erotica, we might focus on mutual agreement and mutual benefit. If we use these criteria, pornography may be defined as materials that favorably show subordination and degradation of a person such as presenting sadistic behaviors as pleasurable, brutalizing and pain as enjoyable, and forced sex or abuse as positive. Erotica, on the other hand, depicts consensual sexual activities that are sought by and pleasurable to all parties involved (MacKinnon, 1987). These distinctions are important, since it has been well established that graphic sexual material itself is not harmful, while sexually violent materials appear to be (Donnerstein, Linz, & Penrod, 1987).

Pornographic films are a big business, outnumbering other films by 3 to 1 and grossing over $365 million a year in the United States alone (Wolf, 1991). The primary themes characteristic of pornography as a genre are extremes of those in media generally: sex, violence, and domination of one person by another, usually women by men (Basow, 1992, p. 317). More than 80% of X-rated films in one study included scenes in which one or more men dominate and exploit one or more women; within these films, three-fourths portray physical aggression against women, and fully half explicitly depict rape (Cowan et al., 1988). That these are linked to viewers' own tendencies to engage in sexual violence is no longer disputable. According to recent research (Demare, Briere, & Lips, 1988; Donnerstein et al., 1987; Malamuth & Briere, 1986), viewing sexually violent material tends to increase men's beliefs in rape myths, raises the likelihood that men will admit they might themselves commit rape, and desensitizes men to rape, thereby making forced sex more acceptable to them. This research suggests that repeated exposure to pornography influences how men think about rape by transforming it from an unacceptable behavior with which they do not identify into one they find acceptable and enticing. Not surprisingly, the single best predictor of rape is the circulation of pornographic materials that glorify sexual force and exploitation (Baron & Straus, 1989). This is alarming when we realize that 18 million men buy a total of 165 different pornographic magazines every month in the United States (Wolf, 1991, p. 79).

It is well documented that the incidence of reported rape is rising and that an increasing number of men regard forced sex as acceptable (Brownmiller, 1993; Soeken & Damrosch, 1986). Studies of men (Allgeier, 1987; Koss & Dinero, 1988; Koss, Dinero, Seibel, & Cox, 1988; Koss, Gidycz, & Wisniewski, 1987; Lisak & Roth, 1988) have produced shocking findings: While the majority of college men report not having raped anyone, a stunning 50% admit they have coerced, manipulated, or pressured a woman to have sex or have had sex with her after getting her drunk; 1 in 12 men at some colleges has engaged in behaviors meeting the legal definition of rape or attempted rape; over 80% of men who admitted to acts that meet the definition of rape did not believe they had committed rape; and fully one-third of college men said they would commit rape if they believed nobody would find out.

Contrary to popular belief, we also know that men who do commit rape are not psychologically abnormal. They are indistinguishable from other men in terms of psychological adjustment and health, emotional well-being, heterosexual relationships, and frequency of sexual experiences (Segel-Evans, 1987). The only established difference between men who are sexually violent and men who are not is that the former have "hypermasculine" attitudes and self-concepts—their approval of male dominance and sexual rights is even stronger than that of nonrapists (Allgeier, 1987; Koss & Dinero, 1988; Lisak & Roth, 1988; Wood, 1993a). The difference between sexually violent men and others appears to be only a matter of degree.

We also know something about women who are victims of rape and other forms of sexual violence. Between 33% and 66% of all women have been sexually abused before reaching age 18 (Clutter, 1990; Koss, 1990). The majority of college women—up to 75%—say they have been coerced into some type of unwanted sex at least once (Koss, Gidycz, & Wisniewski, 1987; Poppen & Segal, 1988; Warshaw, 1988). A third of women who survive rape contemplate suicide (Koss et al., 1988). It is also clear that the trauma of rape is not confined to the time of its actual occurrence. The feelings that accompany rape and sexual assault—fear, a sense of degradation and shame, anger, powerlessness, and depression—endure far beyond the act itself (Brownmiller, 1975; Wood, 1992b, 1993f). Most victims of rape continue to deal with the emotional aftermath of rape for the rest of their lives (Marhoefer-Dvorak, Resick, Hutter, & Girelli, 1988).

What causes rape, now the fastest growing violent crime in the United States (Doyle, 1989; Soeken & Damrosch, 1986)? According to experts (Costin & Schwartz, 1987; Koss & Dinero, 1988; Koss, Gidycz, & Wisniewski, 1987; Scott & Tetreault, 1987; Scully, 1990), rape is not the result of psychological deviance or uncontrollable lust. Although rape involves sex, it is not motivated by sexual desire. Authorities agree that rape is an aggressive act used to dominate and show power over another person, be it a man over a woman or one man over another, as in prison settings where rape is one way inmates brutalize one another and establish a power hierarchy (Rideau & Sinclair, 1982). Instead, mounting evidence suggests that rape is a predictable outcome of views of men, women, and relationships between the sexes that our society inculcates in members (Brownmiller, 1975; Costin & Schwartz, 1987; Scott & Tetreault, 1987; South & Felson, 1990).

Particularly compelling support for the cultural basis of rape comes from cross-cultural studies (Griffin, 1981; Sanday, 1986), which reveal that rape is extremely rare in cultures that value women and feminine qualities and that have ideologies that promote harmonious interdependence among humans and between them and the natural world. Rape is most common in countries, like the United States, that have ideologies of male supremacy and dominance and a disrespect of women and nature. Cultural values communicated to us by family, schools, media, and other sources constantly encourage us to believe men are superior, men should dominate women, male aggression is acceptable as a means of attaining what is wanted, women are passive and should defer to men, and women are sex objects. In concert, these beliefs legitimize violence and aggression against women.

While the majority of media communication may not be pornographic, it does echo in somewhat muted forms the predominant themes of pornography: sex, violence, and male domination of women. As we have seen, these same motifs permeate media that are part of our daily

M Y T H S   A N D   F A C T S   A B O U T   R A P E

Myth	Fact
Rape is a sexual act that results from sexual urges.	Rape is an aggressive act used to dominate another.
Rapists are abnormal.	Rapists have not been shown to differ from nonrapists in personality, psychology, adjustment, or involvement in interpersonal relationships.
Most rapes occur between strangers.	Eighty percent to 90% of rapes are committed by a person known to the victim (Allgeier, 1987).
Most rapists are African-American men, and most victims are Caucasian women.	More than three-fourths of all rapes occur within races, not between races. This myth reflects racism.
The way a woman dresses affects the likelihood she will be raped.	The majority—up to 90%—of rapes are planned in advance and without knowledge of how the victim will dress (Scully, 1990).
False reports of rapes are frequent.	The majority of rapes are never reported (Koss, Gidycz, & Wisniewski, 1987). Less than 10% of rape reports are judged false, the same as for other violent crimes.
Rape is a universal problem.	The incidence of rape varies across cultures. It is highest in societies with ideologies of male dominance and a disregard for nature; it is lowest in cultures that respect women and feminine values (Griffin, 1981).

lives, which generally portray males as dominating in number, status, authority, and will. Substantial violence toward women punctuates movies, television—including children's programming—rock music, and music videos, desensitizing men and women alike to the *unnaturalness* and unacceptability of force and brutality between human beings. Thus, the research that demonstrates connections between sex-stereotypical media and acceptance of sexual violence is consistent with that showing relationships between more extreme, pornographic media and acceptance of and use of violence....

REFERENCES

Adams, C. (1991, April). The straight dope. *Triangle Comic Review*, p. 26.

Allgeier, E. R. (1987). Coercive versus consensual sexual interactions. In V. P. Makosky (Ed.), *The G. Stanley Hall Lecture Series* (Vol. 7, pp. 7–63). Washington, DC: American Psychological Association.

Baron, L., & Straus, M. A. (1989). *Four theories of rape in American society.* New Haven, CT: Yale University Press.

Basow, S. A. (1992). *Gender: Stereotypes and roles* (3rd ed.). Pacific Grove, CA: Brooks/ Cole.

The best in the house. (1988, October 19). *New York Times*, p. 52Y.

Boyer, P. J. (1986, February 16). TV turns to the hard-boiled male. *New York Times*, pp. H1, H29.

Bretl, D., & Cantor, J. (1988). The portrayal of men and women in U.S. commercials: A recent content analysis and trend over 15 years. *Sex Roles, 18,* 595–609.

Brown, J. D., & Campbell, K. (1986). Race and gender in music videos: The same beat but a different drummer. *Journal of Communication, 36,* 94–106.

Brown, J. D., Campbell, K., & Fisher, L. (1986). American adolescents and music videos: Why do they watch? *Gazette, 37,* 9–32.

Brownmiller, S. (1975). *Against our wills: Men, women, and rape.* New York: Simon and Schuster.

Brownmiller, S. (1993, January 4). Making female bodies the battlefield. *Newsweek*, p. 37.

Carter, B. (1991, May 1). Children's TV, where boys are king. *New York Times*, pp. A1, C18.

Clutter, S. (1990, May 3). Gender may affect response and outrage to sex abuse. *Morning Call*, p. D14.

Costin, F., & Schwartz, N. (1987). Beliefs about rape and women's social roles: A four-nation study. *Journal of Interpersonal Violence, 2,* 46–56.

Courtney, A. E., & Whipple T. W. (1983). *Sex stereotyping in advertising.* Lexington, MA: D. C. Heath.

Cowan, G., Lee, C., Levy, D., & Snyder, D. (1988). Dominance and inequality in X-rated videocassettes. *Psychology of Women Quarterly, 12,* 299–311.

Cowan, G., & O'Brien, M. (1990). Gender and survival vs. death in slasher films: A content analysis. *Sex Roles, 23,* 187–196.

Craft, C. (1988). *Too old, too ugly, and not deferential to men: An anchorwoman's courageous battle against sex discrimination.* Rockland, CA: Prima.

Davis, D. M. (1990). Portrayals of women in prime-time network television: Some demographic characteristics. *Sex Roles, 23,* 325–332.

Demare, D., Briere, J., & Lips, H. M. (1988). Violent pornography and self-reported likelihood of sexual aggression. *Journal of Research in Personality, 22,* 140–153.

Dieter, P. (1989, March). *Shooting her with video, drugs, bullets, and promises.* Paper presented at the meeting of the Association of Women in Psychology, Newport, RI.

Donnerstein, E., Linz, D., & Penrod, S. (1987). *The question of pornography: Research findings and policy implications.* New York: Free Press.

Doyle, J. A. (1989). *The male experience* (2nd ed.). Dubuque, IA: William C. Brown.

Evans, D. (1993, March 1). The wrong examples. *Newsweek*, p. 10.

Faludi, S. (1991). *Backlash: The undeclared war against American women.* New York: Crown.

Feldman, N. S., & Brown, E. (1984, April). *Male vs. female differences in control strategies: What children learn from Saturday morning television.* Paper presented at the meeting of the Eastern Psychological Association, Baltimore, MD. (Cited in Basow, 1992.)

Foreit, K. G., Agor, T., Byers, J., Larue, J., Lokey, H., Palazzini, M., Patterson, M., & Smith, L. (1980). Sex bias in the newspaper treatment of male-centered and female-centered news stories. *Sex Roles, 6,* 475–480.

Gray, H. (1986). Television and the new black man: Black male images in prime-time situation comedies. *Media, Culture, and Society, 8,* 223–242.

Greene, R., & Dalton, K. (1953). The premenstrual syndrome. *British Medical Journal, 1,* 1007–1014.

Greer, G. (1992). *The change: Women, aging, and menopause.* New York: Alfred Knopf.

Griffin, S. (1981). *Pornography and silence: Culture's revenge against nature.* New York: Harper and Row.

Hansen, C. H., & Hansen, R. D. (1988). How rock music videos can change what is seen when boy meets girl: Priming stereotypic appraisal of social interactions. *Sex Roles, 19,* 287–316.

Haskell, M. (1988, May). Hollywood Madonnas. *Ms.*, pp. 84, 86, 88.

Horovitz, B. (1989, August 10). In TV commercials, men are often the butt of the jokes. *Philadelphia Inquirer*, pp. 5b, 6b.

The implant circus. (1992, February 18). *Wall Street Journal*, p. A20.

Koss, M. P. (1990). The women's mental health research agenda: Violence against women. *American Psychologist, 45,* 374–380.

Koss, M. P., & Dinero, T. E. (1988). Predictors of sexual aggression among a national sample of male college students. In V. I. Quinsey & R. Orentky (Eds.), *Human sexual aggression* (pp. 133–147). New York: Academy of Sciences.

Koss, M. P., Dinero, T. E., Seibel, C. A., & Cox, S. L. (1988). Stranger and acquaintance rape: Are there differences in the victim's experience? *Psychology of Women Quarterly, 12,* 1–24.

Koss, M. P., Gidycz, C. J., Wisniewski, N. (1987). The scope of rape: Incidence and prevalence of sexual aggression and victimization in a national sample of higher education students. *Journal of Consulting and Clinical Psychology, 55,* 162–170.

Leland, J., & Leonard, E. (1993, February 1). Back to Twiggy. *Newsweek*, pp. 64–65.

Lichter, S. R., Lichter, L. S., & Rothman, S. (1986, September/October). From Lucy to Lacey: TV's dream girls. *Public Opinion*, pp. 16–19.

Lichter, S. R., Lichter, L. S., Rothman, S., & Amundson, D. (1987, July/August). Prime-time prejudice: TV's images of blacks and Hispanics. *Public Opinion*, pp. 13–16.

Lisak, D., & Roth, S. (1988). Motivational factors in nonincarcerated sexually aggressive men. *Journal of Personality and Social Psychology, 55,* 795–802.

Lott, B. (1989). Sexist discrimination as distancing behavior: II. Prime-time television. *Psychology of Women Quarterly, 13,* 341–355.

MacKinnon, C. A. (1987). *Feminism unmodified: Discourses on life and law.* Cambridge, MA: Harvard University Press.

Malamuth, N. M., & Briere, J. (1986). Sexual violence in the media: Indirect effects on aggression against women. *Journal of Social Issues, 42,* 75–92.

Marhoefer-Dvorak, S., Resick, P., Hutter, C., & Girelli, S. (1988). Single-versus multiple-incident rape victims: A comparison of psychological reactions to rape. *Journal of Interpersonal Violence, 3,* 145–160.

Maslin, J. (1990, June 17). Bimbos embody retro rage. *New York Times*, pp. H13, H14.

Masse, M. A., & Rosenblum, K. (1988). Male and female created they them: The depiction of gender in the advertising of traditional women's and men's magazine's. *Women's Studies International Forum, 11,* 127–144.

Mattell offers trade-in for "Teen Talk" Barbie. (1992, October 13). *Raleigh News and Observer*, p. A3.

McCauley, C., Thangavelu, K., & Rozin, P. (1988). Sex stereotyping of occupations in relation to television representations and census facts. *Basic and Applied Social Psychology, 9,* 197–212.

Menopause. (1992, May 25). *Newsweek*, pp. 71–80.

Mills, K. (1988). *A place in the news: From the women's pages to the front page.* New York: Dodd, Mead.

Modleski, T. (1982). *Loving with a vengeance: Mass-produced fantasies for women.* New York: Methuen.

Muro, M. (1989, April 23). Comment: New era of eros in advertising. *Morning Call*, pp. D1, D16.

The new traditionalist. (1988, November 17). *New York Times*, p. Y46.

Nigro, G. N., Hill, D. E., Gelbein, M. E., & Clark, C. L. (1988). Changes in the facial prominence of women and men over the last decade. *Psychology of Women Quarterly, 12,* 225–235.

O'Connor, J. J. (1989, June 6). What are commercials selling to children? *New York Times*, p. 28.

Pareles, J. (1990, October 21). The women who talk back in rap. *New York Times*, pp. H33, H36.

Parlee, M. B. (1973). The premenstrual syndrome. *Psychological Bulletin, 80,* 454–465.

Parlee, M. B. (1979, May). Conversational politics. *Psychology Today*, pp. 48–56.

Peirce, K. (1990). A feminist theoretical perspective on the socialization of teenage girls through *Seventeen* magazine. *Sex Roles, 23,* 491–500.

Rakow, L. F. (1986). Rethinking gender research in communication. *Journal of Communication, 36,* 11–26.

Richmond-Abbott, M. (1992). *Masculine and feminine: Gender roles over the life cycle.* New York: McGraw-Hill.

Rideau, W., & Sinclair, B. (1982). Prison: The sexual jungle. In A. Scacco, Jr. (Ed.), *Male Rape* (pp. 3–29). New York: AMS Press.

Russell, D. E. H. (Ed.). (1993). *Feminist views on pornography.* Colchester, VT: Teachers College Press.

Sanday, P. R. (1986). Rape and the silencing of the feminine. In S. Tomaselli & R. Porter (Eds.), *Rape* (pp. 84–101). Oxford, UK: Basil Blackwell.

Sanders, M., & Rock, M. (1988). *Waiting for prime time: The women of television news.* Urbana, IL: University of Illinois Press.

Scott, R., & Tetreault, L. (1987). Attitudes of rapists and other violent offenders toward women. *Journal of Social Psychology, 124,* 375–380.

Scully, D. (1990). *Understanding sexual violence: A study of convicted rapists.* Boston, MA: Unwin Hyman.

Segel-Evans, K. (1987). Rape prevention and masculinity. In F. Abbott (Ed.), *New men, new minds: Breaking male tradition* (pp. 117–121). Freedom, CA: Crossing Press.

Sights, sounds and stereotypes. (1992, October 11). *Raleigh News and Observer*, pp. G1, G10.

Silverstein, B., Perdue, L., Peterson, B., & Kelly, E. (1986). The role of the mass media in promoting a thin standard of bodily attractiveness for women. *Sex Roles, 14,* 519–532.

Soeken, K., & Damrosch, S. (1986). Randomized response technique: Application to research on rape. *Psychology of Women Quarterly, 10,* 119–126.

South, S. J., & Felson, R. B. (1990). The racial patterning of rape. *Social Forces, 69,* 71–93.

Spitzack, C. (1993). The spectacle of anorexia nervosa. *Text and Performance Quarterly, 13,* 1–21.

Stroman, C. A. (1989). To be young, male and black on prime-time television. *Urban Research Review, 12,* 9–10.

Study reports sex bias in news organizations. (1989, April 11). *New York Times*, p. C22.

Tavris, C. (1992). *The mismeasure of woman.* New York: Simon and Schuster.

Texier, C. (1990, April 22), Have women surrendered in MTV's battle of the sexes? *New York Times*, pp. H29, H31.

Unger, R., & Crawford, M. (1992). *Women and gender: A feminist psychology.* New York: McGraw-Hill.

Warshaw, R. (1988). *I never called it rape.* New York: Harper and Row.

Wolf, N. (1991). *The beauty myth.* New York: William Morrow.

Women in media say careers hit "glass ceiling." (1988, March 2). *Easton Express*, p. A9.

Wood, J. T. (1992b). Telling our stories: Narratives as a basis for theorizing sexual harassment. *Journal of Applied Communication Research, 4,* 349–363.

Wood, J. T. (1993a). Engendered relationships: Interaction, caring, power, and responsibility in close relationships. In S. Duck (Ed.), *Processes in close relationships: Contexts of close relationships* (Vol. 3). Beverly Hills, CA: Sage.

Wood, J. T. (1993c). *Who cares: Women, care, and culture.* Carbondale, IL: Southern Illinois University Press.

Wood, J. T. (1993f). Defining and studying sexual harassment as situated experience. In G. Kreps (Ed.), *Communication and sexual harassment in the workplace.* Cresskill, NJ: Hampton Press.

Woodman, S. (1991, May). How super are heros? *Health*, pp. 40, 49, 82.

Don't Blame TV

JEFF GREENFIELD

Jeff Greenfield is a correspondent for ABC's Nightline *and a syndicated columnist.*

ONE OF THE enduring pieces of folk wisdom was uttered by the 19th-century humorist Artemus Ward, who warned the readers: "It ain't what you don't know that hurts you; it's what you know that just ain't so."

There's good advice in that warning to some of television's most vociferous critics, who are certain that every significant change in American social and political life can be traced, more or less directly, to the pervasive influence of TV.

It has been blamed for the decline of scores on scholastic achievement tests, for the rise in crime, for the decline in voter turnout, for the growth of premarital and extramarital sex, for the supposed collapse of family life and the increase in the divorce rate.

This is an understandable attitude. For one thing, television is the most visible, ubiquitous device to have entered our lives in the last 40 years. It is a medium in almost every American home, it is on in the average household some seven hours a day, and it is accessible by every kind of citizen from the most desperate of the poor to the wealthiest and most powerful among us.

If so pervasive a medium has come into our society in the last four decades and if our society has changed in drastic ways in that same time, why not assume that TV is the reason why American life looks so different?

Well, as any philosopher can tell you, one good reason for skepticism is that you can't make assumptions about causes. They even have an impressive Latin phrase for that fallacy: *post hoc, ergo propter hoc.* For instance, if I do a rain dance at 5 P.M. and it rains at 6 P.M., did my dance bring down the rains? Probably not. But it's that kind of thinking, in my view, that characterizes much

of the argument about how television influences our values.

It's perfectly clear, of course, that TV *does* influence some kinds of behavior. For example, back in 1954, *Disneyland* launched a series of episodes on the life of Davy Crockett, the legendary Tennessee frontiersman. A song based on that series swept the hit parade, and by that summer every kid in America was wearing a coonskin cap.

The same phenomenon has happened whenever a character on a prime-time television show suddenly strikes a chord in the country. Countless women tried to capture the Farrah Fawcett look a decade ago when *Charlie's Angels* first took flight. Schoolyards from Maine to California picked up — instantly, it seemed — on such catch phrases as "Up your nose with a rubber hose!" (*Welcome Back, Kotter*). "Kiss my grits!" (*Alice*) and "Nanu-nanu!" (*Mork & Mindy*). Today, every singles bar in the land is packed with young men in expensive white sports jackets and T-shirts, trying to emulate the macho looks of *Miami Vice*'s Don Johnson.

These fads clearly show television's ability to influence matters that do not matter very much. Yet, when we turn to genuinely important things, television's impact becomes a lot less clear.

Take, for example, the decline in academic excellence, measured by the steady decline in Scholastic Aptitude Test scores from 1964 to 1982. It seemed perfectly logical to assume that a younger generation spending hours in front of the TV set every day with Fred Flintstone and Batman must have been suffering from brain atrophy. Yet, as writer David Owen noted in a . . . book on educational testing, other equally impassioned explanations for the drop in scores included nuclear fallout, junk food, cigarette smoking by pregnant women, cold weather, declining church attendance, the draft, the assassination of President Kennedy and fluoridated water.

More significant, SAT scores stopped declining in 1982: they have been rising since then. Is TV use declining in the typical American home? On the contrary, it is increasing. If we really believed that our societal values are determined by news media, we might conclude that the birth of MTV in 1981 somehow caused the test scores to rise.

Or consider the frequently heard charge that the increase in TV violence is somehow responsible for the surge in crime. In fact, the crime rate nationally has been dropping for three straight years. It would be ludicrous to "credit" television for this: explanations are more likely to be found in the shift of population away from a "youth bulge" (where more crimes are committed) and improved tracking of career criminals in big cities.

But why, then, ignore the demographic factors that saw in America an enormous jump in teen-agers and young adults in the 1960s and 1970s? Why *assume* that television, with its inevitable "crime-does-not-pay" morality, somehow turned our young into hoodlums?

The same kind of problem bedevils those who argue that TV has triggered a wave of sexually permissible behavior. In the first place, television was the most sexually conservative of all media through the first quarter-century of its existence. While Playboy began making a clean breast of things in the mid-1950s, when book censorship was all but abolished in the "Lady Chatterly's Lover" decision of 1958, when movies began showing it all in the 1960s, television remained an oasis—or desert—of twin beds, flannel nightgowns and squeaky-clean dialogue and characters.

In fact, as late as 1970, CBS refused to let Mary Tyler Moore's Mary Richards character be a divorcée. The audience, they argued, would never accept it. Instead, she was presented as the survivor of a broken relationship.

Why, then, do we see so many broken families and divorces on television today? Because the networks are trying to denigrate the value of the nuclear family? Hardly. As *The Cosby Show* and its imitators show, network TV is only too happy to offer a benign view of loving husbands, wives, and children.

The explanation, instead, lies in what was happening to the very fabric of American life. In 1950, at the dawn of television, the divorce rate was 2.6 per 1000 Americans. By 1983, it had jumped to five per thousand; nearly half of all marriages were ending in divorce. The reasons range from the increasing mobility of the population to the undermining of settled patterns of work, family and neighborhood.

What's important to notice, however, is that it was not television that made divorce more ac-

ceptable in American society: it was changes in American society that made divorce more acceptable on television. (Which is why, in her new sitcom, Mary Tyler Moore can finally play a divorced woman.) In the mid 1980s, divorce has simply lost the power to shock.

The same argument, I think, undermines most of the fear that television has caused our young to become sexually precocious. From my increasingly dimming memory of youthful lust, I have my doubts about whether young lovers really need the impetus of *Dallas* or *The Young and the Restless* to start thinking about sex. The more serious answer, however, is that the spread of readily available birth control was a lot more persuasive a force in encouraging premarital sex than the words and images on TV.

We can measure this relative impotence of television in a different way. All through the 1950s and early 1960s, the images of women on TV were what feminists would call "negative"; they were portrayed as half-woman, half-child, incapable of holding a job or balancing a checkbook or even running a social evening. (How many times did Lucy burn the roast?) Yet the generation of women who grew up on television was the first to reject forcefully the wife-and-homemaker limitations that such images ought to have encouraged. These were the women who marched into law schools, medical schools and the halls of Congress.

The same was true of the images of black Americans, as TV borrowed the movie stereotypes of shiftless handymen and relentlessly cheerful maids. We didn't begin to see TV blacks as the equal of whites until Bill Cosby showed up in *I Spy* in 1966. Did the generation weaned on such fare turn out to be indifferent to the cause of black freedom in America? Hardly. This was the generation that organized and supported the civil-rights sit-ins and freedom rides in the South. Somehow, the reality of second-class citizenship was far more powerful than the imagery of dozens of television shows.

I have no argument with the idea that television contains many messages that need close attention: I hold no brief for shows that pander to the appetite for violence or smarmy sexuality or stereotyping. My point is that these evils ought to be fought on grounds of taste and common decency. We ought not to try and prove more than the facts will bear. Television, powerful as it is, has shown precious little power over the most fundamental values of Americans. Given most of what's on TV, that's probably a good thing. But it also suggests that the cries of alarm may be misplaced.

Violence on TV

No topic touches a nerve in American homes as does violence on television, especially its effect on children.

What do we know in 1992 that we didn't know 20 or even 10 years ago? Is there any question that violence has an effect on kids—and on society at large?

In this special issue, the editors of TV GUIDE present the results of a special study on how much violence is out there, what leading experts think about its effects, and what can be done.

How Much Violence?

What we found in an eye-opening study

Neil Hickey

More televised violence than at any time in the medium's history is flowing into American homes. It's coming from many more sources than ever before—home video, pay-per-view, and cable, as well as from the broadcast networks and stations. The overwhelming weight of scientific opinion now holds that televised violence is indeed responsible for a percentage of the real violence in our society. What is new is that psychologists, child experts, and the medical community are just now beginning to treat televised violence as a serious public health issue—like smoking and drunk driving—about which the public needs to be educated for its own safety and well-being.

How much violence is there on American television?

How is it more virulent now than in recent years? Where is it coming from? What are its effects? What can parents, educators, the industry, and public officials do about it?

To attack those questions systematically, we commissioned a study of one day in the life of TV—and convened an expert panel whose comments begin on page 220.

To snap our day-in-the-life-of-TV photo, we enlisted the Center for Media and Public Affairs, a nonprofit monitoring company whose business is fashioning statistical portraits of how American society is depicted in the media. We asked for and received a nonjudgmental, bias-neutral content analysis of one typical day of American television.

During 18 hours (6 A.M.-midnight) on April 2, 1992, in

Washington, D.C., the center taped, tabulated, computerized, and analyzed the programs on 10 channels: the affiliates of ABC, CBS, NBC, Fox and PBS; one non-affiliated station, WDCA, the USA Network, MTV, and HBO. The program schedules, it turned out, were notable only for their ordinariness: no untypically violent movies like "Rambo" or "Scarface" were shown; even the news on that date was light on violent events such as wars, civil disorders, and local crime. The results of the study were an eye-opener. In those 180 hours of programming, we observed:

A total of 1,846 individual acts of violence; 175 scenes in which violence resulted in one or more fatalities; 389 scenes depicting serious assaults; 362 scenes involving gunplay; 673 depictions of punching, pushing, slapping, dragging, and other physically hostile acts; 226 scenes of menacing threats with a weapon.

Newer program forms like music videos and reality shows, it turns out, are significantly increasing the amount of violence on our screens. And commercials for violent theatrical movies and TV series have become a major source of televised violence.

News broadcasts, in their heightened competitive fervor, are peddling strong doses of murder, muggings, and mayhem as ratings-getters.

In fictional programming alone, we found more than 100 violent scenes per hour across the 10 outlets studied. Well over a third of all the violence (751 scenes) involved some sort of life-threatening assault. Cartoons were the most violent program form, with 471 scenes.

(A note: child experts agree that violent cartoons are inadvisable for very young children, 2 to 5, who may not distinguish between animated violence and the real thing, so they were included in our tabulations. Also, our study shows a glut of superhero-style cartoons that feature more "human" characters than earlier Tom & Jerry type fare; these realistic cartoons may have an even stronger influence on children.) Promos for television shows were next (265), then movies (221), toy commercials (188), music videos (123), ads for theatrical films (121), TV dramas (69), news (62), reality shows like *Top Cops* and *Hard Copy* (58), sitcoms (52), and soap operas (34).

The outlet purveying the most violence on that particular spring day was the unaffiliated station: 376 scenes, or one every three minutes. The rest of the list:

WTBS—321 scenes (18 per hour)
HBO—257 scenes (14 per hour)
USA Network—209 scenes (12 per hour)

Does TV Violence *Cause* Real Violence?

There's no shortage of major studies on the effect of televised violence. Among them: the National Commission on the Causes and Prevention of Violence (1968): the Surgeon General's Report (1972); the National Institute of Mental Health's (1982); and the U.S. Attorney General's Task Force on Family Violence (1984). The NIMH states the consensus: "Violence on television does lead to aggressive behavior by children and teenagers who watch the programs. . . ."

One of the most ambitious and conclusive studies (conducted by Dr. Leonard D. Eron and others) examined a group at ages 8, 19, and 30 in a semirural county of New York State. The findings: the more frequently the participants watched TV at age 8, the more serious were the crimes they were convicted of by age 30; the more aggressive was their behavior when drinking; and the harsher was the punishment they inflicted on their own children. Essentially the same results emerged when the researchers examined another large group of youths for three years in a suburb of Chicago. And when they replicated the experiment in Australia, Finland, Israel, and Poland, the outcome was unchanged: as Dr. Eron states it, "There can no longer be any doubt that heavy exposure to televised violence is one of the causes of aggressive behavior, crime, and violence in society. The evidence comes from both the laboratory and real-life studies. Television violence affects youngsters of all ages, of both genders, at all socioeconomic levels, and all levels of intelligence."

MTV—202 scenes (11 per hour)
Fox—182 scenes (10 per hour)
CBS—175 scenes (10 per hour)
ABC—48 scenes (three per hour)
NBC—39 scenes (two per hour)
PBS—37 scenes (two per hour)

WTBS's high total is partly explained by a high incidence of Tom & Jerry-type cartoons and old movies and TV series.

Unmeasured in our survey, of course, were the many hundreds of hours of VCR-watching that went on in that city on the day—much of it devoted to theatrical films with violent content.

Thus, the study's conclusion: violence remains a pervasive, major feature of contemporary television programming and it's coming from more sources and in greater volume than ever before.

(continued)

The Experts Speak Out

TV Guide's Panel: 'The New Face of violence on TV'

To learn the latest, the best, and most authoritative thinking on the subject of television, TV GUIDE invited a blue-ribbon panel of experts (see box) to convene in New York before an invited audience in the auditorium of the Center for Communication, a nonprofit media forum which cosponsored the event. Neil Hickey, senior editor of TV GUIDE, was the moderator. A transcript of the panel's remarks, edited for space, follows:

TVG: Let's start off with a brief quote from a 1992 survey by the American Psychological Association called "Big World. Small Screen." It says: "Since 1955, about 1,000 studies, reports, and commentaries concerning the impact of television violence have been published. . . . The accumulated research clearly demonstrates a correlation between viewing violence and aggressive behavior—that is, heavy viewers behave more aggressively than light viewers." Any comment on that?

SLABY: Yes, the research does show that television violence is a contributing cause to violence in our society. Years of research evidence has gone into establishing television violence as a contributing cause—and the word "cause" is not used lightly by scientists.

GERBNER: Television, in my opinion, is one of the factors, but to attribute the violence in our society to television alone is a form of scapegoating—considering that we have growing joblessness and an undeclared civil war in our cities. Violence is used as a solution to problems by people who otherwise cannot get ahead or get attention.

Also, television trains us to be victims. Our studies, as confirmed by many independent investigators, show that the most pervasive, long-term consequence of growing up in a media cult of violence is a sense of pervasive insecurity, what we call "the mean-world syndrome." It's a sense of feeling vulnerable, of dependence, of needing protection.

And children's television programming on the weekend is saturated with violence. The number of cartoon programs has increased over the last three years from 31 to 40 and our research shows that the amount of violent acts per hour has risen from 25.5 in 1988 to 32 last year. That's an all-time high.

TVG: Senator John Glenn, during hearings on youth violence-prevention in March of this year, said, "The United States is the most violent 'civilized' country in the world." Let me also quote briefly from Dr. Prothrow-Stith's book *Deadly Consequences*: "Just as our nation has more violent crime than any other industrialized nation, so too is our popular culture more violent than that of other countries. . . . In the media world, brutality is portrayed as ordinary and amusing."

PROTHROW-STITH: I think that the impact of television violence is small on most of us, but it's quite large on some of us. And I agree that it's one of the factors, particularly among urban poor children who don't have male role models countering the television superhero who's solving problems with violence.

TVG: Dr. Leonard Eron of the University of Illinois said recently in testimony before Congress that there is no longer any doubt that heavy exposure to televised violence is one of the causes of aggressive behavior, crime, and violence in society, and he estimates that fully 10 percent of the actual violence in our society is attributable to the viewing of violence on television.

WEINMAN: But I think the first thing we need to do is define what we mean by "television."

TVG: This symposium, for good reason, is called "The new Face of Television Violence." And we're defining "television" as anything and everything that comes through the television screen into the home, from whatever source: the networks, local stations, cable, premium channels, pay-per-view channels, direct broadcast satellites, laser disc players, videocassette players. There's the violence on news programs and music videos. The new courtroom television channel televises live the trial of Jeffrey Dahmer, with the most lurid descriptions of his bestial acts.

WOLF: I hate to be the fly in the ointment here, but I've seen a lot of research over the last 15 years, and to say that the case is closed on the effects of TV violence is incredibly misleading.

WEINMAN: That's right, there isn't really a consensus, and there's actually very little violence on ABC, NBC, and CBS.

CHARREN: How about cable?

WEINMAN: Cable is a different subject.

TVG: The network's Standards and Practices departments, headed by people like Dr. Weinman, cut out a certain amount of violence. Most other program providers do not. Dr. Aletha Huston, co-director of the Center for Research on the Influence of Television on Children at the University of Kansas, testified before Congress that " . . . cable and videotape recorders . . . have altered our television experience drastically. . . . Children and adults have easy access to R- and X-rated films, many of which contain very graphic, explicit violence."

CHARREN: But even if you can prove that TV violence has an effect on causing you to be more aggressive, what are you going to do about it? I have taken the position for 24 years that, yes, it has an effect, but in a democracy you still shouldn't censor it. So not being a researcher, I don't care whether it has an effect or not.

GERBNER: Well, I *do.* And not only do I care whether it has an effect, but I care about trying to characterize accurately this new age into which our children are born. There has never been a situation like this. They are born into homes in which the TV set is on seven hours a day. They start viewing as infants. Most of the stories they hear are not told by the parents, the school, the church, or neighbors. They are told by a handful of conglomerates who have something to sell. That has a powerful effect. An average of six and eight acts of violence—physical, overt violence, hurting or killing people—per hour in prime time. In Saturday children's programming, between 20 and 25 acts of violence per hour. There's never been the type of expertly choreographed brutality that we have at the present time. And what we're dealing with is a kind of pollution that we have to understand and take care of, and let's not deny it.

LEONARD: Look, this culture has always been an extremely violent one compared to European nations. The cult of the frontier, the cult of the superhero, have been part of our popular literature. I'd like to point out that the only country in the world that watches more television that the United States is Japan. The programs are surprisingly violent. The Japanese movie industry is the major distributor throughout Asia of rape and snuff films. And yet all this watching of television and all this emphasis on violence doesn't have the effect of murder and mayhem in the Japanese culture that it does in our country.

It's not TV that's killing people. It's guns and drugs and cuts in federal aid to big cities, and we've allowed our public school system to degenerate. We throw away portions of our society, and that they should respond

"There's never been the expertly choreographed brutality [on TV] that we have at the present time."
—George Gerbner

THE PANEL

Peggy Charren President, Action for Children's Television

George Gerbner Dean-emeritus, Annenberg School of Communication, University of Pennsylvania

Rosalyn Weinman VP of Broadcast Standards and Practices, NBC

Dick Wolf Television producer (Law & Order, Miami Vice)

Ronald Slaby Senior scientist, The Education Development Center, and lecturer, Harvard University

Deborah Prothrow-Stith, M.D. Harvard School of Public Health

John Leonard Television critic, CBS Sunday Morning, New York magazine

with violence makes sense. I noticed the week after all that violence in Los Angeles that for the first time I was seeing very interesting and heretofore unknown black people on my society that I'd never heard about. Violence did one thing. It got those people onto the TV screen for the first time.

"If you let them, children will rent from the video store the worst bloody stuff."
—Peggy Charren

GERBNER: We did a comparative study and found that Japanese violence, unlike ours, is not happy violence. It's painful, it's awful, it teaches a very different lesson.

WOLF: I want to put something in perspective here. Violence as entertainment has been around as long as we have. The ancient Greeks had it. People have wanted it from the Middle Ages, from the Romans to Milton, Shakespeare, and everybody else. "Hamlet" is one of the most violent stories ever conceived. We can get into all kinds of psychological claptrap about why people enjoy watching drama that has life-and-death effects. The real problem here is—I have an 8-year-old and a 5-year-old child. They've never seen any of the shows I've ever produced. They shouldn't be watching them. They're not allowed to watch Saturday-morning cartoons.

PROTHROW-STITH: Why not?

WOLF: Why not? Because they're extremely violent.

PROTHROW-STITH: Do you think it has an impact on them?

WOLF: I don't know. But I don't think that 5-year-old little girls should be watching superheroes beat the c—

> "[To combat TV violence] we need to use health education, the same way we did with smoking."
>
> —Deborah Prothrow-Stith

out of people. The issue here is, when are you going to stop blaming the media and recognize that parents are supposed to monitor what their children are watching? When you blame television in a society that is the most violent on earth, that has taken the six-shooter and made it an object of erotic desire for 150 years, to claim now that it's television that is setting people on this course from the time they were born, is unrealistic.

GERBNER: This is argument by setting up straw men to knock them down. We were very careful to point out that we are not blaming television alone. And the notion that, sure, there is violence in fairy tales, there is violence in Shakespeare, and therefore we shouldn't be concerned about it is a powerfully misleading notion.

We have to make a distinction between violence that is selectively used, violence that is handcrafted to show its tragic consequences, to show the pain and to show the suffering and the tragedy that follows. That's not what we're talking about. We're talking about mass-produced, cheap, industrial violence that's injected into every home whether they like it or not. That is an entirely new phenomenon. It's not like Shakespeare, it's not like fairy tales. And that is the critical, or at least the most troublesome, aspect of the situation.

CHARREN: Let me say that this is a price you pay for freedom of speech and diversity of TV sources. We now have cable, we have home video, we have fiber optics coming with 200 channels. When you have that kind of diversity, you're going to get some stuff that's terrible. If you let them, children will rent from the video store the worst bloody stuff that ever hit the market. It's all very well and good to talk about this incredibly violent culture that we have, but I don't know how we can make all of this stuff coming onto our screen completely benign. You have a lot of new sources feeding us, some of which are bad, some of which, like CNN and C-SPAN, are very good.

SLABY: Beyond all else, television is a teacher. We know that because advertisers pay several billion dollars a year in order to get the teaching effect and to sell their products. It's such an effective teacher, and it's teaching the wrong message to young children.

TVG: In that connection, Dr. Carole Lieberman, who is chairperson of the National Coalition on Television Violence, has pointed out that since everybody agrees that *Sesame Street* can teach the alphabet, why don't TV people admit that children can learn the ABC's of murder and mayhem from gratuitously violent entertainment?

GERBNER: The fact is, most highly rated dramatic programs are nonviolent. Then why is violence produced? I'll tell you why it's produced. If you can cheapen the product, you don't need to have the most popular programs and you can still make money. Violence is a cheap, industrial ingredient. It reduces time for writing.

WOLF: I don't know who you've been speaking to, but that is absolutely fallacious. The most expensive form of entertainment ever devised is the one-hour television drama. To say that people who make fictional dramas are putting violence in because it's cheaper is just untrue!

GERBNER: It's profitable to put on violence instead of other, more diversified, creative solutions to problems which require more talent, more time, and more money. Violence is a formula that's relatively cheap to inject into programs.

PROTHROW-STITH: Let me move to another aspect—to the different way we think of sex in the media versus violence in the media. Do we know that a 5-year-old watching intercourse is going to be harmed in some way? No, we don't know that. There are no causal relationships established. Yet we make sure, as best we can, that sex is not portrayed to our children. We don't do that with violence. People are making money off of violence and are callous about it, and I think we need to start calling some people to task.

WEINMAN: There are responsible people at all three networks who are not callous. That's why we have in place a set of guidelines that deal not only with sex but, very specifically, with violence. One of the seminal, important issues we deal with every day is, how do you find a balance between sanitizing violence and sensationalizing it?

TVG: In view of those guidelines, I'd like to know how the interaction works between Dr. Weinman and Mr. Wolf. Dr. Weinman's job is to review Mr. Wolf's scripts for objectionable content before they get on the air. Now, he is a producer of very, very successful television programs. In effect, he's an 800-pound gorilla.

WEINMAN: Nine hundred, this year.

TVG: OK, 900. So he comes to you and says, "Look, if you take this violent scene out, you'll ruin my show! I'm going to have you fired!" What happens then?

WOLF: Let me answer, because it's very interesting. I think that what's instructive is that Roz and I have never failed to reach agreement, that there have obviously been spirited discussions—very spirited discussions.

WEINMAN: Very late at night.

WOLF: Very late at night, very early in the morning. It goes on and on. And some episodes have taken literally weeks to get into shape for broadcast approval. My feeling is, if you're going to show someone being shot, then show them writhing on the ground in pain, see them in a hospital three days later, still writhing in pain. Don't make it glamorous.

GERBNER: Remember that much of the revenue of TV and movies come from outside the United States. And in

"How do you find a balance between sanitizing violence and sensationalizing it?"
—Rosalyn Weinman

the trade, the slogan is, "Violence travels well, humor doesn't." Violence doesn't need much explanation, and therefore, from the point of view of global marketing, is an excellent commodity and highly profitable.

TVG: Dr. Prothrow-Stith, you mentioned in your book that children in inner cities watch more television because they have little money to do anything else, the streets are dangerous, and there are fewer recreational opportunities.

PROTHROW-STITH: I think one of the things that came through quite clearly in the Los Angeles revolt was that teens have learned that if you think you have a cause to justify, violence is the way to do it. When characters like Rambo get angry, they blow people away. So children have learned that violence is the way to solve problems. And the challenge I would put to the TV industry is to show, in an appealing way, how people can solve their problems and achieve success nonviolently.

TVG: That doesn't tend to happen much in big-hit theatrical movies, which everybody agrees are the most violent in the history of the film industry. A *New York Times* movie critic counted 74 dead in "Total Recall," 81 dead in "Robocop 2," 106 dead in "Rambo III," and 264 dead in "Die Hard 2." [Earlier this month, an accused serial killer of six women in New York State said he was copying scenes in "Robocop 2."] All those movies show up in home video.

PROTHROW-STITH: That brings up liability by the filmmakers or networks, and that's a can of worms—establishing a copycat, causal relationship.

TVG: Meaning a victim could sue a broadcaster, you mean. But so far that argument has been rejected by the courts.

What about the copycat issue in a situation like the Los Angeles riots, where people saw what was happening, and joined in?

GERBNER: I think Ted Koppel was right, for once anyway, when he said that live, unedited telecasting of the Los Angeles riots spread the virus from one part of the city to another. I think it was done in a reprehensible way. The lesson for broadcasters in such situations is to be very careful about live, real-time telecasting of violent scenes.

CHARREN: There's a point to be made about the looting that went on in Los Angeles and how that relates to television. The advertising that interrupts most TV programs conveys the message that everybody can afford these products. But most of those inner-city people can't. And a lot of those people who looted stores were not reacting to the Rodney King tape, but were saying,

"Where is it written that I can't have all these things that television tells me I need, but which I can't afford?"

WOLF: The desire for objects advertised on television is much more destructive to children and adolescents than it is for adults. And the children's shows on Saturday morning *are* too violent and that's something that has to be corrected, but I don't know how you do it. Not legislatively, because that's censorship.

TVG: I want to ask Dr. Weinman about the NBC series *I Witness Video*. When it came on NBC last February, it showed a replay of murders that had been captured on tape by amateur camcorder operators. We wrote about it in TV GUIDE at the time, saying, "For the first time in TV history, a major network started programming death as entertainment." How about that, Dr. Weinman?

WEINMAN: It doesn't relate to my department. That's a program that is produced by NBC News. I think the whole question about tabloid, reality-based programs is a whole other issue.

TVG: Yes, and they are a new and very popular program form—series like *America's Most Wanted, Inside Edition,* and *Top Cops.*

WEINMAN: The only good news is that very few kids watch those kinds of programs.

TVG: As popular as some of those new reality shows are, what does it say that almost all the top shows—*Roseanne, Murphy Brown, Cheers, Home Improvement, Designing Women*—are comedies and thus almost entirely nonviolent?

LEONARD: Well, I'd like to see Dr. Gerbner do a study—similar to his violence profiles—on how much hugging there is on TV. Hugs are all over prime time, in these family comedies, perhaps far more than they are in our own families. Yet we're not more peaceful, as far as I can tell. We have to talk about all of TV. We surf, we pick and choose. We want to laugh sometimes, and we want violence and quick solutions other times.

"[My children] have never seen any of the shows I've produced. They shouldn't be watching them."
—Dick Wolf

WOLF: Picking up on Roz Weinman's point about standards and practices, three years ago, several producers, myself among them, were approached by a network—specifically, NBC—and asked whether we wanted them to disband the standards and practices department. I was quite vehement about it. No, I didn't want that, because for better or worse, I don't want that responsibility. And I don't consider it censorship. I consider it a business decision, and a way to make sure that the product has the most chance of staying on the air.

TVG: But is everything related to TV violence done merely for a business reason? Is there a moral issue involved here, or is everything just economics and money?

WOLF: I think that most producers of shows that have survived have a kind of internal moral gyroscope, so that they are not just catering to the basest instincts of the audience. This isn't bread and circuses.

"The crime is: TV has potential that it's not using to solve the problem of violence."
—Ronald Slaby

CHARREN: The thing is, censorship would be terrific if I made all the decisions about what goes on and is taken off. I'm trying to put through a media-literacy merit badge for the Boy Scouts and Girl Scouts. It's a way to teach kids that the violence you see on television is not the solution to problems.

GERBNER: Well, there is another law on the books, which may or may not provide an opportunity, and that's Senator Paul Simon's bill, the Television Violence Act. What it does is provide an exemption for the networks and cable companies for a period of three years from any prosecution under the antitrust laws if they agree to some kind of self-regulatory mechanism pertaining to violence.

TVG: Yes, but Senator Simon made a speech on the Senate floor on June 30 lambasting the networks for not taking advantage of the Television Violence Act. And he said that he continues to get statements from TV-industry people insisting that television violence doesn't do any harm.

LEONARD: I don't *want* to see a three-year exemption so that the networks can get together and decide how they're going to handle these problems. I don't want anything more that looks to me like censorship, no matter whether you call it business decisions or whether you call it taste. I think violence and sex and political dissent are all in bed together, and if you start messing with one, you end up messing with the rest of them. We already have too many gentlemen's agreements that have, in effect, wiped out political dissent.

PROTHROW-STITH: Why is violence the only area where we have no such agreements?

LEONARD: We do, all the way along, in little ways. And this is what happens when people get together and decide what the country needs to be protected from. It's exactly the same thing that's wrong with political correctness on too many college campuses. I don't think anybody should get together and say, "Here's how we can work it out."

TVG: Yet another source of TV violence, and a fairly recent one, is music videos. Dr. Prothrow-Stith has written that "the subjects of heavy-metal songs are sex, violence, death, Satan, and alienation." She adds that "in rap song after rap song, young black men brag about owning guns, using guns, and killing." There aren't any studies showing cause-and-effect with music videos, but what do you advise?

PROTHROW-STITH: My favorite strategy is the strategy of making that sort of thing unpopular, as we did with smoking and drunk driving. We said: we want the TV industry to help, through sitcoms and other shows, to teach our children that this is bad and dangerous behavior. So I think we can make violent music videos unpopular. People recognize that the music itself is nice, upbeat, kind of bopping music. The lyrics, though, are often horrible.

TVG: On another front, the National Coalition on Television Violence puts out a monitoring report occasionally, and the most recent one says that the most violent network shows—for the spring of 1991—were, in order: *Young Riders, The Flash, In the Heat of the Night, Black Jack Savage, Top Cops, MacGyver, America's Most Wanted, American Detective, DEA, Hunter,* and *Unsolved Mysteries.* All of those had 20 or more violent acts per hour, and *Young Riders* had 55. But let's ask the question: should anything be done to lessen gratuitous brutality, murder, and mayhem on television, from whatever source: networks, cable, home video? Do the broadcasters' rights of free speech on the public-owned airwaves supersede the public's right—and desire—for some modicum of protection?

CHARREN: We can educate children, we can educate parents. We can have seminars like this. We can have seminars like this. We can try to help parents understand something that this panel has tried to articulate, namely that it's important for parents to pay attention to what their children watch. I sometimes tell parents: suppose a complete stranger came into your home carrying two bags—one containing a lot of products for sale, and the other a lot of stories. And he said to you, "You look tired. Why don't you just leave, and I'll talk to your kids here on the couch." How many of us would say, "Go right ahead?" You have to help parents understand that that box in the living room is not always a friend of the family.

SLABY: In its listings for the premium cable channels like HBO and Showtime, TV GUIDE tells you if a movie is violent. That can help parents decide which movies to watch and which not.

GERBNER: That's good for highly educated, upper-middle-class parents who control the set. Most parents do not look at either ratings or advisories.

SLABY: I did a quick count of the premium cable movies listed last week in TV GUIDE. Over half of them were labeled "violence." So we're talking about the really new look, the new face of media violence.

PROTHROW-STITH: I think that the media can expect that the public may come around to demanding the same regulations for television as are in place for other professions. You wouldn't want doctors and hospitals to be unlicensed and unregulated.

CHARREN: But the potential for closing down free speech in this country from ideas like this—liability for speech—is so horrendous that I'd rather put up with the violence on television.

PROTHROW-STITH: Well, there is a middle ground, and if we reach it without censorship, we'll be in a lot better shape.

CHARREN: There's almost no information-based programming for kids on commercial television in this country, and it's the biggest blot on the landscape of American broadcasting that ever was.

TVG: What does that have to do with the problem of violence on television?

CHARREN: We could use that kind of program to help kids understand what televised violence really is. Television should also stop putting on the air as promotional announcements the most violent 30 seconds of upcoming movies and miniseries. And running those promos adjacent to children's shows. It's an industry problem.

TVG: Some experts say schools should teach that real violence actually hurts, that there's no such thing as violence without consequences.

PROTHROW-STITH: Yes. Television certainly isn't telling 12- and 14-year-olds shooting each other to death in our cities that death is permanent, final, tragic. We had a young man in the emergency room at Boston City Hospital who was surprised that his gunshot wound hurt. And I thought, boy, he's really stupid, anybody knows that if you get shot it's going to hurt. But it dawned on me that what he sees on television is that when the superhero gets shot in the arm, he uses that arm to hold onto a truck going 85 miles an hour around a corner. He overcomes the driver and shoots a couple of hundred people while he's at it.

It's important, I think, to differentiate the kind of violence you see in movies like "Boyz N the Hood" and "The Killing Fields" and "Glory," where you are saddened by it, and where the pain is obvious, where there are consequences to the violence.

WOLF: I agree with you. I'd go further. Dr. Weinman and I occasionally have arguments because, when I depict violence on a show, my desire is always to show it much worse than the network or the advertisers have any desire to see it. If somebody gets shot, they should be writhing on the ground screaming in pain, with gallons of blood running out of them. We're not allowed to show that. I agree that if you show violence, show it the way it is, do not glamorize it.

TVG: Another problem seems to be that women are too often the victims in TV scenes of violence. Some people argue that violent TV is written almost exclusively by white males, and that men—not necessarily women—want violent entertainment.

GERBNER: Many years of study have led me to the

conclusion that broadcasting policy is held very tightly by a handful of men imposing rather strict controls. If there is only one thing I would say to do, it is—hire more women, both on screen and off. And the minute you do that, the world will begin to change and be more fair, more just and less violent.

As it is, there is an unwritten policy that is very consistent, that is highly prejudiced, that encourages violence and victimization on a very unequal scale, showing certain people—mostly women and minorities—as more vulnerable.

WEINMAN: But we hope there are times when we actually put programs on which enlighten on this subject and do more than entertain; for example, "The Burning Bed." By and large, what you see on television and in the movies is basically what people are interested in watching, and these are cultural reflections.

PROTHROW-STITH: But we treat violence and sex very differently. We have no evidence that watching sex does any damage to children, and yet we go on and on about the sexual content of television and movies, and about regulations relating to sex.

We protect our children from a variety of things via regulatory mechanisms, and I think we need to do some protection in the area of violence—particularly of those children whose parents aren't able to or don't do it. And I think that if the industry, particularly the networks,

---

"I don't want anything more that looks to me like censorship."

—John Leonard

---

continues to be as sensitive as they have been to this problem, and if that spills over into the movie industry, we'll be successful. When it's unpopular, it won't make money.

LEONARD: As someone who actually watches a lot of TV, I think prime-time commercial TV has been more responsible than other parts of the culture. It's been the miniseries and TV-movies about date rape, child abuse, alcoholism, AIDS—and not movies or newspaper or schools—that have done the most to air these issues. But the best kind of education on TV won't do any good in a terrible home environment. We begin as always with providing bread and jobs, then a culture begins to create grander cultures in its imaginary forms. That's where I would begin.

GERBNER: Yes, education is very important, but it's like saying there are problems in our environment, so let's teach children to wear gas masks, and maybe not to breathe too much. It's not enough.

PROTHROW-STITH: You've got to have policy that

protects people and you've got to have education to help them deal with the situation. What changed our attitude about smoking? It was education in the classroom. It was working with the media. We banned the advertising of cigarettes on television.

TVG: How does that relate to media violence?

PROTHROW-STITH: We have to use health education, relating to violence, in the classroom—the same way we did with smoking. We have to use the media to deglamorize violence, and to show that nonviolence can be productive.

SLABY: I was going to say that one thing that resonates with me is the rather sad commentary that Dick Wolf says his children aren't allowed to watch any of the programs he has made, or even any of the Saturday-morning programs.

WEINMAN: But critics aren't coming down on the kinds of productions Mr. Wolf makes. They're talking about slasher movies kids are renting at the local video store, and, more and more, the pay-per-view button that gets similar material. HBO shows uncut movies at 8 at night as well as 11 in the morning.

GERBNER: I want to urge parents to participate in children's viewing, so they know something about what they criticize. They shouldn't use TV as a form of punishment or reward because that teaches indiscriminate viewing. I think teaching critical viewing should be a central task in our schools.

SLABY: I think public education on violence through TV is the missing ingredient. All of us would agree there's a great deal known about media violence. There are good suggestions on how to teach the public about guns, alcohol, drugs—and their relation to violence. The media can play a major role, consistent with other public-health areas.

I think that we American citizens would like to see the television industry—including cable and independent producers—pull together with researchers, and all of us get together and solve this problem once and for all. Certainly, Congress is calling for the industry to solve it. And I think the American people are calling for us to solve it. The crime is that TV has such potential that it's not using to try to solve this problem of violence. And I would like to see that happen in the next decade.

Summing Up: What We Can Do

A few modest proposals to mitigate, moderate, and minimize the effects of televised violence on viewers

The American Psychological Association suggests four steps parents can take:
1) Watch at least one episode of programs the child watches to know how violent they are.
2) When viewing together, discuss the violence with the child: why the violence happened and how painful it is. Ask the child how the conflict could have been solved without violence.
3) Explain to the child how violence in entertainment is "faked" and not real.
4) Encourage children to watch programs with characters that cooperate, help, and care for each other. These programs have been shown to influence children in a positive way.

OTHER POSSIBLE STEPS

• Urge the broadcaster, cable, and home video industries to adopt a unified ratings system of advisories to parents, labeling programs and movies as to their violence content.
• Urge TV and cable industry executives to take full advantage of The Television Violence Act, permitting them to work collectively toward reducing media violence.
• Make TV violence part of the public health agenda (as with smoking and drunk driving), publicizing—through a vigorous public information campaign in all informational media—its perils and effects.
• Establish courses in "critical viewing skills" as a regular aspect of school curricula, to help young people become more discriminating viewers.
• Inquire of elected officials their views and policies on televised violence; and then vote accordingly in November.
• Promote passage of a law requiring that, eventually, all new television sets be manufactured with built-in time-channel lock circuitry allowing parents to "lock out" channels and programs containing high levels of violence.
• Support the resolution of the American Psychological Association urging the broadcast and cable industries "to take a responsible attitude in reducing direct, imitable violence" in live-action children's shows and "violent incidents on cartoons."

Frankenstein Must Be Destroyed

Chasing the Monster of TV Violence

Brian Siano

Brian Siano is a writer and researcher living in Philadelphia. His column, "The Skeptical Eye," appears regularly in The Humanist. *He can be contacted via E-mail at revpk@cellar.org.*

Here's the scene: Bugs Bunny, Daffy Duck, and a well-armed Elmer Fudd are having a stand-off in the forest. Daffy the rat-fink has just exposed Bugs' latest disguise, so Bugs takes off the costume and says, "That's right, Doc, I'm a wabbit. Would you like to shoot me now or wait until we get home?"

"Shoot him now! Shoot him now!" Daffy screams.

"You keep out of this," Bugs says. "He does not have to shoot you now."

"He does *so* have to shoot me now!" says Daffy. Full of wrath, he storms up to Elmer Fudd and shrieks, "And I *demand* that you shoot me now!"

Now, if you *aren't* smiling to yourself over the prospect of Daffy's beak whirling around his head like a roulette wheel, stop reading right now. This one's for a very select group: those evil degenerates (like me) who want to corrupt the unsullied youth of America by showing them violence on television.

Wolves' heads being conked with mallets in Tex Avery's *Swing Shift Cinderella*. Dozens of dead bodies falling from a closet in *Who Killed Who?* A sweet little kitten seemingly baked into cookies in Chuck Jones' *Feed the Kitty*. And best of all, Wile E. Coyote's unending odyssey of pain in *Fast and Furrious* and *Hook, Line, and Stinker*. God, I love it. The more explosions, crashes, gunshots, and defective ACME catapults there are, the better it is for the little tykes.

Shocked? Hey, I haven't even gotten to "The Three Stooges" yet.

The villagers are out hunting another monster—the Frankenstein of TV violence. Senator Paul Simon's hearings in early August 1993 provoked a fresh round of arguments in a debate that's been going on ever since the first round of violent kids' shows—"Sky King," "Captain Midnight," and "Hopalong Cassidy"—were on the air. More recently, Attorney General Janet Reno has taken a hard line on TV violence. "We're fed up with excuses," she told the Senate, arguing that "the regulation of violence is constitutionally permissible" and that, if the networks don't do it, "government should respond." Reno herself presents a fine example, given her rotisserielike tactics with the Branch Davidian sect in Waco, or her medieval record on prosecuting "satanic ritual abuse" cases in Florida. (At least she wasn't as befuddled as Senator Ernest Hollings, who kept referring to "Beavis and Butt-head" as "Buffcoat and Beaver.")

Simon claims to have become concerned with this issue because, three years ago, he turned on the TV in his hotel room and was treated to the sight of a man being hacked apart with a chainsaw. (From his description, it sounds like the notorious scene in Brian de Palma's *Scarface*—itself censored to avoid an X-rating—but Simon never said what network, cable, or pay-per-view channel he saw it on.) This experience prompted him to sponsor a three-year antitrust exemption for the networks, which was his way of encouraging them to voluntarily "clean house." But at the end of that period, the rates of TV violence hadn't changed enough to satisfy him, so Simon convened open hearings on the subject in 1993.

If Simon was truly concerned with the content of television programming, the first question that comes to mind is why he gave the networks an antitrust exemption in the first place. Thanks to Reagan-era deregulation, ownership of the mass media has become steadily more concentrated in the hands of fewer and fewer corporations. For example, the Federal Communications Commission used to have a "seven-and-seven" rule, whereby no company was allowed to own more than seven radio and seven television stations. In 1984, this was revised to a "12-and-12-and-12" rule: 12 FM radio stations, 12 AM radio stations, and 12 TV stations. It's a process outlined by Ben Bagdikian in his fine book *The Media Monopoly*. The net result is a loss of dissident, investigative, or regional voices; a mass media that questions less; and a forum for public debate that includes only the powerful.

This process could be impeded with judicious use of anti-trust laws and stricter FCC controls—a return to the "seven-and-seven" rule, perhaps. But rather than hold hearings on this subject—a far greater threat to the nation's political well-being than watching *Aliens* on pay-per-view—Simon gave the networks a three-year *exemption* from antitrust legislation.

There's a reason we should be concerned about this issue of media ownership: television influences people. That's its *job*. Advertisers don't spend all that money on TV commercials because they have no impact. Corporations don't dump money into PBS shows like "The McLaughlin Group" or "Firing Line" unless they are getting their point across. *Somebody* is buying stuff from the Home Shopping Network and keeping Rush Limbaugh's ratings up. Then, too, we all applaud such public-service initiatives as "Don't Drink and Drive" ads, and I think most of us would be appalled if Donatello of the *Teenage Mutant Ninja Turtles* lit up a Marlboro or chugged a fifth of Cutty Sark. So it's not unreasonable to wonder whether violent television might be encouraging violent behavior.

The debate becomes even more impassioned when we ask how children might be affected. The innocent, trusting little tykes are spending hours bathed in TV's unreal colors, and their fantasy lives are inhabited by such weirdos as Wolverine and Eek the Cat. Parents usually want their kids to grow up sharing their ideals and values, or at least to be well-behaved and obedient. Tell parents that their kids are watching "Beavis and Butt-head" in their formative years and you set off some major alarms.

There are also elitist, even snobbish, attitudes toward pop culture that help to rationalize censorship. One is that the corporate, mass-market culture of TV isn't important enough or "art" enough to deserve the same free-speech protection as James Joyce's *Ulysses* or William Burrough's *Naked Lunch*. The second is that rational, civilized human beings are supposed to be into Shakespeare and Scarlatti, not Pearl Jam and "Beavis and Butt-head." Seen in this "enlightened" way, the efforts of Paul Simon are actually for *our own good*. And so we define anything even remotely energetic as "violent," wail about how innocent freckle-faced children are being defiled by such fare as "NYPD Blue," and call for a Council of Certified Nice People who will decide what the rest of us get to see. A recent *Mother Jones* article by Carl Cannon (July/August 1993) took just this hysterical tone, citing as proof "some three thousand research studies of this issue."

Actually, there aren't 3,000 studies. In 1984, the *Psychological Bulletin* published an overview by Jonathan Freedman of research on the subject. Referring to the "2,500 studies" figure

bandied about at the time (it's a safe bet that 10 years would inflate this figure to 3,000), Freedman writes:

> The reality is more modest. The large number refers to the complete bibliography on television. References to television and aggression are far fewer, perhaps around 500. . . . The actual literature on the relation between television violence and aggression consists of fewer than 100 independent studies, and the majority of these are laboratory experiments. Although this is still a substantial body of work, it is not vast, and there are only a small number of studies dealing specifically with the effects of television violence outside the laboratory.

The bulk of the evidence for a causal relationship between television violence and violent behavior comes from the research of Leonard Eron of the University of Illinois and Rowell Huesmann of the University of Michigan. Beginning in 1960, Eron and his associates began a large-scale appraisal of how aggression develops in children and whether or not it persists into adulthood. (The question of television violence was, originally, a side issue to the long-term study.) Unfortunately, when the popular press writes about Eron's work, it tends to present his methodology in the simplest of terms: *Mother Jones* erroneously stated that his study "followed the viewing habits of a group of children for twenty-two years." It's this sort of sloppiness, and overzealousness to prove a point, that keeps people from understanding the issues or raising substantial criticisms. Therefore, we must discuss Eron's work in some detail.

The first issue in Eron's study was how to measure aggressiveness in children. Eron's "peer-nominated index" followed a simple strategy: asking each child in a classroom questions about which kids were the main offenders in 10 different categories of classroom aggression (that is, "Who pushes or shoves children?"). The method is

There are elitist and snobbish attitudes toward pop culture that help to rationalize censorship.

consistent with other scales of aggression, and its one-month test-retest reliability is 91 percent. The researchers also tested the roles of four behavioral dimensions in the development of aggression: *instigation* (parental rejection or lack of nurturance), *reinforcement* (punishment versus reward), *identification* (acquiring the parents' behavior and values), and *sociocultural norms*.

Eron's team selected the entire third-grade population of Columbia County, New York, testing 870 children and interviewing about 75 to 80 percent of their parents. Several trends became clear almost immediately. Children with less nurturing parents were more aggressive. Children who more closely identified with either parent were less aggressive. And children with low parental identification who were punished tended to be *more* aggressive (an observation which required revision of the behavioral model).

Ten years later, Eron and company tracked down and re-interviewed about half of the original sample. (They followed up on the subjects in 1981 as well.) Many of the subjects—now high-school seniors—demonstrated a persistence in aggression over time. Not only were the "peer-nominated" ratings roughly consistent with the third-grade ratings, but the more aggressive kids were three times as likely to have a police record by adulthood.

Eron's team also checked for the influences on aggression which they had previously noted when the subjects were eight. The persistent influences were parental identification and socioeconomic variables. Some previously important influences (lack of nurturance, punishment for aggression) didn't seem to affect the subjects' behavior as much in young adulthood. Eron writes of these factors:

Their effect is short-lived and other variables are more important in predicting later aggression. Likewise, contingencies and environmental conditions can change drastically over 10 years, and thus the earlier contingent response becomes irrelevant.

It's at this stage that Eron mentions television as a factor:

One of the best predictors of how aggressive a young man would be at age 19 was the violence of the television programs he preferred when he was 8 years old. Now, because we had longitudinal data, we could say with more certainty, on the basis of regression analysis, partial correlation, path analysis, and so forth, that there indeed was a cause-and-effect relation. *Continued research, however, has indicated that the causal effect is probably bidirectional: Aggressive children prefer violent television, and the violence on television causes them to be more aggressive.* [italics added]

Before we address the last comment, I should make one thing clear. Eron's research is sound. The methods he used to measure aggression are used by social scientists in many other contexts. His research does not ignore such obvious factors as the parents' socioeconomic status. And, as the above summary makes clear, Eron's own work makes a strong case for the positive or negative influence of parents in the development of their children's aggressiveness.

Now let's look at this "causal effect" business. Eron's data reveals that aggressive kids who turn into aggressive adults

like aggressive television. But this is a correlation; it is not proof of a causal influence. If aggressive kids liked eating strawberry ice cream more often than the class wusses did, that too would be a predictor, and one might speculate on some anger-inducing chemical in strawberries.

Of course, the relation between representational violence and its influence on real life isn't as farfetched as that. The problem lies in determining precisely the nature of that relation, as we see when we look at the laboratory studies conducted by other researchers. Usually, the protocol for these experiments involves providing groups of individuals with entertainment calibrated for violent content, and studying some aspect of behavior after exposure—response to a behavioral test, which toys the children choose to play with, and so forth. But the results of these tests have been somewhat mixed. Sometimes the results are at variance with other studies, and many have methodological problems. For example, which "violent" entertainment is chosen? Bugs Bunny and the "Teenage Mutant Ninja Turtles" present action in very different contexts, and in one study, the Adam West "Batman" series was deemed nonviolent, despite those *Pow! Bam! Sock!* fistfights that ended every episode.

Many of the studies report that children do demonstrate higher levels of interpersonal aggression shortly after watching violent, energetic entertainment. But a 1971 study by Feshbach and Singer had boys from seven schools watch preassigned violent and nonviolent shows for six weeks. The results were not constant from school to school—and the boys watching the *nonviolent* shows tended to be more aggressive. Another protocol, carried out in Belgium as well as the United States, separated children into cottages at an institutional school and exposed certain groups to violent films. Higher aggression was noted in *all* groups after the films were viewed, but it returned to a near-baseline level after a week or so. (The children also rated the less violent films as less exciting, more boring, and sillier than the violent films—indicating that maybe kids *like* a little rush now and then.) Given the criticisms of the short-term-effects studies, and the alternate interpretations of the longitudinal studies, is this matter really settled?

Eron certainly thinks so. Testifying before Simon's committee in August, he declared that "the scientific debate is over" and called upon the Senate to reduce TV violence. His statement did not include any reference to such significant factors as parental identification—which, as his own research indicates, can change the way children interpret physical punishment. And even though Rowell Huesmann concurred with Eron in similar testimony before a House subcommittee, Huesmann's 1984 study of 1,500 youths in the United States, Finland, Poland, and Australia argued that, assuming a causal influence, television might be responsible for 5 percent of the violence in society. At *most*.

This is where I feel one has to part company with Leonard Eron. He is one of the most respected researchers in his field, and his work points to an imperative for parents in shaping and sharing their children's lives. But he has lent his considerable authority to such diversionary efforts as Paul Simon's and urged us to address, by questionable means, what only *might* be causing a tiny portion of real-life violence.

Some of Eron's suggestions for improving television are problematic as well. In his Senate testimony, Eron proposed restrictions on televised violence from 6:00 AM to 10:00 PM—which would exclude pro football, documentaries about World War II, and even concerned lawperson Janet Reno's proudest moments. Or take Eron's suggestion that, in televised drama, "perpetrators of violence should not be rewarded for violent acts." I don't know what shows Eron's been watching, but all of the cop shows I remember usually ended with the bad guys getting caught or killed. And when Eron suggests that "gratuitous violence that is not necessary to the plot should be reduced or abandoned," one has to ask just *who* decides that it's "not necessary"? Perhaps most troubling is Eron's closing statement:

> For many years now Western European countries have had monitoring of TV and films for violence by government agencies and have *not* permitted the showing of excess violence, especially during child viewing hours. And I've never heard complaints by citizens of those democratic countries that their rights have been violated. If something doesn't give, we may have to institute some such monitoring by government agencies here in the U.S.A. If the industry does not police itself, then there is left only the prospect of official censorship, distasteful as this may be to many of us.

The most often-cited measure of just how violent TV programs are is that of George Gerbner, dean of the Annenberg School of Communications at the University of Pennsylvania. Few of the news stories about TV violence explain how this index is compiled, the context in which Gerbner has conducted his studies, or even some criticisms that could be raised.

Gerbner's view of the media's role in society is far more nuanced than the publicity given the violence profile may indicate. He sees television as a kind of myth-structure/religion for modern society. Television dramas, situation comedies, news shows, and all the rest create a shared culture for viewers, which "communicates much about social norms and relationships, about goals and means, about winners and losers." One portion of Gerbner's research involves compiling "risk ratios" in an effort to discern which minority groups—including children, the aged, and women—tend to be the victims or the aggressors in drama. This provides a picture of a pecking order within society (white males on top, no surprise there) that has remained somewhat consistent over the 20-year history of the index.

In a press release accompanying the 1993 violence index, Gerbner discusses his investigations of the long-term effects of television viewing. Heavy viewers were more likely to express feelings of living in a hostile world. Gerbner adds, "Violence is a demonstration of power. It shows who can get away with what against whom."

In a previous violence index compiled for cable-television programs, violence is defined as a "clear-cut and overt episode of physical violence—hurting or killing or the threat of hurting and/or killing—in any context." An earlier definition reads: "The overt expression of physical force against self or other compelling action against one's will on pain of being hurt or killed, or actually hurting or killing." These definitions have been criticized for being too broad; they encompass episodes of physical comedy, depiction of accidents in dramas, and even violent incidents in documentaries. They also include zany cartoon violence; in fact, the indexes for Saturday-morning programming tend to be substantially higher than the indexes for prime-time programming. Gerbner argues that, since he is analyzing cultural norms and since television entertainment is a deliberately conceived expression of these norms, his definition serves the purposes of his study.

> *Stories of media-inspired violence are atypical of the norm; the vast majority of people don't take a movie or TV show as a license to kill.*

The incidents of violence (total number = R) in a given viewing period are compiled by Gerbner's staff. Some of the statistics are easy to derive, such as the percentage of programs with violence, the number of violent scenes per hour, and the actual duration of violence, in minutes per hour. The actual violence index is calculated by adding together the following stats:

$\%P$ — the *percentage* of programs in which there is violence;

$2(R/P)$ — twice the number of violent episodes per program;

$2(R/H)$ — twice the number of violent episodes per *hour*;

$\%V$ — percentage of *leading characters* involved in violence, either as victim or perpetrator; and

$\%K$ — percentage of leading characters involved in an actual *killing*, either as victim or perpetrator.

But if these are the factors used to compile the violence profile, it's difficult to see how they can provide a clear-cut mandate for the specific content of television drama. For example, two of the numbers used are averages; why are they arbitrarily doubled and then added to percentages? Also, because the numbers are determined by a definition which explicitly separates violence from dramatic context, the index says little about actual television content outside of a broad, overall gauge. One may imagine a television season of nothing but slapstick comedy with a very high violence profile.

This is why the violence profile is best understood within the context of Gerbner's wider analysis of media content. It does not lend itself to providing specific conclusions or guidelines of the sort urged by Senator Paul Simon. (It is important to note that, even though Simon observed little change in prime-time violence levels during his three-year antitrust exemption, the index for all three of those years was *below* the overall 20-year score.)

Finally, there's the anecdotal evidence—loudly trumpeted as such by Carl Cannon in *Mother Jones*—where isolated examples of entertainment-inspired violence are cited as proof of its pernicous influence. Several such examples have turned up recently. A sequence was edited out of the film *The Good Son* in which MacCaulay Culkin drops stuff onto a highway from an overhead bridge. (As we all know, nobody ever did this before the movie came out.) The film *The Program* was re-edited when some kids were killed imitating the film's characters, who "proved their courage" by lying down on a highway's dividing line. Perhaps most notoriously, in October 1993 a four-year-old Ohio boy set his family's trailer on fire, killing his younger sister; the child's mother promptly blamed MTV's "Beavis and Butt-head" for setting a bad example. But a neighbor interviewed on CNN reported that the family didn't even have cable television and that the kid had a local rep as a pyromaniac months before. This particular account was not followed up by the national media, which, if there were no enticing 'Beavis and Butt-head" angle, would never have mentioned this fire at a low-income trailer park to begin with.

Numerous articles about media-inspired violence have cited similar stories—killers claiming to be Freddy Kreuger, kids imitating crimes they'd seen on a cop show a few days before, and so forth. In many of these cases, it is undeniably true that the person involved took his or her inspiration to act from a dramatic presentation in the media—the obvious example being John Hinckley's fixation on the film *Taxi Driver*. (Needless to say, Bible-inspired crimes just don't attract the ire of Congress.) But stories of media-inspired violence are striking mainly because they're so *atypical* of the norm; the vast majority of people don't take a movie or a TV show as a license to kill. Ironically, it is the *abnormality* of these stories that ensures they'll get widespread dissemination and be remembered long after the more mundane crimes are forgotten.

Of course, there are a few crazies out there who will be unfavorably influenced by what they see on TV. But even assuming that somehow the TV show (or movie or record) shares some of the blame, how does one predict what future crazies will take for inspiration? What guidelines would ensure that people write, act, or produce something that *will not upset a psy-*

chotic? Not only is this a ridiculous demand, it's insulting to the public as well. We would all be treated as potential murderers in order to gain a hypothetical 5 percent reduction in violence.

In crusades like this—where the villagers pick up their torches and go hunting after Frankenstein—people often lose sight of what they're defending. I've read reams of statements from people who claim to know what television does to kids; but what do *kids* do with television? Almost none of what I've read gives kids any credit for thinking. None of these people seems to remember what being a kid is like.

When *Jurassic Park* was released, there was a huge debate over whether or not children should be allowed to see it. Kids like to see dinosaurs, people argued, but this movie might scare them into catatonia. There was even the suspicion that Steven Spielberg and company were being sneaky and underhanded by making a film about dinosaurs that was terrifying. These objections were actually taken seriously. But kids like dinosaurs because they're big, look really weird, and scare the hell out of everything around them. Dinosaurs *kick ass*. What parent would tell his or her child that dinosaurs were *cute*? (And how long have these "concerned parents" been *lying* to their kids about the most fearsome beasts ever to shake the earth?)

Along the same lines, what kid hasn't tried to gross out everyone at the dinner table by showing them his or her chewed-up food? Or tried using a magnifying glass on an ant-hill on a hot day? Or clinically inspected the first dead animal he or she ever came across? Sixty years ago, adults were terrified of *Frankenstein* and fainted at the premiere of *King Kong*. But today, *Kong* is regarded as a fantasy story, *Godzilla* can be shown without the objections of child psychologists, and there are breakfast cereals called Count Chocula and Frankenberry. Sadly, there are few adults who seem to remember how they identified more with the monsters. Who wanted to be one of those stupid villagers waving torches at Frankenstein? That's what our *parents* were like.

But it's not just an issue of kids liking violence, grossness, or comic-book adventure. About 90 percent of the cartoon shows I watched as a child were the mass-produced sludge of the Hanna-Barbera Studios—like "Wacky Races," "The Jetsons," and "Scooby Doo, Where Are You?" I can't remember a single memorable moment from any of them. But that Bugs Bunny sequence at the beginning of this article (from *Rabbit Seasoning*, 1952, directed by Chuck Jones) was done from memory, and I have no doubt that it's almost verbatim.

I know that, even at the age of eight or nine, I had some rudimentary aesthetic sense about it all. There was something hip and complex about the Warner Bros. cartoons, and some trite, insulting *sameness* to the Hanna-Barbera trash, although I couldn't quite understand it then. Bugs Bunny clearly wasn't made for kids according to some study on social-interaction development. Bugs Bunny was meant to make adults laugh as much as children. Kids can also enjoy entertainment ostensibly created for adults—in fact, that's often the most rewarding kind. I had no trouble digesting *Jaws*, James Bond, and Clint Eastwood "spaghetti westerns" in my preteen years. And I'd have no problems with showing a 10-year-old *Jurassic Park*, because I know how much he or she would love it.

Another example: Ralph Bakshi's brilliant "Mighty Mouse" series was canceled after the Reverend Donald Wildmon claimed it showed the mouse snorting coke. Kids don't organize mass write-in campaigns, and I hate to see them lose something wonderful just because some officious crackpot decides it was corrupting their morals. Perhaps aspartame-drenched shows like "Barney and Friends" or "Widget" (a purple, spermy little alien who can do magic) encourage children to be good citizens, but they also encourage kids to be docile and unimaginative—just the sort of "good citizens" easily manipulated by the likes of Wildmon.

I don't enjoy bad television with lots of violence, but I'd rather not lose *decent* shows that use violence for good reason. Shows like "Star Trek," "X-Men," or the spectacular "Batman: The Animated Series" can give kids a sense of adventure while teaching them about such qualities as courage, bravery, and heroism. Even better, a healthy and robust spirit of irreverence

can be found in Bugs Bunny, "Ren and Stimpy," and "Tiny Toons." Some of these entertainments—like adventure stories and comic books of the past—can teach kids how to be really *alive.*

Finally, if we must have a defense against the pernicious influence of the mass media, it cannot be from the Senate's legislation or the pronouncements of social scientists. It must begin with precisely the qualities I described above—especially irreverence. One good start is Comedy Central's "Mystery Science Theater 3000," where the main characters, forced to watch horrendous movies, fight back by heckling them. Not surprisingly, children love the show, even though most of the jokes go right over their curious little heads. They recognize a kindred spirit in "MST 3000." Kids want to stick up for themselves, maybe like Batman, maybe like Bugs Bunny, or even like Beavis and Butt-head—but always against a world made by adults.

You know, *adults*—those doofuses with the torches, trying to burn up Frankenstein in the old mill.

Ethical Dilemmas of Prosocial Television

William J. Brown and Arvind Singhal

William J. Brown (Ph.D., University of Southern California, 1988) is an Assistant Professor in the Department of Speech, University of Hawaii, Honolulu, HI 96822.

Arvind Singhal (Ph.D., University of Southern California, 1990) is an Assistant Professor in the College of Communication at Ohio University, Athens, Ohio 45701.

The present article examines the ethical dilemmas associated with the use of entertainment television for prosocial development. During the 1980s, the production of entertainment television programs for consumption worldwide was unprecedented. While entertainment television is generally created to attract large audiences and sell commercial products, many countries are producing entertainment-educational programs that are intended to diffuse prosocial messages. U.S. television producers are increasingly pressured by various lobby groups to address social issues on prime-time television. The promotion of prosocial beliefs and behaviors through television raises important ethical dilemmas, four of which are discussed here: (1) the ethics of distinguishing prosocial television content from antisocial television content, (2) the ethics of depicting socio-cultural equality through television programs, (3) the ethics of limiting the unintended effects of television programs, and (4) the ethics of using television as a persuasive tool to guide social development.

KEY CONCEPTS *Communication ethics, prosocial messages, entertainment television, development communication.*

The use of television to promote social development has generated ethical dilemmas that will affect several billion television viewers during the 1990s. *Development* is defined as a widely participatory process of directed social change in a society, intended to bring about both social and material advancement (Rogers, 1976). Television has a greater potential impact on social development now than ever before in human history. Several countries are systematically producing television programs with prosocial messages. *Prosocial* television content refers to televised performances that depict cognitive, affective, or behavioral activities considered to be socially desirable by most members of a television audience (Rushton, 1982). Ethical concerns regarding the responsible use of television are prompting television producers and officials to reduce the antisocial effects of television by increasing the prosocial content of television programs.

While the use of prosocial television programs raises several ethical dilemmas (as we will show later in this essay), literature on television ethics is severely limited. Television ethics represents a relatively neglected and undeveloped field of inquiry. Existing research focuses primarily on specialized themes such as television news ethics (Cooper, 1988). The purpose of the present article is (1) to investigate the use of prosocial television, (2) to review relevant theory on communication ethics, and (3) to address several important ethical dilemmas that television producers, educators, government officials, and communication scholars should consider as television's influence grows during the 1990s.

TELEVISION'S GROWING INFLUENCE

The use of communication satellites has rapidly expanded television audiences worldwide. In Third World nations, the percentage of the world's total number of television sets increased from 5 percent in 1965, to 10 percent in 1975, to 20 percent in 1984, and to 40 percent in 1988. During the eight year period from 1980 to 1987, the number of television sets increased by 15 times in the People's Republic of China, and by 10 times in India. Television now reaches 550 million of China's 1.1 billion people (50%), about 120 million people in India (15%), and about 70 million people in Mexico (87%). Sharp increases in the size of television audiences have also occurred in other countries.

As television audiences increase, entertainment television is rapidly replacing educational television. *Entertainment television* is comprised of televised performances intended to capture the interest or attention of individuals, giving them pleasure and/or amusement. *Educational television* refers to a televised program of instruction and training intended to develop an individual's mental, moral, or physical skills to achieve a particular end. Entertainment programs are highly popular in Third World countries. In India, television began as an educational service (in 1959), but in the late 1980s entertainment

From *Communication Quarterly,* Vol. 38, No. 3, Summer 1990, pp. 268-280. © 1990 by the Eastern Communication Association. Reprinted by permission.

television crowded out educational programs. This same trend is occurring in other countries because entertainment programs attract larger audiences, are viewed for longer periods, and generate greater profits than do educational programs.

Despite the sustained growth of entertainment television, little is known about the prosocial effects of entertainment television programs. There are several reasons for this limited knowledge. First, television programs are commonly categorized into a dichotomy that separates entertainment television from educational television. In the past four decades this dichotomy has been reified in the way television and its effects have been discussed and researched. For example, before cable television, "entertainment television" was often referred to as "commercial television" and "educational television" was called "public television."

These arbitrary labels complicate research on the effects of television programs. Educational programs like *Sesame Street* and *The Electric Company* can be highly entertaining, and entertainment programs like *Shogun* and *The Day After* can be highly educational (Kulman & Akamatsu, 1988; Palmer, 1978; Shatzer, Korzenny, & Griffis-Korzenny, 1985). The prevailing notion that "entertainment television entertains rather than educates" limits a researcher's framework by underestimating the importance of entertainment television's educational and social influence.

A second reason for the paucity of research on the prosocial effects of entertainment television is the emphasis on studying television's antisocial effects. *Antisocial* is defined as cognitive, affective, or behavioral activities considered to be socially undesirable by most members of a social system. Of the many thousands of studies conducted on antisocial television effects, we identify four major research strains: (1) the harmful effects of television violence (Andison, 1980; Donnerstein, 1980; Donnerstein & Berkowitz, 1981; Malamuth & Donnerstein, 1984; Phillips, 1982; Phillips & Hensley, 1984; Zillmann & Bryant, 1982), (2) the effects of promoting inaccurate health-related information on television (Barnum, 1975; Cassata, Skill, & Boadu, 1979; Long, 1978; Lowry & Towles, 1989; Smith, 1972; Tan & Tan, 1986), (3) the portrayal of negative (and often discriminating) images of women and children on television (Cassata & Skill, 1983; Downing, 1974; Goldsen, 1975; Liebert, Neale, & Davidson, 1973; Noble, 1975; Tuchman, Daniels, & Benet, 1978), and (4) the unrealistic depiction of interpersonal and social relationships on television (Alexander, 1985; Buerkel-Rothfuss & Mayes, 1981; Estep & MacDonald, 1985; Greenberg, Abelman, & Neuendorf, 1981; Greenberg & D'Alessio, 1985; Lowry, Love, & Kirby, 1981; Sutherland & Siniawsky, 1982).

In contrast, relatively few studies have focused on the prosocial effects of entertainment television (see Amato & Malatesta, 1987; Brown, 1988; Ball-Rokeach, Rokeach, & Grube, 1984; Ball-Rokeach, Grube, & Rokeach, 1981; Berrueta, 1986; Gunter, 1984; Harvey, Sprafkin, & Rubinstein,

1979; Lovelace & Huston, 1982, Porter & Ware, 1989; Sabido, 1981; Singhal & Rogers, 1988a, 1989a, 1989b). Therefore much less is known about the effects of television programs that are intended to have positive social impacts than is known about the unintended antisocial effects of entertainment television.

The Growth of Prosocial Television

The idea of producing entertainment television programs for prosocial purposes is not new. However, the use of human communication theories to promote specific prosocial beliefs and behaviors through entertainment television programs (not just commercials) is a relatively new practice (Brown, 1989; Brown, Singhal, & Rogers, 1989).

Mexico was the first country to develop a theoretical framework for producing prosocial television programs. From 1975 to 1981, Televisa, Mexico's private national television network, produced six series of *telenovelas* (soap operas) in order to promote adult literacy, family planning, and gender equality. The Mexican soap operas, also called *pro-development soap operas*, utilized an entertainment-education communication strategy to induce cognitive and behavioral changes in their viewers (Brown, Singhal, & Rogers, 1989; Rogers et al., 1989; Sabido, 1981).

Miguel Sabido, Vice-President of Research at Televisa, utilized the principles of (1) Bandura's (1977) social learning theory, (2) Bentley's (1964) dramatic theory, (3) Jung's (1970) theory of archetypes and stereotypes and (4) his own theory of tones (Sabido, 1982) to create prosocial messages in each of the six Mexican soap operas.

Inspired by Sabido's soap opera methodology, Indian media officials produced India's first long-running television soap opera, *Hum Log* ("We People"), to promote women's status, family harmony, and family planning (Brown, 1988; Singhal & Rogers, 1988a). *Hum Log* became one of the most popular programs in the history of Indian television (Jain, 1985; Mitra, 1986; Singhal & Rogers, 1989a). Research on the effects of *Hum Log* indicated that the program positively influenced viewers' beliefs regarding the status of women in India, made people more dependent on television, and led to the proliferation of indigenously-produced dramatic television serials on Indian television (Brown, 1988, Singhal & Rogers, 1988a).

In 1987, encouraged by the success of *Hum Log* in India, Kenya began broadcasting an indigenously-produced entertainment soap opera designed to promote family planning. Kenya's soap opera, *Tushauriane* ("Let's Discuss"), which ended in 1988, was the most popular television program in the history of Kenyan television. Other examples of prosocial entertainment television programs are Nigeria's *Cock Crow at Dawn*, a dramatic serial that promoted the adoption of modern agricultural practices (Ume-Nwagbo, 1986), *In a Lighter Mood*, another Nigerian series that promoted family planning (Winnard, Rimon, & Convisser, 1987), *High Stakes*, a Brazilian soap opera that encouraged viewers to overcome alcoholism, *Sparrows Don't Migrate*, a Turkish family planning soap opera, and *Polite Society*, a Mexican soap opera promoting sexual responsibility (Rogers et al., 1989).

On several occasions, U.S. television producers have incorporated prosocial messages into entertainment television programs. During the 1970s, Norman Lear launched the popular CBS television series *All in the Family* to address ethnic prejudices and encourage racial harmony in America. The highly acclaimed ABC miniseries *Roots*, viewed by 32 million U.S. households, and its sequel, *Roots: The Next Generation*, viewed by 22.5 million U.S. households, promoted the value of egalitarianism (Ball-Rokeach, Grube, & Rokeach, 1981). Another television mini-series studied, *Shogun*, positively affected viewers' attitudes toward the Japanese; the series increased viewers' knowledge of the Japanese language, history, and customs, and increased their desire to be socially closer to the Japanese people (Shatzer, Korzenny, & Griffis-Korzenny, 1985).

Research indicates that exposure to even a single prosocial television program can produce enduring cognitive and behavioral changes in viewers. The television movie *The Day After* significantly increased viewers' attitudes about preventing nuclear war (Kulman & Akamatsu, 1988). *The Great American Values Test*, a 30-minute television special designed to promote prosocial values, significantly increased viewers' proenvironmental and proegalitarian beliefs and behaviors (Ball-Rokeach, Rokeach, & Grube, 1984). Although most of the studies of prosocial television programs indicate only modest effects, they reveal the potentially beneficial impact of prosocial television content.

Numerous organizations maintain a presence in Hollywood in order to influence U.S. television producers to include social issues in an episode of a television series. These "Hollywood lobbyists" (social cause groups) occasionally are successful in getting their issue presented on prime-time television, and thus raise public consciousness about that issue (Montgomery, 1989).

Educational institutions also have made contributions to the production of prosocial messages. For example, the Harvard University School of Public Health instigated the "designated driver" television campaign to prevent drinking and driving. By March 1989, the designated driver concept appeared in 35 different prime-time series on U.S. network television (Rogers et al., 1989). As social problems facing many countries become more acute, as is expected with the growing AIDS crisis and widespread drug abuse, more prosocial television content is likely to be broadcast during the 1990s.

ETHICAL THEORY AND PROSOCIAL MEDIA

The expanding use of television worldwide for social development raises important ethical concerns that need to be discussed by television producers, government officials, and media scholars. First, we discuss perspectives provided by several key ethical theorists to define and evaluate the ethics of prosocial media.[1] Then we discuss four ethical dilemmas associated with prosocial television.

Aristotle's (1960) "golden mean" concept suggests that messages should be tailored to address an audience in the "prime of life," balancing the extreme characteristics of young people and old people. Aristotle emphasized that ethical conduct is attained by actions that are intermediate between extremes, and that moral knowledge and ethics are produced collectively (Johnstone, 1980). Consistent with Aristotle's ethical theory, several media planners have created prosocial messages that are addressed to the "golden mean" of modern societies, focusing on the common needs of most people. However, using prosocial media to address only these audiences may lead media planners to ignore needs of other demographic groups, especially minorities.

Other media planners have created prosocial messages consistent with John Stuart Mill's (1957) "principle of utility," which judges an action to be ethically appropriate only when it produces the greatest amount of good for the greatest number of people in a society (Merrill & Barney, 1975, p. 11). Creating prosocial messages that produce the greatest good for the greatest number of people is difficult to implement because someone must define what constitutes the "greatest good." For example, the Communist Party in the People's Republic of China may decide the "greatest good" is achieved when citizens place the State before self and are loyal to the communist doctrine. Not only does a majority group impose their perceptions of the "greatest good" on minorities, but often a ruling minority government, for example, the White South African government, can impose their perceptions of the "greatest good" on the Black majority of the country.

Immanuel Kant's (1964) ethic of the "categorical imperative" has also influenced ethical theory in the media (Christians, 1977). Kant believed that a good act was one which the actor would be willing to see universalized and that every person should be considered as an end rather then as a means to an end (Merrill, 1974, p. 5). Media policy based on Kant's view would suggest that every individual in society should have an equal opportunity to receive beneficial media messages, and that the focus of such messages should be first to help the individuals, not just to change the individuals to achieve a government's objectives.

The ethical view presented in the present article is closely related to Kantian philosophy. We suggest that common human values should be considered in producing prosocial media messages. Minnick (1980) noted that Albert Schweitzer defined ethics as nothing more than reverence for life. Schweitzer's definition implies that moral judgments are built upon commonly accepted values. Ethics emerge from enduring social values rather than from logically defensible propositions (Minnick, 1980). Thus, ethical communication has a dimension of social identity (Chesebro, 1969).

We define *ethical communication* as that which upholds and protects an individual's freedom, equality, dignity, and physical and psychological well-being. Communication media are ethically employed when they are not the limiting factor in addressing individual and social needs (Martin, Byrne, & Wedemeyer, 1977). If the media fail to uphold and protect basic human values, or limit people's access to resources that provide their basic needs, then it is used unethically.

Ethical Dilemmas of Prosocial Television

An evaluation of prosocial television according to our definition of ethical communication has revealed four important ethical dilemmas: (1) the prosocial content dilemma, that is, how to distinguish prosocial from antisocial television content; (2) the socio-cultural equality dilemma, that is, how to ensure that prosocial television upholds socio-cultural equality among viewers; (3) the unintended effects dilemma, that is, how to respond to the unintended consequences of prosocial television; and (4) the prosocial development dilemma, that is, how to respond to those who argue it is unethical to use television as a persuasive tool to guide social development.

The Prosocial Content Dilemma

Previously we defined prosocial television as televised performances that depict "cognitive, affective, and behavioral activities considered to be socially desirable or preferable by most members of a particular social system." Distinguishing prosocial content, however, is difficult when people do not have common moral and ethical values. There is some consensus about certain prosocial issues in most societies. For example, almost everyone would agree that child abuse is wrong, that violence against women should be stopped, and that it is good to "say no" to illegal drugs. However, the best ways to prevent the abuse of women and children or to prevent drug abuse are hotly disputed, and a lack of consensus exists regarding many social issues.

During the past two decades one of the most controversial social issues in the U.S. has been abortion. In a 1972 episode of *Maude*, the middle-aged star of the television series decided to get an abortion rather than bear an unwanted child. This episode set off a controversy with right-to-life organizations in the U.S., who demanded equal television attention to their position on abortion. In 1985, an episode of *Cagney and Lacey* showed a right-to-life group picketing an abortion clinic, causing tremendous consternation among pro-abortion groups in the U.S. For those favoring abortion, the *Maude* episode was considered to be prosocial (based on freedom of choice to abort

a child), but for those against abortion, the *Maude* episode was considered to be antisocial (based on the right to life of an unborn child). Similarly, picketing the abortion clinic in *Cagney and Lacey* was viewed as prosocial by right-to-life advocates. Ted Turner, an outspoken abortion-rights advocate, invigorated this controversy once again when he recently broadcast *Abortion: For Survival* on his TBS network. Turner's opponents want equal time on TBS.

At the heart of the prosocial content dilemma is determining "*who* will decide for *whom, what* is prosocial and what is not." In most Third World nations, including the ones broadcasting prosocial television programs, the government overseeing the media usually decides what is prosocial. History reveals horrendous abuses by governments who have used the media to promote antisocial beliefs and behaviors, leading many countries to limit or eliminate government regulation of the media. Yet in many countries governments have used the media ethically and responsibly for prosocial purposes.

Unfortunately, the assurance that the media will be used for prosocial purposes is not greater in nations where the responsibility for prosocial media is left to television producers and commercial advertisers. Such a responsibility shift creates problems for television producers and advertisers who usually avoid addressing controversial social and educational issues. For example, U.S. television networks have resisted the broadcast of condom advertisements. While entertainment television programs depict numerous sexual behaviors every day in the U.S., the depiction of condom use is virtually nonexistent (Lowry & Towles, 1989). Although Americans want to reduce teenage pregnancy and the AIDS epidemic, the networks' policy on condom advertising exists because people disagree about the consequences of making condoms the answer to these problems.

The reconciliation of prosocial programming in free market economies like the U.S. (where television systems are commercially driven) is in itself an ethical dilemma.[2] The ongoing contention against commercial television's depiction of tobacco and alcohol use in the U.S. illustrates the difficulties encountered when judging the prosocial and antisocial content of media messages. Many Americans feel that they should have the freedom to decide whether or not to use alcohol and tobacco products, and that restricting information regarding the use of such products is wrong. However, others feel that it is unethical to promote products that encourage potentially harmful beliefs and behaviors.

In summary, the prosocial content ethical dilemma results from differing views about what beliefs and behaviors benefit society and which ones are detrimental. Regulation of television content, as is often the case in Third World countries, is vehemently resisted in the U.S. Yet if the decision about prosocial television content is left to commercial networks, some of the most important prosocial messages may never reach millions of American television viewers. Balancing the freedom of the broadcast media with the need for more prosocial television is an ethical dilemma every nation must face.[3]

The Socio-Cultural Equality Dilemma

A second ethical dilemma in using prosocial television concerns the problem of ensuring socio-cultural equality, that is, providing an equal treatment on television of various social and cultural groups. Socio-cultural equality means regarding each social and cultural group with the same value or importance (Gudykunst & Kim, 1984, p. 5). In nations with a high homogeneity index, a measure of a country's socio-cultural diversity, there is a high degree of consensus regarding a society's normative beliefs and behaviors. In Japan, where the homogeneity index is 99 percent, people have fewer problems agreeing on what is prosocial than do people in the U.S., where the homogeneity index is 50 percent (Kurian, 1979).

Ensuring socio-cultural equality through prosocial television is especially important and problematic in socio-culturally diverse countries, for example, India. The popular Indian television soap opera, *Hum Log*, attacked the dowry system of marriage and challenged traditional beliefs about women's status in Indian society. Research on the effects of *Hum Log* indicated that ethnicity, geographical residence, gender, and Hindi language fluency of *Hum Log* viewers were significant determinants of beliefs about gender equality (Brown, 1988; Singhal & Rogers, 1989a). The subservience of women is considered to be socially and culturally appropriate by many Indians, but not by all. So television's treatment of all viewers as socio-culturally "equal" in India is an ethical dilemma.

The socio-cultural equality dilemma is heightened when prosocial television programs are exported to other countries. Television programs are imbued with the socio-cultural values of the society where they are produced. The threat of "cultural imperialism" generates great concern about the socio-cultural impact of imported television programs. For example, the influence of Western entertainment television programs was one factor that contributed to the Iranian Revolution (Tehranian, 1980). Disdain for the "immoral" sexual relations depicted by several American-produced dramatic television serials fueled the Iranian fundamentalist movement against Westernized secularism.

It is difficult to predict that certain viewers may be offended by a television program, even if the program is considered to be prosocial. After the Iranian Revolution, Iran was careful to only allow broadcasts of programs considered to be "prosocial" in the Islamic sense. A very popular Japanese soap opera, *Oshin* (a Japanese name), was imported into Iran and dubbed in Farsi (the lingua franca of Iran) because its values did not conflict with Islamic values and the program was a non-Western production (Mowlana, 1988). *Oshin* became so popular in Iran that Teheran traffic fell to a minimum while the

program was broadcast (Tehranian, in press). The heroine of the series, Oshin, a poor laundry women, achieved dignity and social success through her hard work and determination. Oshin became so well-liked by Iranians that some women began naming their newborn daughters Oshin.

When the Ayatollah Khomeini heard that an Iranian woman on a radio talk show had admitted that Oshin was a more important role model to her than Fatemeh Zahra, the Prophet Muhammad's daughter, he punished the Director of Iran's broadcasting agency with 50 lashes (Tehranian, in press). Iran's radio officials had little idea that allowing discussions about the morally acceptable soap opera *Oshin* would eventually prove disastrous.

The Unintended Effects Dilemma

A third ethical dilemma brought about by the use of prosocial television is the problem of unintended effects. Social development is a complex phenomenon whose consequences are not easily predictable. Undesirable and unintended consequences can result from the diffusion of prosocial messages, as officials in Iran discovered. Reluctance to depict condom use on U.S. television, as mentioned earlier, demonstrates how a fear of unintended consequences can discourage broadcasts of prosocial content. Many parents fear that television content intended to encourage sexual responsibility might encourage sexual promiscuity instead.

As evidenced by the thousands of studies on antisocial television effects, unintended consequences of entertainment television programs are common. To illustrate this problem worldwide, the present discussion will focus on four popular television series: (1) *Miami Vice* and *All in the Family* in the U.S., (2) *Ven Conmigo* ("Come With Me") in Mexico, and (3) *Hum Log* ("We People") in India. Of these series, *Ven Conmigo* and *Hum Log* were overtly prosocial, *All in the Family* was intended to be somewhat prosocial, and *Miami Vice* was not intended to be either prosocial or antisocial.

In the early 1970s, CBS broadcast a mildly prosocial and highly acclaimed situation comedy, *All in the Family*. The series focused on ethnic prejudices through the depiction of a highly bigoted character, Archie Bunker. While the program attempted to point out to viewers the absurdities of their own ethnic prejudices, some already-prejudiced viewers became even more prejudiced in their beliefs (Vidmar & Rokeach, 1974). Similar findings resulted from studies on the impact of the television miniseries *Roots* (Hurr & Robinson, 1978) and *Roots: The Next Generation* (Ball-Rokeach, Grube, & Rokeach, 1981). Viewers of these two television series became more aware of racial issues, but did not become less prejudiced.

NBC's popular crime-drama series, *Miami Vice*, illustrates that even seemingly insignificant events in entertainment programs may lead to sizable unintended behavioral effects on television viewers. U.S. gun-shop owners noticed a remarkable effect on the gun-buying behaviors of *Miami Vice* viewers during the 1980s. Shortly after Detective Sonny Crockett began sporting a shark-gray Australian-made 5.5 6-mm. Steyr AUG, a semi-automatic assault rifle, on episodes of *Miami Vice*, gun shops across the U.S. were flooded with customer calls asking how they could buy one (Alexander & Stewart, 1989). Although *Miami Vice's* producers never claimed they were trying to promote social responsibility, NBC was likely surprised to learn the degree to which *Miami Vice* promoted gun sales and had become the fashion leader in assault weaponry in the U.S.

The third example of an entertainment television program's unintended effects resulted from broadcasts of *Ven Conmigo*, a Mexican prosocial television series that promoted adult literacy. In 1976, an episode of *Ven Conmigo* announced the location of a government warehouse in Mexico City where free literacy booklets were available. However, Mexican officials greatly underestimated the prosocial effects of this episode. Requests for literacy booklets far exceeded the warehouse supply, resulting in mass frustration and huge traffic jams near the warehouse in Mexico City.

The prosocial Indian television soap opera *Hum Log* also had some unintended effects. Bhagwanti, the mother in the *Hum Log* family, was suppose to be a negative role model for female equality: a subservient, self-sacrificing traditional Indian woman who endured great abuse and hardship, especially from her male chauvinist husband. However, a national survey of *Hum Log* viewers indicated 80 percent of the viewers who chose Bhagwanti as a positive role model were women (Singhal & Rogers, 1989a). As with the character Archie Bunker, Bhagwanti became a positive role model for viewers.

Another unintended effect of *Hum Log* was the commercialization of Indian television and the proliferation of other dramatic serials sponsored by advertisers (Singhal & Rogers, 1988b, 1989a). The profits generated by the program demonstrated that prosocial television programs can be commercially successful. However, many Indians believe the commercialization of Indian television will broaden the communication gap between the information-rich and the information-poor and create frustration among disadvantaged viewers who are unable to purchase the advertised consumer goods (Katzman, 1974).

These four examples of unintended consequences from *All in the Family*, *Miami Vice*, *Ven Conmigo*, and *Hum Log* demonstrate how entertainment (and often prosocial) television programs can produce powerful unintended effects.

The Prosocial Development Dilemma

Even if a society agrees on a set of prosocial beliefs and practices, can maintain a reasonable degree of socio-cultural equality, and can control unintended effects of prosocial television, is it ethical to systematically attempt to use television as a persuasive tool to guide social development?

Past research on television effects indicates that we should be concerned about the antisocial effects of television. Thoman (1989) notes that the popular myth describing entertainment television as "mindless entertainment" perpetuates the idea that entertainment programs have little impact on viewers' beliefs and behaviors. It is virtually impossible to produce "value-free" or "socially innocuous" entertainment programs.

The idea that persuasive communication is unethical and, therefore, should be avoided in television production denies the reality of what past research indicates. Television persuades people; how much, is debatable. Even if 1 percent of a population is persuaded to change a belief or behavior on account of watching television, that is still an important change. Persuasive communication can not and should not be eliminated in a democratic society (Bettinghaus & Cody, 1987, p. 14). Therefore, arguing that it is unethical to use television to promote prosocial beliefs and behaviors seems unreasonable and inconsistent with democratic freedoms.

However, unequivocal promotion of prosocial television for social development can also represent an untenable ethical position. When there is disagreement about the "rightness" or "wrongness" of certain social beliefs and behaviors, it becomes obvious that what is considered to be "prosocial" by any group of people, whether that group represents the majority of a population or the highest court of the land, should not be uncritically promoted on television. Whether or not it is ethical to produce prosocial television depends on a number of factors, including the nature of the belief or behavior being promoted, who decides the prosocial status of a certain belief or behavior, and what effects the promotion of a certain belief or behavior are likely to have on an audience. Thus, the ethics of using television as a persuasive tool for social development is inextricably intertwined with the three other ethical dilemmas that were discussed earlier.

CONCLUSION

In summary, we have discussed four ethical dilemmas associated with the use of prosocial television: (1) the ethics of distinguishing prosocial and antisocial content in television programs, (2) the ethics of ensuring socio-cultural equality in prosocial programs, (3) the ethics of dealing with the unintended effects of prosocial television, and (4) the ethics of using television as a tool to guide social development. As television audiences expand in Third World countries, and as the number of prosocial programs increase, an understanding of these ethical dilemmas becomes crucially important.

Promoting prosocial change through television requires responsible communication which demands a commitment to the moral responsibility of protecting the public (Weiser, 1988). Since television is already used as a persuasive tool, the ethical use of television calls for the provision of accurate, timely, and freely distributed information that protects the voluntary choices of television viewers (Jaksa & Pritchard, 1988, p. 33).

Entertainment television has a complex social impact on its viewers. If societies are to use television for social development, then the production of prosocial television content should not be discouraged, despite the ethical dilemmas associated with its effects. Television consumers who are unhappy with the antisocial effects of entertainment television should become more actively involved in determining the kind of content they desire.

Prosocial television can improve the quality of our lives, but if we are to encourage its use, then the responsibility for television content cannot remain on the shoulders of commercial sponsors and networks prone to avoid prosocial programing content, or on government officials who can arbitrarily decide what is prosocial and what is not. The ethical use of media must be based upon the imperative of protecting our freedom, equality, dignity, and physical and psychological well-being. In the case of prosocial television, ultimately, the ethical dilemmas will be decided by television viewers.

NOTES

1. We would like to thank our anonymous reviewers for their helpful contributions to our discussion on ethical theory.
2. The unique dilemma of producing prosocial media messages in free market economies represents an important subject that requires an in-depth analysis beyond the scope of our present discussion. We would like to thank one of our anonymous reviewers for articulating this dilemma, which we hope will be addressed in future research.
3. A version of this article, presented at the 40th Annual Conference of the International Communication Association, June 23–29, 1990, in Dublin, Ireland, contains an expanded discussion of this dilemma.

REFERENCES

Alexander, A. (1985). Adolescents' soap opera viewing and relational perceptions. *Journal of Broadcasting & Electronic Media, 29*(3), 295–308.

Alexander, A., & Stewart, J. (1989, September 19). Detective Sonny Crockett: Leader in fashion weaponry. *The Honolulu Star-Bulletin*, p. B-1.

Amato, P. P., & Malatesta, A. (1987). Effects of prosocial elements in family situation comedies. Paper presented at the 37th Annual Conference of the International Communication Association, Montreal.

Andison, F. S. (1980). Television violence and viewer aggression. In G. C. Wilhoit & H. de Bock (Eds.), *Mass communication review yearbook 1* (pp. 555–572). Beverly Hills, CA: Sage.

Aristotle. (1960). The rhetoric of Aristotle (L. Cooper, Trans.). New York: Appleton-Century-Crofts.

Ball-Rokeach, S. J., Rokeach, M., & Grube, J. W. (1984). *The great American values test: Influencing behavior and belief through television.* New York: The Free Press.

Ball-Rokeach, S. J., Grube, J. W., & Rokeach, M. (1981). "Roots: The Next Generation"—Who watched and with what effect? *Public Opinion Quarterly, 45,* 58–68.

Bandura, A. (1977). *Social learning theory.* Englewood Cliffs, N.J.: Prentice-Hall.

Barnum, H. J., Jr. (1975). Mass media and health communications. *Journal of Medical education, 50,* 25.

Bentley, E. (1964). *Life of the drama.* New York: Atheneum.

Berrueta, M. C. G. (1986). The soap opera as a reinforcer of social values. Unpublished master's thesis, Iberoamericana University, Mexico City.

Bettinghaus, E. P., & Cody, M. J. (1987). *Persuasive communication* (4th ed.). New York: Holt, Rinehart, & Winston.

Brown, W. J. (1988). Effects of "Hum Log," a television soap opera on prosocial beliefs in India. *Dissertation Abstracts International, 50,* 01A, 20.

Brown, W. J. (1989, May). The role of entertainment television in development communication. Paper presented at the 39th Annual Conference of the International Communication Association, San Francisco, CA.

Brown, W. J., Singhal, A., & Rogers, E. M. (1989). Pro-development soap operas: A novel approach to development communication. *Media Development, 36*(4), 43–47.

Buerkel-Rothfuss, N. L., & Mayes, S. (1981). Soap opera viewing: The cultivation effect. *Journal of Communication, 31*(3), 108–115.

Cassata, M. B., Skill, T. D., & Boadu, S. O. (1979). In sickness and in health. *Journal of Communication, 29*(4), 73–80.

Cassata, M. B., & Skill, T. D. (1983). *Life on daytime television: Tuning-in American serial drama.* Norwood, N.J.: Ablex.

Chesebro, J. W. (1969). A construct for assessing ethics in communication. *The Central States Speech Journal, 20,* 104–114.

Christians, C. G. (1977). Fifty years of scholarship in media ethics. *Journal of Communication, 27*(4), 19–29.

Cooper, T. W. (1988). Ethics, journalism and television: Bibliographic constellations, black holes. *Journalism Quarterly, 65*(2), 450–455, 496.

Donnerstein, E. (1980). Pornography and violence against women. *Annals of the New York Academy of Sciences, 347,* 227–288.

Donnerstein, E., & Berkowitz, L. (1981). Victim reactions in aggressive-erotic films as a factor in violence against women. *Journal of Personality and Social Psychology, 41,* 710–724.

Downing, M. (1974). Heroine of a daytime TV serial. *Journal of Communication, 24*(2), 130–137.

Estep, R., & MacDonald, P. T. (1985). Crime in the afternoon: Murder and robbery on soap operas. *Journal of Broadcasting & Electronic Media, 29*(3), 323–331.

Goldsen, R. K. (1975). Throwaway husbands, wives, and lovers. *Human Behavior, 4,* 64–69.

Greenberg, B. S., Abelman, R., & Neuendorf, K. (1981). Sex on the soap opera: Afternoon delight. *Journal of Communication, 31*(3), 83–89.

Greenberg, B. S., & D'Alessio, D. (1985). Quantity and quality of sex in the soaps. *Journal of Broadcasting & Electronic Media, 29,* 309–321.

Gudykunst, W. B., & Kim, Y. Y. (1984). *Communicating with strangers.* Reading, MA: Addison-Wesley.

Gunter, B. (1984). Television as a facilitator of good behavior amongst children. *Journal of Moral Education, 13,* 69–77.

Harvey, S. E., Sprafkin, J. N., & Rubinstein, E. A. (1979). Primetime television: A profile of aggressive and prosocial behaviors. *Journal of Broadcasting, 23,* 179–189.

Hurr, K. K., & Robinson, J. P. (1978). The social impact of "Roots." *Journalism Quarterly, 55,* 19–24.

Jain, M. (1985, April 14–20). Be Indian, see Indian. *Sunday,* pp. 24–27.

Jaksa, J. A., & Pritchard, M. S. (1988). *Communication ethics: Methods of analysis.* Belmont, CA: Wadsworth.

Johnstone, C. L. (1980). An Aristotelian trilogy: Ethics, rhetoric, politics, and the search for moral truth. *Philosophy & Rhetoric, 13*(1), 1–24.

Jung, C. G. (1970). *Archetypes and the collective unconscious.* Buenos Aires, Argentina: Paidos.

Kant, I. (1964). *Groundwork of the metaphysics of morals* (H. J. Paton, Trans.). New York: Harper Torch books.

Katzman, N. (1974). The impact of communication technology: Some theoretical premises and their implications. *Ekistics, 225,* 125–130.

Kulman, R. I., & Akamatsu, J. T. (1988). The effects of television on large-scale attitude change: Viewing "The Day After." *Journal of Applied Social Psychology, 18*(13), 1121–1132.

Kurian, G. T. (1979). *The book of world rankings.* New York: Facts on File.

Liebert, R. M., Neale, J. M., & Davidson, E. S. (1973). *The early window: Effects of television on children and youth.* New York: Pergamon.

Long, M. C. (1978). Television: Help or hindrance to health education? *Health Education, 9*(3), 32–34.

Lovelace, V. O., & Huston, A. C. (1982). Can television teach prosocial behavior? *Prevention in Human Services, 2*, 93–106.

Lowry, D. T., Love, G., & Kirby, M. (1981). Sex on the soap operas: Patterns of intimacy. *Journal of Communication, 31*(3), 90–96.

Lowry, D. T., & Towles, D. E. (1989). Soap opera portrayals of sex, contraception, and sexually transmitted diseases. *Journal of Communication, 39*(2), 77–83.

Malamuth, N. M., & Donnerstein, E. (Eds.). (1984). *Pornography and sexual aggression.* New York: Academic Press.

Martin, T. M., Byrne, R. B., & Wedemeyer, D. J. (1977). Balance: An aspect of the right to communicate. *Journal of Communication, 27*(2), 158–162.

Merrill, J. C. (1974). *The imperative of freedom: A philosophy of journalistic autonomy.* New York: Hastings House.

Merrill, J. C. (1975). Ethics and journalism. In J. C. Merrill & R. D. Barney (Eds.), *Ethics and the press: Readings in mass morality* (pp. 8–17). New York: Hastings House.

Mill, J. S. (1957). *Utilitarianism.* New York: Liberal Arts Press, Bobbs-Merrill.

Minnick, W. (1980). A new look at the ethics of persuasion. *The Southern Speech Communication Journal, 65*, 352–362.

Mitra, S. (1986, January 15). *"Hum Log"*: The final flourish. *India Today*, pp. 142–143.

Mowlana, H. (1988, September). Communication and cultural development: A report from Iran. Paper presented at the Annual Conference of the International Institute of Communications, Washington, D.C.

Montgomery, K. C. (1989). *Target: Primetime: Advocacy groups and the struggle over entertainment television.* New York: Oxford University Press.

Noble, G. (1975). *Children in front of the small screen.* Beverly Hills, CA: Sage.

Palmer, E. L. (1978, June). A pedagogical analysis of recurrent formats on "Sesame Street" and "The Electric Company." Paper presented at the International Conference on Children's Television, Amsterdam.

Phillips, D. P. (1982). The behavioral impact of violence in the mass media: A review of evidence from laboratory and non-laboratory investigations. *Sociology and Social Research, 66*, 386–398.

Phillips, D. P., & Hensley, J. E. (1984). When violence is rewarded or punished: The impact of mass media stories on homicide. *Journal of Communication, 34*(3), 101–115.

Porter, W. J., & Ware, W. (1989). The frequency and context of prosocial acts on primetime television. *Journalism Quarterly, 66*(2), 359–366, 529.

Rogers, E. M. (1976). Communication and development: The passing of the dominant paradigm. In E. M. Rogers (Ed.), *Communication and development: Critical perspectives* (pp. 121–133). Newbury Park, CA: Sage.

Rogers, E. M., Aikat, S., Soonbum, C., Poppe, P., & Sopory, P. (1989, April 1). *Proceedings from the conference on entertainment-education for social change.* Los Angeles, CA: Annenberg School of Communications, University of Southern California.

Rushton, J. P. (1982). Television and prosocial behavior. In D. Pearl, L. Bouthilet & J. Lazar (Eds.), *Television & behavior: Ten years of scientific progress and implications for the eighties* (Vol. 2, pp. 248–258). MD: National Institute of Mental Health.

Sabido, M. (1981). Towards a social use of soap operas. Paper presented at the International Institute of Communication, Strassbourg, France.

Sabido, M. (1982). *Handbook of social value reinforcement.* Mexico City: Televisa.

Shatzer, M. J., Korzenny, F., Griffis-Korzenny, B. A. (1985). Adolescents viewing "Shogun": Cognitive and attitudinal effects. *Journal of Broadcasting & Electronic Media, 29*(3), 341–346.

Singhal, A., & Rogers, E. M. (1988a). Television soap operas for development in India. *Gazette, 41*, 109–126.

Singhal, A., & Rogers, E. M. (1988b). *India's information revolution.* New Delhi: Sage.

Singhal, A., & Rogers, E. M. (1989a). Prosocial television for development in India. In R. E. Rice & C. Atkin (Eds.), *Public communication campaigns* (2nd ed.)(pp. 331–350). Beverly Hills, CA: Sage.

Singhal, A., & Rogers, E. M. (1989b). Entertainment-education communication strategies for family planning. *Populi 16*(2), 38–47.

Smith, F. A. (1972). Health information during a week in television. *New England Journal of Medicine, 286*, 516.

Sutherland, J. C., & Siniawsky, S. J. (1982). The treatment and resolution of moral violations on soap operas. *Journal of Communication, 32*(2), 67–74.

Tan, A. S., & Tan, G. K. (1986). Television use and mental health. *Journalism Quarterly, 63*(1), 107–113.

Tehranian, M. (1980). Communication and revolution in Iran: The passing of a paradigm. *Iranian Studies, 13*, 1–4.

Tehranian, M. (in press). Communications. In E. Yarshater (Ed.), *Encyclopedia Iranica.* London: Routledge, Kegan, & Paul.

Thoman, E. (1989). Media education: Agenda for the 90s. *Media Ethics Update, 2*(1), 8–9.

Tuchman, G., Daniels, A. K., & Benet, J. (Eds.). (1978). *Hearth and home: Images of women in the mass media.* New York: Oxford University Press.

Vidmar, N., & Rokeach, M. (1974). Archie Bunker's bigotry: A study in selective perception and exposure. *Journal of Communication, 24*(1), 36–47.

Weiser, D. (1988). Two concepts of communication as criteria for collective responsibility. *Journal of Business Ethics, 7*, 735–744.

Winnard, K., Rimon, J. G., & Convisser, J. (1987). The impact of television on the family planning attitudes of an urban Nigerian audience: The NTA/Enugu experience. Paper presented at the Annual Conference of the American Public Health Association, New Orleans.

Ume-Nwagbo, E. N. E. (1986). "Cock Crow at Dawn," a Nigerian experiment with television drama in development communication. *Gazette, 37*(3), 155–167.

Zillmann, D., & Bryant, J. (1982). Pornography, sexual callousness, and the trivialization of rape. *Journal of Communication, 32*(4), 10–21.

Credits/ Acknowledgments

Cover design by Charles Vitelli

1. Living with Media
Facing overview—Photo by the Sony Corporation of America.

2. The Source's Perspective
Facing overview—The Dushkin Publishing Group, Inc. photo by Pamela Carley.

3. Commercial Considerations
Facing overview—Photo by Rebecca Holland.

4. Legal and Regulatory Restraints on Media Content
Facing overview—Photo by EPA Documerica.

5. Information and Influence
Facing overview—United Nations photo by F.B. Grunzweig.

6. The Power of Images
Facing overview—United Nations photo.

7. Ethical Questions
Facing overview—Photo by Criminal Justice Publications, NY.

8. Media and Politics
Facing overview—Photo by AP/Wide World Photos.

9. Implicit Lessons
Facing overview—Photo by Apple Computer.

ANNUAL EDITIONS ARTICLE REVIEW FORM

■ NAME: _____ DATE: _____

■ TITLE AND NUMBER OF ARTICLE: _____

■ BRIEFLY STATE THE MAIN IDEA OF THIS ARTICLE: _____

_____

_____

_____

_____

■ LIST THREE IMPORTANT FACTS THAT THE AUTHOR USES TO SUPPORT THE MAIN IDEA:

_____

_____

_____

_____

_____

■ WHAT INFORMATION OR IDEAS DISCUSSED IN THIS ARTICLE ARE ALSO DISCUSSED IN YOUR TEXTBOOK OR OTHER READING YOU HAVE DONE? LIST THE TEXTBOOK CHAPTERS AND PAGE NUMBERS:

_____

_____

_____

_____

_____

■ LIST ANY EXAMPLES OF BIAS OR FAULTY REASONING THAT YOU FOUND IN THE ARTICLE:

_____

_____

_____

_____

■ LIST ANY NEW TERMS/CONCEPTS THAT WERE DISCUSSED IN THE ARTICLE AND WRITE A SHORT DEFINITION:

_____

_____

_____

_____

_____

*Your instructor may require you to use this Annual Editions Article Review Form in any number of ways: for articles that are assigned, for extra credit, as a tool to assist in developing assigned papers, or simply for your own reference. Even if it is not required, we encourage you to photocopy and use this page; you'll find that reflecting on the articles will greatly enhance the information from your text.

ANNUAL EDITIONS: MASS MEDIA 95/96
Article Rating Form

Here is an opportunity for you to have direct input into the next revision of this volume. We would like you to rate each of the 42 articles listed below, using the following scale:

1. **Excellent: should definitely be retained**
2. **Above average: should probably be retained**
3. **Below average: should probably be deleted**
4. **Poor: should definitely be deleted**

Your ratings will play a vital part in the next revision. So please mail this prepaid form to us just as soon as you complete it.
Thanks for your help!

Annual Editions revisions depend on two major opinion sources: one is our Advisory Board, listed in the front of this volume, which works with us in scanning the thousands of articles published in the public press each year; the other is you—the person actually using the book. Please help us and the users of the next edition by completing the prepaid article rating form on this page and returning it to us. Thank you.

Rating	Article	Rating	Article
	1. Television: The Shared Arena		23. What the Jury Saw: Does the Videotape Lie?
	2. As the Dial Turns		24. When Pictures Drive Foreign Policy
	3. The Trouble with Television		25. Photographs That Lie: The Ethical Dilemma of Digital Retouching
	4. TV as Boob Tube: Bad Rap		26. Ethics and Society
	5. Why Blame TV?		27. Legislating Ethics
	6. Power Structure of the American Media		28. Feeding Frenzy
	7. Media Habits of Media Tycoons		29. When a Story Subject Threatens Suicide: "I'm Going to Kill Myself!"
	8. Democratic Media		30. To "Out" or Not to "Out"
	9. Sitcom Politics		31. Bad News Bearers
	10. Advertiser Influence		32. Churning Whitewater
	11. Sex, Lies, and Advertising		33. The Trouble with Spots
	12. Hollywood the Ad		34. The Power of Talk
	13. Newspaper Advocacy Advertising: Molder of Public Opinion?		35. The Make-Believe Media
	14. Hollywood Can No Longer Ignore Watchdog Groups		36. Battle for Your Brain
	15. "If I Don't Like It, You Can't See It"		37. Hollywood's Poison Factory: The Movies' Twisted Image
	16. Media Accountability for Real-Life Violence: A Case of Negligence or Free Speech?		38. Gendered Media: The Influence of Media on Views of Gender
	17. The Tangled Webs They Weave		39. Don't Blame TV
	18. Media Con Games		40. Violence on TV
	19. Make-Your-Own Journalism: The Trend toward Fabricating the News		41. Frankenstein Must Be Destroyed: Chasing the Monster of TV Violence
	20. Media Pervasiveness		42. Ethical Dilemmas of Prosocial Television
	21. Summer's Top Crime Drama, Continued		
	22. Old News Is Good News		

(Continued on next page)

ABOUT YOU

Name_____ Date_____

Are you a teacher? ☐   Or student? ☐

Your School Name _____

Department _____

Address _____

City _____ State _____ Zip _____

School Telephone # _____

YOUR COMMENTS ARE IMPORTANT TO US!

Please fill in the following information:

For which course did you use this book? _____

Did you use a text with this Annual Edition?   ☐ yes   ☐ no

The title of the text? _____

What are your general reactions to the Annual Editions concept?

Have you read any particular articles recently that you think should be included in the next edition?

Are there any articles you feel should be replaced in the next edition? Why?

Are there other areas that you feel would utilize an Annual Edition?

May we contact you for editorial input?

May we quote you from above?

ANNUAL EDITIONS: MASS MEDIA 95/96